COMPUTER GRAPHICS

Volume 20 • Number 4 • August 1986
A publication of ACM SIGGRAPH
Production Editor John C. Beatty

SIGGRAPH '86 Conference Proceedings
August 18-22, 1986, Dallas, Texas
Edited by David C. Evans and Russell J. Athay

Sponsored by the Association for Computing Machinery's
Special Interest Group on Computer Graphics

The Association for Computing Machinery, Inc.
11 West 42nd Street
New York, New York 10036

**SIGGRAPH '86 is sponsored by the Association for
Computing Machinery's Special Interest Group on
Computer Graphics in cooperation with the IEEE Technical
Committee on Computer Graphics.**

Additional copies may be ordered prepaid from:

ACM Order Department
P.O. Box 64145
Baltimore, MD 21264
ACM Order Number: 428860

Price:
Members : $30.00
All Others: $40.00

Manufactured By K Graphics, Inc.

Printed in the U.S.A.

Contents

Thursday, 21 August 1986

Friday, 22 August 1986

Panels

Preface

Welcome to SIGGRAPH '86. This is the Thirteenth Annual Conference on Computer Graphics and Interactive Techniques. The papers presented at SIGGRAPH '86 are published in these proceedings as a special issue of *Computer Graphics*. These 35 papers were selected from 140 submitted papers by the Technical Program Committee.

The papers were distributed to the members of the Technical Program Committee (listed in the next next section), who acted as senior reviewers. In addition to their own review, each senior reviewer solicited at least two outside reviews for each paper. The full committee then met for two days to consider each paper, discuss its merits, and make the final decision. Every effort was made to make the review process as fair as possible and to select the best previously unpublished papers for presentation at SIGGRAPH '86. We feel that the papers selected are of the highest quality and report important research results.

We thank the members of the Technical Program Committee for the many hours they devoted to reviewing papers, arranging additional reviews, gathering results and participating in the selection meeting. Without their willing and expert help, this whole process would not have been possible. We also thank those who reviewed papers; their names are also listed in the next next section.

We give special thanks to John Beatty, who is the production editor for these proceedings, and to Image Network in Mountain View, California, who made their troff production facilities available. Finally, thanks go to Janet Athay, who cheerfully and expertly handled the administrative chores associated with the Technical Program.

Dave Evans
Russ Athay
Technical Program Committee Co-Chairs

Conference Committee

CONFERENCE CO-CHAIRS

Ellen Gore   Raymond L. Elliott
(ISSCO)   (Los Alamos National Laboratory)

CONFERENCE COMMITTEE CHAIRS

Michelle L. Amato, *Electronic Theatre*
(Cranston/Csuri Productions, Inc.)

Beverly Aquino, *Exhibits*

Russell J. Athay, *Technical Program*
(Biosym Technologies Inc.)

Michael H. Bigbee, *Controller*
(ISSCO)

Kerry G. Brix, *Aural/Visual*

Bruce Eric Brown, *Slides*
(The Quail Group)

David C. Evans, *Technical Program*
(Evans and Sutherland Computer Corporation)

John E. French, Jr., *Special Interest Groups*
(Exxon Production Research Co.)

Andy Goodrich, *Student Volunteers*
(University of Michigan Computing Center)

Michael W. Herman, *Conference Materials*
(Optical Recording Corporation)

Susan Keeley, *Exhibits*

David D. Loendorf, *Courses*
(Duke University)

Linda Lucas, *Public Relations / Local Arrangements*
(Mary Kay Cosmetics, Inc.)

Adele Newton, *Registration*
(University of Waterloo)

Richard L. Phillips, *Panels*
(University of Michigan)

Patric Prince, *Art Show*
(California State University, Los Angeles)

Virginia Romero, *Speaker Slides*
(Los Alamos National Laboratory)

Sharon Wilhelmy, *Treasurer*
(Los Alamos National Laboratory)

CONFERENCE PLANNING COMMITTEE

Pat Cole (Hewlett-Packard)
Raymond L. Elliott (Los Alamos National Laboratory)
Robert A. Ellis, *Chair* (GE/Calma Company)
Ellen Gore (ISSCO)
Richard Mueller (Control Data Corporation)
Jim Thomas (Battelle Northwest)
Richard A. Weinberg (University of Southern California)
Bob Young (Mission Computer Associates)

TECHNICAL PROGRAM COMMITTEE

Russell J. Athay, *Co-Chair* (Biosym Technologies, Inc.)
Mike Bailey (Megatek)
Brian A. Barsky (University of California, Berkeley)
John C. Beatty (University of Waterloo)
R. Daniel Bergeron (University of New Hampshire)
Jim Blinn (Jet Propulsion Laboratories)
Bruce Eric Brown (The Quail Group)
Edwin E. Catmull (Pixar)
Louis Crain (PDA Engineering)
Franklin C. Crow (Xerox PARC)
David C. Evans, *Co-Chair* (Evans and Sutherland Computer Corp.)
A. Robin Forrest (University of East Anglia)
Henry Fuchs (University of North Carolina, Chapel Hill)
Ambros S. Hoffmann (Avco-Lycoming)
Tom Jensen (Evans and Sutherland Computer Corp.)
Gearold R. Johnson (Shape Data, Ltd.)
James T. Kajiya (California Institute of Technology)
Jeffrey M. Lane (Daisy Systems Corp.)
Dave Rogers (United States Naval Academy)
Gary Rogers (Superset)
Maureen Stone (Xerox PARC)
Spencer Thomas (University of Utah)
Fujio Yamaguchi (Waseda University)

TECHNICAL PROGRAM REVIEWERS

Gregory Abram	Rob Cook
Rick Adams	Sabine Coquillart
Bill Appelbe	John Danskin
Dennis Arnon	Mark Dippé
Chuck Athey	Jim Donahue
Norm Badler	Tom Duff
Ron Baecker	Rich Ehlers
Alan Barr	Carl Ellison
Rick Beach	Nick England
Stephen Benton	Jerry Evans
Frank Bliss	Gerald Farin
Jules Bloomenthal	Russell Fish
Sara Bly	Patrick Fitzhorn
Rod Bogart	Jim Foley
Kevin Borg	Alain Fournier
Russ Brown	Issei Fujishiro
Bill Buxton	Don Fussell
Stu Card	Steve Gabriel
Wayne Carlson	Andrew Glassner
Loren Carpenter	John Gould
Malcolm Casale	Charles Grant
Brad Castalia	Eric Grant
Bill Charlesworth	Alan Grayer
Hiroaki Chiyokura	Leo Guibas
Richard Chuang	Charlie Gunn
Elizabeth Cobb	Karl Guttag
Jim Cobb	Pat Hanrahan
Elaine Cohen	Paul Heckbert

(TECHNICAL PROGRAM REVIEWERS, continued)

Franz Herbert
Bert Herzog
Ian Hirschsohn
Larry Hodges
Ambrose Hoffmann
James Hunter
Masanori Igoshi
Dan Ingalls
Andy Ingersoll
John Jacko
Erik Jansen
Gearold Johnson
Mike Jones
Robert Judd
Brian Kantor
Lou Katz
Steven Kensinger
Fumihiko Kimura
Brian Kirschner
Myke Klucewicz
Louis Knapp
Toshiyasu Kunii
Junnosuke Kutsuzawa
Gary Laroff
Mark Lavin
Steve Levine
Mark Levoy
Henry Lieberman
Richard Littlefield
Robert Magedson
Nadia Magenat-Thalmann
Robert Marchot
Nelson Max
David McAllister
Jock McKinley
Glenn McMinn
Donald Meagher
Even Mehlum
Jim Michener
Gene Miller
Jim Miller
Lance Miraco
Don Mitchell
Hans Moravec
Henry Moreton
Avi Naiman
Gregory Nelson
Koichi Ohmura
Eben Ostby
Fred Parke
Kenneth Perlin
Mike Pique
Dave Plunkett

Tom Porter
Michael Potmesil
Michael Propen
Dick Puk
Peter Quarendon
Michael Rarick
Bill Reeves
Ari Requicha
Henry Rich
Alyn Rockwood
Stephen Rogers
Patrick Rooney
Judson Rosebush
David Rosenthal
Candace Rush
Malcolm Sabin
Ray Sarraga
Tim Schreiner
Andrew Schulert
Tom Sederberg
Carlo Sequin
Takao Shibuya
John Sibert
Phil Skolmoski
John Staudhammer
Garland Stern
Cliff Stoll
Dan Swinehart
Peter Tanner
Jim Thomas
Shinji Tomita
Edwin Tripp
Ken Turkowski
Mike Ullner
Tim Van Hook
John Van Rosendale
Bill Verplank
Mitch Wade
Michael Wahrman
Gary Watkins
R. E. Webber
Marceli Wein
Richard Weinberg
Lee Westover
Dan Whelan
Turner Whitted
Mary Whitton
Lance Williams
Peter Willis
John Woodwark
Burkard Wordenweber
Fujio Yamaguchi

PROFESSIONAL SUPPORT

ACM SIGGRAPH Conference Coordinator
Betsy Johnsmiller

Art Show Administrative Assistant
Deborah Colman

Aural/Visual Management
(Video Research Consultants)
Mark Fausner
Alex Halkin
Johnie Horn
Doris Kochanek
Phil Morton
Lucy Petrovich
Sally Rosenthal

ACM SIGGRAPH '86 Conference Coordinator
Connie Martiny

Conference Management / National Public Relations
(Smith Bucklin and Associates, Inc.)
John Fetters
Ellen Frisbie
Sheila Hoffmeyer
Joy Lee
Cynthia Stark

Courses Executive Assistant
Mary Shingleton

Decorator/Drayage
(Andrews-Bartlett and Associates, Inc.)
Bob Borsz
Betty Fuller
Ken Gallagher
Barby Patronski
John Patronski

Exhibition Management
(Robert T. Kenworthy, Inc.)
Robert T. Kenworthy
Hank Cronan
Barbara Voss

Graphic Design
(Pirtle Design)
Woody Pirtle
Alan Colvin
Wing Chan

Local Public Relations
(The Oakley Company)
Joann Martindale

Technical Program Administrative Assistant
Janet Athay

Treasurer Administrative Assistant
Kay Keszler

Exhibitors

Abekas Video Systems, Inc.
Abel Image Research
Academic Press, Inc.
ACS International Inc.
Adage, Inc.
Addison-Wesley Publishing Company, Inc.
Advanced Electronics Design, Inc.
Advanced Technology Center
Alias Research Inc.
A.M.A.P.
American Small Business Computers Inc.
AMF Logic Sciences, Inc.
Ampex Corporation
Amtron Corporation
Animatic Comparetti
Antics Enterprises Inc.
Apollo Computer Inc.
Arcanal
Artel Communications
Artronics Inc.
Association for Computing Machinery
AT&T Computer Systems Center
Autodesk, Inc.
Autographix, Inc.
AVAX Inc.
AV Video
AZTEK
Barco Industries, Inc.
Bell & Howell, Quintar Division
BNW, Inc.
Robert Bosch Corporation
Brooktree Corporation
Business Computer Systems
CalComp
Celco (Constantine Engineering Laboratories Company)
CH Products
Chyron Corporation
ColorGraphics Systems, Inc.
Computer-Aided Engineering
Computer Graphics Laboratories, Inc.
Computer Graphics Today
Computer Graphics World
Computer Pictures Magazine
Computer Retail News
Computer Support Corporation
Computer Systems News
Cray Research, Inc.
Cromemco, Inc.
Crossfield Electronics
CSP, Inc.
Cubicomp Corporation
Daikin U.S. Corporation
Daikiri
Dalim
Datacube Inc.
Data Translation, Inc.
Decision Images Inc.
DEC Professional
DE GRAFE

DICOMED Corporation
Digital Equipment Corporation
Digital Review
Dubner Computer Systems
Dunn Instruments
DYNAIR Electronics, Inc.
Eastman Kodak Company
EDN Magazine
EIKONIX Corporation
Electrohome Limited
Electronic Business
Elographics, Inc.
Equitable Life Leasing Corporation
Evans & Sutherland Computer Corporation
Flamingo Graphics
Floating Point Systems, Inc.
Flying Moose Systems & Graphics Ltd.
French Expositions in the U.S. Inc.
General Electric Company
General Electric Company, Silicon Systems Technology Dept.
General Parametrics Corporation
Genigraphics Corporation
Geoscan, Inc.
Getris Image
Gigatek Limited
Gould, Inc., Imaging & Graphics Division
G.R.A.C.E.
Grafpoint
Graftel, Inc.
Graphic Controls Corporation
Graphic Resources Corporation
GraphOn Corporation
Greyhawk Systems, Inc.
GTCO Corporation
GTI Corporation
Karl Gutmann Inc.
Hardcopy Magazine, Seldin Publishing, Inc.
Hewlett-Packard Company
Hitachi America, Ltd.
Houston Instrument, A Division of Ametek
Howe Industries
Human Designed Systems Inc.
Ibis Systems, Inc.
IEEE Computer Society
Ikegami Electronics (USA), Inc.
Imagen Corporation
Images II
Imaging Technology Inc.
Imagraph Corporation
I.N.A.
Inflight Services Inc.
INI Computer Products
Inmos Corporation
Inovion Corporation
Intecolor
Integrated Technologies, Inc.
Interactive Machines, Inc.
International Imaging Systems (I2S)
Ioline Corporation

I.S.G. Technologies Inc.
Island Graphics Corporation
ISSCO
I.T.F. (Images Transfert France)
King Concept Corporation
Kloss Vido Corporation
kms Advanced Products, Inc.
KMW Systems Corporation
Koh-I-Noor Rapidograph, Inc.
Kontron Electronics, Inc.
Kurta Corporation
Lazerus Productions
Lear Siegler Inc.
Lundy Electronics & Systems, Inc.
Lyon Lamb VAS Inc.
Machine Design
Management Graphics, Inc.
Mangum Sickles Industries Inc.
MASSCOMP
Matrix Instruments, Inc.
Matrox Electronic Systems Ltd.
Measurement Systems Inc.
Media Cybernetics, Inc.
Megascan Technology, Inc.
Megatek Corporation
Meiko Limited
Mercury Computer Systems, Inc.
Meret, Inc.
Metheus Corporation
Microfield Graphics, Inc.
MicroTouch Systems, Inc.
Mini-Micro Systems
Minolta Corporation
Mitsubishi Electronics America, Inc.
Mitsubishi International Corporation
Mitsui & Company (U.S.A.), Inc.
Modgraph Inc.
Moniterm Corporation
Monitronix Corporation
Motion Analysis Corporation
Multiwire Division, Kollmorgen Corporation
National Semiconductor Corporation
NCGA
NEC Electronics Inc.
NEC Information Systems
Neo-Visuals, Inc.
New Media Graphics Corporation
Nicolet's Computer Graphics Division
N.I.S.E., Inc.
Nova Graphics International
Number Nine Computer Corporation
Numonics Corporation
Oasys Office Automation Systems, Inc.
OCLI, Inc.
Omnicomp Graphics Corporation
Oxberry Div. of Richmark Camera Service, Inc.
Panasonic Industrial Company, Computer Components Division
Panasonic Industrial Company
Pansophic Systems of Canada Ltd.
Parallax Graphics Inc.
PC Products
PC Week
Perceptics Corporation
Pericom Inc.
Peritek Corporation
PIXAR, Inc.
Polhemus Navigation Sciences Division, McDonnell Douglas Corporation
Princeton Graphics Systems
PRIOR Data Sciences
Proteon Inc.
QMS, Inc.
Quadram Division, Intelligent Systems Corporation

Quantel
Quantum Data Inc.
Qume Corporation/ITT
Ramtek Corporation
Raster Technologies Inc.
Recognition Concepts, Inc.
Saber Technology Corporation
Sampo Corporation of America
Scan Group International, A CLAL Company
Science Magazine
Scriptel Corporation
Seiko Instruments USA Inc., Graphic Devices & Systems Division
S.F.P. Societe Francaise de Production
Shima Seiki Manufacturing Ltd.
Silicon Graphics, Inc.
SlideTek Inc.
Small System Design, Inc.
Sogitec Audiovisual
Springer-Verlag New York, Inc.
SPSS Inc.
Stereographics Corporation
Storage Concepts, Inc.
Summagraphics Corporation
Sun Microsystems, Inc.
Superset
Symbolics, Inc.
Synergy Computer Graphics Corporation
SysScan, Inc.
Talaris Systems Inc.
TAT Graphics Group, Inc.
Techexport, Inc.
Technology Business Communications, Inc.
Teledyne Post
Telmat
Template, The Software Division of Megatek Corporation
Texas Instruments Semiconductor Group
Texas Memory Systems, Inc.
Thomson Digital Image
Time Arts Inc.
Transformations
Trident International, Inc.
Uniras A/S
UNIX/World Magazine
Vectrix Corporation
Versatec, A Xerox Company
Versicolor Corporation
Vertex Inc.
Vertigo Systems International Inc.
Via Visuals Inc.
Video Monitors Inc.
Visual Engineering
Visual Horizons, Inc.
VLSI Design
VMI
Wasatch Computer Technology
Wavefront Technologies
West End Film, Inc.
Westward Technology Inc.
The Winsted Corporation
xePIX Inc.
The Xerox Corporation
Xtar Electronics Inc.
Zenith Electronics Corporation

ACM/SIGGRAPH Award

Computer Graphics Achievement Award

Dr. Turner Whitted

Dr. Turner Whitted is being recognized for his important contribution to ray tracing. In computer graphics, and computing in general, many techniques are implemented but await higher-speed hardware and larger-sized memory to achieve acceptable or improved performance. Often such techniques have flaws which must be overcome by complex exceptions or consideration of special cases. That was the situation in the early applications of ray tracing.

Turner Whitted did not invent ray tracing. Instead, he contributed what so many wish to contribute: a simple and elegant algorithm which, in this case, made the ray tracing technique not only scrutable but also more efficient. The need for special cases was eliminated; he was the first to show the world how to do it. His papers, and his film *The Compleat Angler*, inspired thousands of people to write their own ray tracing programs. By making a complicated problem simple Whitted made it possible for practitioners and students alike to gain first-hand experience with synthetic image processing. They could realize a working solution, and recognize significant principles of computing and computer graphics, without having to code for many months. Essentially all the beautiful ray tracing pictures and animations that exist today are based on the original work of Turner Whitted.

Dr. Whitted was educated at Duke University, receiving a BSE degree in electrical engineering in 1969 and an MS degree the following year. He was granted the PhD degree in electrical engineering by North Carolina State University in 1978. For the next five years he was a Member of the Technical Staff at the Computer Systems Research Laboratory of Bell Laboratories.

In 1983 he "returned home" to North Carolina as founder and Technical Director of Numerical Design, Ltd., a firm which produces image rendering software. Since 1982 he has been an Adjunct Associate Professor of Computer Science at the University of North Carolina at Chapel Hill.

His achievements go beyond the ray tracing algorithm. An important 1980 paper[1] on scan line methods for display of parametric surfaces was editorially crafted from the work of three different sets of authors, of whom Whitted was one. With Rubin, he published a paper[2] showing the importance of a consistent treatment of coherence to optimize the speed of ray tracing. Despite numerous attempts this result has not been supplanted. Whitted published an article[3] in *Science* that brought computer graphics to the attention of perhaps the largest single readership of scientists.

Turner Whitted has shown us the importance of simplicity and elegance. As a colleague has said: "Turner is an extraordinarily humble and generous person, and an example of non-stop creativity."

SIGGRAPH recognizes the contributions of Dr. Turner Whitted by presenting him the 1986 ACM/SIGGRAPH Computer Graphics Achievement Award.

[1] James F. Blinn, Loren C. Carpenter, Jeffrey M. Lane and Turner Whitted, "Scan Line Methods for Displaying Parametrically Defined Surfaces," *Communications of the ACM*, volume 23, number 1, January, 1980, pages 23-34.

[2] Turner Whitted, and Steven M. Rubin, "A 3-Dimensional Representation for Fast Rendering of Complex Scenes," *Computer Graphics*,

SIGGRAPH '86

Proceedings of SIGGRAPH '80, volume 14, number 3, July, 1980, pages 110-116.

[3] Turner Whitted, "Some Recent Advances in Computer Graphics," *Science*, Special Issue on Electronics and Computers, volume 215, 12 February 1982, pages 767-774.

REAL-TIME SHADED NC MILLING DISPLAY

TIM VAN HOOK

Trancept Systems Inc.

521F Uwharrie Court

Raleigh, NC 27606

Abstract

The real-time shaded display of a solid model being milled by a cutting tool following an NC path is attained by the image-space Boolean subtraction of solid objects. The technique is suitable for implementation in microcode in a raster graphic display processor. Update rates of 10 cutting operations per second are typical.

Problem

The integration of computer aided design (CAD) and computer aided manufacturing (CAM) into computer integrated manufacturing (CIM) places increasing emphasis on the design of tools and paths for numerically controlled (NC) milling machines.[1] An NC path consists of a list of tool positions and orientations which directs a milling machine to cut the desired part out of a block of material. In CIM, NC paths are generated from solid models designed with CAD systems. The path must be verified for gouging, clamp interference, speeds, feeds, depths, elapsed time, as well as whether the part is actually produced as designed. As path generation becomes more automated and less the responsibility of skilled human parts programmers, the need for verification increases.

Shaded computer graphics is central to the design of solid models, but NC paths are commonly displayed as line drawings. Line drawings don't completely describe the three-dimensional solid being milled (figure 1). Since the milling operation is equivalent to a Boolean (logical) subtraction of the tool solid from the block solid for each position of the tool along the path, constructive solid geometry (CSG) modelers, such as MAGI

Synthavision, have been used to generate shaded images of NC milling. Ray tracing is typically used as a display technique for CSG models. A ray for each pixel intersects each solid object in the scene and generates a line segment. These line segments are bounded by the points at which the ray enters and exits the objects. Boolean operations, such as subtraction for milling, can then be simply performed on these one-dimensional line segments.[2] However, in contrast to a CSG solid model, which might consist of dozens of Boolean operations between primitive solids, a typical NC path contains many hundreds of tool positions. Execution times for that number of intersection calculations are many hours on mainframe computers, especially if a continuous animation sequence of the part being milled is generated. The display of NC milling can also be implemented by the calculation of the surface intersections of the block with each position of the tool or with the swept volume of the tool path, but the number of calculations is not less than by ray tracing.

Because of the time and expense of graphical simulation, NC paths are commonly verified on an actual milling machine, using a material softer than the final product. The expense and hazard of testing on a costly production machine are undesirable, especially during the early debugging of a path or a path generation routine.

Background

The Z buffer is the most common commercial approach to the interactive shaded display of solid models. A Z buffer is an extended frame buffer. A frame buffer consists of a matrix of memory locations which refresh a raster display. Each memory location, commonly called a pixel, contains a color number. In addition to a matrix of color numbers, a Z buffer contains a corresponding matrix of Z or depth values of the nearest or visible surface at each pixel. [3] Z buffered visible surface processing is simple. Each surface element is converted into pixels with a color and a Z value, often by stepping through each X pixel for each Y line (scan conversion). Each of these pixels is conditionally written to the Z buffer if its Z value is nearer the viewpoint than the Z value of the corresponding pixel in the Z buffer. The simplicity of Z buffered visible surface processing is suitable for bit-slice microcode or hardware implementation. Because the Z buffer is basically a large memory, it benefits greatly from the continuing increases in semiconductor memory density and decreases in price.

Several graphics techniques have extended the Z buffer to include more information than depth and color at each pixel. Lucasfilm [4] maintains a list of the subpixel fragments of surfaces at each pixel for use in anti-aliasing calculations. Soft shadows are generated from a list of potentially shadowing objects at each pixel. [5] An extended depth buffer stores both a near and far depth at each pixel with a hole count and primitive identifiers for CSG modeling in the TIPS system. [6] Atherton [7] described an object buffer matrix of depth vectors for cutaway and section views, translucency, and shadows.

In these and other applications, the Z buffer is generalized from a display memory and visible surface method, to a spatial data structure which is indexed by the X and Y pixel address, and contains graphic, spatial, and modeling information. The use of spatial data structures is more common in voxel (volume cell) representations, which are often organized in octrees. [8] The ability to access model geometry with an index of a spatial location can simplify both display and intersection calculations, and polygonal data as well as solid volume elements can be organized in octree structures. [9] Ray tracing intersection calculations can be reduced by selecting probable objects to intersect from an octree structure indexed by the position of the ray. [10]

Algorithm

Real-time shaded NC milling display is accomplished with an extended Z buffer data structure. Each pixel is a rectangular solid extending along the Z axis, and consists of a near Z depth, a far Z depth, a color, and a pointer. In keeping with the convention of the names pixel and voxel, this rectangular solid is called a dexel, or depth element. The dexels are organized in an X by Y matrix called a dexel structure, which corresponds to the raster display frame buffer. Each cell in the matrix may contain one of the following: no dexel, with a background color and near Z depth of maximum Z; one dexel, with a null pointer; or more than one dexel, with a pointer to another dexel in a linked list data structure (figure 2). Multiple dexels in a cell are maintained in near to far Z order. The dexel structure is directly displayed just like an ordinary frame buffer, because the color of a dexel in the X Y matrix is the visible surface color at that pixel location.

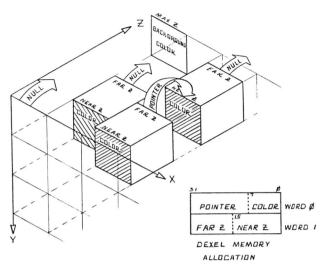

FIGURE 2

The dexel structure is created by scan conversion of surface data much like scan conversion for a conventional Z buffer, except that the Z value of the farthest surface, as well as the Z value of the nearest surface, is stored at each dexel. After scan conversion of an object, the dexel structure consists of one dimensional segments on the Z axis similar to those created by intersecting rays with objects. One dimensional Boolean operations can then be performed on these segments like those done in CSG ray tracers, but with the efficiency of the coherence of scan conversion, instead of individual ray to object intersections. Similar efficiencies have been noted in scan-line CSG algorithms. [11] For NC milling operations, cutting tools and blocks of material are often convex solids without internal concavities, so multiple dexels are created in a cell only by the cutting operation. For more general data types, scan conversion creates a linked list of surfaces in Z order at each pixel which are grouped in pairs to form dexels as a post process.

The tool is a negative solid which will be subtracted from the block or positive solid. The only difference between the tool and block dexel structures lies in the dexel color. The tool is an inverse visible surface image, in that the color of the farthest surface is stored in the dexel. The surface normals of the tool solid are inverted for shading so that they point inside the solid. When the tool is subtracted from the block, the far surface of the tool becomes the new near surface of the block, and the inversely shaded tool color is the properly shaded new block color.

The cutting procedure consists of three nested loops which step through each Y and X tool dexel, and subtract it from each block dexel in the linked list. In order to subtract an object with internal voids, a fourth loop can be added to step through the linked list of dexels in the tool. This capability would provide a general CSG subtraction operation, but it is unnecessary in NC milling display where the tool is a convex solid of revolution. The offsets in X and Y from the tool dexel to the block dexel, along with the Z offset of the tool, are three degrees of freedom in the cutting procedure. For more than three degrees of freedom, the tool dexel structure is recreated from a transformed tool surface description. Since the tool is typically small in proportion to the entire scene, and the recreation is equivalent to scan conversion, 5 or 6 axis milling can be effectively displayed.

The cutting procedure in pseudo-code (below) shows that the algorithm can be implemented in read, write, compare, and conditional branch instructions, without any geometric computation. This simplicity, and an appropriate processor with direct access to a large memory, yield real-time performance. Linked list management turns out to be a relatively small proportion of the operation, and the linked list is under 50K dexels in a typical 512 by 512 resolution display. The logical states of the operation are referenced to eight different cases (figures 3 and 4) of the intersection of two dexels.

```
procedure cut ( tool_x_min, tool_y_min, tool_x_max, tool_y_max,
                block_x_off, block_y_off, tool_z_off)
[
structure tool_dexel [
                tool_near_z, tool_far_z, tool_ptr, tool_clr ]
structure block_dexel [
                block_near_z, block_far_z, block_ptr, block_clr ]

for tool_y = tool_y_min to tool_y_max [

     for tool_x = tool_x_min to tool_x_max [

              read tool_dexel (tool_x : tool_y);
CASE 1:       if tool_near_z = background then next tool_x;

              tool_near_x += tool_z_off;
              tool_far_x += tool_z_off;
              block_ptr = tool_x = block_x_off :
                                tool_y + block_y_off;

         while block_ptr != null [

CASE 8:          read block_dexel(block_ptr);
                 if block_near_z = background then next tool_x;

CASE 2:          if tool_far_z < block_far_z [
                      if tool_far_z < block_near_z
                           then next tool_x;
CASE 3:               else if tool_near_z < block_near_z
                           then update block_near_z
                                        and block_clr;
CASE 5:               else create block_dexel;
                      next tool_x;
                      ]
                 else [
CASE 7:               if tool_near_z > block_far_z
                           then next block_ptr;
CASE 6:               else if tool_near_z > block_near_z
                           then update block_far_z;
CASE 4:               else delete block_dexel;
                      next block_ptr;
                      ]
                 ]
            ]
        ]
    ]
```

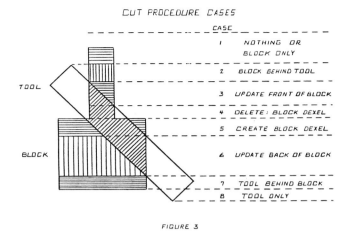

CUT PROCEDURE CASES

```
                                    CASE
                               1   NOTHING  OR
                                   BLOCK ONLY
                               2   BLOCK BEHIND TOOL
                               3   UPDATE FRONT OF BLOCK
                               4   DELETE : BLOCK DEXEL
                               5   CREATE BLOCK DEXEL
                               6   UPDATE BACK OF BLOCK
                               7   TOOL BEHIND BLOCK
                               8   TOOL ONLY
```

FIGURE 3

Implementation

The cutting operation is implemented on an Adage 3000 raster display system in Icross, a C-like microcode compiler for the Adage GPS bit-slice processor. The cutting function is a part of SOLID 3000, a set of Fortran-callable graphics functions for the solid model display [12]. A 100 by 100 pixel tool can be subtracted from a block at 10 updates per second, providing a continuous shaded animation of an NC path for a 3-axis machine. A new tool can be generated and subtracted at 2 updates per second for multiple cutters or for a 6-axis machine. Tools and blocks can be modeled with any SOLID 3000 data types, including bicubic surface patches and polygonal meshes.

Figure 5 shows a sequence of stages in the milling of a part. The path consists of 490 tool positions, which are linearly interpolated to 8179 steps. At each step, the cutting operation is invoked. The number of steps between each pair of tool positions depends on the distance between the positions and a programmable interpolation tolerance. A finer interpolation produces a smoother part, and a coarser interpolation more quickly follows the path. The part requires 7 cutter tools, each of which is converted into a dexel structure when it is specified in the path. The total time to mill the part at an interpolation tolerance of 3 screen units is 780 seconds for the 8179 steps, or slightly over 10 cutting operations per second.

Limitations

The view of the final part at the completion of the milling path cannot readily be redisplayed from another viewpoint. The milled part exists only as an image-resolution data structure, without any object-space surface description. Although voxel-based view transforms can be applied, the results are of the quality associated with voxel data, generally lower than that expected of solid model display. Shading for a new view by calculating new surface normals based on the dexel structure is much less accurate than the surface descriptions of the tool and its path. However, since the milling display runs in real-time, a new view can be generated by running the path from a different viewpoint, or running a path from multiple viewpoints in different image windows at the same time (figure 6).

The view of the final part at the completion of the milling is an image-resolution model that does not provide tolerancing verification or mass properties. The cutting function will not entirely replace object-space intersection calculations on general purpose computers, or test runs on the actual milling machine. However, it will limit those expensive operations to visually verified paths, and encourage interactive experiment and optimization to better use production resources. Image space verification on color raster displays is being developed by other researchers [13]. If a boundary model of the part is available to the user, it could be converted into a dexel structure and then intersected with the milled part in a matter of seconds.

Extensions

The visualization of voxel data is possible through ray-tracing techniques [14], and voxel data structures are used to optimize ray-tracing primitive intersection selection [15]. A straightforward extension of the dexel structure for milling changes the dexel color to a general attribute. This attribute can be the name of the primitive or element which created that dexel, such as a polygon, a surface patch, a quadratic, or the number of the tool position in the NC path. A ray-tracing display approach intersects each ray with the dexel structure and finds the object space element with which to perform a precise intersection. This approach retains the efficiency of the dexel structure and adds the capabilities of arbitrary viewing angles and precise surface verification.

Figures 7 and 8 are examples of ray-traced images of dexel structures with attributes as pointers to object-space surface elements. Figure 7 is a 426 surface patch scene, equivalent to approximately 9000 polygons, and figure 8 is a 13,500 polygon scene. The ray tracing display program includes reflection, refraction, shadows, and anti-aliasing entirely in a microcoded integer display processor. Each ray averages less than ten intersection calculations, instead of the equivalent thousands of potential intersections in the scene, because of the spatial locality of the dexel structure.

Acknowledgments

I'd like to thank Nick England of Trancept Systems for creating an environment at Adage which made this work possible, and Alan Coles of Northrop for the support and test data which made this work practical.

REFERENCES

[1] Pratt, Mike, "Interactive Geometric Modelling for CAD/CAM", Eurograph 84 course notes, 1984.

[2] Roth, S. D., "Ray Casting for Modeling Solids", Computer Graphics and Image Processing, Vol 18, 1982.

[3] Catmull, E., "Computer Display of Curved Surfaces", Proc. IEEE Conf. on Computer Graphics, Pattern Recognition, and Data Structures, May 1975, Los Angeles.

[4] Carpenter, Loren, "The A-buffer, an Antialiased Hidden Surface Method", Computer Graphics, Vol 18 No 3, July 1984, ACM, NYNY.

[5] Brotman, Lynne Shapiro, and Badler, Norman I., "Generating Soft Shadows with a Depth Buffer Algorithm", IEEE Computer Graphics and Applications, Vol 4 No 10, October 1984.

[6] Okino, Norio, et al., "Extended Depth-Buffer Algorithms for Hidden Surface Visualization", IEEE Computer Graphics and Applications, Vol 4 No 5, May 1984.

[7] Atherton, Peter R., "A Method of Interactive Visualization of CAD Surface Models on a Color Video Display", Computer Graphics, Vol 15 No 3, August 1981, ACM, NYNY.

[8] Doctor, Louis, and Torborg, John, "Display Techniques for Octree-Encoded Objects", IEEE Computer Graphics and Applications, Vol 1 No 3, July 1981.

[9] Carlbom, Ingrid, et al., "A Hierarchical Data Structure for Representing the Spatial Decomposition of 3D Objects", Computer Graphics Tokyo 84 Proceedings, April 1984, Japan Management Association, Tokyo Japan.

[10] Glassner, Andrew, "Space Subdivision for Fast Ray Tracing", IEEE Computer Graphics and Applications, Vol 4 No 10, October 1984.

[11] Atherton, Peter R., "A Scan-line Hidden Surface Removel Procedure for Constructive Solid Geometry", Computer Graphics, Vol 17 No 3, July 1983, ACM, NYNY.

[12] Van Hook, Tim, "Advanced Techniques for Solid Modeling", Computer Graphics World, Vol 7 No 11, November 1984.

[13] Oliver, James, and Goodman, Erik, "Color Graphic Verification of NC Milling Programs for Sculptured Surfaces", Proceedings of the Automotive Computer Graphics Conference, December 1985, Detroit.

[14] Schusselberg, Daniel, Smith, Wade, and Woodward, Donald, "Three-Dimensional Display of Medical Image Volumes", NCGA Conference Proceedings, May 1986, Anaheim.

[15] Fujimoto, Akira, Tanaka, Takayuki, and Iwata, Kansei, "ARTS:Accelerated Ray-Tracing System", IEEE Computer Graphics and Applications, Vol 6 No 10, April 1986.

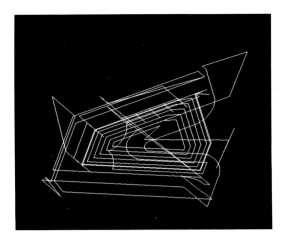

[1] An NC milling path displayed with lines connecting tool positions. Data courtesy of Northrop Corporation.

[4] The relation between a block of material and a cutting tool at one tool position. The block and tool as solid objects (left), the subtraction of the tool from the block (right), and the cutting operation for that subtraction (bottom).

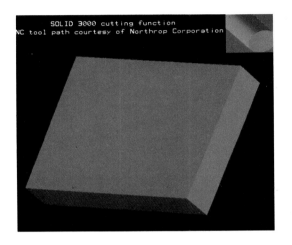

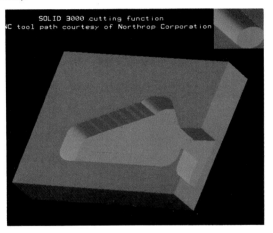

[5] A sequence of positions in the real-time shaded display of a solid model being milled. Data courtesy of Northrop Corporation.

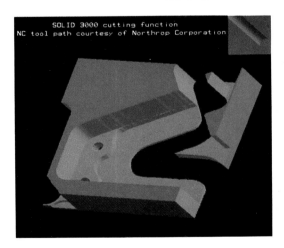

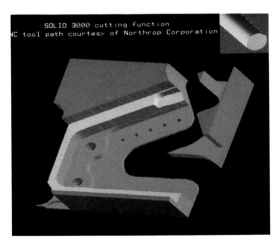

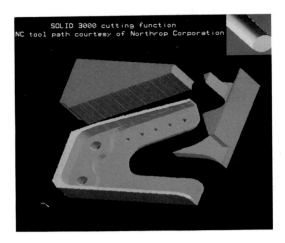

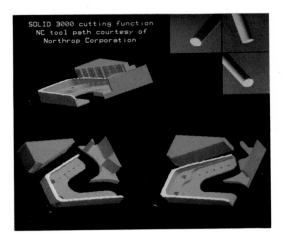

[6] Simultaneous milling display from multiple viewpoints. Data courtesy of Northrop Corporation.

[7] Ray traced display of dexel structure. Bicubic patch data courtesy of PDA Engineering.

[8] Ray traced display of dexel structure. CAM-I test part data courtesy of Matra Datavision.

A Differential Compiler for Computer Animation

Michel J. Denber
Xerox Corp.
800 Phillips Rd.
Webster, N.Y. 14580

Paul M. Turner
Consultant
287 Ravenwood Ave.
Rochester, N.Y. 14619

Abstract

A program for the real-time display of computer animation on a bit-mapped raster display is presented. The differential compiler performs temporal domain image data compression using frame replenishment coding on successive frames of animation stored in memory as bitmaps and saves only the differences. A small run-time interpreter then retrieves and displays the differences in real-time to create the animated effect. This results in a significant reduction in storage requirements, and allows animation on general purpose computers which would otherwise be too slow or have insufficient memory. Frame creation is both device and method independent. An animation environment supports interactive editing capabilities, reconstructing any arbitrary desired frame for later modification. Frames can be added, modified, or deleted, and the animated sequence can be viewed at any point during the session. The compiler is automatically called as needed; its operation is transparent to the user. The compiler is decribed in detail, both in terms of data compression and the requirements of interactive animation editing.

CR Categories and Subject Headings: I.3.2 [Graphics Systems]; I.3.3 [Picture/Image Generation]; I.3.4 [Graphics Utilities]; I.4.2 [Image Processing - Compression (coding)]; J.5 [Arts and Humanities]
General Terms: Computer Graphics, Animation
Additional Keywords and Phrases: Real-time animation, Storage compression techniques, Interactive systems, Picture editing, Raster displays

Introduction

Animation is the creation of the illusion of movement from a series of static images. If the images are displayed rapidly enough, the result is perceived as motion due to the factor of persistence of vision of the human eye. The smoothness of motion is determined both by the frame rate (the number of complete images presented to the viewer per second) and the relative velocity of objects moving in the image. Flicker results from an insufficient frame rate, although it can be aggravated by various psychological and physiological factors [7].

Traditional animation was done by drawing and painting individual images on celluloid sheets or cels, and then photographing each drawing one at a time on movie film. The amount of effort that goes into the creation of a feature-length animated film is difficult to comprehend. The nature and number of repetitive tasks involved make animation an ideal application for computerization [3]. However, although computers have eased the burden of certain administrative and bookkeeping tasks in traditional animation, animation by computer presents a variety of new problems related to image data storage requirements and user interaction [21].

There are two main types of 2-D computer animation: character (or cartoon) animation, and modelled (or object-oriented) animation [11]. *Character* animation systems duplicate traditional animation steps on a computer and provide in addition certain features such as editing and pencil test (animation preview) facilities. However, the actual creation of the animated movement is left up to the operator of the system, thus much of the work of traditional animation remains. Some systems have features to do automatic inbetweening (missing frame interpolation), given two key frames [17]. However, inbetweening is a difficult problem in itself and no fully general solution presently exists.

Object-oriented systems shift the burden of motion generation to the computer itself. The animation is controlled in two main ways, either procedurally or "by example". In *procedural animation*, a program (often using a special animation language) generates the desired motion analytically. Although this eliminates the need for moving objects by hand, it requires the ability to describe the motion to the computer. The animator has in effect become a programmer. Many existing systems in fact take this approach [6, 9, 15, 19]. However, it is difficult to describe complex motions (such as human movement) procedurally.

Animation by example is a technique in which the motion is shown to the computer, for example by tracing a trajectory with a mouse or touch screen [14]. The computer then stores the trajectory for subsequent playback. This method is limited by the amount of detail which can be presented to the computer.

Real-time display

Once an animated sequence has been created, it can be displayed either in *real-time* or *off-line*. In off-line display, each frame is recorded on film or video tape for later viewing. In real-time display, the animation is shown directly by the computer. Real-time raster-based display creates space and time problems. Consider space: a modest one-minute film at 24 frames per second using 512 x 512 x 1 bit frames uses more than 47 million bytes of storage. Consider time: each frame (32K bytes) must be retrieved and displayed in 1/24th second (a data rate of over 6 million bits per second). Even recently, real-time raster display has been considered infeasible [13].

A number of different approaches have been taken in the past to achieve real-time display. Generally, special-purpose hardware is used [2], or some form of image data compression is performed in order to relieve the burden on memory size and bandwidth. Sometimes clever use can be made of hardware originally designed for other purposes to achieve limited animation as in the method of color-map cycling [20]. Some graphics terminals have features, such as pan or zoom registers that can be used for limited animation. Some systems use *feature coding* (higher level object-oriented representations which make use of knowledge about objects in a scene) [10]. Image data compression typically is performed on individual frames using techniques from the field of signal processing such as run coding, predictive coding, or pulse-code modulation [18].

Data compression is attractive in principle but is difficult to achieve in practice because it requires the system to restore each compressed frame in the available inter-frame interval (typically 1/24th or 1/30th second). This is a serious problem because many image data compression algorithms are quite expensive computationally. The linear transformation with the smallest mean-square error of all (the Karhunen-Loeve transform), for instance, requires computation proportional to N^4 for an N x N image [16]. Faster transforms (such as the Fourier) operate at the expense of accuracy of image reconstruction, and still require considerable computation. Even simple techniques such as run-length encoding may be too slow, depending on image complexity.

Our animation system is based on a temporal domain data compression technique known as *frame replenishment coding* [18]. Just as spatial image data compression takes advantage of the high degree of spatial similarity in local picture regions, we take advantage of the statistical redundancy between successive frames of animation. On average, this redundancy is high since it is a requirement for achieving the illusion of smooth movement.

The system consists of three parts: an *animation environment*, the *differential compiler* and a *real-time interpreter*. The animation environment provides the user with a variety of paint and editing tools. The real-time interpreter displays the animation. The focus of this paper is on the operation of the remaining element, the differential compiler.

Compiler Implementation

To achieve sustained real-time raster display, our system uses a *differential compiler* to perform temporal domain encoding of animation image data. Rather than save each entire frame as it is created, the compiler saves only the differences between frames. Our system is unusual in that it implements frame difference (or inter-frame) compression on bitmap images using only bit-level operations. The entire system is written in Interlisp-D (a window-based Interlisp implementation developed by Xerox Corp.).

The differential compiler does not compile a language, although it has features similar to a traditional compiler. The compiler consists of two main parts: a *comparison* phase and a *merging* phase. In the comparison phase, the differences between an input frame and its predecessor are computed. For example, Figure 1 shows a box which has moved down between frames 1 and 2. The differences between these two frames are shown in the frame labelled D. The open rectangle in D is an area which has been erased and the solid rectangle is an area which has been added.

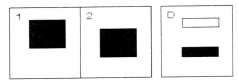

Figure 1: The difference (D) between frames 1 and 2.

Only the regions where the two frames differ are saved; the original frames are discarded. Then in the merging phase, the saved difference-regions are combined by merging adjacent regions into one. Merging these regions simplifies the operation of the run-time interpreter.

Frame comparison

In the comparison phase, the compiler traverses both frames looking for differences. (The compiler can deal with frames of any size, however, all frames in a given sequence must be the same size). The comparison is done in *primitive blocks* 16 bits wide to take advantage of the 16 bit word size of the machine. There is little point in trying to identify changes at the individual pixel level when we can process sixteen pixels at once for the same cost. Also, *bitblt* (the *bit block transfer* instruction, described in appendix B) works faster when transferring bitmaps to a destination that is aligned on full word boundaries. The height of each primitive block can in theory be set to any value; we use 16, producing square blocks. This simplifies the merging process described in the next section.

When a difference is noted, the block and its location are added to a list of changes for this frame. This process continues for the entire bitmap. At the end, this *change list* may contain hundreds of primitive blocks identifying the locations of changes in the two frames. This is sufficient to establish the frame differences, but it is inefficient to reconstruct the frame this way because the set-up time required by *bitblt* is independent of the size of the bitmap being transferred to the display. (Appendix B shows the relationship between bitmap size and display time.) To minimize overhead, the frame comparison is followed by a process that merges primitive blocks into larger bitmaps.

Primary merging

This merging operation is done in two steps: *primary* and *secondary* merging. Primary merging finds primitive blocks which are immediately adjacent to each other either horizontally or vertically; these are merged into one larger rectangular *merged-block* (Figure 2).

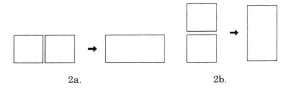

2a. 2b.

Figure 2: Primary merging of horizontally (2a) and vertically (2b) adjacent blocks.

It is always advantageous to do this since displaying one rectangular bitmap saves the additional overhead that would be required to display its component sub-rectangles individually.

Figure 3: Merging order of primitive blocks.

In actual operation, the compiler performs primary merging in two passes. It merges all horizontally adjacent blocks first. Then it merges as many blocks as possible vertically. In Figure 3, blocks *a* and *b* would be merged first. This order minimizes *bitblt* scanline overhead. Block *ab* takes less time to display than block *ac*, although both contain the same number of bits, because *ab* contains fewer scan lines. When as many adjacent primitive blocks as possible have been combined, the compiler does secondary merging. Figure 4 illustrates primary merging on a more complex image [5]. To demonstrate the segmentation and merging process, we assume that the entire image in 4a is to be considered changed, as it would if it followed a blank frame. In 4b, the primitive blocks are identified. In 4c, they are merged horizontally, and in 4d they are merged vertically.

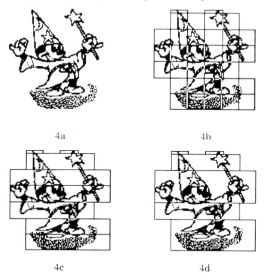

4a   4b

4c   4d

Figure 4: Primary merging of primitve blocks.

Secondary merging

Primary merging greatly reduces the number of blocks on the change list (in Figure 4, it goes from 33 to 6). However, depending on the complexity of the image, we sometimes still end up with more blocks than could be displayed in the time available between frames. This is tested by doing a "trial blt" of the change list. The list is "displayed" to an off-screen buffer with a timer running. If the display time exceeds the inter-frame time, the change list contains too many bitmaps.

Secondary merging is used in this case to further reduce the number of bitmaps which have to be displayed. This can only be done at the expense of including regions of no change between the two frames being compiled. For example, the three blocks from Figure 3 are reduced to two in primary merging. How could we merge these two blocks ab and c, into one new larger "superblock"? Recall that primitive blocks represent areas of change. If we are willing to include the corner represented by the dotted line in Figure 5b, we could produce a single block (bitmaps always have to be rectangular). The disadvantage is that this new block represents a decrease in compression efficiency, since one quarter of it (the dotted area) is a region in which no changes occurred between frames.

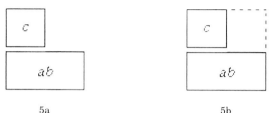

5a   5b

Figure 5: Secondary merging of ab with c.

To measure compression efficiency, we define an efficiency term e, as

$$e = N_p / S_b \, ,$$

where N_p is the number of primitive blocks in a block and S_b is the total size (in multiples of primitive blocks) of the block.

The primitive blocks a, b, and c from Figure 3 all have $e = 1.0$ by definition. Since merged-blocks are assumed to be maximally compressed (they are the result of directly combining primitive blocks), block ab also has an e of 1.0. Merging ab with c yields a superblock with an e of 0.75 (because it is made up of three primitive blocks, plus the space of a fourth).

The efficiency factor e is used to control secondary merging, by indicating which blocks are suitable candidates for merging. The user can change the default threshold for e (0.5) at any time. Setting it to 1.0 results in no secondary merging taking place (since each block then has to be composed entirely of primitive blocks), while an e of 0.0 would cause every block to be merged together into one superblock equal to the original bitmap (all blocks are candidates for merging).

Figures 6a and 6b show two frames of a more complex image. The animation involves Alice going "through the looking glass" [4] and in Figure 6b, her arm begins to fade from view as she reaches through the mirror. The differences (the compressed representation of 6b) are shown in Figure 6c.

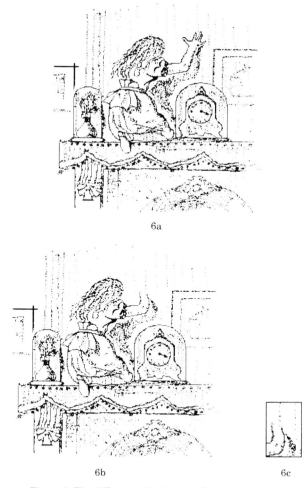

6a

6b   6c

Figure 6: The difference (6c) between frames 6a and 6b.

How merging works

Although it is conceptually simple, the actual process of finding an optimal secondary merging strategy for blocks is very difficult. It is in fact NP-complete, being an instance of the rectilinear picture compression problem [8]. Our approach to secondary merging is essentially a best-fit algorithm. Starting with the change list of all merged-blocks remaining after primary merging, each block is compared to every other block. The pair of blocks with the largest e value is selected for merging. The resulting superblock is added to the change list and the two original blocks are discarded. If no combination can be found satisfying the desired compression efficiency, the current block is assumed to be unmergable (isolated too far from any other block) and is removed from further consideration.

As blocks are merged, the change list is updated to reflect the locations of the new superblocks formed, as well as their efficiencies for use in any further merging required. When no more merging is possible (because the e would drop too low), the compilation is complete. The compiler returns the change list which is saved along with a tag identifying the frame from which it was derived. Although secondary merging is the most time-consuming part of the compiler, the overhead is distributed by being performed immediately as each frame is completed. It can be further reduced by executing the merge phase as a separate process which proceeds in parallel with picture editing, which is largely I/O bound.

Playback

When the user is ready to run the animation, the run-time interpreter is called. It uses the change list created by the compiler for each successive frame, copying the appropriate superblocks into the specified locations in the animation window.

A delay mechanism is applied in the display process to those frames which are displayed in less time than the desired inter-frame interval, to obtain a constant frame rate. Optionally, the user may specify a greater or lesser delay for individual frames. This is used for example, to display a title frame where it is desired to leave a static image visible for several seconds or to allow time for a narration. In conventional animation, the same frame is repeated on the film as long as necessary. Since there are no differences, the run-time interpreter uses the delay loop to achieve the same effect. In this case the subsequent identical frames require no storage at all.

There is a clear division of labor between compression and decompression in this system. Because of the real-time requirements of playback, the run-time interpreter is designed to be as simple as possible. All of the complexity is placed in the compiler, which has more time available for execution. Appendix A gives a pseudo-code description of the compiler in an Algol-like language.

The Animation Environment

The animation environment is the system's user interface. We discuss it here in the context of user interface problems in relation to the compiler. For example, it is important to maintain a "virtual frame illusion" for the user. That is, the system should present the illusion that the animated sequence being created consists of a series of full frames that can be accessed at any time for subsequent editing. Of course, the system has really only saved lists of differences between frames. This creates a problem in reconstructing an arbitrary frame in a given sequence.

Maintaining consistency

How then, do we deal with editing operations? When the user wants to view a particular frame, the run-time interpreter is called. It "plays back" the sequence from the beginning at high speed without displaying it, until the desired frame is reached. The user sees only one frame appear. It is now easy to modify that frame. Any of a number of different graphics tools can be called to make whatever changes are needed. When the changes are complete, the compiler takes the changed frame and its immediate predecessor and recompiles the changed frame, overwriting its previous definition. Then it recompiles the changed frame's successor.

As an example of this process, consider Figure 7, which shows a simple five-frame animation sequence of a bouncing ball.

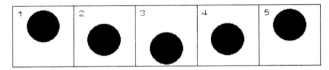

Figure 7: A bouncing ball.

Suppose we want this to be a rubber ball, and decide to change frame 3 to make the ball squash out on impact with the ground. Figure 8 shows the desired result.

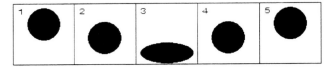

Figure 8: A bouncing ball, with squash.

Using the editor, we display frame 3 and modify the ball. The editor also saves adjacent frames 2 and 4 in their decompressed form. Frame 3 is then recompiled against frame 2 to link it back into the sequence. Now frame 4 is compiled against the modified frame 3, yielding a new change list for frame 4. It is important to note that the "buck stops here." *It is not necessary to recompile frame 5 against frame 4.* This is often a source of confusion for the casual observer, who might assume that since each frame is derived from its predecessor, a change in any frame means that all subsequent frames have to be recompiled. It is obvious that editing frame 3 means that it will have to be recompiled. It is not so obvious that by *then* recompiling frame 4, the entire sequence is once again consistent.

Because the time needed to recreate a frame is directly proportional to its distance from the start of a sequence, it is desirable in long sequences to cache certain checkpoint frames at regular intervals (for example, every 500 frames). This cache does not have to be saved with the sequence; it can be created at the beginning of an edit session and discarded upon completion. The system keeps the full definition of cached frames; then it is only necessary to back up to the last checkpoint to reconstruct a particular frame for editing.

Frame editing

The animation environment provides several different editing operations on frames. Frames may be changed, added, deleted, or copied. Copying is the default operation when creating a new frame. The system copies the previous frame so that the user can make changes while maintaining overall image registration. New frames can be created in any order. It is sometimes desirable to create frames in reverse order. For example, the user may want to show an object in the foreground moving to reveal a scene in the background. Rather than draw in the background elements revealed by the moving foreground object with each new frame, it is easier to draw the last frame containing the background first, and then move the foreground object backwards, gradually obscuring the background. Then each preceding frame can be generated simply by moving the object and erasing the part of the background newly obscured. Also, it is sometimes useful to be able to copy a previous frame into a later position. From the user's point of view, these operations are similar to those in text editing.

The frame-difference technique lends itself well to modular design. In particular, the choice of input medium can be left up to the designer or user of the system. It makes no difference to the compiler how the image to be compiled was created, as long as it is placed in the frame window. In our system, the user can draw with the mouse or graphics tablet, or use images retrieved from an optical scanner.

A good user interface should provide helpful feedback. This is especially important in animation where the motion must be built up from a series of static images. In our system, the user can do a pencil test at any time during the editing session (although only in a forward direction). The entire sequence or any part of it can be played back, either once or in a loop.

Results

Frame rate

One important measure of a real-time animation system is how fast it can display animation. Unfortunately the definition of "frame rate" becomes somewhat blurred in a system which uses data compression. A motion picture projector always displays discrete frames at a constant rate as complete images on film. However, our system uses a varying length of time to reconstruct frames, depending on the size of their change lists, and may leave each frame visible for varying times (as set by the user). Our "frame rate" is bounded by the time needed for the interpreter to display change lists. For example, for a rate equivalent to 24 distinct frames per second, the interpreter has 1/24th second to put up all of the differences between the current frame and the next one. This "frame rate" can be changed by adjusting the delay between frames. Consider the technique of "shooting on twos", that is, repeating each frame twice to reduce the number of drawings that have to be made. In our system, this is accomplished simply by doubling the frame delay time.

The frame rate of our system then depends on the complexity of the change-list plus the overhead of the run-time interpreter itself. This overhead is given by the formula:

$$o_{rti} = (t_f - N_k * t_k) / N_k$$

where t_f is the inter-frame time, N_k is the number of bitmaps of size k the interpreter can display in time t_f, and t_k is the time *bitblt* takes to display one bitmap of size k.

For example, by running a timer we find that the interpreter can display 27 16 x 16 bitmaps in 1/24 sec. (41.7 msec.). Since *bitblt* alone takes 1.48 msec. to display a 16 x 16 bitmap, we find o_{rti} = (41.7 - 27 * 1.48) / 27 = 64.4 μsec. per bitmap per frame. This figure is independent of the size or number of bitmaps in the change list.

The general frame rate is then simply

$$r = 1 / (o_{rti} * n + \sum_{i=1}^{n} t_i)$$

where *n* is the number of bitmaps in the change list and t_i is the time it takes to *bitblt* the *n*th bitmap. From this one can find the upper bound on frame rate, which would result from displaying a change list containing a single 16 x 1 bitmap (the smallest possible block). *Bitblt* transfers this bitmap in 1.21 msec., therefore, r_{max} = 1 / (0.064 + 1.21) = 0.785, or 785 frames per second. A more typical example is Figure 8, which can be run at up to 139 frames per second.

Data rate

Also of interest is the maximum amount of data which can be displayed per frame. This depends not only on the number of bitmaps in the change list, but also on their shape, because of the set-up time per scan line associated with *bitblt*. Assuming as an average, a square shape, in 41.7 msec. the interpreter can display a bitmap of size 445 x 445. This is an area approximately 1/4 the size of the screen of an 1108 (1024 x 808) and is the upper bound on frame size in the limit case where every pixel is changed between frames (a very rare occurrence). In practice, the order of primary merging causes the compiler to generate more wide blocks (which can be displayed faster) than tall blocks.

The exact amount of compression obtained depends on the complexity of the motion within the scene being animated. Complexity here refers to the degree of redundancy between successive frames, rather than the analytical description of the motion itself. On average, this complexity is directly proportional to the spatial complexity of the individual images, because of their lower spatial correlation. For simple animation the savings can be very large. For example, the original frame size of the five frame sequence in Figure 8. was 400 x 300 pixels (15,000 bytes), for a total size of 75,000 bytes. After compiling with a 0.5 efficiency, the compressed sequence used 15,255 bytes, an 80% reduction. For a longer sequence of 125 frames (frame size = 400 x 225 pixels), the full frame representation used 1.4 megabytes; the compressed version (0.5 efficiency) used 85,636 bytes, a 94% savings.

The total length of animation possible is limited by the hardware. For example, on an 1108 with 3.5 Mb. of real memory, assuming 500 bytes per frame, and allowing 1/2 Mb. for system code, one could display 6291 frames, or 4.16 minutes at 24 fps. If we include the maximum virtual memory size of 32 Mb., less 8 Mb. for system code, we could display an additional 50,331 frames, although the maximum frame rate would be lower due to swapping considerations.

Compilation time

The length of time it takes to compile a frame is proportional to the complexity of the changes between the two frames being compared, not necessarily the complexity of the images themselves. For example, the bouncing ball in Figure 8 took 3.8 seconds per frame to compile. Figure 9 shows a six frame cycle of a dancer performing a fouette [12]. This used 25.9 seconds per frame.

Figure 9: A fouette turn.

Conclusions

Frame difference data compression can be used to make animation possible on a general purpose computer. It is attractive because, by using *bitblt*, the total time for compression and decompression can be largely shifted to the compression phase, making it possible to restore the images quickly.

This project demonstrates several basic programming principles of particular interest to graphics programmers:

1. *When time is limited, shift the execution burden to a less critical section.* The operation of the run-time interpreter was kept as simple as possible by having the compiler do the hard work. This leaves free cycles for the later addition of new features which might need to be done at run-time.

2. *Use parallelism wisely.* Bitblt is a powerful operation for moving large areas of memory within the computer with a single instruction. However, the straight-forward use of *bitblt* to do animation by superimposing whole frames is wasteful of space.

3. *Demonstrating is better than calculating.* To decide if secondary merging is required, we initially thought to calculate the time required from the change list to see if it is less than the interframe interval. However, it is simpler to actually do a trial display of the frame to a scratch area, running a timer on it. Having the computer do this work provides an existence proof that the frame can or cannot be reconstructed in the required interval, and is less work than calculating the expected display time from a formula. This method automatically accounts for different processor speeds, future microcode upgrades, etc.

The system is still under active development. Several optimizations can be made to the code. For example, *bitblt* is a complex instruction that handles many special cases, most of which are not used for animation display. We could increase the display rate by using a customized *bitblt* without the special case code. Greater space compression could be obtained by applying simple image processing techniques to the images before being compared. For example, the inputs could be low-pass filtered, reducing the contribution of isolated pixels.

Two new features need to be added to make the system easier to use. The first is to allow cels to exist on multiple planes, as in traditional animation. The second is to add object-oriented animation to the environment. Objects present a challenge to the animation compiler because they reflect a fundamentally different paradigm. The motion of an object in a scene is a property of the object itself. Objects move independently without regard to the fact that the system views the animation as a series of frames. In order to determine where an object would appear in a particular frame, the compiler has to execute the motion assigned to the object and calculate its location based on its speed.

The system as currently implemented has been used successfully by professional technical illustrators who were not familiar with programming or with the Interlisp-D environment. They were able to produce drawings using the paint portion of the system after about a half hour of familiarization under the guidance of one of the implementors, and created simple animated sequences in less than two hours.

Although the frame difference technique has disadvantages, we have shown that it can be used to create a viable animation tool on a computer which would otherwise be unable to support animation of such complexity. The versatile programming environment provided by Interlisp-D was of great help in programming our system. The use of powerful interactive languages including Lisp and Smalltalk is still relatively uncommon in computer animation [1, 18]. We believe that the advantages to the programmer are significant, especially where extensive user interaction is required.

Acknowledgements

The authors gratefully acknowledge the valuable technical comments and suggestions offered by Jules Bloomenthal, Xerox PARC, and the Siggraph reviewers. Bill Anderson, Xerox Webster, was of great help in editing the paper. Dave Ingalls, Xerox Webster, helped out with implementation issues and integrated the system into Trillium, a user-interface design tool developed by Austin Henderson at PARC. I want to thank Chris Brown, University of Rochester Computer Science Dept., for sharing his insight and enthusiasm for computer graphics. Finally, special thanks to Jim Iverson, Xerox Webster, for his continuing support and encouragement of our work, which made it all possible.

Appendix A: Compiler pseudocode

The compiler takes two bitmaps BM_1 and BM_2, a maximum inter-frame time t_i, and a user-set efficiency threshold u, and returns the compressed representation of BM_2 in the change list L.

```
L ← empty-list ;
begin "scan and save differences "
   for Y from 1 to bitmap-height by 16 (ie. block height) do
      for X from 1 to bitmap-width by 16 do
         get a 16 x 16 block B₁ at X,Y from BM₁ ;
         get a 16 x 16 block B₂ at X,Y from BM₂ ;
         if B₁ ≠ B₂ then add B₂ to change list L ;
      end "for x" ;
   end "for y" ;
end "scan and save differences" ;
begin "combine regions (merge phase)"
   begin "primary merge"
      for i from 1 to length L - 1 do
         if block Bᵢ in L is horizontally adjacent to Bᵢ₊₁ then
            replace Bᵢ and Bᵢ₊₁ with Bᵢ ← Bᵢ + Bᵢ₊₁ ;
      end "for i" ;
      for i from 1 to length L - 1 do
         if block Bᵢ in L is vertically adjacent to Bᵢ₊₁ then
            replace Bᵢ and Bᵢ₊₁ with Bᵢ ← Bᵢ + Bᵢ₊₁ ;
      end "for i" ;
   end "primary merge" ;
   timer-count ← timer ("display" (off-screen) the blocks in L) ;
   if timer-count > inter-frame time tᵢ then

   until no space-efficient blocks can be formed do "secondary
      merge"
      for i from 1 to length L do
         for j from 1 to length L when i ≠ j do
            if Bᵢ + Bⱼ is the most efficient combination so far
                  then Bₘₐₓ ← Bᵢ + Bⱼ ;
         end "for j" ;
      end "for i" ;
      if e (efficiency factor) of Bₘₐₓ > user-set threshold u then
            replace Bᵢ and Bⱼ in L with Bᵢ ← Bᵢ + Bⱼ ;
   end "secondary merge" ;
end "combine regions (merge phase)" ;
Attach a default frame delay time (0) to L ;
return L.
```

Notes: The "sum" $B_i + B_j$ is the smallest bounding rectangular block around B_i and B_j. Loop indices (such as "length L") are recomputed each time through the loop.

Appendix B: Speed of bitblt

Bitblt is short for *bit block transfer*. This instruction treats memory as rectangular blocks and moves blocks of any size to any location. If the destination corresponds to the machine's display memory, an image will appear on the screen. The user can specify how the source and destination bits should be logically combined before being displayed. This gives the effect of replacement, erasure, addition, or inversion of pixels.

The Xerox 1108 has a 17 inch bit-mapped raster display with a resolution of 1024 x 808 pixels. The following timings were obtained using *bitblt* to transfer various word-aligned bitmaps into a window on the display in *replace* mode:

time (*msec.*)	bitmap size (bits w x h)
0.70	0 x 0
1.48	16 x 16
3.01	64 x 64
16.9	256 x 256
1.21	16 x 1
1.26	256 x 1
4.95	1 x 256
1.54	32 x 16
1.78	16 x 32

References

1. Baecker, Ronald M., "A conversational extensible system for the animation of shaded images", *Computer Graphics* (Proc. Siggraph 76), **10**:2, 1976, 32-39

2. Baecker, Ronald M., "Digital video display systems and dynamic graphics", *Computer Graphics* (Proc. Siggraph 79), **13**:2, Aug. 1979, 48-56

3. Catmull, Edwin, "The problems of computer-assisted animation", *Computer Graphics* (Proc. Siggraph 78), **12**:3, July 1978, 348-353

4. Carroll, Lewis, *The Annotated Alice*, World Publishing Co., New York, 1960, p. 184 (illustration by John Tenniel).

5. Disney, Walter, *Fantasia*, 1940. Drawing digitized and then modified from a frame in the "Sorcerer's Apprentice" section of this film.

6. Feiner, S., D. Salesin, T. Banchoff, "Dial: a diagrammatic animation language", *IEEE Computer Graphics and Applications*, **2**:7, Sept. 1982, 43-53

7. Fox, David, Mitchell Waite, *Computer Animation Primer*, McGraw-Hill, New York, 1984

8. Garey, Michael R., David S. Johnson, *Computers and Intractability: A Guide to the Theory of NP-Completeness*, W.H. Freeman & Co., San Francisco, 1979

9. Kahn, Kenneth M., "An Actor-based computer animation language", *Proc. ACM-SIGGRAPH Workshop on User-Oriented Design of Computer Graphics Systems*, Pittsburgh, Pa., Oct. 1976

10. Karshmer, Arthur I., "A motion directed picture segmentation system to support network graphics applications", *Proc. 1979 IEEE Computer Society Conference on Pattern Recognition and Image Processing*, Aug. 1979, 630-637

11. Lansdown, R.J., "Computer animation: A concise review", *Computer Graphics 82, Proceedings of the Online Conference*, 1982, 279-290

12. Laws, Kenneth, "Physics and dance", *American Scientist*, **73**:5, Sept.-Oct. 1985, 426-431. Drawings digitized from photographs by Martha Swope of Lisa de Ribere.

13. Magnenat-Thalmann, Nadia, Daniel Thalmann, *Computer Animation: Theory and Practice*, Springer-Verlag, Tokyo, 1985

14. Minsky, Margaret R., "Manipulating simulated objects with real-world gestures using a force and position sensitive screen", *Computer Graphics* (Proc. Siggraph 84), **18**:3, July 1984, 195-203

15. O'Donnell, T.J., Arthur J. Olson, "GRAMPS: A graphical language interpreter for real-time, interactive, three-dimensional picture editing and animation", *Computer Graphics* (Proc. Siggraph 81), **15**:3, Aug. 1981, 133-142

16. Oppenheim, Alan V., ed., *Applications of Digital Signal Processing*, Prentice-Hall, Englewood Cliffs, N.J., 1978

17. Palyka, Duane M., "A brief description of an inbetween system (using drawings by Francis Glebas)", NYIT CGL, July 1983, in *Siggraph 84 Animation Tutorial Notes*, 82-87

18. Pratt, William K., *Digital Image Processing*, John Wiley & Sons, New York, 1978

19. Reynolds, Craig W., "Computer animation with Scripts and Actors", *Computer Graphics* (Proc. Siggraph 82), **16**:3, July 1982, 289-296

20. Shoup, Richard G., "Color table animation", *Computer Graphics* (Proc. Siggraph 79), **13**:2, Aug. 1979, 8-13

21. Thomas, Frank, "Can classic Disney animation be duplicated on the computer?", *Computer Pictures*, July/Aug. 1984, 20-26

Image Rendering by Adaptive Refinement

Larry Bergman, Henry Fuchs, Eric Grant
University of North Carolina at Chapel Hill

Susan Spach
Hewlett-Packard Laboratories
Palo Alto, California

Abstract

This paper describes techniques for improving the performance of image rendering on personal workstations by using CPU cycles going idle while the user is examining a static image on the screen. In that spirit, we believe that *a renderer's work is never done*. Our goal is to convey the most information to the user as early as possible, with image quality constantly improving with time. We do this by first generating a crude image rapidly and then adaptively refining it where necessary as long as the user does not change viewing parameters. The renderer operates in a succession of phases, first displaying only vertices of polygons, next polygon edges, then flat shading polygons, then shadowing polygons, then Gouraud shading polygons, then Phong shading polygons, and finally anti-aliasing. Performance is enhanced by each phase using results from previous phases and trimming the amount of data needed by the next phase. In this way, only a fraction of the pixels in an image may be Phong shaded while the rest may be Gouraud or flat shaded. Similarly anti-aliasing is performed only on pixels around which there is significant color change. The system features fast response to user intervention, encourages user intervention at any moment, and makes useful the idle cycles in a personal computer.

CR Categories and Subject Descriptors: I.3.3 [Computer Graphics]: Picture/Image Generation -- Display algorithms, I.3.7 [Computer Graphics]: Three-Dimensional Graphics and Realism -- Visible line/surface algorithms,

General Terms: algorithms, computer graphics,

Additional Keywords: image synthesis, 3-D rendering, hidden-surface elimination, interaction, anti-aliasing.

1. Introduction

Computer image generation algorithms can be divided roughly into two application areas: interactive and non-interactive. Non-interactive algorithms typically generate high-quality still images or animated sequences, whereas interactive algorithms seek to generate the image in near real-time. In this paper we describe algorithms which unify the two approaches: the best possible image is generated subject to the near real-time constraint, but the image improves with time to a level of quality usually not found in interactive applications.

This paper describes an implementation of a general purpose polygon-based renderer with the above goals. We use the term *refinement* to indicate that the image is constantly being improved, and *adaptive* to indicate that the improvement adapts to the particular nature of the image -- the polygons and pixel locations whose further processing is likely to make the greatest improvement in the picture quality. We have at this time only heuristic measures of picture quality, but hope that the techniques described in this paper will apply even more dramatically with more precise measures of image quality.

2. Related Work

Progressive Transmission of Images

A number of researchers [SLOAN79,KNOWLTON80,HILL83] have addressed the problem of transmitting images over low bandwidth lines. Images are encoded and transmitted so that the user first sees a rough, low resolution representation of the complete image. As time passes, the image is refined until the source image is seen. The user may abort transmission at any time. This provides an efficient means for browsing through an image database.

Our research shares a similar goal: to convey the most information as early as possible, with image quality improving in time. Instead of starting with a complete image at the far end of a communication channel, however, we start with a scene description (e.g., a collection of polygons) and must generate the final image.

Level of Detail Management

The time required to render an image is related to the complexity of the scene description. Two methods have been used to control the size of the rendered data set.

The first method is to generate adaptively the scene description at image generation time based on constraints. Subdivision algorithms [CATMULL74, LANE80, FOURNIER82] are examples of procedure models whose output varies based on view information.

The second method is to store a hierarchy of object descriptions, and choose the most appropriate representation at display time. Clark [CLARK76] recognized the value of this approach, which apparently had been used in flight simulators for many years.

The flight simulator application, however, differs from our application in at least two significant ways. Designing a database for a flight simulator is a one-time task, hence it is reasonable to hand-tune a database. Secondly, many of the objects are procedurally modeled, and can be generated to varying levels of detail by varying the parameters of a single procedure. Medical imaging, one of our applications, must often deal with new data sets that are not procedurally modeled, such as models reconstructed from CT scans. It is possible to generate less detailed versions of these data sets as a post-process [MACDOUGAL84], but in general this is a more difficult problem than generating these versions at original object-definition time (such as with data sets for flight simulators).

Oct-trees [HUNTER78, JACKINS80, MEAGHER80, SAMET84], because of their natural hierarchy, are well-suited for rendering at various levels of refinement; rendering can take place to the desired level of definition. Although we might explore oct-trees for some of our medical applications, we have found polygonal surface representations to be more compact than oct-trees; they also allow very high quality rendering directly.

Multiple Pass Refinement

There are undoubtedly hundreds of implementations of what we will call the two pass approach. In the two pass approach, the user initially manipulates a crude (typically wire-frame) representation of the object and selects a particular view. A more time-consuming, high quality rendering of the scene is then performed. A problem with this approach is that the crude representation may not provide enough information for positioning. Moreover, the higher quality rendering must usually complete in a reasonable amount of time, and hence is frequently not chosen to be of the highest quality possible. The quality levels are determined *a priori* by the graphics system implementor. We prefer to let the user determine when the image is sufficiently detailed.

Forrest [FORREST85] proposed a system with a predefined number of quality levels. A scene is first rendered at level zero, the lowest quality level. If the scene parameters do not change, the scene is then progressively rendered at levels one, two, and so forth. He noted that in some cases the higher levels can be achieved with a small amount of additional computation. The first three of his five quality levels for lines are 1) whatever the hardware can draw, 2) anti-aliased lines without readback, 3) anti- aliased lines with readback. He noted that for smooth-shaded 3-D objects anti-aliasing is needed only in silhouette edges. In addition, he presented a fact that forms a foundation for our work; if the user is working on a personal workstation, there is no reason not to take advantage of idle CPU cycles to improve the quality of the image. We are extending this approach to allow automatically a continuum of quality levels without user definition, to allow efficient image improvement by cutting down on the amount of data remaining

for each successively higher level routing (flat, Gouraud, Phong shaders), and suggest refinement methods without any fixed highest level.

Numerous rendering systems first generate a low resolution image, then refine it. For instance, UNC graduate student Andrew Glassner has implemented arbitrary slicing through a 3D density distribution (typically an anatomical structure described by a stack of CT images), by generalizing Crow's sum tables [CROW84]. His algorithm first generates a crude 64x64-pixel image, then refines it to 128x128, then refines that to 256x256 pixels. In general, rendering algorithms that compute pixels independently (e.g., ray tracers) are well suited to this type of operation, while others such as list priority algorithms are not.

The UNC Pixel-Planes project [FUCHS85] proposed a multiple pass approach to anti-aliasing. The image is initially sampled at display resolution. In subsequent passes, the image is also sampled at display resolution, but with samples taken at subpixel offsets from the original samples. The samples at the end of each pass are merged with previous samples to form an anti-aliased image.

An alternative approach to anti-aliasing is described in [BLOOMENTHAL83]. Edges detected using image-processing methods are smoothed during a post-processing step. This post-processing edge inference is useful because they render a variety of object types (polygons, quadrics, patches) and keeping track of pixels to be anti-aliased is difficult in such circumstances.

Objects in the UNC vibrating ("varifocal") mirror system [FUCHS82, MILLS84] are represented as a large set of points. It was noted that the general position of the object can be determined by a small fraction of the points. The system takes advantage of this by rendering the data set in a random order. If the user moves the joystick, a new image is started. If the joystick remains stationary, the image continues to fill in until the entire data set has been rendered.

Adaptive Rendering

Efficient rendering techniques adapt to scene characteristics to minimize the amount of computation performed. Whitted, Lee, Redner, and Uselton [WHITTED80, LEE85] described techniques for adapting the number of rays cast by a ray-tracer to the complexity of the area being sampled.

Cook [COOK84] described a shading system in which a separate shader may be associated with each surface. This permits arbitrarily complex shading computations to be applied where required, without performing extra computation on surfaces where a very simple model is sufficient. Our method also adapts the renderer to the complexity of the surface, with the binding is done at the individual polygon and pixel level. The decision is made on the fly, depending on time available for the rendering process. A single surface of polygons may have a fraction of its polygons flat-shaded, another fraction Gouraud shaded, and another fraction Phong shaded.

The Brown Graphics Group [STRAUSS84] uses a scene format that can be interpreted by a variety of rendering systems. This permits a different renderer to be used on the same data on different workstations [VANDAM86]. The Cornell testbed [HALL83] similarly permits various rendering modules to be interfaced to a common modeler.

3. Our Methods

Our new methods concentrate on the rendering process itself, rather than on object representation techniques. We do this because our applications of medical imaging and molecular modeling impose severe restrictions on the use of certain techniques such as procedural data set generation and multiple, hierarchical representations.

From the user's perspective, the quality of the image from a standard renderer improves with time roughly as shown in one of the curves in Figure 1. Of course, the "quality" of a synthetic image is not easy to quantify, and we do not propose any metric for it here; we simply note that certain operations improve the quality of the image and certain renderers generate higher quality images than others. Any rendering process improves the image quality in time as the rendering progresses to completion; the image then remains constant. Two problems are immediately apparent:

1) the image may not be useful in early stages when perhaps only a few polygons or a few scanlines have been rendered, and

2) the image doesn't improve (obviously) once the rendering is complete.

Our approach seeks to ameliorate both of these weaknesses. For the early phases of the rendering, we restructure the tasks to display some results (vertices, edges) on the screen as soon as possible. The renderer then begins shading the object by scan-converting the object polygons and optionally, the precomputed shadow polygons. The polygon data structure is traversed more frequently than is usual; it is traversed each time there is either more data to display (for instance, polygon edges instead of merely vertices) or a more refined rendering to be performed (for instance, Gouraud instead of flat shading). Our rendering techniques adapt to the specific data set being rendered by performing operations only on "needed polygons" and "needed pixels." This technique prevents the implementation from becoming simply a sequence of increasingly sophisticated renderers; such a naive structure's execution time would be the sum of the times of all the renderers in the sequence.

The next section details our currently implemented techniques. These techniques address only the first of the two problems listed above, that of generating useful images as early as possible. They do not address, for we are still investigating, the second problem -- the renderer never stops, but "keeps improving the image forever."

We have adopted the following guidelines:

- we try to follow the image quality curves of various renderers (Figure 1) by always doing whatever (we estimate) improves the image most at that particular point in time-- painting another point, another edge, another polygon with Phong highlighting, etc.,

- we start a new image whenever new user input is received in order to achieve fast user interaction,

- we perform only necessary work at each phase before going on to the next: Gouraud shading only those polygons that are not "flat", Phong shading only those polygons that have high specular component, anti-aliasing only pixels around which the color changes significantly,

- we use results from previous phases to reduce calculations in later phases, and

- we aim to use all available CPU cycles (a picture is never finished -- "a renderer's work is never done")

4. Implementation

We first preprocess the three dimensional data set by randomly ordering the polygons and converting to a winged-edge data structure format [BAUMGART75]. From the winged-edge data structure, our testbed builds a polygon list, an edge list, a vertex list, and a vertex normal list. The normals require a separate list, since multiple normals may be associated with each vertex, depending on the polygons (flat and/or smooth-shaded) to which the vertex belongs. This format enables fast traversal of the data set for vertices and points, and also provides necessary connectivity information.

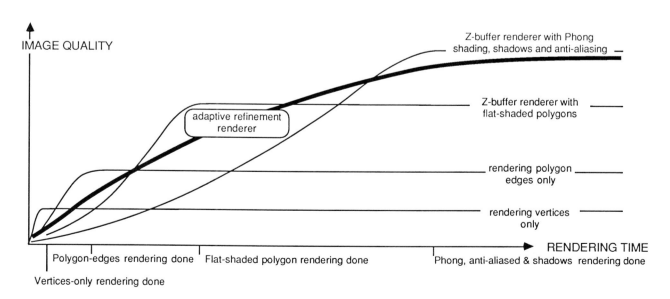

Figure 1: "Image Quality" vs. Rendering Time

In addition to this permanent, viewpoint independent information, our data structure provides storage for values calculated during the rendering process. For example, we save the transformed vertices during vertex display so that transformation need not be repeated during subsequent processing.

Our rendering system provides standard viewing and lighting features. The user can select the view position, viewing angle, hither/yon clipping planes, and light source position, along with the user-specified rendering options detailed in the steps below. The renderer displays shadows if precomputed shadow polygons are provided in the original data set.

Our adaptive rendering system proceeds as follows (Figure 2):

1) **Vertex display** We transform the vertices, build the 6-bit, three-dimensional Cohen-Sutherland clip code [NEWMAN73], and display (with depth cueing) the resulting visible points.

2) **Edge display** We clip the edges of the visible polygons as line segments. The visible edges are displayed with depth cueing using the workstation hardware vector draw.

3) **Flat shading** We complete polygon clipping by joining the clipped edge segments. We then scan-convert the polygons with flat shading using a Z-buffer for hidden surface elimination. A polygon identifier buffer is built to identify the polygon visible at each pixel. This buffer is used by later scan conversion and shadow processing phases. The user may set parameters that control the display of back facing polygons and dithering of color values at each pixel (to enhance the display on workstations with a limited number of colors).

4) **Shadow display** If the data set contains precomputed shadow polygons, we scan-convert these shadow polygons. A pixel is in shadow if the shadow polygon identifier matches the value stored in the polygon identifier buffer. We attenuate the intensity of that pixel by a user specified scaling factor. We also mark that the pixel is in shadow in a pixel attribute buffer (a bit-map which may be stored in either main or non-displayable frame buffer memory). This allows us to adjust the shadow intensity during later processing.

5) **Gouraud shading** We perform Gouraud shading only on those polygons where the range of intensity of a polygon's vertices exceeds a user-specified threshold. We include only the ambient and diffuse components of our lighting model at this stage. Since visibility has already been performed at earlier stages, the process here merely checks the polygon identifier buffer to determine whether or not to display the current polygon at a particular pixel.

6) **Phong shading** We perform Phong shading on those polygons for which the direction of the specular reflectance (highlight) vector at any vertex is within a user-specified tolerance of the direction of maximum highlight. Ideally, this threshold is chosen so that Phong shading is performed only on polygons with noticeable highlights.

7) **Anti-aliasing** We compute a threshold pixel-map that designates which pixels need to be anti-aliased. A

pixel is anti-aliased if the maximum range of variance in intensity in the three by three pixel neighborhood around it exceeds a pre-defined threshold. We then build polygon fragments for the designated pixels and perform anti-aliasing with the A-buffer hidden surface algorithm [CARPENTER84].

We note that with some enhancements to the implementation, the above order could be modified under user control.

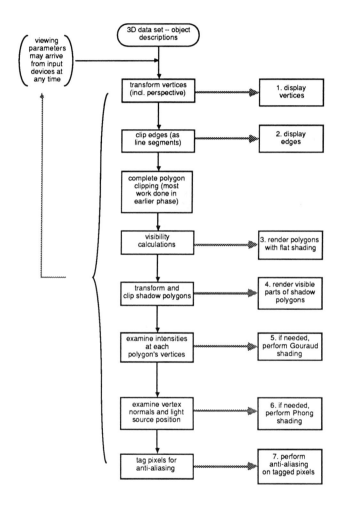

Figure 2: Rendering pipeline modified for adaptive refinement

5. Experimental Results

Since this conference paper is but the first report on this work, the results thus far are very tentative. However, we already find useful the display of even a small fraction of the vertices whenever these points are updated fast enough for perceptible motion.

We have also found useful the partially completed images early in the rendering process, with polygon edges and a few flat-shaded polygons -- such as the scene illustrated in Figure 3.

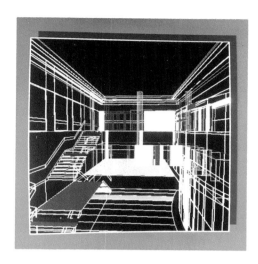

Figure 3: Image in early rendering phase, showing polygon edges and a few flat-shaded polygons (view of lobby of UNC's future Computer Science building).

We have been surprised that the threshold settings for Gouraud and Phong shading have such a major effect on the amount of work being done; the fraction of pixels displayed with Phong shading can easily vary from 5 to 50% depending on the threshold setting. Unfortunately we have not yet had time to characterize these results. We have already found, however, that since the light source direction strongly effects the number of pixels needing Phong shading for specular light component calculations, the user needs to be able to control easily and interactively the location and orientation of the light source in the three-dimensional scene.

The software runs on three different configurations, all running under UNIX: a Masscomp MCS 500 workstation, a DEC VAX-780, and an HP-9000 Series 500. All images except Figures 14 through 19 were photographed directly from the Masscomp screen. The execution times vary from one frame per second (user set) for a fraction of the vertices to about 20 minutes for the Phong shaded image. Figures 14 through 19 show images generated from the implementation running on the HP-9000.

6. Extensions

We hope to add textures and transparency as a later phase similar to the one just described for shadows. We are also eager to try these techniques with some high-speed hardware to see if they could apply in a more structured setting than in our current general purpose workstation environment. In particular, we hope to use some of these techniques on the Pixel-planes system currently under construction [POULTON85, FUCHS85].

Our ultimate goal in this exploration is to find what we call a "golden thread", a single step that if repeated a few times will generate a crude image, one which repeated many times will generate a high quality image, and one which could be repeated indefinitely to yield ever higher quality images. Our current hope is that some form of ray-tracing [WHITTED80,LEE85] with an ever increasing number of rays (and ever deeper "ray" trees) will yield such a "golden thread." Although these notions are purely speculative at the moment, we're encouraged that some of the current calculations may prove useful: the initial ray casting is essentially done by the Z-buffer, and the anti-aliasing bit-map indicates pixels likely to need the most rays.

7. Conclusions

Image generation by adaptive refinement provides an encouraging combination of rendering speed, user convenience, and high quality pictures. The major cost appears to be the large amount of main memory required to store the data set and the intermediate values. With increasing memory capacity for workstations, however, the techniques presented in this paper should become increasingly easy to adopt. Indeed, with more personal, dedicated workstations having spare computing cycles, one may yet develop a renderer whose work is never done.

Acknowledgements

We thank Fred Brooks, Stephen Pizer, and Turner Whitted for many stimulating and useful discussions and for their leadership of many cooperating projects. We thank Julian Rosenman, Edward Chaney, and George Sherouse of the UNC School of Medicine, Department of Radiology for the CT data of the head, and Brian Whitney and Sukumar Ramanathan for generating the polygon description of the Head from the CT data. We thank Dana Smith and Greg Abram for the building data.

We gratefully acknowledge the support of this work in part by the Defense Advanced Research Projects Agency Contract DAAG29-83-K-0148 (monitored by the US Army Research Office, Research Triangle Park, NC), the National Institutes of Health Grant R01-CA39060, and the National Science Foundation Grant ECS-8300970.

References

[ATHERTON78] Atherton, Peter, Kevin Weiler, and Donald Greenberg *Polygon Shadow Generation.* **Computer Graphics**, 12, No. 3 August 1978 pp. 275-281.

[BAUMGART75] Baumgart, Bruce G. *A Polyhedron Representation for Computer Vision.* **NCC 1975**, pp. 589-596.

[BLOOMENTHAL83] Bloomenthal, Jules *Edge Inference with Applications to Antialiasing.* **Computer Graphics**, 17, No. 3 July 1983 pp. 157-162.

[CARPENTER84] Carpenter, Loren *The A-buffer, an Antialiased Hidden Surface Method.* **Computer Graphics**, 18, No. 3 July 1984 pp. 103-108.

[CATMULL74] Catmull, Edwin E. *A Subdivision Algorithm for Computer Display of Curved Surfaces.* Ph.D. Diss. University of Utah December 1974.

[CLARK76] Clark, James H. *Hierarchical Geometric Models for Visible Surface Algorithms.* **Communications of the ACM**, 19, No. 10 October 1976 pp. 547-554.

[COOK84] Cook, Robert L. *Shade Trees.* **Computer Graphics**, 18, No. 3 July 1984 pp. 223-231.

[CROW84] Crow, Franklin C. *Summed-Area Tables for Texture Mapping.* **Computer Graphics**, 18, No. 3 July 1984 pp. 207-212.

[FORREST85] Forrest, A.R. *Antialiasing in Practice* in **Fundamental Algorithms for Computer Graphics**, Ed. Earnshaw, R.A. in Proc. of NATO ASI Series. Springer-Verlag, 1985 pp. 113-134.

[FOURNIER82] Fournier, Alain, Don Fussell, and Loren C. Carpenter *Computer Rendering of Stochastic Models.* **Communications of the ACM**, 25, No. 6 June 1982 pp. 371-384.

[FUCHS82] Fuchs, H., S.M. Pizer, E.R. Heinz, L.C. Tsai, and S.H. Bloomberg *Adding a True 3-D Display to a Raster Graphic System.* **IEEE Computer Graphics and Applications**, 2, No. 7 September 1982 pp. 73-78.

[FUCHS85] Fuchs, Henry, Jack Goldfeather, Jeff P. Hultquist, Susan Spach, John D. Austin, Frederick P. Brooks, Jr., John G. Eyles, and John Poulton *Fast Spheres, Shadows, Textures, Transparencies, and Image Enhancements in Pixel- Planes.* **Computer Graphics**, 19, No. 3 July 1985 pp. 111-120.

[HALL83] Hall, Roy A., and Donald P. Greenberg *A Testbed for Realistic Image Synthesis.* **IEEE Computer Graphics and Applications**, 3, No. 8 November 1983 pp. 10-20.

[HILL83] Hill, F.S., Jr., Sheldon Walker, Jr., and Fuwen Gao *Interactive Image Query System Using Progressive Transmission.* **Computer Graphics**, 17, No. 3 July 1983 pp. 323-330.

[HUNTER78] Hunter, G.M. *Efficient Computation and Data Structures for Graphics.* Ph.D. Diss. Princeton University 1978.

[JACKINS80] Jackins, C., and Tanimoto, S.L. *Oct-trees and Their Use in Representing Three-Dimensional Objects.* **Computer Graphics and Image Processing**, 14, No. 3 November 1980 pp. 249-270.

[KNOWLTON80] Knowlton, Ken Progressive *Transmission of Grey-Scale and Binary Pictures by Simple, Efficient, and Lossless Encoding Schemes.* **Proceedings of the IEEE**, 68, No. 7 July 1980 pp. 885-896.

[LANE80] Lane, Jeffrey M., Loren C. Carpenter, James F. Blinn, and Turner Whitted *Scan Line Methods for Displaying Parametrically Defined Surfaces.* **Communications of the ACM**, 23, No. 1 January 1980 pp. 23-34.

[LEE85] Lee, Mark E., Richard A. Redner, and Samuel P. Uselton *Statistically Optimized Sampling for Distributed Ray Tracing.* **Computer Graphics**, 19, No. 3 July 1985 pp. 61-67.

[MACDOUGAL84] MacDougal, Paul D. *Generation and Management of Object Description Hierarchies for Simplification of Image Generation.* Ph.D. Diss. Ohio State University August 1984.

[MEAGHER80] Meagher, D. *Octree: A New Technique for the Representation, Manipulation and Display of Arbitrary 3-D Objects by Computer.* Technical Report IPL-TR-80-111. Rensselaer Polytechnic Institute. 1980.

[MILLS84] Mills, Peter H., Henry Fuchs, and Stephen M. Pizer *High-Speed Interaction on a Vibrating Mirror 3D Display.* **Proceedings of SPIE**, 507 August 1984 pp. 93-101.

[NEWMAN73] Newman, William M. and Robert F. Sproull **Principles of Interactive Computer Graphics** 1st Edition, McGraw-Hill 1973 pp. 123-124.

[POULTON85] Poulton, John, Henry Fuchs, John D. Austin, John G. Eyles, Justin Heinecke, Cheng-Hong Hsieh, Jack Goldfeather, Jeff P. Hultquist, Susan Spach *PIXEL-PLANES: Building a VLSI-Based Graphic System* **Proceedings of the 1985 Chapel Hill Conference on VLSI** Computer Science Press pp. 35-60.

[SAMET84] Samet, Hanan *The Quadtree and Related Hierarchical Structures.* **ACM Computing Surveys**, 16, No. 2 June 1984 pp. 187-260.

[SLOAN79] Sloan, Kenneth R., Jr., and Steven L. Tanimoto *Progressive Refinement of Raster Images.* **IEEE Transactions on Computers**, c-28, No. 11 November 1979 pp. 871-874.

[STRAUSS84] Strass, P., M. Shantis, and D. Laidlaw *SCEFO: A Standard Scene Format for Image Creation and Animation.* Brown University Graphics Group Memo, 1984.

[VANDAM86] Van Dam, A. *Personal communication.* 1986.

[WHITTED80] Whitted, Turner *An Improved Illumination Model for Shaded Display.* **Communications of the ACM**, 23, No. 6 June 1980 pp. 343-349

Figure 4: User with image after vertex-display phase.

Figure 5: 10% of vertices displayed at ~1Hz. update rate.

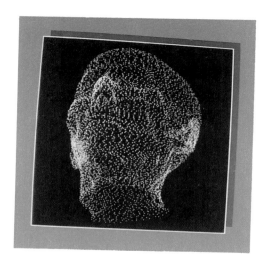

Figure 6: All 8,029 vertices displayed.

Figure 7: User with image after "flat-shaded polygons" phase.

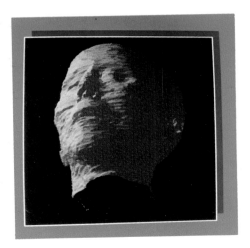

Figure 8: Image after "flat-shaded polygons" phase.

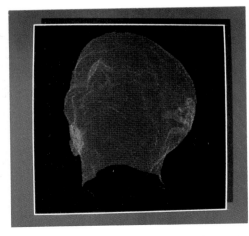

Figure 9: "Cost image" showing computation cost at each pixel for generating Figure 8.

Figure 10: Image after "Gouraud-shaded polygons" phase.

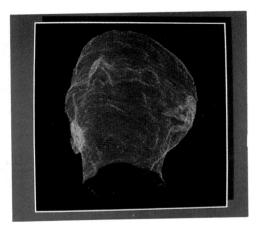

Figure 11: "Cost image" showing computation cost at each pixel for generating the image of Figure 10. Recall that Gouraud shading is performed on a polygon only if the intensity difference among its vertices exceed the user-defined threshold.

Figure 12: Image after "Phong-shaded polygons" phase.

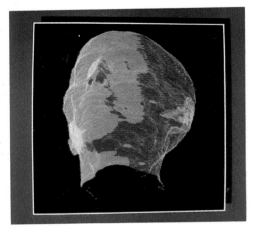

Figure 13: "Cost image" showing the computation expense at each pixel for generating Figure 12. In this case, the user-defined threshold for proceeding with Phong shading passed about 50% of the front-facing polygons.

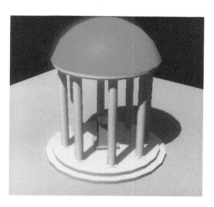

Figure 14: Rendering of the UNC "Old Well" through the Phong-shading phase. 125,459 pixels rendered within the 400 x 400 pixel image.

Figure 15: Extreme closeup of one of the column bases showing the deleterious effects of simple, non-anti-aliased rendering.

Figure 16: Anti-aliasing map of Figure 14, showing the 13,037 pixels (about 10% of those originally rendered) that will receive anti-aliasing computations.

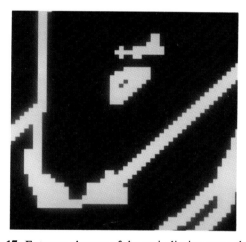

Figure 17: Extreme closeup of the anti-aliasing map, showing same area as Figure 15.

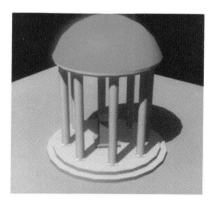

Figure 18: Image of Figure 14 after anti-aliasing computations on the pixels shown in Figure 16. These computations generated 50,722 fragments for the A-buffer-based anti-aliasing.

Figure 19: Extreme closeup of Figure 18, showing the same area as Figures 15 and 17.

The Definition and Rendering of Terrain Maps

Gavin S. P. Miller

Cambridge University Engineering Department

Cambridge, England.

Abstract

This paper examines three methods, two existing and one new, for the generation of fractals based on recursive subdivision. Both existing methods are found to have defects, which are not present in the new method. A parallel processing algorithm is proposed for the rendering of height fields which is exact and distributes the load evenly between the processors. A method is described for the 'fan-tracing' of height fields to allow the realistic simulation of water reflections.

Key words and phrases: computer graphics, terrain, height fields, fractals, scanline algorithms, parallel algorithms.

1. Introduction

The rendering of terrain models using computer graphics is an important problem because of its relevance to flight simulation, animation and CADCAM, to mention but a few applications. Special problems are posed by the realistic rendering of landscape because of the amount of detail required. Fractal methods have been proposed to allow database amplification, which is the generation of controlled random detail from a fairly sparse description [9].

An alternative approach is to use texture mapping methods on a few simple primitives. The texturing is defined procedurally, which means that the textured elements may be expanded without loss of high frequency detail, or shrunk without the occurrence of aliasing artifacts. Such texturing helps to blend together the crude approximate surfaces [12].

However problems remain. Fractal subdivision methods are slow and generate defects due to what is known as the 'creasing problem' which is the occurrence of creases or slope discontinuities along boundaries. Texture map methods, on the other hand, display visible discontinuities in texture gradient where two surfaces intersect. Also the outlines are smooth rather than irregular.

True parallax cues are important in generating a sense of movement and visual realism. Unfortunately, the texture mapping of a few simple primitives does not give correct local height variations. A typical state-of-the-art flight simulator can render about 5000 polygons in real time whereas a detailed terrain may consist of one quarter of a million elements. To achieve this degree of detail in real time will require a careful partitioning of the computational load between hundreds of processors working in parallel. Fortunately the special geometrical properties of height fields allow this.

2. A New Fractal Method

Recursive subdivision methods are preferable to Fourier transform methods because they are linear in time with the number of elements rather than NlogN. Recursion also allows the computation of a surface to varying degrees of detail in different regions based on the current projection. The two methods current in the literature are triangular edge subdivision, and what for this paper will be called diamond-square subdivision [9].

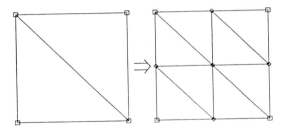

□ Iteration N
◇ Iteration N+1

Figure 1   Triangle Edge Subdivision.

Triangular edge subdivision is illustrated in Figure 1. Each triangle is divided into four new ones. The edges are each divided equally into two. The midpoint then has a Gaussian random variable added to it. The standard deviation of this is given by:

$$S = k2^{-iH}$$

Where i is the iteration level, k is a scale factor and H is the fractal dimension.

No information is passed between adjacent triangles, so this may be termed to be a 'context independent' method [18]. This is important since it leads to what is known as the creasing problem. An important measure of a randomising interpolant is what it looks like if the randomisation is turned off, i. e. k is set to zero. For the sake of later comparison a simple test case is considered. The fractals are defined to be periodic and to have their control points lying on a square matrix. The vertices of the square and the edge midpoints are all set to a constant level. The midpoint of the square is raised above the constant level.

Image 1a illustrates the effect of subdivision for k equal to zero. A pyramid is the result. This is because below the first level of subdivision each triangle is merely divided into other triangles which are coplanar with it. Thus rather than rolling hills we have 'rolling pyramids' which are unsatisfactory for terrain. Also note that the original control points had square symmetry whereas the surface is skewed. The skewness can be overcome by placing the control points on an equilateral triangular mesh rather than on a rectangular one, but the discontinuities in slope will remain.

Image 1b indicates a plan view of a randomised version of the pyramid with H equal to 1.0. The shading model used is a simple scaling of the X-component of the surface normal. The creases parallel to the X and Y axes and along the diagonal are all too apparent. However, rotated by 60 degrees about the X-axis with Cosine Law shading the mountains look quite respectable and very detailed. See Image 1c. Indeed the creasing artifacts do much to make the mountains dramatic. However it would be more desirable to have random detail generated which could be considered to look natural from all directions.

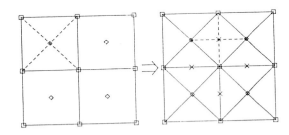

□ Iteration N
◇ Iteration N+1
× Iteration N+2

Figure 2   Diamond - Square Subdivision.

The second method in [9] was the diamond-square lattice illustrated in Figure 2. Rather than subdividing only edges a square is used to generate its centre point which then leaves holes which are surrounded by data in a diamond arrangement. The diamond is used to generate its centre point and this level of subdivision is complete. This method of subdivision does take values from neighbouring regions and so it is 'context dependent'. However, because of the two tier iteration scheme artifacts do occur. Again with the randomisation turned off Image 2a indicates the rather peculiar surface which results. Note that the original control points have the surface passing through them. The surface is very pointed towards the peak and there are bumps and dents in the surface depending on the local curvature. These are, of course, innate in the interpolant and nothing to do with fractal randomisation which is not present. Image 2b again indicates the X-component of the surface normal. Tell-tale vertical streaks indicate a persistent creasing problem and Image 2c shows pointed peaks not only at the control points but also at other intermediate points as well.

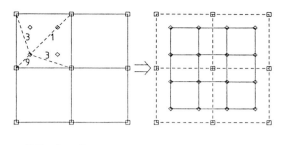

□ Iteration N
◇ Iteration N + 1

Figure 3   Square - Square Subdivision.

The new method here proposed is one adapted from the field of CADCAM. In order to gain first order continuity in the interpolant we sacrifice the requirement of having the surface passing through the control points. Figure 3 illustrates the square-square subdivision rule of [4] and [7]. The new points are generated on a square which is half the size of an existing square. The new values are taken in the proportion 9:3:3:1, the nearer points having the greater weighting. This leads to an interpolant which in the limit is a biquadratic surface. This is a surface which is smooth and continuous in surface normal. Note that with this method the control points deflect the surface but do not normally lie on it.

Image 3a indicates the form of the interpolant. First order continuity is achieved but the surface is rather conservative in the way it is deflected by the control points. Image 3b shows no creasing artifacts and Image 3c is well behaved. However the surface looks rather bland compared with Image 1c, but the value of H can always be decreased to create more roughness, and the control points may be exaggerated in Z to make a more pronounced peak. With this square-square fractal method we may generate terrain which is anything from rolling hills to rough mountains, since the roughness is due to the fractal statistics and is not produced by the underlying interpolant.

Whilst so far we have only considered the use of fractals for terrain, the generation of cloud filled skies is also an important problem. As demonstrated later the new fractal method leads to the generation of acceptable clouds, because of the lack of unnatural artifacts. It is worth noting, however, that for texturing purposes, fractal subdivision methods may be replaced by Perlin's stochastic modelling approach [17].

3. A Parallel Algorithm for Rendering Height Fields

For the purposes of this paper a height field is a surface which in object space coordinates is defined by a single value of Z for every X and Y. We have a viewpoint $\underline{P}$ and a view direction $\underline{V}$. We wish to be able to compute an image of the height field for any view direction and position. The usual approach to this is to consider a plane image whose surface is perpendicular to the view direction vector. A 4x4 transformation matrix is sufficient to project from the object space into the image space. The surface elements are transformed into perspective and then rendered into the image. The use of occlusion-compatible ordering allows the elements to be rendered from back to front with pixel overwrite, or from front to back for antialiasing [5]. A general polygon-based system explicitly computes this order from the polygon data, or derives it from a precomputed data structure [11]. With height fields, however, we may divide the surface into four rectangular regions within which the ordering can be generated trivially. We split the object X-Y plane into four regions using lines parallel to the X-axis and Y-axis which intersect vertically beneath the viewpoint. Each region may then be rendered using polygons generated in the correct row by row or column by column order [1]. We then need a fast method of scan-conversion, but this may be difficult to distribute evenly between parallel processors. In particular, a height field in perspective may not project to singly valued screen y coordinates. The importance of this is explained later. Another problem with this method is that if several different view directions are required, then the visibility calculations must be recomputed. Similarly it is difficult to process scenes for which the view angle is greater than 180 degrees.

An established technique for the projection of planar textures into perspective is to use a row-column access method. In this approach pixels are read, transformed and stored for each row in turn. The columns are then each accessed and transformed. The net result is a planar texture which has been transformed into perspective with antialiasing [3]. This scheme may be thought of as a parallel algorithm since each row could be processed by a different processor at the same time. Each column could then be processed similarly. The advantage of this method is that there is no executive processor allocating fragments of the entire image to each subprocessor. Also each processor does not need to store the entire image, but only a single row or column. The difficulty with this method is the dual access of the data first for the rows and then for the columns. If the processors are connected by a common bus then the image may be flipped about a diagonal in one frame time.

It would be attractive to apply a row-column algorithm to the rendering of height fields. The rows would be stretched laterally in accordance with the perspective projection and then the columns would be transformed to the correct view. Unfortunately this approach is only exact for perspective projections if the view vector is parallel to the X-Y plane. For other view directions the projected height field is not singly valued in screen y coordinate. Indeed the process collapses if the view vector is straight down along the object space Z-axis. However this inexact approach has been used to good effect in [10].

The new approach presented in this paper is to abandon the planar projection and to use an intermediate viewing sphere. (This is an extension of the method described in [8] which was restricted to having view directions parallel to the X-Y plane). We consider the viewpoint to be surrounded by a sphere onto which have been projected the surfaces from all directions. This sphere may then be transformed into screen coordinates for viewing on a flat screen or directly projected onto a spherical screen for wide angle work.

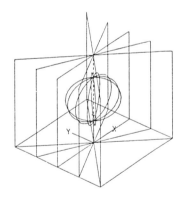

Figure 4   Viewing Sphere with Axial Planes

The advantage of this method is that the visible surface calculation for the viewing sphere is independent of the viewing direction and the processing may use planes which pass vertically through the terrain map. See Figure 4. If we consider the family of planes which pass through a line dropped vertically from the viewpoint, then the planes will have intersections with the terrain which are singly valued in Z.

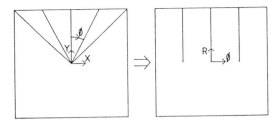

Figure 5   Cartesian to Polar Conversion.

A way to achieve this with a row-column algorithm is to split the object plane into wedge quadrants. These are + or - 45 degrees from either the X or Y axes. We stretch each row until the vertical planes of constant Phi become columns. See Figure 5.

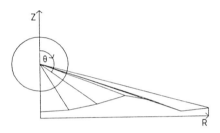

Figure 6   Projection of Slice onto Viewing Sphere.

To project onto the viewing sphere we then process each column using inverse trigonometric functions to compute values of Theta. See Figure 6. From a Phi-Theta representation of the viewing sphere we proceed to project onto the viewing plane. See Figure 7.

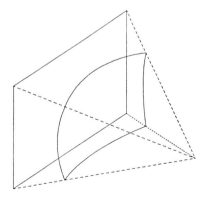

Figure 7   Projection of Viewing Sphere onto Image Plane.

Image 4 illustrates this process. Top left is the original terrain map with areas within the wedge quadrants of interest highlighted in grey. Top right is the same terrain after it has been expanded row by row in X by a factor of 1/Y. Bottom left is the same region after a subsequent column stretch by a factor of 1/Cos(X), where X has been scaled to lie between -Pi/4 and Pi/4. Note that the bottom half of the data was then flipped vertically. The top and bottom halves now correspond to two opposite wedge quadrants. Bottom right is a polar representation of half of the viewing sphere. Phi is along X, Theta is along Y. The two wedge quadrants have been projected onto the viewing sphere. The lack of visual detail for near parts of the terrain is readily apparent.

Image 5 demonstrates the additional use of a two-dimensional version of Perlin's fractal texturing technique. In this a bandwidth-limited function of X and Y is successively scaled and superimposed in accordance with the viewing transformation. This is used to compute a normal perturbation for the shading function. With this near elements remain detailed despite their expansion by the spherical projection. Top right is an orthogonal spherical projection taken along the Y-axis. Top left is the same projection taken looking straight down along the Z-axis. Image 6 shows a perspective projection of the viewing sphere taken along the X-axis.

If the viewing sphere is transformed such that the polar axis lies along the current rotation axis of the observer, then rotational motion blur may be computed. A block or ramp filter is applied along the Phi direction of the polar representation of the viewing sphere. Image 7 is the same scene as that shown in Image 6, but with motion blur due to a barrel roll about the view vector. Image 8 shows a wide angle projection of the viewing sphere after it has been tilted about the X-axis by 45 degrees. Image 9 is a perspective projection of the rotated viewing sphere.

The details of the row-column algorithms for arbitrary spherical-to-spherical and spherical-to-planar transformations will be the subject of a later work [15]. However it should now be apparent that by using a spherical projection as an intermediate representation it is possible to construct a row-column algorithm for the perspective rendering of height fields.

4. The Fan-tracing of Height Fields

Recently some work has been done on ray-tracing fractal surfaces defined by the triangle edge subdivision technique [2] and [14]. While these methods work

they are slow and restricted to a certain class of surfaces. In general the key uses in terrain modelling for ray-tracing like effects would be the calculation of shadows and reflections in water. Usually where shadows are required the sun may be considered to be a point light source. This is equivalent to computing a second hidden surface calculation. A more difficult problem is the reflection of light in water. For distant regions there may be many water waves per pixel. Thus many rays per pixel will be required for raytracing rippling water. Also each ray must be separately traced against the whole terrain.

The approach adopted here is to assume that rays may be perturbed vertically by the water but not laterally. This allows us to model the actual appearance of reflections of distant hills in lakes quite realistically whilst reducing a 3-D ray trace to a 2-D one. Since these vertical planes are equivalent to those in the previous section this procedure may be implemented in parallel as a natural part of the hidden surface algorithm. Since reflected light is scattered vertically but not horizontally, the light which will be scattered towards an observer lies within a range of vertical angles from the point on the water surface. This may be thought of as a 'fan' of light rays incident on the water. The reflected light intensity is merely the integral of the incident light lying within the range of the fan.

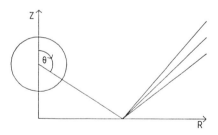

Figure 8   The Beam Geometry of Water Reflection

To ease the computational load the water is treated as flat with a normal perturbation. The waves are modelled as superimposed sine waves which aids clamping, i. e. the bandwidth-limiting of the normal perturbation texture [16]. However since we are interested in reflections of a fan rather than the projection of a texture the waves have two effects. The first is to perturb the centre of the fan based on the slope of the wave surface. The second is to spread the fan based on the curvature of the wave. See Figure 8. The fan centre perturbation is clamped to zero for distant waves whilst the fan spread is set to maximum. An alternative to superimposed sine waves would have been the wave model in [17]. Perlin's model uses several point sources of disturbance and so avoids the periodicity inherent in the sine wave approach. It gives very realistic pictures and the incorporation of that method into this system is an area for future work.

If there were none of the height field protruding above the water level then the intensity for a fan could be computed from an environment map of the sky. For each vertical slice this environment map would be one-dimensional, and a precomputed integral table could be used to speed calculations [6]. However, since the height field can obstruct all or part of the sky contribution to the fan, a more complicated approach is required.

For each water pixel a fan is generated based on the projection distance, the perturbation and the spread of the wave. The plane slice of the height field is projected and clipped to that fan and the intensities are averaged over the fan. Thus there is one fan per water pixel rather than many rays. For Image 10, the view direction was taken parallel to the negative Y-axis. Also the height field was painted onto piecewise flat vertical elements for rapidity of projection. This latter simpification did lead to unnatural vertical streaks for some images and is not recommended. However the results were quite encouraging. The clouds were generated using the new fractal method as were the mountains. The snow line was prevented from being too regular by the use of normal as well as height data to determine the snow threshold.

By dividing a 3-D problem into a 2-D problem a great speed saving was achieved thus allowing the simulation of quite realistic effects on a small machine. Image 10 took 6 hours on a Prime 250 for 512x512 resolution, including the time for the generation of the terrain data.

5. Conclusions and Future Developments.

This paper has presented a new method for the generation of fractals by recursive subdivision, which does not create the artifacts of previously published methods. It has also presented a parallel algorithm for the perspective rendering of height fields which uses an intermediate spherical projection. This algorithm was extended to include an approximate but convincing method for the simulation of reflections of terrain and sky in water.

The common bus architecture mentioned in this paper may be replaced by a more complex one, to speed up the diagonal flip process.

Also, the height field rendering algorithm as given does not allow the inclusion of collections of trees or bushes. By allowing more data to be stored in the rows and columns it may be possible to include features such as the textured ellipsoids of Gardner [12] and [13].

Acknowlegments

Thanks to Jon Hunwick who designed the yacht in Image 10 on the DUCT surface modeller. Thanks to my Ph. D. supervisor Dr. D. P. Sturge for encouragement and support and to Deltacam Systems Ltd and Sigmex Ltd for the loan of equipment.

References

[1] Anderson D. P., Hidden Line Elimination in Projected Grid Surfaces, A.C.M. Trans. Graphics, Vol. 1, No. 4, Oct 1982, pp 274-288.

[2] Bouville C., Bounding Ellipsoids for Ray-Fractal Intersection, SIGGRAPH '85, Computer Graphics, Vol. 19, No. 3 (July 1985).

[3] Catmull E. and A. R. Smith, 3-D transformations of images in scanline order, Computer Graphics, Vol. 14, No. 3, pp 279-284, 1980.

[4] Catmull E. and J. Clark, Recursively generated B-spline surfaces on arbitrary topological meshes, CAD Vol. 10, pp 350-355, 1978.

[5] Coquillart S. and M. Gangnet, Shaded Display of Digital Maps, IEEE Computer Graphics and Applications, Vol. 4, No. 7. July 1984.

[6] Crow F. C., Summed-area tables for texture mapping. Computer Graphics, Vol. 1, No. 3 (July 1984), pp 207-212.

[7] Doo D. and M. Sabin, Behaviour of recursive division surfaces near extraordinary points, CAD Vol. 10, pp 356-362, 1978.

[8] Fishman B. and B. Schecter. Computer Display of Height Fields. Computers and Graphics Vol. 5 (1980) pp53-60.

[9] Fournier A., D. Fussell, L. Carpenter, Computer Rendering of Stochastic Models. Comm. of the A.C.M., 25, 6, (June 1982), pp 371-384.

[10] Fournier A. and T. Milligan, Frame Buffer Algorithms for Stochastic Models. IEEE Computer Graphics and Applications. October 1985. Vol. 5, No. 10.

[11] Fuchs H., G. D. Abram and E. D. Grant. Near Real-Time Shaded Display of Rigid Objects, Computer Graphics, Vol. 17, No. 3 (July 1983).

[12] Gardner G. Y., Simulation of Natural Scenes Using Textured Quadric Surfaces. Computer Graphics Vol. 18, No. 3 (July 1984) pp 11-20.

[13] Gardner G. Y., Visual Simulation of Clouds, Computer Graphics, Vol. 19, No. 3 (July 1985), pp 297-303.

[14] Kajiya J. T., New Techniques for Ray Tracing Procedurally Defined Objects, Computer Graphics, Vol. 17, No. 3, (July 1983).

[15] Miller, G. S. P., Author's unpublished Ph. D. dissertation - work in progress.

[16] Norton A., A. P. Rockwood and P. T. Skolmoski, A Method of Antialiasing Textured Surfaces by Bandwidth Limiting in Object Space. Computer Graphics Vol. 16, No. 3 (July 1982).

[17] Perlin K., An Image Synthesizer, SIGGRAPH '85, Computer Graphics, Vol. 19, No. 3 (July 1985).

[18] Smith A. R., Plants, Fractals and Formal Languages. Computer Graphics, Vol. 18, No. 3 (July 1984).

Triangular Interpolant.

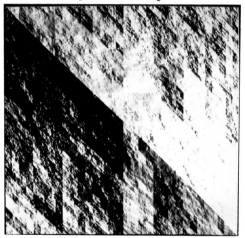

1b.   Triangular Fractal Normal Map.

1c.   Triangular Fractal Mountain.

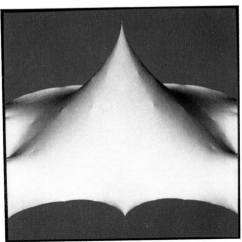

2a. Diamond-Square Interpolant.

3a. Square-Square Interpolant.

2b. Diamond-Square Fractal Normal Map.

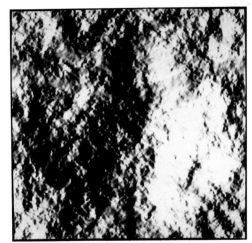

3b. Square-Square Fractal Normal Map.

2c. Diamond-Square Fractal Mountain.

3c. Square-Square Fractal Mountain.

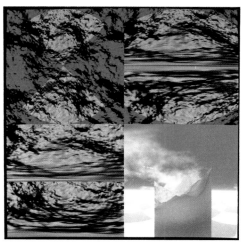

4. Wedge Quadrants to Viewing Sphere.

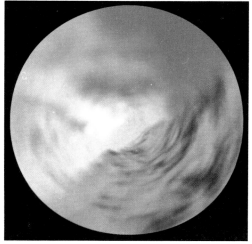

7. View Along X with Motion Blur.

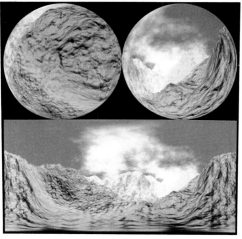

5. Viewing Sphere With Texture.

8. Wide Angle View Down Incline.

6. Perspective View Along X.

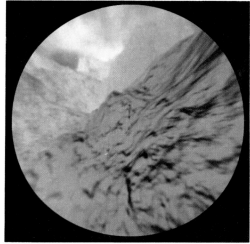

9. Perspective View Down Incline.

10. Sailing By.

The Synthesis of Cloth Objects

Jerry Weil
AT&T Bell Laboratories
Murray Hill, New Jersey 07974

Abstract

In image synthesis, cloth objects such as clothes are most often modelled as textures mapped onto rigid surfaces. However, in order to represent such objects more realistically, their physical properties must be examined. This paper describes a method for modelling cloth material hanging in three dimensions when supported by any number of constraint points. The cloth synthesized with this model contains folds and appears more realistic than simple texture mapping. This paper also describes a method for rendering the cloth once its free-hanging shape has been determined.

The computation of the surface of a free-hanging cloth is performed in two stages. The first stage approximates the shape of the surface which is interior to the constraint points, and the second stage performs a relaxation process on all points on the surface to arrive at a close approximation to its shape. The rendering of the surfaces is done using a ray-tracer which treats the surface as a mesh of line segments.

Introduction

In the field of computer graphics, objects made of cloth are usually modelled as rigid surfaces with textures mapped onto them [1,2,3,4]. These surfaces do not have the properties of cloth, such as folds, and they therefore lack a degree of realism. Taking into account the physical properties of such objects would lead to more realistic looking scenes. Not only is the shape of the surface important in achieving realism, but the method for rendering the cloth objects in an image is also important.

The applications for modelling cloth accurately are varied. Aside from the industrial applications in the fashion and textile industries, realistic looking clothes and other cloth objects could enhance computer generated animation or computer synthesized advertisements. The research described in this paper relates to methods for modelling arbitrary cloth objects, but the focus of the paper deals with one specific problem.

The Problem

This paper examines one solution to a very specific problem. A piece of cloth exists in three dimensions, and it is fixed in location at chosen constraint points. The problem is to determine a possible solution to the way in which the cloth will hang from these constraint points. Determining a smooth surface for the cloth will not suffice, since, in reality, folds may occur in the cloth.

The Method

First, it is necessary to find a way to represent the cloth to be modelled. For the purposes of this paper, the cloth will be assumed rectangular, and will be represented as a grid, or two-dimensional array, of three-dimensional coordinates. The grid is treated as a two-dimensional coordinate system, the axes of which consist of the row and column axes. The grid coordinate system should not be confused with the object's coordinate system, which is a standard three-dimensional system with x, y and z axes. By increasing the density of the grid, greater resolution of the surface model may be obtained.

There are two stages to the method described here. In the first stage, an approximation is made to the surface within the convex hull of the constraint points in the grid coordinate system. Some natural constraints of the cloth are ignored during this stage of processing, therefore the folds which would in reality appear over the surface may not appear after the completion of this stage. The constraints of the cloth are applied during the second stage of processing, which involves an iterative relaxation process [7]. The relaxation of points is iterated over the surface until the maximum displacement of the points during one pass falls below a predetermined tolerance.

Surface Approximation

A differentiation must be made between the *interior* and *exterior* points on the grid. The interior points are those which lie within the convex hull formed by the constraint points in the grid coordinate system, and the remaining points are considered as exterior points. The surface approximation stage is completed when all interior points have been positioned somewhere in three dimensions by the method described below. At the start of this process, only the constraint points have been positioned, therefore we begin by positioning points lying between pairs of constraint points.

For a piece of cloth made of woven threads, the positioning of points along any given thread can be determined by examining the physics of such a model. The curve which an ideal thread naturally follows when suspended by two points is called a catenary [8], and is of the form:

$$y = \frac{a}{2}\left(e^{\frac{x}{a}} + e^{-\frac{x}{a}}\right) = a\cosh\left(\frac{x}{a}\right)$$

By tracing catenaries between each pair of constraint points [13], the grid points which lie along the lines between constraint points can be positioned. A line between constraint points refers to the (*row,column*) coordinates through which a line scan-converted from one point to the other would pass in the grid coordinate system. Thus, if one constraint point was at grid coordinate (2,3) and another was at (5,3), the line between the two points would include grid coordinates (3,3) and (4,3). What should be done in the case of a grid coordinate through which more than one such line passes? **Figure 1** illustrates such a case. In reality, the correct position for the point through which the lines pass may be somewhere between the two curves traced along those lines, thus adding a new constraint point to the model. To avoid the computational complexity of adding such new points each time two curves cross, one of the two curves will simply be removed. Ignoring the forces which the two crossing curves may apply to each other, the points along each curve have been positioned as low as they will naturally fall (by definition of the catenary curve). According to this model, no point on the upper curve can move any lower; therefore, the lower of the two curves is chosen to be eliminated, and the upper one remains.

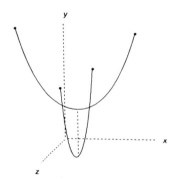

Figure 1. Two crossing catenary curves

The surface approximation stage consists of this tracing of catenary curves. In the first step, a curve is traced from each constraint point to each other constraint point. The curve equation can be found from the two endpoints and the length of the thread hanging between (see **Appendix** for derivation of this equation). One result of the process of positioning points between constraint points is a series of triangles of connected constraint points. As constraint points are connected (by tracing catenaries between them), these triangles are created and added to a database of such triangles. This list of triangles will be used in the next step of the surface approximation stage. Of course, if a curve is removed due to a crossing, any triangle utilizing the removed curve as an edge must also be removed.

A similar process to the one described above is now performed on each triangle in the current list. Each triangle, which represents a section of the cloth, is treated as a separate entity, and will be repeatedly subdivided until each grid point in its interior has been positioned. To determine how to subdivide the triangle, three catenaries are traced, one from each vertex to the midpoint of its opposite edge. The *highest* of the three is chosen to subdivide the triangle. Each triangle is subdivided by this process until all interior points have been positioned. **Figure 2** illustrates a sample of such processing. After every triangle has been processed this way, the interior surface will be closely approximated.

Relaxation

The next step in the process of determining the surface of the cloth involves an iterative relaxation stage. The relaxation of the surface is achieved by propagating the displacement of grid points over the surface until the maximum displacement in a single pass falls below a certain tolerance. The displacement of the points during each pass is determined through approximations to physical constraints. This is by no means an exact solution, but it is merely meant to achieve a reasonable looking surface through straightforward means.

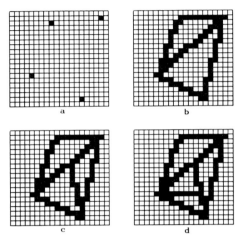

a) original constraint points
b) triangles formed by connecting constraint points
c) subdivision of triangle
d) subdivision of newly formed triangle

Figure 2. Four stages of surface approximation

For the sake of simplicity, gravity is ignored during the relaxation process. In order to achieve a hanging effect in the direction of gravity, the exterior points are initially placed at $y = -\infty$. This simulates a downward pull, and the relaxation process gradually repositions these points upward until the constraints are met. The effects of gravity have already been accounted for by catenary modelling of the interior region. If the cloth is not free-falling, the exterior points may be initially placed at some other locations. For example, to model a cloth being lifted from a flat surface, the exterior points would be placed at their initial locations on that surface.

To determine the displacement of each point, the constraints of the cloth must be examined. The placement of any given point on the surface is one unit distance from each of its four-connected neighbors (without stretching). In order to determine the displacement of a point in a given pass, displacement vectors are determined to position the point at the correct distance from each of its neighbors. By adding these vectors, the direction of displacement is found. The optimal magnitude for the final displacement vector is difficult to determine, since it would be necessary to predict the displacement of the future points to be examined. To emphasize the influence of larger displacement vectors, the squares of the magnitudes of the vectors are averaged, and the square root of this result is used as the final magnitude. It is possible that, following the displacement of a grid point, the surface will intersect itself. For simplicity, surface intersections are neither tested for nor corrected in this implementation, and this has not proven to be a problem in the cases tested.

Some materials are stiffer than others, and therefore will

not bend as much. This property is easily incorporated into the technique already described. One way to accurately model the property of stiffness is to measure the angle formed by three consecutive grid points; the stiffer the cloth, the less the angle may deviate from 180° — a completely stiff material would not allow this angle to deviate at all. This calculation would be fairly costly, and even more difficult would be determining how to rotate the points in order to increase the angle if necessary. A simpler solution which achieves a similar result is to examine the distance between each grid point and the points two rows or columns away. This distance must be greater than a certain minimum distance, determined by the stiffness of the cloth. An added advantage to this method is that it fits in perfectly with the method described above for determining displacement vectors. If a point is determined to be too close to another point two rows or columns away, another vector is added which places it at the minimum distance from that point.

Several times, the tolerance for relaxation has been mentioned. This value is more or less arbitrary, depending on the accuracy desired. However, this tolerance is somewhat related to the constraints placed on the cloth. For example, the stiffer the cloth is modelled to be, the more iterations may be necessary for convergence. We do not attempt to establish a relationship between the degree of stiffness and the value chosen for the tolerance; the tolerance values for this research have been determined by experimentation.

Although the surface approximation stage can be completely eliminated, using only the relaxation stage, the initial approximation can greatly reduce the number of iterations necessary during the relaxation stage. There are situations when it is more practical to use the relaxation stage by itself. One such example is in animation, when the constraint points are gradually moved for each frame. In this case, computing each frame could consist of updating the positions of the constraint points followed by relaxation processing on the remaining points. The relaxation stage would also be useful by itself if the cloth had already taken on some general shape - the shape of the human body if modelled as clothing, or the shape of furniture if modelled as upholstery.

Rendering

Once the surface of the cloth has been relaxed, it can be easily converted to a polygonized surface, ready for any of several rendering techniques. Rendering the surface in this manner may appear realistic for some materials, but, in general, the surface will still not have a cloth-like quality. A cloth texture can be mapped onto the surface, but the translucent effect of some types of cloth may still not be achieved. There are other ways to render the cloth more realistically, such as using Kajiya's recent work with anisotropic surfaces [9], but probably the most realistic way to render the cloth is to actually render each thread individually. This is certainly computationally more expensive than the other methods mentioned, but this kind of detail allows for realistic close-ups of the cloth.

The rendering technique used here is a ray-tracer [14] which treats the cloth as a collection of line segments, the endpoints of which are four-connected neighboring points in the grid. These lines are not treated as one-dimensional lines, but as shapes with thickness and depth. In reality, the threads of a piece of cloth are somewhat cylindrical in shape. As will be seen, this cylindrical shape is simulated by the perturbation of normals [2].

In order to achieve a surface which does not appear like a fish net, a very fine mesh of lines must be fit to the surface. However, the surface approximation and relaxation stages become computationally intensive when run on a fine grid of points. Furthermore, there is not much difference between the overall structure of a surface calculated on a very fine grid from that calculated on a much coarser grid. Therefore, the two-stage process described above is run on a relatively coarse grid, and the remaining points are filled in by fitting splines to the calculated

grid coordinates [12]. A finer mesh is created by first fitting splines to the grid points along each column of the grid. Corresponding points along each of these splines are then used as the knots for splines to be fit along the rows. The points along this last set of splines are used as the surface points by the ray-tracer (**Figure 3**).

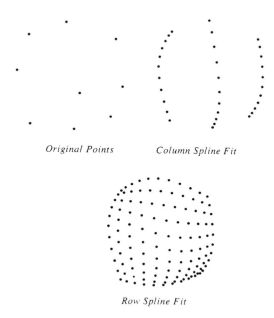

Original Points   *Column Spline Fit*

Row Spline Fit

Figure 3. Spline fitting of surface

Next, the necessary information for each line is placed into a database. This information includes the endpoints of the line as well as three shading values for each endpoint. Three shading values are used to model the line as a cylinder. The three values are computed based on three normal vectors, which are determined in the following manner. The directions of the first two normal vectors are found by projecting the line segment onto the $z=0$ plane and then finding the two oppositely directed vectors which lie in that plane and are perpendicular to the projection, i.e. $(-dy, dx, 0)$ and $(dy, -dx, 0)$. The third normal lies along the vector which is perpendicular to the line segment as well as the first two normal vectors. These three directional vectors are all treated as normal vectors, and thus the three shading values can be computed (**Figure 4**).

Assuming the scene has been normalized to a rectangular view volume, rays can be cast into the scene perpendicular to the viewing plane to be tested for intersections with the threads in the scene. To determine if a ray intersects a thread, the minimum distance is found from the ray to the line segment representing the thread. If this distance is within a chosen tolerance, the ray intersects a cylinder surrounding the line segment and therefore intersects the thread. This distance tolerance represents the radius of the cylinder, and it can be altered to represent various thicknesses of cloth - the larger the tolerance, the thicker the threads, and, therefore, the thicker the cloth. Since calculating the exact distance from the ray to the line is a bit time consuming, this distance is approximated. Only the horizontal or vertical distance from the ray to the line is found, depending on the slope of the line. This approximation will result in variations of the thicknesses of the cylinders by a factor of $\sqrt{2}$, but this variation is hardly noticeable because of the size and density of the threads in the cloth. This approximation also results in the cylinders appearing two-dimensionally as parallelograms rather than rectangles. Again, this factor is hardly noticeable in the final image. To compute the distance from a ray at location (x,y) to a line from (x_1, y_1, z_1) to (x_2, y_2, z_2), two cases are possible:

$$dx = (x_2 - x_1)$$

$$dy = (y_2 - y_1)$$

$$dz = (z_2 - z_1)$$

Case 1: $|dy| > |dx|$

$$t = \frac{y - y_1}{dy}$$

$$distance = x - \left(x_1 + t\, dx \right) \qquad \text{(Distance)}$$

$$z = z_1 + t\, dz \qquad \text{(z-intersection)}$$

Case 2: $|dy| \le |dx|$

$$t = \frac{x - x_1}{dx}$$

$$distance = y - \left(y_1 + t\, dy \right) \qquad \text{(Distance)}$$

$$z = z_1 + t\, dz \qquad \text{(z-intersection)}$$

If the computed distance is within the chosen tolerance, the distance is normalized to lie between -1 and 1, and, by linearly interpolating between the three shade values, an appropriate shade can be determined. Nonlinear interpolation could be used to model other three-dimensional surfaces as well. Note that division by zero is a special case.

Conclusion

The techniques outlined in this paper lead to the creation of more realistic looking images of cloth objects. Many of the methods described involve approximations rather than exact solutions; however, the approximations achieve results which appear realistic. A very specific problem has been addressed here, which is to model the appearance of a piece of cloth which is suspended at certain constraint points. The algorithms described for solving this problem can be extended for other uses, such as for modelling clothes or for use in animating cloth objects. A method for rendering cloth has also been described in which a ray-tracer is used to render a mesh of line segments. Improvements might be made toward the time and space efficiency of such an algorithm.

Several enhancements can be made to the algorithms described here for more general situations. Such enhancements could include the addition of propagating forces to create wave patterns in animation, or additional constraints which would allow the cloth to be draped over solid objects.

Appendix

Solution to finding the catenary equation between two points:

Assume the two endpoints are (x_1, y_1) and (x_2, y_2) and the length is L. To solve for the equation of the catenary passing between the two points, $y = c + a \cosh\left(\frac{x - b}{a} \right)$:

$$y_2 = c + a \cosh\left(\frac{(x_2 - b)}{a} \right) \qquad (1)$$

$$y_1 = c + a \cosh\left(\frac{(x_1 - b)}{a} \right) \qquad (2)$$

$$L = a \sinh\left(\frac{(x_2 - b)}{a} \right) - a \sinh\left(\frac{(x_1 - b)}{a} \right) \qquad (3)$$

By subtracting (2) from (1), squaring, and subtracting (3) squared,

$$\frac{L^2 - [y_2 - y_1]^2}{2a^2} = \cosh\left(\frac{(x_2 - x_1)}{a} \right) - 1 \qquad (4)$$

By the half angle formula and some rearranging,

$$\sqrt{L^2 - [y_2 - y_1]^2} = 2a \sinh\left(\frac{(x_2 - x_1)}{2a} \right) \qquad (5)$$

This can be rewritten as $K = A \sinh\left(\frac{C}{A} \right)$, and A can be found numerically. Since $a = \frac{A}{2}$, from (3) we find that

$$\frac{L}{a} = \cosh\left(\frac{b}{a} \right) \left[\sinh\left(\frac{x_2}{a} \right) - \sinh\left(\frac{x_1}{a} \right) \right]$$

$$- \sinh\left(\frac{b}{a} \right) \left[\cosh\left(\frac{x_2}{a} \right) - \cosh\left(\frac{x_1}{a} \right) \right] \qquad (6)$$

Letting:

$$M = \sinh\left(\frac{x_2}{a} \right) - \sinh\left(\frac{x_1}{a} \right) \qquad (7)$$

$$N = \cosh\left(\frac{x_2}{a} \right) - \cosh\left(\frac{x_1}{a} \right) \qquad (8)$$

it follows that:

$$\frac{L}{a} = M \cosh\left(\frac{b}{a} \right) - N \sinh\left(\frac{b}{a} \right) \qquad (9)$$

If $N > M$,

$$\mu = \tanh^{-1}\left(\frac{M}{N} \right) \qquad (10)$$

$$Q = \frac{M}{\sinh(\mu)} = \frac{N}{\cosh(\mu)} \qquad (11)$$

$$b = a \left[\mu - \sinh^{-1}\left(\frac{L}{Qa} \right) \right] \qquad (12)$$

If $M > N$,

$$\mu = \tanh^{-1}\left(\frac{N}{M} \right) \qquad (13)$$

$$Q = \frac{M}{\cosh(\mu)} = \frac{N}{\sinh(\mu)} \qquad (14)$$

$$b = a \left[\mu - \cosh^{-1}\left(\frac{L}{Qa} \right) \right] \qquad (15)$$

Knowing a and b, the solution for c is straightforward.

Acknowledgements

I would like to thank Larry O'Gorman for his continued help, advice and criticism with this research. Special thanks to John Hughes of Brown University for supplying the derivation in the **Appendix** and thanks to David Laidlaw for organizing it. I would also like to thank Dave Hagelbarger for introducing me to the catenary.

References

(1) Blinn, J., *Computer Display of Curved Surfaces*, University of Utah, Salt Lake City, December 1978.

(2) Blinn, J., "Simulation of Wrinkled Surfaces," *Computer Graphics*, Vol. 12, No. 3, August 1978, pp. 286-292.

(3) Blinn, J. and Newell, M., "Texture and Reflection on Computer Generated Images," *Communications of the ACM*, Vol. 19, No. 10, Oct. 1976, pp. 542-547.

(4) Catmull, E., *A Subdivision Algorithm for Computer Display of Curved Surfaces*, University of Utah, Salt Lake City, December 1974.

(5) Foley, James D. and van Dam, Andries, *Fundamentals of Interactive Computer Graphics*, Addison-Wesley, Reading, Massachusetts, 1982.

(6) Hathorne, Berkeley L., *Woven Stretched and Textured Fabrics*, Interscience Publishers, New York, 1964.

(7) Hsu, M.B., "An Interactive Graphics Program For The Equilibrium Shape Determination For Tensioned Fabric Structures," *Engineering Software for Microcomputers, Proceedings of the First International Conference*, Venice, Italy, 1984, pp. 227-237.

(8) Irvine, H. M., *Cable Structures*, M.I.T., 1981.

(9) Kajiya, James T., "Anisotropic Reflection Models," *Computer Graphics*, Vol. 19, No. 3, July 1985, pp. 15-21.

(10) Miller, L., "Computer Graphics and the Woven Fabric Designer," *Computers in the World of Textiles, Annual World Conference*, Hong Kong, Sept. 1984, pp. 634-644.

(11) *Physical Methods of Investigating Textiles*, Edited by R. Meredith and J.W.S. Hearle, Textile Book Publishers, Inc., New York, 1959, pp. 211-278.

(12) Rogers, David F. and Satterfield, Steven G., "B-Spline Surfaces for Ship Hull Design," *Computer Graphics*, Vol. 14, No. 3, July 1980, pp. 211-217.

(13) *Tensile Structures*, Edited by Frei Otto, M.I.T. Press, Cambridge, Massachusetts, 1967.

(14) Whitted, Turner, "An Improved Illumination Model for Shaded Display," *C. .C.M.*, Vol. 23, No. 6, June 1980, pp. 343-349.

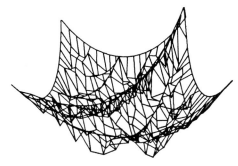

Surface Approximation

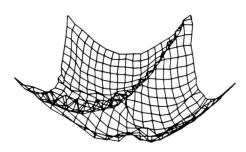

6 Iterations of Relaxation

Spline Fit

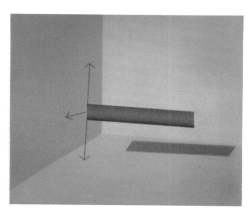

Figure 4. Rendering of single thread showing three normals used to compute shading values

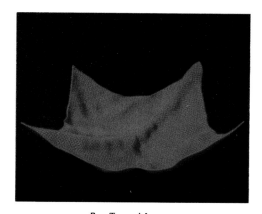

Ray Traced Image
Figure 5. Four stages in synthesis of cloth suspended at corners

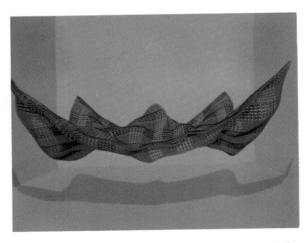

Figure 6. Cloth lifted by five points (corners and center)

Figure 7. Three stages of cloth lifted by corners (only relaxation was used)

Figure 8. Image with varying coarseness and thickness of threads (bars are threads also)

Real Time Design and Animation of Fractal Plants and Trees

Peter E. Oppenheimer
New York Institute of Technology
Computer Graphics Lab

ABSTRACT

The goal of science is to understand why things are the way they are. By emulating the logic of nature, computer simulation programs capture the essence of natural objects, thereby serving as a tool of science. When these programs express this essence visually, they serve as an instrument of art as well.

This paper presents a fractal computer model of branching objects. This program generates pictures of simple orderly plants, complex gnarled trees, leaves, vein systems, as well as inorganic structures such as river deltas, snowflakes, etc. The geometry and topology of the model are controlled by numerical parameters which are analogous to the organism's DNA. By manipulating the *genetic* parameters, one can modify the geometry of the object in real time, using *tree based* graphics hardware. The random effects of the environment are taken into account, to produce greater diversity and realism. Increasing the number of significant parameters yields more complex and evolved species.

The program provides a study in the structure of branching objects that is both scientific and artistic. The results suggest that organisms and computers deal with complexity in similar ways.

CR CATAGORIES AND SUBJECT DESCRIPTORS: C.3 [Special-Purpose and Application-Based Systems]: Real-time systems; G.3 [Probability and Statistics]: Random number generation; I.3.3 [Computer Graphics]: Computational Geometry and Object Modeling; I.3.7 [Computer Graphics]: Three-Dimensional Graphics and Realism; I.6.0 [Computer Graphics]: Simulation and Modeling; J.3 [Life and Medical Sciences]: Biology; J.5 [Arts and Humanities]: Arts, fine and performing.

ADDITIONAL KEY WORDS AND PHRASES: plant, tree, fractal, real time, DNA, genetics animation, recursion, stochasitic modeling, natural phenomena

1. INTRODUCTION

Benoit Mandelbrot recognized that the relationship between large scale structure and small scale detail is an important aspect of natural phenomena. He gave the name *fractals* to objects that exhibit increasing detail as one zooms in closer. [12][13] If the small scale detail resembles the large scale detail, the object is said to be self-similar.

The geometric notion of fractal self-similarity has become a paradigm for structure in the natural world. Nowhere is this principle more evident than in the world of botany. Recursive branching at many levels of scale, is a primary mechanism of growth in most plants. Analogously, recursive branching algorithms, are fundamental to computers. Many high performance processing engines specialize in tree data structures.

Computer generation of trees has been of interest for several years now. Examples of computer generated trees include

Benoit Mandelbrot (1977)(1982)   [12],[13]
Marshall,Wilson,Carlson (1980)   [14]
Craig Reynolds, (1981)   [19]
Yoichiro Kawaguchi (1982)   [10]
Geoff Gardiner (1984)   [9]
Aono,Kunii (1984)   [2]
Alvy Ray Smith, Bill Reeves (1984)(1985)   [21][18]
Jules Bloomenthal (1985)   [4]
Demko,Hodges,Naylor (1985)   [6]
Eyrolles, Francon, Viennot (1986)   [8]
among others.

Not all of the above used recursive tree data structures. Mandelbrot is largely responsible for the growing awareness of recursion as a process in nature. He and Kawaguchi each used minimal recursive topologies and added simple geometric relationships to generate complex images of branching plants and other objects. Alvy Ray Smith applied the theory of formal languages to generate more complex and systematized tree topologies, while emphasizing the separation between topology and geometry.

Each attempt at modeling trees takes a new approach, and thereby captures some different aspect of branching phenomena.

2. THE TREE MODEL

The tree model presented in this paper has the following features:

- A detailed parameterization of the geometric relationship between tree nodes.

- Real Time Design and Animation of tree images using high performance hardware.

- Application of Stochastic (random) Modeling to both topological and geometric parameters.

- Stochastic modeling of tree bark.

- High Resolution (2024 x 1980) Shaded 3D Renderings.

Here's how the model works:

This program implements a recursive tree model. Each tree generated satisfies the following recursive tree node definition:

```
tree :=
{
        Draw Branch Segment

        if (too small)
                Draw leaf
        else
        {
                # Continue to Branch
                {
                        Transform Stem
                        "tree"
                }
                repeat n times
                {
                        Transform Branch
                        "tree"
                }
        }
}
```

Paraphrased, a tree node is a branch with one or more tree nodes attached, transformed by a 3x3 linear transformation. Once the branches become small enough, the branching stops and a *leaf* is drawn. The trees are differentiated by the geometry of the transformations relating the node to the branches and the topology of the number of branches coming out of each node. These branching attributes are controllable by a set of numerical parameters. Editing these parameters, changes the tree's appearance. These parameters include:

- The angle between the main stem and the branches

- The size ratio of the main stem to the branches

- The rate at which the stem tapers

- The amount of helical twist in the branches

- The number of branches per stem segment

Figure 1 shows a simple example.

3. RANDOM NUMBERS IN FRACTAL MODELING

If the parameters remain constant throughout the tree, one gets a very regular looking tree such as a fern. This tree is strictly self similar; that is, the small nodes of the tree are identical to the top level largest node of the tree.

If the parameters vary throughout the tree, one gets an irregular gnarled tree such as a juniper tree. In order to achieve this, each parameter is given a mean value and a standard deviation. At each node of the tree, the parameter value is regenerated by taking the mean value and adding a random perturbation, scaled by the standard deviation. The greater the standard deviation, the more random, irregular, and gnarled the tree. The resulting tree is *statistically* self-similar; not *strictly* self-similar.

There are several reasons for the stochastic approach. First, adding randomness to the model generates a more natural looking image. Large trees have an intrinsic irregularity (caused in part by turbulent environmental effects). Random perturbations in the model reflect this irregularity. Second, random perturbations reflect the diversity in nature. A single set of tree model parameters can generate a whole forest of trees, each slightly different. This increased database amplification is one of the hallmark features of fractal techniques.

When generating random numbers, one must be careful about consistency and reproducibility. Simply reseeding the random number generator at the outset is not enough. For example, if one decreases the *minimum branch size* parameter, one would like the new tree to be a simple extension of the old tree. However, the order in which these new branch nodes are generated is intermixed with the old branch nodes. This could potentially scramble the random number generator, drastically changing the shape of the resulting tree. To avoid this, the random perturbations corresponding to a given node, should be determined by the *topological branch address* of the node, and not the order in which it is generated.

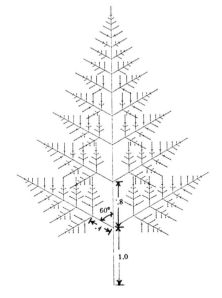

Figure 1	stem/stem ratio	= .8
	branch/stem ratio	= .4
	branching angle	= 60°

Fallen Leaf - An exaggerated image of vein branching in a fall leaf. The external boundary shape is the limit of growth of the internal veins. (512x480)

Snowflakes - Self similar branching occurs in the inorganic world as well.(512x480 resolution)

Fractal Fern - The classic organic self similar form. Every branch point looks the same -- but at different scales. (1024 x 960)

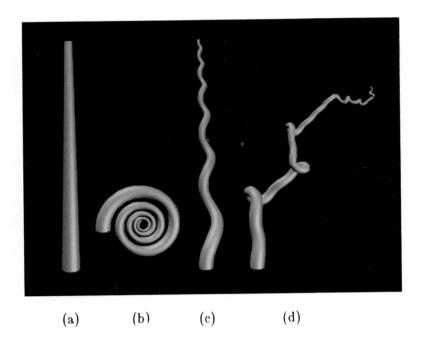

(a)   (b)   (c)   (d)

Figure 2   Spirals & Helixes

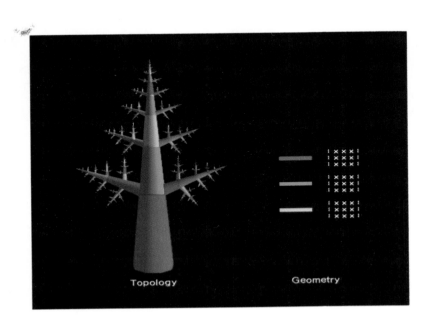

Figure 3   The Display List

Decreasing the *minimum branch size* parameter can also cause branches to *POP* on the tree, causing a disturbing effect in animations. This can be avoided by drawing partial branch segments whenever scaling a branch segment would cause it to be smaller than the *minimum branch size*. Using this method causes the branches to grow smoothly as the minimum branch size parameter is decreased, rather than *popping on*.

4. MODELING STEM SHAPE

By stripping all of the branches one is left with just a stem. By varying the transformation between stem segments, one derives the class of *spirals and helizes* and their random perturbations. These shapes appear in all forms of growth, organic and inorganic -- from the inner ear, sea shells, and plant sprouts, to spiral galaxies. *Spirals and helizes* are in some sense degenerate self similar sets. They are the atomic units that make up the fractal trees.

Figure 2 shows 4 typical *stem* shapes.

a) *cylinder*: the transformation is a translation and a scale.

b) *spiral*: one performs a rotation perpendicular to the stem axis, in addition to a scale and translation.

c) *helix*: one performs an additional rotation along the stem axis.

d) *squiggle* By randomly changing the transformation from segment to segment, case c) becomes case d).

Branches are simply stem shapes attached to the main stem and each other.

5. RENDERING THE FRACTAL

A variety of geometric elements can be used to render the branch segments. The simplest primitive is one single vector line per tree node. Antialiased vector lines with variable thickness allow one to taper the branches towards the tip. This method is satisfactory for leaves, ferns and other simple plants, for small scale detail in complex scenes, or for more abstract stylized images. Varying the vector color provides depth cuing and shading, and can also be used to render blossoms or foliage. Antialiased vectors are similar to particle systems used by Bill Reeves in his forest images. [18]

The thicker branches of a tree require a shaded 3D primative. Bump mapped polygonal prisms are used to flesh out the trees in 3D. The program makes sure that the polygons join continuously along each limb. The branches emanating from a limb simply interpenetrate the limb. For a more curvilinear limb shape, one can link several prisms together between branch points.

Shaded polygon limbs are far more computationally expensive than antialiased vectors. Since the number of branches increases exponentially with branching depth, one can spend most of an eternity rendering sub pixel limb tips, where bark texture and shading aren't visible anyway. In addition to being faster, sub pixel vectors are easier to antialias than polygons on our available rendering package. So for complex trees with a high level of branching detail, polygonal tubes were used for the large scale details, changing over to vectors for the small stuff. One can notice the artifacts of this technique. Overall, however, the eye ignores

this inconsistency if the cutover level is deep enough. Thinner branches require fewer polygons around the circumference; in fact triangular tubes will do for the smallest branches.

6. BARK

Sawtooth waves modulated by Brownian fractal noise are the source for the simulated bark texture. This texture is bump mapped onto the tree limbs. More specifically,

$$bark\ (x,y) = saw\ [\ N * [x + R * noise\ (x,y)]]$$

where

$$saw\ (t) = \begin{cases} 2 * fraction(t) & \text{if } fraction(t) < .5 \\ 2 * (1 - fraction(t)) & \text{if } fraction(t) > .5 \end{cases}$$

noise (x,y) is a periodic (ie wrapping) fractal noise function.

N is the number of bark ridges, and
R is the roughness of the bark.

Paraphrased, bark is generated by adding fractal noise to a ramp, then passing the result through a sawtooth function. A close up view of the bark would look like the ridges of a fractal mountain range. By adding the noise before the sawtooth function, the crests of the sawtooth ridges become wiggly. Note that bark(x,y) wraps in x and y.

7. REAL TIME FRACTAL GENERATION

Complex tree images can take 2 hours or more to render on a VAX 780. Editing tree parameters at this rate is not very effective. Near real time feedback is needed to allow one to freely explore the parameter space, and design the desired tree. Since vertex transformation cost is high for a complex fractal tree, hardware optimized for linear transformations was used for the real time editor. The Evans and Sutherland MultiPictureSystem generates vector drawings of complex 3D display lists in near real time. The display lists on the MPS look a lot like our tree nodes: primitive elements, transformed by linear transformations, and linked by pointers to other nodes. For a strictly self similar tree, the transformation is constant, therefore the entire display list can share a single matrix. To modify the tree one only has to change this one matrix, rather than an entire display list. This makes updating the tree display list very fast. For non-strictly self similar trees, the transformations are not the same. However a lookup table of less than a dozen transformations, is adequate to provide the necessary *pseudo* randomness. [21]

Figure 3 illustrates the logic of the display list.

The left side of the display list contains the topological description of the tree. Each node contains pointers to offspring nodes plus a pointer to the transformation matrix which relates that node to its parent node. This part of the display list is purely topological: it contains no geometric data. The geometric information is contained in the small list of transformation matrices on the right. To edit a tree, one can create a large topology list once and then rapidly manipulate only the small geometry list. Alvy Ray Smith in his research on *graftals*, recognized the separation of the topological and geometric aspects of trees. He calls these components the graph, and the interpretation respectively. His work deals primarily with specification of the tree topology, ignoring interpretation for the most part [21]. The

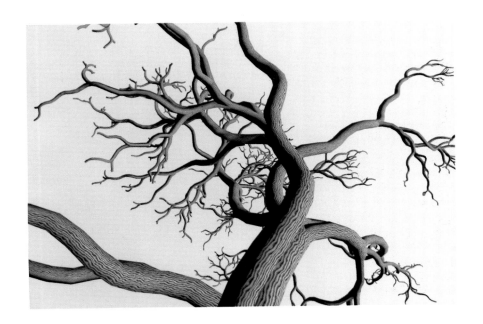

Views I - By randomly perturbing the branching parameters, one generates a more naturalistic gnarled tree. (2048x1920)

Blossomtime - The bark of this cherry tree is made with bump mapped polygonal tubes. The blossoms are colored vectors (particle systems) Instead of modeling blossoms, one can simply *dip* the branches in pink paint. (1024x960)

Raspberry Garden at Kyoto - The leaves and branches are generated by the fractal branching program. Berries are based on symmetry models by Haresh Lalvani, with added random perturbations. Non-self similar features such as berries, require genetic specialization. (1024x960) paper presented here emphasizes the geometric interpretation. The thesis of this paper is that the key to realistically modeling the diversity of trees lies in controlling the geometric interpretation. Many different topologies were used in this project. But by varying the geometric interpretation of a *single* topology, one could still generate a wide variety of trees each with its own distinct taxonomic identity.

The real time generation of fractal trees has been packaged as an interactive editing system. This multi-window system allows one to edit the tree parameters, (both geometric and topological) via graphically displayed sliders. A vector image of the tree responds in real time. To see all the parameters change at once one performs keyframe interpolation of the parameters. Each tree parameterization is written to a keyframe file. A cubic spline program, interpolates these parameters to create the inbetween frames. In the resulting animation, the tree metamorphoses from key to key. A simple *tree growth* animation is achieved by interpolating the trunk width parameter, and the recursion size cutoff parameter. Modifying additional parameters makes the growth more complex and natural looking. For example, many plants uncurl as they grow. A metamorphosis animation is achieved by interpolating parameters from different tree species. Growing and metamorphosing tree animations appear in *The Palladium* animation produced at NYIT. [1]

8. FRACTALS, COMPUTERS, AND DNA

The economic advantage of this program is that a highly complex structure is generated from a simple concise kernel of data which is easy to produce. (Such large database amplification is a primary advantage of fractal techniques in general.) How does the representation of complexity by computers compare with complex expression in nature itself?

Presumably, complexity in nature has evolved because it can bestow benefits on an organism. But, as with computers, complexity must not be a burden. Genetic economy demands that intricate structures be described by a limited supply of DNA. This struggle to simplify genetic requirements, determines the geometric structure of the plant. Form follows genetic economics.

This suggests a natural explanation as to why self-similarity abounds in the natural world: evolution has resolved the tension between complexity and simplicity in the same way that computer science has -- with recursive fractal algorithms. If fractal techniques help the computer resolve the demands of database amplification, then presumably organisms can benefit as well. For genes and computers alike, self-similarity is the key to thrifty use of data. [16][13]

The parameters of the tree program are numerical counterparts to the DNA code that describes a tree's branching characteristics. The logic of the gene is mimicked although the mechanism is different. The early stages of the model contained only 3 changeable parameters. The resulting images were of very simple fern like plants. New species were generated by controlling the parameter values, rerolling the dice of mutation and then selecting the forms that would be allowed to proliferate. As the model became more complex with the inclusion of more parameters, the program created images of more genetically complex trees such as cherry trees, higher on the evolutionary scale. Whereas natural selection of organisms is based on survival value, this aesthetic selection is based upon resemblance to the forms of nature.

9. CONCLUSION

Of course any scientific model is simply an attempted translation of nature into some quantifiable form. The success of the model is measured by some qualifyably predictive result. In experimental science, the success of a theory is measured by the degree to which the predicative model matches experimental data. Computer graphics now provides another style of predictive modeling. The success of a computer simulation is reflected in how well the image resembles the object being modeled. If one can model a complex object through simple rules, one has mastered the complexity. What appeared to be complex, proves to be primitive in the end. And the proof (although subjective) is in the picture.

10. ACKNOWLEDGEMENTS

Thanks go to all the members of NYIT staff and management for their help in the production of this work. Particular mention goes to Paul Heckbert and Lance Williams for software support and consultation. Kevin Hunter's Brownian Fractal Noise Texture was used to generate the bark. Haresh Lalvani contributed the original symmetry models for the raspberries. Design and direction by Rebecca Allen made the *Palladium* Animation possible. Special thanks go to Jane Nisselson and Robert Wright for editing, and to Ariel Shaw, Cydney Gordon, and the NYIT photo department, for film support.

Special thanks go to Benoit Mandelbrot, who has been a tremendous inspiration and influence.

Winter - Snow Algorithm by Lance Williams.
One renders the tree twice. Once with a side
light source. Once with an overhead *snow*
source. The snow *sticks* to the bump-mapped
texture.

Views II - (2048 x 1920)

REFERENCES

[1] Allen, R., Oppenheimer, P., *The Palladium* (Video), New York Institute of Technology, 1985

[2] Aono, M., Kunii, T.L., *Botanical Tree Image Generation*, IEEE Computer Graphics and Applications, Vol. 4, No. 5, May 1984

[3] Bentley, W.A., Humphreys, W.J., *Snow Crystals*, Dover Publications Inc.,New York, 1962 (Originally McGraw Hill, 1931)

[4] Bloomenthal, J., *Modeling the Mighty Maple*, Computer Graphics, Vol. 19, No. 3, July 1985.

[5] Bloomenthal, J., *Nature at New York Tech*, IEEE Computer Graphics and Applications, Vol. 6, No. 5, May 1986

[5] Cole, V.C., *The Artistic Anatomy of Trees*, Dover Publications Inc., New York, 1965 (Originally Seeley Service & Co, London, 1915)

[6] Demko, S., Hodges, L., Naylor, B., *Construction of Fractal Objects with Iterated Function Systems*, Computer Graphics, Vol. 19, No. 3, July 1985.

[7] De Reffye, P., Edelin, C., Francon, J., Puech, C., *L'Atelier de Modelisation de L'Architecture des Plantes*, (illustrated manuscript),1986

[8] Eyrolles, G., Francon, J., Viennot, G., *Combinatoire pour la Synthese d'Images de Plantes*, Cesta: Deuxieme Colloque Image, Vol. 2, Nice, April 1986

[9] Gardiner, G., *Simulation of Natural Scenes Using Textured Quadric Surfaces*, Computer Graphics, Vol. 18, No. 3, July 1984.

[10] Kawaguchi, Y., *A Morphological Study of the Form of Nature*, Computer Graphics, Vol. 16, No. 3, July 1982.

[11] Klee, P.,*On Modern Art*, (tr. Paul Findlay) Faber Ltd., London, 1948

[12] Mandelbrot, B., *Fractals: Form, Chance and Dimension*, W.H. Freeman and Co., San Francisco, 1977.

[13] Mandelbrot, B., *The Fractal Geometry of Nature*, W.H. Freeman and Co., San Francisco, 1982.

[14] Marshall, R., Wilson, R., Carlson, W., *Procedural Models for Generating Three-Dimensional Terrain*, Computer Graphics, Vol. 14, No. 3, July 1980.

[15] Oppenheimer, P., *Constructing an Atlas of Self Similar Sets* (thesis) Princeton University, 1979.

[16] Oppenheimer, P., *The Genesis Algorithm*, The Sciences, Vol 25, No 5., 1985.

[17] Queau, P., *Eloge de la Simulation*, Champ Vallon, France, 1986

[18] Reeves, W., *Particle Systems--A Technique for Modeling a Class of Fuzzy Objects*, Computer Graphics, Vol. 17, No. 3, July 1983.

[19] Reynolds, C., *Arch Fractal*, Computer Graphics (Front Cover), Vol. 15, No. 3, August 1981.

[20] Serafini, L., *Codex Seraphinianus*, Abbeville, New York, 1983.

[21] Smith, A.R., *Plants, Fractals, and Formal Languages*, Computer Graphics, Vol. 18, No. 3, July 1984.

[22] Stevens, P.S., *Patterns in Nature*, Little, Brown, and Co. Boston, 1974.

Modeling Waves and Surf

Darwyn R. Peachey

Department of Computational Science
University of Saskatchewan
Saskatoon, Canada

ABSTRACT

Although modeling natural phenomena is recognized as one of the greatest challenges of computer graphics, relatively little time has been spent on modeling ocean waves. The model presented in this paper is suitable for the rendering and animation of waves approaching and breaking on a sloping beach. Waveforms consist of a phase function which correctly produces wave refraction and other depth effects, and a wave profile which changes according to wave steepness and water depth. Particle systems are used to model the spray produced by wave breaking and collisions with obstacles. A scanline algorithm for displaying the wave surface is presented, along with a method of integrating separately rendered particle systems with other surfaces. Hidden surface removal for both waves and particles is done using a novel variation of the A-buffer technique. Methods of implementing the model are presented and compared with previous rendering techniques.

CR Categories and Subject Descriptors: I.3.3 [**Computer Graphics**]: Picture/Image Generation; I.3.5 [**Computer Graphics**]: Computational Geometry and Object Modeling; I.3.7 [**Computer Graphics**]: Three-Dimensional Graphics and Realism.

Additional Key Words and Phrases: A-buffer, clamping, particle systems, stochastic modeling, surf, water, wave refraction, waves.

1. Introduction

Modeling natural phenomena has always been among the most challenging problems in computer graphics, because natural phenomena have an inherent complexity far beyond that of most man-made objects. Significant progress has been made in modeling a variety of phenomena, including terrain [5], clouds [7], fire [14, 17], trees [1, 18, 19], and grass [18]. Relatively little time has been spent in modeling the appearance and behavior of the oceans.

Turner Whitted, in his film "The Compleat Angler", was among the first to attempt to render waves in water. Using ray tracing [21] Whitted animated realistic reflections from ripples in a small pool.

The ripples were created by bump mapping the flat pool surface, perturbing the surface normal according to a single sinusoidal function [22]. Another early effort was the Pyramid Films leader produced by Information International in 1981, which used a similar technique with cycloidal waveforms. More recently, Ken Perlin [14] has used bump mapping with a richer texture map to convincingly simulate the appearance of the ocean surface as one might see it from an aircraft well out to sea. Perlin used a set of 20 cycloidal waveforms, each radiating in a circular fashion from a randomly placed center point.

Although bump mapping is inexpensive and has been effectively used to simulate waves in the cases cited above, bump mapping is not sufficient to simulate waves in general. Since the actual surface is flat, bump mapped waves do not exhibit realistic silhouette edges or intersections with other surfaces. Another limitation of bump mapped waves is that they cannot shadow one another or cast shadows on other surfaces.

To avoid these shortcomings, Nelson Max [10] used a "height field" algorithm to render explicitly modeled wave surfaces for his film "Carla's Island". His wave model consisted of several superimposed linear sinusoidal waves simulating ocean waves of low amplitude.

In this paper we present a model of ocean waves which is capable of simulating the appearance and behavior of waves as they approach a sloping beach, steepening, breaking, and producing a spray of water droplets from the crests of the waves. Wavefronts are correctly refracted by the transition to shallow water, so that they align themselves parallel to the beach. The model is also capable of simulating spray resulting from the collision of waves with partially submerged obstacles. To our knowledge, no computer graphics model of these phenomena has previously been presented, although Fournier and Reeves [6] are involved in similar research.

2. Wave Fundamentals

A rich body of theory and observation exists concerning the behavior of waves in general, and water waves in particular [9, 11, 20]. There are several classes of water waves observed in the ocean:

- the tides, which have very long wavelengths and periods.
- seismic waves (tsunamis)
- internal waves
- surface gravity waves
- capillary (surface tension) waves, which have very short wavelengths and periods

Surface gravity waves and capillary waves generally result from the action of wind on the surface of the water, so they are collectively called "wind waves". Since our goal is to produce realistic pictures of waves and surf as they might be seen from the beach, we will deal only with surface gravity waves, which are usually the most noticeable waves on the beach during any short period of observation. (Small capillary wave ripples may be bump mapped on the wave surface for additional detail.)

The simplest surface gravity wave in water is a sinusoidal function of the form:

$$(1) \quad f(x,t) = A \, \cos(\frac{2\pi \, (x - Ct)}{L})$$

where x is the distance from an origin point, A is the amplitude of the wave, L is the wavelength, C is the propagation speed, and t is the time. The period, T, is the time between successive crests of the wave passing a particular point. The wavelength, period, and speed are related by the equation $C = L/T$. The frequency of the wave is $1/T$. The wave number of the wave, which is the spatial analog of the frequency, is $\kappa = 2\pi/L$. The magnitude of a water wave is often specified in terms of its height, H, rather than its amplitude, where $H = 2A$ for the simple sine wave. The steepness of a wave is the ratio $S = H/L$.

The motion of the wave must be distinguished from the motion of the water through which the wave is propagating. While the wave moves past a given point, the water at that point moves in a circular or elliptical orbit as shown in Figure 1. The water in the crest of the wave moves in the same direction as the wave, while the water in the trough of the wave moves in the opposite direction. The net motion of the water is zero in an ideal sinusoidal wave. The water must complete one orbit in the same time that it takes for a complete wavelength of the wave to pass a given point, namely the period of the wave, T. Since the diameter of the orbit is H, the average orbital speed of the water is:

$$(2) \quad Q_{avg} = \frac{\pi H}{T} = \frac{\pi H C}{L} = \pi S C$$

A wave breaks at the crest when the orbital speed Q of the water at the crest exceeds the speed C of the wave itself. This limits the steepness of a stable wave, since Q grows as S grows. Typical values for the steepness of ocean waves have been observed to be between 0.05 and 0.1.

Various hydrodynamic models of wave motion have been constructed by assuming that sea water is a perfectly nonviscous, incompressible fluid. The general model is nonlinear and has no convenient solutions [20]. Therefore, many simplified or idealized models are used for various situations. One of the more commonly used hydrodynamic models is the Airy model of sinusoidal waves of small (negligible) amplitude. The Airy model is linear, and

predicts that the propagation speed and wavelength of a wave will depend on the depth of the water, d, as follows:

$$(3a) \quad C = \sqrt{\frac{g}{\kappa} \tanh(\kappa d)} = \sqrt{\frac{gL}{2\pi} \tanh(\frac{2\pi d}{L})}$$

$$(3b) \quad L = CT$$

where g is the acceleration of gravity at sea level, 9.81 m/sec^2. In deep water, $\tanh(\kappa d)$ approaches 1, so C approaches $gL/2\pi$. In shallow water, $\tanh(\kappa d)$ approaches κd, so C approaches $\sqrt{gd}$. To achieve five percent accuracy in these approximations, it is sufficient for "deep" to mean $d \geq L/4$ and for "shallow" to mean $d \leq L/20$ [9].

As surface gravity waves are driven to large amplitudes by the wind, their shapes change, with the crests becoming more sharply peaked and the troughs becoming shallower and flatter. The Gerstner/Rankine wave model [9] gives an exact solution to the hydrodynamic equations for a wave of non-negligible amplitude in deep water. This model predicts a trochoidal or cycloidal waveform, approaching sinusoidal shape when the wave steepness is small. Another popular model is the Stokes wave model [9, 20] which is an infinite Fourier series which resembles the trochoidal wave up to the third order terms. The Stokes model predicts a slight dependence of wave speed on steepness, and a maximum wave steepness of 0.142. Nelson Max [10] used only the first-order term of the Stokes model for most of his waves, and used the first and second-order terms for the wave with the largest amplitude.

As waves approach the shore from deep water, the crests of the waves tend to become parallel to the shoreline regardless of their initial orientation. This is a result of *wave refraction*, a bending of the waves due to the dependence of propagation speed on the depth of the water. Since waves move more slowly in shallower water, the part of a wave which enters shallow water first will be retarded, and the remainder of the wave which is still in deeper water will move faster. This tends to turn the wave crest to be parallel to the line of transition to shallower water. Wave models which ignore refraction may produce "impossible" situations, such as the wave crests running perpendicular to the beach in [10].

Although the speed and wavelength of a wave are reduced as it enters shallower water, the period remains constant and the amplitude remains the same or increases slightly. The orbital speed of the water, which is directly related to the period and amplitude of the waves, stays the same even as the wave speed declines. This leads to a change in the shape of the waves, with the front of the crests becoming steeper and eventually breaking when the speed of the wave drops below the orbital speed of the water. When breaking occurs, droplets of water moving faster than the wave leave the wave surface in the form of spray. The existing hydrodynamic wave models do not adequately describe the breaking of waves.

3. A Model of Waves and Surf for Computer Graphics

The goal of our model of waves and surf is to allow us to synthesize convincing images of ocean waves as they might be seen on a beach. Moreover, the model must be suitable for animation, since it is the motion of waves and spray which give the strongest impression of realism to the viewer. Since no existing hydrodynamic model can claim to fully and realistically describe the behavior of any real ocean waves, we will not attempt to use such a model directly. However, we will depend on the predictions of the Airy model for the relationship between the depth of the water and the speed and wavelength of waves (even though many of our waves are neither sinusoidal nor of small amplitude).

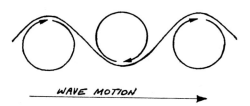

Figure 1: Orbital motion

3.1 Basic Model

We represent the ocean surface as a single-valued function of three variables:

$$y = f(x, z, t)$$

where (x, y, z) is the usual 3D Cartesian modeling space with the Y axis directed upwards, and t is the time, which is advanced for each successive frame of an animation. The use of a single-valued height function for the wave model means that we are prevented from producing waves whose crests actually curl forward. On the other hand, this representation of the surface permits us to easily combine numerous waves into one surface by superposition (simply adding together the heights of the individual wave components).

Our wave function f is a sum of several long-crested linear waveforms W_i with amplitudes A_i propagating in various directions from various origin points:

$$(4) \quad f(x, z, t) = \sum_{i=1}^{n} A_i W_i(x, z, t)$$

Instead of using W_i directly, we prefer to split W_i into a composition of two functions:

$$W_i(x, z, t) = w_i \left(fraction \left[\theta_i(x, z, t) \right] \right)$$

The functions w_i are called *wave profiles*, and are single-valued periodic functions of one parameter with a value between 0 and 1. This parameter value is the fractional part of the *phase* function, $\theta_i(x, z, t)$. The separation of W_i into a wave profile and a phase function makes it easier to describe and change the wave profile to give different wave shapes. It also allows us to address phase-related problems without concern for the final shape of the waveform. We discuss the phase function in the next section, and delay the discussion of wave profiles until section 3.3.

Each wave component can be completely characterized by giving its period T_i, its amplitude A_i, its origin, and its direction. Since each component may have a different origin and direction, the phase functions θ_i have a simpler form if expressed in a per-component coordinate system in which the wave starts at the coordinate system origin and propagates in the +X direction. A simple 2D transformation may be used to convert the coordinates of the point (x, z) into the corresponding coordinates $(\bar{x}_i, \bar{z}_i)$ in the coordinate system of component i.

3.2 The Phase Function

The phase function has a very simple dependence on the time t. Just as each wave component has the same constant period T_i at all points in space, it is also true that the wave component has the same constant rate of phase change at all points in space, namely the frequency:

$$\frac{\partial \theta_i}{\partial t} = -\frac{1}{T_i}$$

(The negative sign of the derivative is necessary to make the waves propagate in the direction of increasing phase values.) If we know the phase at a particular time $\theta_i(x, z, t_0)$ for all points (x, z), we can compute the phase for any frame of an animation by using the rule:

$$(5) \quad \theta_i(x, z, t) = \theta_i(x, z, t_0) - \frac{t - t_0}{T_i}$$

We will ignore the time-dependence of θ_i in the following discussion, and describe the phase at a fixed time t_0, assuming that the phase is 0 at the component origin point at time t_0 (which we can arrange, if necessary, by moving the origin point).

Unfortunately, the dependence of the phase on (x, z) is not nearly so tractable. It is necessary for our graphics model to include the effects of depth on wavelength and speed, in order to produce realistic wave refraction effects, such as the alignment of crests parallel to the beach, and in order to accurately depict the motion of the waves in shallow water. The implication of the dependence of wavelength and speed on depth is that the phase function depends on the cumulative effects of the depth of the water between the wave origin and the point of interest. In general, there is no simple expression for the phase function in water of varying depth. If the depth of the water is constant, then according to the Airy model (equation 3) the wavelength and speed are also constant. In this case, the phase function (expressed in the per-component coordinate system) is simply:

$$(6) \quad \theta_i(\bar{x}_i, \bar{z}_i) = \frac{\bar{x}_i}{L_i}$$

Since the wavelength L_i is variable in water of varying depth, it appears that the phase function must be evaluated as an integral of a depth-dependent phase-change function over the distance from the origin to the point of interest. In one-dimensional terms:

$$(7) \quad \theta_i(\bar{x}_i) = \int_0^{\bar{x}_i} \theta_i'(u) \, du$$

In the constant-depth case, the derivative is:

$$(8) \quad \theta_i'(u) = \frac{1}{L_i} = \frac{1}{C_i T_i}$$

where C_i or L_i may be computed from the Airy model of equation 3. Note that this equation may be obtained by differentiating equation 6.

Without justification, we use the same derivative (phase-change function) in water of varying depth. We must integrate this function as suggested by equation 7 in order to obtain a phase function will which give us the wave refraction effects we want. We numerically integrate from the origin of each component along the direction of propagation in deep water to obtain a grid of phase values. The grid for each component is stored in a file and is loaded during rendering of the wave surface in order to look up phase values for the component. Bilinear interpolation among grid values is used to produce phase values between grid points. This interpolation procedure does not seem to produce objectionable artifacts in the final images, because the interpolated phase is not rendered directly, but rather is used as the parameter of the wave profile function. Of course, a time adjustment for the particular frame being rendered must be subtracted from the phase (equation 5). It should be emphasized that the expensive numerical integration of the phase function for each component is done only once, not once for each frame.

3.3 Wave Profiles

The wave profile functions introduced in section 3.1 are single-valued periodic functions of one parameter:

$$w_i(u), \; 0 \leq u < 1$$

The values of w_i are interpreted as vertical displacements of the ocean surface from the rest position. In order for the wave amplitude A_i to have its desired effect, it is normally required that the values of w_i range over the interval $[-1, 1]$. The crest of the wave is conventionally located at $u = 0$, so $w_i(0) = 1$. In order that the wave surface be continuous, it is required that the function be continuous on $[0, 1)$ and that:

$$\lim_{u \to 1} w_i(u) = w_i(0) = 1$$

The simplest method of handling wave profiles is to use a fixed function for all w_i in all situations. For example, the function $w_i(u) = \cos(2\pi u)$ meets all of the requirements for a wave profile and will give a simple sinusoidal wave shape.

For greater realism, the wave profile function is changed according to the wave steepness, S, and the ratio, δ, between the depth of the water and the deep-water wavelength L_i^{deep}.

$$L_i^{deep} = \frac{gT_i^2}{2\pi}$$

$$\delta = \frac{d}{L_i^{deep}}$$

The steepness controls a linear blending between a sinusoidal function (when the steepness is small) and a sharp-crested quadratic function (when the steepness is large). The sharp-crested function is:

$$w_i(u) = 8\,|\,u - \frac{1}{2}\,|^2 - 1$$

This function superficially resembles a cycloid; we do not use an actual cycloid because it has no convenient formulation as an explicit function of the phase. The change of the wave profile as a function of steepness produces a realistic change in appearance from long smooth swell with rounded crests to short choppy waves with sharp crests.

The depth ratio, δ, controls the asymmetry of the wave profile. When δ is large, the wave profile is evaluated normally. When δ is small, the parameter u is exponentiated to shift its values toward the low end of the interval $[0, 1)$. This has the effect of steepening the front of the wave crest and stretching out the back of the crest. Similar asymmetry in wave profiles is easily observed as waves enter the shallow water near a beach and approach the breaking point. Figure 2 illustrates the different wave profiles produced by this model.

Since waves break and dissipate much of their energy as they enter very shallow water, our wave model reduces the amplitude of each wave component so that the vertical displacement of the ocean surface never exceeds the depth of the water. This reduction only takes effect when the depth of the water is comparable to the sum of the various amplitudes A_i.

3.4 Spray

Spray from breaking waves and from the collision of waves with partially submerged obstacles is an important aspect of modeling waves and surf. Particle systems [17] are a natural mechanism to use to simulate the behavior of the population of water droplets which make up the spray.

As mentioned earlier, waves break when the speed of circular motion of the water in the crest of the wave exceeds the speed of the wave itself. Based on the assumption of uniform circular motion, breaking would occur when $Q_{avg} > C$. From equation 2, $Q_{avg} = \pi S C$, so the condition becomes $\pi S > 1$ or $S > 1/\pi$. Clearly the assumption of uniform circular motion is incorrect, since the maximum steepness actually observed is much smaller, in the neighborhood of 0.1. The water in a steep wave moves faster in the crest than would be predicted by the uniform motion assumption. A "corrected" particle speed Q is computed by multiplying Q_{avg} by the factor $1/\pi S_{max}$ where S_{max} is the desired maximum steepness at the breaking point.

Generation of the particle system for a given breaking wave crest is relatively straightforward. The initial position of each particle is at the crest of the wave. The initial velocity of the particle is in approximately the same direction as the wave motion, with a speed of Q. A stochastic perturbation with a Gaussian distribution is added to the particle velocity to avoid excessively uniform particle behavior. An increasing number of particles is generated as the speed differential between the wave speed and Q increases.

Notice that the criterion for the generation of spray due to breaking is entirely dependent on wave steepness and not on the depth of the water. Usually breaking will result from the reduction in wavelength and consequent steepening when a wave enters shallow water. In this case, the generation of spray will be accompanied by an asymmetric wave profile as described in the previous section. However, it is also possible for waves to break in deep water when the amplitude becomes sufficiently large (storm conditions). In this case, the wave profiles will be symmetrical and sharp-crested, approximating a cycloid.

A similar particle system model is used to simulate the spray resulting from waves striking obstacles (rocks, piers, etc.) along the beach. Particles are generated when the crest of a wave is near the seaward face of the obstacle. The crest is the relevant part of the wave for spray generation because the water in the crest is moving toward the beach with its maximum speed, and therefore generates the most spectacular spray.

The rate of particle generation increases from zero at a time slightly before the crest meets the obstacle, to a maximum value when the crest is at the obstacle, and then falls back toward zero as the crest passes the obstacle. The initial positions of the particles lie approximately on the curve along which the wave surface intersects the obstacle. The initial velocities of the particles are chosen stochastically, with a magnitude that is a constant fraction of the speed Q at which the water is striking the obstacle, and a direction which is the reflection direction for an ideal elastic collision, plus a Gaussian perturbation (Figure 3).

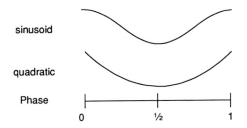

Figure 2: Wave profiles

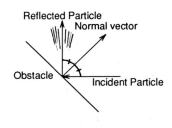

Figure 3: Obstacle impact

Once a particle has been generated as a result of wave breaking or obstacle impact, its behavior is simulated according to gravitational kinematics as described in section 4.3.

3.5 Designing the Beach

Since so much of the wave and spray model depends on the depth of the water at a given point, the final images are greatly affected by the shape of the terrain which makes up the beach, and especially by the submarine contours of the terrain. The images in this paper are based on a hypothetical beach called "Babbage Beach". Figure 4 is a topographic map of Babbage Beach with yellow indicating high cliffs, green indicating low beach, white and light blue indicating shallow water, and darker blue indicating deep water. The water at the top of the map averages 10 meters deep. Adjacent lines of the black grid are 100 meters apart. The red bands indicate the crests of a wave component with a period of six seconds. Wave refraction effects are clearly visible in the shape of these bands. Figure 5 is a perspective view of the terrain without water.

The Babbage Beach terrain was entered as a coarse grid of manually generated elevations. This data was smoothed and interpolated with some stochastic variation to produce a much finer grid of elevations. At present, the resulting terrain is rendered as a collection of triangles with the grid points as vertices. Bilinear interpolation is used to determine the elevation at an arbitrary point for use by the wave and spray model. Alternatively, an interpolating spline surface could be passed through the grid points for smoother interpolation and a more realistic appearance.

If a beach is to be designed without simply digitizing a contour map of a real beach, some study of coastal geomorphology [15] is useful in determining realistic landforms and submarine contours. The slope of the beach depends on the type of sand particles or rocks which make up the beach. Larger particles lead to steeper beaches; a slope between 1:10 and 1:30 is typical for sandy beaches, while beaches made of stones or slate-like "shingle" can be as steep as 1:2 or 1:3. The nature of the beach also depends on the steepness of the large waves which strike it. Steep winter storm waves tend to erode the above-water part of the beach while building up underwater sand bars. The lower waves of the summer season move the sand landward and build up an above-water hill called a "berm".

4. Rendering

The model described in section 3 has been implemented as part of two image synthesis systems, a ray tracing system called "Portray" [13] and an A-buffer-like system called "Pixie". The ray tracing implementation does not include the particle system model of spray.

4.1 Ray Tracing Waveforms

In the Portray ray tracing system, a modified *regula falsi* iterative root-finding technique was used to solve the ray-surface intersection equation directly. The advantage of ray tracing as a means of rendering the wave surface is that it easily and correctly handles the images of the sky and of objects reflected in the water. However, these reflections usually can be simulated by the use of reflection environment maps in non-ray tracing systems. The surface of the ocean is usually so rough that reflections cannot be seen very clearly, and an approximation to the correct reflection will suffice. The disadvantages of ray tracing are its immense cost (nearly 30 CPU hours on a Pyramid 90x for some wave surfaces), the difficulty of rendering complex procedural models such as particle systems, and the tendency for aliasing to arise from point sampling distant waves near the horizon. Stochastic sampling is a possible, but expensive, solution to the latter problem.

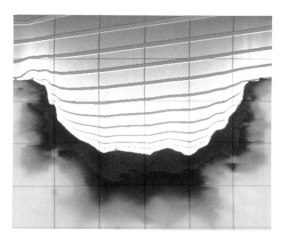

Figure 4: Topographic map of Babbage Beach

Figure 5: Beach terrain without water

4.2 Scanline Rendering of Waveforms

Because ray tracing is expensive and inconvenient for rendering complex ocean phenomena, we would like to develop a hidden surface technique more suited to the task. The Z-buffer hidden surface technique [3] seems to offer the greatest modeling freedom, since any element of a model may be rendered at any convenient time. Unfortunately, the Z-buffer technique requires a great deal of memory and is very prone to aliasing.

The A-buffer technique has been proposed [2] as an anti-aliased alternative to the Z-buffer. Unfortunately, the A-buffer does not really offer the same degree of rendering freedom as the Z-buffer. A pixel of the A-buffer is equivalent to a pixel of the Z-buffer when the pixel is entirely covered by an opaque surface. However, when a pixel is only partially covered or the covering surface is not opaque, the A-buffer stores the sub-pixel information as an arbitrarily long linked list of "fragment" structures, each of which is 28 bytes long in the original implementation. If the model being rendered produces a large number of such complex pixels, the memory consumption of the A-buffer may become prohibitive, and the paging of virtual memory may severely impact performance. To alleviate these problems, the A-buffer system pages the pixel array in software and renders surfaces in "approximately scanline order".

Since it is necessary to render in approximately scanline order to make practical use of the A-buffer, we decided to build an A-buffer-like system, Pixie, in which rendering takes place in *strictly* scanline order. Although the basic A-buffer techniques are still used at each pixel, our approach has a number of advantages. Instead of a buffer array with one entry per image pixel, we need only a single row buffer with one entry per image column. The vastly reduced storage requirements eliminate any need to page the A-buffer in software, and free us to store more information per pixel. In particular, there is no need to use the smaller 8-byte per pixel Z-buffer-like data structure for completely covered pixels. Even pixels which are covered by a single opaque surface are represented as a fragment list. This simplifies the algorithms and allows us to maintain 12 bits of color resolution and both minimum and maximum Z values for *all* pixels. An 8×8 bit pixel mask is used instead of the 4×8 mask originally proposed. The buffer itself is simply an array of fragment list pointers, with a NULL pointer indicating an empty pixel. When all rendering for the current scanline has been completed, an output routine is called to pack the fragment list (if any) at each pixel of the scanline, write the final color and coverage information out to the image files, and reclaim the fragment storage, setting the buffer fragment list pointers back to NULL.

Given the design of the Pixie rendering system, it was necessary to develop a scanline display algorithm for rendering wave surfaces. The algorithm is an adaptation of the general Lane/Carpenter parametric surface subdivision algorithm [8]. Our wave model may be viewed (in the appropriate coordinate system) as a function $y = f(x, z)$ at a particular time t. The form of this function is described in section 3. A suitable parametric representation of the surface in terms of parameters (u, v) is:

$$x(u, v) = u$$

$$y(u, v) = f(u, v)$$

$$z(u, v) = v$$

The algorithm maintains a set of polygons to be rendered and a set of wave surface patches to be rendered. Each set consists of a linked list for each scanline. The algorithm begins with the x and z coordinates of the initial wave surface in the modeling coordinate system. This initial wave patch is inserted in the linked list for the scanline on which the patch is first visible. As each scanline is reached, the algorithm checks each patch in the list for the scanline to see whether it can be accurately represented by a single polygon. If so, the patch is discarded and the appropriate polygon is inserted in the polygon display list to be rendered by an anti-aliased polygon scan conversion algorithm. If the patch is still too large to render as a polygon, the patch is subdivided into four subpatches, and each of these patches is inserted in the linked list for the scanline on which it first appears. Subdivision of the patch is done according to the perspective projection of the patch into screen space, in such a way that each of the four subpatches covers an approximately equal area on the screen. A patch is rendered as a polygon only when the patch covers approximately one pixel or less.

To implement the Lane/Carpenter scanline display algorithm requires that we are able to determine a fairly tight lower bound on the screen space Y coordinate of a given surface patch (assuming the Y coordinates increase going down the screen beginning with scanline 0 at the top). For any wave surface patch, a lower bound on the screen Y coordinate (scanline number) of the visible part of the patch may be found by transforming the modeling space coordinates (x_i, A, z_i) into screen space for each patch corner (x_i, z_i).

This is true because the amplitude A gives an upper bound on the height of the wave function. Assuming the camera (eyepoint) is located above the plane $y = A$ in modeling space, the screen Y coordinate of the point $(x_i, f(x_i, z_i), z_i)$ cannot be less than the screen Y coordinate of (x_i, A, z_i).

Aliasing of distant waves is prevented by a form of "clamping" [12] which reduces the amplitude of waves which are very short relative to the pixel diameter. Waves shorter than two pixel diameters are completely ignored (their amplitude is zero).

It is interesting to compare this wave rendering algorithm to the "height field" algorithm used by Max [10] and originally proposed by Fishman and Schachter [4]. The height field algorithm renders a single-valued function of two variables by scanning columns of the image from bottom to top. Thus the algorithm would not be directly applicable to a scanline-oriented rendering system such as Pixie. A more serious problem is that the permissible viewing geometry is quite restricted with the height field algorithm. The camera must be above the top of the waves (maximum height field value), the viewing direction must lie in a horizontal ($y = k$) plane (the camera cannot be pointed somewhat upward or downward), and the camera must be upright (cannot be tilted from side to side). Our algorithm, as an adaptation of the general Lane/Carpenter technique, has no such viewing restrictions. However, a slightly more complex scanline bounding test must be used when the camera lies below the $y = A$ plane or is tilted very sharply to one side.

4.3 Rendering Spray

Our model of spray consists of the particle systems described in section 3.4. It is very difficult to directly render particle systems in scanline order. Instead, the particle systems are simulated by a separate program which contains the same wave model as the main Pixie rendering program. This program outputs a file of pixel information in scanline order which is used by Pixie to combine particles with the other elements of the scene and determine which surfaces are visible in each pixel.

The particle program advances through time in steps of ½-frame (1/48th second). At each step, new particles are generated according to the rules for wave breaking and obstacle impact. A data structure is allocated for each new particle to store its current position, its previous position, and its velocity. Each old particle is moved according to its average velocity during the step, and the velocity is updated so that the particle accelerates downward with the correct acceleration of gravity. Particles are deleted if they drop below the lower bound of the wave surface. No attempt is made to determine the actual wave level in the vicinity of the particle, since hidden surface removal will later be done by Pixie.

The particle population usually stabilizes after about ½ second, so that the number of new particles being generated is roughly equal to the number of particles being deleted. In order to ensure that all particles that could appear in the image have been generated, it is necessary to start the model far enough back in time that a particle generated in the initial step with the maximum upward velocity will have fallen below the lower bound of the wave surface by the time of the image.

When the particle population at the time of the desired frame has been generated, the particles are clipped to the viewing volume and transformed into screen space using exactly the same perspective projection used in Pixie to render the other elements of the scene. Each particle is drawn as an anti-aliased line segment joining its positions at the beginning and end of the ½-frame interval. This effectively provides temporal anti-aliasing (motion blur) for the particles, which are the fastest moving objects in each image. (The waves move and change relatively slowly and smoothly so temporal aliasing is not a serious problem.)

The particles are drawn into a "sparse Z-buffer" in the particles program. The sparse Z-buffer consists of a linked list of pixel structures for each scanline of the image. When some particle is drawn in a given pixel, the appropriate scanline list is searched for the pixel, and a new pixel is added to the list if no other particle has previously been drawn into that pixel. In practice, the particles cover a relatively small portion of the entire image, so only about 10% of the total image pixels appear in the sparse Z-buffer. Because space consumption is quite small, it is possible to keep the color, coverage, and maximum and minimum screen Z value (perspective depth) for each pixel. Pixel data which overlap in Z value are stored in the same pixel structure; data with disjoint depths are stored in separate structures even if they appear in the same scanline and column of the image. Coverages of particles are determined from the distance to the particle and its velocity. The coverages of all particles in a pixel are added together subject to a maximum value of 1. The colors of particles are combined using a sum weighted by their coverages. Finally, the maximum and minimum Z values are updated according to each new particle in the pixel.

When all particles have been drawn into the sparse Z-buffer, the contents of the buffer are written into a temporary file. This file is read by Pixie during the rendering of the other elements of the scene. Since the particle file is in scanline order, Pixie can easily read the information (if any) which is relevant to the scanline currently being rendered. Each pixel in the particle file is passed to the A-buffer hidden surface routines, using the color, coverage (opacity), and maximum and minimum Z values which were determined by the particles program. Using this information, Pixie can determine whether the particles obscure or are obscured by other surfaces in the scene, such as the wave surface or the surface of an obstacle.

In the original work on particle systems [17], the particles were rendered by a separate program which produced color and coverage information for each image pixel in the form of an RGBα image [16]. This image was combined with other image elements using a digital compositing scheme. For images of waves and surf, it would be very difficult to determine clear depth relationships between particles and the surfaces in the scene, so that compositing of images could be used. The combination of particle information with other surface information in the A-buffer at the time of rendering solves this problem by automatically determining where surfaces or particles are visible.

Our current illumination model for spray particles is quite primitive. Particles are treated as small white spheres. Since it is prohibitively expensive to determine which particles are in the shadow of the waves or other particles, all of the particles are shaded the same color. To achieve a more realistic appearance, a random component is used to vary the shade a little. A slight darkening of the particles based on the magnitude of their downward velocity is used to simulate the shadowing of the particles by other particles and objects. This trick has worked fairly well, but clearly it would be easy to construct counter-examples where the effect would be quite unrealistic.

5. Examples

Figures 6 through 10 were produced using Pixie and the wave and surf model described in section 3. Figure 6 shows a group of moderately high waves approaching the beach. Figure 7 shows a similar group of waves with a three times larger amplitude. The increased amplitude makes these waves steep enough to break and

Figure 6: Waves on Babbage Beach

Figure 7: Breaking waves

generate spray when the wavelength is reduced in shallow water. Figure 8 is the same as Figure 7, with the addition of an pyramid-shaped rock as an obstacle. A small plume of spray is produced from the impact of a wave with the obstacle. Figures 9 and 10 show a sunward view of the beach in the late afternoon and at sunset.

These examples were produced using only three wave components, the main waves with a period of 6 seconds and two secondary components with periods of 2 and 2.5 seconds. Realism would be enhanced by the addition of a time-dependent bump-mapped texture pattern of small ripples.

Each of the examples was generated in approximately one hour of CPU time on a Pyramid 90x computer (comparable to a VAX-11/785 FPA). The implementation has not yet been carefully tuned or optimized. The simulation and rendering of the particle systems took approximately 10 CPU minutes with 2.5 megabytes of virtual

Figure 8: Breaking waves with obstacle

memory to simulate an active population of 56000 particles from a total of 95000 particles that were generated. Pixie took about 40 CPU minutes and 3 megabytes of virtual memory to render the wave surface and terrain, and to determine the visible surfaces at each pixel, including the particle coverage and depth information supplied by the particle program. The generation of the numerically integrated phase function table for each wave component consumed from 2 to 5 CPU minutes.

6. Conclusions and Future Research Directions

We have presented a graphical model of waves and surf which is capable of rendering and animating realistic images of these ocean phenomena. This is one of the first attempts to model breaking waves and surf in the field of image synthesis. In our model the shapes of waves change as they approach the shore, with the fronts of the waves steepening markedly as the depth of the water decreases. When the waves break, spray is simulated by a particle system in order to give the appearance of "whitecaps". Particle system spray is also used to model the impact of waves on obstacles. Wave refraction effects and the change of speed and wavelength in shallow water are simulated using a numerically integrated phase function which need only be computed once for a given wave component, even if many frames of animation are generated.

The rendering of the wave model is done by an adaptation of the Lane/Carpenter subdivision algorithm for parametric surfaces to the particular case of single-valued functions of two variables. This is a scanline algorithm, and does not suffer from the restrictions on viewing geometry inherent in Max's height field algorithm. The wave rendering algorithm is incorporated in a novel implementation of the A-buffer, with performance and simplicity advantages over the original A-buffer scheme. Particle systems are rendered by a separate program which produces a scanline sorted file of pixel information suitable for the A-buffer.

This allows us to integrate particle systems with other surfaces at low cost and with greater flexibility than can be achieved using compositing techniques.

This work has concentrated on modeling the geometry and motion of waves, surf, and spray. Further work on illumination models is needed, especially to approximate shadowing of spray particles, refraction of light from spray particles, and transmission of light through steep wave crests. Texturing of wave surfaces might be used to simulate foam, but care must be taken that such texture maps behave sensibly from frame to frame of animation. The effectiveness of particle systems in modeling spray suggests that they might be used to model fountains, waterfalls, and perhaps even rapids.

In our model each wave component is long-crested and has a fixed amplitude. To more realistically model the ocean surface, it would be desirable to add the concept of "wave groups" to the model. A wave group would consist of a phase offset and an amplitude function which would produce a moving "bump" of short-crested waves which could be out of phase with other wave groups of the same wave component. The wave group would move at one-half the wave speed as predicted by theory, in the same general direction as the waves themselves. Several wave groups could share a single phase function.

Acknowledgements

This research was supported by the Natural Sciences and Engineering Research Council of Canada through infra-structure grant no. A2527. The work could not have been done without the support and facilities of the Department of Computational Science and the University of Saskatchewan. The encouragement and assistance of my wife, Judy, was vital to the completion of this paper.

Figure 9: Sunset

Figure 10: Late afternoon

References

[1] Bloomenthal, J. Modeling the mighty maple, *Computer Graphics 19*, 3 (July 1985), 305-311.

[2] Carpenter, L. The A-buffer, an antialiased hidden surface method, *Computer Graphics 18*, 3 (July 1984), 103-108.

[3] Catmull, E. *A Subdivision Algorithm for Computer Display of Curved Surfaces*, University of Utah, December 1974.

[4] Fishman, B. and Schachter, B. Computer display of height fields, *Computers and Graphics 5* (1980), 53-60.

[5] Fournier, A., Fussell, D., and Carpenter, L. Computer rendering of stochastic models, *Commun. ACM 25*, 6 (June 1982), 371-384.

[6] Fournier, A. and Reeves, W. A simple model of ocean waves, *Computer Graphics 20*, 3 (August 1986).

[7] Gardner, G. Visual simulation of clouds, *Computer Graphics 19*, 3 (July 1985), 297-303.

[8] Lane, J. and Carpenter, L. A generalized scan line algorithm for the computer display of parametrically defined surfaces, *Computer Graphics and Image Processing 11* (1979), 290-297.

[9] Kinsman, B. *Wind Waves: their generation and propagation on the ocean surface*, Prentice-Hall, Englewood Cliffs, N.J., 1965.

[10] Max, N. Vectorized procedural models for natural terrain: waves and islands in the sunset, *Computer Graphics 15*, 3 (August 1981), 317-324.

[11] Milne-Thomson, L. *Theoretical Hydrodynamics, 5th edn.*, Macmillan & Co., London, 1968.

[12] Norton, A., Rockwood, A., and Skolmoski, P. Clamping: a method of antialiasing textured surfaces by bandwidth limiting in object space, *Computer Graphics 16*, 3 (July 1982), 1-8.

[13] Peachey, D. PORTRAY—an image synthesis system, *Proc. Graphics Interface '86*, Vancouver, May 1986.

[14] Perlin, K. An image synthesizer, *Computer Graphics 19*, 3 (July 1985), 287-296.

[15] Pethick, J. *An Introduction to Coastal Geomorphology*, Edward Arnold Ltd, London, 1984.

[16] Porter, T. and Duff, T. Compositing digital images, *Computer Graphics 18*, 3 (July 1984), 253-259.

[17] Reeves, W. Particle systems — a technique for modelling a class of fuzzy objects, *Computer Graphics 17*, 3 (July 1983), 359-376.

[18] Reeves, W. and Blau, R. Approximate and probabilistic algorithms for shading and rendering structured particle systems, *Computer Graphics 19*, 3 (July 1985), 313-322.

[19] Smith, A. Plants, fractals, and formal languages, *Computer Graphics 18*, 3 (July 1984), 1-10.

[20] Stoker, J. *Water Waves: The Mathematical Theory with Applications*, Interscience Publishers, New York, 1957.

[21] Whitted, T. An improved illumination model for shaded display, *Commun. ACM 23*, 6 (June 1980), 343-349.

[22] Whitted, T. The hacker's guide to making pretty pictures, SIGGRAPH '85 Course Notes: Image Rendering Tricks, July 1985.

A Simple Model of Ocean Waves

Alain Fournier †

Department of Computer Science
University of Toronto
Toronto, Ontario

William T. Reeves

Animation Research and Development
PIXAR
San Rafael, CA

ABSTRACT

We present a simple model for the surface of the ocean, suitable for the modeling and rendering of most common waves where the disturbing force is from the wind and the restoring force from gravity.

It is based on the Gerstner, or Rankine, model where particles of water describe circular or elliptical stationary orbits. The model can easily produce realistic waves shapes which are varied according to the parameters of the orbits. The surface of the ocean floor affects the refraction and the breaking of waves on the shore. The model can also determine the position, direction, and speed of breakers.

The ocean surface is modeled as a parametric surface, permitting the use of traditional rendering methods, including ray-tracing and adaptive subdivision. Animation is easy, since time is built into the model. The foam generated by the breakers is modeled by particle systems whose direction, speed and life expectancy is given by the surface model.

To give designers control over the shape of the ocean, the model of the overall surface includes multiple trains of waves, each with its own set of parameters and optional stochastic elements. The overall "randomness" and "short-crestedness" of the ocean is achieved by a combination of small variations within a train and large variations between trains.

Rendered examples of oceans waves generated by the model are given and a 10 second animation is described.

CR Categories and Subject Descriptors: I.3.3 [**Computer Graphics**]: Picture/Image Generation - Display Algorithms; I.3.5 [**Computer Graphics**]: Computational Geometry and Object Modeling - Curve, surface, solid and object representations - Modeling Packages; I.3.7 [**Computer Graphics**]: Three-dimensional Graphics and Realism - Animation - Colour, shading, texture.

General Terms: Waves, Model, Algorithms.

Additional Keywords and Phrases: Ocean Waves, Wave Refraction, Surf and Spray.

---

†Address for 1985-1986: Department of Computer Science, Stanford University.

1. Introduction

There is no longer a need to justify the modeling of natural phenomena and no need to restate the seemingly limitless complexity of nature. One natural object especially interesting to model, and important because, to give only one reason, it covers two-thirds of the surface of the earth, is the ocean.

Compared to other natural objects and phenomena, the sea is both easier and more difficult to model. It is easier because it is relatively homogeneous, and more difficult because it moves. In fact, if it did not move, the surface would be flat, and we would be left with only a rendering problem (albeit not a simple one, due to water transparency and reflectance). Because of the homogeneity, we do not have to worry about widely different shapes (such as in species of trees) or different shaping mechanisms (such as in tectonic phenomena). We can hope to find a model that will be satisfactory for a wide range of sea conditions. Because the sea moves, the model has to include time explicitly in the surface description.

Looking at the sea (and this is where it should always begin and end), we can observe a wide range of "basic" familiar wave shapes, with typical crests and troughs, but it is hard to identify distinct individual waves or distinct trains of waves. In fact, individual waves are short-lived and all different, and the sea often appears to be made of randomly distributed waves. Our model must deal with this mixture of randomness and regularity.

We can, at the outset, establish a wish list of what we hope our model to accomplish. The model should:
- produce shapes similar to the shape of real waves;
- generate realistic motion;
- give a range of waves from very low ripples to high storm waves;
- make the surface take the shape of the shore;
- show the effect of shallow bottoms, such as refraction and breaking;
- identify the areas where breakers occur;
- allow an interface to a user-specified "wind field"; and
- include parameters to allow departure from "earth" conditions.

From the point of view of rendering, the model should:
- accommodate some, if not all, of the familiar rendering techniques;
- be easy to compute (in terms of basic operations and in terms of number of operations per point);
- permit rendering the surface at controllable levels of detail; and
- allow easy spatial and temporal filtering.

We also can list a few characteristics the model should not have:
- It will not be totally stochastic, even though stochastic elements are necessary.

In other words there is a strong deterministic element among the noise. Waves do roll in parallel to the shore and there are trains (the swell from storms thousands of miles away can be felt).
- It will not be a "fractal" model.

The reason given above is enough, but even considered as a random process the ocean surface does not have the characteristics of fractal noises. Figure 1 gives the energy spectrum of the sea. It is only a "generic" spectrum to give a qualitative idea. The figure also includes some of the typology of waves. It is obvious that it is not the spectrum of a fractal, which is characterized by a slow decay of the energy in the high frequencies. Nevertheless, fractals have been used to model water surface [Ogde85]. In fact, in the range we will attempt to model, that is waves of periods from about 0.5 to 30 seconds, where the major disturbing force is due to the wind, and the major restoring force is due to gravity, the distribution is close to being gaussian. By the same token, the probability distribution for the surface displacement of the sea fits a gaussian very well.[1]

• It will not be a height field.

A height field, which has been used before to model waves [Max81, Scha80], is such that for each pair (x,y) there is at most one z value. Figure 2, which is realistic in its own way, shows us why height fields should be avoided.

• There should not be a net transport of matter as time advances.

We do not want the whole sea, as an object, to march across the landscape. While we certainly want local motion, as in the water lapping against the shore, the sea should globally stay put, as it fortunately does most of the time. There can be a transitory net mass transport, but we

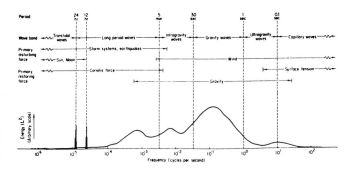

Figure 1
Rough energy spectrum of the sea (from [Kins84]).

Figure 2
The surface of the sea is not a height field.

will neglect this effect.

• We do not expect any "physical" answer from our model.

In fact, we do not ask any question except "does it look like the real thing". So a model which might be useless to an oceanographer might turn out to be good for our purposes. By the same token, we will feel free to adjust coefficients to achieve the needed effect, even if we are not quite sure if doing so has a physical meaning. This is of course extremely bad form when building physical models.

2. Sources and Previous Work

In the time honored tradition of computer graphics, we can now go ahead and steal anything we can get. The literature of hydrodynamics and waves is quite large, but we relied mainly on the books of Crapper [Crap84], Le Mehaute [LeMe76], Leblond [Lebl78] and Kinsman [Kins84], which is a Dover reprint of [Kins65]. The latter book by B. Kinsman, *Wind Waves*, is highly recommended. It is a rarity, a book filled with equations but written by somebody who obviously loves words and uses them superbly.

There have been a few previous attempts to model waves or some aspects of the ocean surface before in computer graphics. The first two are referred to by their appearance in the Siggraph slide sets, since they were not described elsewhere to the best of our knowledge. The first is the "Pyramid" slide, by Gary Demos et al, in the 1981 collection. It appears to use cycloidal waves and it was also animated (see reference in [Max81a]). The other is the "Night Castles" slide, by Ned Green, in the 1982 collection which used sine waves and the "bump mapping" technique [Blin78]. Nelson Max, in his famous *Carla's Island* [Max81b], also used a few terms of a sum of sine waves to approximate Stokes waves [Max81a]. His chosen rendering algorithms required a height field. That was accompanied by partial ray-tracing and imaginative sunset and moonlight effects. Norton, Rockwood and Skolmoski [NoRS82] used frequency limited ("clamped") analytical functions to model waves. The technique was intended for use in a real-time image generator. Schachter [Scha80] used the sum of narrow band noise waveforms, a technique also intended for real-time applications, and which was implemented in hardware.

More recently Perlin [Perl85] describes various types of waves as part of an application of his Pixel Stream Editor. He used, among others, spherical cycloidal waves and, specifically to simulate sea waves, random sources with a constant amplitude-frequency product. Ts'o and Barsky [TsBa85] model the sea surface as a height field from the Stokes model, and fit it with β-splines, adjusting the shape parameters to obtain symmetrical waves. They were the first to have as one their goals the modeling of wave refraction as the ocean floor depth decreases. Peachy [Peac86] models the ocean surface using a height field computed from the Stokes model, with quadric surfaces to introduce asymmetry. He also used particle systems to model the surf, but did not include depth effects.

3. The Basic Model[2]

Fluid motion is generally studied by one of two methods. In the *Eulerian* method, one considers a point (x,y,z) and tries to answer questions about the properties of the fluid at this point as a function of time, such as the speed:

$$U=f(x,y,z,t)$$

In the *Lagrangian* method, one follows the trajectory of a point (x_0,y_0,z_0), given by a reference position. This can be seen as the trajectory of a particle of matter. For instance, we can ask for the speed at time t:

$$V_x=f_x(x_0,y_0,z_0,t)$$
$$V_y=f_y(x_0,y_0,z_0,t)$$
$$V_z=f_z(x_0,y_0,z_0,t)$$

The first method is favored in hydrodynamics, and in the study of waves, especially since the development of stochastic models for the analysis of the sea. The second method looks a priori more useful for graphics modeling. It is more convenient to treat the ocean surface as a graphical primitive and a Lagrangian approach will describe it explicitly.

We will consider that each particle (i.e., each point) on the free surface describes a circle around its rest position (x_0,y_0,z_0). Without loss of generality, we will orient our world coordinates so that the XY plane is the plane of the sea at rest, and the Z axis is pointing up. For the time being, we will only consider the motion in the XZ plane. The equation of the motion of a particle is then:

$$x=x_0+r \times \sin(\kappa x_0-\omega t) \qquad (1a)$$
$$z=z_0-r \times \cos(\kappa x_0-\omega t) \qquad (1b)$$

Looking at the equations above as parametric equations in x_0 for a given t and a constant z_0, one can see that the surface is a *trochoid*, a generalization of a *cycloid*. It can be seen as the curve generated by a point P at a distance r from the center of a circle of radius $\frac{1}{\kappa}$ rolling over a line

---

1. The distribution of the heights of wave crests fits a Raleigh distribution (cf [LeMe76], Appendix A). The distribution of wavelengths is not so easily expressed.

2. A glossary at the end of this paper lists the symbols used.

at distance $\frac{1}{\kappa}$ under the X axis (Figure 3). The parametric equations are, for t=0 and $z_0=0$:

$$x=-\frac{\alpha}{\kappa}-r \times \sin(\alpha)$$

$$z=-r \times \cos(\alpha) \quad \text{where} \quad \alpha=-\kappa x_0$$

The height of the wave is H=2r, the wavelength is $L=\frac{2\pi}{\kappa}$, the period is $T=\frac{2\pi}{\omega}$ and the phase speed (the speed of travel of the crest, for instance) is $c=\frac{L}{T}=\frac{\omega}{\kappa}$. The phase is $\phi=\kappa x_0-\omega t$, assuming a phase of 0 for $x_0=0$. Figure 4 shows the various shapes obtained for $\kappa r=0.2$ which is almost a sine wave, for $\kappa r=0.7$, $\kappa r=1.0$ which is a cycloid, and $\kappa r=1.2$, which leads to self intersection. In fact, the limiting reasonable value for κr is 1, which means that $\frac{H}{L}=\frac{\kappa r}{\pi}=\frac{1}{\pi}$. The ratio $\delta=\frac{H}{L}$, called the *steepness* of the wave, functions as the *shape parameter* of the wave.

The closed circular orbit is not merely a convenient description. It can be derived from the equations of motion for deep water small amplitudes waves [Kins84, LeMe76, FeLS65]. In fact this model was proposed long ago in oceanography, and is called the Gerstner's or Rankine wave [Gers1802, Rank1863], see also [Kins84]. It is seldom used in contemporary oceanography, because it is hard to extract information from it, but it is satisfactory for our purposes. Note that there is no net mass transport.

So this is our basic model. To introduce the needed effects and variations, we will manipulate the parameters of the orbit equations (modifying the radius, the phase angle, turning the circle into an ellipse, etc.).

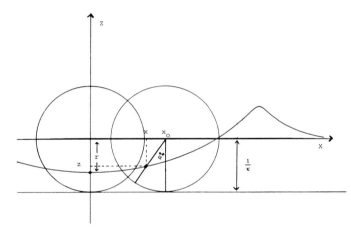

Figure 3
The trochoid.

Most of these parameters are physically related. In deep water (we will see later that *deep* is relative to the wavelength), there is a simple relationship between the period and the wavelength:

$$L=\frac{gT^2}{2\pi} \qquad (2)$$

which can be stated as:

$$c=\frac{gT}{2\pi}$$

The group velocity (the speed at which the energy carried by the wave travels) is then $U=\frac{c}{2}$. These relations are valid only when the basic differential equation for the flow of water can be simplified to be linear, but this is a good approximation for slow motion. We can go a little further, and relate the height of the wave to the wind speed, to provide reasonable defaults. Here again we have to simplify tremendously. If a wind of speed V has been blowing for ever over an infinite *fetch* (the area covered by the wind), we obtain a *fully aroused sea*. One possible formula for the *significant height* of the waves (the average height of the

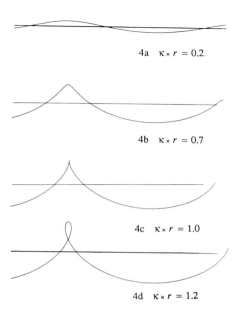

4a $\kappa \times r = 0.2$

4b $\kappa \times r = 0.7$

4c $\kappa \times r = 1.0$

4d $\kappa \times r = 1.2$

Figure 4
Shapes of waves as κr varies.

highest one-third of the waves) is ([Kins84]):

$$\overline{H}_{\frac{1}{3}}=7.065 \times 10^{-3}V^{2.5}$$

The heights are in meters, and the speeds in meters/seconds. We can take this height to be representative, and create a wave of that height if only the wind speed is given. In this case, the average L and T are related by the formula in equation (2), and the frequency at which the maximum in the energy spectrum occurs is given by:

$$\omega=\frac{g}{V}\sqrt{\frac{2}{3}}$$

Thus, only a wind speed has to be supplied to completely define the waves under these simplified conditions. It is important to note that these different relations do not strictly apply to the same definitions of *average*. We can use them only because we are looking for "reasonable" values, and we will not base numerical forecast on them.

4. Special Effects

The first modification to the basic equations (1a) and (1b) is a trivial one. It is to take the direction of the wave into account. Initially the wave fronts are in a direction perpendicular to the wind that created them, and the plane of the orbits is defined by the wind speed vector and the Z axis. Wave fronts keep the same direction even after the wind ceases or blows in another direction. To impose a direction, we perform a two-dimensional rotation on the orbit plane. In this section, we will stay in the original coordinate system, so that the waves progress in the positive X direction, and the crests are parallel to the Y axis.

The second modification can properly be called a *kludge*. To model the effect of the wind on the top of the crests, a third term is added to the expression for the phase angle ϕ, proportional to the height of the wave above the sea level at rest (with the sign included). Thus the phase angle becomes:

$$\phi=\kappa x_0-\omega t-\lambda \Delta z \Delta t$$

The term Δz is $z-z_0$. The term Δt is included because this effect is proportional to time. λ is the coefficient of proportionality. This is a temporary effect on the phase, which does not accumulate, and sums to 0 both in time and in space. It maintains the shape of the orbit but causes the point to accelerate at the top and decelerate at the bottom. The shapes of the waves obtained with various λ are given in Figure 5.

The next modification is to account for the effect of the depth h at the point (x_0, y_0, z_0) measured positively down from the sea level at rest. The first effect of the depth is to alter the wavelength of the wave. It is assumed, and largely true, that the period is not affected. If we call κ_∞ the wave number at infinite depth, a good approximation for the wave number κ at depth h is:

$$\kappa \tanh(\kappa h) = \kappa_\infty \qquad (3)$$

It is unfortunately a transcendental equation in κ. But when $x \to 0$ then $\tanh(x) \to x$. Therefore at small depth (which means when κh is small), the relation becomes:

$$\kappa^2 h = \kappa_\infty \quad \text{or} \quad \kappa = \sqrt{\frac{\kappa_\infty}{h}}$$

When $x \to \infty$, then $\tanh(x) \to 1$, so $\kappa \to \kappa_\infty$, which is to be hoped. Note that since $\kappa h = \frac{2\pi h}{L}$, a ratio $\frac{h}{L}$ of 0.5 gives an argument of π for the tanh which makes it practically equal to 1. Thus for practical purposes, ''deep'' is related to the wavelength, and means a ratio $\frac{h}{L}$ greater than 0.5. A good approximation for equation (3), valid for the entire range within 5% is:

$$\kappa = \frac{\kappa_\infty}{\sqrt{\tanh(\kappa_\infty h)}}$$

Since the wavelength is affected, so is the phase speed, which means: $\frac{c}{c_\infty} = \frac{\kappa_\infty}{\kappa}$ and the waves are refracted as they slow down. In fact one can apply Snell's law:

$$\frac{\sin(\alpha_h)}{\sin(\alpha_\infty)} = \frac{c_h}{c_\infty}$$

to compute the angles the wave fronts make when going from infinite depth to a depth of h (or between any two depths for that matter). Figures 6, 7 and 8 illustrate the refraction of waves caused by two bottoms of constant depth, a gently sloping beach, and an undersea valley. A *decay factor* multiplies the argument of the tanh function; it scales the real depth to control the intensity of the effect. Another parameter allows the user to clamp the effect and limit the shortening of the wavelength.

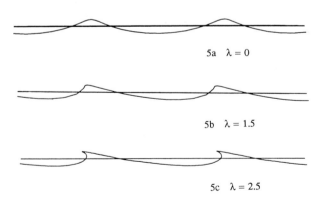

5a $\lambda = 0$

5b $\lambda = 1.5$

5c $\lambda = 2.5$

Figure 5
Shapes of waves for various λ.

The depth effect cannot be computed from local information only, since the phase delay it introduces is cumulative. Now κ is a function of the depth, which in turn is a function of x_0 (and of y_0 in the general case). Assuming that $\phi = 0$ for $x_0 = 0$, and for brevity that λ is zero, the phase equation should now be:

$$\phi = -\omega t + \int_0^{x_0} \kappa(x) dx \quad \text{where} \quad \kappa(x) = \frac{\kappa_\infty}{\sqrt{\tanh(\kappa_\infty h(x))}}$$

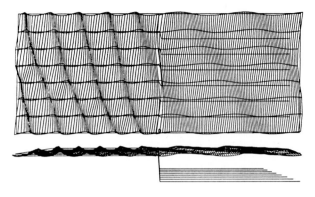

Figure 6
The refraction of waves.
The angle with the X axis is 30° on the deep bottom.
On the shallow bottom to the left the wavelength has been halved.

Since in general we do not even know h(x), an exact solution is not very likely. Furthermore, when considered in two dimensions, the integral along the path followed by the wave varies according to its direction. So precomputing this integral is not practical. Since we want to be able to have several trains of waves passing over a given point, remembering the cumulative depth information at each point for each train would be costly in storage. Even more seriously, we want to be able to compute points in any order and at any spacing, so we do not want to depend on the phase value passed by the neighbors.

The solution is to have the *trains* themselves accumulate and carry the information as they ''sweep'' the bottom. Each train carries a grid (of a resolution chosen to pick up the rough features of the bottom), and for each point of that grid at position x the term:

$$\kappa_\infty \left(-1 + \frac{1}{\sqrt{\tanh(\kappa_\infty h(x))}}\right) \Delta x$$

is added. So the cumulative term D is:

$$D = \sum_0^{x_0} \kappa_\infty \left(-1 + \frac{1}{\sqrt{\tanh(\kappa_\infty h(x))}}\right) \Delta x$$

When computing ϕ for a given x_0 for this train, it is evaluated as:

$$\phi = \kappa_\infty x_0 - \omega t + D$$

which is equal to:

$$\phi = -\omega t + \sum_0^{x_0} \frac{\kappa_\infty}{\sqrt{\tanh(\kappa_\infty h(x))}} \Delta x$$

Thus we have a good approximation of the integral. The cumulative term

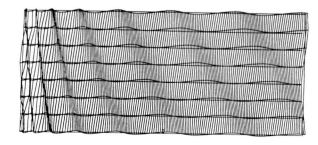

Figure 7
Refraction of waves.
The beach gently slopes down from the left.
The wave fronts align themselves with the beach.

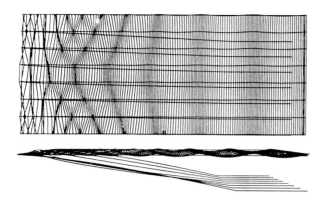

Figure 8
Refraction of waves over an undersea valley.

for x_0 on the sea surface is bilinearly interpolated from the nearest cumulative terms of the train grids. Trains will be described in more detail in the next section.

The last modification models the waves breaking on the shore. Classic theories predict that the orbits will become ellipses in water of intermediate depth, and eventually collapse down to straight line segments as $h \to 0$ (see Le Mehaute, p. 235, for example). More interestingly, Biesel [Bies52], proposed a model where the major axis of the ellipses tends to align itself with the beach as the depth goes to zero. This effect gives a very realistic shape to the breakers. Unfortunately his coefficients are fairly complicated and costly to compute (even though they are only functions of κh, and could be determined by lookup tables). We decide to adopt our own model, which keeps most of the necessary features but is simpler and easier to control. Equations (1a) and (1b) are replaced by:

$$x = x_0 + r \times \cos\alpha \times S_x \times \sin\phi + \sin\alpha \times S_z \times \cos\phi$$
$$z = z_0 - r \times \cos\alpha \times S_z \times \cos\phi + \sin\alpha \times S_x \times \sin\phi$$

ϕ is defined as before, $\sin\alpha$ is given by $\sin\alpha = \sin\gamma e^{-\kappa_o h}$, where γ is the slope of the bottom in the direction of the wave travel. S_x and S_z are:

$$S_x = \frac{1}{1 - e^{-\kappa_x h}} \quad \text{and} \quad S_z = S_x(1 - e^{-\kappa_z h})$$

The κ_o, κ_x and κ_z terms are scaling constants.

The net effect is to flatten the circles into ellipses (down to line segments when $h=0$), to orient their major axis toward the slope of the bottom, and to increase the length of the major axis. Figure 9 shows the influence of this effect on the orbitals, and Figure 10 shows an example of the wave shapes obtained.

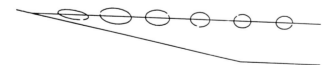

Figure 9
How the depth affects the orbits.
Gaps represent points at the same time.

Figure 10
How the depth affects the shape of the waves.

It should be noted that some models predict a slight decrease in radius before it starts increasing. We decided to neglect this. It is also important to note that $S_x \to \infty$ when $h \to 0$. As before, parameters allow the users to control this effect and clamp them.[3]

5. Breakers, Spray and Foam

One can distinguish two types of breakers, a *plunging* type, which appears on waves whose shapes are similar to the one in Figures 2, 5 or 10, and a *breaking* type, for waves like in Figure 4b and 4c. The exact conditions for breakers are hard to specify, but the consensus seems to be that to cause breakers:

- The particle speed has to be greater then the phase speed, and
- the curvature of the surface has to be high.

Some other conditions are occasionally mentioned, notably that the slope has to be "nearly vertical", as a sufficient condition. A paper by Longuet-Higgins [Long76] contains a picture which proves that it is not so.

It is interesting to note that our model is "aware" of the particle speed, which gives it a better chance to test for breakers, and make informed decisions about what to do. We have experimented with various conditions, but the simplest and the most reliable (as checked by our intuition of where breakers should appear) was to test the curvature, and decide a breaker should appear if it is above a set threshold. In practice a curvature roughly corresponding to an angle of 60° at a surface point seems reasonable.

When a breaker is detected, spray and foam are generated. Spray is generated if the difference between the particle speed and the surface speed projected in the direction of the normal to the surface exceeds a set threshold. The spray is then sent in that direction and follows a trajectory affected by gravity after that (taking air drag into account). It is rendered by particle systems (see section 7).

If the speed threshold is not passed, then foam is sent sliding along the wave surface. Each "unit" of foam is given a lifetime, and is passed from point to point, taking the acceleration of gravity and viscosity into account, until it "dies." The foam is also rendered by particle systems. Figure 11 illustrates the mechanism for foam. Breakers occur on the crests in the lower left hand side. Plus signs indicates points where breakers are generated in this particular frame, and "o"s indicate where there is foam which has been generated earlier. In the case of the second crest, the sources of foam move towards the bottom right. For the first crest, they remain relatively fixed with respect to the crest. The "S" characters indicate where the particle speeds are high enough to generate spray.

Figure 11
Detection of breakers and spray, and generation of foam.
At "+" breakers are detected, at "S" spray
is generated, at "o" foam is "alive".

6. Wave Trains and their Properties

We have described a model for regular, long-crested waves. We have now to introduce the variability and randomness characteristic of the real sea.

Wave trains define groups of similar waves that permit controlled variation both within trains and between trains. A wave train[4] is a rectangular box on the surface of the sea containing waves of the same basic characteristics and of the same phase origin. Thus the heights, periods and

---

3. The model requires the computation of many transcendental functions. Fortunately, they are all in the range 0-1, and all can be computed through lookup tables.

4. A wave train is not to be confused with a *wave packet*. The latter is a convenient mathematical object to study sums of sine waves.

wavelengths of waves within a train are originally the same. The local coordinate system is always such that the direction of motion is towards the positive X axis, the crests are parallel to the Y axis, and the phase is 0 at the origin. The train as a whole has an origin in the world coordinate system, a direction (given by an angle positive counter-clockwise from the world X axis), a size in X and Y, and a speed (as distinct from the speed of the waves it contains). By default the train speed is half of the phase speed, that is, equal to the *group velocity* in deep water. The trains can also be turned off and on if necessary.

To shape the train (rectangular boxes are rare on the sea) an amplitude function gives each train its own *height envelope*. The function takes the local coordinates and returns a local radius (i.e., height). For most trains, the amplitude function is the product of an X-amplitude function and a Y-amplitude function. In the Y direction the function is usually an envelope with a flat top and soft decay on the side. In the X direction, the same function is multiplied by a random component to vary the wave heights within the same train. Figure 12 gives a typical example of a X-amplitude envelope. Of course, other distributions can be used (see footnote 1).

The variation in wavelengths within a train is obtained by transforming from the local x_l to an adjusted value, x_a, such that $\frac{dx_a}{dx_l} > 0$ and the boundary values are the same. Those two effects, variations in height and variations in wavelengths can be made a function of time, so that the "age" of the train is taken into account, although we have not implemented this effect.

To further reduce the regularity of the wave trains, random "holes" are distributed within the trains to interrupt the crests. These holes, whose number is determined for each train by the user, have a diameter on the order of the wavelength, have an inverted bell-shaped height profile, and have a *Poisson disc* distribution.

The trains also carry the cumulative depth effect described in section 4. A grid is defined for each train, and at each time update of the train the incremental depth effect is calculated, interpolating the depth at this point from the terrain grid points (or depth function if there is one). A time decay factor is optional in the cumulative depth factor, to allow for a slow decay of the bottom effect as the train moves on. The train grid can be rather coarse, as the depth effect does not have to give a sharp image of the bottom profile. However, too coarse a grid would cause rather brutal slope discontinuities. Also, interpolation from the grid might make the waves feel the depth ahead of their current position. This can be avoided by not using the train grid points ahead of the waves for interpolation, at a slight cost in precision on the interpolated cumulative term. To initialize the train grid for the depth effect, trains can be backed up a given distance before starting the wave computations, so that they have accumulated enough depth information.

In summary, we compute the position of a point on the ocean surface as the sum of the displacements from the point's rest position due to all active trains covering this point. Our assumption of a linear addition law is accurate enough for our purposes, especially since we do not add the surface displacements, but the Lagrangian displacements.

To create a model, the designer specifies the number of trains and model characteristics for each train. An interactive two-dimensional version of the model demonstrates the effects of the selected parameters. A train with small waves and a high degree of randomness is usually selected for

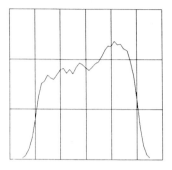

Figure 12
A typical X-amplitude envelope.

a noisy background, then two or three trains with sizeable wave heights generate the interesting features. It is interesting to note that "normal" waves have a fairly low steepness (δ from 0.008 to 0.1), and only about 10% of the waves are above 6 meters in height [Kins84]. One usually has to exaggerate heights and steepness to make things more spectacular.

The use of trains as controllable groups of waves has another advantage. We can easily model the reflection of waves on walls, rocks or high slope shores by generating a second train for the "mirror" image of the reflected one, with the height of the waves reduced as a function of the slope of the shore.

7. Rendering Issues

Our model of ocean waves describes the three-dimensional geometry of the water surface and how it transforms and moves over time. We now wish to render that data into a sequence of color-shaded raster images that resemble as closely as possible the appearance of the real ocean. The surface generated by the model is a parametric surface whose parameters are the (x_0, y_0) of the sea surface at rest, and time. Points on this surface can be computed independently of their neighbors, so a regular grid is not needed, and ray intersection operations, adaptive sampling, and other point driven methods can be applied directly to the surface. Each point on the surface also has a natural bounding volume in the sphere centered at that point and whose radius is the sum of the radii defined by all the waves trains. We had available, however, an outstanding set of rendering software, and it made the rendering considerably easier. We used an anti-aliasing, scan-line oriented, adaptive subdivision rendering system called *reyes* [Cook86] that incorporates a sophisticated shading and texturing system using shade trees [Cook84].

Our first step in rendering a frame is to execute the model at a rectangular grid of points in the x–y plane in the world coordinate system. We then transform the resulting three-dimensional data points describing the surface of the water into a set of three-dimensional surface primitives. Currently, we can interpolate the data with either bi-linear or bi-cubic (Catmull-Rom) patches. Bi-linears are better when debugging and planning a scene as they are faster to compute and use less storage space. Bi-cubics are better for final images as the surfaces are smooth, not faceted. Selecting the right size of grid (and hence the number of patches) is important; we want enough resolution so that the waves in the train with the shortest wavelength do not alias, and yet we do not want so many patches that the scene will take forever to render.

The color and shading of the real ocean surface is derived mainly from the sky. In general, the ocean reflects its surrounding environment. To simulate this, we use an *environment map*. An image of the surrounding world is placed into a series of texture maps that together form a gigantic sphere about the waves. To determine the color of a point on the wave's surface, we perform what amounts to a one-level ray trace, bouncing a ray from the camera position off the surface point according to the rule: the angle of incidence about the surface normal is equal to the angle of reflectance about the surface normal. Where the reflected ray now intersects the enclosing sphere, which is very easy to compute, gives us indices into one of the texture maps and hence a color to be reflected.

The environment map used in Figure 13 models a very simple sky, and is made from a series of ramps going from dark blue (opposite the sun) to orange (behind the sun) and a very bright yellow disk to represent the sun. Clouds were painted unto the sky around the sun. More elaborate environment maps including shorelines and general terrain are possible and easy to add.

The one flaw in this scheme is that the ray trace is only one level. It only intersects the environment map and not other parts of the scene or other parts of the water itself. Nevertheless, it makes interesting pictures and is definitely less expensive computationally than general ray tracing.

The actual shade used for a given point on the surface is:

$$finalcolor = REF*reflcolor*refl(normal, viewer) + \\ watercolor*(AMB*ambient() + DIFF*diffuse(normal) + \\ SP*specular(normal, viewer, ROUGH));$$

where *normal* is the surface normal, and *viewer* the vector from the camera to the surface point. The *refl* routine returns the color from the environment map as reflected off the surface. The shading routines *ambient*, *diffuse* and *specular* return the intensity and color of the ambient, diffuse, and specular components from any light sources in the scene. *Reflcolor* and *watercolor* are two scaling parameters (they are RGB triples) that can be used to selectively filter out different parts of the color spectrum. For example, setting *reflcolor* to (1,.9,.8) filters out some of the green and blue components of the reflected color. The constants *REF*, *AMB*, *DIFF*, and *SP* are other scaling parameters and *ROUGH* sets the roughness or sensitivity of the specular function. Typical values are: $REF=.8$, $AMB=.01$, $DIFF=.1$, $SP=.5$, and $ROUGH=.02$. For the *diffuse* and *specular* functions, we position a light source at the sun. The Fresnel coefficient for reflectance of water is included in *refl()* and *specular()*.

To model water shimmering and other forms of small perturbations like wave chop, we could use several wave trains with very small wavelengths and highly stochastic amplitudes. But this approach requires a very small grid size to represent all the surface detail and greatly increases the number of patches to render. Instead, we use *bump mapping* [Blin78]. The normal to the surface is slightly perturbed at each point when shading it. This affects the *diffuse*, *specular*, and *refl* components of the above shading equation and makes the surface appear more complex than it really is. The amount of perturbation is specified by a *bump map* texture which is mapped onto the surface. For animation purposes, the bump map must move with the wave surface in a natural way. To do so, we actually translate the *bump map* over time just like we translate trains over time.

Figure 13 was computed at 2048 by 1228 pixel resolution. It was modeled with 92,724 bi-cubic patches and took 10 hours and 21 minutes on a Computer Consoles Power 6/32 computer. Figure 14 used 85680 patches and took 2 hours and 21 minutes. To give an idea of modeling time, a 2,400 point grid, which when rendered is modeled with the same number of bicubic patches, takes about 36 seconds per frame to generate on a VAX 11/750.

8. Conclusions

We have shown that a simple basic model can produce a large range of wave shapes and phenomena. This includes the effects of depth such as refraction and surf, and some of the effects of wind. The model also has the advantage of fitting in well with most rendering methods, since it is essentially a parametric surface in two spatial parameters and one time parameter. The model also makes possible the detection of the appearance of spray and foam. The model has been easily interfaced to a completely independent rendering package, to produce the color pictures

Figure 13
Beach at sunset. Notice the breaking of waves on the shore,
and how the crests take the shape of the shore.

All of the above shading calculations are handled with a shade tree in the *reyes* system. It also handles hidden surface and motion blur automatically.

The position, size and speed of each foam and spray "element" is passed to a particle system based program. For the spray, the particles follow the free fall laws of motion. For the foam, the motion is controlled by the model itself, as described above.

One final note about how we modeled the terrain in our images. With a tablet and a simple program, we entered a set of unequally spaced, three-dimensional data points. A surface (a mesh of patches) was then passed through these points using a localized version of Shepard's method [Shep64]. This same data set was used to specify the depth of the ocean floor.

Figure 13 is actually a frame from a ten second animation we are in the process of computing. The most satisfying feature of the sequence is the convincing way the breakers crash and the waves lap up on the beach. Figure 14 is an example of wave refraction due to the ocean floor shallowing near shore. Note how the waves tend to align themselves with the shoreline. The slope of the beach is more gentle on the right hand side, causing more shortening of the wavelength.

Figures 15 and 16 are examples of spray and foam generated by particle systems. Figure 16 shows what happens when the wind factor λ is used to obtain overhanging waves.

illustrating this paper. Few parameters and the inclusion of individually controlled trains of waves allow the designer and the animator to achieve the wanted effects relatively easily. We therefore met most of the goals listed in section 1, with the possible exception of the one concerning simplicity and a small number of the operations. We already mentioned that the square roots, trigonometric and hyperbolic functions can easily be replaced by lookup tables or *ad hoc* approximations. The number of operations per point, though quite large, is not prohibitive, as shown by the time necessary to compute frames.

Some of the effects which where not included, but are relatively easy to add within the model, are the creation of *wakes*, the *ageing* of wave trains, that is the modification in heights and wavelengths they undergo after their creation, and some diffraction. Other effects, such as modeling turbulent flow, additional phenomena due to refraction such as caustics, and the effect of moving ocean floors, would be mostly beyond our model, but then again some of these phenomena do not have very satisfactory physical models either.

We will have reached our goal if, by designing and implementing this basic tool to model many aspects of the ocean, we have included enough features to make it useful, and we have left out enough phenomena so that we will all be challenged to do better.

Figure 14
Wave refraction.

Figure 15
Waves with spray and foam

9. Acknowledgements

Most of this research was performed while Alain Fournier visited and Bill Reeves was employed by the Computer Division of Lucasfilm Limited.

Alain Fournier wants to acknowledge the financial support of Canada's National Science and Engineering Research Council, the hospitality of the Department of Computer Science at Stanford University, and the hospitality of PIXAR during many phases of this project. He also wishes to thank Adrienne, who took him to the ocean.

Bill Reeves wishes to acknowledge Rob Cook for his *reyes* rendering software, Eben Ostby for help with the environment maps, and John Lasseter for the clouds and advice on coloration.

Figure 16
Beneath the Waves of San Rafael

10. Glossary

Symbol	Meaning	Unit	Remarks
L	wavelength	meter	
H	height of wave	meter	
δ	steepness	-	$\delta = \dfrac{H}{L}$
r	radius of orbit	meter	$H = 2 \times r$
T	period	second	
κ	wave number	radian/meter	$L = \dfrac{2 \times \pi}{\kappa}$
ω	angular speed	radian/second	$T = \dfrac{2 \times \pi}{\omega}$
c	phase speed	meter/second	$c = \dfrac{L}{T}$
h	depth	meter	
x_0, y_0, z_0	rest position	meter	
x,y,z	position at time t	meter	
g	acceler. of gravity	meter/second^2	vector
U	group velocity	meter/second	vector
V	wind speed	meter/second	vector
t	time	second	
γ	slope of bottom	-	in direction of wave
ϕ	phase angle	radian	
λ	wind factor	radian/m. × second	
D	cumulative depth effect	radian	

11. References

Bies52 Biesel, F., "Study of Wave Propagation in Water of Gradually Varying Depth," in *Gravity Waves*, U.S. National Bureau of Standards Circular 521, (1952), pp. 243-253.

Blin78 Blinn, J. F., "Simulation of Wrinkled Surfaces," in *Proceedings of SIGGRAPH '78*, also published as Comput. Graphics, *12*, 3, (Aug 1978), pp. 286-292.

Cook84 Cook, R. L., "Shade trees," in *Proceedings of SIGGRAPH '84*, also published as Comput. Graphics, *18*, 3, (July 1984), pp. 223-231.

Cook86 Cook, R. L., "Antialiasing by Stochastic Sampling," accepted to appear in *Transactions on Graphics*, (summer 1986).

Crap84 Crapper, G. D., *Introduction to Water Waves* (Chichester, West Sussex, England : 1984).

FeLS65 Feynman, R. P., Leighton, R. B. and Sands, M., *The Feynman Lecture Notes on Physics*, (Addison-Wesley, 1965).

Gers1802 Gerstner, F. J. v, "Theorie der Wellen," Abh. d. k. bohm. Ges. d. Wiss. *Also reprinted in* Ann. der Physik, 32, (1809), pp. 412-440.

Kins65 Kinsman, Blair, *Wind Waves* (Prentice-Hall, 1965).

Kins84 Kinsman, Blair, *Wind Waves* (Dover, 1984), *reprint of preceding*.

LeBl78 LeBlond, Paul H., *Waves in the Ocean* (Amsterdam, 1978.)

LeMe76 Le Mehaute, Bernard, *An Introduction to Hydrodynamics and Water Waves* (New York, Springer-Verlag, 1976)

Long76   Longuet-Higgins, M. S., "On Breaking Waves," *in Waves on Water of Variable Depth*, Provis, D. G. and Radok, R., *Eds*, Springer-Verlag Lecture Notes in Physics, (1976), pp. 129-130.

Max81a   Max, N., "Vectorized Procedural Models for Natural Terrains: Waves and Islands in the Sunset," in *Proceedings of SIGGRAPH 81*, also published as Comput. Graphics, *15*, 3, (Aug 81), pp. 317-324.

Max81b   Max, N., "Carla's Island," appeared in Issue #5 of the *SIGGRAPH Video Review*, (1981).

Mei83   Mei, Chiang C., *The Applied Dynamics of Ocean Surface Waves* (New York, c1983.)

NoRS82   Norton, A., Rockwood, A. P. and Skolmoski, P. T., "Clamping: A Method of Antialiasing Textured Surfaces by Bandwidth Limiting in Object Space," in *Proceedings of SIGGRAPH 82*, also published as Comput. Graphics, *16*, 3, (July 82), pp. 1-8.

Ogde85   Ogden, J., "Generation of Fractals Using the Burt Pyramid," *presented at the* 1985 Optical Society of America Annual Meeting, Washington, DC, (October 1985).

Peac86   Peachy, D., "Modeling Waves and Surf", *these Proceedings*.

Perl85   Perlin, K., "An Image Synthetizer," in *Proceedings of SIGGRAPH 85*, also published as Comput. Graphics, *19*, 3, (July 85), pp. 287-296.

Rank1863   Rankine, W. J. W., "On the Exact Form of Waves near the Surfaces of Deep Water," Phil. Trans. Roy. Soc., A 153, (1863), pp. 127-138.

Reev83   Reeves, W. T., "Particle Systems-A Technique for Modeling a Class of Fuzzy Objects," Transactions on Graphics, *2*, 2, (April 83), pp. 91-108.

Scha80   Schachter, B., "Long crested wave models," Computer Graphics and Image Processing, *12*, (1980), pp. 187-201.

Shep64   Shepard, D., "A two-dimensional interpolation function for irregularly spaced data," in *Proceedings 1964 ACM National Conference*, (1964), pp. 517-524.

TsBa86   Ts'o, P. Y. and Barsky, B. A., "Modeling and Rendering Waves: Wave-tracing using Beta-splines and Reflective and Refractive Texture Mapping", submitted for publication.

Combining Physical and Visual Simulation -
Creation of the Planet Jupiter for the Film "2010"

Larry Yaeger and Craig Upson
Digital Productions

Robert Myers
Poseidon Research

1. Abstract

By integrating physical simulation, in the form of numerical fluid dynamics, with visual simulation, in the form of particle rendering, texture mapping and traditional polygonal modeling techniques, we have achieved a uniquely realistic and organic special effects sequence of a planetary atmospheric flow. This paper examines the selection, implementation, and application of these techniques, known collectively as VORTEX, to produce the moving images of the planet Jupiter in the film "2010." Details of the generation of the flow field and the fluid dynamic algorithms employed are presented, along with issues relating to the generation and updating of the atmospheric images. We also describe the integration of these techniques with an advanced computer graphics imaging system. The VORTEX system provides a fairly general solution to a class of imaging problems involving two-dimensional fluid flows, and we remark upon its application to other projects. VORTEX, as an example of the marriage of physical simulation to visual simulation, demonstrates the importance of computer graphics to the computational sciences and of the physical sciences to the field of computer graphics.

2. Introduction

The primary significance of this work stems from the integration of well understood physical and computational science techniques with well understood computer graphics techniques. The fluid models we selected are well established; Section 5 provides discussion and references. The particle renderer is a simple two-dimensional algorithm, which is only somewhat related to the three-dimensional particle systems discussed by Reeves [11]. In both Reeves's and our work, particles are moved and re-rendered, though we have replaced Reeves's algorithmic particle trajectories with a more complex physical simulation and use simpler 2-D rendering. Additionally, the output of our particle

renderer is not a final product, but serves as a texture map in a polygonal rendering system. Our texture mapping techniques are based more on the seminal works by Catmull [4] and Blinn and Newell [2] than on later efforts such as Williams [15] and Crow [5]. Our polygonal rendering model is based on a hidden surface algorithm most resembling Bouknight's [3], though any of a variety of other renderers would have served [13, 9, 12, 14]. It is the fact and methodology of combining a complex physical model with high resolution computer graphics that represents a significant development in the field of visual simulation.

The VORTEX project was initiated because of a need to provide very detailed, very high resolution images of the planet Jupiter for the movie "2010". Since much of the action in "2010" occurs in orbit around Jupiter, the appearance of the planet was vital to the setting and believability of the motion picture. We examined motion studies of Jupiter, based on Voyager spacecraft data compiled by NASA's Jet Propulsion Laboratory (JPL), and discussed various approaches to simulating the appearance of the planet. It was realized early on that the fluid motion of the atmospheric features was both the most significant and the most difficult aspect of the planet to be modeled. It was this realization, along with some fortuitous experience in the discipline, that led to the somewhat radical solution of coupling a legitimate numerical fluid dynamics model to our existing graphics software.

The basic technique employed in the digital synthesis of Jupiter consisted of the following:

1) a set of software tools to manipulate texture images and decompose them into particles;

2) a software tool to generate an initial vorticity field (which defines the wind field), derived from encoded symbols marking planetary flow features;

3) a fluid dynamics driver that, on a frame by frame basis, updated both the fluid mechanics quantities and the position of the image-derived particles;

4) a particle renderer that, frame by frame, regenerated an image file from the repositioned particles;

5) graphics software capable of mapping the regenerated images onto an object (a sphere or portion thereof in this case), and of rendering a high resolution, high quality image of the result.

The image manipulation and decomposition tools and the vorticity-field generator were used in a stand-alone fashion, to provide initial conditions for the texture, particle, and vorticity data structures. The fluids driver and the particle renderer were integrated with the existing graphics software at Digital Productions through the existing command parsers along with a new supervisory routine which handled file manipulations and calling sequences.

In use, a scheduled command would cause the main graphics software to invoke the VORTEX supervisory program each frame. This supervisor would then call the first half of the fluids driver, known as TRADE. TRADE would carry out the fluid dynamics modeling, reading in the old vorticity field and creating and writing out the new vorticity field. Back in the supervisor, then, the second half of the fluids driver, known as WINDS, would be invoked. WINDS would apply the new wind field, derived from the new vorticity field, to the particles--reading in the old particle positions and writing out updated particle positions. The supervisor would then call on the particle renderer, DEPICT, to read the updated particle positions and generate the new, updated texture file. The supervisor would then relinquish control and return to the command processor of the main graphics software. At this point, a sequence of scheduled commands would cause the newly generated texture to be mapped onto a spherical object, which would then be positioned, lit, rendered in a traditional fashion, and recorded on film. Re-invoking the VORTEX system (TRADE, WINDS, DEPICT, and their supervisor) and re-rendering the texture-mapped sphere each frame produces an apparently three-dimensional planetary atmospheric flow.

Both VORTEX and the principal rendering algorithm, DP3D, are written in a mixture of CFT and CAL (Cray Fortran and assembly language, respectively).

3.   Initial Texture and Particle Generation

Our original choice for the atmospheric texture map was the large number of Voyager II image mosaics [1]. These mosaics, while quite astounding in terms of scientific data, contained visible linear anomalies, sections with bad data, and were insufficiently detailed (approximately 1500 by 300 pixels) for our purposes. Thus we were forced to select an alternative source for the initial image. From the mosaic of rotation 349 (Fig. 1), an eight-foot long cibachrome print was made. An artist then meticulously airbrushed over the entire image, adding detail at every level (Fig. 2). This process provided the correct amount of feature resolution and color range.

In order to achieve sufficient resolution, consistent with the image size on the 65-mm final film product, multiple overlapping vertical strips from the retouched image were rephotographed with a VistaVision motion picture camera. Multiple copies of each strip were photographed so that four (seemingly) identical images of each portion of the painting could be scan-digitized (at a resolution of 2560 by 2048 pixels) and averaged together to minimize film grain. As film grain is a random variation in intensity, this process very effectively raised the signal-to-noise ratio of the image panels. Care was taken during the rephotographing process to assure uniform lighting, an orthogonal camera/painting geometry, and a constant overlap between adjacent frames.

The scanned, film grain-corrected images were then interactively recomposited in a process whereby one image was allowed to slide (in 2-D) over another until a visual match was made. The two images were then merged in their overlap region with a simple linear blend function. Any visible anomalies were then digitally airbrushed.

Once a single image was composited from several (varying from two to seven) images, color

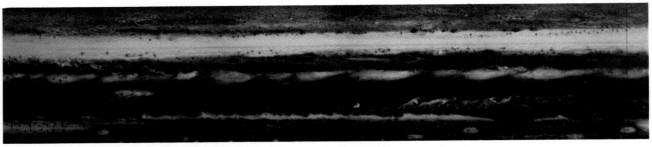

Figure 1. Voyager II mosaic image from rotation 349.

Figure 2. Artist-enhanced, airbrushed image of Voyager II mosaic seen in Fig. 1.

corrected, and cropped to the correct size, it was turned into particles. This process converted a pixel into several particles, each of which contained an (x, y) location with 1/256 subpixel accuracy (up to 20 bits each), and an RGB color triple (8 bits each). Each particle's data structure was thus contained in a single 64-bit word.

The particle location was determined stochastically within the pixel, and the color was chosen such that the average of all particles in a pixel resulted in the original pixel color. We allowed a maximum variation of 5-10 percent in color for particles within the same pixel. The number of particles within a pixel was a quadratic function based on the latitude of the pixel location; thus there was a concentration in the equatorial region leaving poles relatively sparse. The particle-per-pixel density ranged from 1 near the poles to approximately 10 at the equator. The multiple-particle-per-pixel scheme was both an effective antialiasing (via super sampling) technique and also one that retained the largest amount of information throughout the computation. The alternative of advecting pixels (or subpixels) instead of particles whose colors don't change would have been quite diffusive, resulting in a blurred image.

These techniques generated a sufficiently detailed image. Due to the available-memory constraints in the Cray X-MP, however, the final texture map was limited to a resolution of about 1400 by 1000 pixels in the rendering stage. This resulted in the adoption of a new technique for distributing the resolution of the texture map in a "nonlinear" fashion, concentrating pixels near the center of the projected image. A step was introduced between the image generation and the particle generation that supported the creation of this nonlinear texture map. This additional step and its integration with the other VORTEX software elements is described in Section 7.

4. Vorticity Initial Conditions

Several centuries of terrestrial observation and, more importantly, the two Voyager encounters in 1979 with the planet Jupiter, have given scientists a substantial databank of information concerning the major Jovian cloud features. As a result of television coverage of these fly-bys and the subsequent image analysis, the public also has certain expectations about the general behavior of the planet's atmosphere. We had selected a fluid dynamic technique that would deliver this realistic motion. The remaining fluid dynamic requirement was an appropriate set of initial conditions--in our case, an initial vorticity field. The initial condition of the vorticity along with the boundary conditions and certain nondimensional parameters determine (to the accuracy of the method) the time evolution of the flow field in the Navier-Stokes equations. Therefore, this beginning vorticity state is quite important and must match up with the desired visual features to assure the proper advection.

Again, our initial thoughts were to utilize JPL's data obtained from the Voyager missions. The major source of Voyager data available was a compilation of tie point correlations, or discrete fluid patch trajectories, over the major portion of the planet [8]. Determining the vorticity from

this was believed to be difficult, potentially marred by the same anomalies seen in the photographs, and very specific to a single application. The Voyager data also could not match the features of our artist-enhanced source image. Thus, a less rigorous but more general approach was undertaken.

The overall flow field structure of Jupiter may be characterized by the summation of a one-dimensional (east-west) shear flow and numerous smaller-scale disturbances or vortices. Our ad hoc approach was driven by the need for an arbitrarily high resolution vorticity field that would align with the cloud features. To accomplish this, we made a four-foot black and white print of the retouched image, and hand-marked discernible vortex features. The center, horizontal and vertical extents, rotation sense, and model type of each discernible vortex were then encoded on a digitizing tablet.

The contribution of encoded vortex ω_i^G at a point (x, y) in the domain was then approximated as an elliptical Gaussian distribution

$$\omega_i^G(x,y) = \bar{\omega}_i \, \exp -\frac{1}{2}\left[\frac{(x-x_i)^2}{\sigma_{x_i}^2} + \frac{(y-y_i)^2}{\sigma_{y_i}^2}\right],$$

where vortex ω_i^G is centered at (x_i, y_i). The horizontal and vertical extents (the major and minor axes), along with the assignment of a somewhat arbitrary 5 percent of maximum vorticity level at these extents, determined the variances σ_{x_i} and σ_{y_i}. The strength of the encoded vortex was modeled as

$$\bar{\omega}_i = \pm A_i^{1/4}$$

where A_i is the area contained within the perceived elliptical boundaries of the feature. The sign of this strength determined the rotational sense of the fluid. This simple model is sufficient for the majority of the small-scale features, but other local disturbances such as the white ovals and the Great Red Spot are notable exceptions. For these ω_j^P, experimental data was chosen [8] in the form of a vorticity profile across the minor axis of the Great Red Spot.

The shear velocity $u_s(y)$, also approximated from Voyager data [8], was modeled as a cubic spline. Thus the resultant initial vorticity (Fig. 3) is

$$\Omega(x,y) = -\bar{u}_s\frac{du_s(y)}{dy} + \sum_{i=1}^{N}\omega_i^G(x,y) + \sum_{j=1}^{M}\omega_j^P(x,y) .$$

An initial vorticity distribution was constructed for each sequence of frames, or scene, by choosing an appropriate window in this global approximation and discretized onto a 512 by 256 (longitude by latitude) grid. The typical computational domain contained 400 to 800 encoded vortices, with a maximum of 1300.

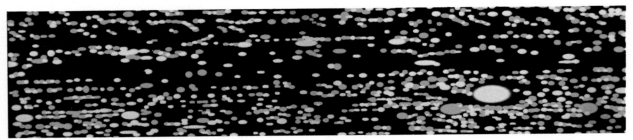

Figure 3. Contour map of the global initial vorticity distribution. Negative vorticity is in blue, positive vorticity in white.

5. Fluid Mechanics

We were interested in simulating the circulation patterns of a planetary atmosphere. Taken quite literally, this would mean that we wanted to do weather forecasting on Jupiter, and the average layperson could predict the success of such an enterprise, given his experience on Earth. Our real interest, however, was to select the simplest model that would give visually reasonable (and interesting) results, without worrying about complete fidelity to the actual physics of a "global circulation model."

The simplest model we could have used would have been a fixed velocity field. Such a model would permit perceived motion of an atmosphere, but would not permit the atmospheric features themselves, such as the cyclonic spots on the surface of Jupiter, to move in a visually reasonable fashion. In particular, the color variations associated with the vortex would move with the flow, while the center of the vortex motion would remain fixed.

The simplest model that permits actual dynamics, i.e., that permits the "weather" at a point to change in time, is the barotropic model [6]. This is the basic model employed in TRADE, the first half of the fluid dynamics driver. An assumption that the atmosphere is incompressible, with no vertical motions, permits us to represent both components of horizontal velocity (u and v) as derivatives of a single stream function ψ

$$u = - \frac{\partial \psi}{\partial y} \; ,$$

$$v = \frac{\partial \psi}{\partial x} \; ,$$

where x and y are the two horizontal dimensions of the planetary surface mapped onto a flat rectangle by means of a cylindrical projection. The north and south poles correspond to $y = \pm L_y/2$ and the equatorial "extremes" (the seam of the mapping) correspond to $x = \pm L_x/2$.

Particles, like smoke, injected into a steady flow would follow constant contours of the stream function ψ, referred to as streamlines. The incompressibility of the flow also allows us to write an equation for ψ in terms of the vorticity Ω

$$\nabla^2 \psi = \Omega \; ,$$

where the vorticity is itself derived from the velocity

$$\Omega = - \frac{\partial u}{\partial y} + \frac{\partial v}{\partial x} \; .$$

All of this would be beautifully, and uselessly, circular, were it not for the fact that the vorticity satisfies a single predictive equation

$$\frac{\partial \Omega}{\partial t} + u \frac{\partial \Omega}{\partial x} + v \frac{\partial (\Omega + f)}{\partial y} = -\nu \nabla^2 \Omega \; ,$$

where we have introduced the Coriolis parameter f for completeness and the kinematic viscosity ν in case it is needed to stabilize the calculation. The Coriolis term represents effects of planetary rotation that are crucial to the correct modeling of global circulation. We could, and did, ignore this term for simulations of sufficiently short time scale. The term involving the kinematic viscosity ν is dissipative and may be used to provide numerical as well as physical damping.

For purposes of efficiency, we elected to use a pseudospectral method [10], rather than finite differences, as our basic numerical method. We intentionally set boundary conditions, periodicity at the left and right boundaries and rigid walls at the top and bottom, that permitted representation of all field variables via finite Fourier series. We could go back and forth from the series representation to a pointwise representation via highly optimized Fourier transform software written expressly for the Cray. In the series representation, evaluation of a derivative is reduced to multiplication by a constant, and solution of the stream-function-vorticity-equation is reduced to division by a constant. A complete fluid mechanics code was written that involved little more than calls to FFT subroutines and some fairly simple DO loops. Since the vast bulk of the work is done in the highly optimized FFT subroutines and since the pseudospectral method is itself economical in the number of points required to achieve a given accuracy, the resulting code is very efficient.

The predictive equations were marched in time using an Adams-Bashforth predictor, which is a two-level scheme that is second order in time. The dissipative term was included to control a known, very weak instability of this method.

The strong zonal or shear flow is an important, and potentially troublesome, part of the flow field. The total velocity and vorticity can be written as the velocity and vorticity of the zonal flow, plus a part that varies in time

$$\Omega(x, y, t) = \Omega_s(y) + \Omega'(x, y, t) \; ,$$

$$u(x, y, t) = u_s(y) + u'(x, y, t) \; .$$

We use this representation in the predictive equation for vorticity to obtain

$$\frac{\partial \Omega'}{\partial t} + (u_s + u') \frac{\partial \Omega'}{\partial x} + v \frac{\partial \Omega'}{\partial y} = -\nu \nabla^2 \Omega' .$$

Notice that we have dropped two terms involving Ω_s. One of these terms, $v \partial \Omega_s / \partial y$, is the source of the Kelvin-Helmholtz instability, an energy bridge between the shear flow and the rotational flow. We simply dropped this term, knowing that, for our purposes, keeping it could only bring trouble. There was also no reason to include a dissipative term for the zonal flow vorticity, and so it too was left out.

The time scale for changes in the actual atmosphere of Jupiter is fairly long, and an orbiting observer would only perceive motion over an extended period of observation. The time scale of our motion was set, in practice, to achieve a desired visual effect, rather than to mimic reality. We also gave ourselves control over the relative magnitude of the zonal flow, as compared to the smaller-scale vortical flows, so that the most desirable visual effect could be achieved through experimentation.

Given the velocity field as output from the fluid mechanics code at each frame, the position of each of several million particles is updated by a separate code, WINDS. In theory, the task of this particle tracking code is very simple; it needs only to integrate the equations

$$dx_i/dt = u[x_i(t), y_i(t), t] ,$$

$$dy_i/dt = v[x_i(t), y_i(t), t] ,$$

where the index i is an arbitrary particle index. Given the position of the particle at time t, the velocity of the particle is determined by bilinear interpolation of the velocity grid output from TRADE. The particle positions are then updated by a simple forward Euler scheme; i.e., distance traveled is computed as the velocity times the time step. For the numerical solution of partial differential equations, the forward Euler scheme is unconditionally unstable. The particle advection, however, is essentially independent of the fluid mechanics, and we were able to get away with such a scheme because the total integration time was always short. The instability and the first-order nature of the integration scheme can and does manifest itself by particles spiralling outward from vortex centers, rather than following closed orbits. If longer integration times are desired, a stable second order Runge-Kutta scheme could be used for the particle advection.

Because of the very large number of particles to be handled in the particle tracking code, attention to efficiency was mandatory. Particle file I/O transfers were asynchronously double-buffered on both input and output, in order to achieve maximum overlap of I/O and computation. I/O buffers were maximally sized at about two disk tracks each to coax a sustained near-peak performance (4 Mbytes/sec) from the drives. The nonvectorizable indexing step of the velocity calculation was isolated, and the remaining operations were organized into separate, vectorizing DO loops.

In order to achieve a "black hole" effect, another feature was added to WINDS, which allowed the superposition of a velocity sink onto the calculated wind field. This was in the form of a circle of velocity vectors all oriented toward the center of the circle. The result was that affected particles developed an overall trajectory toward the circle's center, while still maintaining their vortical motion.

6. Particle Rendering

Once the particle positions have been updated for the current frame, a texture map is constructed by our 2-D particle renderer, DEPICT. While the algorithm to map a particle back into a pixel is extremely simple, the sheer number of particles used in this application again dictated a very efficient technique. In general, eight to ten million particles were generated for a 1.4-million pixel texture map, with an average of six particles initially inhabiting the same pixel. This large number of particles precluded any sorting.

The texture map generation algorithm required an in-memory frame buffer consisting of one 64-bit word per two pixels. The entire frame buffer could not be kept in memory due to its size, thus an alternative scheme was adopted. Since the major direction of flow was horizontal (due to Jupiter's prevailing shear bands), a particle rarely traveled too far from the scan line it was launched upon. This flow coherency allowed a moving window technique to be adopted. Each pixel in this frame buffer contained 8 bits for each color component and an 8-bit particle accumulator. Particles were mapped into single pixels, their colors were averaged into the existing colors and the accumulator was incremented. For a pixel already containing n particles, with average color component value c, the addition of a new particle of color component value c_p resulted in a new pixel color component value of

$$c_{new} = (nc + c_p)/(n + 1) .$$

A scan line of pixels remained in memory until a pixel beyond the bottom of the window was referenced. At this point, as many scan lines as necessary were flushed to disk from the top of the window, filling any holes (pixels without particles) in these scan lines with the prior frame's pixel color. This reliance on frame-to-frame coherence was sufficient given the relatively slow motion. By appropriate indexing, the window was then effectively slid down, and the process continued.

The techniques of mapping particles into a frame buffer also took advantage of positional coherency. Since the average pixel initially contained approximately six particles, and each 64-bit word contained two pixels, a modification of this method capitalized on similar operations on the same pixel and/or word, thus saving computations and memory references. At the end of a scene consisting of several seconds, the average coherency was still above two sequential particles per word.

Large I/O buffers and asynchronous double-buffering were also used in DEPICT for efficiency. In addition, the central kernel of DEPICT was moved into Cray Assembly Language. This made it possible to adopt a technique for differentiation between the nonlinear regions discussed below, using the Cray's Vector Mask register, which allowed the vectorization of calculations not vectorizable within Cray Fortran. A factor of eight overall improvement in the particle rendering time was thus achieved.

7. Nonlinear Texture Mapping

A method for creating and using nonlinear images and their corresponding parametric maps was employed to concentrate the resolution of the texturing image where it was most needed. A new software tool, NLPIC (for NonLinear PICture), was applied to the extremely high resolution images--greater than could ultimately be used in the filming process--that resulted from the merging of the scanned-in photographs. The (cylindrical projection) parametric mapping used to map the texture onto the planet also served as an input to NLPIC. The output consisted of a nonlinear image; a modified parametric map, which would reexpand the compressed boundaries of the texture when it was applied to the sphere; and a small data file containing a set of corresponding constants, which were subsequently used as inputs to the particle generation and particle rendering algorithms. Figures 4a and 4b show linear and nonlinear versions of the same texture map.

The nonlinear mapping was created by breaking the image space into five regions along each axis, with user-specified region boundaries and region pixel counts (Fig. 5). The first and last regions each had constant, large pixel sizes. The center region had a constant, small pixel size. The second and fourth regions contained pixels of linearly varying size, providing a smooth transition between the outer, low-resolution regions and the center high-resolution region. In order to rigorously enforce the smooth transition at region boundaries, the locations of the actual boundaries between regions 1 and 2 and between 4 and 5 were allowed to vary slightly from those input by the user.

Please note that all equations in this section are given in a "mathematical" form rather than a "software" form; for computational purposes, all variables would be treated as real (floating point) numbers, including indices and counts.

Given the definitions

L_{o_i} = the input length of the ith region

L_i = the actual length of the ith region

N_i = the input and actual number of pixels in the ith region,

by selecting

$$L_1 = [2(L_{o_1} + L_{o_2}) - L_3 N_2/N_3]/(2 + N_2/N_1)$$
$$L_2 = (L_{o_1} + L_{o_2}) - L_1$$
$$L_5 = [2(L_{o_4} + L_{o_5}) - L_3 N_4/N_3]/(2 + N_4/N_5)$$
$$L_4 = (L_{o_4} + L_{o_5}) - L_5 ,$$

it may be shown that one has maintained both the position and the length (hence the resolution, given a fixed number of pixels) of the important central region. Only the position of the boundary between the outer regions has been allowed to vary slightly, along with the resolutions in those regions. The above formulas were derived by defining the fixed, known sum of the lengths of the two outlying regions $(L_{o_1} + L_{o_2})$ in terms of the unknown length of the first region (L_1) and the implied length of the second region based on the summation of pixel sizes varying linearly between those in region 1 (L_1/N_1) and those in region 3 (L_3/N_3).

Figure 4a. Example of a linear texture map.

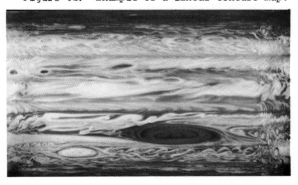

Figure 4b. Example of a nonlinear texture map (same domain as 4a).

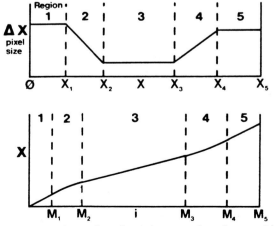

Figure 5. Schematic of region mapping for nonlinear texture definition.

90

This particular form of mapping was chosen partly because it provided a system that was fairly easy to control, and more importantly because it provided an analytically invertible mapping within each region (required for computational efficiency). Accordingly, during the particle generation phase, $\Delta x(i)$, the pixel width, and $x(i)$, the particle position (at pixel center), as functions of pixel index, are determined as follows.

Let $M_j = \Sigma_{i=1}^{j} N_i$ and $X_j = \Sigma_{i=1}^{j} L_i$, being the cumulative pixel counts and lengths of the five regions, respectively. Then

$$\Delta x(i) = \begin{cases} L_1/N_1 = \Delta x_1 , & 0 < i \leq M_1 \\ \Delta x_1 - [(\Delta x_1 - \Delta x_3)/(N_2-1)](i-M_1-1), & M_1 < i \leq M_2 \\ L_3/N_3 = \Delta x_3 , & M_2 < i \leq M_3 \\ \Delta x_3 - [(\Delta x_5 - \Delta x_3)/(N_4-1)](i-M_3-1), & M_3 < i \leq M_4 \\ L_5/N_5 = \Delta x_5 , & M_4 < i \leq M_5 \end{cases}$$

and

$$x(i) = \begin{cases} (i - \tfrac{1}{2})\Delta x_1 & 0 < i \leq M_1 \\ X_1 + \dfrac{\Delta x_1}{2} + \Delta x_1(i-M_1-1) - \dfrac{1}{2}\left(\dfrac{\Delta x_1 - \Delta x_3}{N_2-1}\right)(i-M_1-1)^2 & M_1 < i \leq M_2 \\ (i-M_2 - \tfrac{1}{2})\Delta x_3 + X_2 & M_2 < i \leq M_3 \\ X_3 + \dfrac{\Delta x_3}{2} + \Delta x_3(i-M_3-1) + \dfrac{1}{2}\left(\dfrac{\Delta x_5 - \Delta x_3}{N_4-1}\right)(i-M_3-1)^2 & M_3 < i \leq M_4 \\ (i - M_4 - \tfrac{1}{2})\Delta x_5 + X_4 & M_4 < i \leq M_5 \end{cases}$$

During the particle rendering phase, $i(x)$, the pixel index as a function of particle position is determined by

$$i(x) = \begin{cases} x/\Delta x_1 + 1/2 , & 0 < x \leq X_1 \\ M_1 + 1 + \Delta x_1\left(\dfrac{N_2-1}{\Delta x_1 - \Delta x_3}\right) - \sqrt{\Delta x_1^2\left(\dfrac{N_2-1}{\Delta x_1 - \Delta x_3}\right)^2 - 2[x-(X_1+\Delta x_1/2)]\left(\dfrac{N_2-1}{\Delta x_1 - \Delta x_3}\right)} , & X_1 < x \leq X_2 \\ (x - X_2)/\Delta x_3 + 1/2 + M_2 , & X_2 < x \leq X_3 \\ M_3 + 1 - \Delta x_3\left(\dfrac{N_4-1}{\Delta x_5 - \Delta x_3}\right) + \sqrt{\Delta x_3^2\left(\dfrac{N_4-1}{\Delta x_5 - \Delta x_3}\right)^2 + 2[x-(X_3+\Delta x_3/2)]\left(\dfrac{N_4-1}{\Delta x_5 - \Delta x_3}\right)} , & X_3 < x \leq X_4 \\ (x - X_4)/\Delta x_5 + 1/2 + M_4 , & X_4 < x \leq X_5 \end{cases}$$

(Note: the final index is the nearest integer to the above result.)

The nonlinear image went on to serve as both the initial texture file in the simulation and the source for the particle generation program. The nonlinear parametric map was used in place of the original cylindrical mapping to apply the nonlinear image to the planet's surface. The defining constants were used by both the particle generation and rendering programs to relate linear particle positions to the nonlinear source image. The particle advection step did not require any knowledge of the nonlinear mapping, since each particle retained a linear-space position based on the formulas above.

8.   Integration with the Principal Rendering Algorithm

As described in the Introduction (Section 2), we placed the primary data elements and software elements of the VORTEX system under the control of a supervisory program. All software elements of the VORTEX system, including the supervisor, were added as a major overlay structure to the existing principal rendering software at Digital Productions, known as DP3D. This permitted a sharing of memory space between DP3D and the VORTEX system. Each of the primary elements of the VORTEX system--TRADE, WINDS, and DEPICT--were further overlaid upon each other. This provided maximum memory availability to each software element. Communication between the VORTEX software elements was facilitated by the contents of the main VORTEX data elements--texture, particle, and vorticity files--and the supervisor program. Communication between the VORTEX system and DP3D was effected through the top-level command parser in DP3D, especially through a full function, high-level, procedural programming language called FIFTH, which is used to process and generate command lines for DP3D.

Each of the VORTEX software elements typically expected a pair of file names for each data element it was to process--one for input and one for output. It was necessary to toggle the relationship between input and output for file pairs on even and odd invocations. The issue became more complicated when attempting to compute simultaneously on our X-MP's two cpu's, in two complete invocations of the DP3D--VORTEX system. First, each cpu required its own full set of file pairs. Second, it was necessary for the supervisor to be aware of the number of processors involved in the current simulation, and to take the appropriate double steps in both the fluid dynamics and particle advection stages when in the multiprocessing mode. The logic to handle all of these issues was installed in the VORTEX supervisory program. Additionally, restarts after interruptions were a complicated problem, since the simulation is necessarily dependent upon history to the point of interruption. Special procedures at the FIFTH and supervisor levels were required to handle most restart cases.

DP3D was used, then, to render the final image of Jupiter (Figs. 6a and 6b), at a resolution of 3200 by 1620 pixels (calculated at a resolution of 6400 by 3240 and averaged down). The total time per frame, including all VORTEX and DP3D computations and I/O, was approximately 2 minutes. With some effort this time per frame could be reduced further. The frames were recorded on Digital Productions' custom-built, high-resolution Digital Film Printer Recorder. A total of approximately 2 and 1/2 minutes (3600 frames) of Jupiter simulation was delivered.

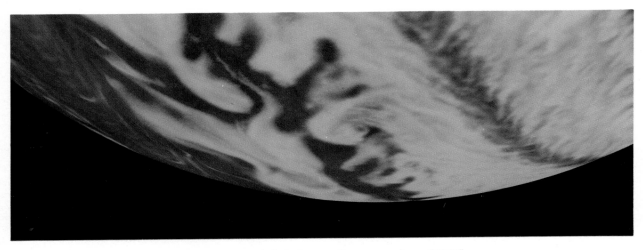

Figure 6a. Initial frame of a scene from "2010".

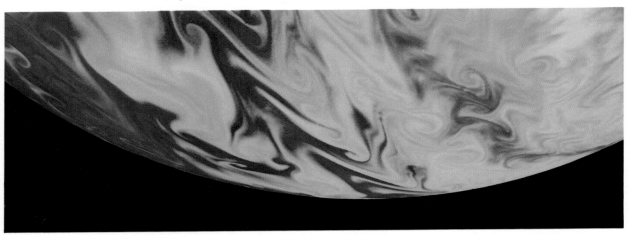

Figure 6b. Evolved state of same planet portion seen in Fig. 6a. Note local vortex motion after several seconds of animation.

9. Concluding Remarks

The work documented herein represents a successful integration of diverse simulation types, and it is this integration that we feel constitutes the work's primary significance. By combining computational models of the physics of fluids with the physics and phenomenology of vision, we have produced strikingly realistic images of a natural, but currently unobservable phenomenon. With the advent of modern supercomputers and a maturing of the computational sciences, it has become possible to incorporate physically realistic models into computer graphics imaging. This approach is one powerful technique available to push visual simulation farther down the road toward one of its longstanding goals--simulation indistinguishable from reality. Automatic, realistic model behavior and modes of interaction between elements composing a scene should play an important role in the future of computer graphics, as it becomes feasible to invest computing power in the solution of these problems.

One of the greatest compliments ever paid to the Jupiter simulation work was to describe the resulting images as having an "organic" feeling, belying their computer graphic origins. Almost everyone has had the occasion to notice an oil slick on moving water, with its swirling rainbow hues, or a dollop of cream poured into a black cup of coffee, with the subsequent rolling filaments of light and dark. These motions are recalled--with good reason, since the physics are similar--when watching the cloud motions of the simulated Jupiter. It is not claimed that the fluid dynamics models utilized in the VORTEX system accurately portray the physics of the atmosphere of Jupiter. Yet the model is not entirely ad hoc either, and it does provide a fundamentally accurate portrayal of fluid motion. It is this natural authenticity that helps viewers to willingly suspend disbelief and to imagine themselves actually watching the great planet Jupiter swirl and churn before their eyes.

Projects other than "2010" have utilized the VORTEX system. In the stereoscopic 3-D footage generated for the Hitachi pavilion at Tsukuba for Japan's Expo '85 (and shown at SIGGRAPH '85), the VORTEX system was used to add a touch of realism to a flight between cloud layers of a Jupiter-like planet. A multipanel view of the Earth from space, with realistic cloud motion supplied by VORTEX, was created for a CircleVision installation entitled "Portraits of Canada," to be seen at Expo '86 in Vancouver. Other uses for VORTEX are planned.

Additionally, the techniques employed in the VORTEX system are amenable to applications other than special effects for movies. Substitution of a scientific researcher's fluids model for TRADE, with an appropriate particle advection scheme in WINDS and utilizing DEPICT precisely as is, could provide a very effective flow visualization technique.

While the fluid dynamics in VORTEX were being used to create a "special effect" (a realistic, though not necessarily accurate, rendition of a fluid phenomenon), we are beginning to see more and more examples of very real, very significant physical simulations coupled to computer graphic display techniques. In industry and in academia (especially through the NSF Supercomputer Initiative) researchers have been using Cray X-MPs and other supercomputers to numerically solve problems that are intractable by any other means. The traditional results of such simulations are countless reams of numbers, which contain some significant answers if one could only find them. Coupling computer graphics to these physical models provides insights and understanding to the researcher and an effective means of communicating these insights to peers. If a picture is worth a thousand words, it must surely be worth a million numbers.

Two-dimensional simulations of a fluid in the vicinity of a black hole, three-dimensional simulations of the evolution of matter distribution in the universe, and complicated deconvolutions of very large radio-array astronomical data are just a few recent examples of important scientific research that has benefited from both the computational power of supercomputers and the interpretive power of computer graphics. Of course, the aerospace industry, the automobile industry, and NASA-Ames's Numerical Aerodynamic Simulation Facility employ large fluid dynamic simulations and stand to benefit greatly from computer flow visualization techniques. All of these (and many more) research areas are representatives of a relatively new branch of science—the experimental and theoretical sciences now have a third partner in their collaborative investigation of the nature of reality—computational science. It is the nature of this science and its computer simulations, aided and abetted by the size and power of today's supercomputers, that guarantees the production of more data than can conceivably be digested in numeric form; computer graphics must provide the answers. The bond between physical and visual simulation can only grow stronger.

10. Acknowledgments

The authors would like to thank the following: Gary Demos and John Whitney, Jr. for their pioneering efforts in CGI; Jim Davis for his support in the writing and publication of this work; Julie Hahn, Dave Wicinas, John Graham, and Kathy Chasen for their assistance in the rapid deployment of this paper; Mitch Wade, Dick McHugh, Phil Chen, David Ruhoff, Jack Green, Don Smith, Jim Rygiel, David Keller, and Lee Dyer for their various efforts, which contributed greatly to the successful completion of this project.

11. References

1. Avis, Charles C., Collins, Stewart A., "Voyager Time-Lapse Cylindrical-Projection Jupiter Mosaics," NASA JPL Publication JPL D-531, Feb. 1983.

2. Blinn, J. and Newell, M., "Texture and Reflection on Computer-Generated Images," Communications of the ACM, 19, 10, Oct. 1976.

3. Bouknight, W.J., "A Procedure for Generation of Three-Dimensional Half-Toned Computer Graphics Representations," Communications of the ACM, 13, 9, Sept. 1970.

4. Catmull, E., "A Subdivision Algorithm for Computer Display of Curved Surfaces," PhD Dissertation, Computer Science Dept., University of Utah, Tech. Report UTEC-CSc-74-133, Dec. 1974.

5. Crow, F., "Summed-Area Tables for Texture Mapping," Computer Graphics, 18, 3, July 1984.

6. Holton, James R., An Introduction to Dynamic Meteorology, Academic Press, 1972.

7. Limaye, S.S., et. al, "Jovian Winds from Voyager 2. Part I: Zonal Mean Circulation," Journal of Atmospheric Sciences, 39, 7, July 1982.

8. Mitchell, J., "The Nature of Large-Scale Turbulence in the Jovian Atmosphere," NASA JPL Publication 82-34, Jan. 1982.

9. Newman, W. and Sproull, R., Principles of Interactive Graphics, 2nd Ed., McGraw-Hill, 1979.

10. Orszag, S.A. and Gottlieb, D., "Numerical Analysis of Spectral Methods," Society for Industrial and Applied Mathematics, 1977.

11. Reeves, W.T., "Particle Systems--A Technique for Modeling a Class of Fuzzy Objects," ACM Transactions on Graphics, 2, 2, April 1983.

12. Sutherland, I.E., Sproull, R.F., and Schumacher, R.A., "A Characterization of Ten Hidden-Surface Algorithms," ACM Computing Surveys, 6, 1, March 1974.

13. Watkins, G.S., "A Real-Time Visible Surface Algorithm," Computer Science Dept. University of Utah, UTEC-CSc-70-101, June 1970.

14. Weiler, K. and Atherton, P., "Hidden Surface Removal Using Polygon Area Sorting," Computer Graphics, 11, 2, Summer 1977.

15. Williams, L., "Pyramidal Parametrics," Computer Graphics, 17, 3, July 1983.

A Fast Shaded-Polygon Renderer

by Roger W. Swanson and Larry J. Thayer

Hewlett-Packard Company
3404 East Harmony Road
Fort Collins, CO 80525
(303) 229-3023 or 229-3048

Abstract

Image rendering is the performance bottleneck in many computer-graphics systems today because of its computation-intensive nature. Described here is a one-chip VLSI implementation of a shaded-polygon renderer which provides an affordable solution to the bottleneck. The chip takes advantage of a unique extension to Bresenham's vector drawing algorithm [1] to interpolate four axes (for Red, Green, Blue and Z) across a polygon, in addition to the X and Y values. Its inherent accuracy and ease of high-speed hardware implementation distinguish this new algorithm from interpolation with incrementing fractions (DDA).

This chip was designed as part of a workstation primarily for mechanical engineering CAD applications. The pipelining and internal bandwidth possible on the chip allows rendering speeds of over twelve-thousand, 1000-pixel, shaded polygons per second, suitable for interactive manipulation of solids. Described in this paper is the derivation of the new algorithm and its implementation in a pipelined, polygon-rendering chip.

CR Categories and Subject Descriptors: B.2.1 [Arithmetic and Logic Structures]: Design Styles – Pipeline; I.3.3 [Computer Graphics]: Picture/Image Generation – Display algorithms.

Additional Key Words and Phrases: image synthesis, shading, interpolation, multiple-axis interpolator, graphics VLSI.

Introduction

Computer-Aided Engineering (CAE) workstations for mechanical engineers need to produce accurate visual cues to the properties of objects to assist engineers in their designs. Typical properties include structure, shape, appearance, thermal gradients, and stress gradients. It is the function of the graphics subsystem of a CAE workstation to produce these images in a form that can be easily understood and manipulated.

With most methods of image synthesis, the image is generated by breaking the surfaces of the object into polygons, calculating the color and intensity at each vertex, and drawing the results into a frame buffer while interpolating the colors across the polygon (Gouraud shading [4]). The color information can be calculated from light source data or computed with thermal or stress analyses.

The interpolation of coordinate and color (or intensity) across each polygon must be performed quickly and accurately. This is accomplished by interpolating the coordinate and color of each quantized point (pixel) on the edges of the polygon and subsequently interpolating from edge to edge to generate the fill lines. If hidden surface removal with a Z buffer is required, then the depth (Z) value for each pixel must also be calculated. Furthermore, since color components can vary independently across a surface or set of surfaces, red, green, and blue intensities must be interpolated independently. Thus, for a general-purpose graphics system, a minimum of 6 different parameters (X, Y, Z, Red, Green, and Blue) must be independently calculated when drawing polygons with Gouraud shading and interpolated Z values.

Generating the pixels has traditionally been the bottleneck in image generation [Fuchs et al 3] because creating images at interactive speeds requires millions of pixels to be drawn per second. Alleviating the bottleneck requires an interpolation algorithm which can be implemented in hardware and extended to include six parameters. To maximize process overlap and minimize cost, it is desirable to have all components of the polygon-rendering pipeline contained on a single chip.

The following is a description of a one-chip VLSI implementation of an interpolator (called the Polygon Rendering Chip, or PRC) capable of performing interpolated polygon fill with six parameters at rates up to 20 million pixels per second. Inputs for the PRC consist of polygon vertex data (X, Y, Z, R, G, B in the form of 16-bit integers) and vertex connectivity information fetched from an external dual-ported RAM. Its outputs are the X, Y, Z, R, G, and B data for each pixel. The PRC is capable of filling shaded polygons with over 2000 convex, concave, and/or crossing sides, and has an address space of 32768 x 32768 pixels.

The interpolation algorithm used in the PRC is an extension of the line-drawing algorithm proposed by Bresenham [1], but uniquely extended to six axes. The use of integer math for speed and ease of hardware implementation is the distinguishing feature of the algorithm.

Multiple-Axis Interpolation

This section contains a discussion of the evolution of raster graphics from line-rendering algorithms through the development of a multiple-axis interpolator. Each step in the derivation is shown in a Pascal-like program. Unless otherwise noted, the following will assume X to be the major axis and increasing in value. (By swapping X,Y and/or mirroring across the X and/or Y axis, any vector can be mapped into this assumption). Xs and Ys will be the starting values for X and Y. Xe and Ye will be the ending values for X and Y.

Digital Differential Analyzer (DDA)

The Digital Differential Analyzer (DDA) [5] permits calculation of the Y value of a line without solving the equation $Y = M*X+C$ (requiring a multiplication) for each value of X. This is accomplished by computing the line differential, or slope (M), as a constant $(Ye-Ys)/(Xe-Xs)$. Once M has been computed, successive X,Y points can be generated by repeatedly incrementing X by 1 and adding M to Y. All Y values still need to be rounded to the nearest integer, but this is easily accomplished by adding 0.5 to the initial Y value and truncating each Y result. A down counter starting at Xe-Xs is also needed to detect the end of the line. Summarizing the above in program form we get:

```
PROCEDURE DDA1(Xs,Xe,Ys,Ye:INTEGER);
  VAR M,Y:REAL;
      N,X:INTEGER;

  BEGIN
  (* SETUP *)
  X := Xs;
  Y := Ys+.5;
  M := (Ye-Ys)/(Xe-Xs);
  N := (Xe-Xs);
  (* INTERPOLATION *)
  PLOT (X,INT(Y));
  WHILE N<>0
  DO BEGIN
     X := X+1;
     Y := Y+M;
     N := N-1;
     PLOT (X,INT(Y));
     END;
  END;
```

The main difficulties in using the DDA are the initial divide to generate M, and the need to use real or fractional binary numbers for M and Y. Not only is the division generally slow, but it is prone to round-off errors. The fractional part of M and Y must have a precision at least equal to the screen precision to be guaranteed of hitting the correct end point, and our empirical data suggest that the precision must be at least twice that of the screen's precision to correctly draw all the points in between.

Bresenham's Algorithm

The DDA can be split into two parts, the integer and the fractional. The integer part includes the count value N, the X value, and the integer part of the Y value. The fractional part includes only the fractional part of the Y value and all of the slope M . Since we initially assumed X to be the major axis, the slope (Ye-Ys)/(Xe-Xs) will always be less than or equal to 1.

The only connection between the fractional values and the integer values is the carry from the Y-fractional part to the Y-integer part. As long as any integer values generated by adding the slope M to the Y-fractional part are transferred to the Y-integer part, the integer and fractional parts can be treated independently. This can be done by subtracting 1 from the Y-fractional part and adding 1 to the Y-integer part whenever the Y-fractional part is greater-than-or-equal-to (GE) 1. Since comparing for GE zero (sign bit interrogation) is usually easier than comparing for GE 1, 1 can be subtracted from the initial Y-fractional part and the GE zero comparison can be used. Letting Yf represent the Y-fractional part, and Yi represent the Y-integer part, our program becomes:

```
PROCEDURE DDA2(Xs,Xe,Ys,Ye:INTEGER);
  VAR M,Yf:REAL;
      N,X,Yi:INTEGER;

  BEGIN
  (* SETUP *)
  X := Xs;
  Yi := Ys;
  Yf := -.5;
  M := (Ye-Ys)/(Xe-Xs);
  N := (Xe-Xs);
  (* INTERPOLATION *)
  PLOT (X,Yi);
  WHILE N<>0
  DO BEGIN
     X := X+1;
     Yf := Yf+M;
     IF Yf>=0
     THEN BEGIN
          Yf := Yf-1;
          Yi := Yi+1;
          END;
     N := N-1;
     PLOT (X,Yi);
     END;
  END;
```

Since the values of the fractional parts are never used outside their own system of equations, they can all be scaled by the constant 2*(Xe–Xs). Only the boolean result of a compare for GE zero is sent out. This has the result of eliminating the initial divide and converting all the fractional variables into integers. This is done without adding any multiplications other than by 2 which can easily be accomplished with a left shift. Our program now becomes:

```
PROCEDURE BRESENHAM(Xs,Xe,Ys,Ye:INTEGER);
  VAR M,Yf,
      N,X,Yi:INTEGER;

  BEGIN
  (* SETUP *)
  X := Xs;
  Yi := Ys;
  Yf := -(Xe-Xs);
  M := 2*(Ye-Ys);
  N := (Xe-Xs);
  (* INTERPOLATION *)
  PLOT (X,Yi);
  WHILE N<>0
  DO BEGIN
     X := X+1;
     Yf := Yf+M;
     IF Yf>=0
     THEN BEGIN
          Yf := Yf-2*(Xe-Xs);
          Yi := Yi+1;
          END;
     N := N-1;
     PLOT (X,Yi);
     END;
  END;
```

The above program is essentially the same as the rules Bresenham presented in his original article [1].

Z, Red, Green, and Blue

When using Bresenham's algorithm in X and Y only, the major axis should always be defined as the axis of greatest delta, thus ensuring that a point will be plotted for each pixel along the major axis. When interpolating along the Z, Red, Green, or Blue axes, the X (or Y) axis should remain the major axis, even though its delta may be smaller than delta Z, delta Red, delta Green, and/or delta Blue. This is due to the fact that the line is projected onto the X,Y plane. For example, it would be absurd to take 10,000 steps along the Z axis when only three pixels are to be drawn! This implies that the slope of the line in the X-Z plane, for example, may be greater than 1, a condition which would exclude using the Bresenham algorithm.

One approach [2,6] many have used to implement Z, Red, Green, and Blue interpolation is to return to the DDA, which doesn't require the slope to be between 0 and 1. They claim that slight inaccuracies due to the DDA in the Z, Red, Green, and Blue values are not as critical as those in X and Y.

However, a transformation similar to the one used above can be done without requiring the slope to be between 0 and 1. If the slope is unrestricted, then it will have an integer part and a fractional part which must be split up just as the Y value was. Modifying DDA1, we now get:

```
PROCEDURE DDA3(Xs,Xe,Zs,Ze:INTEGER);

  VAR Mf,Zf:REAL;
      N,Mi,X,Zi:INTEGER;

  BEGIN
  (* SETUP *)
  X := Xs;
  Zi := Zs;
  Zf := -.5;
  Mi := (Ze-Zs) DIV (Xe-Xs);
  Mf := FRACT((Ze-Zs)/(Xe-Xs));
  N := (Xe-Xs);
  (* INTERPOLATION *)
  PLOT (X,Zi);
  WHILE N<>0
  DO BEGIN
     X := X+1;
     Zi := Zi+Mi;
     Zf := Zf+Mf;
     IF Zf>=0
     THEN BEGIN
          Zf := Zf-1;
          Zi := Zi+1;
          END;
     N := N-1;
     PLOT (X,Zi);
     END;
  END;
```

As with DDA2, all fractional parts can be changed to integers by scaling with the constant 2*(Xe-Xs). The following Multiple-Axis Interpolator (MAI) assumes X to represent the major axis and Z to represent any of the other axes. Note that B MOD A = A*FRACT(B/A).

```
PROCEDURE MAI1(Xs,Xe,Zs,Ze:INTEGER);

    VAR Mf,Zf,
        N,Mi,X,Zi:INTEGER;

    BEGIN
    (* SETUP *)
    X := Xs;
    Zi := Zs;
    Zf := -(Xe-Xs);
    Mi := (Ze-Zs) DIV (Xe-Xs);
    Mf := 2*((Ze-Zs) MOD (Xe-Xs));
    N := (Xe-Xs);
    (* INTERPOLATION *)
    PLOT (X,Zi);
    WHILE N<>0
    DO BEGIN
        X := X+1;
        Zi := Zi+Mi;
        Zf := Zf+Mf;
        IF Zf>=0
        THEN BEGIN
            Zf := Zf-2*(Xe-Xs);
            Zi := Zi+1;
            END;
        N := N-1;
        PLOT (X,Zi);
        END;
    END;
```

At first glance, the MAI looks worse than the DDA. There is a DIV and a MOD function in the MAI while DDA has only one division. However, the DIV in the MAI is an integer division which is much simpler than the real division in the DDA. The MOD function is free as this value is simply the remainder from the DIV done in the line above. Since the integer remainder is not thrown away, there is no round-off error as in the DDA. In a hardware implementation, the adders required for the Zi and Zf additions require the same, or fewer, bits than are required for the real value Z in the DDA.

Since all operations use simple integer arithmetic, the required resolution can be precisely specified. The needed resolution is determined by that of the delta terms (Xe-Xs and Ze-Zs), which require one bit more than the number of bits in the X or Z range. For example, if the desired X or Z range is 0 to 32767, then 16 bits of resolution are required to ensure no loss of information.

Implementation in Hardware

Implementation of the MAI
The above algorithm can easily be modified to plot one pixel every clock period for hardware implementation by rolling part of the interpolation loop calculation into setup and precomputing the constant Mf2.

```
PROCEDURE MAI2(Xs,Xe,Zs,Ze:INTEGER);

    VAR Mf,Zf,
        N,Mi,X,Zi:INTEGER;

    BEGIN
    (* SETUP *)
    X := Xs;
    Zi := Zs;
    Mi := (Ze-Zs) DIV (Xe-Xs);
    Mf := 2*((Ze-Zs) MOD (Xe-Xs));
    Mf2 := Mf-2*(Xe-Xs);
    Zf := -(Xe-Xs)+Mf;
    N := (Xe-Xs);
    (* INTERPOLATION *)
    PLOT (X,Zi);
    WHILE N<>0
    DO BEGIN
        X := X+1;
        IF Zf>=0
        THEN BEGIN
            Zf := Zf+Mf2;
            Zi := Zi+Mi+1;
            END
```

```
    ELSE BEGIN
        Zf := Zf+Mf;
        Zi := Zi+Mi;
        END;
    N := N-1;
    PLOT (X,Zi);
    END;
END;
```

The interpolation loop can now generate values at a rate of 1 pixel per clock if two adders per axis are used, one for Zf, and one for Zi. Since the data flow from the setup to the interpolation loop is unidirectional, the two routines can easily be pipelined. The entire setup procedure can be accomplished using one adder per axis and doing a shift-and-add type divide in 20 to 34 clocks. Since our data show the typical fill vector length to be about 30 pixels, there is a good speed match between the setup and the pixel drawing and there is little need for any special divide hardware. The parameters for interpolation are calculated in the SETUP functional block on the PRC. Pixel drawing takes place in the INTERPOLATOR functional block.

Six interpolators are used in the PRC. Even though one of X or Y could always be handled with an up/down counter, extra bookkeeping would be required to keep track of which parameter was where and the routing of the chip would be more complex. Adding another copy of the interpolator engine running in parallel with the other axis is a much simpler solution.

Polygon Fill Functions
The PRC begins the polygon fill process by reading an instruction and a pointer out of an external dual-ported RAM. The instruction indicates what kind of figure (polygon or vector) is to be drawn and if a linetype pattern is to be used. The pointer indicates the location of the first edge data packet for the polygon. Each packet contains a pointer to the next packet.

The first pointer is passed to the EDGE functional block. The EDGE block builds up an ordered list of active edges (in the order to be used) and then reads the data packets of the first two edges to be drawn. As they are read, they are passed to the SETUP block and then on to the INTERPOLATOR. When the INTERPOLATOR block finishes one scan line of each edge, the packets are passed back to the EDGE block.

If there are only two active edges, they are both stored in the EDGE block's registers. If there are more than two active edges, EDGE swaps the appropriate edges in and out of the external dual-ported RAM. The EDGE block also dynamically maintains the active edge list, adding edges as the current scan line reaches them, and deleting edges as they are completed. EDGE will also re-sort the order of the active edge list whenever two edges cross. This permits the drawing of non-planar, concave, twisted polygons which may contain holes.

As the INTERPOLATOR steps along each edge, the output is sampled by the FILL block. The FILL block saves the starting and ending points of each edge's contribution to the scan line. From these, it generates fill vectors which are passed on to SETUP. FILL also needs to keep track of whether or not each edge is just starting or ending so as to properly handle vertices. Since EDGE, FILL, INTERPOLATOR, and SETUP are all pipelined, the setup of the fill vector will happen in parallel with the interpolation of the next edge segment. The data flow described in this section can be seen in Figure A.

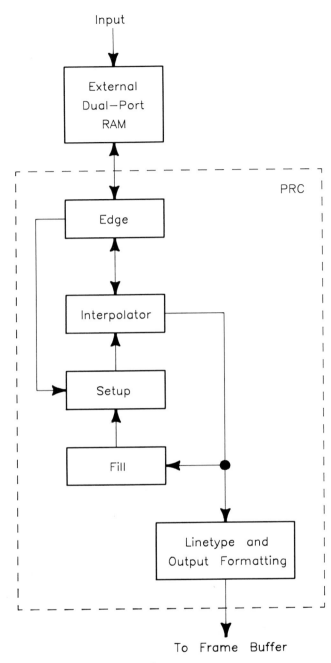

Figure A.

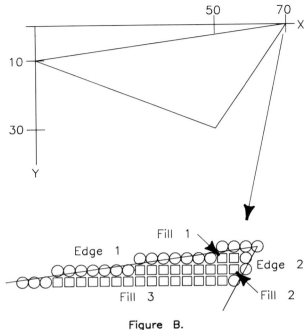

Figure B.

Polygon Fill Example
One way to maximize performance is to pipeline the different parts of the fill and shading algorithm. The PRC is designed to have the EDGE, SETUP, INTERPOLATOR, and FILL functional blocks running in parallel. Furthermore, by having the functional blocks all on one chip, the data can be transferred from one block to another in only one clock via extremely wide busses.

A polygon rendering example to illustrate how this pipelining works is shown in the top of Figure B. Each vertex of this polygon has unique color and depth data. It takes about 90 microseconds to draw this 1030-pixel triangle.

The bottom of Figure B shows the first four lines of pixels drawn. The pixels in the edge are represented with circles and the pixels making up the fill lines are shown as squares.

Figure C shows how the functional blocks interact to generate the edges and the fill lines. Time is shown on the vertical axis in units of chip clock cycles (approx. 20 MHz). The columns under each label show when each functional block is active. For simplification, the FILL routine (which determines the fill lines) is not explicitly shown. It is in operation when edges are being drawn.

Notice that the first block activated is EDGE, which must set up the list of active edges then read in the data for the first two edges. After the first edge (Edge 1) is read, the SETUP block prepares Edge 1 for the interpolation process. This is done in parallel with Edge 2 being read.

Once the setup for Edge 1 is complete, its packet of data is sent to the INTERPOLATOR and the first row of pixels in the edge is drawn. Then the packet is sent to the EDGE block. EDGE then compares its X and Y values to verify that the third edge does not yet have to be activated. After Edge 2 is set up, its first pixel is drawn and its packet is sent on to EDGE. Then the next horizontal row of pixels in Edge 1 is drawn, followed by the next pixel in Edge 2. Notice that Edge 1 has several pixels drawn per line, while Edge 2 has only one.

The data from the second line of the edges are sent to EDGE for comparison and to SETUP for building the data for the first fill line (Fill 1). The fill line is then drawn between the inside pixels of each edge. While Fill 1 is being set up, the two edges are again incremented in the Y direction and the next row of pixels in the edges is drawn. While Fill 1 is being drawn, Fill 2 is already in SETUP. Fill lines are drawn at a rate of one pixel every 50-nanosecond state.

Note that the first fill lines are short, so it takes more time to do the set-up operation than it takes to draw the line. As the fill lines become longer, the set-up process no longer is the bottleneck in the rendering process and the INTERPOLATOR is almost continuously drawing pixels.

Also note that very little time is spent transferring the data from one functional block to another, making pipelining very efficient. By putting all the blocks on one chip, the blocks can be interleaved within data stacks. This way, all the data (as much as 480 bits) for each edge or fill line can be moved from one functional block to another in one clock cycle via register-to-register transfers.

Since the data output speed is so fast, it is necessary to have an external "pixel cache" so frame buffer writes and Z buffer accesses can be done for several pixels in parallel.

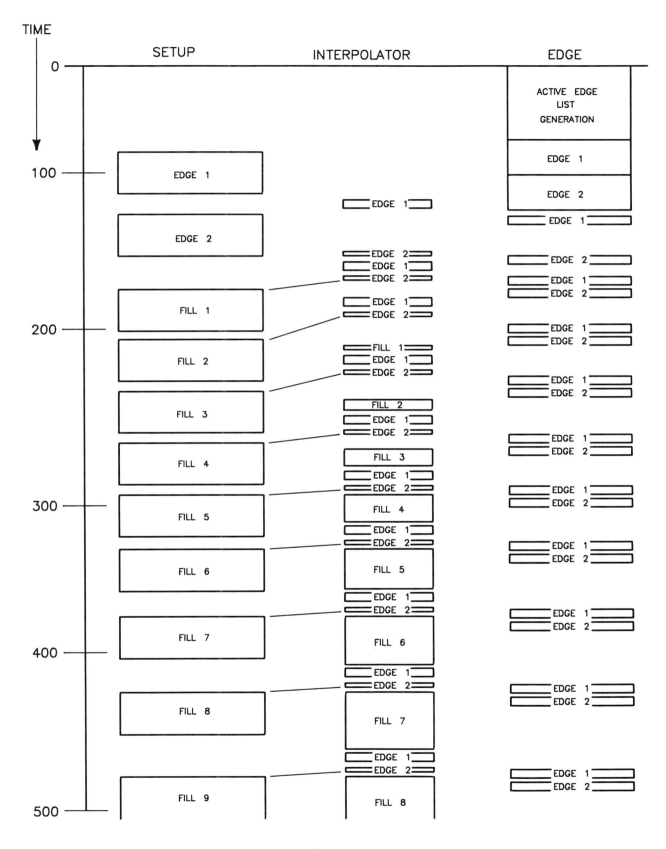

Figure C.

Conclusions

We have presented a multiple-axis interpolation algorithm which has been implemented in a general-purpose, single-chip polygon renderer. We have demonstrated how the different parts of the algorithm can be pipelined for maximum polygon-drawing performance. The polygon example illustrates how the different internal functional blocks interact. Figures D, E, and F show photographs and drawing times of some images generated by the PRC.

The chip is built with an HP-proprietary poly-gate NMOS process using two layers of metal and 1.7-micron minimum channel lengths. Both the polysilicon layer and first metal layer have a minimum trace pitch of 2.5 microns. The PRC measures 8300 x 8300 microns and contains approximately 150,000 transistors (Figure G). It is currently being used in a mechanical CAD workstation.

Acknowledgements

The design work of Bill Cherry, Mark D. Coleman, Darel N. Emmot, and Jim Jackson was essential to the successful completion of the project. The management support of Don Stewart, Dan Griffin, and Dave Maitland is also greatly appreciated.

References

[1] Bresenham, J.E. Algorithm for computer control of a digital plotter.

IBM Systems Journal 4, 1 (1965),25-30.

[2] Foley, James D., Andreis Van Dam.

Fundamentals of Interactive Computer Graphics. Addison-Wesley Publishing Company, Reading, Massachusetts, 1982. 560-561.

[3] Fuchs, Henry, Jack Goldfeather, Jeff P. Hultquist, Susan Spach, John D. Austin, Fredrick P. Brooks, Jr., John G. Eyles, and John Poulton. Fast spheres, shadows, textures, transparencies, and image enhancements in Pixel-Planes.

Computer Graphics 19, 3 (1985), 111 (Proc. SIGGRAPH 85).

[4] Gouraud, H., Continuous shading of curved surfaces.

IEEE Transactions on Computers C-20, 6 (June, 1971), 623-629.

[5] Newman, William M., and Robert F. Sproull,

Principles of Interactive Computer Graphics. McGraw-Hill Book Company, New York, 1973. 41-45.

[6] Sato, Hiroyuki, Mitsuo Ishii, Keiji Sato, Morio Ikesaka, Hiroaki Ishihata, Masanori Kakimoto, Katsuhiko Hirota, Kouichi Inoue. Fast image generation of constructive solid geometry using a cellular array processor.

Computer Graphics 19, 3 (1985), 99 (Proc. SIGGRAPH 85).

Figure D.
1 polygon
1 million pixels
Drawing time: 54 msec

Figure F.
400 polygons
128072 pixels
Drawing time: 30 msec
(Image courtesy of Dave Cooper)

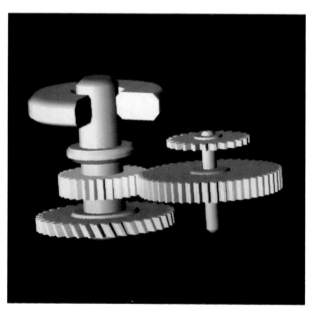

Figure E.
2191 polygons
417947 pixels
Drawing time: 82 msec

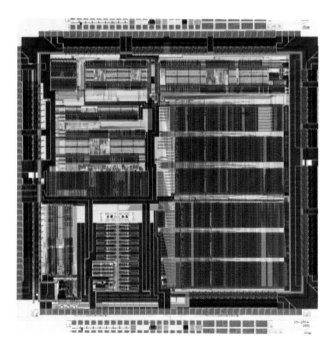

Figure G.
Polygon Rendering Chip

Fast Phong Shading

Gary Bishop
Room 4E-626

David M. Weimer
Room 4F-637

AT&T Bell Laboratories
Crawfords Corner Road
Holmdel, NJ 07733

Abstract

Computer image generation systems often represent curved surfaces as a mesh of planar polygons that are shaded to restore a smooth appearance. Phong shading is a well known algorithm for producing a realistic shading but it has not been used by real-time systems because of the 3 additions, 1 division, and 1 square-root required per pixel for its evaluation. We describe a new formulation for Phong shading that reduces the amount of computation per pixel to only 2 additions for simple Lambertian reflection and 5 additions and 1 memory reference for Phong's complete reflection model. We also show how to extend our method to compute the specular component with the eye at a finite distance from the scene rather than at infinity as is usually assumed. The method can be implemented in hardware for real-time applications or in software to speed image generation for almost any system.

Introduction

Most computer image generation (CIG) systems represent curved surfaces as a mesh of planar polygons because polygons can be transformed and rendered quickly with well known algorithms. Since the polygonal representation is an artifact of the image generation method and is usually of no interest to viewers, (see Figure 1), these systems attempt to restore a smooth appearance to surfaces by varying the intensity across polygons. The efficiency of this shading operation is critical to the performance of a CIG system because it must be performed for one million or more pixels per image. Although algorithms for realistic shading of polygons are well known, real-time CIG systems have not used them because of the large amount of computation they require per pixel. This paper describes a new formulation of Phong shading that drastically reduces the amount of computation compared to previously known formulations. While the new formulation is well suited to implementation with special hardware for real-time display, it is also appropriate for implementation with software for a variety of display systems. Readers who are unfamiliar

with surface representation or shading are referred to one of the standard graphics texts for more information, [Newman and Sproull, 1979; Foley and Van Dam, 1983].

Background

Assume, for simplicity, that the input to the shader consists of triangles, in screen coordinates, with normals, $\vec{N}$, to the original curved surface specified at each vertex. The formulations can be extended to polygons with four or more sides.

The shading algorithm must determine the intensity of each point within a triangle from the surface normals, and a vector to the light source, $\vec{L}$. The light source is assumed to be at infinity so that $\vec{L}$ is independent of the point on which the light shines. We will start with diffuse reflection,

$$I_{diffuse} = \frac{\vec{L} \cdot \vec{N}}{|\vec{L}||\vec{N}|},$$

and later show how to extend the results to include Phong's highlight model and an extended highlight model.

Gouraud Shading. The most commonly used shading method in real-time systems, Gouraud shading [Gouraud, 1971], computes the intensity at each point by linear interpolation of the intensities at the vertices. These intensities are determined using the reflection equation above with the normals given at the vertices. The method is popular for real-time systems because it produces images of acceptable quality with only 1 addition per pixel, but the shading has several disturbing characteristics. (1) Moving objects tend to "flatten out" at certain viewing angles, (2) surfaces appear dull or chalky, and (3) images show pronounced Mach bands, exaggerations of intensity change at discontinuities. Figure 2 is a Gouraud shaded chess piece.

Phong Shading. Phong shading, [Phong, 1973], eliminates "flattening out" and dull surfaces and reduces Mach bands but has not, to my knowledge, been used in any real-time system because of the large amount of computation required for its usual formulation. Phong's method determines the intensity of each point using an approximate surface normal that is linearly interpolated from the true surface normals specified at the vertices.

$$\vec{N}(x,y) = \vec{A}x + \vec{B}y + \vec{C}$$

where $\vec{A}$, $\vec{B}$, and $\vec{C}$ are chosen to interpolate the normal across the polygon. Interpolating for successive values of x and y and evaluating the illumination model requires 7 additions, 6 multiplications, 1 division and 1 square root per pixel. Phong proposed a complicated circuit for evaluating this function but it has not, to my knowledge, been implemented. Figure 3 is a Phong shaded chess piece.

Tom Duff has shown, in [Duff, 1979], that Phong shading can implemented more efficiently by combining the interpolation and reflection equations.

$$I_{diffuse}(x,y) = \frac{\vec{L}}{|\vec{L}|} \cdot \frac{\vec{A}x + \vec{B}y + \vec{C}}{|\vec{L}||\vec{A}x + \vec{B}y + \vec{C}|}.$$

Which can be rewritten as

$$I_{diffuse}(x,y) = \frac{\vec{L}\cdot\vec{A}x + \vec{L}\cdot\vec{B}y + \vec{L}\cdot\vec{C}}{|\vec{L}||\vec{L}\cdot\vec{A}x + \vec{L}\cdot\vec{B}y + \vec{L}\cdot\vec{C}|}.$$

Performing the indicated dot products and expanding the vector magnitude yields

$$I_{diffuse}(x,y) = \frac{ax + by + c}{\sqrt{dx^2 + exy + fy^2 + gx + hy + i}}$$

with

$$a = \frac{\vec{L}\cdot\vec{A}}{|\vec{L}|},$$
$$b = \frac{\vec{L}\cdot\vec{B}}{|\vec{L}|},$$
$$c = \frac{\vec{L}\cdot\vec{C}}{|\vec{L}|},$$
$$d = \vec{A}\cdot\vec{A},$$
$$e = 2\vec{A}\cdot\vec{B},$$
$$f = \vec{B}\cdot\vec{B},$$
$$g = 2\vec{A}\cdot\vec{C},$$
$$h = 2\vec{B}\cdot\vec{C}, \text{ and}$$
$$i = \vec{C}\cdot\vec{C}.$$

Using forward differences, this form can be evaluated for successive values of x and y with 3 additions, 1 division and 1 square root per pixel. This is a substantial savings over Phong's formulation but the division and square root are still too expensive for real-time use.

A New Approach

For display purposes we need not evaluate the reflection equation exactly; a good approximation will suffice. The "error" introduced by the approximation will be of no consequence since Phong's normal interpolation and the reflection equation are already approximations. The one-dimensional form of Taylor's series is widely used for approximating functions, such as sine and log, with polynomials. The less widely used, two-dimensional form will serve to approximate the reflection equation.

Taylor's series for a function of two variables is

$$f(a+h, b+k) = f(a,b) + \left(h\frac{\delta}{\delta x} + k\frac{\delta}{\delta y}\right)f(a,b) + \cdots$$
$$+ \frac{1}{n!}\left(h\frac{\delta}{\delta x} + k\frac{\delta}{\delta y}\right)^n f(a,b) + \cdots$$

Shifting the triangle so that $(0,0)$ lies at its center, and expanding in a Taylor series to the second degree produces

$$I_{diffuse}(x,y) = T_5 x^2 + T_4 xy + T_3 y^2 + T_2 x + T_1 y + T_0$$
with
$$T_5 = \frac{3ig^2 - 4cdi - 4agi}{8i^2\sqrt{i}},$$
$$T_4 = \frac{3cgh - 2cei - 2bgi - 2ahi}{4i^2\sqrt{i}},$$
$$T_3 = \frac{3ch^2 - 4cfi - 4bhi}{8i^2\sqrt{i}},$$
$$T_2 = \frac{2ai - cg}{2i\sqrt{i}},$$
$$T_1 = \frac{2bi - ch}{2i\sqrt{i}}, \text{ and}$$
$$T_0 = \frac{c}{\sqrt{i}}.$$

Using this expansion and forward differences, the intensity can be evaluated with only 2 additions per pixel.

The method can be extended to handle Phong's specular reflection model, $I_{specular} = (\vec{N}\cdot\vec{H})^n$, by using Taylor's series to evaluate the dot product and table lookup to do the exponentiation. (A table of 1k bytes will allow exponentiation to powers up to 20 with less than 1 percent error and a table of 8k bytes allows powers up to 164.) $\vec{H}$ is a vector in the direction of maximum highlight which is halfway between the light direction, $\vec{L}$, and the eye direction, $\vec{E}$.

$$\vec{H} = \frac{\vec{E}+\vec{L}}{|\vec{E}+\vec{L}|}.$$

The eye, like the light source, is assumed for the present to be at infinity. Phong's reflection equation, $I = I_{ambient} + I_{diffuse} + I_{specular}$, can now be evaluated with only 5 additions and 1 memory access per pixel (the ambient component can be rolled into the series for the diffuse component and the series for the specular component can be scaled to allow direct addressing of the exponentiation table). It should be simple to configure hardware to do these operations in less than 100 nanoseconds per pixel.

The additional computation required to determine the T_i for our new method is offset by the greatly reduced computation per pixel for polygons with 10 or more pixels. This estimate is based on the following assumptions: (a) the algorithms are implemented on sequential processors of conventional design, (b) with modern hardware, the time for floating point addition, multiplication, and memory references are all about equal, (c) the computation of $1/\sqrt{x}$ requires about 10 operations, and (d) common subexpressions have been removed from the formulas for T_i. Timings and analysis of the method as implemented in the raster testbed [Whitted and Weimer, 1982] also support a 10 pixel break-even point. The break-even point would be much lower if some simple hardware were added to do the additions and table look-up for our method in parallel. Of course, special hardware could be built for the other methods but it would be much more complicated and probably not as fast.

The images we have produced with this approximation are indistinguishable from those produced with Phong's method. For polygons with more than about 60 degrees of curvature, this new expansion will produce shadings that are noticeably different from Phong shading but curvatures this large should never be represented by a single polygon.

Going Further

Since the form of the polynomial we have to evaluate at each pixel is independent of the original reflection equation, we can use more elaborate models. One useful extension is to provide for finite eye distance, thus requiring that the vector to the eye, $\vec{E}$, vary across the scene. The resulting variation in the specular component produces more natural looking illumination for scenes rendered with perspective. This is most obvious when there are planar surfaces in the scene because Phong shading with the eye at infinity, like flat shading, renders all parallel surfaces with the same intensity. Figure 4 is a comparison of Phong shading with the eye at infinity and with the eye at the true perspective distance. The reflection equation for the specular component with the eye at a finite distance now becomes

$$I_{specular}(x,y) = \frac{\vec{N}(x,y) \cdot \vec{H}(x,y)}{|\vec{N}(x,y)||\vec{H}(x,y)|},$$

where $\vec{H}(x,y) = \vec{E}(x,y) + \vec{L}$ and $\vec{E}(x,y)$ interpolates the eye vector across the triangle. This can be expanded just as before.

$$I_{specular}(x,y) = \frac{(\vec{A}x + \vec{B}y + \vec{C}) \cdot (\vec{D}x + \vec{E}y + \vec{F})}{|(\vec{A}x + \vec{B}y + \vec{C})||(\vec{D}x + \vec{E}y + \vec{F})|}$$

After performing the dot products and expanding the vector magnitude as before.

$I_{specular}(x,y)$
$$= \frac{ax^2 + bxy + cy^2 + dx + ey + f}{\sqrt{(gx^2 + hxy + iy^2 + jx + ky + l)(mx^2 + nxy + oy^2 + px + qy + r)}}$$
with
$$a = \vec{A} \cdot \vec{D},$$
$$b = \vec{A} \cdot \vec{E} + \vec{B} \cdot \vec{D},$$
$$c = \vec{B} \cdot \vec{E},$$
$$d = \vec{A} \cdot \vec{F} + \vec{C} \cdot \vec{D},$$
$$e = \vec{B} \cdot \vec{F} + \vec{C} \cdot \vec{E},$$
$$f = \vec{C} \cdot \vec{F},$$
$$g = \vec{A} \cdot \vec{A},$$
$$h = 2\vec{A} \cdot \vec{B},$$
$$i = \vec{B} \cdot \vec{B},$$
$$j = 2\vec{A} \cdot \vec{C},$$
$$k = 2\vec{B} \cdot \vec{C},$$
$$l = \vec{C} \cdot \vec{C},$$
$$m = \vec{E} \cdot \vec{E},$$
$$n = \vec{D} \cdot \vec{D},$$
$$o = 2\vec{D} \cdot \vec{E},$$
$$p = 2\vec{D} \cdot \vec{F},$$
$$q = 2\vec{E} \cdot \vec{F}, \text{ and}$$
$$r = \vec{F} \cdot \vec{F}.$$

And expanding in Taylor's series about $(0,0)$.

$$I(x,y) = T_5 x^2 + T_4 xy + T_3 y^2 + T_2 x + T_1 y + T_0$$

with

$$T_5 = \frac{8al^2r^2 - 4djlr^2 - 4fglr^2 + 3fj^2r^2 - 4dl^2pr + 2fjlpr - 4fl^2mr + 3fl^2p^2}{8l^2r^2\sqrt{lr}},$$

$$T_4 = \frac{4bl^2r^2 - 2dklr^2 - 2ejlr^2 - 2fhlr^2 + 3fjkr^2 - 2dl^2qr}{4l^2r^2\sqrt{lr}}$$
$$+ \frac{-fjlqr - 2el^2pr + fklpr - 2f^2nr + 3fl^2pq}{4l^2r^2\sqrt{lr}},$$

$$T_3 = \frac{8cl^2r^2 - 4eklr^2 - 4filr^2 + 3fk^2r^2 - 4el^2qr + 2fklqr - 4fl^2or + 3fl^2q^2}{8l^2r^2\sqrt{lr}},$$

$$T_2 = \frac{2dlr - fjr - flp}{2lr\sqrt{lr}},$$

$$T_1 = \frac{2elr - fkr - flq}{2lr\sqrt{lr}}, \text{ and}$$

$$T_0 = \frac{f}{\sqrt{lr}}.$$

Summary

We have shown that computer image generation systems can use Phong shading with only a little more computation per pixel than is required for Gouraud shading. This result should allow real-time systems to generate more realistic scenes and conventional systems to produce images more rapidly.

To test the method, we have implemented it as a shader subroutine for the raster testbed. The cpu time for rendering Figure 4 with 14620 polygons at 2048x2048 resolution on a DEC microVAX-II are:

Shading Method	CPU Time	Notes
Gouraud	406s	
Taylor (infinite)	767s	incl 119s for Taylor coeffs
Taylor (finite)	850s	incl 202s for Taylor coeffs
Duff	2597s	incl 1420s in sqrt
Phong	3900s	incl 1405s in sqrt

Acknowledgements

Tom Duff and the reviewers provided many helpful suggestions.

References

Duff, T. 1979. "Smoothly Shaded Renderings of Polyhedral Objects on Raster Displays," *ACM Computer Graphics*, vol. 13, no. 2, pp. 270–275.

Foley, J. D. and A. Van Dam. 1983. *Fundamentals of Interactive Computer Graphics*, Addison Wesley, Reading, MA.

Gouraud, H. June 1971. "Continuous Shading of Curved Surfaces," *IEEE Transactions on Computers*, vol. 20, no. 6, pp. 623–628.

Newman, W. N. and R. F. Sproull. 1979. *Principles of Interactive Computer Graphics*, McGraw-Hill, New York, NY.

Phong, B. T. July 1973. *Illumination for Computer-Generated Images*, Ph.D. Dissertation, Department of Computer Science, University of Utah, Salt Lake City. Gov. ordering no. AD-A008 786.

Whitted, T. and D. Weimer. 1982. "A Software Testbed for the Development of 3D Raster Graphics Systems," *ACM Transactions on Graphics*, vol. 1, no. 1, pp. 43–58.

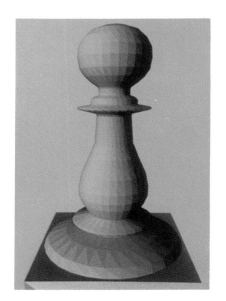

Figure 1: Flat shading.

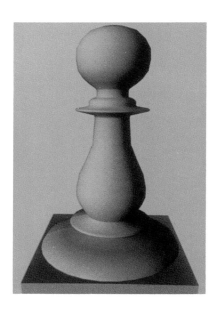

Figure 2: Gouraud shading.

Figure 3: Phong shading.

Figure 4: Phong shading with finite (left) and infinite eye distance.

Fast Constructive Solid Geometry Display in the Pixel-Powers Graphics System

Jack Goldfeather
Carleton College, Northfield, MN

Jeff P.M. Hultquist
Henry Fuchs
University of North Carolina at Chapel Hill

ABSTRACT

We present two algorithms for the display of CSG-defined objects on Pixel-Powers, an extension of the Pixel-Planes logic-enhanced memory architecture, which calculates for each and every pixel on the screen (in parallel) the value of any quadratic function in the screen coordinates (x, y). The first algorithm restructures any CSG tree into an equivalent, but possibly larger, tree whose display can be achieved by the second algorithm. The second algorithm traverses the restructured tree and generates quadratic coefficients and opcodes for Pixel-Powers. These opcodes instruct Pixel-Powers to generate the boundaries of primitives and perform set operations using the standard Z-buffer algorithm.

Several externally-supplied CSG data sets have been processed with the new tree-traversal algorithm and an associated Pixel-Powers simulator. The resulting images indicate that good results can be obtained very rapidly with the new system. For example, the commonly used MBB test part (at right) with 24 primitives is translated into approximately 1900 quadratic equations. On a Pixel-Powers system running at 10MHz (the speed at which our current Pixel-Planes memories run), the image should be rendered in about 7.5 milliseconds.

MBB test part from Pixel-Powers simulator.
The Pixel-Powers graphics system should render this image in 7.5 milliseconds.

CR Categories and Subject Descriptors: I.3.1 [Computer Graphics]: Hardware Architecture — *raster display devices*; I.3.3 [Computer Graphics]: Picture/-Image Generation — *display algorithms*; J.7 [Computer Applications]: Computer-Aided Engineering — *computer-aided design*;

General Terms: algorithms

Additional Key Words and Phrases: constructive solid geometry, SIMD processor, frame buffer

I. Introduction

We are designing Pixel-Powers, an enhancement of the Pixel-Planes graphics system [2][6], by replacing the multiplier tree that evaluated linear expressions by one that evaluates quadratic expressions [3]. This Quadratic Expression Evaluator (QEE) is used to evaluate expressions of the form $Ax^2 + Bxy + Cy^2 + Dx + Ey + F$ simultaneously for each pixel (x, y) on the screen. We estimate that the QEE will calculate bit-sequentially a 30 bit value of this expression for each and every pixel on the screen in under 4 microseconds. The speed at which Pixel-Powers will render convex polyhedra, as well as smooth-shaded cylinders, cones, and ellipsoids, has led us to explore the possibility of using Pixel-Powers for real-time rendering of smooth-shaded Constructive Solid Geometry objects constructed from quadratic primitives. A CSG object is defined by starting with a set of solid primitives and constructing an expression tree in which the leaves are primitives and the non-leaf nodes are set operations. The CSG object is constructed recursively by performing each set operation on the objects defined by its left and right subtrees [7].

In this paper we describe a general method for displaying any CSG object using a frame buffer that is 128 bits deep. Our method differs from other CSG display methods [1] in that we compute on the fly the boundary representation of each primitive in terms of the viewpoint. While this can be a disadvantage in some systems, we will show how it can be implemented efficiently in Pixel-Powers by making use of the Quadratic Expression Evaluator and the general parallelism of the system. In particular, we will describe an algorithm for fast rendering of smooth-shaded CSG objects based on quadratic primitives. Our approach, parallel on all pixels but processing CSG primitives sequentially, contrasts with another system by Kedem [4] that allocates a processing element for each primitive and renders the images sequentially by pixel in raster-scan order.

Just as in the development of the Pixel-Planes system, we have implemented software simulators that enable us to develop display algorithms before the actual chip is completely designed and committed to silicon. All of the images in this paper are from the Pixel-Powers simulator.

II. A Simple Example

In this section we describe a method for displaying any CSG object with the aid of a deep frame buffer. The present working Pixel-Planes system has a 72 bit deep frame buffer. A Pixel-Powers system with a depth of 128 bits was our model when we were analyzing the problem, but the algorithm should be implementable in any computer with a deep frame buffer. The memory requirements are:

- Three flag registers: F1, F2, and F3
  (one bit each)
- Two depth buffers: ZTEMP and ZMIN
  (20-30 bits each)
- One color buffer: COLOR
  (24 bits)
  (If double buffering is desired,
  two color buffers are needed.)

We defer until Sections III and IV the discussion of the particular Pixel-Powers implementation of these algorithms for CSG objects defined with convex primitive solids whose boundary surfaces can be defined using quadratic or linear equations in x, y, and z (e.g. cylinders, ellipsoids, and cones). In this section we outline a general method of display that will work for any set of convex primitives and any display system that can do both of the following:

(a) Scan convert front- and back-facing surfaces of each primitive in screen space. That is, a flag F at each pixel can be set to 1 if it is inside the region on the screen determined by the projection of the surface on the screen. Note that the front and back face of a surface depends on the viewpoint. The front surface of a cylinder consists of all points on the cylinder surface (including the ends) which face toward the viewer.

(b) Calculate and store in each pixel memory with F=1 the depth and color values of the front- or back-facing surfaces of a primitive.

In Section III, a general algorithm is derived based only on the assumptions (a) and (b) above. We illustrate the ideas behind this algorithm by examining the simple cases of union, difference, and intersection of two cylinders.

II.a. *Cylinder1* ∪ *Cylinder2*

This is displayed by applying the standard Z-buffer algorithm. If *Front(obj)* denotes the (viewpoint dependent) visible part of an object's surface, then *Front(Cylinder1)* will, in general, be the visible part of the curved portion of the cylinder together with one of the two planar ends. We begin by calculating the Z values and color values of *Front(Cylinder1)* and storing them in ZMIN and COLOR. Since later in this paper we will be decomposing more complicated objects into unions of simpler ones, we will describe carefully how *Cylinder2* is added to the partial image:

Step 1: At each pixel, set the flag F1 if it is inside the region determined by *Front(Cylinder2)*, and clear it otherwise (figure 1a).

Step 2: Calculate and store Z values for *Front(Cylinder2)* in ZTEMP.

Step 3: For each pixel with F1 set, compare ZTEMP to ZMIN and if ZTEMP > ZMIN then clear F1 (figure 1b).

Step 4: For each pixel with F1 still set, replace the contents of COLOR with the color of *Front(Cylinder2)* and replace ZMIN by ZTEMP (figure 1c).

Note that this algorithm does not require that the unioned objects be primitive. As long as scan conversion, depth values, and colors can be calculated, any objects can be unioned together by this simple method. This technique of composing objects with Z-buffers has been used in many previous systems.

II.b. *Cylinder1* − *Cylinder2*

This can be displayed by first recognizing that its image is identical to the image of:

$$(Front(Cylinder1) - Cylinder2) \quad \cup$$
$$(Back(Cylinder2) \cap Cylinder1).$$

The general algorithm for generating such decompositions is described in Section IV. As we saw in the union process above, it suffices to generate the first term in the union and then add the second term to this partial image. The first term, *Front(Cylinder1)* − *Cylinder2* is rendered as follows:

Step 1: Set F1 for all pixels inside the projection of *Cylinder1* onto the screen (figure 2a).

Step 2: For pixels at which F1 is set, store the depth of *Front(Cylinder1)* in ZTEMP.

Step 3: Set F2 everywhere. Clear F2 at any pixel outside *Cylinder2*. A pixel (x, y) is outside *Cylinder2* if its ZTEMP does not lie between the values of *Front(Cylinder2)* and *Back(Cylinder2)* (figure 2b). Replace F1 by (F1 *xor* F2) (figure 2c).

Step 4: We now transfer the value of ZTEMP to ZMIN for each pixel at which F1 is set. For these same pixels, we update the contents of COLOR with the color of *Front(Cylinder1)* at that location.

Front(Cylinder1) − *Cylinder2* is now finished. Next we add *Back(Cylinder2)* ∩ *Cylinder1* to this partial image.

Step 5: Set F1 for all pixels inside the projection of *Back(Cylinder2)* on the screen (figure 2d).

Step 6: For those pixels in which F1 is set, set ZTEMP to the depth of *Back(Cylinder2)*.

Step 7: Clear F2 everywhere. Set F2 for all pixels which are inside *Cylinder1* in a manner similar to step 3 (figure 2d). Replace F1 by (F1 *and* F2). F1 is now set for all pixels which display the back wall of the hole which *Cylinder2* bores into *Cylinder1* (figure 2e).

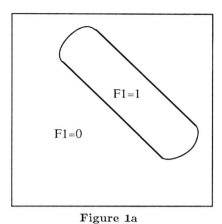

Figure 1a

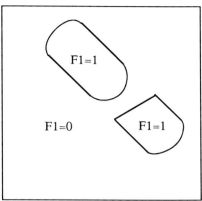

Figure 1b

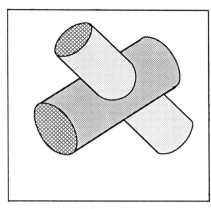

Figure 1c

Step 8: For these pixels, we clear F1 if ZTEMP > ZMIN. We now transfer the value of ZTEMP to ZMIN for each pixel at which F1 remains set. For these same pixels, we update the contents of COLOR with the color of *Back(Cylinder2)* at that location (figure 2f).

II.c. *Cylinder1* ∩ *Cylinder2*

This can be decomposed into

$$(Front(Cylinder1) \cap Cylinder2) \quad \cup$$
$$(Front(Cylinder2) \cap Cylinder1)$$

The terms in this union are generated in a manner similar to the terms in the decomposition of the difference of the cylinders.

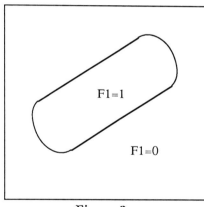

Figure 2a

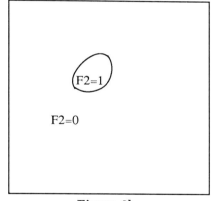

Figure 2b

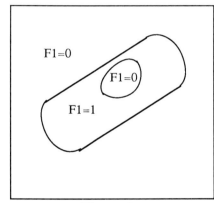

Figure 2c

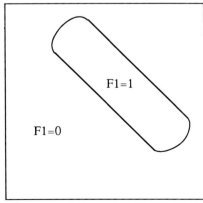

Figure 2d

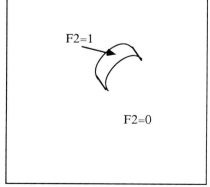

Figure 2e

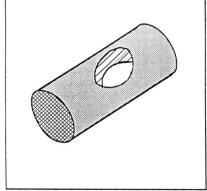

Figure 2f

III. Example Implemented with Pixel-Powers

We will see in the following sections that this method is particularly suitable for implementation in a machine such as Pixel-Powers that has a small fixed amount of memory at each pixel. The dramatic speed in Pixel-Powers is due in large part to the Quadratic Expression Evaluator which evaluates quadratic expressions in x and y simultaneously at each pixel. The architecture of this Evaluator is more fully described in [3]. For the purposes of this discussion, it is sufficient to assert that the Pixel-Powers system will consist of a enhanced frame buffer memory. Each pixel is located at a leaf of the Evaluator, which receives the coefficients A,B,C,D,E, and F as input and evaluates the expression $Q(x, y) = Ax^2 + Bxy + Cy^2 + Dx + Ey + F$. The speed of Pixel-Powers is due in large part to the fact that this calculation is done simultaneously at each pixel when the coefficients are broadcast to the system. One bit of the function value is calculated for each and every pixel at each clock cycle. As with the current Pixel-Planes chips in 3 micron nMOS, we expect a 100 nsec clock cycle. Each pixel will have a single-bit ALU and 128-bits of randomly-addressable memory. This memory is also scanned out by the video controller.

For the particular algorithms described here, the memory is logically configured into ZMIN, ZTEMP, and COLOR registers, and also one-bit flags F1, F2, and F3. The Host processes the CSG tree to produce a sequence of instructions that drive the Evaluator and the ALUs. All geometric transformations and clipping are calculated in the host as well as the translating of the information in the CSG tree into the sequence of opcodes and the quadratic equations.

In this section, we will describe a way to implement in Pixel-Powers the basic operations listed in Section II:

- Scan conversion of primitives
- Computation of depth values
- Determination of "inside" or "outside"
- Calculation of color

We illustrate the procedure with part of the preceeding example: *Front(curved part of Cylinder1) − Cylinder2.* We omit the calculations involving the end of the cylinder as they are similar.

Step 1: Scan Conversion

We begin by writing the equations of the bounding curves of *Front(Cylinder1)* in screen coordinates (x, y) (figure 3a). The elliptical ends are defined by quadratic equations $Q_1(x, y) = 0$ and $Q_2(x, y) = 0$. The lines of intersection of the front- and back-facing surfaces have linear equations $L_1(x, y) = 0$ and $L_2(x, y) = 0$. The lines L_3 and L_4 indicated in figure 3a have linear equations $L_3(x, y) = 0$ and $L_4(x, y) = 0$. We combine L_1 and L_2 to create the quadratic equation $Q(x, y) = L_1(x, y)L_2(x, y) = 0$, and we combine L_3 and L_4 to create the quadratic equation $Q_3(x, y) = L_3(x, y)L_4(x, y) = 0$.

Each of the curves Q, Q_1, Q_2, Q_3 separate the plane into pieces and a pixel can determine which piece it is in by simply checking the sign of the result. Different choices of the coefficients will produce different signs for these expressions, so the selection must be made to conform to the signs indicated in figure 3a. The Host computes the coefficient sets for each of the four quadratic curves and broadcasts them to the Quadratic Expression Evaluator. Three one-bit flags are used to enable or disable pixels according to the sign of the evaluated expression at that location.

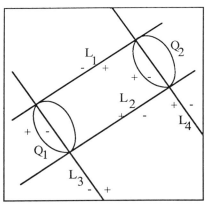

Figure 3a

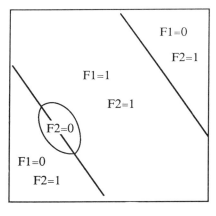

Figure 3b

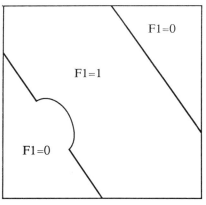

Figure 3c

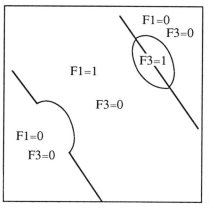

Figure 3d

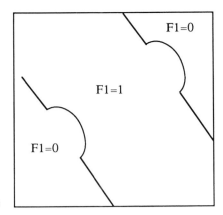

Figure 3e

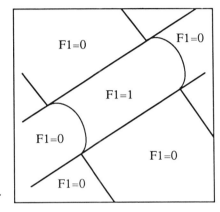

Figure 3f

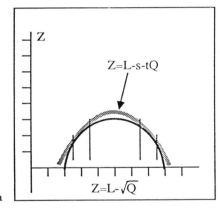

Figure 4a

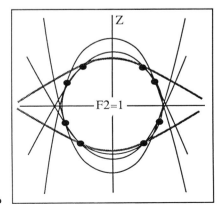

Figure 4b

The specific sequence in our example is:

(a) Clear flags F1, F2, and F3 everywhere.

(b) For each pixel (x, y), set F1 if $Q_3(x, y) > 0$, and set F2 if $Q_1(x, y) > 0$. Replace F1 by (F1 *and* F2) (figures 3b and 3c).

(c) For each pixel (x, y), set F3 if $Q_2(x, y) < 0$. Replace F1 by (F1 *or* F3) (figures 3d and 3e).

(d) For each pixel (x, y), clear F1 if $Q(x, y) < 0$ (figure 3f).

Note that this scan conversion process requires that the coefficient sets for Q, Q_1, Q_2, and Q_3 be broadcast only once each.

Step 2: Z-Buffer

The equation of *Front*(*curved part of Cylinder1*) when solved for z is of the form $z = L - \sqrt{Q}$, where L is linear and Q is quadratic in x and y. (The function Q is the same one from step 1.) Since the QEE cannot evaluate square roots directly, an approximation to $\sqrt{Q}$ must be made. This approximation is of the form $s + tQ$ where s and t are constants, and we replace $z = L - \sqrt{Q}$ by $Zapprox = L - s - tQ$ which is quadratic in (x, y). By choosing s and t carefully, this approximation is very accurate in strips down the length of the cylinder. Geometrically, the surface with equation $Zapprox = L - s - tQ$ is a "parabolic" cylinder. Figure 4a illustrates how it passes near to the actual cylinder surface. The magnitude of the error tolerance determines the size of the strips in which the approximation is within this tolerance.

We begin by choosing an error tolerance for the Z approximation. The Host determines the number of strips needed to guarantee this accuracy across the entire scan converted region. The constants s and t are computed for each such strip pair. Geometrically, the set of parabolic cylinders (one for each (s, t)) forms an "envelope" of the actual cylinder. Further, as indicated in figure 4b, for each (x, y), the largest $Zapprox$ is the one that best approximates the actual Z for that pixel (x, y). The Host simply broadcasts the coefficients for all of the parabolic cylinder approximations and each pixel (x, y) saves in ZTEMP the largest $Zapprox$ for that pixel. Note that for back facing surfaces, the pixel saves the smallest $Zapprox$.

The number of strips needed depends on the size of the object in screen space. It might seem that many strips would be needed to guarantee reasonable accuracy, but in many images that we have generated using the functional simulator, sufficient accuracy can be achieved with a small number of strips (1 to 8). This small number is due to the fact that we are approximating a curved surface by another curved surface, so that we do not need nearly as many subdivisions as would be necessary if we were approximating the same surface with polygons.

Step 3: Subtracting *Cylinder2*

(a) Subdivide *Cylinder2* into strips for accurate Z calculation as in Step 2. Compute the quadratic expressions Q_i that represent the parabolic cylinder approximations for these strips.

(b) Set F2 at each pixel. For each parabolic cylinder C_i, broadcast the coefficients of Q_i and clear F2 if the ZTEMP stored at the pixel (x, y) is less than $Q_i(x, y)$ and C_i is front-facing or if ZTEMP $> Q_i(x, y)$ and C_i is back-facing (figure 4b).

(c) Only those pixels with both F1 and F2 still set are inside *Cylinder2*. Replace F1 with (F1 *xor* F2).

Step 4: Shading

If we compute the exact diffuse shade at (x, y) using the unit normal to the surface then the expression we have to evaluate is of the form $shade(x, y) = (L + \sqrt{Q})/\sqrt{W}$ where L is linear, Q is quadratic in (x, y) and W is a relatively complicated expression in (x, y) that comes from turning an arbitrary normal to the surface into a unit vector. We approximate the numerator as in the Z-buffer step except that we only use a single parabolic cylinder for Q. We approximate the denominator by a single constant. Although these approximations may seem coarse, the effect is smooth shaded.

IV. Tree Restructuring

In this section we describe a method for transforming any CSG tree into an equivalent one that is a union of simpler subtrees. (Similar work is briefly discussed in [8].) We will then describe how each of these simple subtrees can be displayed by further dividing them into the union of pieces which can be displayed by starting with the boundary of a primitive and paring it with other primitives, using the set operations of intersection and difference. This transformation and display process builds up the image without the use of large amounts of intermediate information stored at each pixel. This method is particularly appropriate for a system like Pixel-Powers with limited memory available at each pixel.

There are two major difficulties with trying to display arbitrary CSG trees without any transformation. First, the paring part, that is, the piece that is subtracted or intersected with a previously constructed piece, might be complicated. In particular, it might be hard to determine the inside or outside in an efficient manner. Second, paring may reveal parts of an object previously obscured. Both of these difficulties can be overcome by the transformation process that restructures the CSG tree into an equivalent one in which the paring objects are always primitives.

The transformation produces a new tree which we call a *normal form* for the tree which has the properties (i) at every node where there is an intersection or difference the right branch is primitive, and (ii) no node where there is a union is on a path from a difference or intersection. This new tree can be broken into simpler subtrees that are unioned together. Although the transformation process may increase the size of the tree, each of the simple subtrees can be displayed with a minimum of calculation and merged into a single image using the union process described in Section II. The simple subtrees are of the form:

$$X_0 \, op_1 \, X_1 \, op_2 \, ... \, op_k \, X_k$$

where each X_i is a primitive, op_i is either $-$ or $\cap$, and the absence of parentheses indicates that association is from left to right. A normal form for a CSG tree is created using the 8 basic equivalences in figure 5 together with the following recursive algorithm. The execution of this algorithm is demonstrated in figure 6.

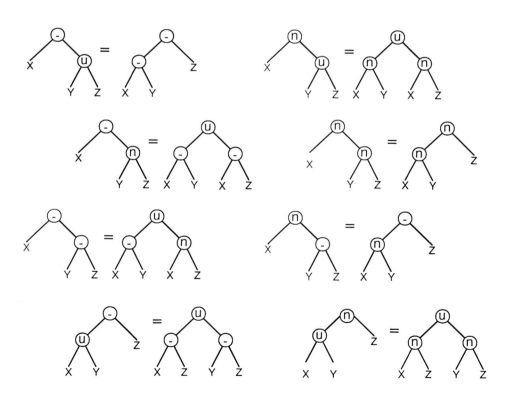

Figure 5. In each pair, the tree on the left can be transformed to the equivalent form to its right. The new tree will have the same image as the original.

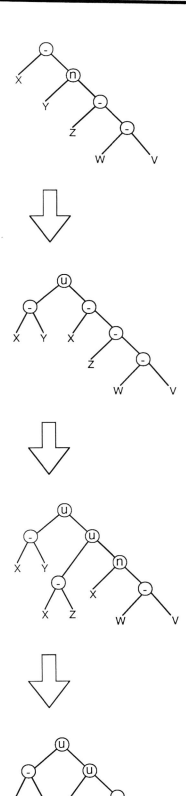

```
procedure Normalize (T);
begin
   Redo(T);
   case (T.type) of begin
      primitive:
         return T;
         break;
      ∪ :
         Normalize (T.L);
         Normalize (T.R);
         break;
      −,∩ :
         while (T.type ≠ primitive) and
               (T ≠ ∪) and
               (T.R.type ≠ primitive) do begin
            Redo (T);
         end;
         Normalize (T.R);
         Normalize (T.L);
         Redo(T);
         break;
   end;
end;
```

```
procedure Redo(T)
begin
   if T does not have any of the patterns
     in figure 5 then begin
      return T;
   end else begin
      restructure the top nodes of T
        using equivalent patterns in figure 5;
      return newT;
   end;
end;
```

Figure 6. The trees on this page demonstrate the execution of the code above using the equivalences shown in figure 5 (at left). At each step, one interior node of the tree is restructured. This processing continues recursively until the tree is in normal form.

Once the tree has been normalized, the problem of display is reduced to that of simple trees. Let $D(X)$, $D_f(X)$, and $D_b(X)$ denote the boundary of a solid X, the front-facing boundary of X, and the back-facing boundary of X, respectively. In order to display a solid X it suffices, of course, to display $D(X)$. We are left then with the problem of displaying

$$D(X_0 \ op_1 \ X_1 \ op_2 \ ... \ op_k \ X_k)$$

In order to derive the general display algorithm, it is necessary to know how the CSG operations interact with the boundary operators D, D_f, and D_b.

Theorem 1: From the point of view of 2-D display:

(a) $D(X) = D_f(X)$
(b) $D(X \cup Y) = D_f(X) \cup D_f Y$
(c) $D(X \cap Y) = (D_f(X) \cap Y) \cup (D_f(Y) \cap X)$
(d) $D(X - Y) = (D_f(X) - Y) \cup (D_b(Y) \cap X)$

For example, if we want to display the tree A-B-C, we apply Theorem 1(d) twice and use the set identity $X \cap (Y - Z) = X \cap Y - Z$:

$$D(A - B - C)$$
$$= (D_f(A - B) - C) \ \cup$$
$$(D_b(C) \cap (A - B))$$

by applying Theorem 1(d) with $X = A - B$ and $Y = C$

$$= (D_f(A) - B - C) \ \cup$$
$$(D_b(B) \cap A - C) \ \cup$$
$$(D_b(C) \cap A - B)$$

by applying Theorem 1(d) again and using the above set identity.

The terms in the union are rendered one at a time and merged into the partial object being built up. The first term is rendered by storing $D_f(A)$ and paring it down with the objects B and C. This is essentially how the example in Section II was done. The other terms are rendered similarly.

We will adopt the convention that there is an operator op_0 equal to $\cap$ preceding X_0 in the simple tree $X_0 \ op_1 \ x_1 \ op_2 \ ... \ op_k \ X_k$ and define for each $i = 0, ..., k$:

$$D_p(X_i) = \begin{cases} D_f(X), & if \ op_i = \cap \\ D_b(X), & if \ op_i = - \end{cases}$$

Then we can apply the theorem recursively to obtain:

Theorem 2: $D(X_0 \ op_1 \ X_1 \ ... \ op_k \ X_k)$ is the union ($i = 0, ..., k$) of:

$$D_p(X_i) \ op_1 \ X_1 \ ... \ op_{i-1} \ X_{i-1} \ op_{i+1} \ X_{i+1} \ ... \ op_k \ X_k$$

The individual terms in this union are displayed as in the example in Section II. To summarize, the normalization process that reduces an arbitrary CSG tree to a union of simple trees together with the further subdivision using Theorem 2 produces a decomposition that allows images to be drawn without sending anything more complicated than a primitive to the system. This is essential for graphics systems with limited frame buffer memory.

V. Results

We have implemented (in C on a VAX-11/780 running 4.2bsd UNIX) and show results here of (1) a tree traverser that processes a union of "simple" trees and generates opcodes and quadratic coefficients to a Pixel-Powers memory system, and (2) a simulator for a Pixel-Powers memory system that accepts opcodes and quadratic coefficients and generates for each pixel the various image buffer-related values ((r,g,b), z, flags, etc.) for display on a conventional raster screen. This set of software modules was exercised with externally supplied data sets from the US Army Ballistic Research Laboratory and Hokkaido University [5].

We have been surprised to find no need yet for the CSG restructuring algorithm, so we have not as yet implemented it. Of the handful of data sets we have received we have found none yet whose CSG tree needed to be restructured before processing for Pixel-Powers. That is, all the trees were already "simple" according to the definition given in Section IV above. Thus the tree traverser could process all of these data sets directly and generate opcodes and coefficients for Pixel-Powers.

We ran the tree traverser on the various data sets and ran the Pixel-Powers simulator on the output from the tree traverser. Table 1 gives, for various data sets, the number of Pixel-Powers operations generated by the tree traversal process and the estimated time for Pixel-Powers to generate the images from these data sets shown in the photographs. It is important to note when considering these results, however, that the estimated image generation times given in the table are for the 10MHz Pixel-Powers logic-enhanced memories themselves. It is assumed that the rest of the system, the "front end" (the viewing transformation engine and the tree traverser) can run fast enough to keep up with the 10MHz Pixel-Powers memories. We hope to achieve this by transferring the implementation to our fast arithmetic processors, which are Mercury Systems ZIP 3232s.

Part Name	Source	Primitives	Opcodes	Equations	Time
Union	local	2	54	46	.19 msec
Difference	local	2	182	170	.68
Intersection	local	2	178	170	.68
Tube	[Okino 84]	11	1205	1065	4.3
Cut Tube	[Okino 84]	12	1969	1733	7.0
MBB	[Okino 84]	24	2139	1854	7.5
Tie Rod	BRL	17	2660	2309	9.3

Table 1: Estimated Image Generation Time

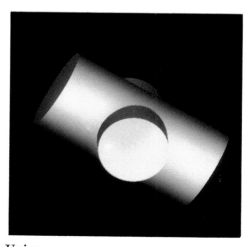

Union
estimated time: 0.19 msec

Tube
estimated time: 4.3 msec

Difference
estimated time: 0.68 msec

Cut Tube
estimated time: 7.0 msec

Intersection
estimated time: 0.68 msec

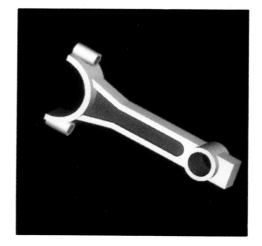

Tie Rod
estimated time: 9.3 msec

Images from Pixel-Powers Simulator

VI. Future Work

We hope to implement a Pixel-Powers system in stages by enhancing the next generation Pixel-Planes chips and by casting much of the CSG tree traverser into microcode for our fast arithmetic processors. The enhancement to the Pixel-Planes chips involves substituting the Quadratic Expression Evaluator tree for the current Linear Expression Evaluation tree and increasing the memory per chip from the 72 bits in the present Pixel-Planes chips to 128 bits.

We also hope to develop more sophisticated algorithms for CSG-defined objects: algorithms for generating shadows and algorithms for calculating shadings on curved surfaces more rapidly according to more sophisticated lighting models such as the popular one due to Phong. We also hope to develop techniques for rendering higher order surfaces such as cubic patches. Already two approaches for this are evident: the quadratic expression evaluator on the memory chip could be expanded into a cubic expression evaluator (we can already see how to do this, but the size would be enormous) or we can approximate each of the cubic curves by combination of many quadratic curves. We also plan to implement with the CSG restructuring algorithm the well-known "bounding-box" techniques to trim the restructured tree to the smallest possible size. For example, if the bounding boxes of A and B do not intersect, then $(A - B)$ is equivalent to A.

VII. Summary

We have shown that CSG-defined objects can be efficiently rendered in a logic-enhanced frame buffer memory with fast quadratic expression evaluation for each pixel. Such rendering can be efficiently generated by first restructuring the tree, if necessary, into a union of simple trees and then traversing these trees to generate a sequence of quadratic coefficients and operation codes for the logic-enhanced memories. Resulting images from a software implementation of the tree traverser and display simulator illustrate the methods and allow estimation of its speed with an expected hardware implementation. The method's speed promises real-time interactions for complex CSG objects and the ability to handle objects of arbitrary complexity by building up the image during the traversal of the CSG tree.

VIII. Acknowledgements

We thank the other members of the Pixel-Planes team — particularly John Poulton, John Eyles, John Austin, and Wayne Dettloff — for stimulating discussions and suggestions. We thank John Eyles also for developing a detailed logic-level simulator of the Quadratic Expression Evaluator and improving the QEE design in the process.

We also wish to thank our colleagues who graciously sent us CSG data sets: Paul Stay and Paul Deitz of the US Army Ballistic Research Laboratory and Professor Ari Requicha, Director of the Production Automation Project at the University of Rochester. Testing our algorithms on these externally-supplied data sets considerably increased our confidence in the algorithms and their implementations. Also we thank Norio Okino and his colleagues for publishing their data.

This research was supported in part by the DARPA contract DAAG29-83-K-0148 (monitored by the US Army Research Office, Research Triangle Park, NC) and the NSF Grant ECS-8300970. Jeff Hultquist was supported with a grant from the UNC Board of Governors.

Finally, we thank Mary Hultquist for her help with the photographs and text.

IX. References

[1] Atherton, P.R., "A Scan-line Hidden Surface Removal Procedure for Constructive Solid Geometry" *Computer Graphics*, Vol. 17, No. 3, pp. 73–82, 1983. (Proceedings of SIGGRAPH '83)

[2] Fuchs, H., J. Goldfeather, J.P. Hultquist, S. Spach, J. Austin, F.P. Brooks, Jr., J. Eyles, and J.Poulton. "Fast Spheres, Textures, Transparencies, and Image Enhancements in Pixel-Planes" *Computer Graphics*, Vol. 19, No. 3, pp. 111–120, 1985. (Proceedings of SIGGRAPH '85)

[3] Goldfeather, J., H. Fuchs. "Quadratic Surface Rendering on a Logic-Enhanced Frame-Buffer Memory" *IEEE Computer Graphics and Applications*, pp. 48–59, January, 1986.

[4] Kedem, G., J.L. Ellis. "Computer Structures for Curve-Solid Classification in Geometric Modelling" Technical Report TR84-37, Microelectronic Center of North Carolina, Research Triangle Park, N.C., 1984.

[5] Okino, N., Y. Kakazu, M. Morimoto. "Extended Depth Buffer Algorithms for Hidden Surface Visualization" *IEEE Computer Graphics and Applications*, pp. 79–88, May, 1984.

[6] Poulton, J., H. Fuchs, J.D. Austin, J.G. Eyles, J. Heinecke, C. Hsieh, J. Goldfeather, J.P. Hultquist, and S. Spach. "PIXEL-PLANES: Building a VLSI Based Raster Graphics System" *Proceedings of the 1985 Chapel Hill Conference on VLSI*, pp. 35–60.

[7] Requicha, A.A.G. "Representation for Rigid Objects: Theory, Methods, and Systems" *ACM Computing Surveys*, Vol. 12, No. 4, Dec. 1980, pp. 437–464.

[8] Sato, H., H. Ishihata, M. Ishii, M. Kakimoto, K. Sato, K. Hirota, M. Ikesaka, K. Inoue. "Fast Image Generation of Constructive Solid Geometry Using A Cellular Array Processor" *Computer Graphics*, Vol. 19, No. 3, pp. 95–102, 1985. (Proceedings of SIGGRAPH '85)

Atmospheric Illumination and Shadows

Nelson L. Max
Lawrence Livermore National Laboratory

Abstract

The shadow volume algorithm of Frank Crow was reorganized to provide information on the regions of illuminated space in front of each visible surface. This information is used to calculate the extra intensity due to atmospheric scattering, so when the atmosphere is partly in shadow, columns of scattered light will be visible. For efficiency in sorting the shadow edges, the image is computed in polar coordinates.

Key Words

Shadows, atmospheric scattering, Watkins hidden surface algorithm, polar coordinates, shadow polygon.

Introduction

Sunlight scattering from water or dust in the air causes the atmosphere to glow. This glow is particularly visible in beams or columns of light in an otherwise shadowed environment. The goal of this work is to simulate these atmospheric shadow effects.

To compute the glow from the scattering along a ray from the eye, one must know which parts of the ray are illuminated and which are in shadow. The hidden-surface/shadow algorithm must be able to provide the extra information.

There are five basic types of shadow algorithms in current use.

(1) *Z buffer* (Williams [1]). Compute the light-source and viewpoint images by depth buffer algorithms. Transform the viewpoint image to the light-source image and compare depths. If the visible point at a pixel is farther from the light than the corresponding depth in the light-source image, it is in shadow.

(2) *Area subdivision* (Atherton and Weiler [2]). In both the viewpoint and light-source projections, divide the image into polygonal regions in which a single surface is visible. Transform the illuminated regions in the light source view into object space and paint them as surface detail before the viewpoint projection is rendered.

(3) *Shadow volumes* (Crow [3]). Create shadow polygons, which, together with the polygons in the original data base, bound the volume of space shadowed by each object. The new shadow polygons lie in planes joining the light source to edges in the data base. Include these shadow polygons in the z sort of a scan-line hidden-surface algorithm, and count the parity of the shadow polygons in front of a visible surface to see if it is in shadow.

(4) *Preprocessing* (Nishita, Okamura, and Nakamae [4], Bouknight and Kelly [5]). Compare a given object to every other, to get a list of objects which can cast shadows on the given object. Use this list to determine the shadows while rendering the objects in scan line order.

(5) *Ray tracing* (Whitted [6], Cook, Porter, and Carpenter [7]). At each sampled surface point, trace a ray towards the light source and see if it hits any other objects first.

The first three methods can readily provide the necessary information for atmospheric shadow effects. To use the first method, transform the ray from the eye into the light-source view, and as it crosses each pixel, compare its depth with that in the Z buffer to see whether it is in shadow. As in the original cast-shadow application, there are aliasing problems which are aggravated because the sampling in the two views does not correspond. In general, the Z-buffer algorithms are not good at anti-aliasing, but have the advantage of handling diverse object types easily. Every pixel on each transformed ray must be considered, which makes the atmospheric shadow computation of order n^3, if the two views are n by n.

To use the second method, the ray is again transformed to the light-source view and compared in depth to the plane equation of each subdivided polygon it crosses in that view, in order to determine the regions of illumination. There are now no sampling problems, because the area subdivision is defined with floating point accuracy instead of at some image resolution. There is also some coherency from the polygons crossed by the transformed ray, so the computation is not necessarily of order n^3, but depends instead on the complexity of the scene. It is a challenging computational geometry problem for future research to create a data structure for the area subdivision which can be efficiently intersected with the transformed rays.

The first two methods both require a finite, flat, light-source view, which may not be possible if the light source is inside the window visible from the viewpoint.

I have chosen to implement the third method, modified by reorganizing the sorting and scan line processing to provide the atmospheric shadow information more efficiently.

Although the last two methods are capable of rendering the penumbras from area light sources, the information necessary for atmospheric shadows is not readily available.

1. Polar coordinate scan lines

I wanted to render forest scenes with shadows of many small leaves. In such scenes, every line segment on a leaf edge generates a shadow polygon, and there are no savings from considering only contour edges as suggested by Crow [3]. In the usual orientation, most of the leaves are at the top half of the frame, and their shadow polygons extend past the bottom. Therefore, for a horizontal scan line in the lower half of a scene containing N leaf edges, all N shadow polygons must be considered and sorted in x and in z. Normally, a scan-line algorithm gains efficiency because in a complex scene with many small polygons, most polygon edges can be expected to cross only a few scan lines. This expected efficiency is negated by the situation described above.

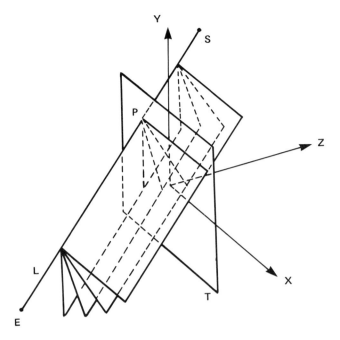

Figure 1. Four scan planes, meeting at the line L between the eye E and the light source S. They intersect the picture plane T in four lines, meeting at the point P, which is the projection of the light source.

However, if the sun is directly overhead and the picture plane is vertical, the efficiency can be regained by using vertical scan lines. The scan planes corresponding to these scan lines all meet in a vertical line through the viewer's eye. Since the sun direction also lies in this vertical line, the shadow polygon generated by an edge will cross only those scan planes that the edge itself crosses.

It is possible to generalize this situation by using radial scan lines in polar coordinates. Consider the line L between the eye E and the light source S, or in the direction of an infinite light source. As shown in Figure 1, this line intersects the picture plane T in a point P, and a family of scan planes meeting in the line L intersect T in a family of lines meeting at P. As above, since each scan plane contains both the eye and the light source, the only shadow polygons intersecting a scan plane come from edges which also intersect that scan plane. This technique greatly simplifies the sorting of shadow polygons and should be useful even if atmospheric shadows are not required.

The point P is the origin for a system of polar coordinates on the image, with radial scan lines. P may lie inside or outside the image window. The case just discussed, where the sun is exactly overhead, is a degenerate one where P is at infinity because the line L is parallel to T, and is not handled in the implementation reported here.

2. The θ-r (z, shadow) sort

My algorithm is a polar coordinate modification of an existing Watkins hidden-surface algorithm available at LLNL (see Watkins [8], Newman and Sproull [9], Rogers [10] and the acknowledgment section below). It sorts first in θ, next in r, and then separately and simultaneously in z and a shadow distance parameter.

The angular coordinate θ goes counterclockwise and edges are sorted into buckets according to the greatest θ of their two endpoints. Scan lines are processed by decreasing θ in analogy to the standard video scan with decreasing y. If P lies outside the image window, there is an interval of possible θ values, but if P lies inside, there is a whole circle of values. In this latter case, scan line processing starts at $\theta = \pi$ and ends at $\theta = -\pi$. Edges which cross from positive to negative θ must be broken into two parts, one extending from $\theta = \pi$

Segment block data structure

1. Pointer to previous segment block in r sort.

2. Pointer to next segment block in r sort.

3. Polygon number.

4. Pointer to next segment in active segment list.

5. Pointer to next segment on test list.

6. Left edge data for θ, r, z, color, normals, and u, v texture parameters.

7. Right edge data for θ, r, z, color. . .etc.

8. Left shadow edge block.
   a. shadow sort parameter
   b. shadow polygon plane equation
   c. pointer to next 0/many change
   d. pointer to next 0/1/many change
   e. value (0, 1, or 2) of current shadow multiplicity

9. Right shadow edge block (same data as for left edge).

10. Bit which is 1 if the polygon is front lit.

11. Name of texture map.

12. U and V partial derivative vectors, for bump mapping.

13. Plane equation of polygon with sun on positive side.

Table 1.

to the endpoint with positive θ, and one from the other endpoint until $\theta = -\pi$. They are thus entered into two different θ buckets.

A further problem exists if a polygon's projection contains P in its interior. If P is inside the polygon, an extra edge surrounding P must be created, going from $\theta = \pi$ to $\theta = -\pi$, with r = 0. The depth and shading attributes at P are found by intersecting the line L of Figure 1 with the polygon, and are entered at both endpoints of the new edge.

The endpoint depth and shading information for each edge are converted to integers and packed efficiently into the 64-bit words of the Cray-1. They are unpacked when the edges are removed from the bucket sort and placed in the appropriate entries in the data blocks for scan line processing of the scan-plane/polygon intersection segments. These *segment blocks* contain r, depth, and shading information for the left and right edges of the segment, as shown in Table 1, and various pointers discussed below.

Since a straight polygon edge projection in the picture plane T intersects the radial polar coordinate lines in a non-linear way, the r, z, and shading information cannot be updated from one scan line to the next by the usual incremental addition. Instead, the edge's intersection with each scan line is computed explicitly, and the other data are interpolated from their values at the edge endpoints. The hidden-surface processing then proceeds as in the Watkins algorithm, with the r sort taking the place of the traditional x sort, and the scan plane x – z sort turning into an r – z sort. An r sorted list of segment blocks is maintained from one scan line to the next, using pointers (items 1 and 2 in Table 1). The scan line is rendered as a sequence of *spans*, along which a single polygon is known to be visible. Polygons potentially affecting the current span are kept in an *active segment list* (item 4 in Table 1). For further details on the Watkins algorithm, see [8], [9], or [10].

3. The shadow sort

Every polygon edge defines a shadow plane containing it and the light source, and a semi-infinite *shadow polygon* in this plane. (See Crow [3].) The shadow polygons intersect a given scan plane in

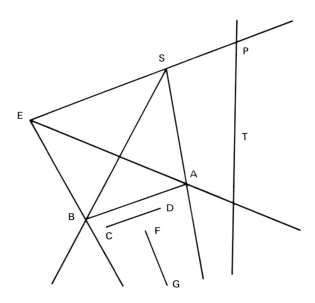

Figure 2a. A scan plane through the viewpoint E and the light source S, intersecting the view plane in line T, and three polygons in segments AB, CD, and FG. The light source is in front of the viewpoint.

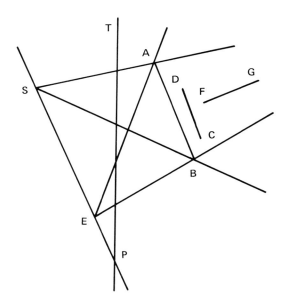

Figure 2b. Same data as in Figure 2a, rotated so that the light source is behind the viewpoint.

shadow edges, and the plane equations for the shadow polygons are stored in *shadow edge blocks*, which are physically part of the segment blocks, but are also linked into separate lists. (See Table 1, items 8 and 9.)

In order to compute the atmospheric shadows, these shadow edges must be sorted in the order of increasing distance from the eye. Since the shadow edges are all parallel, or all radiate from the light source, they never cross except (possibly) at the light source. Therefore they can be sorted in an order which remains valid from one viewing ray to the next along a scan plane.

When the light source is at infinity, the parameter for the shadow sort is the perpendicular distance between the shadow edge and the eye. If the light source is finite, the extended shadow edge passes through it, and the sort parameter is the angle between the shadow edge direction and the line L from the light source to the eye. The shadow edges are linked into the shadow sort list by a separate shadow sort pointer, which identifies the shadow edge block with the next highest sort parameter marking a transition between light (0 shadows) or darkness (1 or more shadows). (See Table 1, item 8c.)

We can think of the scan plane as made up of a collection of rays from the eye, ordered by the r sort in increasing angles away from the sun direction. Along these rays are regions in shadow, bounded at the shadow sort parameters of the shadow edges. These regions determine the shadowed surfaces when rendering a span, and also the shadowed regions in the atmosphere.

At the appropriate time, as discussed below, each polygon in turn must have its shadow edges merged into the shadow sort. This could result in no change, if the new shadow region is already in shadow, or in one or two new shadow edges, depending on the overlap with existing shadows. Old shadow edges overlapped by the new region are unlinked from the sort list, which can thus grow shorter. If care is taken to join shadow regions which exactly abut, then after a network of polygons defining a continuous surface has been processed, the result in the shadow sort is the same as if only shadow polygons for the profile edges had been entered. (See Crow [3].)

Consider the scan plane through the eye E and the light source S, as shown in Figures 2a and 2b. In Frank Crow's algorithm, the shadow edges would be considered together with the polygon segments during the two-dimensional sort constituting the hidden surface algorithm on this plane. Here, we treat the shadow edges separately, in the simpler one-dimensional merge/sort just described, which accounts only for the sort parameter of a shadow edge, and not

the position at which it begins.

In order for this to work, the scan plane must be swept out in order by rays from the eye making increasing angles α with the light source direction, so that before a polygon is rendered, all polygons which could cast shadows on it have been considered and merged into the shadow sort.

In the case shown in Figure 2a, the light source is in front of the viewer, and increasing α corresponds to increasing r, so the Watkins algorithm proceeds in the order of increasing r. However, in the case of Figure 2b, where the light source is behind the viewer, the situation is reversed, and the algorithm must proceed in the order of decreasing r.

Suppose segment AB is the current span to be rendered. In both Figures 2a and 2b, any polygon which can cast a shadow on AB must interest the triangle SAB. By the time this current span is reached, any polygons contained in the semi-infinite angle SEA have already been merged into the shadow sort. But we must treat carefully polygons intersecting the angle AEB, and in particular, the segment AB itself.

We say a polygon is *front lit* if the side facing the viewer also faces the light source, as is true for polygon AB in the figures. In this case, the segment AB is merged into the shadow sort only after the r processing has completely passed it; otherwise it would shadow itself. The neglected shadows caused by this delay will not affect the final picture, because segments like CD and EF, which should have been shadowed by AB, are hidden by AB.

It is also necessary to refrain from merging segments CD and EF until AB has been rendered, otherwise they will cast backwards shadows onto AB. Since CD is front lit, it is delayed by the rule already mentioned for AB. Back lit segments like FG are merged when one of the following conditions becomes true: (a) the segment FG overlaps the span to be rendered and lies at least partly on the sunlit side of the polygon visible in the span, (b) the segment FG is itself about to be rendered, or (c) the r processing has completely passed FG.

When a polygon is entered into the active segment list, its plane equation is computed and entered into its segment block, as coefficients of an affine function which is positive on the side of the polygon containing the light source. (See item 13 in Table 1.) Also a bit (item 10) is set to 1 if the viewpoint is on the positive side of this plane, so that the polygon is front lit. Segments with this bit set are merged into the shadow sort at the time they are removed from the active segment list.

Not-yet-merged back lit active segments are linked into a sublist called the test list (item 5 in Table 1), to facilitate checking conditions (a), (b), and (c) before each span is rendered. The test for (a) uses the plane equation (item 13) for the currently visible segment.

4. Translucency

In a forest, the leaves are translucent and light falling on the sunlit side causes the other side to glow. (A shadow is still cast, however, because the light is scattered in all directions, rather than being partially transmitted along a unique refracted direction.) To get this effect, I could not merely delay entering back lit translucent segments into the shadow sort, to prevent them from shadowing themselves, because they must still shadow other polygons.

Instead, I maintain a "0/1/many" shadow counter, which is 0 for regions with no shadows, 1 for a single shadow, and 2 (representing many) for regions blocked from the sun by more than one polygon. In each shadow edge block is an entry for the count of the region beyond that shadow edge (item 8e in Table 1). The shadow sort pointer discussed above treats 2 the same as 1 in deciding how to merge a new segment into the sort, so I call this the "0/many" list. If a scene has any translucent polygons, a separate 0/1/many list pointer (item 8d) is maintained for the potentially longer sort of 0/1/many shadow regions, and all segments are merged into both linked lists. To do both merges at once, the merge subroutine traces through the 0/many pointers until the 0/many region containing the first shadow edge of the new segment has been found. It then follows the 0/many and 0/1/many pointers separately from this point, and adjusts the lists accordingly. If the 0/many list has N entries, the first search step takes time of order N.

Translucent polygons add 1 to the count of the regions they shadow. When the back lit side of a translucent segment is rendered, 1 is subtracted from the count to determine which regions are glowing. Opaque polygons and front lit translucent polygons add 2 to the count and are thus more likely to shorten the 0/1/many list.

When a visible segment of a polygon is rendered, its endpoints define a region of the shadow sort list, whose counts are used to determine the shadows on the segment. During the sequential search for this region in the 0/many list, the plane equations for all shadow polygons up to and including this region are copied into linearly ordered data arrays. These arrays are then used by the Cray-1 in a vectorized ray/plane intersection computation to determine the illuminated intervals along each ray from the eye. Since this ordered data is needed, a more sophisticated search taking time of order log N cannot be used.

5. Atmospheric illumination

We must now calculate the integrated atmospheric glow along a ray from the eye. This computation varies depending on whether the distance to the light source is finite or infinite.

First, assume the light source, like the sun, is at infinity. In Figure 3, U is a unit vector from the eye along a viewing ray R, with the eye at the origin O, and H is a height above which no data in the model extends. Also, V is a unit vector in the direction of the sun, φ is the angle between the sun direction and the vertical and θ is the angle between the ray R and the vertical. We wish to compute the scattered light reaching the eye from a non-shadowed interval AB on the ray R. We first consider the absorption of the sunlight due to the haze above a point P on the interval AB.

Assume that the haze has constant density and absorbs a fraction b dr of the light along an infinitesimal length dr of the ray R. If I(r) is the intensity at distance r through the haze, then [d I(r)]/I(r) = $-$ b dr, and by integration I(r) = I(0) exp ($-$br). Let I_0 represent the sunlight intensity at altitude H. In Figure 3, the z coordinate at P is s cos θ, so the distance r from P to T is r = PG sec φ = (H $-$ s cos θ) sec φ, and the intensity reaching P is I_0 exp [$-$b (H $-$ s cos θ) sec φ].

In this paper, we assume a single scattering model for light diffusion through haze, as described in Blinn [11] and Max [12]. (For a more sophisticated model of light scattering, see Kajiya [13].) According to the single scattering model, the dust particles or water droplets in the air will scatter an amount ρds of the light at P towards the eye. The scattering coefficient ρ depends on the density and al-

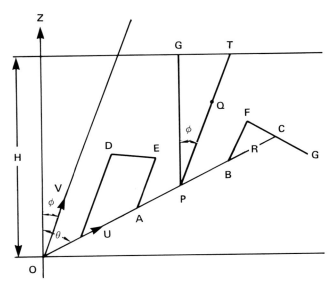

Figure 3. A vertical plane through a ray R between the eye at O and a first polygon intersection point C. For clarity, the figure shows the case when the unit direction vector V to the sun lies in the same vertical plane, so the parallel lines making an angle of φ with the vertical all represent sun rays or shadow edges. The ray R makes an angle of θ with the vertical and U is a unit vector along the ray. DE and FG represent polygon segments casting shadows, and AB is an illuminated interval on the ray between the shadows. P = sU is a typical point in this interval. Q = sU + tV is a typical point on the ray from P towards the sun.

bedo of the particles, and on the scattering angle (see Blinn [11]). The point P is at a distance s from the eye, so this scattered light is further attenuated by a factor exp ($-$bs). Therefore, the light reaching the eye, scattered from the infinitesimal ray segment of length ds at P, is ρI_0 exp [$-$ b (H $-$ s cos θ) sec φ] exp ($-$bs) ds.

The total light reaching the eye, scattered from the interval between A = s_iU and B = s_{i+1} U is

$$\int_{s_i}^{s_{i+1}} \rho I_0 \exp [-b H \sec \varphi - bs (1 - \cos \theta \sec \varphi)] \, ds$$

$$= \rho I_0 \exp (-bH \sec \varphi) \int_{s_i}^{s_{i+1}} \exp [-bs(1 - \cos \theta \sec \varphi)] \, ds$$

$$= \rho I_0 \exp (-bH \sec \varphi) \frac{\exp [-bs (1 - \cos \theta \sec \varphi)]}{-b (1 - \cos \theta \sec \varphi)} \Big|_{s_i}^{s_{i+1}}$$

which is of the form C $\{$exp [$-$D (s_{i+1})] $-$ exp [$-$D (s_i)]$\}$.

The constants C and D depend on the ray, but not on the distances s_i, so the sum of the scattered light reaching the eye from all the illuminated intervals on a ray can be computed in a vectorizable loop, using a vectorized exponential function.

This calculation can be generalized for the case of layered fog, whose density b(z) is a function of only the altitude z above sea level. Perlin [14] suggests that the integral g(z) = $\int_0^z$ b(u) du be precomputed and tabulated. Then, to find the total density between the eye and the point P = sU in Figure 3, we need only look up g (s cos θ) and multiply by sec θ.

Assume that the scattering coefficient ρ satisfies $\rho = \beta$ b(z), with the constant β depending only on the angle between the viewing ray and the sun direction. Then, because of the lucky identity

$$d/dz \{\exp [-g(z)]\} = -dg/dz \{\exp [-g(z)] = -b(z) \exp [-g(z)]\},$$

it turns out that the analysis above for constant density can be repeated for layered fog, giving a total scattering intensity of the form C sec θ $\{$exp [$-$Dg $(s_{i+1} \cos \theta)$] $-$ exp [$-$Dg $(s_i \cos \theta)$]$\}$ with C and

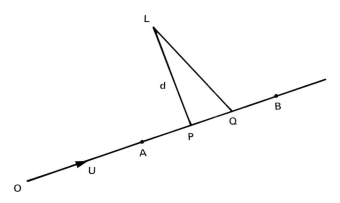

Figure 4. An illuminated interval AB on a ray. The eye is at the origin O, and the light source L is at a finite distance. The line LP is perpendicular to the ray, meeting it at P. The length d of LP is the shortest distance from L to the ray. If U is a unit vector along the ray, then P = s_oU, where s_o is the length of the segment OP.

D depending on φ, H, and β.

In the case of a finite light source, we must take into account the inverse square law, and I only have an easy answer for the case of constant density, no absorption, and constant albedo independent of the angles, which now change even along a single ray. Suppose a point source is at position L, as shown in Figure 4, and a ray from the eye approaches its closest distance d to L at point P = s_o U. Let Q = sU be any other point on the ray. The distance from Q to L is $\sqrt{d^2 + (s - s_o)^2}$. By the inverse square law, assuming no absorption, the intensity at Q is $K/[d^2 + (s - s_o)^2]$.

So the intensity along an interval between A = s_i U and B = s_{i+1} U is

$$\int_{s_i}^{s_{i+1}} \frac{K \, ds}{d^2 + (s - s_o)^2} = \frac{K}{d} \int_{s_i}^{s_{i+1}} \frac{\frac{ds}{d}}{1 + \left(\frac{s - s_o}{d}\right)^2}$$

$$= \frac{K}{d} \int_{t_i}^{t_{i+1}} \frac{dt}{1 + t^2} = K\left[\tan^{-1}(t_{i+1}) - \tan^{-1}(t_i)\right]/d$$

where $t_i = (s_i - s_o)/d$.

Using any of the above methods, the total scattered energy, E, is found by adding up the integrals from each of the illuminated segments along the ray from the eye to a surface point.

6. Composite colors and their cubic interpolation

The final composite color of a surface as influenced by the haze along a ray depends on several quantities: the total scattered energy E as computed above, the surface color (s_r, s_g, s_b) as determined from the illumination and surface shading models, and a haze transmission factor T. The use of a "fog factor" T is already common in computer imagery. If the fog has constant density, with absorption coefficient b, then the transmission factor is T = exp (– bs) where s is the distance from the eye to the surface. For layered fog, T = exp [– sec θ g (s cos θ)], where θ is as shown in Figure 3, and g is the integral of the fog density along a vertical line as discussed above.

Even if the ray is entirely in shadow, the fog still imparts a color (h_r, h_g, h_b) from its ambient illumination. In this case, the standard method for finding the output color (f_r, f_g, f_b) is

$$(f_r, f_g, f_b) = T (s_r, s_g, s_b) + (1 - T) (h_r, h_g, h_b).$$

Now let (i_r, i_g, i_b) represent the color of the haze when illuminated, so that (e_r, e_g, e_b) = (i_r, i_g, i_b) – (h_r, h_g, h_b) is the extra glow. Then if a ray is partly illuminated, the output color is

$$(f_r, f_g, f_g) = T(s_r, s_g, s_b) + (1 - T)(h_r, h_g, h_b) + E(e_r, e_g, e_b),$$

where E is the total scattering energy computed in section 5. (Care must be taken so that this extra term does not cause the color to exceed the displayable range.)

The output of the hidden-surface/shadow algorithm is a collection of visible surface segments, separated into illuminated or shadowed intervals. Each color component f_c, for c = r,g,b, must be interpolated across every interval as a function of the radius parameter r along a radial scan line. These functions may be highly non-linear since s_r, s_g, s_b, T, and E all vary across the surface, and the perspective projection and exponential absorption are non-linear.

The functions $f_c(r)$ must be accurately approximated, or else the color may change suddenly where a new polygon or shadow edge interrupts a longer interval from the previous scan line. I chose to approximate the f_c using a hermite cubic interpolation polynomial t_c, which matches the values of f_c and its derivatives at the interval end points. (See Mortenson [15], Rogers and Adams [16].)

At a division point between a region of shadow and light on the same visible surface, only s_r, s_g, and s_b change suddenly. T and E remain continuous, and need be computed only once. Their derivatives are estimated from finite differences, by evaluating T and E at nearby points.

The endpoint color components and their derivatives are used to calculate the interpolated values $t_c(1/2)$ of the hermite polynomials at the interval midpoint using the identity $t_c(1/2) = f_c(0)/2 + f_c(1)/2 + f'_c(0)/8 - f'_c(1)/8$.

The actual colors at the interval midpoint are also computed by evaluating T, E, and (s_r, s_g, s_b). If all three actual colors agree with their interpolated values to within a specified tolerance, the corresponding hermite polynomial is used for the interval. Otherwise, the interval is subdivided recursively using the actual values found at the midpoint (and at a nearby point for the finite difference) until the tolerance criterion is met or the maximum permitted recursion level is reached.

7. Scan conversion with anti-aliasing

This polynomial shading information must now be scan converted into a standard rectilinear image. If the data were sampled at discrete radial points into a polar coordinate array, it could be resampled by the methods of Catmull and Smith [17]. But this would mean sacrificing the extra accuracy available in the continuous radial direction. Instead, I have used gaussian filtering on an image which is black except on the infinitely thin radial scan lines, where the intensity is given by the polynomials. An explanation of this filtering will appear in a forthcoming paper [18].

8. Clipping

For a perspective view without shadows, all polygons are usually clipped to a view volume, as shown in Figure 5.

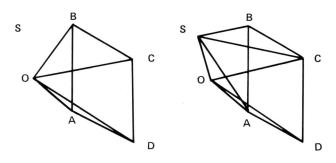

Figure 5. Left: A view pyramid, bounded by four slanted triangles, and a far clipping plane ABCD. From the point of view of the light source S, only faces OAB and OBC are visible, and the profile is the broken line OCBAO. Right: The larger clipping volume for shadows is formed by removing faces OAB and OBC, and adding faces SOC, SCB, SBA, and SAO. The removed planes OAB and OBC, and the near clipping plane, will later be used to separate off the visible polygons.

This eliminates polygons which are invisible and prevents vertices behind the eye from being incorrectly projected. For a view with shadows, such clipping might eliminate polygons which could cast shadows on visible ones. Unless the light source is within the view volume, a larger shadow-casting volume must be found, which includes all polygons which could cast shadows into the view volume.

The planes bounding the shadow casting volume come from two lists: a) the faces of the view volume whose outward normal points away from the light source, and b) planes formed by joining the light source direction to profile edges of the view volume. The profile edges can be identified as those which appear exactly once among the edges of the faces in list a). A third list c) contains the faces of the view volume not in list a), as well as a near clipping plane used to avoid division by zero.

All polygons are clipped to the planes in lists a) and b) to remove polygons or parts of polygons which are irrelevant to the image. Then the planes in list c) are used to break the resulting polygons into two groups: the visible polygons and the shadow-only polygons.

The shadow-only polygons are entered into the θ bucket sort. They need not be entered into the Watkins $r - z$ sort, but they must be merged together as non-translucent segments in the shadow sort lists, before the $r - z$ sort is started.

9. Summary

Put all edges into θ buckets.
For all buckets, in order of decreasing θ:
   Enter all edges from bucket θ into r sort segment blocks.
   Merge all shadow-only segments into shadow sort.
   For each visible span generated by the Watkins $r - z$ sort:
      Merge back lit polygon segments which satisfy conditions (a), (b), or (c) of section 3 into shadow sort.
      Find intervals of light and shade on the visible span.
      For each interval, approximate color functions by recursively defined piecewise cubic polynomials, and scan convert each piece into rectilinear pixel array.
      Merge front lit polygon segments which end during the span into shadow sort.
   Remove edges which terminate at this θ from active r sort.
   Update edges for next radial scan line.
Output final picture.

10. Results

Figure 6 shows a jack-o-lantern, lit by a candle inside it. The finite light source is within the view volume. It took approximately 20 seconds to compute on the Cray-1, at 512 by 512 resolution. Figure 7 shows vertical columns of light coming through a hole in the clouds. The sun is at infinity directly overhead, and the methods of Max [12] were used to compute the atmospheric shadows from the partially transparent clouds.

Figure 8 shows three polygons casting shadows on each other, on the ground below, and in the atmosphere. The contrast in the atmospheric illumination is most apparent where there is a shadow polygon almost parallel to the line of sight. The light is at infinity above and behind the viewer, so the atmospheric shadows appear smaller near the ground, due to the perspective forshortening. Figure 9 shows several trees, designed by Jules Bloomenthal (see [19]), with shadow-mapped bark (see [20]).

These results show that it is possible to integrate atmospheric illumination efficiently into a scan line hidden-surface algorithm, if radial scan lines are used.

Acknowledgments

This work was performed under the auspices of the U.S. Department of Energy by Lawrence Livermore National Laboratory (LLNL) under contract number W-7405-ENG-48.

The algorithm was adapted in incremental fashion from a direct descendant of the original Fortran program written by Gary Watkins to test his proposed hardware hidden surface algorithm. It was rewritten by Mike Achuleta at LLNL and later modified by Bruce Brown, Paul Renard, and Gene Cronshagen. I found incremental changes to an existing program easier than planning a new algorithm from scratch, because I could use the pictures to debug each new feature. I wish to thank Jules Bloomenthal for the tree trunk data and bark texture, Maria Lopez for typing this paper, and Charles Grant for carefully reading and commenting on it.

References

[1] Williams, Lance, "Casting Curved Shadows on Curved Surfaces," SIGGRAPH '78 proceedings, pp. 270–274.

[2] Atherton, Peter, Weiler, Kevin, and Greenberg, Donald, "Polygon Shadow Generation," SIGGRAPH '78 proceedings, pp. 275–281.

[3] Crow, Franklin, "Shadow Algorithms for Computer Graphics," SIGGRAPH '77 proceedings, pp. 242–248.

[4] Nishita, Tomoyuki, Okamura, Isao, and Nakamae, Eihachiro, "Shading Models for Point and Linear Sources," ACM Transactions on Graphics, Vol 4 no. 2 (1985), pp. 124–146.

[5] Bouknight, J., and Kelly, K., "An algorithm for producing half-tone computer graphics presentations with shadows and movable light sources," SJCC, AFIPS, Vol 36 (1970), pp. 1–10.

[6] Whitted, Turner "An Improved Illumination Model for Shaded Display," Communications of the ACM, Vol 23 (1980), pp. 343–349.

[7] Cook, Robert, Porter, Thomas, and Carpenter, Loren, "Distributed Ray Tracing," SIGGRAPH '84 proceedings, pp. 137–145.

[8] Watkins, Gary, "A real-time visible surface algorithm," Ph.D. Thesis, University of Utah (1970) UTECH-CSc-70-101.

[9] Sproull, Robert, and Newman, William, "Principles of Interactive Computer Graphics" (first edition is better on this subject), McGraw Hill, New York (1973).

[10] Rogers, David, "Procedural Elements for Computer Graphics," McGraw Hill, New York (1985).

[11] Blinn, James, "Light Reflection Functions for Simulation of Clouds and Dusty Surface," SIGGRAPH '82 proceedings, pp. 21–29.

[12] Max, Nelson, "Light Diffusion through Clouds and Haze," Computer Vision Graphics, and Image Processing, Vol 33 (1986), pp. 280–292.

[13] Kajiya, James, and Von Herzen, Brian, "Ray Tracing Volume Densities," SIGGRAPH '84 proceedings, pp. 165–174.

[14] Perlin, Ken, "State of the Art in Image Synthesis '85 Course Notes," ACM SIGGRAPH '85, course 11.

[15] Mortenson, Michael, "Geometric Modelling," John Wiley and Sons, New York (1985).

[16] Rogers, David, and Adams, J. A., "Mathematical Elements for Computer Graphics," McGraw Hill, New York (1976).

[17] Catmull, Ed, and Smith, Alvey Ray, "3-D Transformations of Images in Scanline Order," SIGGRAPH '80 proceedings, pp. 279–285.

[18] Max, Nelson "Anti-Aliasing Scan Line Data" to be submitted to IEEE Computer Graphics and Applications.

[19] Bloomenthal, Jules, "Modelling the Mighty Maple," SIGGRAPH '85 proceedings, pp. 305–311.

[20] Max, Nelson, "Shadows for Bump Mapped Surfaces," in Advanced Computer Graphics: Proceedings of Computer Graphics Tokyo '86, T. L. Kunii, ed., Springer Verlag, Tokyo (1986), pp. 145–156. To be revised and submitted to The Visual Computer.

Figure 6.   A jack-o-lantern, lit by a candle.

Figure 8.   Three polygons casting atmospheric shadows.

Figure 7.   Sunlight coming through a break in the clouds.

Figure 9. Several trees.

CONTINUOUS TONE REPRESENTATION OF THREE-DIMENSIONAL OBJECTS
ILLUMINATED BY SKY LIGHT

Tomoyuki Nishita   and   Eihachiro Nakamae

Fukuyama University   Hiroshima University
Higashimura, Fukuyama   Saijocho, Higashihiroshima
729-02, Japan   724, Japan

Abstract

Natural lighting models to date have been limited to calculation of direct sunlight. However, this paper proposes an improved model for natural lighting calculations that adequately considers both direct sunlight and scattered light caused by clouds and other forms of water vapor in the air. Such indirect natural light is termed skylight and can be an important factor when attempting to render realistic looking images as they might appear under overcast skies.

In the proposed natural lighting model, the sky is considered to be a hemisphere with a large radius (called the sky dome) that acts as a source of diffuse light with nonuniform intensity. In order to adequately take into account the nonuniform intensity of such skylight, the sky dome is subdivided into bands. The light intensity within individual bands can be assumed to be transversely uniform and longitudinally nonuniform and therefore the total luminance emanating from each band can be calculated more accurately.

The proposed method significantly improves the realism of natural lighting effects. Its advantages are particularly apparent when simulating lighting under an overcast sky or when rendering surfaces that fall within a shadow cast by an obstruction lit by direct sunlight.

CR Categories and Subject Descriptors: I.3.7 [Computer Graphics]: Three-Dimensional Graphics and Realism; I.3.3 [Computer Graphics]: Picture/Image Generation

General Terms : Algorithms

Additional Key Words and Phrases: shading, sky light, shadows, interreflection of light, daylight factor, distributed light source

1. INTRODUCTION

Recently, various display techniques have been developed by numerous researchers, for such things as trees, natural terrain, clouds and fog effects [1-5]. Still other algorithms have been developed to treat such problems as texture mapping, reflection, refraction and transparency [6,7]. Much of this research has been designed to facilitate generation of more and more realistic looking simulations of various environments.

The visual appearance of such simulated environments depends to a great extent on the lighting model used to illuminate the objects in the environment. In this connection, researchers have already developed lighting models for various types of light sources [8-9] as well as algorithms that take into account the effect of interreflection among objects [10-12].

However, to date, lighting models have been limited to either artificial light sources or direct sunlight. In fact, though, a high percentage of the environments to be simulated are naturally lit by what is commonly called daylight; i.e. a combination of direct sunlight and skylight. One of the most troublesome problems when using only direct sunlight as a light source is that objects in shadow appear to be unnaturally dark. One common solution to this problem is to add a uniform ambient light to the lighting model. But this tends to hide any surface unevenness of the objects in shadow since all parts of the surface are lit evenly. Another common approach is to add a secondary light source coincident with the viewer's eye point. While this is a convenient solution, it detracts from the realism of shaded renderings. In order to overcome such problems in a general way, this paper proposes a lighting model for skylight which, when combined with direct sunlight, allows increased realism when rendering natural environments.

Fundamentally, skylight can be thought to emanate from the sky dome which surrounds the earth. The sky dome can be treated as a hemisphere of very large radius. However, skylight intensity is not uniform accross the entire surface of the sky dome and will also vary greatly with the weather (e.g., clear sky or overcast sky). In order to handle such nonuniformity in a consistent manner, the paper introduces the idea of subdividing the sky dome into light emanating bands whose intensity is uniform within its boundaries; the idea that the intensity of an entire band can be approximated by calculating the intensity of sample lines located at the center of such bands; and the idea of alternative methods for calculating such intensities under either clear or overcast skies.

2. ASSUMPTIONS AND FUNDAMENTAL IDEAS

As already mentioned, daylight is a combination of direct sunlight and diffuse skylight. This paper will only discuss how to handle skylight. Direct sunlight can be handled in the normal way, which is to treat it as a parallel light source.

Intensity of skylight (also called sky luminance) is not uniform and its distribution varies significantly depending on whether the sky is clear or overcast. Such variations due to weather conditions are discussed in this paper.

The color of skylight is also not uniform and its spectral distribution varies significantly depending on solar altitude. This is most obvious at sunrise and sunset when the sun is low on the horizon. Although some of the most beautiful natural lighting effects occur at these times of the day, the issue of spectral distribution is not discussed in this paper. However, spectral distribution is suggested as topic for future research within the conceptual framework of the model for skylighting proposed here.

Before beginning the calculation of illuminance at a given point in the scene, it is necessary to test for obstructions and the resulting shadows. The shadow boundaries that would be caused by direct sunlight on a clear day are determined by an overlap test of objects on the perspective plane when viewed from the sun (see [13]).

The illuminance from skylight can be calculated by determining the area of the sky visible from the given point in the scene. In the proposed lighting model, the skydome is divided into bands which themselves do not necessarily have uniform luminance. Therefore, the total luminance from a visible area of the sky must be derived by summing the luminances of the visible areas of the individual bands.

The illuminance at a given point in the scene is a combination of light from the sky and light reflected from the ground and/or surrounding objects. The ratio between skylight and reflected light from the ground depends on the declination of the plane including the given point in the scene.

Interreflection of light between objects in the scene must also be considered in order to acheive an accurate simulation of natural lighting. This is particularly important when creating interior scenes with many objects in a room. In such cases, the interreflection luminance can be determined by first subdividing the faces of the objects in the scene (such as walls, furniture, etc.) into a suitable number of subsurfaces and then calculating the interreflection at the vertices of each subsurface (see [11]).

The ground and all other objects in the scene are assumed to be sets of convex polyhedra and convex polygons. The surfaces of all polyhedra are assumed to be Lambertian surfaces; i.e., perfectly diffuse. The ground itself is treated as a large area surface with uniform luminance.

3. ILLUMINANCE CALCULATION FOR SKY LIGHT

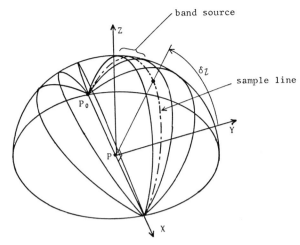

Fig. 1 Subdivision of the sky dome to band sources (P:the calculation point).

If the intensity of sky light were uniform, it has been shown that the illuminance at a given point can be calculated by using a configuration factor. A configuration factor is the ratio of the area of the visible sky projected onto the base of the sky dome vs. the total area of the base of the sky dome(This ratio is also called the sky factor). Illuminance at a given point is then obtained by the multiplication of the configuration factor and the sky luminance. The configuration factor is usually obtained by contour integration of the visible areas of the sky (refer to Ref. [9] for the contour integration method for area sources).

However, the distribution of sky luminance is nonuniform in most cases. The distribution of the sky luminance varies depending on sites, time, and seasons. In order to deal with varied distributions, the following methods might be considered:

(a) Generate many sample points on the sky dome, and set the weighting factor proportional to sky luminance of each point.

(b) Subdivide the sky dome into many finite elements (e.g., rectangular elements).

(c) Subdivide the sky dome into many band elements (we call these elements "band sources").

In methods (a) or (b), both the illuminance calculation and the visibility test used to calculate the effect taking account of obstructions have to be done for each point or each element, respectively. Method (c) is less costly compared with the other methods for the following reasons (see Fig.1).

(1) The calculation point can always be handled as the effective center of the sky dome hemisphere because of the dome's very large radius. (2) The luminance of band sources is assumed to be continuously varying with respect to the longitudinal direction of the band source. (3) The center line of the band source is called a "sample line" and a plane consisting of the sample line and the center of hemisphere is called a "sample plane". The sample plane of the ℓth band source, S_ℓ, is defined as the intersection line between the hemisphere and the plane whose tilt angle is δ_ℓ. The visible parts of the band sources are determined by using these sample lines. Then the illuminance can be obtained by adding the

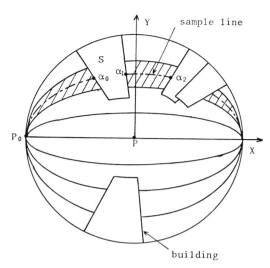

Fig. 2 Calculation of visible areas of a band source by using a sample line.

illuminances of the visible parts of the band sources (Fig.2 shows the visible parts of sample lines on the orthogonal projection); the intersections between obstacles and sample lines can be obtained by testing the intersections between the obstacles and the sample planes in the object space (see 3.3).

3.1 Illuminance Calculation from only Sky Light

The calculation method of illuminance on skyward-facing horizontal surfaces, which are top surfaces of objects such as the ground, is discussed here. In this case, taking reflected light from the ground into account is unnecessary.

3.1.1 Illuminance from Unobstructed Sky

As mentioned before, the calculation point can always be handled as the center of the sky dome. For simple calculation, we define the coordinate system so that the horizontal plane including the calculation point is the X-Y plane, which is coincident with the base of the sky dome with a radius r; the calculation point is the origin of the coordinate system.

The sample planes are determined as declined planes which include the X-axis and whose elevation angles are δ_ℓ ($\ell=1,2,...,N$; N=the number of subdivisions) (see Fig.3). The band source may be broken down into small "sky elements", each of which may be considered to have a constant luminance. By treating the sky elements as a point source P_e, the inverse-square law may be applied for illuminance at a calculation point P. By expressing the position of P_e with angle α from X-axis (PP_0) to sky element and angle δ from horizontal plane to sky element, the illuminance at P due to the sky element represented by P_e is given by

$$dE = L(\alpha,\delta)\cos\theta/r^2 dA \quad , \qquad (1)$$

where L is the sky luminance at P_e, θ is the angle from the zenith to P_e ($\cos\theta = \sin\alpha\sin\delta$), r corresponds to the distance between P and P_e, and

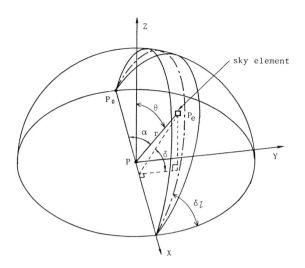

Fig. 3 Distribution of sky luminance.

dA is the area of the sky element ($dA=(rd\alpha) \cdot (rd\delta\sin\alpha)$) (see Fig.3). By integrating equation (1) with respect to α and δ, the illuminance due to the band source between 0 and α is given by

$$E_\ell(\alpha) = \int_0^\alpha \int_{\delta_\ell'}^{\delta_{\ell+1}'} L(\alpha,\delta) \sin\delta\sin\alpha^2 d\delta d\alpha \quad , \qquad (2)$$

where $\delta_\ell' = \delta_\ell - \Delta\delta$, $\delta_{\ell+1}' = \delta_\ell + \Delta\delta$, $2\Delta\delta$ is the angular width of a band source.

Let's consider the case of a uniform sky luminance first. In this case, $L(\alpha,\delta)=L_0$ (i.e., constant), then equation (2) becomes the following equation.

$$E_\ell(\alpha)=0.5d_\ell(\alpha-\cos\alpha\sin\alpha)L_0 \quad , \qquad (3)$$

where $d_\ell=(\cos\delta_\ell'-\cos\delta_{\ell+1}')$. In this paper, we set the angle of the sample plane, δ_ℓ ($\ell=1,2,...,N$), as $d_\ell=1/N$ (constant).

In the case of nonuniform sky luminance, if it is assumed that the luminance in the small width, $\delta_\ell' < \delta < \delta_{\ell+1}'$, is constant, then $L(\alpha,\delta)$ is represented by $L(\alpha,\delta_\ell)$. Thus, equation (2) becomes the following equation.

$$E_\ell(\alpha)=d_\ell \int_0^\alpha L(\alpha,\delta_\ell)\sin\alpha^2 d\alpha \quad . \qquad (4)$$

Empirical formulas for calculating the luminance of both overcast skies and clear skies have been determined by the CIE for international use; the distribution is defined as the relative luminance to the luminance of the zenith.

a) the overcast sky (the CIE Standard sky luminance function[14])

$$L(\theta)=Lz(1+2\cos\theta)/3 \quad , \qquad (5)$$

Lz: luminance of the zenith,
θ : the angle from the zenith to a sky element,

where Lz is the function of the solar altitude, but $L(\theta)$ is independent to the sun position. The above equation means that the sky luminance is the highest at the zenith and the lowest around the horizon.

b) the clear sky (the CIE Standard sky luminance function[15])

$$L(\theta,\phi)=L_z \frac{(.91+10\exp(-3\gamma)+.45\cos^2\gamma)(1-\exp(-.32\sec\theta))}{0.274(0.91+10\exp(-3z_0)+0.45\cos^2 z_0)} \quad (6)$$

γ : the angle from the sun to a sky element;
  ($\cos\gamma=\cos z_0\cdot\cos\theta+\sin z_0\cdot\sin\theta\cdot\cos(\phi-\phi_0)$)
z_0: the angle from the zenith to the sun,
ϕ : the azimuth angle from X-axis to the sky element,
ϕ_0: the azimuth angle from X-axis to the sun.

The above mentioned equation means that the sky luminance varies with the sun position. Sky luminance is highest in the region of the sun and lowest at about 90° from it.

3.1.2 Illuminance Calculation Taking Account of Obstructions

$E_\ell(\alpha)$ in equation (2) is the illuminance due to the region between 0 and α in a band source. Therefore, if the region between α_1 and α_2, where $\alpha_1 \leq \alpha_2$, is visible from the calculation point, P (see Fig.2), the illuminance by the source in this region can be easily obtained as $E_\ell(\alpha_2)-E_\ell(\alpha_1)$. The visible parts detection method is described in the section 3.3 of this paper. It is convenient to precalculate values of $E_\ell(\alpha)$ and store them in look up tables. In this paper, values are prepared every ten degrees, and the E_ℓ at an arbitrary α is computed by linear interpolation.

In case such as a partly cloudy sky which fall between a completely overcast sky and a completely clear sky, we can blend the results of equations (5) and (6) even though the approximation precision is not very accurate because of the varied distribution of clouds. Using a distribution of measured data would be better. Look up tables could be obtained for any particular kind of sky

conditions if the distribution was given. And if the measured data included spectral distributions, it would be possible to compute illuminance taking into account spectral variations by preparing look up tables as functions of the spectrum.

3.2 Illuminance Calculation Taking into Account Reflected Light

Reflected light is composed of light reflected from the ground, light reflected from buildings, and the interreflection of light between buildings, ground and other objects (see Ref.[11,12] for interreflection of light). First, we describe the reflected light from the ground.

Sloped surfaces are usually illuminated by reflected light from the ground. Assuming that the ground is a large surface with a uniform brightness, the illuminance on the sloped surfaces can be obtained by inclining the hemisphere (see Fig.4-a). That is, the upper part of the hemisphere above the horizontal plane including the calculation point has the sky luminance, and the lower part has the luminance of the ground. The illuminance of the ground is obtained by the product of the sky illuminance and the ground reflectance, where the illuminance on the ground is assumed to be the illuminance from the unobstructed sky.

When the inclined angle of the face S_f is β, the illuminance on S_f can be calculated with a look up table, $E_{\ell\beta}(\alpha)$ which is pre-calculated by inclining $L(\alpha,\delta)$ by the angle β. The part of $L(\alpha,\delta)$ under the horizontal plane is set as the luminance of the ground (the dotted area in Fig.4-b shows the luminance of the ground).

In order to simplify the calculation, we assume that the illuminance of each face is uniform (the area, which can't be assumed uniform, may be subdivided into subsurfaces). Let's consider the reflected light from a face S in Fig. 4-b, the face S exists between α_1 and α_2 on the sample line, then

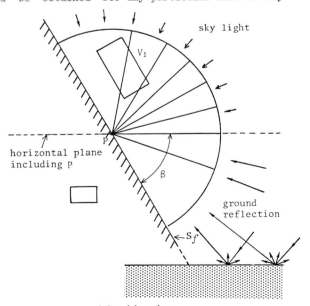

(a):side view

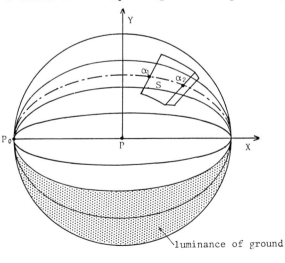

(b):projection onto the base of the hemisphere

Fig. 4 Illuminance calculation for a sloped plane
(the origin of the coordinate system is the calculation point P;
the X-axis is parallel to the horizontal plane)

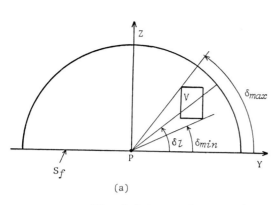

(a)   (b)

Fig. 5 Intersection test between sample planes and objects.

the illuminance due to this region can be obtained by substituting Lo in equation (2) to the luminance of S. This calculation is done only for faces visible from the calculation point, and can be omitted for small and low reflectance faces.

3.3 Calculation of the Visible Parts of the Sky

In order to consider the effect of obstructions, the visible parts of the sky viewed from the calculation point must be determined. The illuminance at a point P on a face S_f can be obtained by extracting the visible sections of the band sources; the procedure is as follows:

1) Extract the objects that cast shadows on the face S_f (i.e., objects existing in front of S_f; e.g., V_1 in Fig.4-a).

2) Transform the coordinates of these objects in order to set S_f as the base of hemisphere (see Fig.5-a).

3) Calculate the existing range of each object (the range is defined by the elevation angle; e.g., δ_{min} and δ_{max} in Fig.5-a).

4) Extract the contour lines of each object when viewed from the calculation point.

5) Execute the following calculation sequence for each sample plane;

   i) Extract the objects intersecting with the sample plane by using the range solved in 3) and the elevation angle of the sample plane.

   ii) Calculate the intersections between the contour line of each object and the sample plane, and get the angles, $\alpha_i(i=1,2,..,m)$, corresponding to the intersections (in Fig.5-b, α_1 is obtained by the inner product of vectors PP_1 and PP_0).

   iii) Extract the visible sections of the sample line (e.g., the section $\alpha_1\alpha_2$ in Fig.2, see [16] for hidden line elimination).

   iv) Calculate the illuminance due to each visible section by using the look up table, E_ℓ.

3.4 Illuminance Calculation for Naturally Lit Interiors

The illuminance at a calculation point in a room is usually influenced not only by the sky light and the ground light coming in through the windows but also by interreflection of light between objects in the room. Therefore, in the first step, the illuminance due to the light source from the windows is calculated, and then the interreflection is calculated by using the direct illuminance from windows (see Ref.[11] for the calculation of interreflection).

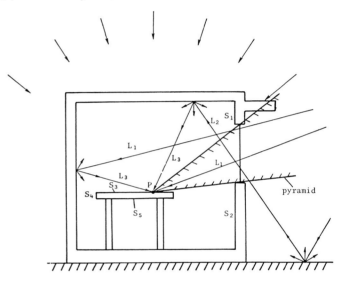

Fig. 6 Components of light in a room.
(L$_1$:direct light from sky, L$_2$:reflected light from the ground, L$_3$:interreflection of light)

It is unnecessary to consider the whole sky for the shading calculation of an interior because of the limited regions of the windows.

Therefore, for the calculation of the direct component from the sky light, the following terms should be considered for interiors :

a) The illuminance on a face, from which all windows are invisible, is zero (e.g., the window is on the back side of the faces such as S_1, S_2, S_4, S_5 in Fig.6).

b) Sample planes are only required to be generated within the range of the windows.

c) For shadow calculations, it is enough to extract the objects only within the pyramids composed by the windows and the calculation point (see Fig.6).

4. DAYLIGHT FACTORS

The illuminance from windows depends on the sky luminance. Therefore, the daylight factor is usually used for lighting design in daytime: it is defined as the ratio between the daylight illuminance at a point in the interior and the simultaneous exterior illuminance available on a horizontal plane from an unobstructed sky expressed as a percentage.

Superimposing the color belts of the daylight factor on the shaded images is used in the examples here; each color corresponds to the value of its daylight factor (see examples in Fig.10). With this depiction method, we can easily grasp the numerical values and the scene simultaneously.

5. EXAMPLES

Fig.7 shows the shaded images of a simple object. Picture (a) shows the object with only direct sunlight, (b): uniform skylight, (c): an overcast sky, (d): a clear sky (only skylight), and (e): a clear sky (including direct sunlight).

Fig.8 shows the outdoor scenes of a building under various conditions. Picture (a) shows the building with direct sunlight and uniform ambient light. Pictures (b) and (c) are with an overcast sky and a clear sky, respectively. Pictures in this sequence take into account reflected light from the ground and other objects.

In the previous methods, shadows under an overcast sky are ignored. As shown in Fig.8-b and c, there are penumbrae which means that the boundaries of shadows are not sharp. These penumbrae are more realistic and make it easy to recognize the shapes of objects in shadows. In Fig. 8-a and Fig.7-a, it is difficult to grasp the shapes of objects in the shadows because only direct sunlight and uniform ambient light are considered.

Fig.9 shows the interior of a computer room illuminated by a clear sky; in this figure the interreflection of light from walls and objects is taken into account. Notice that the parts of the walles farther from the window are also bright.

(All sample images found in this paper were made in this room.)

Fig.10 shows examples of daylight factors. Pictures (a) and (b) show the distribution of daylight factors with an overcast sky and with a clear sky, respectively; the daylight factor is defined only for sky light, then (b) does not include direct sunlight. Picture (c) shows the distribution of daylight factors with a clear sky. The color belts on the images show that the distribution of illuminance caused by the sky light is very complex and depends greatly on the sun's position. However, using the proposed method, we can design the daylighting of the room accurately.

Table 1 shows the computation times for Fig.8(b) and Fig.9. All computation was performed on a TOSBAC DS-600/80 32bit minicomputer. In this paper, the multi-scanning method is used for anti-aliasing (see section 2.5 in Ref.[17]). In these examples, Mach bands are slightly visible, because the illuminance at the calculation point is sampled along the sample lines.

In these examples, the ground reflectance is 0.25, and the number of sample planes (see section 3) for Fig.8 and Fig.9 are 20 and 200, respectively. Note that the effective sample planes for Fig.9 are limited (see 3.4).

These examples make clear that accounting for sky light and its shadow effects is very useful for generating realistic images, especially in cloudy weather, and is helpful for designing buildings and lighting interiors.

6. CONCLUSION

A representation method for three-dimensional objects illuminated by sky light has been proposed.

The following conclusions can be stated from the

(a) (b) (c)

(d) (e)

Fig. 7 Example for a simple shaped object.
a:direct sunlight, b:uniform skylight, c:overcast sky,
d:clear sky, e:clear sky(including direct sunlight)

(a)

(b)

(c)

Fig. 8 Examples for exterior scene.
    a: direct sunlight, b: overcast sky
    c: clear sky (including direct sunlight)

Fig. 9 Example for interior scene.

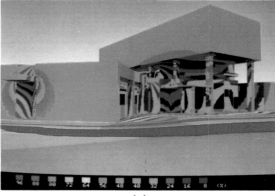

(a)

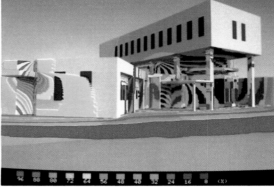

(b)

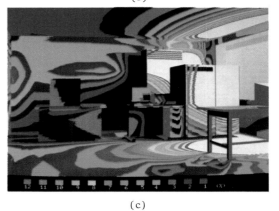

(c)

Fig. 10 Examples for daylight factors.
    (a:overcast sky, b:clear sky, c:clear sky)

Table 1. Computation times

	number of faces	image size	modeling and hidden-surface removal(min.)	shading(min.)	
				direct illumination	interreflection of light
Fig.8(b)	239	480x317	1.56	27.67	6.90*
Fig.9	231	480x325	1.81	20.91	16.08

*only the 1st order of reflection is considered.

results.

(1) Images are much realistic using sky light and its reflections. The proposed method especially improves the realism of buildings under both overcast skies and clear skies, as well as interiors illuminated by sky light through windows.

(2) The illuminance from sky light can be obtained by considering the sky as a hemisphere with a large radius. Subdividing the hemisphere into band sources allows us to compute the illuminance due to nonuniform sky luminance.

(3) The effect of sky light obstructed by objects can be computed by summing the illuminances due to the visible parts of each band source viewed from the calculation point; the illuminance for each visible part can be easily calculated by a look up table for integrated illuminance.

(4) The effect of light reflected from the ground to sloped surfaces can be computed by the ground luminance for the under part of the horizontal plane including the calculation point.

(5) Displaying daylight factor considering the distribution of sky luminance is useful for lighting design.

ACKNOWLEDGEMENT

The authors wish to thank Laurin Herr for his helpful advice.

REFERENCES

[1] Gardner G.Y.: Simulation of Natural Scenes Using Textured Quadric Surfaces, Computer Graphics, Vol.18, No.3(1984) pp.11-20.

[2] Gardner, G.: Visual Simulation of Clouds, Computer Graphics, Vol.19, No.3(1985) pp.297-303.

[3] Cook, R.C.: Shade Tree, Computer Graphics, Vol. 18, No. 3 (1984) pp.223-231.

[4] Aono, M. and Kunii,L.: Botanical Tree Image Generation, IEEE CG and A, Vol.4, No.5 (1984) pp.10-29.

[5] Fournier,A.,Fussell,D.,and Carpenter L., Computer Rendering of Stochastic Models, Comm.

[6] Blinn, J.F. and Newell, M.E.: Texture and Reflection in Computer Generated Images, Comm. ACM, Vol.19, No.10(1976) pp.542-546.

[7] Cook,R.L. and Torrance,K.E.: A Reflectance Model for Computer Graphics, ACM Trans. on Graphics, Vol.1, No.1(1982) pp.7-24.

[8] Nishita,T., Okamura,I. and Nakamae,E.: Shading Models for Point and Linear Sources, ACM Trans. on Graphics, Vol.4, No.2(1985) pp.124-146.

[9] Nishita,T. and Nakamae,E.: Half-Tone Representation of 3-D Objects Iluminated by Area Sources or Polyhedron Sources, IEEE, Proc. of COMPSAC(1983) pp.237-241.

[10] Goral,C.M., Torrance, K.E., Greenberg,D.P. and Battaile,B.: Modeling the Interaction of Light Between Diffuse Surfaces, Computer Graphics, Vol.18, No.3 (1984) pp.66-75.

[11] Nishita,T. and Nakamae,E.: Continuous Tone Representation of Three-Dimensional Objects Taking Account of Shadows and Interreflection, Computer Graphics, Vol.19, No.3(1985)pp.23-30.

[12] Cohen,M.F. and Greenberg,D.P.: The Hemi-cube: a Radiousity Solution for Complex Environments, Computer Graphics, Vol.19, No.3(1985) pp.31-41.

[13] Nishita,T. and Nakamae,E.: An Algorithm for Half-Tone Representation of Three-Dimensional Objects, Information Processing in Japan, Vol.14 (1974) pp.93-99.

[14] IES Daylighting Comittee: Recommended Practice of Daylighting, Lighting Design & Application, Vol.9, No.2(1979) pp.45-58.

[15] CIE Technical Comittee 4.2: Standardization of Luminance Distribution on Clear Skies, CIE Publication, No.22, Comission International de l'Eclairaze, Paris (1973) pp.7.

[16] Nakamae, E. and Nishita, T.: An Algorithm for Hidden line Elimination of Polyhedra, Information Processing in Japan, Vol.12 (1972) pp.134-141.

[17] Nakamae, E., Harada, K., Ishizaki, T. and Nishita,T.: A Montage Method; The Overlaying of The Computer Generated Images onto a Background Photograph, Computer Graphics, Vol.20, No.3 (1986).

A RADIOSITY METHOD FOR NON-DIFFUSE ENVIRONMENTS

David S. Immel, Michael F. Cohen,
Donald P. Greenberg
Cornell University
Ithaca, N.Y.   14853

ABSTRACT

A general radiosity method accounting for all interreflections of light between diffuse and non-diffuse surfaces in complex environments is introduced. As contrasted with previous radiosity methods, surfaces are no longer required to be perfectly diffuse reflectors and emitters. A complete, viewer independent description of the light leaving each surface in each direction is computed, allowing dynamic sequences of images to be rendered with little additional computation per image. Phenomena such as "reflection tracking", reflections following a moving observer across a specular surface are produced. Secondary light sources, such as the light from a spotlight reflecting off a mirror onto a wall are also accounted for.

CR Categories and Subject Descriptors: I.3.7 [Computer Graphics]: Three-Dimensional Graphics and Realism: I.3.3 [Computer Graphics]: Picture/Image Generation

General Terms: Algorithms

Additional Keywords and Phrases: Radiosity, intensity, bi-directional reflectance, hidden-surface, depth buffer, non-diffuse reflection.

INTRODUCTION

The production of realistic images requires the ability to simulate the propagation of light in an environment. This requires two steps: modeling the interaction of light with an individual surface and combining the effects of emission, transmission and reflection between all the surfaces in the environment. In the past, computer generated pictures were obtained by simulating how light is reflected from an individual surface, ignoring the interreflections from surface to surface. A number of reflection models were developed, ranging from a simple Lambertian diffuse

model in which all light is reflected with equal intensity in all directions, to more complex models including non-uniform specular distributions based on geometric and electromagnetic properties of the surface. For any given reflection model, images were created by determining the visible surface at each screen pixel location, and then computing the intensity of light leaving that surface in the direction of the eye. This intensity was typically found from the geometric relationships between the visible surface, the light sources, and the eye.

Ray-tracing was the first method introduced which attempted to include the effects of shadowing and reflections from neighboring surfaces [1]. In ray-tracing, an additional intensity contribution from secondary reflected and transmitted rays is added from the mirror and refracted directions. The fact that a limited number of rays are traced from the eye into the environment precludes the ability to completely account for the global illumination arising from complex interreflections within the environment.

Although ray-tracing techniques have been able to produce strikingly realistic images, only radiosity methods can account for the complex diffuse interreflections within an environment. The radiosity method, borrowed from thermal engineering techniques [2] [3], was introduced in the context of computer graphics by Goral in 1984 [4] and was extended for use in complex environments by Cohen [5] [6] and Nishita [7]. This method is based on the fundamental Law of Conservation of Energy within closed systems. It entails performing a simultaneous global solution for the intensity of light leaving each surface by constructing and solving a set of linear equations describing the transfer of diffuse light energy between all surfaces. Calculations are performed independently for any number of discrete wavelength bands. The advantages of this method are the increased accuracy in simulating the global illumination effects and the fact that all of the intensity calculations are independent of viewing parameters, thus allowing efficient rendering of dynamic sequences.

An underlying assumption in all previous radiosity methods has been that all surfaces exhibit perfect Lambertian diffuse reflections. Environments could not contain surfaces with specular properties. This paper demonstrates a method which removes this restriction by generalizing the radiosity formulation to include directional reflection properties, while still maintaining the advantages of accurate global illumination and view independence.

To correctly determine the illumination of an environment, one must simulate the spatial and spectral intensity distribution of light leaving each differential surface area (or point) within the environment. There are two requirements to predict this intensity distribution. First, the spatial and spectral distribution of the light arriving at the point must be specified. This "incident" light is a function of the point's geometric relationship to all other surfaces in the environment and the light leaving those surfaces in the direction of the point. Second, a reflection model must be specified which describes how light of any spectral content, which arrives from any arbitrary direction, is scattered from the surface. This may include transmission as well as reflection and is usually referred to as the bidirectional reflectance of a surface. Since the light arriving at any surface is a function of the light leaving all other surfaces, it is apparent that a simultaneous solution for the global illumination must be performed.

The solution would contain all of the information necessary to render an image of any part of the environment from any viewpoint. As with standard diffuse radiosity solutions, the complex interreflections within an environment are correctly modeled, yielding "color bleeding" effects, which occur when one surface acts to illuminate another surface, as well as soft shadows and penumbrae, which are associated with area light sources. The new procedure for non-diffuse environments inherently contains additional directional phenomena such as specular reflections, which follow the viewer as the eye position changes. This "reflection tracking" can be seen by moving your head from side to side while looking at a shiny surface. Secondary light sources, such as the light from a spot light bouncing off a mirror onto the floor, are also accounted for. This source of secondary illumination has been ignored by all previous image synthesis methods.

THEORETICAL CONCEPTS

The intensity of a point in a certain direction, or "directional intensity", is the sum of the total reflected intensity from the point in that direction and, if the surface is an emitter, the light intensity emitted from the point in that direction:

$$I_t(\Psi_o) = I_e(\Psi_o) + I_r(\Psi_o) \qquad (1)$$

Figure 1 shows the hemisphere of directions surrounding the normal to a point, or differential area, dA_1, through which and from which it receives and reflects light. The intensity emitted directly from dA_1 in outgoing direction o is simply:

$$I_e(\Psi_{o,1}) = \varepsilon_1(\Psi_{o,1}) \qquad (2)$$

The subscript 1 has been added to indicate that the emittance and reflected intensity terms emanate from surface 1.

Table 1
Definition of Terms

Ψ represents a vector direction to or from a surface.

$\Psi_{i,1}$ = incoming direction to surface 1
$\Psi_{i,2}$ = incoming direction to surface 2
$\Psi_{o,1}$ = incoming direction from surface 1
$\Psi_{o,2}$ = incoming direction from surface 2
θ_1 = angle away from the normal to surface 1
ε_1 = directional emission from surface 1
ρ_1'' = bidirectional refletance of surface 1
$d\omega_1$ = differential solid angle around surface 1
$E_{i,1}$ = energy incident to surface 1
$I_{r,1}$ = intensity reflected from surface 1
$I_{e,1}$ = intensity emitted from surface 1
$I_{t,1}$ = total directional intensity leaving surface 1
$I_{t,2}$ = total directional intensity leaving surface 2
$\Omega_{1,2}$ = total solid angle encompassing surface 2
 when viewed from surface 1

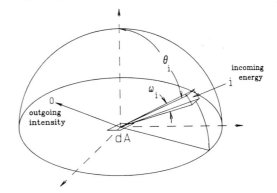

Hemisphere of Directions to a Differential Area
FIGURE 1

The spectral and spatial distribution of the reflected light is a function of the material properties of the surface from which it reflects. The light intensity reflected from a point can be found given a full description of the light arriving at that point and the surface's bidirectional reflectance. The bidirectional reflectance of a surface defines the relationship between the light energy arriving at some point and the intensity of light leaving that point:

$$\rho'' = \frac{I_r}{E_i} \qquad (3)$$

The total incoming energy is a function of the incoming intensity I_i, the solid angle $d\omega_i$ through which it arrives, and the projected differential area. The incoming energy per unit area from direction Ψ_i is thus:

$$E_i(\Psi_i) = I_i(\Psi_i)cos\theta_i d\omega_i \qquad (4)$$

The reflected intensity in direction Ψ_o from energy incident from direction Ψ_i is therefore:

$$I_r(\Psi_o, \Psi_i) = \rho''(\Psi_o, \Psi_i)I_i cos\theta_i d\omega_i \qquad (5)$$

Consider an environment consisting of only two surfaces, A_1 and A_2 (Figure 2). Intensity radiates from differential area dA_1 in direction o due to both emission and reflection. The reflected intensity in the outgoing direction results from energy arriving at dA_1 from A_2. Let $I_{i,1}$ be the incident intensity through solid angle $d\omega_1$. By integrating Equation 5 over the solid angle encompassing area A_2, the total intensity reflected in direction o due to the light energy arriving from A_2 is:

$$I_r(\Psi_{o,1}) = \int_{\Omega_{1,2}} \rho_1''(\Psi_{o,1}, \Psi_{i,1}) I_{i,1}(\Psi_{i,1}) cos\theta_{i,1} d\omega_{i,1} \quad (6)$$

In Equation 6, the incoming intensities, $I_{i,1}$, result from and are equal to the outgoing intensities, $I_{t,2}$, from A_2:

$$I_{i,1}(\Psi_{i,1}) = I_{t,2}(\Psi_{o,2}) \quad (7)$$

Substituting the outgoing intensities from A_2 for the incoming intensities to dA_1, Equation 6 becomes:

$$I_r(\Psi_{o,1}) = \int_{\Omega_{1,2}} \rho_1''(\Psi_{o,1}, \Psi_{i,1}) I_{t,2}(\Psi_{o,2}) cos\theta_{i,1} d\omega_{i,1} \quad (8)$$

Therefore, the directional intensity from surface dA_1 in direction o is the sum of the emitted intensity (Equation 2) and the reflected intensity (Equation 8):

$$I_{t,1}(\Psi_{o,1}) = \varepsilon_i(\Psi_{o,1}) + \int_{\Omega_{1,2}} \rho_1''(\Psi_{o,1}, \Psi_{i,1}) I_{i,1}(\Psi_{i,1}) cos\theta_{i,1} d\omega_{i,1}$$
$$(9)$$

Similar equations define intensities leaving dA_1 for all other directions within the hemisphere in the simple two-surface environment considered above. Each outgoing directional intensity from dA_1 is a function of the directional intensities leaving area A_2. In an equivalent manner, the directional intensities leaving each differential area of A_2 are a function of the directional intensities leaving area A_1. Thus, all of the outgoing directional intensities from both surfaces must be solved simultaneously.

In addition to the directional variation, intensities may vary continuously according to spatial position across a surface, or according to wavelength across the visible spectrum, since the spectral distributions and bidirectional reflectances are wavelength dependent. Thus, there are theoretically an infinite number of unknown intensity values to be simultaneously solved.

The problem is made tractable by discretizing the surfaces, the visible spectrum, and the hemisphere of incoming and outgoing directions. As with previous radiosity approaches, surfaces are divided into small discrete areas, or "patches", with the assumption that for each direction, the intensities arriving and leaving the patch are constant over the whole patch. The visible spectrum is likewise divided into a small number of wavelength bands. Each wavelength band is assumed to be independent from each other, allowing a separate solution for the light interation for each band.

The hemisphere above the patch is also discretized into a finite number of directions, or solid angles. Thus, for a particular patch, the

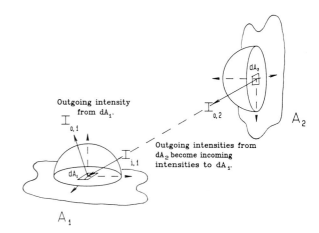

A simple environment of two surfaces, each with its own set of directions.

FIGURE 2

directional intensity in direction f then becomes its emission in direction f plus the sum of the reflected intensities from discrete directions d, which encompasses the hemisphere above the patch (Equation 10). d^{-1} represents the outgoing directions from patch 2 which point towards patch 1, and are thus in the opposite direction from d.

$$I_{t,1}(f) = \varepsilon_1(f) + \sum_{d=1}^{D} \rho_1''(f,d) I_{t,2}(d^{-1}) cos\theta_d \omega_d \quad (10)$$

Figure 3 shows the results of two incoming directions with several outgoing directions from a patch.

A set of simultaneous linear equations can now be formed, defining the unknown directional intensities for all directions, given the bidirectional reflectivities and emissions of each patch.

So far, the method has been illustrated by an environment consisting of only two surfaces. The form of the relationships remains the same for more complex environments except that light

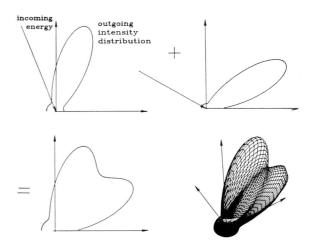

The outgoing distributions from all incoming energies are summed, resulting in an aggregate distribution.

FIGURE 3

arrives at a patch from many surfaces. An additional problem arises from the possible occlusion of one patch from another due to intervening surfaces. Thus, the directional intensities of each patch depend on the directional intensities of all other patches and the visibility between them. Let N be the number of patches in an environment and D be the number of directions on the hemisphere. The outgoing intensity of a patch i is given by:

$$I_{t,1}(f) = \varepsilon_i(f) + \sum_{j=1}^{N} \sum_{d=1}^{D} \rho_i''(f,d) I_{t,j}(d^{-1}) \cos\theta_d \omega_d HID(i,j,d)$$

(11)

where

$$HID(i,j,d) = \begin{cases} 1 & \text{Patch } i \text{ sees patch } j \text{ in direction } d \\ 0 & \text{Otherwise} \end{cases}$$

(12)

for environments with hidden surfaces.

At first glance, Equation 11 appears immensely more complicated than previous radiosity solutions, since intensities must be solved for each patch for each direction. However, certain properties of the matrix and the environment can be effectively exploited to obtain tractable solutions. For example, if in an environment, there are 1000 patches, and the hemisphere of directions is divided into 1000 small solid angles, then there are 1,000,000 unknowns and 1,000,000 squared or 10^{12} matrix coefficients. Fortunately, this matrix is VERY sparse. This can easily be seen since each patch receives energy from only 1000 directions. Thus, each row of the coefficient matrix has only 1000 non-zero HID terms, and the matrix is 99.9% sparse. In addition, if some surfaces are diffuse, each of their patches will exhibit a single constant directional intensity over all directions, and the 1000 directional equations can be reduced to a single linear equation. These facts are taken advantage of in the implementation, which is described in the following sections.

PROGRAM OVERVIEW

The directional radiosity analysis is comprised of a series of separate steps analogous to previous diffuse radiosity methods (Figure 4). First, the environment geometry and material properties such as the bidirectional reflectance must be specified. An additional initial requirement for radiosity analyses is that each surface must be subdivided into discrete surface patches.

The second step is to determine the geometric and visibility relationship between every pair of patches in the environment.

Given the set of equations, a simultaneous solution for the directional intensities of each patch is then performed. This global patch solution is then used along with the vertex to patch visibility relationships to determine the directional intensity distribution at each vertex grid point on every surface. The resulting full description of the intensity leaving each surface in all directions provides the means to render an image of the environment from any given viewpoint.

Given an eye position and viewing direction, the intensities pointing back to the eye from each vertex are used to render an image. Successive images of the environment can be rendered from different viewpoints.

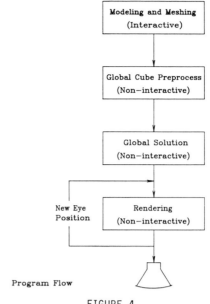

FIGURE 4

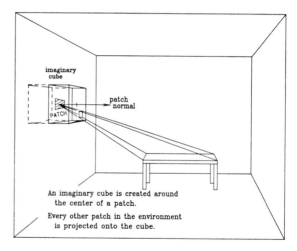

An imaginary cube is created around the center of a patch.

Every other patch in the environment is projected onto the cube.

FIGURE 5

THE GLOBAL CUBE

The light leaving a patch depends on the light arriving at it and the direction(s) from which it arrives. This impinging light is the result of light leaving the other patches in the environment, and thus a determination must be made of which patches are visible from each patch. Each patch has a view of its environment across the hemisphere of directions surrounding its normal. This continuum of directions is approximated by finding the visible patches in a finite number of discrete solid angles which cumulatively are equivalent to the hemisphere.

The hemisphere can be replaced by the upper half of a cube, or "hemi-cube" (Figure 5), creating five separate 90 degree viewing frustums through which to project the environment [5].

Each surface of the cube becomes an imaginary screen which can be divided into small square cells. Each of these cells defines a small solid angle of view from the patch at the center of the cube. Depth buffer algorithms are performed for each frustum to determine the patch "seen" through each cell. To obtain an accurate view of the environment from a patch, a series of sample points within the patch from which to view the environment are selected. A grid is established on the patch defining a series of sub-patches or "elements". A view is taken from each grid vertex and may vary across the grid. The final view of the environment from a patch is taken as a weighted average of the views from the individual grid vertices. This is analogous to the "substructuring" described in [6].

The hemi-cube can be oriented so that the patch normal always coincides with the center of the hemi-cube's top face. This allows for the same set of small solid angles to be located in the same directions relative to each patch. However, since the orientations are always in the patch's local coordinate system, there is no single directional relationship between hemi-cubes (Figure 6). In previous diffuse radiosity methods, since each patch was defined to have a single intensity equal in all directions, the directional relationship was unimportant.

When the intensities are allowed to vary directionally, it is important to equate the incoming directions of the receiving patch with the reciprocal outgoing directions from the sending patches. Rather than reorienting a hemi-cube for each patch, a full cube surrounding each vertex is maintained, oriented along the global axes (Figure 7). The advantage lies in the fact that if patch i sees patch j through the cell oriented in the X,Y,Z direction, then the reciprocal cell from patch j is simply in the -X,-Y,-Z direction. The cube is stored as a vector of visible patch identification numbers. If the faces of the cube are oriented as in Figure 8a and the vector is ordered as in Figure 8b, then the reciprocal global cube locations may be trivially calculated. For a global cube with D discrete directions, the cell with the reciprocal direction from a cell with index c ($0 <= C <= D-1$) will simply have index $D - c - 1$.

The projection of the environment on a "global cube" surrounding a vertex solves the hidden surface problem providing the HID terms in equation 11. The θ terms are found by the dot product of the patch normal and the global orientation of the cell. A small solid angle, ω, is associated with each cell, providing the necessary information to simultaneously solve for the directional radiosities of each patch.

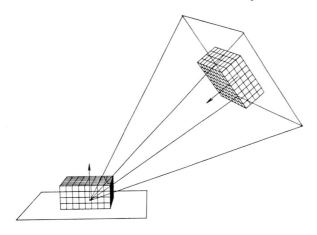

Each hemi—cube has its own local orientation.

FIGURE 6

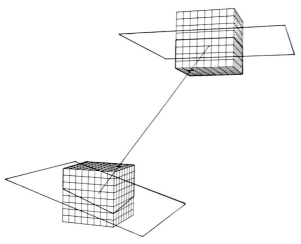

Each global cube is placed in a global orientation.

FIGURE 7

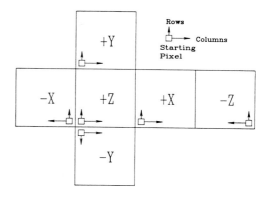

The cells within the faces of the global cube are ordered so that the reciprocal global cube locations may be trivially calculated.

(a)

Vector of cube locations ⟶					
+X	+Y	+Z	-Z	-Y	-X

The ordering within each face is in row major order. The rows and columns are determined by the diagram above.

(b)

FIGURE 8

BIDIRECTIONAL REFLECTANCE

Until now, the actual bidirectional reflectance, which is derived from a model describing how light scatters from a surface, has not been specified. The choice of a specific reflection model is independent of the methods introduced in this paper. However, in this context there are two requirements a reflection model must satisfy. The first requirement is that the model must exhibit reciprocity. That is, the fraction of outgoing intensity to incoming energy for any pair of directions must be the same if the incoming and outgoing directions are reversed.

In other words:

$$\rho''(\Psi_r, \Psi_i) = \rho''(\Psi_i, \Psi_r) \qquad (13)$$

The second requirement is that energy must be conserved. The total amount of incident energy to a patch must be greater than or equal to the total amount of reflected energy from the patch. A patch cannot reflect more energy than it receives. Thus,

$$E_i \geq \int_{\Omega_h} E_r = \int_{\Omega_h} I_r \cos\theta d\omega \qquad \Omega_h = \text{hemisphere} \quad (14)$$

Two different bidirectional reflectance relationships were tested. One relationship is a mirror-like reflection, in which the incoming intensity leaves in the mirror direction tempered only by a reflectance between 0 and 1. The other relationship is based on work done by Phong [8]. The "Phong-like" bidirectional reflectance used is:

$$\rho'' = \frac{k_d}{S_d} + \left[\frac{k_s}{S_s}\right] \cos^n\phi \qquad (15)$$

where k_d = the fraction of energy diffusely reflected, and k_s = the fraction of energy specularly reflected: $k_d + k_s \leq 1$. ϕ is the angle between the mirror direction and the reflection direction, r, and S_d and S_s are constant factors which must be included to conserve energy:

$$S_d = \int_{\Omega_h} d\omega = \pi \quad \text{and} \quad S_s = \int_{\Omega_h} \cos^{(n+1)}\phi d\omega \quad (16)$$

GLOBAL SOLUTION

A simultaneous solution to the matrix of Equations 11 is required to find all of the directional radiosities for all of the surfaces of an environment. The matrix to be solved is too large to be solved using direct solution methods. However, the Gauss-Siedel iterative technique, which was found effective for previous radiosity methods is well suited for this problem [9]. The iteration method allows the matrix coefficients to be computed as they are needed. The solution converges in a small number of iterations since the matrix is diagonally dominant.

An initial estimate for the radiosity solution is set equal to the emissions of the light sources with all other patch radiosities initially zero. The global cube analysis provides the patches and directions from those patches which illuminate a particular patch. Based on this information and the current solution estimate, a global cube of incoming intensities to a patch

through all directions is assembled. From Equation 11, each outgoing intensity can be computed from these incoming intensities and the given bidirectional reflectance of the patch. These new directional patch radiosities are used in the current solution estimate for subsequent patches. Every patch is solved in turn, and the whole process iterates until the solution converges.

After every iteration step, each patch receives a more accurate set of incoming intensities, and therefore, reflects a more accurate set of outgoing intensities (Figure 9). Every directional intensity value is compared with the same directional intensity value from the previous iteration. If no pair of values differ by more than a prespecified margin, the solution process is said to have converged, and no further iterations are required. In pseudo-code, the procedure is as follows:

```
/* Initial estimate for directional intensities */
    FOR each direction d and patch p DO
        Int[p][d] = Emiss[p][d]
    END
    FOR each iteration DO
        FOR each patch p DO
        /* Set each new intensity to be its emission */
            FOR each direction d DO
                Newint[p][d] = Emiss[p][d]
            END
        /* Take energy from incoming directions in and */
        /* distribute it to all outgoing directions out */
            FOR each direction in DO
            /* Calculate energy from in */
                Energy[in] = Int[Cube[p][in]][D-in-1] cosθω[in]
                For each direction out DO
                    Newint[p][out] += ρ''(p, in, out)Energy[in]
                END
            END
        /* Replace old intensities with new and test */
        /* for convergence */
            FOR each direction d DO
                Compare Int[p][d] with Newint[p][d]
                Int[p][d] = Newint[p][d]
            END
        END
    END
```

The number of iterations required for convergence of the patch solution depends on the order in which patch equations are solved since the incoming intensities to a patch result from the outgoing intensities of previously solved patches. It thus makes sense to solve for the patches in roughly the same order that light is propagated through the environment (Figure 10). Thus, the emitters are solved first, because they are the originators of energy for the solution; next, the patches that see the emitters are solved, and thus become secondary emitters; next, those that see the secondary emitters; etc. The results of the global cube provide the visible surfaces seen from each surface. A list is compiled of the secondary light sources by examining the global cubes of the primary emitters. Analogously, a list of tertiary light sources is compiled from the global cubes of the secondary sources, etc.

The patch solution provides the intensity of light leaving each patch in each direction. At this point, an analogous solution must be found for each grid vertex, as it is the vertex directional intensities that will be used during the rendering process. Each grid vertex has an associated global cube of visible patches, from the original global cube analysis. A cube of directional intensities for each grid vertex is filled by back substitution of the previously solved patch intensities. The outgoing intensities are calculated from the incoming intensities and the bidirectional reflectance of the vertex's surface.

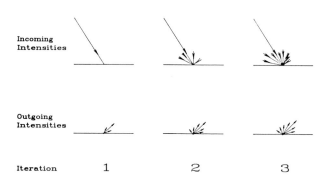

After each iteration, each patch receives a more accurate set of incoming intensities, and therefore, reflects a more accurate set of outgoing intensities.

FIGURE 9

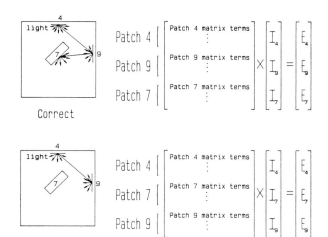

To decrease the number of iterations, solve for the patches in roughly the same order that light is propogated through the environment.

FIGURE 10

RENDERING

At this point, a view independent radiosity solution has been calculated. The final rendering stage is simply a post process to display intensities pointing in the direction of the eye. To render an image, an eye position and viewing direction are specified which establishes the directions from each vertex back to the eye. The particular intensities pointing to the eye are extracted from the global cubes of directional intensities (Figure 11). These are obtained by bilinearly interpolating between the nearest vertex cube directional intensities. This results in a single intensity value for each grid vertex in the environment from that viewpoint. At this point the rendering process becomes identical to the process described in [6], where the pixel intensities are bilinearly interpolated from the vertex intensities. Additional views of the environment are rendered from the same global radiosity solution simply by specifying a new view point.

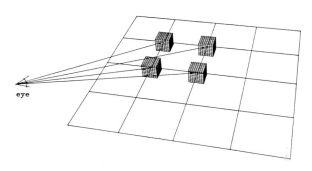

The particular intensities pointing to the eye are extracted from the global cubes of directional intensities.

FIGURE 11

RESULTS

The following images were rendered from two global solutions of the same environment. Each set of figures contains a series of views (a) illustrating the view independence of the solution. Notice the reflections in the floor tracking the eye as the viewer position is changed. The two larger images (b and c) in each set are enlargements from the series above them. The primary difference between the two sets of images is the bidirectional reflectance models. The algorithms outlined in this paper are independent of any particular reflectance model. The solution for the images in Figure 12 used the Phong-like reflectance model. For Figure 13, the solution used the simpler mirror-like bidirectional reflectance.

The environmental modeling and meshing for the images was performed using the testbed image synthesis system at Cornell's Program of Computer Graphics. The system was written in C under a VMS operating system and ran on a VAX 11/780. An Evans and Sutherland picture system was used for the modeling and meshing, a Floating Point Systems FPS264 attached to a VAX 11/750 was used for the solution process, and the pictures were displayed using a Rastertek 1280x1024x24 bits frame buffer.

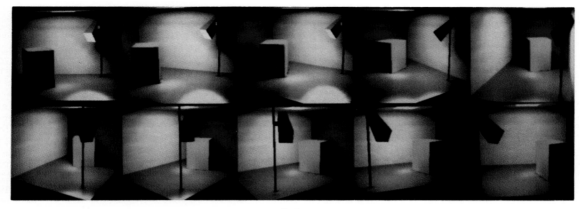

(a)

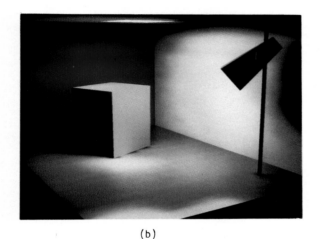

(b)

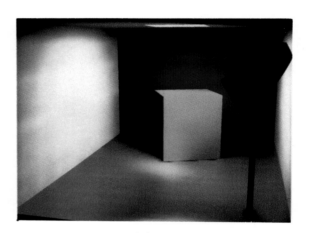

(c)

PHONG-LIKE REFLECTION

			PROCESS	CPUTIME (Hrs)
Number of Specular Patches	:	64		
Number of Diffuse Patches	:	93		
Number of Specular Vertices	:	1089		
Number of Diffuse Vertices	:	1400	Visible Surfaces	8
Number of Cube Directions	:	24576	Solution	192
Number of Wavelengths	:	4	Render	1

FIGURE 12

As can be seen from the statistics listed below each set of images, the computation time, particularly for the solution process, is non-trivial. The time required for the solution process is a function of the number of cube directions and the number of patches and vertices, more specifically, the number of specular patches and vertices. The amount of time is significantly reduced by using the simpler mirror-like reflection model in Figure 13 since incoming energy is not scattered in all directions.

An artifact due to the nature of the algorithm becomes visible when the reflection becomes more mirror-like. Recall that the rendering is based on the vertex solution which is in turn based on the patch solution. Thus, the discrete patches become visible in the reflection. This resulted in the increased number of diffuse patches in Figure 13.

CONCLUSION

A general radiosity method which accounts for all interreflections from both diffuse and non-diffuse surfaces has been introduced. The procedure computes an intensity distribution for every surface in an environment, consisting of directional intensities for a number of discrete directions. The rendering process then becomes one of only looking up the intensities that point back to the eye and displaying them.

This method makes it possible to precalculate the energy leaving specular surfaces regardless of the viewing direction. Since this global solution is view independent, successive views of the same environment can be calculated using the same directional intensity information, and the phenomenon of reflection tracking can be observed.

The addition of specular surfaces to the radiosity method is significant, since radiosity methods need no longer be limited to environments

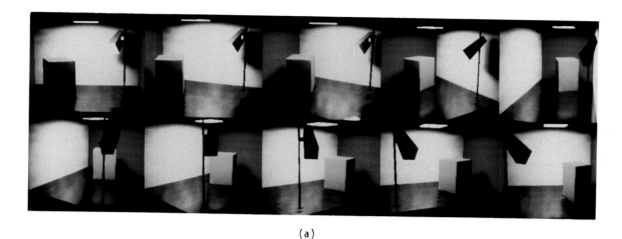

(a)

(b)

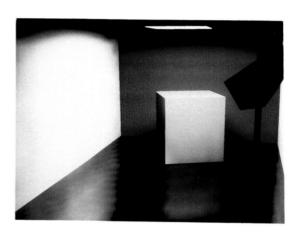

(c)

MIRROR-LIKE REFLECTION

		PROCESS	CPU TIME (Hrs)
Number of Specular Patches	: 64		
Number of Diffuse Patches	: 237		
Number of Specular Vertices:	1089		
Number of Diffuse Vertices	: 1400	Visible Surfaces	7
Number of Cube Directions	: 15000	Solution	25
Number of Wavelengths	: 4	Render	1

FIGURE 13

containing only purely diffuse surfaces. The methodology is independent of a particular reflection model, thus any reflection model which relates incoming energy from one direction to outgoing intensity in another direction can be used. The only restriction placed on the model is that it must conform to the physical laws of reciprocity and the conservation of energy as discussed in the paper.

A few problems exist that must be dealt with in the future. Errors in approximation occur because environments have been discretized. Discretizing the number of directions on the global cube results in misrepresenting the incoming energy because of aliasing on the faces of the global cube. Reflections from a highly reflective surface may appear blurred due to discretizing the surface, as well as interpolating between outgoing intensities in rendering.

Future work should include the addition of non-planar and textured surfaces, as well as transparent and translucent surfaces. The framework of the method is general enough to accomodate these additions by simply using different reflection functions. Although this method currently requires very large computational resources for complex environments due to the volume of information that must be processed, this research was undertaken to provide a scientific basis for modeling complex interreflections within an environment. In the future, as storage and computational power increases, global solutions of more complex environments will be within reach.

ACKNOWLEDGMENTS
The authors would like to thank all those who helped in the preparation of the article. Thanks go to Professor Kenneth Torrance, Holly Rushmeier, and Kevin Koestner for their help in laying the theoretical groundwork. Thanks also go to Dan Baum, Janet Brown-Aist, and Emil Ghinger for their help in coding and preparation of the article. This research was conducted at the Cornell University Program of Computer Graphics, under a grant from the National Science Foundation #DCR-8203979. The VAX computers used were made possible by a large grant from the Digital Equipment Corporation and use of the Floating Point Systems Advanced Processor through Cornell University's Center for Theory and Simulation in Science and Engineering.

REFERENCES

[1] Whitted, Turner, "An Improved Illumination Model for Shaded Display," Communications of the ACM, Vol. 23, No. 6, June 1980, pp. 343-349.

[2] Siegel, Robert and John R. Howell, Thermal Radiation Heat Transfer, Hemisphere Publishing Corp., Washington DC., 1981.

[3] Sparrow, E. M. and R. D. Cess, Radiation Heat Transfer, Hemisphere Publishing Corp., Washington DC., 1978.

[4] Goral, Cindy M., Kenneth E. Torrance, Donald P. Greenberg, Bennet Battaile, "Modeling the Interaction of Light Between Diffuse Surfaces," ACM Computer Graphics (Proceedings 1984), pp. 213-222.

[5] Cohen, Michael F. and Donald P. Greenberg, "A Radiosity Solution for Complex Environments," ACM Computer Graphics (Proceedings 1985), pp. 31-40.

[6] Cohen, Michael F., Donald P. Greenberg, David S. Immel, Philip J. Brock, "An Efficient Radiosity Approach for Realistic Image Synthesis," IEEE Computer Graphics and Applications, March 1986.

[7] Nishita, Tomoyuki, and Eihachiro Nakamae, "Continuous Tone Representation of Three-Dimensional Objects Taking Account of Shadows and Interreflection," ACM Computer Graphics (Proceedings 1985), pp. 22-30.

[8] Phong, Bui Tuong, Illumination for Computer Generated Images, Ph.D. Dissertation, University of Utah, 1973.

[9] Hornbeck, Robert W., Numerical Methods, Quantum Publishers, New York, NY, 1974, pp. 101-106.

THE RENDERING EQUATION

James T. Kajiya
California Institute of Technology
Pasadena, Ca. 91125

ABSTRACT.   We present an integral equation which generalizes a variety of known rendering algorithms. In the course of discussing a monte carlo solution we also present a new form of variance reduction, called Hierarchical sampling and give a number of elaborations shows that it may be an efficient new technique for a wide variety of monte carlo procedures. The resulting rendering algorithm extends the range of optical phenomena which can be effectively simulated.

KEYWORDS: computer graphics, raster graphics, ray tracing, radiosity, monte carlo, distributed ray tracing, variance reduction.

CR CATEGORIES: I.3.3, I.3.5, I.3.7

1. The rendering equation

The technique we present subsumes a wide variety of rendering algorithms and provides a unified context for viewing them as more or less accurate approximations to the solution of a single equation. That this should be so is not surprising once it is realized that all rendering methods attempt to model the same physical phenomenon, that of light scattering off various types of surfaces.

We mention that the idea behind the rendering equation is hardly new. A description of the phenomenon simulated by this equation has been well studied in the radiative heat transfer literature for years [Siegel and Howell 1981]. However, the form in which we present this equation is well suited for computer graphics, and we believe that this form has not appeared before.

The rendering equation is

$$I(x, x') = g(x, x') \left[\epsilon(x, x') + \int_S \rho(x, x', x'') I(x', x'') dx'' \right]. \quad (1)$$

where:
$I(x, x')$ is the related to the intensity of light passing from point x' to point x
$g(x, x')$ is a "geometry" term
$\epsilon(x, x')$ is related to the intensity of emitted light from x' to x
$\rho(x, x' x'')$ is related to the intensity of light scattered from x'' to x by a patch of surface at x'

© 1986   ACM 0-89791-196-2/86/008/0143 $00.75

The equation is very much in the spirit of the radiosity equation, simply balancing the energy flows from one point of a surface to another. The equation states that the transport intensity of light from one surface point to another is simply the sum of the emitted light and the total light intensity which is scattered toward x from all other surface points. Equation (1) differs from the radiosity equation of course because, unlike the latter, no assumptions are made about reflectance characteristics of the surfaces involved.

Each of the quantities in the equation are new quantities which we call *unoccluded multipoint transport* quantities. In section 2 we define each of these quantities and relate them to the more conventional quantities encountered in radiometry.

The integral is taken over $S = \bigcup S_i$, the union of all surfaces. Thus the points x, x', and x'' range over all the surfaces of all the objects in the scene. We also include a global background surface S_0, which is a hemisphere large enough to act as an enclosure for the entire scene. Note that the inclusion of a enclosure surface ensures that the total positive hemisphere for reflection and total negative hemisphere for transmission are accounted for.

As an approximation to Maxwell's equation for electromagneticseq. (1) does not attempt to model all interesting optical phenomena. It is essentially a geometrical optics approximation. We only model time averaged transport intensity, thus no account is taken of phase in this equation—ruling out any treatment of diffraction. We have also assumed that the media between surfaces is of homogeneous refractive index and does not itself participate in the scattering light. The latter two cases can be handled by a pair of generalizations of eq. (1). In the first case, simply by letting $g(x, x')$ take into account the eikonal handles media with nonhomogenous refractive index. For participating propagation media, a integro-differential equation is necessary. Extensions are again well known, see [Chandrasekar 1950], and for use in a computer graphics application [Kajiya and von Herzen 1984]. Elegant ways of viewing the eikonal equation have been available for at least a century with Hamilton-Jacobi theory [Goldstein 1950]. Treatments of participatory media and of phase and diffraction can be handled with path integral techniques. For a treatment of such generalizations concerned with various physical phenomena see [Feynman and Hibbs 1965]. Finally, no wavelength or polarization dependence is mentioned in eq. (1). Inclusion of wavelength and polarization is straightforward and to be understood.

2. Discussion of transport quantities

We discuss each of the quantities and terms of equation (1). This equation describes the intensity of photon transport for a simplified model. $I(x, x')$ measures the energy of radiation passing from point x' to point x. We shall name $I(x, x')$ the *unoccluded two point transport intensity* from x' to x, or more compactly the *transport intensity*. The transport intensity $I(x, x')$ is the energy of radiation per unit time per unit area of source dx' per unit area dx of target.

$$dE = I(x, x') \, dt \, dx \, dx'. \tag{2}$$

The units of I are joule/m^{4}sec,

The term $g(x, x')$ is a geometry term. This term encodes the occlusion of surface points by other surface points. If in the scene, x' and x are not in fact mutually visible then the geometry term is 0. On the other hand if they are visible from each other then the term is $1/r^2$ where r is the distance from x' to x. Note that an occluding perfectly transparent surface can make $g(x, x')$ to be equal 0. For, in fact, the transparent surface, intercepts the radiation and reradiates it on the other side.

The emittance term, $\epsilon(x, x')$ measures the energy emitted by a surface at point x' reaching a point x. We shall call it the *unoccluded two point transport emittance* from x' to x. It gives the energy per unit time per unit area of source and per unit area of target. That is,

$$dE = \frac{1}{r^2} \epsilon(x, x') dt \, dx \, dx'. \tag{3}$$

The units of $\epsilon(x, x')$ are joule/m^{2}sec,

Finally the scattering term $\rho(x, x', x'')$ is the intensity of energy scattered by a surface element at x' orginating from a surface element at x'' and terminating at a surface element at x. We shall call it the *unoccluded three point transport reflectance* from x'' to x through x'.[†] The term ρ is a dimensionless quantity. So the energy reaching x is given by

$$dE = \frac{1}{r^2} \rho(x, x', x'') I(x', x'') \, dt \, dx \, dx' \, dx'' \tag{4}$$

We now relate the transport quantities to more conventional radiometric quantites. We shall do this by equating the energy transported by each quantity for the given geometric configuration.

Ordinary radiometric intensity is defined as energy per unit time per unit of projected area of source per unit of solid angle

$$dE = i(\theta', \phi') d\omega \, dx'_p \, dt. \tag{5}$$

To relate these quantities we look at the imaging geometry in figure 1.

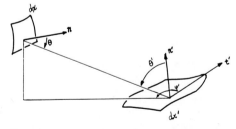

Figure 1. Two point imaging geometry. A frame is attached to each surface element giving a normal, tangent, and binormal vector.

From the figure we obtain

$$\begin{aligned}
r &= \|x - x'\| \\
dx'_p &= dx' \cos \theta \\
\cos \theta &= \frac{1}{r} \langle \mathbf{n}, x - x' \rangle \\
\cos \theta' &= \frac{1}{r} \langle \mathbf{n}', x - x' \rangle \\
\cos \phi' &= \frac{1}{r} \langle \mathbf{t}', x - x' \rangle
\end{aligned} \tag{6}$$

where:

[†] This term also covers the transmittance of light through surfaces as well. To simplify the ensuing discussion we will ignore transmission scattering altogether.

$\mathbf{n}$ is the normal to surface element dx
$\mathbf{n}'$ is the normal to surface element dx'
$\mathbf{t}'$ is the tangent vector to the element dx'
r is the distance from x' to x

The solid angle subtended by a surface element dx is the fractional area of a sphere of radius r taken up by the projected area dx_p of dx.

$$d\omega = \frac{dx_p}{r^2} = \frac{1}{r^2} \cos \theta \, dx. \tag{7}$$

Thus substituting eq. (7) in eq. (5) we get

$$dE = i(\theta', \phi') \frac{1}{r^2} \cos \theta \cos \theta' dt \, dx \, dx'. \tag{8}$$

Equating eq. (2) and eq. (5) gives the relationship between transport intensity and ordinary intensity

$$I(x, x') = i(\theta', \phi') \frac{1}{r^2} \cos \theta \cos \theta'. \tag{9}$$

The relation between transport emittance and ordinaryemittance is derived likewise. Assuming that there are no occluding surfaces, the energy transmitted by emission from surface element dx' to dx is given by eq. (3). Using the definition of ordinary emittance we can follow exactly the same procedure as above to obtain

$$\epsilon(x, x') = \epsilon(\theta', \phi') \cos \theta \cos \theta' \tag{10}$$

Finally, we relate the transport reflectance to the ordinary radiometric total bidirectional reflectance function $\rho(\theta', \phi', \psi', \sigma')$ from the definition

$$i(\theta', \phi') = \rho(\theta', \phi', \psi', \sigma') i(\psi', \sigma') d\omega'' \cos \psi' \tag{11}.$$

Where the imaging geometry appears in figure 2.

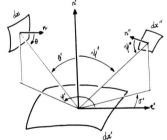

Figure 2. Three point imaging geometry.

From the diagram we obtain in addition to equations (6) and (7), the following

$$\begin{aligned}
r'' &= \|x' - x''\| \\
dx''_p &= dx'' \cos \psi'' \\
\cos \psi' &= \frac{1}{r''} \langle \mathbf{n}', x' - x'' \rangle \\
\cos \psi'' &= \frac{1}{r''} \langle \mathbf{n}'', x' - x'' \rangle \\
\cos \sigma' &= \frac{1}{r''} \langle \mathbf{t}', x' - x'' \rangle \\
d\omega'' &= \frac{dx''_p}{r''^2} = \frac{1}{r''^2} \cos \psi'' dx''
\end{aligned} \tag{12}$$

where:

$\mathbf{n}''$ is the normal to surface element dx''
r'' is the distance from x'' to x'
$d\omega''$ is the solid angle subtended by surface element dx''

Combining eqs.(2),(8),(9),(11), and (12) we obtain the relationship between the unoccluded three point transport reflectance and the ordinary total bidirectional reflectance

$$\rho(x, x', x'') = \rho(\theta', \phi', \psi', \sigma') \cos\theta \cos\theta' \qquad (13)$$

3. Methods for approximate solution

In this section we shall review approximations to the solution of the rendering equation. It appears that a wide variety of rendering algorithms can be viewed in a unified context provided by this equation. During the course of this discussion, many other untried approximations may occur to the reader. We welcome additional work on this area. This territory remains largely unexplored, since the bulk of the present effort has concentrated solely on the solution methods to be presented below.

Neumann series

One method of solving integral equations like eq.(1) comes from a well known formal manipulation, see [Courant and Hilbert 1953]. We rewrite it as:

$$I = g\epsilon + gMI$$

where M is the linear operator given by the integral in eq.(1). Now if we rewrite this equation as

$$(1 - gM)I = g\epsilon$$

where 1 is the identity operator, then we can formally invert the equation by

$$\begin{aligned} I &= (1 - gM)^{-1} g\epsilon \\ &= g\epsilon + gMg\epsilon + gMgMg\epsilon + g(Mg)^3\epsilon \cdots \end{aligned} \qquad (2)$$

A condition for the convergence of the infinite series is that the spectral radius of the operator M be less than one. (Which is met in the case of interest to us). A physical interpretation of the Neumann expansion is appealing. It gives the final intensity of radiation transfer between points x and x' as the sum of a direct term, a once scattered term, a twice scattered term, etc.

The Utah approximation

For lack of a better name, we shall call the classical method for rendering shaded surfaces the Utah approximation. In this approximation we approximate I with the two term sum:

$$I = g\epsilon + gM\epsilon_0$$

Thus the Utah approximation ignores all scattering except for the first. The geometry term is by far the most difficult to compute. The Utah approximation computes the g term only for the final scattering into the eye. This is, of course, the classical hidden surface problem studied by many early researchers at the University of Utah. Note that in the second term, the operator M does not operate on $g\epsilon$ but rather directly on ϵ_0. Thus this approximation ignores visibilty from emitting surfaces: it ignores shadows. The ϵ_0 term is meant to signify that only point radiators are allowed. No extended lighting surfaces were allowed. This simplification reduces the operator M to a small sum over light sources rather than an integration over x''.

Since that time many extensions have appeared, most notably shadow algorithms and extended light sources.

The Ray Tracing approximation

Whitted [1980], proposed a different approximation:

$$I = g\epsilon + gM_0 g\epsilon_0 + gM_0 gM_0 g\epsilon_0 + \cdots$$

In this famous approximation, M_0 is a scattering model which is the sum of two delta functions a cosine term. The two delta functions of course represent the reflection and refraction of his lighting model. The cosine term represents the diffuse component. Note that he gives $g\epsilon_0$: shadows but with point radiators. Whitted's ambient term translates directly to the ϵ term. Again the operator M can be approximated by a small sum.

The distributed ray tracing approximation

In 1984, Cook [Cook et al 1984], introduced distributed ray tracing. This approximation uses an extension of the three component Whitted model resulting in a more accurate scattering model. This extension necessitated the evaluation of an integral in computing the operator M. In this model M is approximated by a distribution around the reflection and refraction delta functions. The innovation that made this possible was the use of monte carlo like techniques for the evaluation. As is well known, the ability to evaluate integrals has widely extended the range of optical phenomena captured by this technique. A proper treatment of the ambient term, however, remained elusive to distributed ray tracing.

The radiosity approximation

In 1984, Goral, Torrance, and Greenburg [Goral et. al. 1984, Cohen and Greenburg 1985, Nishita and Nakamae 1985] introduced radiosity to the computer graphics world. This is a major new rendering technique which handles the energy balance equations for perfectly diffuse surfaces. That is, surfaces which have no angular dependence on the bidirectional reflectance function

$$\rho(\theta', \phi', \psi', \sigma') = \rho_0. \qquad (14)$$

The *radiosity* $B(x')$ of a surface element dx' is the energy flux over the total visible hemisphere. It is the energy per unit time per unit (unprojected) area, measured in watts per meter squared. It is defined by

$$\begin{aligned} dB(x') &= dx' \int_{hemi} i(\theta', \phi') \cos\theta' d\omega \\ &= dx' \int_{hemi} \frac{I(x, x')r^2}{\cos\theta} d\omega \\ &= dx' \int_S I(x, x')dx \end{aligned} \qquad (15)$$

Thus to calculate hemispherical quantities we may simply integrate over all the surfaces in the scene. So from eq.(1) and (15) we obtain

$$dB(x') = dx' \int \Big\{ g(x, x')\epsilon(x, x') \\ + g(x, x') \int \rho(x, x', x'')I(x', x'')dx'' \Big\} dx \qquad (16)$$

If there is an occlusion between x and x' then the contribution of the emmitance term is zero. Otherwise the contribution is

$$\begin{aligned} dB_e(x') &= dx' \int \frac{\epsilon(x, x')}{r^2} dx \\ &= dx' \int \epsilon(\theta', \phi') \cos\theta' \frac{\cos\theta dx}{r^2} \\ &= dx' \int \epsilon(\theta', \phi') \cos\theta' d\omega \\ &= dx' \pi \epsilon_0 \end{aligned} \qquad (17)$$

Where ϵ_0 is the hemispherical emittance of the surface element dx'.

Similarly for the reflectance term, the contribution to radiosity is again zero for an occluded surface. Otherwise we get

$$
\begin{aligned}
dB_r(x') &= dx' \int \frac{1}{r^2} \int \rho(x,x',x'') I(x',x'') dx'' dx \\
&= dx' \int \frac{1}{r^2} \rho(\theta',\phi',\psi',\sigma') \cos\theta \cos\theta' dx \\
&\quad \times \int I(x',x'') dx'' \qquad (18) \\
&= dx' \rho_0 \int \cos\theta \, d\omega \int I(x',x'') dx'' \\
&= dx' \rho_0 \pi H(x')
\end{aligned}
$$

Where H is the hemispherical incident energy per unit time and unit area. In this derivation we switched the order of integration and used identities (13),(12), and (14). Now using equations (17) and (18) in (16) we see that the rendering equation becomes

$$ dB(x') = \pi[\epsilon_0 + \rho_0 H(x')] dx' \qquad (19) $$

Which is equation (4) in Goral et. al. [1984].

Calculating the total integrated intensty H is essential to calculate the final F_{ij} matrix in radiosity. This requires a visibility calculation which may be quite expensive. Since the matrix equation is solved by a number of relaxation steps, is essentially equivalent to summing the first few terms of the Neumann series: propagating the emitters across four or so scatterers. To use relaxation requires that the full matrix be calculated. Relaxation also gives all the intensities at all the surfaces in the scene. While in certain cases this may be an advantage, it is suggested that the monte carlo method outlined below may be quite superior.

4. Markov chains for solving integral equations

The use of Markov chains is perhaps the most popular numerical method for for solving integral equations. It is used in fields as diverse as queuing theory and neutron transport. In fact, the use of monte carlo Markov chain methods in radiative heat transfer has been in use for quite some time, [Siegel and Howell 1981]. In the heat transfer approach, a packet of radiation of specified wavelength is emitted, reflected, and absorbed from a configuration of surfaces in some enclosure. Counting the number of packets absorbed by each surface after a run gives an estimate of the geometric factors whose exact calculation would pose an intractible problem. This is similar to ray tracing a scene from the light sources to the eye. Rather than follow these methods, we will choose to solve eq.(1) more directly going back to an early monte carlo method first put forth by von Neumann and Ulam [Rubenstein 1981].

Finite dimensional version

By way of introduction we first present the method in a finite dimensional context. This simplifies the notation and makes obvious the essential ideas involved. Again we note that this example method may possibly hold many advantages over the currently used relaxation schemes popular in radiosity: intensities at only visible points need be computed, and calculation of the full radiosity matrix may be exchanged for a very much smaller set of selected matrix elements.

Suppose we wish to solve the vector equation:

$$ x = a + Mx $$

where x and a are n-dimensional vectors, x an unknown, and $M = (m_{ij})$ is an $n \times n$ matrix.

Now from a Neumann expansion we see that for M a matrix with

eigenvalues lying within the unit circle, the solution x is given by

$$ x = a + \sum_{k=1}^{\infty} M^k a $$

The method evaluates this sum by averaging over paths through the matrix multiplies. That is, it follows a path through rows and columns that comprises an iterated matrix product. For each point in the path we get a row or column which can be indexed by an integer from 1 to n.

Construct a probability space Ω where each point ω is a path visiting one of n points at each discrete time, viz. $\omega = (n_0, n_1, \ldots, n_k)$ where each n_i is an integer from 1 to n. The length $k = l(\omega)$ of the path ω is finite but otherwise arbitrary and corresponds to an entry in the kth matrix power. Each path is assigned a probability $p(\omega)$.

If we wish to calculate the value of one coordinate of x, say x_1, then we calculate the quantity

$$ \hat{x}_1 = \left(\prod_{i=0}^{l(\omega)} m_{n_{i-1} n_i} \right) a_{n_{l(\omega)}} \frac{1}{p(\omega)} $$

averaged over all paths $\omega \in \Omega$. Simply taking expected values verifies that this quantity gives the desired quantity.

The probability space of paths is most easily constructed using Markov chains. A (stationary) discrete Markov chain consists of a set of states X, and an assignment of a *transition probability* $p(x,x')$ from one state $x' \in X$ to another $x \in X$, and an initial probability density of states $p(x)$. Some subset of states may be designated as *absorbing* in that no transitions out of an absorbing state are permitted.

The probability of a path generated by a Markov chain is simply the the product of the initial state and all the transition probabilities until an absorbing state is reached. So for a path

$$ \omega = (x_0, x_1, \ldots, x_{l(\omega)}) $$

we have the probability is

$$ p(\omega) = p(x_{l(\omega)}, x_{l(\omega)-1}) \cdots p(x_2, x_1) \cdot p(x_1, x_0) \cdot p(x_0) $$

In the finite dimensional case we let the state set of the Markov chain be the set of indices into the vector or matrix, $X = \{1, \ldots, n\}$. Note that although we are allowed wide lattitude in choosing the transition probabilities, they must be positive for the corresponding nonzero entries in the matrix. In the limit our estimate of the solution is quite independent of the probability distribution of the paths. But the rate of convergence to the limit is highly dependent on the manner of choosing the transition probabilities. Section 5 gives a set of new techniques for choosing the transition probabilities.

Infinite dimensional solution

Extending the monte carlo Markov chain method to infinite dimensional equations is straightforward. For the equation at hand, we note that it is a variant of a Fredholm equation of the second kind. The passivity of surfaces in reflecting and transmitting radiation assures the convergence of the Neumann series. We simply replace the state set by the set of points x on a surface. The procedure for calculating the points is thus:

1. Choose a point x' in the scene visible through the imaging aperture to a selected pixel x on the virtual screen.
2. Add in the radiated intensity.
3. For the length of a Markov path do
   3.1 Select the point x'' and calculate the geometrical factor $g(x,x')$.
   3.2 Calculate the reflectance function $\rho(x,x',x'')$ and multiply by $\epsilon(x',x'')$.
   3.3 Add this contribution to the pixel intensity.

Note that calculating the emittance and scattering factors is simply a matter of consulting texture maps and lighting models. Calculating the geometrical factor is, in fact, the ray-object intersection calculation of ray tracing. Note also, that by choosing the next point x'' on the Markov path by shooting a ray at an chosen angle and finding the closest intersection point, we in effect perform a powerful importance sampling optimization. That is, we do not bother to calculate the integral for points x', x'' which are occluded by another surface because we know the integral will be zero. This is in contrast to the relaxation procedure in radiosity which always takes energy contributions from all surfaces.

5. Hierarchical sampling

We now present a number of new variance reduction techniques invented for solving the rendering equation. We hasten to point out, however, that the variance reduction techniques exposed here are of much wider scope. Generally they will have utility in all manner of monte carlo integration problems in which the integrand is particularly difficult. In this situation, the increased overhead beyond previously known methods becomes negligible. We present five methods which take increasing advantage of precious samples of the integrand. All the techniques outlines below were inspired by stratified sampling.

Sequential uniform sampling

The first sampling technique stems from a common sequential sampling strategy. Often samples of the integrand are repeatedly collected until the sample variance of the integral estimate falls below a fixed threshold. This strategy has been shown to be of advantage in [Lee, Redner and Uselton 1985], where many samples were collected at interesting parts of the image while few were collected at uninteresting parts.

Unfortunately, this sequential strategy is incompatiblewith stratified sampling. In the stratified sampling technique, the domain of interest is divided into subcells. Lee, et. al. used a fixed subdivision of 8 cells per pixel and randomly collected samples within each cell. Ideally, better convergence is obtained when one sample per cell is collected, where the cells uniformly divide the domain—this is the so called jitter sampling method, where ordinarily we think of the centers of the cells as forming a lattice. The incompatibility between sequential and jitter sampling arises because a uniform subdivision of the domain is impossible until it is known precisely how many samples will be collected.

Sequential uniform sampling achieves this by keeping a tree of cells of varying sizes. Each time a sample is to be cast, a cell is first chosen and then divided into cells. The old sample of the original cell must lie in one of the new subcells. The new sample is chosen to lie in the opposite cell. A simple example will illustrate this technique.

Suppose we are sampling a unit interval and have already cast 5 samples. The cells chosen with sample points appear thus:

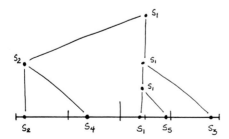

To cast a new sample point we traverse the tree until a leaf cell is encountered. We then split the leaf cell in half and cast the sample into the empty half cell.

REFINE A NODE
1. If the node is an internal node
  1.1 Choose a subnode
  1.2 Refine the chosen subnode
  1.3 Return
2. Else, split the leaf node
3. Propagate the old sample into the subleaf containing it.
4. Cast a new sample in the remaining empty subleaf

How can we assure that the most uniform possible subdivision is computed? One way would be to traverse the sampling tree in breadth first order. Splitting each leaf node at every level before splitting deeper nodes. This strategy produces highly nonrandom sample distributions, essentially scanning across the interval. A better method is to split nodes breadth first in random order. The following criteria effect this strategy

CHOOSE A SUBNODE
1. If either is a leaf choose it.
2. Choose left node if
    level(left)<level(right) and left is balanced
3. Choose right node if
    level(right)<level(left) and right is balanced
4. Choose randomly otherwise.

Note that this strategy will in effect perform a random search throughout the interval, without concentrating on any particular area.

The multidimensional case

The above algorithm is easily extended to higher dimensions simply by using a data structure known as a *k-d tree* due to Bentley [Bentley 1979]. In this data structure, the domain is succesively divided into two halves by a hyperplane perpendicular to successive coordinate axes. Thus for say a unit square, the k-d tree subdivides first along a vertical line, then on the next level down along the horizontal. The uniform subnode choice rules above ensure a uniform subdivision without any modification. Generalization to path spaces is straightforward.

Hierarchical integration

The third version of the above technique takes advantage of the fact that the cells for each sample are recorded with each sample. In this way we may compute a Riemann sum using the volume of the cell and the value of the cast sample as integrand. Yakowitz [Yakowitz et al 1978] has proposed a variant of this method (using the samples themselves as boundary points with no stratification). He has reported a variance of $O(n^{-4})$ in the one dimensional case, and a variance of $O(n^{-2})$ in the two dimensional case. This is in vastly superior to the $O(n^{-1})$ of simple monte carlo. The analysis of our technique is still under investigation, and will appear in a companion paper. But due to the stratification of our samples, early evidence suggests that this is a superior technique for integration.

Each time a leaf cell is split, its contribution to the total integral is divided in half. The new integrand sample is multiplied by the volume of empty cell. After splitting and sampling has occurred, the path from the leaf to the root is traversed, updating the integral stored at each node to be the sum of the integrals of its subnodes. By keeping the integral of nonroot internal nodes we are able to automatically scale the by the density of the samples to maintain a constant measure.

Figure 3 shows the convergence of a two dimensional integral as compared to the conventional monte carlo technique. The value of the integral estimate is plotted versus number of samples cast. The conventional estimator is shown above and the hierarchical integrator is shown below. We are integrating a simple step function on a connected region of the plane.

Adaptive hierarchical integration

The fourth elaboration of this technique concerns other criteria besides uniformity of samples in the domain. In this variation, we seek to concentrate samples in interesting parts of the domain and to sparsely sample those areas in which the integrand is nearly constant.

We seek criteria for selecting interesting parts of the tree to undergo further refinement. How can these criteria be included in the algorithm? It is easy to think of the subnode selection rules of the uniform sequential sampler as a way of setting probability thresholds. Choose a uniform random number in the unit interval. The uniform rule calculates a threshold ϕ_u which is either 1 or 0 if the rule says to choose left or right subnode. If the rule says to choose randomly, the threshold is set to 0.5.

Now let us calculate a number of thresholds $\phi_1, \ldots, \phi_k$. To take all these threshold functions into account an effective scheme is to form the convex combination of them as the global threshold, that is the global threshold ϕ is given by

$$\phi = c_1\phi_1 + c_2\phi_2 + \cdots + c_k\phi_k$$

$$\sum_{i=1}^{k} c_i = 1$$

where $c_i \geq 0$ for every i. Each c_i provides a weight for its corresponding threshold function so that the total strategy can undergo tuning.

What are the useful threshold functions? We have found a few, but it is clear that the number of useful criteria left to be discovered is many. Among the threshold functions we have found useful are 1) the uniform sampling threshold; 2) The totally random threshold ($\phi = .5$); 3) The difference of integrals of the two subnodes; 4) A history of the activity of change in this subnode (which may be the variance, or some weighted time history of the integral); and 5) *A priori* functions that can predict where large illumination components will be.

So far our experiments in finding adaptive criteria have not been terribly successful. We have not used adaptation in computing the final images.

Again we note as in the last section, that recording the volumes of the cells in each node automatically provides the normalization that is needed when the sampling distribution is skewed. This is often problematical in adaptive sampling schemes.

Figure 4 shows the unit square subdivided according to criterion 1) and 3) in equal proportion. This is a snapshot of the subdivision when 165 samples have been cast.

Nonuniform sampling: Importance sampling analogs

Finally, the fifth technique takes into account importance sampling. Instead of dividing a leaf cell exactly in half, it is possible to divide it along a hyperplane that represents the median of some probability density function. The hyperplane chosen is given by the level of the k-d tree in the second technique. Representing the probability density as an integrated distribution function makes it easy to choose the median hyperplane by a quick binary search: to find the median of a probability density $f(x)$ we simply search for the point at which $F(x) = .5$.

Importance sampling is a very important variance reduction technique which can be used to great advantage in solving the rendering equation.

6. Application to the rendering equation

The monte carlo algorithms presented above can all be applied to a solution of the rendering algorithm. For example, sequential uniform sampling is used to sample the aperture for depth of field blur. Adaptive hierarchical integration is used to subsample the pixel. Importance sampling by splitting along the medians is used in choosing a direction to shoot the next ray. We store the lighting model as a summed area table [Crow 1985], giving a probability distribution function which can undergo binary search to find the median in a reflectance cell. Since we search for a median hyperplane of the lighting model, nonlinear transformations of the domain are not particularly important. We simply project the pair of input and output hemispheres onto the tangent plane.

It is interesting to compare the path solution to the conventional ray tracing algorithm. It is in fact quite easy to convert a conventional ray tracer to this algorithm. We essentially perform a conventional ray tracing algorithm, but instead of branching a tree of rays at each surface, we follow only one of the branches to give a path in the tree. We always shoot toward known light sources, which, of course, may be extended areas. Thus a schematic of ray tracing versus the integral equation method appears thus:

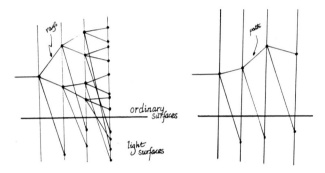

Now an important phenomenon is pointed out by this diagram. Due to the passivity of surfaces, it is widely known that the first generation rays as well as the light source rays are the most important to in terms of variance that they contribute to the pixel integral. Second and higher generation rays contribute much less to the variance. But conventional ray tracing expends the vast bulk of the work on precisely those rays which contribute least to the variance of the image, it shoots too many rays of higher generations. The integral equation method is not prone to this criticism. Because a path is a tree with branching ratio 1, there are as many different first generation rays as there are higher generation rays. This is very important for variance reduction for motion blur, depth of field, and other effects in distributed ray tracing.

This diagram also points out an alternative algorithm for conventional distributed ray tracing. Rather than shooting a branching tree, just shoot a path with the rays chosen probabilistically. For scenes with much reflection and refraction, this cuts down vastly on the number of ray object intersections to be computed for a given pixel and performs a remarkable speed up of ray tracing for very little programming work. However, for this new fast form of ray tracing—called *path tracing*—we have found that it is very important to maintain the correct proportion of reflection, refraction, and shadow ray types contributing to each pixel. Rather than choosing the ray type randomly, there are two alternatives. First, keep track of of the number of each type shot. Make sure the sample distribution of ray types closely matches the desired distribution by varying the the probability of each type so that it is more certain that the sample distribution matches. This is the approach we have actually implemented. A second approach is to let the ray types be chosen randomly but to scale the contribution of each ray type by the ratio of desired distribution to the resulting weighted sample distribution.

7. Results

Figures 5 and 6 show resulting images from the integral equation technique. At each surface element hit, a random variable was calculated from a distribution determined by the specular, diffuse, and transmission coefficients. This random variable was used to choose the shooting of one ray from the surface element. A random point was chosen on each light source to serve as a target for. an illumination ray. The variance reduction methods actually used were multidimensional sequential sampling for choosing the diffuse direction, specular direction, and refracted direction of a new ray. Multidimensional sequential sampling was also used to choose points on the light sources and imaging aperture. Hierarchical integration was used for antialiasing the pixel values. No adaptive or nonuniform sampling was used for either of these images. It is clear that importance sampling would improve the variance of the image considerably. Although implementation of importance sampling is simple and straightforward it has not yet been done. Also, keeping track of the variance of each pixel and collecting sequential has shown to be a significant speed up. However, our program did not do this for these images, we shot a constant 40 paths per pixel.

Figure 5 shows a model rendered via two techniques. On the left side is the model rendered via the standard ray tracing technique (albeit with ambient coefficient set to 0 and the single branching ratio speedup mentioned above). The right image shows the result of rendering via the integral equation. Both images are 256 by 256 pixels with a fixed 40 paths per pixel. The images were computed on an IBM-4341. The first image took 401 minutes of CPU time, the second image 533 minutes. Note that the area of the sphere in shadow is picking up ambient illumination missing in the ray tracing picture. Also light is bouncing off the bottom of the sphere and lighting up the base plane.

In figure 6 we show an image illustrating the power of the integral equation technique. All objects in the scene are a neutral grey except for the green glass balls and the base polygon (which is slightly reddish). Any color on the grey objects would be missing from a ray tracing image. Note that the green glass balls cast caustics on objects in the scene. There is color bleeding from the lightly colored base polygon onto the bottom of the oblate spheroid in the upper right. For simplicity and comparison purposes, the opaque surfaces in this scene are lambertian, but there is no restriction on the lighting models that can be used. Figure 6 is a 512 by 512 pixel image with 40 paths per pixel. It was computed on an IBM 3081 and consumed 1221 minutes of CPU time. Al Barr provided the model for this image.

ACKNOWLEDGMENTS Thanks to Al Barr, Tim Kay, RobCook, Jim Blinn, and the members of CS286 Computer Graphics Seminar, for technical discussions. I am grateful to IBM, Juan Rivero of the Los Angeles Science Center and Alan Norton of Yorktown Heights Research for donating large numbers of mainframe cycles to Caltech. I also wish to thank the reviewers for their many thoughtful comments.

References

J.L. BENTLEY, J.H. FRIEDMAN "Data structures for range searching", ACM Comp. Surv., 11,4, pp.397-409., 1979.

S. CHANDRASEKAR *Radiative Transfer*, Oxford University Press, 1950.

M.F. COHEN, D.P. GREENBURG "The Hemi-cube: a Radiosity solution for complex environments", Computer Graphics 19,3, pp.31-40, 1985.

R.L. COOK, T. PORTER, L CARPENTER "Distributed ray tracing", Computer Graphics18,3, pp.137-146,1984.

R.L. COOK, "Stochastic sampling in computer graphics", to appear in ACM Transactions of Graphics

R. COURANT AND D. HILBERT, *Methods of mathematical physics* 2 vols., Interscience, New York 1953, 1962.

F.C. CROW "Summed area tables for texture mapping", Computer Graphics 18,3, pp.207-212, 1984.

R.P. FEYNMAN AND A.P. HIBBS *Quantum Mechanics and Path Integrals,* McGraw-Hill, New York 1965.

H. GOLDSTEIN *Classical Mechanics* Addison-Wesley, Reading, Mass. 1950.

C. M. GORAL, K.E. TORRANCE, D.P. GREENBURG "Modeling the interaction of light between diffuse surfaces", Computer Graphics 18,3, pp.213-222, 1984.

I.H. HALTON "A retrospective and prospective survey of the monte carlo method", SIAM Rev. 12, pp.1-63, 1970.

J.T. KAJIYA, B. VON HERZEN "Ray tracing volume densitites", Computer Graphics 18,3, pp.165-174, 1984.

M.E. LEE, R.A. REDNER, S.P. USELTON "Statistically Optimized Sampling for distributed ray tracing" Computer graphics v.19,3 pp.61-67.

T. NISHITA, E. NAKAMAE "Continuous tone representation of three dimensional objects taking account of shadows and interreflection", Computer Graphics19,3, pp.23-30, 1985.

R.Y. RUBENSTEIN *Simulation and the Monte Carlo Method*, J.Wiley, New York, 1981.

R. SIEGEL, J.R. HOWELL *Thermal Radiation Heat Transfer*, McGraw Hill, New York, 1981.

T. WHITTED "An improved illumination model for shaded display", Comm. ACM, 23,6, pp.343-349, June 1980.

S. YAKOWITZ, *et. al.* "Weighted monte carlo integration", SIAM J. Num. An. 15,6, pp.1289-1300, 1978.

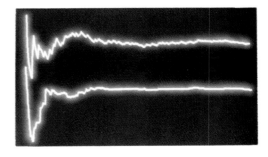

Figure 3. Convergence of naieve monte carlo vs. hierarchical integration. Shown are integral estimates as a function of number of samples cast. Naieve monte carlo is the top curve.

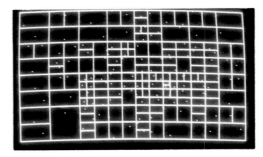

Figure 4. Subdivision of domain by adaptive hierarchical integration.

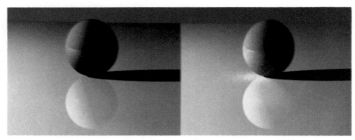

Figure 5. A comparison of ray tracing vs. integral equation technique. Note the presence of light on the base polygon scattered by the sphere from the light source.

Figure 6. A sample image. All objects are neutral grey. Color on the objects is due to caustics from the green glass balls and color bleeding from the base polygon.

Free-Form Deformation of Solid Geometric Models

Thomas W. Sederberg
Scott R. Parry[‡]

Brigham Young University
Provo, Utah 84602

ABSTRACT

A technique is presented for deforming solid geometric models in a free-form manner. The technique can be used with any solid modeling system, such as CSG or B-rep. It can deform surface primitives of any type or degree: planes, quadrics, parametric surface patches, or implicitly defined surfaces, for example. The deformation can be applied either globally or locally. Local deformations can be imposed with any desired degree of derivative continuity. It is also possible to deform a solid model in such a way that its volume is preserved.

The scheme is based on trivariate Bernstein polynomials, and provides the designer with an intuitive appreciation for its effects.

CR Categories and Subject Descriptors: I.3.5 [**Computer Graphics**]: Computation Geometry and Object Modeling - Curve, surface, solid, and object representations; Hierarchy and geometric transformations.

KEYWORDS: Solid geometric modeling, free-form surfaces, deformations.

1. INTRODUCTION

The fields of solid modeling and surface modeling have been developing rather independently over the past fifteen years [Requicha '82], [Varady '84]. Surface modeling has dealt primarily with parametric surface patches. These patches are generally referred to as free-form surfaces, or sculptured surfaces, which suggest that they can be shaped with flexibility akin to clay in a sculptor's hands. For this reason, planes, quadrics and tori are generally not considered to be free-form. Most solid modeling systems use surfaces that are planar, quadric or

toroidal. Recently, the capability of defining fillets and blended surfaces has also been introduced [Hoffmann '85], [Middleditch '85], [Rockwood '86].

The problem of defining a solid geometric model of an object bounded by free-form surfaces has long been identified as an important research problem. Most of the approaches to this problem can be classified into one of three categories:

1. Combining *existing* free-form surface and solid modeling techniques. This extends the surface domain of a solid modeling system to include free-form parametric surface patches. It is currently the most popular approach and some applications can be found in [Kalay '82], [Jared '84], [Chiyokura '83], [Varady '84], [Riesenfeld '83], [Sarraga '84], [Steinberg '84], [Thomas '84], and [Kimura '84]. This method must overcome several difficulties such as ensuring representational validity in using the free-form surfaces in a general manner. These problems are described in [Requicha '82].

2. Trivariate parametric *hyperpatch*. The hyperpatch is used as a solid modeling primitive. This method has been used for years by the analysis community and has many applications such as finite element mesh generation [Stanton '77], [Casale '85]. [Farouki '85] discusses adding a fourth parameter of time to create a time-space swath useful for motion definition.

3. Implicit surfaces. There has been limited investigation of modeling directly with volumes bounded by implicit or algebraic surfaces. Calculating curves of surface intersection and deciding whether a point lies inside a volume is easier with this definition, especially when the surfaces are of low degree. However, free-form shape definition lends itself more naturally to parametric equations

[‡]Current address:

Milliken & Co.

LaGrange, GA. 30241

than to implicit equations. Sabin was one of the early investigators of modeling with algebraic surfaces [Sabin '68]. [Ricci '73], [Barr '81], [Rockwood '86], [Owen '86], [Hoffmann '85] and [Blinn '82] explore modeling implicit surfaces other than quadrics. [Sederberg '85] discusses modeling with piecewise algebraic surface patches.

This paper presents an approach to free-form solid modeling which does not fall cleanly into any of the above three categories, although it developed most directly out of the ideas in [Sederberg '85]. This technique is referred to as free-form deformation or FFD, and can be thought of as a method for sculpturing solid models. It is shown to be of value both as a design method, and as a representation for free-form solids. Indeed, the sculpturing metaphor is stronger for solids than for surfaces because a lump of clay or a block of marble is a solid.

Several researchers have promoted this sculpturing metaphor for geometric modeling, noting that it is a natural and familiar mode of thought for a designer or stylist. For example, [Parent '77] discusses a "computer graphics sculptor's studio" for defining polygonal objects, and [Brewer '77] describes a planar shaping tool for manipulating sculptured surfaces. Other "lump-of-clay" modeling techniques are surveyed in [Cobb '84]. None of these sculpturing techniques are directly applicable to solid geometric modeling. Parent's paper deals with polygonal data, and Brewer's work deals with a class of parametric surface patches.

FFD involves a mapping from R^3 to R^3 through a trivariate tensor product Bernstein polynomial. An earlier use of R^3 to R^3 mapping is found in Barr's innovative paper on regular deformations of solids [Barr '84]. While not a free-form modeling technique, Barr's idea of twisting, bending and tapering of solid primitives is a powerful and elegant design tool. Brief mention of deformation is also made in [Sabin '70] and in [Bézier '74]. Trivariate hyperpatches also are an R^3-R^3 map, but the result is a distorted cube with six four sided faces.

FFD is a remarkably versatile tool. It can be applied to CSG based solid models as well as those using Euler operators. It can sculpt solids bounded by *any* analytic surface: planes, quadrics, parametric surfaces patches, or implicit surfaces. Furthermore, its application is not restricted to solid models, but it can also sculpt surfaces or polygonal data.

FFD can be applied locally while maintaining derivative continuity with adjacent, undeformed regions of the model. It can also be applied hierarchically, with each application being analogous to a sweep of the sculptor's hands. Constraints can be placed on the FFD to control the degree to which the volume of the solid changes, and in fact, there exist free-form deformations which are perfectly volume preserving.

[Veenman '82] suggests that the free-form surfaces used in practical engineering design fall into four categories: Aesthetic surfaces (the main design requirement is visual appearance); fairings or duct surfaces (a surface transition between two other surfaces of different cross-section); blends and fillets (smooth the intersection of two other surfaces); and functional or fitted surfaces (high geometric constraint imposed to satisfy some functional requirement, such as a turbine blade). FFDs can create aesthetic surfaces and fairings. It is also possible to synthesize fillets in certain situations, but a general fillet and blending capability is not claimed. However, FFD can be used in conjunction with any fillet and blend formulation, such as those discussed in [Hoffmann '85], [Middleditch '85] and [Rockwood '86]. Functional surfaces are not discussed, although [Sabin '70] reports that a type of small displacement FFD is useful in the design of airplane wings.

This paper assumes that the reader is familiar with Bezier curves and surface patches. Necessary background can be found in [Boehm '84]. Basic understanding of solid modeling is also presumed, such as discussed in [Requicha '82].

Section 2 presents the mathematical formulation of FFD. Section 3 discusses local deformations and continuity control. Section 4 looks at volume change, and Section 5 presents several examples which illustrate the flexibility of FFD. Section 6 summarizes.

2. FORMULATING FREE-FORM DEFORMATIONS

A good physical analogy for FFD is to consider a parallelpiped of clear, flexible plastic in which is embedded an object, or several objects, which we wish to deform. The object is imagined to also be flexible, so that it deforms along with the plastic that surrounds it.

Figure 1 illustrates this analogy using several objects embedded in clear, flexible plastic. In Figure 2, the plastic has been deformed and the embedded spheres and cubes are deformed in a manner that is intuitively consistent with the motion of the plastic.

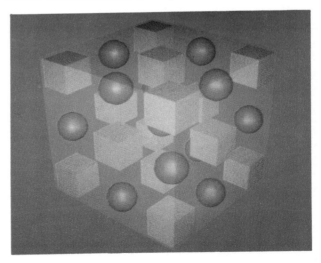

Fig 1. Undeformed Plastic

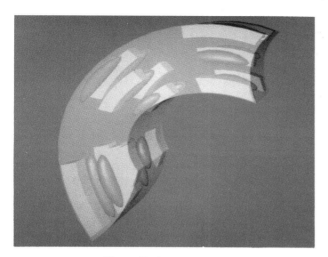

Fig 2. Deformed Plastic

Mathematically, the FFD is defined in terms of a tensor product trivariate Bernstein polynomial. We begin by imposing a local coordinate system on a parallelpiped region, as shown in Figure 3. Any point $\mathbf{X}$ has (s,t,u) coordinates in this system such that

$$\mathbf{X} = \mathbf{X}_0 + s\mathbf{S} + t\mathbf{T} + u\mathbf{U}.$$

The (s,t,u) coordinates of $\mathbf{X}$ can easily be found using linear algebra. A vector solution is

$$s = \frac{\mathbf{T}\times\mathbf{U}\cdot(\mathbf{X}-\mathbf{X}_0)}{\mathbf{T}\times\mathbf{U}\cdot\mathbf{S}}, \; t = \frac{\mathbf{S}\times\mathbf{U}\cdot(\mathbf{X}-\mathbf{X}_0)}{\mathbf{S}\times\mathbf{U}\cdot\mathbf{T}}, \; u = \frac{\mathbf{S}\times\mathbf{T}\cdot(\mathbf{X}-\mathbf{X}_0)}{\mathbf{S}\times\mathbf{T}\cdot\mathbf{U}} \quad (1)$$

Note that for any point interior to the parallelpiped that $0 < s < 1$, $0 < t < 1$ and $0 < u < 1$.

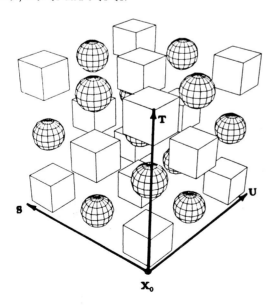

Fig. 3 s,t,u Coordinate System

We next impose a grid of control points $\mathbf{P}_{ijk}$ on the parallelpiped. These form $l+1$ planes in the $\mathbf{S}$ direction, $m+1$ planes in the $\mathbf{T}$ direction, and $n+1$ planes in the $\mathbf{U}$

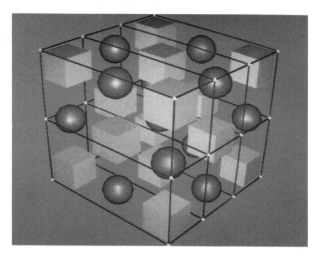

Fig. 4 Undisplaced Control Points

direction. In Figure 4, $l=1$, $m=2$, and $n=3$. The control points are indicated by small white diamonds, and the red bars indicate the neighboring control points. These points lie on a lattice, and their locations are defined

$$\mathbf{P}_{ijk} = \mathbf{X}_0 + \frac{i}{l}\mathbf{S} + \frac{j}{m}\mathbf{T} + \frac{k}{m}\mathbf{U}.$$

The deformation is specified by moving the $\mathbf{P}_{ijk}$ from their undisplaced, latticial positions. The deformation function is defined by a trivariate tensor product Bernstein polynomial. The deformed position $\mathbf{X}_{ffd}$ of an arbitrary point $\mathbf{X}$ is found by first computing its (s,t,u) coordinates from equation (1), and then evaluating the vector valued trivariate Bernstein polynomial:

$$\mathbf{X}_{ffd} = \sum_{i=0}^{l}\binom{l}{i}(1-s)^{l-i}s^i\left[\sum_{j=0}^{m}\binom{m}{j}(1-t)^{m-j}t^j\left[\sum_{k=0}^{n}\binom{n}{k}(1-u)^{n-k}u^k\mathbf{P}_{ijk}\right]\right] \quad (2)$$

where $\mathbf{X}_{ffd}$ is a vector containing the Cartesian coordinates of the displaced point, and where $\mathbf{P}_{ijk}$ is a vector containing the Cartesian coordinates of the control point.

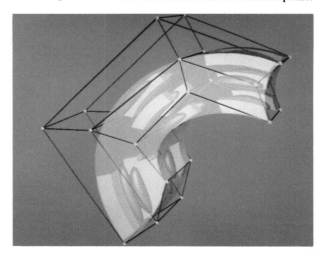

Fig. 5 Control Points in Deformed Position

The control points $\mathbf{P}_{ijk}$ are actually the coefficients of the Bernstein polynomial. As in the case of Bezier curves and surface patches, there are meaningful relationships between the deformation and the control point placement. Note from Fig. 5 that the 12 edges of the parallelpiped are actually mapped into Bezier curves, defined by the control points which initially lie on the respective edges. Also, the six planar faces map into tensor product Bezier surface patches, defined by the control points which initially lie on the respective faces.

This deformation could be formulated in terms of other polynomial bases, such as tensor product B-splines or non-tensor product Bernstein polynomials. We feel that the basis we have chosen provides the clearest discussion.

2.1. Deformation Domain

Consider the versatility of this FFD. Although the purpose of this paper is to establish FFD as a viable tool for solid modeling, we note that it can be applied to virtually any geometric model. Figures 6 and 7 show

Fig. 6 Undeformed Polygons

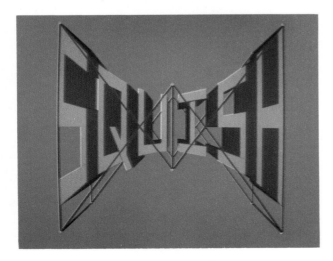

Fig. 7 Deformed Polygons

deformed polygonal data. Only the polygon vertices are transformed by the FFD, while maintaining the polygon connectivity. Deformation of polygonal data is discussed more thoroughly in [Sederberg '86].

Figures 8 and 9 illustrate a sphere intersected by a plane, both deformed simultaneously by the same FFD. The sphere and the plane could each be expressed in parametric equations, or in implicit equations. The FFD can be applied with equal validity to either representation. A very important characteristic of FFD is that a deformed parametric surface remains a parametric surface. This is easy to see. If the parametric surface is given by $x = f(\alpha,\beta)$, $y = g(\alpha,\beta)$ and $z = h(\alpha,\beta)$ and the FFD is given by $\mathbf{X}_{ffd} = \mathbf{X}(x,y,z)$, then the deformed parametric surface patch is given by $\mathbf{X}_{ffd}(\alpha,\beta) = \mathbf{X}(f(\alpha,\beta),g(\alpha,\beta),h(\alpha,\beta))$. This is a simple composition.

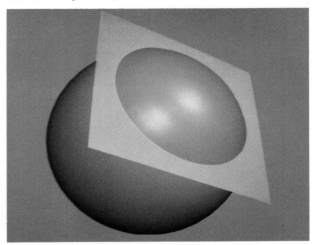

Fig. 8 Sphere and Plane

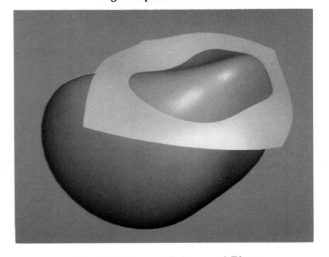

Fig. 9 Deformed Sphere and Plane

An important corollary to this is that parametric curves remain parametric under FFD. In Figure 8, the curve of intersection between the sphere and plane is a circle, which can be expressed parametrically in terms of quadratic rational polynomials. In Figure 9, that deformed circle is still a parametric curve. This fact suggests important possibilities for solid modeling. For example, if one performs FFD in a CSG modeling environment only after all boolean operations are performed, and the primitive surfaces are planes or quadrics, then all intersection curves would be parametric, involving rational polynomials and possibly square roots.

Quadrics and planes make excellent primitives because they possess both implicit and parametric equations. The parametric equation enables rapid computation of points on the surface, and the implicit equation provides a simple point classification test - is a point inside, outside, or on the surface. To classify a point on a deformed quadric, one must first compute its s,t,u coordinates and substitute them into the implicit equation. The s,t,u coordinates can be found by subdividing the control point lattice, or by trivariate Newton iteration (see [Parry '86]). This inverse mapping requires significant computation, and can be a source of robustness problems, especially if the Jacobian of the FFD changes sign (see section 4).

3. CONTINUITY CONTROL

It is possible to apply two or more FFDs in a piecewise manner so as to maintain cross-boundary derivative continuity. We will discuss this continuity in terms of a local surface parametrization. This covers the general case, since all surfaces possess a local parametrization. Denote the local parameters by v,w and the surface by $(s,t,u) = (s(v,w),t(v,w),u(v,w))$. Imagine two adjacent FFDs $\mathbf{X}_1(s_1,t_1,u_1)$ and $\mathbf{X}_2(s_2,t_2,u_2)$ which share a common boundary $s_1 = s_2 = 0$. The first derivatives of the deformed surface can be found using the chain rule:

$$\frac{\partial \mathbf{X}_1(v,w)}{\partial v} = \frac{\partial \mathbf{X}_1}{\partial s} \cdot \frac{\partial s}{\partial v} + \frac{\partial \mathbf{X}_1}{\partial t} \cdot \frac{\partial t}{\partial v} + \frac{\partial \mathbf{X}_1}{\partial u} \cdot \frac{\partial u}{\partial v}$$

$$\frac{\partial \mathbf{X}_1(v,w)}{\partial w} = \frac{\partial \mathbf{X}_1}{\partial s} \cdot \frac{\partial s}{\partial w} + \frac{\partial \mathbf{X}_1}{\partial t} \cdot \frac{\partial t}{\partial w} + \frac{\partial \mathbf{X}_1}{\partial u} \cdot \frac{\partial u}{\partial w}.$$

Note that $\frac{\partial s}{\partial v}$, $\frac{\partial t}{\partial v}$, $\frac{\partial u}{\partial v}$, $\frac{\partial s}{\partial w}$, $\frac{\partial t}{\partial w}$ and $\frac{\partial u}{\partial w}$ are all independent of the deformation. Thus, sufficient conditions for first derivative continuity are that

$$\frac{\partial \mathbf{X}_1(0,t,u)}{\partial s} = \frac{\partial \mathbf{X}_2(0,t,u)}{\partial s},$$

$$\frac{\partial \mathbf{X}_1(0,t,u)}{\partial t} = \frac{\partial \mathbf{X}_2(0,t,u)}{\partial t}, \qquad (3)$$

$$\frac{\partial \mathbf{X}_1(0,t,u)}{\partial u} = \frac{\partial \mathbf{X}_2(0,t,u)}{\partial u}.$$

These conditions (and those for higher derivative continuity) can be shown to be straightforward extensions of the continuity conditions for Bezier curves and tensor product Bezier surfaces, which are explained in [Boehm '84]. We will denote continuity by C^k, which means that two adjacent FFDs are geometrically continuous to the kth derivative.

Consider the two adjacent undeformed FFD lattices in the upper right of Figure 10 which have a plane of control points in common. These two FFDs are C^0 if the common control points remain coincident, as in the upper left of Figure 10a. Sufficient conditions for C^1 are illustrated in the bottom of Figure 10a.

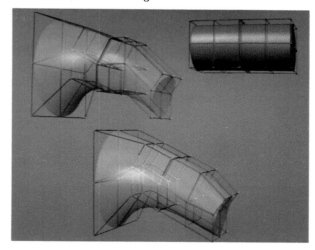

Fig. 10a Control Points for C^0 and C^1 FFDs

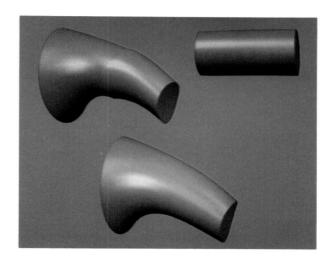

Fig. 10b C^0 and C^1 FFDs

3.1. Local Deformations

A special case of continuity conditions enables us to perform a local, isolated deformation. In this case, we might imagine that the neighboring FFD with which we wish to maintain C^k is simply an undeformed lattice. We consider the problem of maintaining C^k along the plane where one face of the FFD intersects the geometric model. It is easy to show that sufficient conditions for a C^k local deformation are simply that the control points on the k planes adjacent to the interface plane are not moved. This is illustrated in Figures 11 and 12. Of course, C^k can be maintained across more than one face by imposing these conditions for each face that the surface intersects.

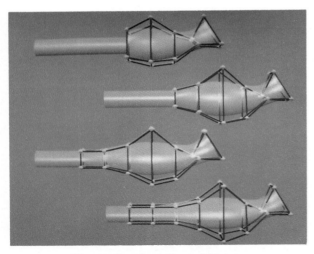

Fig. 11 Local C^k Control Points

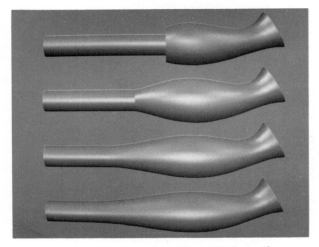

Fig. 12 C^{-1}, C^0, C^1 and C^2 Local Deformations

This local application lends to the FFD a capability which makes the technique strongly analogous to sculpting with clay. These local deformations can be applied hierarchically, which imparts exceptional flexibility and ease of use to the technique.

4. VOLUME CHANGE

Another reason that FFD is so nicely applicable to solid modeling is that it provides us with control over the volume change that a solid experiences under FFD. The volume change that a FFD imposes on each differential element is given by the Jacobian of the FFD. If the FFD is given by

$$\mathbf{F}(x,y,z) = (F(x,y,z), G(x,y,z), H(x,y,z))$$

then the Jacobian is the determinant

$$Jac(\mathbf{F}) = \begin{vmatrix} \frac{\partial F}{\partial x} & \frac{\partial F}{\partial y} & \frac{\partial F}{\partial z} \\ \frac{\partial G}{\partial x} & \frac{\partial G}{\partial y} & \frac{\partial G}{\partial z} \\ \frac{\partial H}{\partial x} & \frac{\partial H}{\partial y} & \frac{\partial H}{\partial z} \end{vmatrix}$$

If the volume of any differential element before deformation is $dx \cdot dy \cdot dz$, then after deformation, its volume is $Jac(\mathbf{F}(x,y,z)) \cdot dx \cdot dy \cdot dz$. The volume of the entire deformed solid is simply the triple integral of this differential volume over the volume enclosed by the undeformed surface. Thus, if we can obtain a bound on $Jac(\mathbf{F})$ over the region of deformation, we will have a bound on the volume change. Such a bound is conveniently provided if $Jac(\mathbf{F})$ is expressed as a trivariate Bernstein polynomial. Then, the largest and smallest polynomial coefficients provide upper and lower bounds on the volume change.

A noteworthy result is that there exists a family of *volume preserving* FFDs, which means $Jac(\mathbf{F}) \equiv 1$. Any solid model will retain its original volume under such a transformation. Figures 13a and 13b illustrate a 12 oz. Coke can before and after a volume preserving FFD. The deformed can still holds exactly 12 oz.! Space limitations prevent a more complete discussion here of volume preservation, but the details can be found in [Sederberg '86b]. The usefulness of the set of volume preserving FFDs is yet to be determined.

Fig. 13a 12 oz. Coke Can

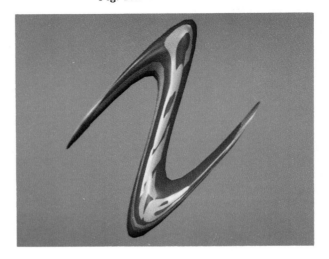

Fig. 13b Still 12 oz.

5. APPLICATIONS

We conclude by demonstrating some of the flexibility of FFD. Figures 14-16 demonstrate how the technique can be applied hierarchically to mold a rounded bar into a telephone handset. Figure 14 shows a local C^1 FFD which draws a mouthpiece from the undeformed bar. The earphone is formed in like manner, and Figure 15 shows a global FFD to impart a slight curvature to the handset. Figure 16 shows the final result. Note that the final telephone is a *free-form solid model*. The original bar in Figure 14 is modeled as a solid using an implicit equation, and each FFD merely modifies the geometry, without altering the integrity of the solid model. Thus, the hierarchical FFD formulation fully enables the computation of mass properties and point classification. We are also impressed by the ease with which the phone was designed. With only a few hours of experience under our belts, the phone was produced in a single design iteration!

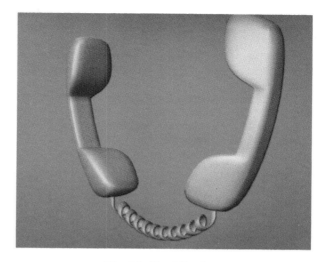

Fig. 16   Final Product

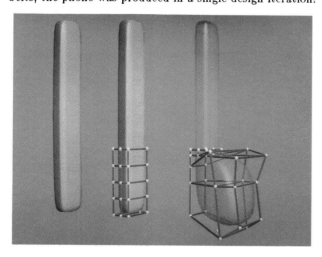

Fig. 14   Local FFD

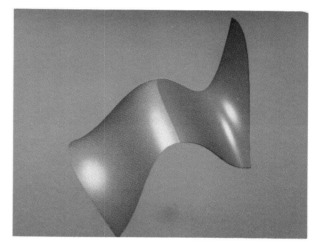

Fig. 17   Two C^1 Bicubic Patches

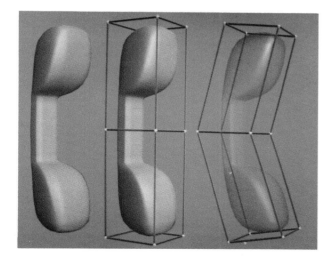

Fig. 15   Global FFD

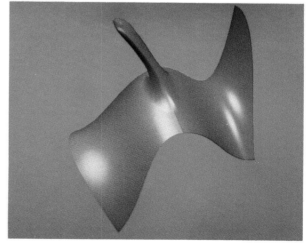

Fig. 18 C^1 FFD

Figures 17 and 18 further illustrate the "lump of clay" metaphor. Two slope continuous bicubic patches have an FFD applied which straddles the common boundary of the two patches. The resulting "tongue" is slope continuous with both patches, and the seam along the tongue is also slope continuous. Each half of the tongue itself is also a parametric surface! This example illustrates another important characteristic of FFD: it cares little about the underlying surface patch topology. To understand the importance of this, consider how the tongue would be created using conventional surface patches. It would probably require 6-8 patches, some of which may have to be non-four sided.

Fig. 19 Trophy

Figure 19 shows a trophy whose handles were created by applying a single FFD to a cylinder. The handles were then joined to the surface of revolution using a boolean sum. Again, the handles are modeled as solids. Since the underlying cylinder primitive has both a parametric and an implicit formulation, the handle surface has a parametric expression as well.

Figures 20-22 show how FFD can be used as a fairing or duct surface. The two cylinders, one with an elliptical cross-section, and the other with a peanut shaped cross-section, were both formed using FFDs applied to circular cylinders. The transitional duct surface is also created by applying a FFD to a circular cylinder, so as to be C^1 with the two neighbors.

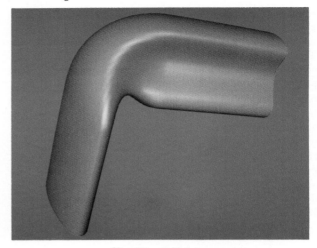

Fig. 21 C^1 Fairing

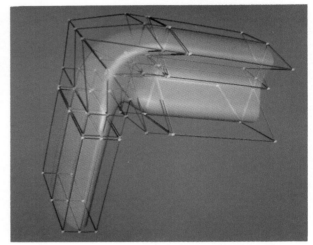

Fig. 22 Control Points

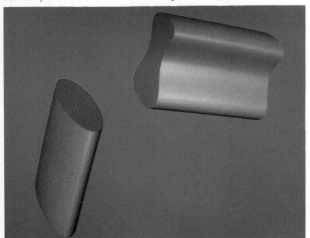

Fig. 20 Dissimilar Cylinders

Fig. 23 It's the Real Thing

Finally, Figure 23 shows an artistic display of a deformed and undeformed Coke can and bottle.

6. CONCLUSIONS

Our brief experience with FFDs persuades us that they have great potential for defining free-form solid models. It's strength and versatility can be summarized as follows:

1. It can be used with any solid modeling scheme.

2. It works with surfaces of any formulation or degree.

3. It can be applied locally or globally, and with derivative continuity.

4. We have found it to be very easy to use. The informal response of some professional stylists is that the strong sculpturing metaphor seems natural and familiar to them.

5. In addition to solid modeling, it can be applied to surfaces or polygonal models.

6. It provides indication of the degree of volume change, and a class of FFDs are even volume preserving.

7. Parametric curves and surfaces remain parametric under FFD.

8. It can be used for aesthetic surfaces, many fairing surfaces, and probably many functional surfaces.

There are limitations to the technique. We can currently identify the following:

1. It cannot perform general filleting and blending.

2. Local FFD forms a planar boundary with the undeformed portion of the object. To create an arbitrary boundary curve, one would have to begin with a FFD which is already in a deformed orientation, and then deform it some more. This would be quite costly.

3. Operations on trivariate Bernstein polynomials, such as subdivision, are much more costly than operations on bivariates.

With more experience, the lists of strengths and weaknesses will both undoubtedly grow.

Due to page limits, several important topics have not been discussed, such as display techniques. This can be found in [Parry '86].

Acknowledgements

Valuable discussions with Ron Goldman, Malcolm Sabin and Alyn Rockwood are gratefully acknowledged. The images were all created using MOVIE.BYU. The first author was sponsored by General Electric Company during the initial stages of the work. The second author was sponsored by the BYU Engineering Computer Graphics Lab.

References

Barr, A. H. Superquadrics and angle-preserving transformations, *IEEE Computer Graphics and Applications,* 1 (January 1981), 11-23.

Barr, A. H. Global and Local Deformations of Solid Primitives, *Computer Graphics* 17,3 (July 1984), pp 21-30.

Bézier, P. Mathematical and practical possibilities of UNISURF, in *Computer Aided Geometric Design,* R. E. Barnhill and R. F. Riesenfeld, eds., Academic Press (1974), New York, pp 127-152.

Blinn, J. A generalization of algebraic surface drawing, *ACM Transactions on Graphics,* 1 (July 1982), 235-256.

Boehm, W., Farin, G. and Kahmann, J. A survey of curve and surface methods in CAGD. *Computer Aided Geometric Design* 1,1(July 1984), 1-60.

Brewer, J. A. and Anderson, D. C. Visual interaction with Overhauser curves and surfaces. *Computer Graphics* 11, 2 (July 1977), 132-137.

Casale, M.S. and Stanton, E. L., An overview of analytic solid modeling, *IEEE Computer Graphics and Applications,* 5 (February 1985), 45-56.

Chiyokura, H. and Kimura, F., Design of solids with free-form surfaces, *Computer Graphics,* 17 (July 1983), 289-298.

Cobb, E. S. *Design of Sculptured Surfaces using the B-spline Representation.* Ph.D. Dissertation, Department of Computer Science, University of Utah, June 1984.

Farouki, R. T. and Hinds, J. K., A hierarchy of geometric forms, *IEEE Computer Graphics and Applications,* 5 (May 1985), 51-78.

Hoffmann, C. and Hopcroft, J. Automatic surface generation in Computer Aided Design. TR 85-661, Dept. of Computer Science, Cornell University, January 1985.

Jared, G. E. M., Synthesis of volume modeling and sculptured surfaces in BUILD, *CAD84, Computers in Design Engineering Conference Proceedings,* (1984), 481-495.

Kalay, Y. E., Modeling polyhedral solids bounded by multi-curved parametric surfaces, *ACM IEEE Nineteenth Design Automation Conference Proceedings* (June 1982), 501-507.

Kimura, F., Geomap-III: Designing solids with free-form surfaces, *IEEE Computer Graphics and Applications,* 4 (1984), 58-72.

Middleditch, A. E. and Sears, K. H. Blend surfaces for set theoretic volume modelling systems. *Computer Graphics* 19, 3 (July 1985), 161-170.

Owen, J. and Rockwood, A. P., General implicit surfaces in geometric modeling, in *Geometric Modeling,* G. Farin, editor, SIAM, to appear (1986).

Parent, R. E. A system for sculpting 3-D data. *Computer Graphics* 11, 2 (July 1977), 138-147.

Parry, S. R. Free-form deformations in a constructive solid geometry modeling system, Ph.D. Dissertation, Department of Civil Engineering, Brigham Young University, April 1986.

Requicha, A. A. G. and Voelcker, H. B. Solid modeling: A historical summary and contemporary assessment. *IEEE Computer Graphics and Applications* 2,2(March 1982), 9-24.

Ricci, A., A constructive geometry for computer graphics, *Computer Journal* 16 (1973), 157-160.

Riesenfeld, R. F., A view of spline-based solid modelling, *Proceedings, Autofac V,* Detroit, MI (November 1983), 75-83.

Rockwood, A. P. and Owen, J. Blending surfaces in solid modeling, in *Geometric Modeling,* G. Farin, editor, SIAM, to appear (1986).

Sabin, M. A. The use of potential surfaces in numerical control, British Aircraft Corporation, Weybridge VTO/MS/153 (1968).

Sabin, M. A. Interrogation techniques for parametric surfaces, Proceedings, Computer Graphics '70, Brunel University, April 1970.

Sarraga, R. F and Waters, W. C., Free-form surfaces in

GMSolid: Goals and issues, in *Solid Modeling by Computers from Theory to Applications,* M. S. Pickett and J. W. Boyse, editors, Plenum Press (1984), 187-204.

Sederberg, T. W. and Parry, S. R., Free-form deformation of polygonal data, *Proceedings, International Electronic Image Week,* Nice, France (April 1986), 633-639.

Sederberg, T. W. and Ferguson, H. R. P. Volume preserving deformations. unpublished notes (1986b).

Stanton, E. L., Crain, L. M. and Neu, T. F., A parametric cubic modeling system for general solids of composite material, *International Journal of Numerical Methods in Engineering,* 11 (1977), 653-670.

Steinberg, H. A., A smooth surface based on biquadratic patches, *IEEE Computer Graphics and Applications,* 4 (September 1984), 20-23.

Thomas, S. W., Modeling volumes bounded by B-spline surfaces, Ph.D. Thesis, Dept. of Computer Science, University of Utah, (1984).

Varady, T. and Pratt, M. J. Design techniques for the definition of solid objects with free-form geometry. *Computer Aided Geometric Design* 1,3 (Dec. 1984), 207-225.

Veenman, P. R., The design of sculptured surfaces using recursive subdivision techniques, in: *Proc. Conf. on CAD/CAM Technology in Mechanical Engineering,* MIT, Cambridge (March 1982).

Constructive Solid Geometry for Polyhedral Objects

David H. Laidlaw
W. Benjamin Trumbore
Department of Computer Science

John F. Hughes
Department of Mathematics

Brown University
Providence, RI 02912

Abstract

Constructive Solid Geometry (CSG) is a powerful way of describing solid objects for computer graphics and modeling. The surfaces of any primitive object (such as a cube, sphere or cylinder) can be approximated by polygons. Being able to find the union, intersection or difference of these objects allows more interesting and complicated polygonal objects to be created. The algorithm presented here performs these set operations on objects constructed from convex polygons. These objects must bound a finite volume, but need not be convex. An object that results from one of these operations also contains only convex polygons, and bounds a finite volume; thus, it can be used in later combinations, allowing the generation of quite complicated objects. Our algorithm is robust and is presented in enough detail to be implemented.

1. Introduction

The algorithm presented finds the polygonal boundaries of the union, intersection, or difference of two polyhedral solids. Our presentation differs from others in the literature [REQ85, TUR84] in several ways. We differ from [REQ85] by presenting an exhaustive analysis of all types of intersections, rather than discussing only generic cases, and by efficiently addressing the difficulties which arise when dealing with coplanar polygons. We differ from [TUR84] by restricting object boundaries to be convex polygons, by subdividing polygons without introducing non-essential vertices, and by allowing objects that are not manifolds. We also sketch an argument showing that the algorithm terminates.

"Constructive Solid Geometry" [REQ80a] operations are defined on surfaces that bound a volume of finite extent. These surfaces may be constructed from several pieces, with very weak constraints on how these pieces touch one another. As a result these objects can be more general than the standard polyhedral surfaces found in mathematics. For example, a single object can consist of two cubes joined along an edge and a third cube that is not connected to the first two (Figure 3.1a). The shared edge touches four faces and cannot be an edge of a polyhedral surface, but the object is still valid. Many other CSG systems will not allow this type of object. The union, intersection, and difference operations on the solids bounded by each object give rise to corresponding operations on the boundaries. We identify these boundaries with the same names as the objects. The *union* of two objects is defined as the boundary of the volume contained in either or both of the objects, while the *intersection* is defined as the boundary of the volume that they have in common. The *difference* of two objects is defined as the boundary of the volume contained in the first object but outside of the second. Using primitive objects like cubes, spheres, and cylinders, this algorithm can construct more complicated objects that in turn can be used to construct even more complex objects.

Our algorithm is part of a set of rendering and solid modeling programs developed at Brown. SCEFO, a language developed at Brown to describe animations and static scenes, describes CSG combinations of objects using a binary tree, with a primitive object at each leaf and a set operation at each internal node [STR84]. From this description renderers create images of the objects. Figure 1.1 (after section 10) shows the CSG construction of a spoon using primitive objects. The images are rendered polygonally, using this algorithm.

A ray-tracer and a polygonal renderer can render an object described as a binary tree of CSG combinations of primitives. Ray-tracers intersect a ray with each primitive object and perform the CSG operation along the ray [ROT82], while polygonal renderers use our algorithm to produce polygonal versions of CSG combinations and then render them as polygons. Using renderers that understand SCEFO, we can quickly render polygonal versions of objects to preview an image and later ray-trace them to produce a more polished image (see Figure 10.1).

The basic ideas of the algorithm have been suggested in other sources [REQ80a, REQ80b], but were not described in enough detail to be implemented. We will present the algorithm so that it may not only be implemented but also verified. As long as the polygons of an object bound a volume of finite extent and each polygon is convex, the algorithm will work and will produce a new object that satisfies the same restrictions.

The paper is organized as follows: first, we present an overview of the algorithm. Then the data structure used by the algorithm is described, followed by a detailed description of the algorithm. A discussion of results, problems and extensions concludes the paper.

2. Overview

Our algorithm operates on two objects at a time. The routines can be called successively using the results of earlier operations to create more complicated objects. Each object is represented as a collection of polygons and vertices; each spatially distinct vertex is represented exactly once, and each polygon contains a list of references to vertices. Each polygon also contains a normal that points outwards from the object. Each vertex contains a list of references to other vertices connected to it by an edge.

This research was sponsored in part by the Digital Equipment Corporation and the Office of Naval Research under contract N00014–78–C–0396, Andries van Dam, principal investigator.

The algorithm first subdivides all polygons in each of the objects so that no two polygons intersect. Two non-coplanar polygons *intersect* if a vertex of one lies in the interior of a face or edge of the other, or if an edge of one crosses an edge or face of the other. Polygons that share a vertex or an edge, or that are coplanar, do not intersect. The logic for not intersecting coplanar polygons is described in the last paragraph of section 4.

Once the polygons of both objects have been subdivided, the polygons of each object are classified with respect to the surface of the other object. A polygon in one object may lie inside, outside, or on the boundary of the other object. Vertex adjacency information is used here so that the same classification can be assigned to polygons that are adjacent and do not cross the surface of the other object. This avoids comparing all polygons in one object with all polygons in the other object. The boundary of the combination of the objects will be a subset of all the polygons in both objects. Each polygon's classification is determined by casting a ray from the polygon through the other object and testing the intersection point and surface normal of the nearest intersecting polygon in the other object. The algorithm uses the classification of each polygon to retain or delete it according to the set operation being performed.

As the algorithm proceeds it modifies the objects until, finally, the set of all polygons in both modified objects forms the resulting object.

3. Object Data Structure

While these CSG routines are flexible enough to operate on many different types of objects, the objects must satisfy certain restrictions. Because we are performing operations on the boundaries of volumes, each object must be constructed of polygons that form the topological boundary of the closure of an open set of finite extent in R^3 [REQ80]. More simply, an object must be the surface of a volume and must not have dangling faces or edges. This restriction enables us to efficiently distinguish the interior of the object from the exterior. Planes and other surfaces that do not enclose a volume are not valid objects, but can often be modified to bound some volume. Figure 3.1 shows examples of two valid and two invalid objects.

Each polygon in an object must satisfy five restrictions. (1) It must be planar and convex. (2) No three vertices in the polygon may be collinear. (3) It may not contain the same vertex twice. (4) The vertices must be ordered clockwise when viewed from outside the object, so that cross-products using the directed edges of the polygon may be used to determine the interior of the object. (5) No polygon may intersect any other polygon in the object. A simple verification program can check that the order of the vertices in each polygon agrees with the direction of the normal, and verify that all polygons are convex and planar. Combining two valid objects always produces a new valid object which therefore does not need to be verified.

The vertex data structure contains the spatial location of the vertex as well as a list of pointers to adjacent vertices and a "status" field. Initially, the status field is set to UNKNOWN, but as the algorithm proceeds, this field changes to indicate whether the vertex is INSIDE, OUTSIDE, or on the BOUNDARY of the other object. The list of adjacencies is used for traversing the edges of the object to find connected regions of vertices with identical status. This adjacency informations calculated after the objects have been intersected with each other.

The polygon structure includes a list of pointers to the vertices of the polygon, the plane equation, and the extent of the polygon. The plane equation is used as the polygon normal, and is also used when intersecting polygons. The extent is used to determine quickly if two polygons do not intersect.

The object structure consists of the extent of the object, an array of vertices, and an array of polygons. Again, the extent is used to determine quickly when a polygon does not intersect the object. The data structures for objects, vertices, and polygons are shown in Figure 3.2.

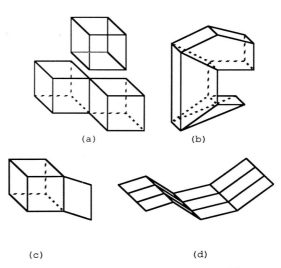

(a) (b)

(c) (d)

Fig. 3.1: Objects (a) and (b) are valid; objects (c) and (d) are not

Object Structure
  array of vertices
  array of polygons
  object extent (minimum and maximum x,y,z)

Vertex Structure
  spatial location (x, y, z)
  array of pointers to adjacent vertices
  status (inside, outside, boundary, or unknown)

Polygon Structure
  array of pointers to vertices
  polygon extent (minimum and maximum x,y,z)
  polygon plane equation (x,y,z,d)

Fig 3.2: Data structures

4. Intersecting the Objects

The first step in the algorithm is splitting both objects so that the polygons in each do not intersect. In this discussion, we will refer to the object which is to be split as objectA and to a polygon in that object as polygonA. Similarly, polygonB is a polygon in objectB, the other object.

The first part of Figure 4.1 explains how pairs of objects are subdivided. When polygonA is split, new edges will be introduced into objectA, and a face that is split will become two or more new faces. The new edges in objectA may intersect the interiors of faces of objectB, possibly requiring further subdivision of polygons in objectB.

When the splitting routine is initially called, the first object is objectA and the second is objectB. After this initial splitting, no face of the second object intersects the interior of any face of the first object. So on the second pass, the new faces that are generated by splitting faces of the second object create no further intersections with interiors of faces in the first object; only new edge intersections are created.

Consequently on the third pass (the first object is once again objectA), polygons in objectA will only be changed by splitting edges at points where these edges intersect new edges of the second object. This will, as before, introduce no new edges that intersect faces in objectB. It also will not introduce any new edge-edge intersections, since the only new edges that are added come in the interiors of polygonAs, and these never intersect the faces or edges of polygonBs. Thus there is no need to make a fourth pass; the algorithm is finished.

Subdividing Objects

split the first object so that it doesn't intersect the second object
split the second object so that it doesn't intersect the first object
split the first object again, resolving newly introduced intersections

Splitting ObjectA by ObjectB

if extent of objectA overlaps extent of objectB
   for each polygonA in objectA
      if the extent of polygonA overlaps the extent of objectB
         for each polygonB in objectB
            if the extents of polygonA and polygonB overlap
               analyze them as in "5. Do Two Polygons Intersect?"
               if they are not COPLANAR and do INTERSECT
                  subdivide polygonA as in
                    "6. Subdividing Non-Coplanar Polygons"
               else if they do NOT_INTERSECT
               or if they are COPLANAR
               (do nothing)

Fig. 4.1: Splitting objects

The second part of Figure 4.1 explains how all the polygons in one object are split so that they do not intersect a second object. For each pair of polygons with overlapping extents, the routine described in the section "Do Two Polygons Intersect?" determines whether the polygons are COPLANAR, INTERSECT in a line (or possibly a point), or do NOT_INTERSECT. Pairs of polygons that INTERSECT are subdivided as described in the section "Subdividing Polygons." New polygons are added to the end of the the list of polygons in objectA, and are checked against objectB after all original polygons in objectA have been checked. Those that are COPLANAR or do NOT_INTERSECT are not subdivided.

Although COPLANAR pairs of polygons are not subdivided, after the first two subdivisions all groups of adjacent coplanar polygons in one object will have corresponding groups of coplanar polygons in the other object. While the polygons in these groups may not be identical, the regions they cover will be the same. Each edge of a polygon is shared by at least one other polygon. If an edge of polygonB crosses polygonA, then there must be another polygonB which also has that edge. If this polygonB is not coplanar with polygonA, then polygonA will be subdivided when compared to this second polygonB. If the adjacent polygonB is coplanar with polygonA, it either extends beyond polygonA (and will eventually be subdivided by some polygonA), or is contained within polygonA and, again, will not be used to subdivide polygonA.

5. Do Two Polygons Intersect?

This section describes how to determine whether two polygons are coplanar, intersect in a line (or possibly a point), or do not intersect. The first step in determining whether the two polygons intersect is finding the signed distance from each of the vertices in polygonA to the plane of polygonB. The distance is positive if the normal vector points from the plane of the polygon towards the point. If these distances are all zero, then the polygons are coplanar. If they are all positive or all negative, then polygonA lies entirely to one side of the plane of polygonB, and thus the two polygons do not intersect; otherwise they may intersect, and the signed distance from each vertex in polygonB to the plane of polygonA is computed. Again, if the distances are all positive or all negative, then polygonB lies entirely to one side of polygonA, and the two polygons do not intersect. Coplanar polygons would have been discovered by the first test, so the distances cannot all be zero.

If the preceding tests are inconclusive, then we calculate the line of intersection of the two planes. The line of intersection L is determined by a point P and a direction D. Some segment of this line is interior to or on the perimeter of polygonA, and some segment is interior to or on the perimeter of polygonB. If these two

segments overlap, then the polygons intersect. If the segments do not overlap, then the polygons do not intersect.

Data structures for each of the two segments store information that is used to subdivide polygonA and polygonB, if they intersect. This information includes the distance from P to the starting and ending points of the segment, as well as descriptors that record whether each point of the segment corresponds to a vertex of the polygon it spans, a point on its edge, or a point on its face. Because all polygons are convex and contain no collinear vertices, it follows that the intersection is a single line segment and that three descriptors are sufficient to describe the entire segment: one for the starting point, a second for the interior of the segment, and a third for the ending point. A segment that starts at a vertex, crosses a face, and ends at an edge can be represented by the mnemonic vertex-face-edge. Similarly, any type of segment can be represented by a three-word mnemonic.

Only the distances from P to the start and end of the segment are necessary to determine if the polygons intersect. If the segments overlap, then the additional information is used later to subdivide the polygons.

The intersection of L with either polygon must both start and end at a vertex or an edge. In addition to the beginning and ending points on L and the three type descriptors for the segment, the segment structure stores the indices of the vertices preceding the endpoints of the segment (for example, B and E in Figure 6.3a-q). The segment data structure is shown in Figure 5.1.

> distance of start of segment from P
> distance of end of segment from P
> descriptors for starting, middle, and ending points
> index of polygon vertex near start point
> index of polygon vertex near end point

Fig. 5.1: Segment data structure

The remainder of this section and the following sections discuss operations on polygonA; these same operations are also performed on polygonB.

The segment structure is filled in as follows. There are six different ways in which L can intersect polygonA. They are characterized by the types of the starting, middle, and ending points of the intersection segment. Because the polygons are convex, the segment starts at a vertex or edge, continues through a vertex, an edge, or the face, and ends at a vertex or edge. Of the twelve combinations, six are not possible. Vertex-edge-edge, edge-edge-vertex, and edge-edge-edge are impossible because any segment that contains edge points in the middle must begin and end at a vertex; if a segment contains some points on an edge, it must contain all points on the edge, including both endpoints. Similarly, edge-vertex-edge, vertex-vertex-edge and edge-vertex-vertex are impossible. Figure 5.2 gives examples of the six possibilities.

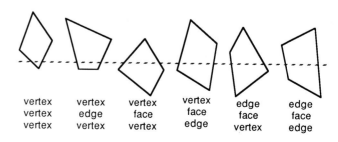

vertex	vertex	vertex	vertex	edge	edge
vertex	edge	face	face	face	face
vertex	vertex	vertex	edge	vertex	edge

**Fig. 5.2: Intersection possibilities of
a polygon and a line in a plane**

The distances of all the vertices of polygonA from the plane of polygonB were calculated for an earlier test; they are now used to find where L crosses polygonA, since the distance from each vertex to the plane of polygonB is proportional to the distance from the vertex to L. Vertices with distance zero lie on L, while adjacent vertices with distances that differ in sign lie on opposite sides of L and thus are endpoints of an edge that crosses L. For a vertex intersection the index of the vertex is saved in the segment structure and the endpoint type is set to VERTEX (B and E in Figure 6.3b). For an edge intersection, the ratio of the calculated vertex distances is used to find the intersection point, and the intersection point is used to find the distance between the intersection point and P along L. The index of the first vertex of the edge is saved and the endpoint type is set to EDGE (B and E in Figure 6.3k).

The midpoint descriptor is determined from the endpoints of the segment. It is set to EDGE if the endpoints of the segment are adjacent vertices in polygonA, and to VERTEX if the endpoints are the same vertex. Otherwise, the middle points must lie in the FACE of the polygon.

6. Subdividing Non-coplanar Polygons

Given two polygons, polygonA and polygonB, that intersect and are not coplanar, we must subdivide them so that the resulting smaller polygons do not intersect and are still legal polygons. We are also given two segment structures, one representing the intersection of polygonA with L, the other representing the intersection of polygonB with L.

To split polygonA so that none of the resulting smaller polygons intersect polygonB, we need to find the intersection of segmentA and segmentB and determine the type of that intersection segment with respect to polygonA. If either end of segmentA is changed, then the type of that end becomes the same type as the middle points (Figure 6.1).

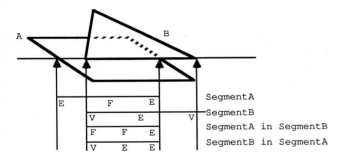

Fig. 6.1: Intersecting two segments

To subdivide polygonA so that the new polygons do not intersect polygonB, the intersection segment must become an edge in the decomposition. The splitting of polygonA is dependent on how the intersection segment cuts across it. Since the starting point can be a vertex, an edge, or a face, as can the midpoints and the endpoint, there are at most $3\times3\times3 = 27$ different kinds of intersection segments. Thirteen of these segment types are impossible, because they have middle point types that are of lower dimension than one of the end types, and in convex polygons that is not possible. Of the remaining fourteen types, four are symmetric to other types with their endpoints swapped. We then need discuss only ten.

In the list of 27 segment types in Figure 6.2, the thirteen impossible types are marked with an "X," and the four symmetric cases are marked with an "S." The remaining ten are numbered to correspond with the discussion that follows. A description of the geometry of the intersection for each of these ten types follows, as does a discussion of the method of splitting polygonA into smaller polygons for each type.

(1)	vertex-vertex-vertex	(X)	edge-edge-face
(X)	vertex-vertex-edge	(S)	edge-face-vertex
(X)	vertex-vertex-face	(8)	edge-face-edge
(2)	vertex-edge-vertex	(9)	edge-face-face
(3)	vertex-edge-edge	(X)	face-vertex-vertex
(X)	vertex-edge-face	(X)	face-vertex-edge
(4)	vertex-face-vertex	(X)	face-vertex-face
(5)	vertex-face-edge	(X)	face-edge-vertex
(6)	vertex-face-face	(X)	face-edge-edge
(X)	edge-vertex-vertex	(X)	face-edge-face
(X)	edge-vertex-edge	(S)	face-face-vertex
(X)	edge-vertex-face	(S)	face-face-edge
(S)	edge-edge-vertex	(10)	face-face-face
(7)	edge-edge-edge		

Fig. 6.2: Identification of valid segment types

The diagrams for each type of segment (Figure 6.3) illustrate the intersection segment and how a polygon with that type of intersection is subdivided. The vertex in the segment structure associated with the beginning of the intersection segment is marked with a "B" and the vertex of the end is marked with an "E." Vertices that are added so that the polygon can be split are marked "M" and "N." The vertices are ordered clockwise in the diagrams.

Note that all subdivisions produce only legal new polygons; no collinear vertices or non-convex polygons are introduced. All vertices that are added must lie on the boundary of objectB, and are thus marked as boundary vertices. These boundary vertices play an important role in selecting polygons for the resultant object (section 8).

(1) Vertex-vertex-vertex — The polygon is intersected at a single vertex and does not need to be subdivided. The vertex is marked as a boundary vertex (Figure 6.3a).

(2) Vertex-edge-vertex — The polygon is intersected along an entire edge and does not need to be subdivided. Both vertices are marked as boundary vertices (Figure 6.3b).

(3) Vertex-edge-edge — The segment intersects the polygon along part of an edge, starting at a vertex and ending in the interior of the edge. The vertex is marked as a boundary vertex. A new vertex is added in the interior of the edge and the polygon is subdivided so that it forms two new polygons (Figures 6.3c and 6.3d).

(4) Vertex-face-vertex — The segment cuts across the polygon starting at a vertex and ending at a vertex. The polygon is cut into two polygons along the line between the two vertices and both vertices are marked as boundary vertices (Figure 6.3e).

(5) Vertex-face-edge — The segment cuts the polygon starting at a vertex, crossing a face, and ending at an edge. The vertex is marked as a boundary vertex. A new vertex is added along the edge and the polygon is divided into two polygons (Figure 6.3f).

(6) Vertex-face-face — The segment crosses part of the polygon, starting at a vertex and ending in the interior of the face. The vertex is marked as a boundary vertex. A new vertex is added in the face. If the segment continued, it would either pass through one of the vertices on the other side of the polygon or miss all of them. If the extended segment passes through a vertex, the polygon is divided into four new polygons to avoid introducing collinear edges or non-convex polygons in the decomposition (Figure 6.3g). If the segment misses the vertices, then the polygon is divided into three new polygons (Figure 6.3h).

(7) Edge-edge-edge — The intersection starts at a point in the interior of an edge and ends at a point in the interior of the same edge, possibly the same point. If the points are not the same, then two new vertices are added along the edge and the polygon is divided into three new polygons (Figure 6.3i). Otherwise, if the intersection is a single point on the edge, then a single new vertex is added along the edge and the polygon is divided into two polygons (Figure 6.3j).

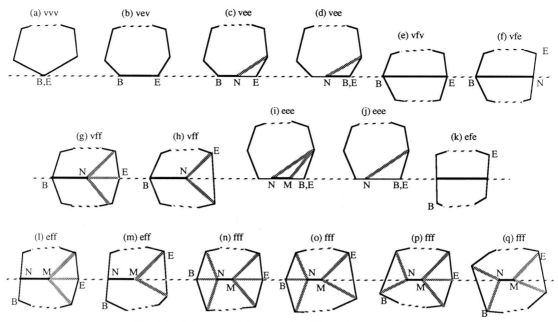

Fig. 6.3: Polygon subdivisions for different segment types

(8) Edge-face-edge — The polygon is cut across its face starting and ending at two different edges. Two new vertices are added along the edges and the polygon is divided into two polygons along the intersection line (Figure 6.3k).

(9) Edge-face-face — The segment cuts across part of the polygon starting at an edge and ending in the interior of the face. Two new vertices are added, one in the face and one along the edge. If the extension of the intersection segment would pass through a vertex, then the polygon is divided into four new polygons, just as with (6) vertex-face-face (Figure 6.3l). Otherwise, the polygon becomes three new polygons (Figure 6.3m).

(10) Face-face-face — In this final case the intersection segment both starts and ends in the interior of the polygon, possibly at the same point. If the intersection is a single point, then one new vertex is added, otherwise two new vertices are added. As with (9) edge-face-face and (6) vertex-face-face, the continuation of the segment will hit either a vertex or an edge of the polygon, this time in both directions. Figures 6.3n-q illustrate how the polygon is divided into four, five, or six new polygons depending on where the segment crosses the perimeter of the polygon.

These descriptions mention several operations that have not yet been explained. Some add a vertex in the interior of an edge, some add a vertex in the interior of a face, and most replace a polygon with several new polygons.

When a vertex must be added in the interior of an edge, the intersection segment structure contains the distance of the new vertex from P on L. By using that distance and the equation for the line of intersection, we can find the coordinates of the point. The intersection segment structure also contains the index of the first vertex of the edge that is intersected. The calculated point, which may have suffered from some floating-point error, is projected onto this edge. If the vertex has coordinates different from all existing vertices, then a new vertex is added to the object; otherwise, nothing is added.

Adding a vertex that lies in the interior of a face is more complicated. Again, the approximate coordinates are found by substituting the distance of the new point along L into the equation of L. The new point is then projected onto the plane of the polygon and the vertex is added just as a new vertex along an edge is added.

In addition to updating edges and adding new vertices, polygons must be replaced with smaller polygons. Figure 6.3 shows how a polygon is subdivided in each case, but if the original polygon has few vertices, the decomposition may produce degenerate polygons containing only two vertices. These polygons should not be added to the object, and are ignored. Figure 6.4 (after section 10) shows wireframe renderings of a pair of overlapping cubes and their state after having been intersected with each other.

7. Classifying Polygons

A routine that determines the position of polygonA relative to objectB is used several times by the algorithm. It is given objectB and a polygonA and returns the position of polygonA with respect to objectB: INSIDE, OUTSIDE, on the boundary of objectB with the normal vector facing in the SAME direction as the normal vector to objectB at that point, or on the boundary of objectB with the normal vector facing in the OPPOSITE direction.

The average of the vertices of a polygon is called the barycenter. A ray is cast from the barycenter of polygonA in the direction of the normal vector to polygonA, and is intersected with every polygonB in objectB. The polygonB that intersects the ray closest to the barycenter is found. If the barycenter does not lie in the plane of the nearest polygonB, then the direction of the normal vector to polygonB determines whether polygonA is inside or outside objectB. If the normal to polygonB points toward polygonA, then polygonA is OUTSIDE objectB; otherwise, polygonA is INSIDE objectB. If no polygons were intersected, then polygonA is OUTSIDE objectB. If the origin of the ray lies in the plane of the nearest polygonB, then polygonA lies in the boundary of objectB. In this case, if the normal vectors of polygonA and polygonB point in the same direction polygonA is classified as SAME; otherwise, it is classified as OPPOSITE. These two classifications are used in the next section.

The ray can intersect each polygonB in objectB in several different ways. To determine an intersection type, we need to know the dot product of the ray being cast with the normal vector of the polygonB being checked, and the signed distance from the barycenter to the plane of polygonB in the direction of the normal vector. Figure 7.1 shows the five possible intersection types.

First, if the signed distance is negative, then polygonB is behind the barycenter and can be ignored.

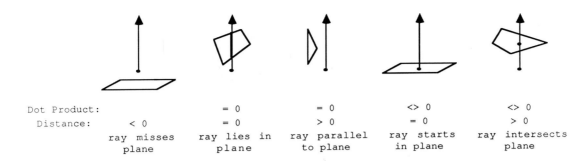

Fig. 7.1: Intersections of a ray and polygonB

Second, if the dot product and the distance are both zero, then the ray lies in the plane of polygonB. Without complicated analysis of all the polygons that the ray intersects, it is impossible to determine the status of polygonA in this case, so the direction of the ray must be perturbed by some small random value and the classification retried for the new direction. Although it is theoretically possible that an infinite number of random perturbations will all lead to invalid directions, in our implementation we have never needed to perturb the direction more than once to find a valid direction.

Third, if the dot product is zero and the distance is positive, the ray is parallel to the plane but never intersects it and therefore does not intersect polygonB.

Fourth, when the dot product is non-zero and the distance is zero, the barycenter lies in the plane of polygonB. If the barycenter lies outside polygonB in that plane, then the ray does not intersect polygonB; otherwise, polygonA lies on the boundary of objectB and this must be the closest intersection.

The fifth case occurs when the dot product is non-zero and the distance is positive. The point of intersection of the ray and the plane of polygonB must be inside polygonB, outside polygonB, or on an edge of polygonB. If an edge is hit, the ray must be perturbed and recast for all polygonBs in objectB. If the ray misses the interior of polygonB, then there is no intersection. Otherwise, the ray intersects polygonB, and this intersection is saved if it is closer than any intersection yet found. Figure 7.2 shows pseudocode for the polygon classification routine.

8. Marking Vertices

Once each object has been split so that none of the polygons in either object intersects any of the polygons in the other object, all the vertices in each object that lie on the boundary of the other object will have been marked as BOUNDARY vertices by the routines that subdivided each polygon. This section describes how the remaining vertices, still marked as UNKNOWN, are classified as lying INSIDE or OUTSIDE the other object so that the set of polygons that make up the resulting object may be found. This resulting set of polygons is a subset of all the polygons in both of the objects. Whether or not each polygon is in this subset depends on whether it lies INSIDE, OUTSIDE, or on the BOUNDARY of the other object. The polygon classification routine could be called to classify each polygon in both objects, but this would be time-consuming. Instead, all the vertices of the object are classified by classifying just a few of the polygons. Once all the vertices have been classified, all of the polygons that have at least one vertex not in the boundary of the other object can be classified, and only the polygons that have exclusively boundary vertices need to make extensive use of the ray-casting routine. This procedure must be executed for both objects.

```
create a RAY starting at the barycenter of polygonA
  in the direction of the normal of polygonA
while no successful cast has been made
  for each polygonB in objectB
    find the DOT PRODUCT of RAY direction
        with the normal of polygonB
    find the DISTANCE from barycenter to the plane of polygonB
    if (DOT PRODUCT = 0) and (DISTANCE = 0)
      cast is unsuccessful — leave loop and perturb
    else if (DOT PRODUCT = 0) and (DISTANCE > 0)
      no intersection
    else if (DOT PRODUCT <> 0) and (DISTANCE = 0)
      if RAY passes through interior or edge of polygonB
        save polygonB — this is closest possible intersection
      else
        no intersection
    else if (DOT PRODUCT <> 0) and (DISTANCE > 0)
      find intersection point of ray with plane of polygonB
      if intersection is closest yet
        if RAY passes through interior of polygonB
          (first check if point is within extent of polygonB)
          save polygonB
        else if RAY hits an edge of polygonB
          cast is unsuccessful — leave loop and perturb
        else
          no intersection
  if cast is unsuccessful
    perturb RAY by a small random value
end while
if there were no intersections
  return OUTSIDE
find the polygonB closest to POINT
find the DOT PRODUCT of closest polygonB normal and RAY
find the DISTANCE to closest polygonB
if (DISTANCE == 0)
  if (DOT PRODUCT > 0)
    return SAME
  else if (DOT PRODUCT < 0)
    return OPPOSITE
else if (DOT PRODUCT > 0)
  return INSIDE
else if (DOT PRODUCT < 0)
  return OUTSIDE
```

Fig. 7.2: Polygon Classification Routine

We first use the edges of the subdivided polygons to calculate the adjacency information for each object. Then begin at the first polygon in the object structure that contains a vertex marked UNKNOWN. The polygon cannot lie in the boundary of the other object, since it contains at least one vertex that does not lie on the boundary; the polygon classification routine determines if the polygon is INSIDE or OUTSIDE the other object. The vertex is marked appropriately, and all UNKNOWN vertices connected by edges to this vertex are marked identically. Since all BOUNDARY vertices were detected when the polygons were split, the vertices of each object have been divided into connected regions: each connected region is separated from other regions by boundary vertices, and all the vertices in a connected region of one object lie on the same side of the other object. Once the entire region has been marked, another polygon with vertices marked UNKNOWN is found. The operation is repeated until all polygons have been checked and all vertices classified. Figure 8.1 shows pseudocode for the region-marking routine.

Region-Marking Routine:
calculate adjacency information for all vertices of objectA
for each polygonA in objectA
    if any vertices are marked UNKNOWN
        call Polygon Classification Routine
            to determine if polygonA INSIDE/OUTSIDE objectB
        for each UNKNOWN vertex in polygonA
            call Vertex Marking Routine

Vertex-Marking Routine:
mark the specified UNKNOWN vertex as INSIDE/OUTSIDE
for each vertexA′ adjacent to vertexA
    if vertexA′ is marked UNKNOWN
        call this routine recursively for vertexA

Fig. 8.1: Region- and vertex-marking routines

9. Selecting Polygons for Output

Once the two objects have been intersected and all vertices have been classified as INSIDE, OUTSIDE, or BOUNDARY, the polygons that comprise the resulting object must be selected. Figure 9.1 shows which polygons are in the set of polygons that comprise the CSG combination of the two objects.

	polygons in A			
	inside	outside	same	opposite
A ∪ B	no	yes	yes	no
A ∩ B	yes	no	yes	no
A − B	no	yes	no	yes

	polygons in B			
	inside	outside	same	opposite
A ∪ B	no	yes	no	no
A ∩ B	yes	no	no	no
A − B	yes	no	no	no

Fig. 9.1: Selecting polygons for output

When a difference is performed, each polygonB inside objectA must have the order of its vertices reversed, and its normal vector must be inverted, since the interior of objectB becomes the exterior of the resulting object. Faces classified as SAME or OPPOSITE in one object exactly match faces in the other object. In the combination, at most one face needs to be added. We have chosen to always take that face from objectA, so polygons in objectB classified as SAME or OPPOSITE are never retained. Once the

appropriate polygons have been deleted from both objects, the objects are combined to form the resulting object.

Most polygons are classified by examining the classifications of their vertices. Polygons that have only boundary vertices are classified by the ray-casting routine described earlier. Vertices classified as INSIDE or OUTSIDE are deleted or kept according to the table in Figure 9.1, although BOUNDARY vertices are never deleted. Once the polygons have been deleted, the normals and vertices reversed if necessary, and the object parts linked together, the CSG operation is complete.

The pseudocode in Figure 9.2 for the polygon selection routine makes use of the polygon classification routine described previously. Figure 9.3 (after section 10) shows wireframe and raster renderings of two cubes which have been unioned, intersected, and differenced.

(called by the union, intersection, and difference control routines)
(deletes polygons in objectA that are STATUS relative to objectB)

for each polygonA in objectA
    for each vertexA in polygonA
        if the status of vertexA is not BOUNDARY
            the status of the polygonA is the status of vertexA
    if no status for polygonA was found
        determine status of polygonA
        using the polygon classification routine
    if polygons of this status should be deleted for this operation
        delete polygonA from objectA

for each vertexA in objectA
    if vertices with this status should be deleted for this operation
        delete vertexA

Fig 9.2: Selecting polygons for output

10. Conclusions

We have presented a straightforward yet robust algorithm for performing CSG operations on polygonal objects. The algorithm runs in $O(V^2 + P^2)$ where V is the total number of vertices and P the total number of polygons in both objects after subdividing. The time can probably be reduced to $O(V \log V + P \log P)$ with suitable sorting of polygons and vertices.

Floating-point granularity must be considered when implementing this algorithm. A CSG combination that strains many commercial solid modellers combines two unit cubes, one rotated N degrees first around the x-axis, then around the y-axis, and finally around the z-axis [JOH86] Most commercial solid modelers fail when $0.5 degree < N < 1 degree$. Our implementation is successful for $N > 0.1 degree$. Rather than failing catastrophically on the test case for smaller values of N, the algorithm detects a potential error and prints an error message. The error is detected when the signed distances from the vertices of one polygon to the plane of another are calculated. A consistency check signals that the calculated distances are impossible.

There are several places where we attempt to correct possible floating point problems. All floating point comparisons are made so that numbers that differ less than a small predefined value are considered equal. For example, when a vertex is added to an object, the list of existing vertices is checked for an equivalent vertex using the approximate comparison above. If a match is found, then the coordinates of the new vertex are set to be identical to the coordinates of the vertex that was found. In addition, when the coordinates of a new vertex that lies on the edge or face of a polygon are calculated, the calculated value is projected onto the edge or face to ensure that small errors will not propogate.

We are currently continuing work on this algorithm in several directions. This algorithm divides polygons up more than is strictly necessary. After several operations, what might have been a single polygon in the resulting object may have instead become 10 or 20. We would like to combine these coplanar faces to reduce the number of polygons in a resulting object. Also, when several CSG operations must be performed to generate an object, the intermediate results are often not of interest. A modification of this algorithm might subdivide all of the sub-objects at once, classifying each polygon with respect to all of the other objects. If the entire operation were performed at one time, a tremendous amount of overhead from individual operations might be saved.

Figure 10.1 shows a spoon described in SCEFO using CSG. The ray-traced image was rendered in 1300 CPU seconds on a VAX 11/780 running 4.2bsd UNIX. The polygonal image was rendered using a Z-buffer algorithm and this CSG algorithm, taking 76 seconds on the same machine. Both images were rendered at a resolution of 640 $\times$ 512 pixels, and the ray-traced image is antialiased. In addition to making quick polygonal renderings possible, this algorithm is used to generate wireframe representations of objects for interactive modeling and animation previewing.

11. Acknowledgements

We would like to thank Trina Avery, Matthew Kaplan, Barbara Meier, Joseph Pato, and Andries van Dam for reading early versions of the paper. Thanks also goes to Andries van Dam and the Brown University Computer Graphics Group for their assistance and support.

12. References

FOL82 Foley, J. D. and A. van Dam, *Fundamentals of Interactive Computer Graphics*, Addison-Wesley, 1982.

REQ80a
Requicha, A. A. G. and H. B. Voelcker, "Constructive Solid Geometry," Production Automation Project Technical Memorandum TM-25, April 1980.

REQ80b
Requicha, A. A. G. and H. B. Voelcker, "Mathematical Foundations of Constructive Solid Geometry: General Topology of Closed Regular Sets", Production Automation Project Technical Memorandum TM-27a, November 1980.

REQ83 Requicha, A. A. G. and H. B. Voelcker, "Solid Modeling: Current Status and Research Directions," *IEEE Computer Graphics and Applications*, 3 (7), October 1983.

REQ85 Requicha, A. A. G. and H. B. Voelcker, "Boolean Operations in Solid Modeling: Boundary Evaluation and Merging Algorithms," *Proceedings of the IEEE* January 1985, pp. 30-44.

ROT82 Roth, Scott, "Ray Casting for Modeling Solids," *Computer Graphics and Image Processing* 18 (1982), pp. 109-144.

STR84 Strauss, P., M. Shantzis and D. Laidlaw, "SCEFO: A Standard Scene Format for Image Creation and Animation," Brown University Graphics Group Memo, Providence, R.I., 1984, 32 pp.

TUR84 Turner, James A., "A Set-Operation Algorithm for Two- and Three-Dimensional Geometric Objects," Architecture and Planning Research Laboratory, College of Architecture, University of Michigan, Ann Arbor, MI, August, 1984.

JOH86 Johnson, Robert H., *Solid Modeling: A State of the Art Report (Second Edition)*, CAD/CIM Alert, Management Roundtable, Inc., 1986.

Volume 20, Number 4, 1986

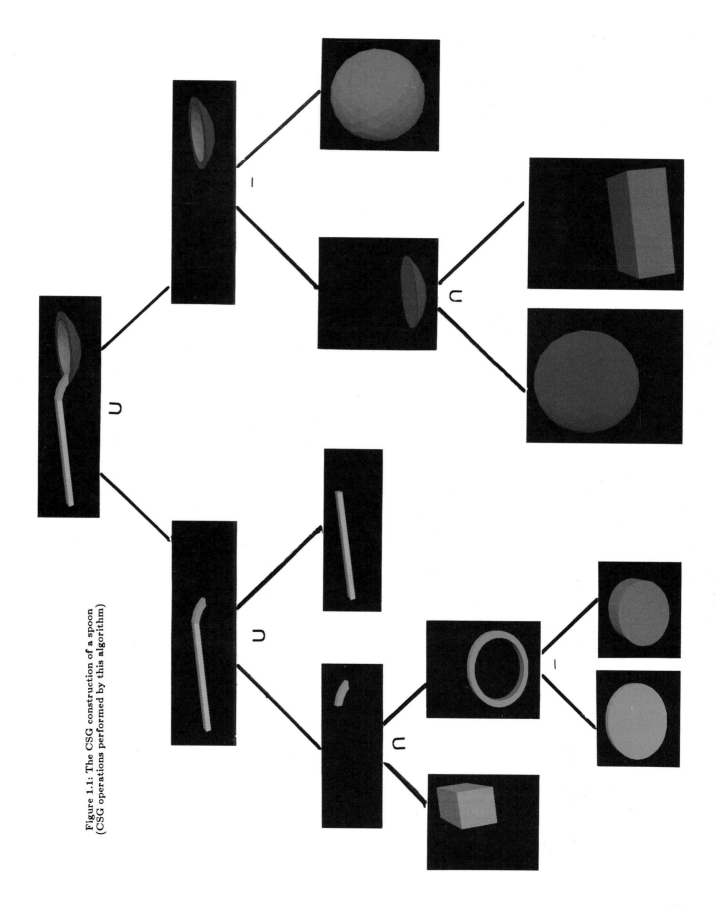

Figure 1.1: The CSG construction of a spoon
(CSG operations performed by this algorithm)

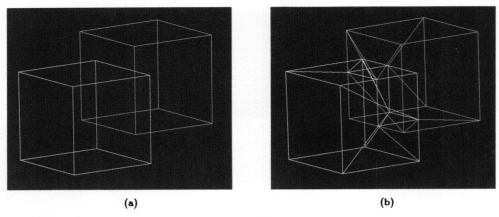

Figure 6.4: (a) Two cubes positioned so that they overlap
(b) The result of splitting the two objects against each other

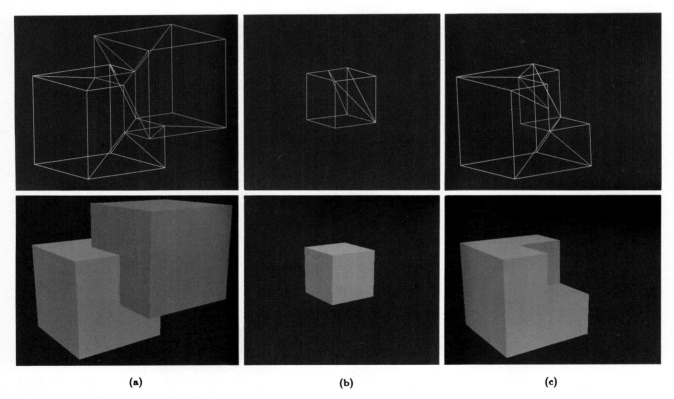

Figure 9.3: Wireframe and raster renderings of two cubes:
(a) union, (b) intersection, (c) difference

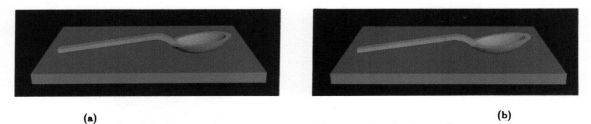

Figure 10.1: (a) was ray-traced and (b) was rendered polygonally
(both images were generated from the same description)

Automated Conversion of Curvilinear Wire-Frame Models
to Surface Boundary Models; A Topological Approach

S. Mark Courter
Engineering Systems Corporation
Baton Rouge, Louisiana 70816

John A. Brewer, III
Mechanical Engineering Department
Louisiana State University
Baton Rouge, Louisiana 70803

ABSTRACT

An algorithm is presented for automatically converting data representing unambiguous, three-dimensional objects in wire-frame form with curvilinear edges into a boundary representation. The method is an important extension to a previously published algorithm based on graph theory and topology. The new method automatically detects and resolves anomalies, such as necks which may appear to be faces, that formerly required human intervention. The topological basis for the solution to this problem is given along with a description of what topological properties a well defined three-dimensional object should have. An implementation has been coded and examples of results are included.

INTRODUCTION

The field of computer graphics has advanced rapidly in recent years and many methods have been developed to represent basic geometric and topological data. The most common of all models is the wire-frame where one represents objects with coordinates and connection information only. Another particularly useful model is the surface boundary representation. This method represents objects by defining the faces forming the boundaries of the object. Boundary representations are generally more useful than wire-frames in geometric modeling applications. Unfortunately, boundary representations are also more difficult to create.

Almost every modeling system has the ability to define wire-frame models since they are initially much easier to specify. A logical approach to creating surface models is to extract surfaces from wire-frame representations. The automatic conversion from wire-frames to surface models has therefore been a research issue for

some time now. The early work in this area has been heavily dependent on geometrical information [IDES73], [LAFU76], [BREW83b], although topological notions are essential in any case. The primary limitation of the geometric approach is that only planar faces can be found.

Methods where topology plays a more important role were introduced very recently [MARK80]. Wesley and Markowski's method makes use of many ideas from topology, both the algebraic and point-set branches. Their algorithm seems to handle just about every type of wire-frame, including holes and ambiguous cases. However, geometric information is still explicitly used (surface normals are calculated) and the faces that are found are required to be planar. Therefore, their method is restricted to objects with straight edges and planar faces.

Strictly topological approaches have been taken by several authors including Dutton and Brigham [DUTT83] and Hanrahan [HANR82]. These methods have the advantage of being able to handle objects with non-planar faces or edges. Fundamentally, these methods use the technique of planar embedding in which the wire-frame is represented as a flat, two-dimensional (2D) edge-vertex graph in which none of the edges intersect except at vertices. The resulting regions created represent the faces of the object. This technique was made possible by the efficient planar embedding algorithm of Tarjan [TARJ71]. The approach is effective for objects with no ambiguities and no holes, however, an object as simple as a brick with a hole in it cannot be handled.

A new topological method for wire-frame translation has been described recently by Ganter and Uicker [GANT83]. Their method is based on earlier work by Cobb [COBB78] and also uses concepts from graph theory. This method also treats the object as an edge-vertex graph which is examined to find a set of independent closed paths called cycles. The set of cycles is then reduced to the set of true faces by combining cycles in a way that reduces edge interaction. The set of faces can then be properly oriented with respect to each other if desired. A deficiency in the Ganter/Uicker implementation, however, is the need for an interactive face editor to handle certain anomalies that can arise with their implementation algorithm. Because there are no inherent limitations in the type of objects that can be handled, as in the previously mentioned algorithms, this method was chosen as the basis for an improved algorithm requiring no human intervention.

THE ALGORITHM

Much of the new algorithm presented here follows Ganter and Uicker's algorithm [GANT83]. Differences occur in the reduction process where fundamental cycles yield actual faces. A major improvement is the addition of logic which automatically identifies and eliminates anomolies, such as invalid faces (necks).

Input

Let us assume that the input for this algorithm is correct and consistent and therefore represents some physically realistic object, although this is not a requirement of the algorithm.

The data required by the algorithm are an edge table (an example is shown in Figure 1), the number of vertices making up the object (v), and the number of edges the object contains (e). The edge table contains pairs of vertices defining each edge of the object. Notice that the actual geometric coordinates of the vertices are not required since only topology is important.

EDGE TABLE

EDGE	END POINTS
1	1 . 2
2	1 . 4
3	1 . 6
4	2 . 3
5	2 . 8
6	3 . 4
7	3 . 9
8	4 . 12
9	5 . 6
10	5 . 12
11	6 . 7
12	6 . 11
13	7 . 8
14	7 . 10
15	8 . 9
16	9 . 10
17	10 . 11
18	11 . 12

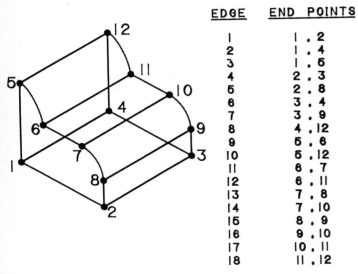

Figure 1. An example object and its data definition.

The input data, which represents a graph, must be converted to a form which is easily manipulated by a computer. Therefore, an adjacency matrix, X, is calculated which represents the graph. This matrix is an v by v symmetric matrix whose elements, $X(i,j)$, are defined such that

$X(i,j)=1$ if there is an edge between vertex i and j
$X(i,j)=0$ if there is no such edge

Finding the Cycles

The first major task is to find a set of linearly independent cycles of the object, which is now represented as a graph. This approach is based on the principle of connectivity from topology, which states that the connectivity of a graph is the maximum number, n, so that the graph has a system of n linear independent cycles. The cycles in this set are called fundamental cycles.

The fundamental cycles are found by first generating a spanning tree of the graph. A spanning tree is a subgraph in which all of the vertices of the original graph remain but some of the edges are removed to eliminate every cycle while keeping the graph in one connected piece. The edges of the graph that are not in the spanning tree are called chords, each one of which will form an independent cycle when added to the tree. Figure 2 shows a spanning tree for the sample object given in Figure 1.

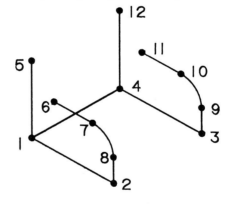

Figure 2. A spanning tree of object generated by Paton's algorithm.

Paton [PATO69] has described an efficient algorithm which combines the process of spanning tree generation with that of cycle formation. Paton's algorithm uses the adjacency matrix for input and performs a breadth-first search (BFS) on the graph to determine which edges will produce a spanning tree. During the process of tree formation, if an edge is found that would form a cycle when added to the tree, the vertices that make up this cycle are recorded as belonging to a fundamental cycle.

Paton's algorithm should be used because it is efficient and because it uses a BFS tree search, which produces low, broad trees and is not dependent on the order of the input data [GANT83]. Low broad trees produce cycles with a minimum number of edges, which is good for most objects encountered in a design environment.

The cycles for the example object found by Paton's algorithm, shown in Figure 3, are stored in the form of a cycle-edge incidence matrix, or more simply, a cycle matrix. The cycle matrix, C, is a q by e unsymmetric matrix, where q is the number of cycles.

An element of C, C(i,j) is defined by:

C(i,j)=1 if edge j is in cycle i
C(i,j)=0 otherwise

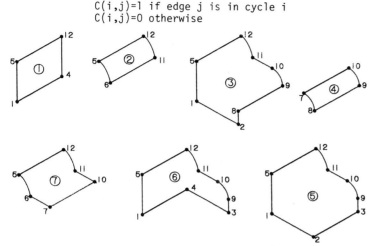

Figure 3. Fundamental cycle set.

Changing Cycles into Faces (The Reduction Process)

In Figure 3 it can be seen that some of the cycles do not represent true faces but are either combinations of true faces or combinations of each other. The process of changing the fundamental cycles to actual faces (the reduction process) constitutes the major part of the wire-frame conversion procedure. This is accomplished by making use of a set operation called the symmetric difference. The symmetric difference of two sets is defined as the union of the sets minus their intersection. For two graphs, G1 and G2, the symmetric difference is a graph consisting of the edges that are in either G1 or G2 but not in both. The symmetric differences analogous to the exclusive-or (XOR) operation found in binary logic.

It is clear that a cycle which is a combination of other cycles can be reduced to a true face if it is replaced by the symmetric difference of it and an appropriate other cycle. The problem, therefore, is to determine the manner in which the cycles can be combined via the symmetric difference in order to produce the true faces of the object. Part of the solution lies in two observations from graph theory [DEO74]:

1. In a graph, there exists a complete set of basic cycles such that no edge appears in more than two of these cycles.

2. When the sum of all edges in all cycles in a graph is a minimum, then the cycles are true faces of the graph.

These results indicate that the goal is to minimize the edge-interaction between cycles. With this in mind, an interactions matrix, Z, is calculated. Each element, Z(i,j), of Z contains the number of edges that face i and face j have in common. This matrix is a q by q symmetric matrix, each element of which is calculated by taking the vector dot product of row i and row j of the cycle matrix. A diagonal element, Z(i,i) contains the number of edges in cycle i.

In order to achieve the maximum possible gain from each reduction, the algorithm requires that the cycle with the highest edge count be checked for reduction by the cycle which has the most number of edges in common with it.

In the following discussion let the symbol i stand for the cycle which has the most number of edges and the symbol j stand for the cycle that has been chosen to reduce cycle i by replacing i with the symmetric difference of cycles i and j.

The cycle with the most edges is found simply by scanning the diagonal elements of Z for the maximum value. The cycle having the highest edge interactivity with i is found by scanning row i (excluding the diagonal element) of matrix Z for a maximum value.

To test the usefulness of reducing cycle i with cycle j a check is made to see if cycle i would have fewer edges after reduction than before. Note that this is an application of observation 1 above.

This test can be expressed mathematically by noting that the number of edges in cycle i before reduction is Z(i,i), while the number after reduction by cycle j is: Z(i,i)-Z(i,j)+Z(j,j)-Z(j,i). The conditional test [GANT83] is therefore:

$$Z(i,i)-Z(i,j)+Z(j,j)-Z(j,i) < Z(i,i)$$
but $Z(i,j) = Z(j,i)$
therefore $Z(j,j) < 2Z(i,j)$

If Z(j,j) = 2 x Z(i,j) then observation 2, a global rather than local criterion, must be used to determine if reduction should occur. This test is accomplished by first summing the elements in row i of Z. A trial reduction is then performed and a new sum of row i and Z calculated. If the new sum is less than the old, then the new cycle is accepted by replacing row i of the cycle and interactions matrix by the trial calculations. If the sum increased then there were no changes made and a new combination of faces are tried.

A question left open by Ganter and Uicker was what to do if the new sum was equal to the old sum. From experiments which were carried out with a variety of objects it was found that allowing a reduction to be done if an equality occurs resulted in a much better performance of the algorithm, with a fewer number of reductions necessary to fully reduce the cycle set.

Another departure from their algorithm was the search routine used to choose which cycles to

combine. Ganter and Uicker used what might be
called a local selection algorithm. When the
first pair of cycles chosen fail the above tests,
the same i is used and j becomes the cycle with
the next highest interactivity with i. If this
in turn fails, then again the next highest
interactive cycle with the same i is chosen and
so on.

An improvement was made by using a more
global selection process. If the first j cycle
chosen fails the tests, then the i,j element of
the interactions matrix is flagged as having been
tried. The entire matrix is then searched for
the largest i having the corresponding largest j.
A major improvement results when several cycles
have the same largest number of edges.

For example, Figure 4 can be used to show
how the two selection approaches would work for a
hypothetical interactions matrix. A local
approach would first attempt to reduce cycle 1
by cycle 4. If that failed, the cycle with the
next highest interactivity with the same cycle 1
(cycle 3) would be tried and so on.

In the approach used here, the first
combination to be tried would be cycle 3 with
cycle 4. If that failed then reducing cycle 1
with cycle 3 would be tried. This approach not
only improves the choice for secondary combinations, but also leads to a better choice of
primary combinations if there are several cycles
with the same maximum number of interactions.

8	1	2	3
1	4	2	2
2	2	8	5
3	2	5	6

Figure 4. A possible interactions matrix.

After a reduction is made, Z is recalculated from C to restore the elements that were
marked. This new algorithm greatly improved the
cycle reduction process, making it faster and
more complete.

The actual reduction process is carried out
by performing an element by element XOR between
rows i and j of the cycle matrix and replacing
row i with the result. The interactions matrix
must be recalculated after each reduction by the
dot product method described earlier. The
reduction process continues until all cycles
have a maximum interactivity of one. The cycle
matrix that results from this process now
defines the true faces in terms of their bounding edges, and the results for the sample object
are shown in Figure 5.

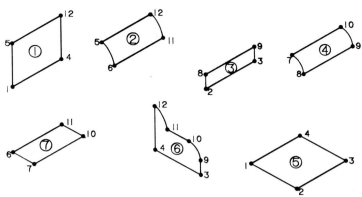

Figure 5. Faces generated from cycle set.

The Closing Face

Recall that the number of fundamental
cycles in a connected graph is e-v+1, while
Euler's Formula states that the number of faces
in a planar graph is e-v+2. The reduction
process minimizes the number of edge-cycle
interactions but does not change the actual
number of cycles present. Where is the missing
face? The answer lies in the fact that a set of
edges can be found which belongs to only one
cycle. These edges form the boundary of the
missing face, which corresponds to the infinite
face of a planar representation of the object.

The "closing face," as it can be called, is
easily found from the cycle matrix by observing
which of its columns contained a single 1. The
column number corresponds to the edge number in
question. These edges define the closing face,
which is included with the other faces by adding
a row to the cycle matrix.

Anomalies

During the process of finding the closing
face it is possible that a set of edges could be
found which belongs to more than two faces.
This indicates that an anomaly has occurred and
the closing face can not be determined until the
conflict has been resolved. Assuming correct
input data, anomalies can occur in three different ways.

The first two forms involve illegal intersections between faces. Since faces can intersect only along edges, any two faces which
contain a point internal to both intersect ille-
gally. The first type of illegal intersection
has two faces intersecting along a line that is
not an edge of the object. This often occurs in
objects with high degrees of symmetry, as shown
in Figure 6(a). The second type has an edge of
one face piercing the interior of the other
face. This often occurs in objects with holes
in them (Figure 6(b)).

The third type of anomaly is the pseudo face, which is caused by a chance alignment of edges in objects with "necks". Although pseudo faces are not involved in any of the illegal face intersections, they are invalid because they cannot separate solid material from empty space. Figure 6(c) shows an example.

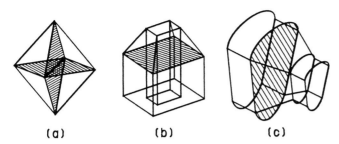

(a)   **(b)**   **(c)**

Figure 6. Invalid face Intersections (a,b) and pseudo face (c).

Automatic Detection and Deletion of Invalid Faces

In order to detect and correct anomalies, common characteristics must be found which signal the presence of such problems. One characteristic is the fact that no more than two faces can meet along any one edge. Conversely, any one edge of the object can belong to no more than two faces. Therefore, the presence of edges belonging to more than two faces signals an anomaly which must be dealt with. Another characteristic is that no vertex in a true face has degree greater than two, when that face is considered by itself.

There are basically two distinct processes involved. The first is to detect and delete the invalid faces which cause conflicts to occur. The second is to replace the deleted faces with valid ones built up from the edges belonging to less than two faces. What follows is a description of how these processes work.

Figure 7 shows a "head on" perspective view of the object in figure 6(c). In this planar view, the shaded regions represent valid faces that have been found up to this point in the algorithm. Cycles 5 and 9, shown in dark outline, are both invalid faces that have taken the place of two actual faces, which are shown as unshaded regions. Notice that one of the unshaded regions represents the closing face.

It can be seen that the edges labeled "a" through "c" belong to more than two faces. This is found by examining each column of the cycle matrix. This set of edges is partitioned into sets of connected components, each of which will be a subset of an invalid face. In Figure 7 there are two such sets The invalid faces are then deleted by zeroing the appropriate row in the cycle matrix. The deleted face number is pushed onto a stack to be used later in restoring valid faces.

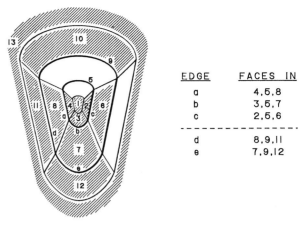

EDGE	FACES IN
a	4,5,8
b	3,5,7
c	2,5,6
d	8,9,11
e	7,9,12

Figure 7. Detection of face conflicts.

Replacing Deleted Faces with Valid Ones

The faces that were deleted must now be replaced with valid ones. When invalid faces are deleted, there is left a set of edges of the object which belong to less than two faces. The idea is to form a graph containing the edges of the object that belong to 0 or 1 face. Figure 8 shows the set of edges remaining from the example of Figure 7.

This graph is then passed to Paton's algorithm where it is again broken down into a set of fundamental cycles which may or may not represent valid faces. For an object with no holes, the number of cycles which are returned will be one more than the number of faces deleted in the previous section. This is because the closing face is found in addition to cycles replacing deleted faces. These cycles are then inserted into the cycle matrix of the object where the deleted faces used to be, and the last face is inserted at the end.

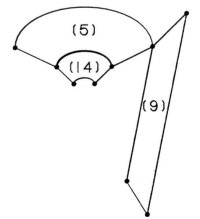

Figure 8. Edges that yield valid faces.

The entire object is then fed back to the cycle reduction routine. If the cycles found by Paton's algorithm correspond to true faces then the conversion process is complete. If however the cycles need further reduction, then the reduction process is used to break the cycles into true faces. Anomalies can't occur this time since the graph passed the Paton's algorithm does not represent a closed three-dimensional object, but a collection of 2-dimensional polygons (topologically) which may or may not be connected.

Results of Implementations of the Algorithm

The following Figures (9 through 12) show the results of implementations of this algorithm for a variety of objects. One version of the algorithm has been incorporated into an existing program called SKETCH [BREW83a, BREW83b] which is used to create wire-frame data from free-hand sketches. A proprietary version of the algorithm has also been developed at Engineering Systems Corporation for use with their computer-aided design and drafting system, DESIGN GRAPHIX (TM). The output of both implementations is in the form of an ordered list of vertices which define the edges of the boundary of each face.

Figures 9 and 10 show the results from the SKETCH implementation. Notice that the faces are all properly oriented with respect toeach other, meaning that each edge is traversed exactly twice, once in each direction. Notice also that the only human interaction involved is to reverse overall orientation of the object, if desired.

Figure 9 shows that the algorithm can handle objects with curved edges and faces. Two edges in this figure are quadratic curves.

Figure 10 shows that an object with potentially invalid faces. If the algorithm finds these faces, they would automatically be removed. However, the spanning tree organization depends to some degree on the order of the original edge table, and, in some cases, the invalid faces may not even be identified as possible faces. This is an example of an object where all of the faces found on the first pass were valid faces, so the anomaly resolution logic was unnecessary.

Figures 11 and 12 show the results of the DESIGN GRAPHIX (TM) implementation, which is used as part of a hidden-line removal package. The hidden-line routine accepts face information in the form of vertex lists which are generated from wire-frame data. Notice that it can handle multiple objects at a time if desired.

Types of Objects Handled

This algorithm will presently handle any wire-frame automatically if it represents a valid 3-D connected object without holes. Pseudofaces and illegal intersections are detected and replaced with valid faces with no human intervention required.

The possibility also exists for ambiguities to occur. If an ambiguous wire-frame is input to the algorithm, one valid solution will always be found, but the user has no control over which solution this will be. The solution found depends on the nature of the original cycle set, which is affected by the order of the edges in the input data.

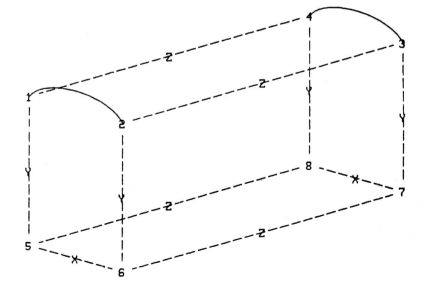

```
0 INVALID FACES FOUND AND RESOLVED
FACES ORIENTED
    NUMBER OF FACES= 6

#     FACE NODES
1:    4    1    5    8    4
2:    5    6    7    8    5
3:    2    1    4    3    2
4:    3    4    8    7    3
5:    1    2    6    5    1
6:    2    3    7    6    2

REVERSE ORIENTATION OF
OBJECT? y
    (ORIENTATION REVERSED)

#     FACE NODES
1:    4    8    5    1    4
2:    5    8    7    6    5
3:    2    3    4    1    2
4:    3    7    8    4    3
5:    1    5    6    2    1
6:    2    6    7    3    2
=
```

Figure 9

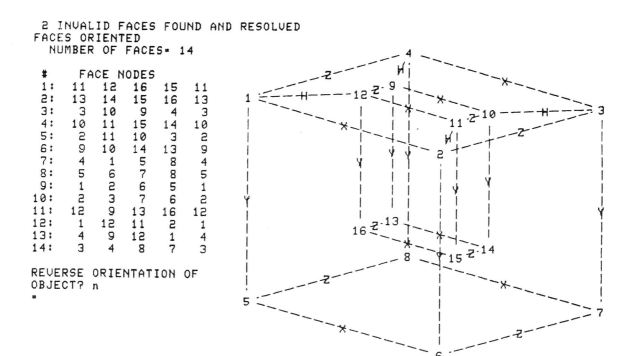

```
2 INVALID FACES FOUND AND RESOLVED
FACES ORIENTED
    NUMBER OF FACES= 14

    #    FACE NODES
    1:   11  12  16  15  11
    2:   13  14  15  16  13
    3:    3  10   9   4   3
    4:   10  11  15  14  10
    5:    2  11  10   3   2
    6:    9  10  14  13   9
    7:    4   1   5   8   4
    8:    5   6   7   8   5
    9:    1   2   6   5   1
   10:    2   3   7   6   2
   11:   12   9  13  16  12
   12:    1  12  11   2   1
   13:    4   9  12   1   4
   14:    3   4   8   7   3

REVERSE ORIENTATION OF
OBJECT? n
```

Figure 10

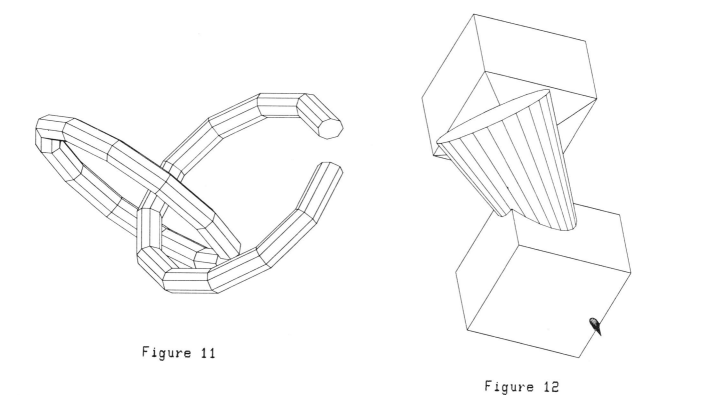

Figure 11

Figure 12

SUMMARY

The problem of converting wire-frame representations to surface boundary representations by using topological methods has been examined. The algorithm is an extension to the method developed by Ganter and Uicker. An implementation has been accomplished and has proven to demonstrate all the features claimed by the authors.

A major deficiency of the Ganter and Uicker method is that it requires human intervention to resolve anomalies. A remedy to this deficiency has been identified and discussed in this paper. A more efficient and functional cycle reduction algorithm was found which reduced the number of iterations needed to get a solution. As an example, the object shown in Figure 10 required 16 reduction iterations with the old method and only 7 using the improved algorithm. In addition, the problem of the equality case of global interactions during the cycle reduction process was addressed and it was found that a reduction should occur if an equality arose.

In summary it is believed that the algorithm for face generation presented here is a significant improvement over present methods in that it allows curved faces to be found just as easily as planar faces and does not require human intervention to deal with face anomalies. This is because the face generation process is totally independent of geometric information concerning edge connections and invalid faces are automatically detected, deleted, and replaced with valid ones.

ACKNOWLEDGEMENTS

This work was funded through a grant from the Army Research Office, Contract Number DAAG29-82-K-0104. Additional support was provided by the Department of Mechanical Engineering and the Computer Graphics Research and Applications Laboratory. Substantial refinement of an implementation of the algorithm has occurred at Engineering Systems Corporation.

REFERENCES

[BREW83a]   Brewer, J. A., "User's Guide: Computer Graphics Program for Generation of Engineering Geometry (SKETCH)", Waterways Experiment Station Report No. k-83-2, June 1983.

[BREW83b]   Brewer, J. A., "Reference Manual: Computer Graphics Program for Generation of Engineering Geometry (SKETCH)", Waterways Experiment Station Report No. k-83-2, September 1983.

[COBB78]   Cobb, E. C., "On the Extraction of Solid Geometry from a Wire Frame Geometric Data Base", M.S. Thesis, University of Wisconsin-Madison, 1978.

[DEO74]   Deo, N., GRAPH THEORY WITH APPLICATIONS TO ENGINEERING AND COMPUTER SCIENCE, Englewood Cliffs, NJ: Prentice-Hall, 1974.

[DUTT83]   Dutton, R. D. and R. C. Brigham, "Efficiently Identifying the Faces of a Solid", COMPUTERS AND GRAPHICS IN MECHANICAL ENGINEERING"-- 7(2): 143-147; 1983.

[GANT83]   Ganter, M. A. and J. J. Uicker, "From Wire-Frame to Solid Geometric: Automated Conversion of Data Representations", COMPUTERS IN MECHANICAL ENGINEERING-- 2(2):40-45 (Sept. '83).

[HANR82]   Hanrahan, P. M., "Creating Volume Models from Edge-Vertex Graphs", ACM COMPUTER GRAPHICS-- 16(3):77-84 (July '82).

[HOCK61]   Hocking, J. G. and G. S. Young, TOPOLOGY, Addison-Wesley, Reading, MA, 1061.

[IDES73]   Idesawa, M., "A System to Generate a Solid Figure from a Three View", BULL. JSME-- 16:216-225 (Feb. '73).

[LAFU76]   Lafue, G., "Recognition of Three-Dimensional Objects from Orthographic Views", PROCEEDINGS 3RD ANNUAL CONFERENCE ON COMPUTER GRAPHICS, INTERACTIVE TECHNIQUES AND IMAGE PROCESSING, ACM/SIGGRAPH, July '76, pp. 103-108.

[MARK80]   Markowski, G. and M. A. Wesley, "Fleshing Out Wire Frames", IBM JOURNAL OF RESEARCH AND DEVELOPMENT -- 24(5):582-597 (Sept. '80).

[PATO69]   Paton, K., "An Algorithm for Finding a Fundamental Set of Cycles of a Graph", COMM OF ACM-- 12(9):514-518 (Sept. '69).

[TARJ71]   Tarjan, R., "An Efficient Planarity Algorithm", Computer Science Department, Report No. CS-244-71, Stanford University, November 1971.

An Adaptive Subdivision Method for Surface-Fitting from Sampled Data

Francis J. M. Schmitt
Brian A. Barsky *
Wen-Hui Du

Laboratoire Image
Ecole Nationale Supérieure des Télécommunications
46, rue Barrault
75634 Paris CEDEX 13
France

Abstract

A method is developed for surface-fitting from sampled data. Surface-fitting is the process of constructing a compact representation to model the surface of an object based on a fairly large number of given data points. In our case, the data is obtained from a real object using an automatic three-dimensional digitizing system. The method is based on an adaptive subdivision approach, a technique previously used for the design and display of free-form curved surface objects. Our approach begins with a rough approximating surface and progressively refines it in successive steps in regions where the data is poorly approximated. The method has been implemented using a parametric piecewise bicubic Bernstein-Bézier surface possessing G^1 geometric continuity. An advantage of this approach is that the refinement is essentially local reducing the computational requirements which permits the processing of large databases. Furthermore, the method is simple in concept, yet realizes efficient data compression. Some experimental results are given which show that the representation constructed by this method is faithful to the original database.

Categories and Subject Descriptors: I.3.5 [**Computer Graphics**]: Computational Geometry and Object Modelling -- Curve, surface, solid, and object representations; Geometric algorithms, and systems; Modelling packages; I.3.4 [**Computer Graphics**]: Graphics Utilities -- Software support; I.3.3 [**Computer Graphics**]: Picture/Image Generation -- Display algorithms; Viewing algorithms

General Terms: Algorithms

Additional Key Words and Phrases: Surface-fitting, adaptive subdivision, geometric modelling, data compression, Bernstein-Bézier patches, geometric continuity, Beta-constraints, shape parameters.

---

* Barsky's permanent address: Berkeley Computer Graphics Laboratory, Computer Science Division, University of California, Berkeley, California 94720, U.S.A.

1. Introduction

1.1. Problem Definition

Computer aided geometric design and modelling (CAGDM) is concerned with the representation, specification, and manipulation of free-form curves and surfaces in an interactive computer environment. For background information on these issues, the reader is invited to consult [Bartels87] [Barsky84] [Boehm84a]. Current research problems were treated in a recent special issue of IEEE Computer Graphics and Applications devoted to this subject [IEEE86]. Much of the research in this field has addressed the development of mathematical techniques for ab initio shape design. The assumption here is that a shape is to be specified by a designer using the tools made available to him or her by the computer system. On the other hand, it is equally important to study the problem of defining mathematical models of already-existing shapes. The idea is that a set of data points is given, from which a model of the curve or surface is to be constructed.

This modelling problem itself can be divided into two types. In the first case, every data point is retained and the number of curve or surface pieces in a piecewise representation is approximately the same as the number of points. When the constructed curve or surface passes through all the points, the data is said to be interpolated. A disadvantage of interpolation is that when there are many data points, the resulting shape representation is cumbersome in both space and computational requirements. When there is a lot of data, it is desirable to have a more compact representation of the shape to achieve data compression. The intent is to begin with a fairly large number of given data points, and approximate them with a curve or surface that is defined by a smaller number of points. This latter approach is referred to as curve- or surface- fitting. It is the problem of surface-fitting from sampled data that is addressed in this paper.

The literature on curve- or surface-fitting is sparse in computer graphics and CAGDM. Some notable exceptions for curve-fitting include the article by Plass and Stone [Plass83] as well as Reeves' dissertation [Reeves81]. For a more approximation theoretic treatment of the curve-fitting problem, the reader is referred to [Chung80], [Cox71], [Dierckx75], [Dierckx82], [Ichida77], [Rice76], and [Rice78].

We would like to model a real-world object from a set of sample points. This database of sample points has a rectangular topology; that is, any non-boundary point is connected to exactly four neighbours (Figure 1).

In our case, this data is obtained from a real object using an automatic three-dimensional digitizing system developed by the Laboratoire IMAGE of the Ecole Nationale Supérieure des Télécommunications [Maître81] [Schmitt85a] (Figure 2) and available commercially from Studec. This micro-processor controlled video-laser data acquisition system is capable of obtaining the coordinates of approxi-

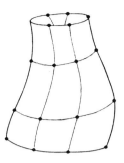

Figure 1. The sample points form a database with a rectangular topology.

Figure 2. The microprocessor-controlled 3D Video-laser data acquisition system.

mately 200,000 points per minute. The goal is to develop a surface-fitting method that is simple in concept, yet capable of realizing significant data compression. Our method is based on an adaptive subdivision approach.

1.2. Subdivision

Subdivision, or splitting, is a type of "divide-and-conquer" technique which has been employed in CAGDM and computer graphics for the design and display of free-form curved surface objects. In this paper, we develop a new use of subdivision: surface-fitting.

For shape design, subdivision has been used as a method of top-down design. The central idea is that the design process is iterative; it starts with a rough overall shape and converges to a final form. This notion corresponds to successive refinement design in CAGDM. At each step, the designer can specify a region which he or she wishes to refine. Through the use of subdivision, additional control vertices defining the shape are created in this region without modifying the current shape. The reader is referred to [Knapp79] for a description of a design scheme based on this approach.

For display of surfaces, subdivision has been used to provide a polygonal approximation to a spline surface. An adaptive subdivision algorithm recursively splits the curve or surface. At each step of the subdivision, a new set of control vertices defining the shape is generated. For all curve and surface representations whose blending functions are continuous, linearly independent, and sum to one, the successive sets of control vertices converge to the original curve or surface. When these vertices are deemed to be sufficiently close to the curve or surface, they can be used as a polygonal approximation of the shape. Of historical interest are the approaches in [Nydegger72] and [Ramer72]. An early algorithm was introduced by Catmull [Catmull75] which subdivides the surface until each piece is no larger than a pixel. More recent algorithms use termination criteria based on bilinearity [Clark79] or flatness [Lane79] [Lane80] [Barsky85a] [Barsky86a]; that is, the recursion stops when the subpolygon is planar to

within a given tolerance. Another early subdivision algorithm was discovered by Chaikin [Chaikin74] which successively chops the corners of a control polygon, yielding a piecewise linear approximation to a quadratic B-spline [Riesenfeld75]. A recursive subdivision algorithm which generates bicubic surfaces of arbitrary topology and which has no closed form is discussed in [Catmull78] [Doo78] [Doo78a].

The mathematical theory of subdivision has been analyzed for various curve and surface representations. A precursor to the development of subdivision of Bernstein-Bézier curves and surfaces was the very early work of de Casteljau [de Casteljau59] who developed the recursion formula for the evaluation of a point on a Bernstein-Bézier curve or surface. This recursive algorithm has recently been generalized for rational curves and surfaces in [Piegl85]. Subdivision algorithms for both polynomial and rational parametric curves were presented in [Koparkar83]. Midpoint subdivision of Bernstein-Bézier curves and surfaces was thoroughly analyzed and proved by Lane and Riesenfeld [Lane80a]. The more general case of arbitrary Bernstein-Bézier subdivision (where the subdivision point is not constrained to be the parametric midpoint) was handled in [Lane81] [Goldman82] [Barsky85]. Catmull [Catmull75] derived a basis which required only additions and shifts to perform a subdivision computation. In [Lane80a], Lane and Riesenfeld also analyzed subdivision of uniform B-splines. Subdivision of the more general non-uniform B-splines has been developed independently by Cohen, Lyche and Riesenfeld in the "Oslo algorithm" [Cohen80] [Riesenfeld81] [Prautzsch84] and by Boehm in the "knot insertion algorithm" [Boehm80] [Boehm84] [Boehm85]. Subdivision of Beta-splines is explained in [Barsky86a] while the subdivision of the special case of Beta2-splines was covered in [Barsky85a]. On a related note, the technique of Wang [Wang84] yields the number of subdivisions necessary to achieve a given tolerance. However, his technique is not adaptive; that is, a full subdivision tree must be constructed.

1.3. Overview of the Method

We use adaptive subdivision to develop an automatic method of surface-fitting from sampled data. The method comprises two basic phases and a testing procedure. The first phase is initialization which defines a rough approximating surface of the sampled data. This is a piecewise polynomial surface; that is, it is defined by stitching together a mosaic of surface patches.

Each patch is then tested to decide if it is sufficiently close to the underlying data. This is determined by a criterion which uses a tolerance level specified by the user. If the criterion is satisfied, the patch is accepted without further processing; otherwise, it undergoes the next phase of adaptive subdivision.

This phase subdivides a patch into four sub-patches thereby creating new vertices which are then positioned so as to achieve a closer approximation of the underlying data. Each of these sub-patches is then tested in the same manner as described above. Any sub-patch that is not accepted at this level is then recursively subdivided. This recursive process continues until all patches are accepted. In the extreme case of a zero tolerance level, the resulting surface interpolates all the data points. The method always converges in a finite number of steps.

1.4. Characteristics of the Database

As previously mentioned, the database is large and has a rectangular topology. Furthermore, in our case, the data acquisition system either translates or rotates the object during the scanning process. These two types of movement engender a database which has either a Cartesian or cylindrical geometry, respectively[+]. In both cases,

---

[+] This restricts the class of objects that can be correctly sampled to those that can be explicitly represented in Cartesian ($z = f(x,y)$) or cylindrical ($r = g(\theta, z)$) coordinates.

the structure of the database is an array, each of whose rows and columns corresponds to a set of coplanar data points. This array can be displayed as an image by setting the gray level of each pixel equal to the distance from the reference plane, in the Cartesian case, or from the axis of rotation, in the cylindrical case. Figure 3 shows such an image in the cylindrical case.

Our method for surface-fitting is based on the topological structure of the database; however, our approach is simplified by exploiting the additional geometric properties outlined above.

In the next section, the methodology for constructing the piecewise parametric polynomial surface is developed. Section 3 describes the adaptive subdivision method in more detail. We illustrate our method in Section 4 using a database obtained from a bust of Victor Hugo (Figure 2).

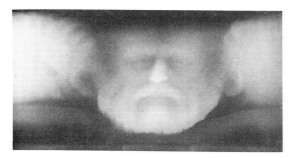

Figure 3. Database array in the cylindrical case displayed as an image.

2. Methodology for Constructing the Piecewise Parametric Polynomial Surface

2.1. Bicubic Bernstein–Bézier Representation

We use the bicubic Bernstein–Bézier representation for each patch. With this formulation, a patch is uniquely specified by a control graph consisting of sixteen control vertices. The resulting surface patch mimics the overall shape of this arrangement of control vertices, but only interpolates the four corner control vertices (see Figure 4). A bicubic Bernstein–Bézier patch $Q(u,v)$ can be expressed as a tensor product of two cubic Bézier curves. Using vector notation, the patch is given by the following expression:

$$Q(u,v) = [\ u^3\ u^2\ u\ 1\ ][Bez][V][Bez]^t[\ v^3\ v^2\ v\ 1\ ]^t$$
$$0 \le u \le 1 \qquad 0 \le v \le 1 \qquad\qquad (1)$$

where [Béz] is the symmetric matrix defining the Bernstein basis functions and [V] is the matrix of control vertices given by:

$$[Bez] = \begin{bmatrix} -1 & 3 & -3 & 1 \\ 3 & -6 & 3 & 0 \\ -3 & 3 & 0 & 0 \\ 1 & 0 & 0 & 0 \end{bmatrix} \qquad [V] = \begin{bmatrix} V_{00} & V_{01} & V_{02} & V_{03} \\ V_{10} & V_{11} & V_{12} & V_{13} \\ V_{20} & V_{21} & V_{22} & V_{23} \\ V_{30} & V_{31} & V_{32} & V_{33} \end{bmatrix}$$

Further details concerning the Bernstein–Bézier representation can be found in [Barsky84] [Barsky85] [Bartels87] [Bézier70] [Bézier74] [Bézier77].

2.2. Geometric Continuity Constraints

The individual Bernstein–Bézier surface patches need to be joined in a smooth fashion. This smoothness is quantified through the use of equations known as continuity constraints. These constraints have traditionally matched parametric derivatives at the borders between patches. Recent research has given rise to the ideas of geometric continuity as a more natural and appropriate means of measuring the continuity of parametric shapes [Barsky81] [Barsky84a] [Barsky86] [Barsky83] [DeRose85]. Geometric

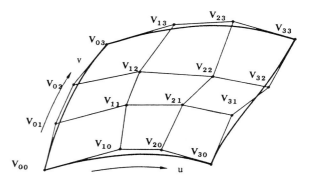

Figure 4. Bicubic Bernstein–Bézier surface patch with its defining control graph.

continuity of Bézier curves is treated in more detail in [Bartels87] and [Fournier85]. In this paper, we restrict our attention to G^1 continuous surfaces; these are surfaces possessing a continuous tangent plane in addition to continuous position.

First, consider the problem of maintaining continuous position across the border between adjacent patches. A border curve of a bicubic Bernstein–Bézier patch can be determined by substituting $v=0$ into equation (1):

$$Q(u,0) = [\ u^3\ u^2\ u\ 1\ ][\ Bez\ ][\ V_{00}\ V_{10}\ V_{20}\ V_{30}\ ]^t \qquad 0 \le u \le 1.$$

Thus, this curve is completely controlled by the four control vertices that comprise this side of the control graph. An analogous analysis reveals a similar situation for the other three sides. From this, it is evident that the constraint of continuous position between adjacent patches reduces to requiring that the four vertices along the common border be identical for the two adjacent patches.

2.3. G^1 Continuity

Consider two adjacent patches, $Q_L(u_L,v_L)$ and $Q_R(u_R,v_R)$ (Figure 5) that share a common border curve segment $C(v)$; that is,

$$C(v) = Q_L(u_L=1,v_L=v) = Q_R(u_R=0,v_R=v) \qquad 0 \le v \le 1.$$

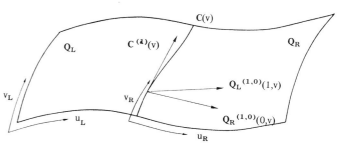

Figure 5. Two adjacent patches meeting with G^1 continuity along a common border curve segment.

The two patches Q_L and Q_R meet with G^1 continuity if the tangent plane is continuous. The tangent plane of a parametric surface $Q(u,v)$ is the plane formed by the two derivative vectors with respect to u and v, denoted by $Q^{(1,0)}(u,v)$ and $Q^{(0,1)}(u,v)$, respectively (Figure 6), where the superscripts in parentheses denote the level of differentiation with respect to u and v, respectively. The two patches Q_L and Q_R meet with G^1 continuity if the first derivative vector along the common border curve segment and the cross-boundary derivative vectors of both patches are coplanar, along the length of this curve segment (see Figure 5). This condition is equivalent to requiring that the determinant formed by these three vectors be zero:

$$\det [\ C^{(1)}(v),\ Q_L^{(1,0)}(u_L=1,v_L=v),\ Q_R^{(1,0)}(u_R=0,v_R=v)\ ] = 0$$
$$0 \le v \le 1.$$

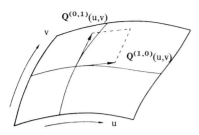

Figure 6. The tangent plane is formed by the two derivative vectors $Q^{(1,0)}(u,v)$ and $Q^{(0,1)}(u,v)$.

Several authors have studied this problem in a general setting [Beeker86] [Bézier70] [Coons67] [DeRose85] [Farin82] [Faux79] [Kahmann83]. Such studies engender piecewise surfaces with a set of constraints which are intertwined and which propagate along the common border curves between adjacent patches. To simplify our approach and to preserve the local nature of our method, we impose a sufficient (although not necessary) condition instead. This previously employed condition requires only the collinearity of the two cross-boundary derivative vectors of the two abutting patches (Figure 5); that is,

$$Q_R^{(1,0)}(u_R=0, v_R=v) \quad 0 \leq v \leq 1 = \beta 1_u Q_L^{(1,0)}(u_L=1, v_L=v) \quad (2)$$

where $\beta 1_u$ is constant along the common border curve segment $C(v)$. For a fixed value $\hat{v}$ of v along this curve, equation (2) expresses G^1 continuity between the two isoparametric curves $Q_L(u_L, v_L=\hat{v})$ and $Q_R(u_R, v_R=\hat{v})$ (see Figure 7). This continuity constraint can be seen to be a first order Beta-constraint as defined in [Barsky84a] [DeRose85]. The multiplicative factor $\beta 1_u$ is the shape parameter known as bias in the Beta-spline which provides further control of the shape [Barsky81] [Barsky86].

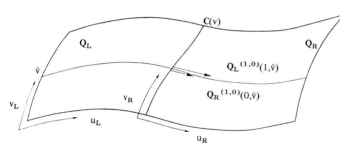

Figure 7. G^1 continuity between the two isoparametric curves $Q_L(u_L, v_L=\hat{v})$ and $Q_R(u_R, v_R=\hat{v})$.

The two derivatives in equation (2) can be obtained from equation (1) as follows. First, we denote the matrices of control vertices for patches Q_L and Q_R by $[V^L]$ and $[V^R]$, respectively. Then the two derivatives are determined by differentiating equation (1) with respect to u, and finally setting $u_L=1$ or $u_R=0$ as appropriate. Substituting the resulting expression into equation (2) yields,

$$[-3\ 3\ 0\ 0][V^R][Béz][\ v^3\ v^2\ v\ 1\ ]^t =$$
$$\beta 1_u[\ 0\ 0\ -3\ 3\ ][V^L][Béz][\ v^3\ v^2\ v\ 1\ ]^t \quad 0 \leq v \leq 1. \quad (3)$$

Since the matrix [Béz] is invertible (it has a nonzero determinant), requiring that equation (3) be satisfied for any value of v is equivalent to:

$$[\ -1\ 1\ 0\ 0\ ][\ V^R\ ] = \beta 1_u[\ 0\ 0\ -1\ 1\ ][\ V^L\ ].$$

This expression corresponds to the following set of equations:

$$V_{1j}^R - V_{0j}^R = \beta 1_u (V_{3j}^L - V_{2j}^L), \quad j = 0,1,2,3. \quad (4)$$

Performing the analogous analysis along a border curve segment $C(u)$ yields:

$$V_{i1}^T - V_{i0}^T = \beta 1_v (V_{i3}^B - V_{i2}^B), \quad i = 0,1,2,3 \quad (5)$$

where $[V^B]$ and $[V^T]$ are the matrices of control vertices for these two adjacent patches.

At each common border curve segment, there is a set of four G^1 Beta-constraints of the form given by equations (4) or (5). These four constraints can be divided into two groups: two "exterior constraints" ((i=0 and i=3) or (j=0 and j=3)) and two "interior constraints" ((i=1 and i=2) or (j=1 and j=2)). Following along a border curve from one segment to the next shows that each of the exterior constraints is common to two sets of G^1 Beta-constraints. This implies that the bias ($\beta 1_u$ or $\beta 1_v$) must be identical in all the G^1 Beta-constraints along a common border curve (along the v or u direction, respectively). Nevertheless, this collection of constraints can be simply regrouped into independent systems of six conditions, each involving the subset of nine control vertices located around the corner formed where four patches meet (Figure 8).

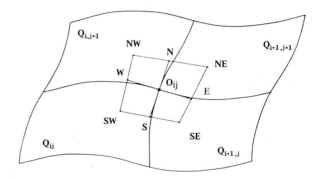

Figure 8. The nine control vertices around a corner.

Consider one of these subsets of nine control vertices shown in Figure 8. Let O_{ij} denote the point of intersection of the four patches $Q_{i,j}$, $Q_{i,j+1}$, $Q_{i+1,j+1}$, $Q_{i+1,j}$, and let $\beta 1_i$ (or $\beta 1_j$) denote the bias parameter $\beta 1_u$ (or $\beta 1_v$) in the u (or v) direction across the border curve parametrized in v (or u) and passing through the point O_{ij}.

We label these unknown vertices according to the directions on a compass, as shown in Figure 8. These vertices must satisfy the G^1 Beta-constraints. These conditions result in the following system of six linear equations:

$$NE - N = \beta 1_i (N - NW) \quad (6-1)$$
$$E - O_{ij} = \beta 1_i (O_{ij} - W) \quad (6-2)$$
$$SE - S = \beta 1_i (S - SW) \quad (6-3)$$
$$NW - W = \beta 1_j (W - SW) \quad (6-4)$$
$$N - O_{ij} = \beta 1_j (O_{ij} - S) \quad (6-5)$$
$$NE - E = \beta 1_j (E - SE) \quad (6-6)$$

These vector equations are linearly dependent, and thus they comprise a system of 15 linear constraints in terms of nine three-dimensional vertices, or equivalently 27 coordinate values. The 27-15=12 degrees of freedom remaining will be used to locally improve the surface-fitting process by positioning the control vertices. After this adjustment phase, the resulting patches are tested, and those that still do not satisfy the criterion are then subdivided. This subdivision creates new sets of nine control vertices which are positioned to further improve the approximation of the sample data.

The positioning of the control vertices as well as the patch testing procedure require a correspondence between a patch Q_{ij} and a set of points in the database. This matching technique forms the subject of the next sub-section. The two sub-sections following that are devoted to the positioning of the vertices and to the testing procedure.

2.4. Matching the Piecewise Surface to the Database

The matching of the real object surface with a mathematical surface requires the definition of a point-to-point correspondence between the two surfaces[+]. However, to have the matching be a simple projection of one surface onto the other requires that the correspondence have a clear geometric interpretation. Such a projection must take into account the characteristics of the object to be fitted. A "natural" approach for determining this projection would be to define it locally as the orthogonal projection of the mathematical surface onto the real object surface. For non-convex objects, the projection can be uniquely defined only inside a volume around the object whose boundaries are defined by radii of curvature of the real object surface. Hence, it can be seen that in the general case, although the determination of such a projection is theoretically possible, it can be quite complex.

In our case, the problem is far simpler due to the characteristics of the acquisition system which samples objects according to either a Cartesian or cylindrical structure. Thus, a projection can be defined that is less "natural" than the orthogonal projection, but much simpler to exploit and that is dependent only on the geometric structure of the data. Specifically, the Cartesian and cylindrical representations correspond to projections which are parallel and perpendicular, respectively, to the z-axis.

Having defined the projection, the matching of the parametric piecewise polynomial surface with the database permits the definition of a partition of the data. For this, we draw on graph theory in the following manner:

Consider the graph whose vertices correspond to the sample points and whose edges link any pair of neighbouring vertices according to the rectangular topology. The projection establishes a correspondence between the mathematical surface and the graph by associating (i) a corner point O_{ij} with the point of the graph that is the closest in projection, (ii) a border curve segment with an 8-connected path of the graph, and (iii) a surface patch Q_{ij} with an inner-region I_{ij} that contains the vertices of the graph delimited by the cycle formed by the four 8-connected paths associated with the four border curve segments of the patch. The set of inner-regions then forms a partition of the set of sample points. This matching technique was originally developed for the case of a polygonal approximation of our databases with triangular faces and is explained in more detail in [Gholizadeh85] [Schmitt85].

2.5. Positioning of Control Vertices

The adjustment of the parametric piecewise polynomial surface is effected by exploiting the twelve remaining degrees of freedom that arose by applying the G^1 Beta-constraints to a subset of nine control vertices (equations (6)). This is done by using some geometric characteristics directly estimated from the database. First the corner control vertex O_{ij} is positioned, then the 4-connected vertices of O_{ij} denoted N, S, E, and W, and finally the remaining four control vertices NE, NW, SE, and SW.

The vertex O_{ij} is displaced by mapping it to the corresponding point P_{ij} in the database, as described above. We denote the row and column of its location in the database by r and c, respectively. This "tacking" of the piecewise surface onto the object database at this point uses three degrees of freedom, leaving nine remaining.

The vertices N, S, E, W, and O_{ij} are constrained by equations (6-2) and (6-5) to lie on two straight lines intersecting at O_{ij}. These vertices will therefore be coplanar, and this plane is the tangent plane to the piecewise surface at O_{ij} (moved to P_{ij}). Using two degrees of freedom, we first adjust this plane by estimating the tangent plane of the object from a subset of sampled points

---

[+] Although the object surface is only known by the set of sample points, we suppose here that a full description of this surface is available.

in the neighbourhood of P_{ij}. The neighbourhood can be very local, consisting of only the points that are 4-connected or 8-connected to P_{ij}. On the other hand, in the cases of noisy data or patches with large inner-regions, it is preferable to use a large neighbourhood and optimization techniques, such as least-squares error fitting, to estimate the tangent plane of the object. For this, the width of the neighbourhood can be calculated as a function of the width of the inner-regions corresponding to the four patches surrounding the control vertex O_{ij}.

Once the tangent plane has been estimated, the positions of the vertices N, S, E, and W are then determined; this is done separately for N and S and for E and W. For each pair, the positioning involves adjusting the direction formed by the two vertices and the distance between them. Considering the E and W pair, the E - W direction is along the unit tangent vector of the border curve in the u direction on the tangent plane. This direction is adjusted using the sampled points in row r in a neighbourhood of point P_{ij}. Due to the specific geometric structure of our data, this direction is simply obtained as the intersection of the estimated tangent plane with the plane containing the points of row r (these are all coplanar and include P_{ij}). This uses one degree of freedom, leaving six remaining. Having set $\beta 1_i$, the ratio of $||E - O_{ij}||$ to $||O_{ij} - W||$ is fixed in equation (6-2). Since O_{ij} is also fixed, vertices E and W can be determined simply by adjusting the scale. This can be done by choosing the Euclidian distance between E and W to be one third of the sum of the lengths of the 8-connected path from $P_{i-1,j}$ to P_{ij} plus the 8-connected path P_{ij} to $P_{i+1,j}$, where $P_{i-1,j}$ and $P_{i+1,j}$ are the sampled points onto which are mapped the corner control vertices $O_{i-1,j}$ and $O_{i+1,j}$, respectively. This degree of freedom is set in this manner to attempt to achieve a homogeneous distribution of the control vertices corresponding to the database. The process is similar for N and S using the points in column c. Two degrees of freedom are thereby used, leaving three remaining.

Finally, the four control vertices NE, NW, SE, and SW are determined with the three remaining independent equations (6-1), (6-3), and (6-4). The unit cross-tangent vector at each border curve is then adjusted to correspond to the tangent direction of the object defined by the rows or columns. Again, due to the geometric structure of our data, these directions can be defined simply by intersecting the estimated tangent plane with the planes defined by the rows or columns. This is accomplished using only two degrees of freedom because of the nature of equations (6). One final degree of freedom remains, and it can be used to mimic the shape characteristics (convex, concave, or saddle-shape) of the object in the neighbourhood of P_{ij}.

2.6. Patch Testing Procedure

To be accepted, the patch Q_{ij} must be compared with its inner-region I_{ij} containing the points of the database onto which Q_{ij} was mapped. The simplest approach is to test whether or not the distance from each point in the inner-region I_{ij} to the patch Q_{ij} is smaller than the user-specified tolerance level. If all these distances satisfy this test, the patch Q_{ij} is accepted and saved; otherwise it will be subdivided.

The distance from a point P to a surface can be geometrically defined as the distance from P to the closest point on the surface. For a parametric polynomial surface patch, we must determine the parameters (u_0, v_0), not necessarily unique, that minimize the Euclidian distance $||Q_{ij}(u,v) - P||$. This can be accomplished by using an iterative technique, such as the multivariate Newton method. A simple approach for estimating an initial approximation for (u_0, v_0) is to measure the relative position of P in the inner-region I_{ij} to which it belongs.

The iterative estimation process for (u_0, v_0) terminates when the difference between the values estimated at two successive iterations is no longer significant, or when the current estimated Euclidian distance no longer exceeds the tolerance level specified by the user. Due to the smooth properties of bicubic patches, this iterative process requires few steps to converge.

3. Description of the Adaptive Subdivision Method

3.1. Initialization Phase

The initial piecewise surface is chosen to have a rectangular topology with n_u by n_v patches in the u and v directions, respectively. This facilitates the initial matching of the surface to the array of data points. Therefore the corner points Q_{ij}, $i=0,1,\ldots,n_u$, $j=0,1,\ldots,n_v$, are located on a mesh consisting of (n_v+1) rows and (n_u+1) columns. An initial surface comprising only a single patch can be defined by setting $n_u=n_v=1$.

The eight control vertices "around" each corner point are then positioned as described in Section 2.5. Around the boundary of the surface, these sets of control vertices are truncated but they are still treated in an identical manner; all that is required is to estimate the geometric characteristics of the object by simply using the available data points. Having defined the patches, the next step is to test each patch using the procedure described in Section 2.6. Any patch not meeting this criterion is then adaptively subdivided.

3.2. Adaptive Subdivision Phase

Our method for surface-fitting using adaptive subdivision can be effected in either a recursive or iterative manner. As described earlier, recursive subdivision of surfaces is commonly performed in CAGDM and computer graphics. However, in our case, the subdivision phase is context-sensitive in the sense that the subdivision of a patch is dependent on whether or not there are neighbouring patches that have already been accepted. Thus, the recursive approach requires a data structure to store the information needed at each level of recursion which is sufficiently sophisticated to avoid repeating the same computation for the neighbouring sub-patches. On the other hand, the iterative approach is simpler to implement, and thus this is the technique that we present herein. There are two steps in each iteration: creation of new control vertices by subdivision and the subsequent positioning of those among them that are free to be moved.

3.2.1. Creation of New Control Vertices

Consider the piecewise surface consisting of a set of patches, accepted or not, obtained from the initialization phase. Figure 9 represents a patch Q_{ij} with its eight neighbouring patches. Each patch that is not accepted is subdivided into four sub-patches separated by the two isoparametric curves $Q_{ij}(u=u^*,v)$ and $Q_{ij}(u,v=v^*)$, where u^* and v^* are constants to be defined. We denote the four sub-patches as Q_{ij}^{00}, Q_{ij}^{01}, Q_{ij}^{11}, Q_{ij}^{10} (Figure 9). These sub-patches are themselves bicubic Bernstein-Bézier patches.

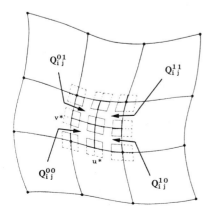

Figure 9. The subdivided patch Q_{ij} with its eight neighbouring patches.

The control vertices of these subdivided patches can be given by a recurrence relation given in [Barsky85]. Since the relation is linear, the recurrence can be unravelled, solved for the vertices of the subdivided patches, and written in matrix form. This is done in [Barsky86a] for the case of subdivision in either the u or v direction. Now, we combine both subdivisions for our case of subdividing into four sub-patches. This yields the following expressions for the matrices of control vertices of the sub-patches in terms of the matrix of control vertices of the original patch,

$$\begin{aligned}
[V^{00}] &= [A(u^*)][V][A(v^*)]^t \\
[V^{01}] &= [A(u^*)][V][Z(v^*)]^t \\
[V^{11}] &= [Z(u^*)][V][Z(v^*)]^t \\
[V^{10}] &= [Z(u^*)][V][A(v^*)]^t
\end{aligned}$$

Applying the subdivision matrices A and Z on the left corresponds to subdivision in u, and multiplying their transposes on the right corresponds to subdivision in v. The matrix A performs subdivision for lower parametric values while Z corresponds to higher values. The elements of A and Z are given by:

$$a_{ij}(t^*) = \binom{i}{j}(t^*)^j(1-t^*)^{i-j}, \qquad i=0,1,2,3; \ j=0,\ldots,i;$$

$$z_{ij}(t^*) = \binom{3-i}{j-i}(t^*)^{j-i}(1-t^*)^{3-j}, \quad i=0,1,2,3; \ j=i,\ldots,3;$$

and zero otherwise. Thus, the matrices are:

$$A(t^*) = \begin{bmatrix} 1 & 0 & 0 & 0 \\ 1-t^* & t^* & 0 & 0 \\ (1-t^*)^2 & 2(1-t^*)t^* & (t^*)^2 & 0 \\ (1-t^*)^3 & 3(1-t^*)^2 t^* & 3(1-t^*)(t^*)^2 & (t^*)^3 \end{bmatrix},$$

$$Z(t^*) = \begin{bmatrix} (1-t^*)^3 & 3(1-t^*)^2 t^* & 3(1-t^*)(t^*)^2 & (t^*)^3 \\ 0 & (1-t^*)^2 & 2(1-t^*)t^* & (t^*)^2 \\ 0 & 0 & 1-t^* & t^* \\ 0 & 0 & 0 & 1 \end{bmatrix}.$$

Since the union of the four sub-patches is identical to the original patch which is a bicubic polynomial, the sub-patches must be C^∞ continuous everywhere, including along their common border curves. This implies that the $\beta 1_u$ and $\beta 1_v$ would be equal to unity provided that the sub-patches were parametrized on the subintervals arising from the above equations. However, since we reparametrize so that all the sub-patches are on $[0,1] \times [0,1]$, the control vertices satisfy the collinearity expressions shown in equations (4) and (5) where $\beta 1_u$ and $\beta 1_v$ must have the values $(1-u^*)/u^*$ and $(1-v^*)/v^*$, respectively.

3.2.2. Positioning the Free Sets of Control Vertices

Having created the new control vertices via subdivision, the mathematical surface can now be improved by positioning those control vertices that are free to be moved. To better understand the process, suppose that Q_{ij} and each of the eight adjacent patches are subdivided into four sub-patches. Then there are nine sets of nine control vertices each as indicated in Figure 9.

The continuity requirements among the four sub-patches in the center of Q_{ij} are local and completely unaffected by those between Q_{ij} and its neighbours. That is, the system of G^1 Beta-constraints that must be satisfied by the set of control vertices in the center of Q_{ij} is completely independent of the G^1 Beta-constraints governing the meeting of Q_{ij} with its neighbouring patches. The only external parameters intervening in this system of equations are $\beta 1_u$ and $\beta 1_v$ which are defined as previously indicated using the values u^* and v^* selected for the subdivision. The independence of this set of control vertices enables the local adjustment of properties from the database with the adjustment process previously described in Section 2.5.

The eight other sets of control vertices situated on the periphery of Q_{ij} share some of their control vertices with the adjacent patches. If one of these sets shares some of its vertices with an already accepted patch, then this set must remain fixed to preserve G^1 continuity as governed by equations (6). Note that, consequently, accepted patches need not be subdivided. On the other hand, if one of these sets has all its control vertices from patches that are not accepted, then the new control vertices are free to be moved with the adjustment process.

The parametric values u^* and v^* at which to subdivide can be freely chosen. However, the set of constraints in equations (4) or (5) requires that the bias shape parameters ($\beta 1_u$ and $\beta 1_v$) be constant along a border curve. Since $\beta 1_u = (1-u^*)/u^*$ and $\beta 1_v = (1-v^*)/v^*$, the value u^* or v^* must be the same along a strip of connected, not-accepted patches in the v or u direction, respectively, that is, along $(\ldots, Q_{i,j-1}, Q_{i,j}, Q_{i,j+1}, \ldots)$ or $(\ldots, Q_{i-1,j}, Q_{i,j}, Q_{i+1,j}, \ldots)$, respectively. Since a local optimization of the values u^* and v^* is not evident, we have simply used $u^* = v^* = 1/2$.

3.2.3. Description of a Complete Iteration

A complete iteration of the adaptive subdivision is performed in a single pass of the data. The data is processed as a sequence of bands along the v direction of the piecewise surface, where each band is a strip along the u direction. Consider now the current band to be treated, the preceding adjacent band having already been processed. Any set of nine vertices that is common to the two bands has already been computed and stored. We need to know only whether or not each of the adjacent patches in the next band has been accepted in order to subdivide the patches in the current band that are not accepted. Then, these patches are subdivided and adjusted. All the resulting sub-patches are subsequently tested and the results stored in a Boolean array. The accepted sub-patches are saved. Their control vertex matrices will no longer be needed for further processing since the necessary information is available in the Boolean array.

The number of iterations necessary to achieve a piecewise surface that satisfies a given tolerance level is finite. In fact, the inner-region I_{ij} associated with a patch Q_{ij} contains a finite number of data points. The adaptive subdivision of the patch Q_{ij} fragments this inner-region into smaller and smaller regions.

As soon as one such region contains only the points associated with the four corners of the patch, the patch is automatically accepted. Thus, the mathematical surface has locally become an interpolating surface.

4. Illustrations and Results

We will illustrate our method using a database obtained from a bust of Victor Hugo analyzed in cylindrical coordinates (see Figure 3). This database contains 8280 points corresponding to 120 meridians and 69 parallels. A wireframe representation of this database is shown in Figure 10. The initialization of the adaptive subdivision algorithm was done with $n_v = 3$ bands, each consisting of $n_u = 6$ patches, all of roughly the same size. The results of the adaptive subdivision are presented for two different tolerance levels in Figures 11 and 12, respectively. These levels are in the relation 10:3. Figures 11.a and 12.a correspond to the initialization. The subimages on the left represent the rectangular support of the patches comprising the piecewise surface; that is, the corner points of each patch are connected by straight line segments. The subimages on the right are views of this surface. The number of points computed for this display is approximately the same as that in the database. Figures 11.b, 11.c, and 11.d show the results of first, second, and third iterations, respectively, for tolerance level 10, and likewise for tolerance level 3 in Figures 12.b, 12.c, and 12.d. The piecewise surfaces shown in Figures 11.d and 12.d have attained the specified tolerance levels. Subjectively, the 192 patches obtained in Figure 11.d do not provide an acceptable representation of Hugo whereas the 756 patches of Figure 12.d produce an excellent G^1 continuous approximation of the database. Figures 13 and 14 show shaded raster images of the final piecewise surface shown in wireframe in Figures 11.d, and 12.d, respectively.

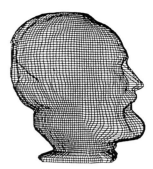

Figure 10. Wireframe representation of our database obtained from a bust of Victor Hugo.

The subimages of the support of the patches shown in Figures 11 and 12 provide a good illustration of the different sizes of accepted patches at different iterations. It is apparent that the deepest levels of subdivision occur where the surface of the object is most complex. These images illustrate the hierarchical nature of the piecewise surface which could be represented with a quadtree structure. Our method of adaptive subdivision obtained rates of data compression, with respect to an interpolating piecewise bicubic surface database, of 42.5 and 10.8, for Figures 11 and 12, respectively[+].

5. Conclusions

We have developed a top down method for the problem of surface fitting from sampled data. The method is based on an adaptive subdivision approach. It begins with a rough approximating surface and progressively refines it in successive steps to adjust the regions where the data is poorly approximated. To our knowledge, this problem has received little attention in computer graphics.

Our method constructs a parametric piecewise polynomial surface representation. The surface-fitting is effected through a novel use of subdivision techniques which had been previously employed for shape design and display. The mathematical surface is adjusted with respect to the sampled data by generating and exploiting new degrees of freedom. The subdivision creates new vertices which are then positioned so as to achieve a closer approximation of the underlying data. An advantage of this approach is that the adjustment is essentially local reducing the computational requirements which permits the processing of large databases. Furthermore, the method is simple in concept, yet realizes efficient data compression.

The surface provided by this local adjustment is suboptimal, however. Nevertheless, this is compensated by the computational efficiency of this algorithm compared to the global methods in approximation theory or the combinatorial methods of dynamic programming. In the latter case, solutions have been proposed only for the curve fitting problem [Cox71, Plass83]. Furthermore, our adaptive subdivision method provides a hierarchical representation of the surface as a quadtree-like structure which is useful for display purposes in computer graphics.

In our case, the data is obtained from a real object using an automatic three-dimensional data acquisition system. The method has been implemented using a surface representation formed by bicubic Bernstein-Bézier patches meeting with G^1 geometric continuity in a rectangular topology.

Future work will address the relaxation of some of these restrictions. It would be of interest to investigate extensions to higher degree Bernstein-Bézier patches with

---

[+] This rate of data compression is the ratio of the number of patches in our surface to that of an interpolating surface.

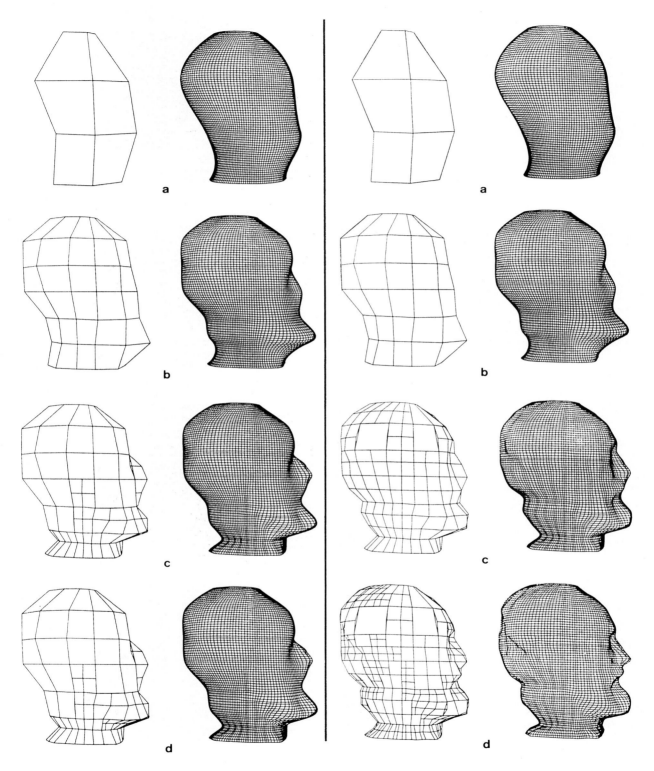

Figure 11. Tolerance level 10.   Figure 12. Tolerance level 3.

Successive iterations of the adaptive subdivision method. The left and right columns of each figure show the support of the patches and the piecewise surface, respectively.

Figure 13. Tolerance level 10.

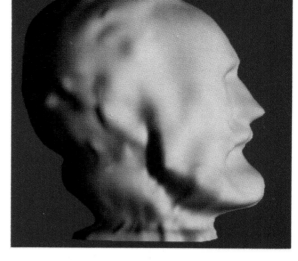

Figure 14. Tolerance level 3.

Shaded raster images of the final surface for two different tolerance levels.

G^2 continuity, exploitation of degrees of freedom for shape parameters such as tension ($\beta 2$), the use of other surface formulations, extensions to higher order geometric continuity, and extensions to piecewise surfaces having a triangular topology.

Acknowledgements

We thank Pascal Leray of the Centre Commun d'Etudes de Télévision et Télécommunications in Rennes for the z-buffer program and Yves Trousset for his help in the preparation of our shaded raster images.

References

[Barsky81] Brian A. Barsky: The Beta-spline: A Local Representation Based on Shape Parameters and Fundamental Geometric Measures, Ph.D. Thesis, University of Utah, Salt Lake City, Utah, December, 1981.

[Barsky84] Brian A. Barsky: "A Description and Evaluation of Various 3-D Models," IEEE Computer Graphics and Applications, Vol. 4, No. 1, January, 1984, pp. 38-52.

[Barsky85] Brian A. Barsky: Arbitrary Subdivision of Bézier Curves, Technical Report No. UCB/CSD 85/265, Computer Science Division, Electrical Engineering and Computer Sciences Department, University of California, Berkeley, California, October, 1985.

[Barsky86] Brian A. Barsky: Computer Graphics and Geometric Modelling Using Beta-splines, Springer-Verlag, Tokyo, 1986.

[Barsky83] Brian A. Barsky and John C. Beatty: "Local Control of Bias and Tension in Beta-splines," ACM Transactions on Graphics, Vol. 2, No. 2, April, 1983, pp. 109-134. Also published in SIGGRAPH'83 Conference Proceedings, Vol. 17, No. 3, ACM, Detroit, 25-29 July, 1983, pp. 193-218.

[Barsky84a] Brian A. Barsky and Tony D. DeRose: Geometric Continuity of Parametric Curves, Technical Report No. UCB/CSD 84/205, Computer Science Division, Electrical Engineering and Computer Sciences Department, University of California, Berkeley, California, October, 1984.

[Barsky85a] Brian A. Barsky and Tony D. DeRose: "The Beta2-spline: A Special Case of the Beta-spline Curve and Surface Representation," IEEE Computer Graphics and Applications, Vol. 5, No. 9, September, 1985, pp. 46-58.

[Barsky86a] Brian A. Barsky, Tony D. DeRose and Mark D. Dippé: "An Adaptive Subdivision Method with Crack Prevention for Rendering Beta-spline Objects," submitted for publication.

[Bartels87] Richard H. Bartels, John C. Beatty and Brian A. Barsky: An Introduction to the Use of Splines in Computer Graphics, to be published by Morgan Kaufmann Publishers, Inc., Los Altos, California, 1987.

[Beeker86] Etienne Beeker: "Smoothing of Shapes Designed with Free-form Surfaces," Computer-Aided Design, Vol. 18, No. 4, May, 1986, pp. 224-232.

[Bézier70] Pierre E. Bézier: "Emploi des machines à commande numérique," Masson et Cie., Paris, 1970. Translated by A. Robin Forrest and Anne F. Pankhurst as Numerical Control -- Mathematical and Applications, John Wiley and Sons Ltd., London, 1972.

[Bézier74] Pierre E. Bézier: "Mathematical and Practical Possibilities of UNISURF," in Computer-Aided Geometric Design, edited by Robert E. Barnhill and Richard F. Riesenfeld, Academic Press, New York, 1974, pp. 127-152.

[Bézier77] Pierre E. Bézier: Essai de définition numérique des courbes et des surfaces expérimentales, Ph.D. Thesis, l'Université Pierre et Marie Curie, Paris, 1977.

[Boehm80] Wolfgang Boehm: "Inserting New Knots into B-spline Curves," Computer-Aided Design, Vol. 12, No. 4, 1980, pp. 199-202.

[Boehm84] Wolfgang Boehm: "On the Efficiency of Knot Insertion Algorithms," Computer-Aided Geometric Design, Vol. 1, 1984.

[Boehm84a] Wolfgang Boehm, Gerald Farin and Juergen Kahmann: "A Survey of Curve and Surface Methods in CAGD," Computer-Aided Geometric Design, Vol. 1, No. 1, July, 1984, pp. 1-60.

[Boehm85] Wolfgang Boehm and Hartmut Prautzsch: "The Insertion Algorithm," Computer-Aided Design, Vol. 17, No. 2, March, 1985, pp. 58-59.

[Catmull75] Edwin E. Catmull: "Computer Display of Curved Surfaces," Proceedings of IEEE Conference on Computer Graphics, Pattern Recognition, and Data Structure, Los Angeles, May, 1975, pp. 11-17.

[Catmull78] Edwin E. Catmull and James H. Clark: "Recursively Generated B-spline Surfaces on Arbitrary Topological Meshes," Computer-Aided Design, Vol. 10, No. 6, November, 1978, pp. 350-355.

[Chaikin74] George M. Chaikin: "An Algorithm for High-Speed Curve Generation," Computer Graphics and Image Processing, Vol. 3, No. 4, December, 1974, pp. 346-349.

[Chung80] Won. L. Chung: "Automatic Curve Fitting Using an Adaptive Local Algorithm," ACM Transactions on

Mathematical Software, Vol. 6, No. 1, March, 1980, pp. 45-57.

[Clark79] James H. Clark: "A Fast Scan-Line Algorithm for Rendering Parametric Surfaces," Computer Graphics, Vol. 13, No. 2, 7-12 August, 1979 [addendum to the SIGGRAPH'79 Conference Proceedings].

[Cohen80] Elaine Cohen, Tom Lyche and Richard F. Riesenfeld: "Discrete B-splines and Subdivision Techniques in Computer-Aided Geometric Design and Computer Graphics," Computer Graphics and Image Processing, Vol. 14, No. 2, October, 1980, pp. 87-111.

[Coons67] Steven A. Coons: "Surfaces for Computer-Aided Design of Space Forms," Report, MAC-TR-41, Massachusetts Institute of Technology, June, 1967.

[Cox71] Morris G. Cox: "Curve Fitting with Piecewise Polynomials," J. Inst. Maths. Applications, Vol. 8, 1971, pp. 36-52.

[de Casteljau59] Paul de Casteljau: "Courbes et surfaces à pôles," S. A. André Citroen, Paris, 1959.

[DeRose85] Tony D. DeRose and Brian A. Barsky: "An Intuitive Approach to Geometric Continuity for Parametric Curves and Surfaces," in Computer-Generated Images -- The State of the Art, edited by Nadia Magnenat-Thalmann and Daniel Thalmann, Springer-Verlag, 1985, pp. 159-175.

[Dierckx75] P. Dierckx: "An Algorithm for Smoothing, Differentiation and Integration of Experimental Data Using Spline Functions," J. Comput. Appl. Math., Vol. 1, 1975, pp. 165-184.

[Dierckx82] P. Dierckx: "Algorithms for Smoothing Data with Periodic and Parametric Splines," Computer Graphics and Image Processing, Vol. 20, No. 2, October, 1982, pp. 171-184.

[Doo78] D. W. H. Doo: "A Subdivision Algorithm for Smoothing down Irregularly Shaped Polyhedrons," in the Proceedings of Interactive Techniques in Computer-Aided Design, Bologna, Italia, 1978, pp. 157-165.

[Doo78a] D. W. H. Doo and M. A. Sabin: "Behaviour of Recursive Division Surfaces Near Extraordinary Points," Computer-Aided Design, Vol. 10, No. 6, November, 1978, pp. 356-360.

[Farin82] Gerald Farin: "A Construction for Visual C^1 Continuity of Polynomial Surface Patches," Computer Graphics and Image Processing, Vol. 20, 1982, pp. 272-282.

[Faux79] Ivor D. Faux and Michael J. Pratt: Computational Geometry for Design and Manufacture, Ellis Horwood Ltd., 1979.

[Fournier85] Alain Fournier and Brian A. Barsky: "Geometric Continuity with Interpolating Bézier Curves (Preliminary Report)," in Computer-Generated Images -- The State of the Art, edited by Nadia Magnenat-Thalmann and Daniel Thalmann, Springer-Verlag, 1985, pp. 153-158.

[Gholizadeh85] Behrouz Gholizadeh: Représentation par triangulation de la surface d'objets tridimensionnels, Thèse de 3e Cycle, Université de Paris-Sud, Centre d'Orsay, December, 1985.

[Goldman82] Ronald N. Goldman: "Using Degenerate Bézier Triangles and Tetrahedra to Subdivide Bézier Curves," Computer-Aided Design, Vol. 14, No. 6, November, 1982, pp. 307-311.

[Ichida77] K. Ichida and F. Yoshimoto: "Curve Fitting by a One-Pass Method with a Piecewise Cubic Polynomial," ACM Transactions on Mathematical Software, Vol. 3, No. 2, 1977, pp. 164-174.

[IEEE86] IEEE Computer Graphics and Applications, Special Issue on Parametric Curves and Surfaces, Vol. 6, No. 2, February, 1986.

[Kahmann83] Juergen Kahmann: "Continuity of Curvature between Adjacent Bézier Patches," Surfaces in CAGD, edited by Robert E. Barnhill and Wolfgang Boehm, 1983, North-Holland Publishing Company, Amsterdam, pp. 65-75.

[Knapp79] Lewis C. Knapp: A Design Scheme Using Coons Surfaces with Nonuniform B-spline Curves, Ph.D. Thesis, Syracuse University, Syracuse, New York, September, 1979.

[Koparkar83] P. A. Koparkar and S. P. Mudur: "A New Class of Algorithms for the Processing of Parametric Curves," Computer-Aided Design, Vol. 15, No. 1, January, 1983, pp. 41-45.

[Lane79] Jeffrey M. Lane and Loren C. Carpenter: "A Generalized Scan Line Algorithm for the Computer Display of Parametrically Defined Surfaces," Computer Graphics and Image Processing, Vol. 11, No. 3, November, 1979, pp. 290-297.

[Lane80] Jeffrey M. Lane, Loren C. Carpenter, J. Turner Whitted and James F. Blinn: "Scan Line Methods for Displaying Parametrically Defined Surfaces," Communications of the ACM, Vol. 23, No. 1, January, 1980, pp. 23-34.

[Lane80a] Jeffrey M. Lane and Richard F. Riesenfeld: "A Theoretical Development for the Computer Generation of Piecewise Polynomial Surfaces," IEEE Transactions on Pattern Analysis and Machine Intelligence, Vol. PAMI-2, No. 1, January, 1980, pp. 35-46.

[Lane81] Jeffrey M. Lane and Richard F. Riesenfeld: "Bounds on a Polynomial," BIT, Vol. 21, No. 1, 1981, pp. 112-117.

[Maître81] Henri Maître, Jaime Lopez-Krahe, Alain Clainchard, and Francis Schmitt: "Appareil automatique pour la numérisation d'une surface tridimensionnelle," BREVET No. 81-24418, 1981.

[Nydegger72] Robert W. Nydegger: A Data Minimization Algorithm of Analytical Models for Computer Graphics, Master's thesis, University of Utah, Salt Lake City, Utah, 1972.

[Piegl85] L. Piegl: "Recursive Algorithms for the Representation of Parametric Curves and Surfaces," Computer-Aided Design, Vol. 17, No. 5, June, 1985, pp. 225-229.

[Plass83] Michael Plass and Maureen Stone: "Curve-Fitting with Piecewise Parametric Cubics," SIGGRAPH'83 Conference Proceedings, Vol. 17, No. 3, ACM, Detroit, 25-29 July, 1983, pp. 229-239.

[Prautzsch84] Hartmut Prautzsch: "A Short Proof of the Oslo Algorithm," Computer-Aided Geometric Design, Vol. 1, No. 1, July, 1984, pp. 95-96.

[Ramer72] Urs Ramer: "An Iterative Procedure for the Polygonal Approximation of Plane Curves," Computer Graphics and Image Processing, Vol. 1, No. 3, November, 1972, pp. 244-256.

[Reeves81] William T. Reeves: Quantitative Representations of Computer Dynamic Shape for Motion Analysis, Ph.D. Thesis, University of Toronto, Toronto, July, 1981. Also Technical Note CSRG-23, University of Toronto, Toronto.

[Rice76] John R. Rice: "Adaptive Approximation," Journal of Approximation Theory, Vol. 16, 1976, pp. 329-337.

[Rice78] John R. Rice: "Algorithm 525 ADAPT, Adaptive Smooth Curve Fitting," ACM Transactions on Mathematical Software, Vol. 4, No. 1, March, 1978, pp. 82-94.

[Riesenfeld75] Richard F. Riesenfeld: "On Chaikin's Algorithm," Computer Graphics and Image Processing, Vol. 4, No. 3, September, 1975, pp. 304-310.

[Riesenfeld81] Richard F. Riesenfeld, Elaine Cohen, Russell D. Fish, Spencer W. Thomas, Elizabeth S. Cobb, Brian A. Barsky, Dino L. Schweitzer, and Jeffrey M. Lane: "Using the Oslo Algorithm as a Basis for CAD/CAM Geometric Modelling," pp. 345-356 in the Proceedings of the Second Annual NCGA National Conference, National Computer Graphics Association, Inc., Baltimore, Maryland, 14-18 June, 1981.

[Schmitt85] Francis Schmitt and Behrouz Gholizadeh: "Adaptive Polyhedral Approximation of Digitized Surfaces," SPIE Proceedings Vol. 595 of Conference on Computer Vision for Robots, Cannes, France, 2-6 December, 1985.

[Schmitt85a] Francis Schmitt, Henri Maître, Alain Clainchard and Jaime Lopez-Krahm: "Acquisition and Representation of Real Object Surface Data," SPIE Proceedings Vol. 602 of Biostereometrics'85 Conference, Cannes, France, 2-6 December, 1985.

[Wang84] Guo-Zhao Wang: "The Subdivision Method for Finding the Intersection between Two Bézier Curves or Surfaces," Zhejiang University Journal, Special Issue on Computational Geometry (in Chinese), 1984.

Managing Geometric Complexity with Enhanced Procedural Models

Phil Amburn
Eric Grant
Turner Whitted

The University of North Carolina at Chapel Hill

Abstract

We illustrate two enhancements to procedural geometric models which allow autonomous procedures to jointly satisfy mutual constraints. One of the techniques adds communications paths between procedures which may affect one another. Conflicts are resolved by modifying communicating procedures as they execute.

The second technique is a generalization of widely used subdivision procedures. The termination test of typical subdivision methods is replaced with a "transition" test. The subdivision procedure is augmented with a "script" in the form of a state transition table which controls the procedures' response to external events as well as to the normal termination conditions.

In the examples we show how effective these techniques are in building complex geometric models with very sparse input.

CR Categories and Subject Descriptors: I.3.5 [Computer Graphics]: Computational Geometry and Object Modeling - Curve, surface, solid, and object representations; I.3.3 [Computer Graphics]: Picture/Image Generation - Display algorithms

General Terms: Geometric models

Additional Keywords and Phrases: procedural models, subdivision, stochastic modeling, parametric surfaces

1. Introduction

The use of procedural models in computer graphics provides an effective means for creating extremely complex shapes semi-automatically. We introduce two enhancements which extend the function of conventional geometric procedures.

The first is a communication mechanism whereby independent procedures may modify the operation of one another. This requires that models have methods which implement the shape modification in response to messages. It also requires a means of pruning the communications paths to avoid a message passing bottleneck. So far we have only applied the new technique to procedures, such as subdivision, which maintain a natural hierarchy that can be used to prune communication paths.

The second enhancement is a generalization of widely used subdivision procedures that supports an extra degree of flexibility in the shapes that it constructs. In addition, we identify generic components of the procedures to allow sharing of common elements among different subdivision techniques.

Both enhancements rely heavily on the inheritance and message passing features of object oriented programming environments. Neither, however, represents a simple application of object oriented programming to geometric modeling.

2. Conventional Procedural Models

In even the simplest geometric modeler, methods are provided for generating swept surfaces or surfaces of revolution. Clearly, as Newell points out [13], the notion of using active (procedural) rather than passive representations of geometric models for computer graphics is a powerful amplifier of a human model maker's effort.

The basic notion of using a sparse set of geometric data as a seed for modeling procedures along with a small set of parameters for the model has been exploited with great success in imitating natural shapes. Some of the more successful applications include terrain [12], [7], trees and plants [18], [3], [16], and fire [15], [14].

In addition to the definition of specific models for specific classes of features, a significant amount of work has been done to devise ways in which models should interact with one another when assembled into groups. Blinn [2] demonstrates that homogeneous collections of amorphous shapes can be used to form models of complex molecules. Our work, however, is concerned with heterogeneous collections. The related work that is most familiar to the computer graphics community is that which is associated with control of animated figures [9], [17], [1], [20]. While most systems for controlling animation rely on an exhaustive centralized script, these permit autonomous action by individual "actors."

Our own work falls into this second category, although it applies to the generation of shape rather than the control of motion. We are aware of others who have pursued similar research [8], [6].

3. Communicating Procedural Models

Two issues arise when programming the interaction between independent models - communication and response. Messages or shared data provide the communication mechanism. In a typical message, one object would inform its neighbors of its position. The response of the neighbor objects would be to adjust their own position to conform.

3.1. Response

Response to a message results in a modification of a model, either by altering its current parameters, by adjusting its current data values, or by modifying the procedure which implements the model. Response is complicated by conflicts between objects. In a simple case, if the procedures which generate two solid objects place them both in the same volume, one must give way.

To illustrate a specific response by a procedural object, consider a stochastic subdivision equation [7] :

$$newPoint = \frac{(pointA+pointB)}{2} + gauss(level)$$

The $gauss()$ function returns a Gaussian distributed random variable scaled by a function of the level of subdivision. An extended subdivision equation is:

$$newPoint = \frac{(pointA+pointB)}{2} + gauss(level) + f(objectC)$$

In this simplified example, object C "pulls" or "pushes" the shape defined by the subdivision procedure (figure 1). The objective, in this instance, is to force the subdivided object to conform to object C.

Resolution of conflicts between objects requires an additional parameter which we call "dominance". If two cooperating processes are attempting to conform to one another, the dominant one will adapt less. If dominance varies in the normal progression of a procedural model, then different objects may dominate at different points in the processes. In the examples given later in the paper, this property is an important factor in creating a realistic model.

In our initial experiments we have represented dominance for an object as a single scalar value. Although this simple representation is inadequate for most real applications, it does have two advantages. First, having a uniform representation means that procedures need not know details of one another. Second, a scalar value never creates loops. (A classic example of a dominance loop is the set of rules for a well known children's game: rock crushes scissors, scissors cut paper, paper covers rock.)

We have considered two techniques of determining a scalar value for dominance: (1) mathematical functions, (2) sets of rules. Both provide a way of encoding heuristics about relationships between the objects being modeled. The simplest function is a constant value. This is appropriate for classes of objects where the inter-relationship is static, i.e., where

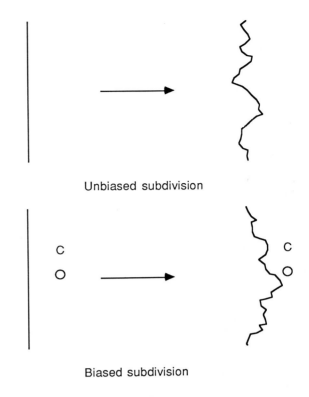

Figure 1. Unbiased and biased subdivision

objects of class A always dominate objects of class B. For some subdividable objects dominance is not static, and in these cases it is encoded as a function of level of subdivision. This provides a way of representing the situation where the relative dominance switches as level of subdivision increases (see figure 2).

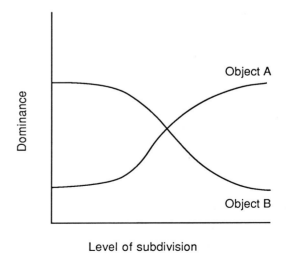

Figure 2. Dominance functions

A more robust, but more difficult technique is to formulate a set of rules that determine dominance for objects. The difficulty is ensuring that the rule set is complete, i.e. it does not produce implausible results.

Consider using dominance in a subdivision procedure (written in something like the C language):

```
while ( this.test(this) != TERMINATE )
{
      this.dominance = this.computeDominance(this);
      for ( each data_point )
      {
            this.adjust(this,this.neighborhood);
      }
      this.expand(this, this.level + 1);
}
```

The *expand*() function performs whatever subdivision is appropriate for the object "this." The routine *computeDominance*() can use either technique described above. The *adjust*() procedure uses the dominance of the neighboring objects relative to the dominance of this object and modifies each data point as necessary. Note that the object's neighborhood has somehow been communicated to the object so that the object can decide how to respond in the *adjust*() procedure.

3.2. Interlocked Hierarchies

Communications can be naively handled by broadcasting messages from all procedures to all other procedures, but in complex assemblies the overhead would be too expensive. Since objects typically interact only within a limited neighborhood, it is more efficient to establish only those communications paths which are essential.

For an analysis of message passing overhead, consider a pair of subdivision procedures - A, which splits each parent element into four subelements and B, which splits into to two subelements. (One of the examples shown in a later section is of this type.) To simplify things, assume a fixed level of subdivision (even though most subdivision procedures are adaptive). For a brute force approach, where each subelement of A is checked against each subelement of B,

$$(m \times 4^k) \times (n \times 2^l)$$

where

m is the number of initial A elements,
k is the level of subdivision for A,
n is the number of initial B elements, and
l is the level of subdivision for B

is the number of message links between subelements at the lowest level.

The total number of links is

$$m \ n \sum_{i=0}^{level} 4^i \ 2^i$$

To maintain message links for elements produced by subdivision procedures, we interlock the hierarchies that result from such procedures. However, if any part of the hierarchy of object A does not overlap some part of the hierarchy of object B, then no message links are required between these parts nor are any needed between any of their descendants. We use this fact to prune the network of message links. The number of message passing links required after pruning is:

$$m \ n \sum_{i=0}^{level} (4f_A)^i (2f_B)^i$$

where

f_A is the fraction of the number of A subelements in a B element's conflict set, and
f_B is the fraction of the number of B subelements in an A element's conflict set.

As shown in figure 3, as the size of the fractions diminish, the effectiveness of pruning increases dramatically.

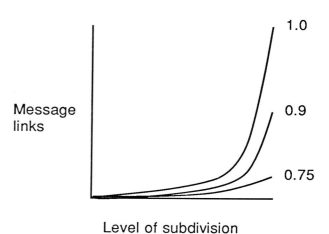

Figure 3. Number of message links-vs-level of subdivision for $f_A = f_B$ =0.75,0.9, and 1.0

4. Expandable Geometry

Our modeling system is designed to support the construction of very complex geometric objects from sparse input. Moreover, it must provide a means for controlling a heterogeneous collection of modeling procedures. As noted in the previous section, the use of adjustments in response to inter-object communication fits nicely into subdivision procedures. This has lead us to further consider the nature of subdivision based procedural models.

We initially abstracted the common elements of subdivision-based procedural models in our attempt to provide a generic subdivision interface. We realized that our abstractions were suitable for more general forms of geometry, and have used these abstractions as the basis for our modeling system. The next sections describe the resulting generalized subdivision scheme.

4.1. Recursive Subdivision

Recursive subdivision is an effective technique for a variety of applications in computer graphics and computer aided design. It has been used for display of parametric surfaces, surface intersection calculation, and more recently for stochastic modeling. In the most basic form, subdivision procedures have three components:

1) a framework
2) a subdivision equation
3) a termination criterion

The subdivision framework is the overall organization of the procedure and controls the order of surface subdivision. For example, Catmull's algorithm for curved surface display uses a stack based framework, a very fast midpoint subdivision equation, and a subpatch extent termination test [4]. The Lane-Carpenter curved surface display algorithm has a scanline oriented framework, a different subdivision equation [10], and a subpatch flatness termination criterion [11]. Fournier, Fussell, and Carpenter [7] use a variety of frameworks and termination tests with a stochastic subdivision equation to model natural features.

Typically the termination condition signals a change of representation. In Catmull's algorithm subpatches are replaced by pixels since the termination criterion guarantees that each subpatch covers only one pixel. In the Lane-Carpenter algorithm, subpatches are replaced by polygons. Clark [5] suggests a useful alternative whereby a more complex termination test modifies the subdivision equation itself, thus effecting a change of representation. We find that additional extensions along this line provide a substantially greater amount of control over shapes that can be produced using conventional subdivision.

4.2. Generalized Subdivision

We generalize the previous subdivision techniques by including state variables and a state transition table in the form of a script along with the control points as instance variables of each object.

Instead of a single subdivision equation, we now have a collection of potential geometric operations. Traditional notions of convergence and closeness of fit are meaningless in this case, and the ability to prune communications links between modeling elements suffers unless extents can be defined not only for the current representation but for all representations that will be encountered in a script.

Each state in the script carries a transition test instead of the conventional termination test. A variety of tests (on size, distance, color, flatness, etc.) may trigger a change of representation. A special transition method, tile, specifies the final transition from geometric entity to rendering primitive.

A script specifies which operations (methods) should be invoked, and when. The script consists of a list of states, with tests and operations to be performed in each state. In its most general form, the script may be included as an instance variable of an object. The other extreme, a hardcoded script, is less flexible but more compact since the script can be shared by all instances of a class of object. Figure 4 summarizes the enhancements of generalized subdivision.

4.3. Change of Representation

Change of representation is invoked by an explicit command to change to a particular representation. The presence of such a command contradicts our goal of freeing the human

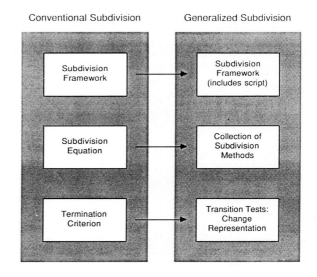

Figure 4. Correspondence between conventional and generalized subdivision structure

modeler from knowing the implementation details of the object. *I.e*, the modeler must know about linear interpolation, stochastic surfaces, bi-cubic patches, etc. We recognize this problem, but find it difficult to express the representations in terms of their properties. The solution that we are currently pursuing uses a set of modeling rules to produce scripts.

Each object is responsible for interpreting the change of representation command. Some intelligence is needed by the object in order to properly implement these transformations. Consider a vase modeled by a collection of polygons. Suppose we send a request to the vase instructing it to change to a Bezier patch representation. A naive implementation would simply pass the change of representation command onto its components (the polygons are themselves objects that can respond to such requests), but when a polygon receives this request it has no knowledge of its own context within the vase, and thus it is difficult to prevent surface smoothness discontinuities.

A more intelligent implementation considers the entire structure of the vase, and effects an alternate conversion based on this global knowledge. For this we introduce methods that exist solely to provide missing context for a change of representation.

4.4. Exploiting Compound Representations

Much of the power of generalized subdivision is derived from the combination of representations. In addition to providing a framework for diverse models, we are now able to form compound surfaces by mixing characteristics of several representations. The complexity of generated surfaces may be further enhanced by exploiting various adaptive transition tests, including stochastic tests and transitions based on non-geometric properties such as color.

4.5. Implementation

Our implementation, and the general notion of a script based modeler, were chosen to meet the following requirements: Objects must be able to access others at intermediate steps of the modeling process. This is necessary for constraint satisfaction among interacting objects. We wish to permit a backtrack mechanism for the modeling process to allow alternate parameters to be used if it is later determined that the object modification (primarily expansion) does not meet specified constraints. We currently keep a history of intermediate results, since we do not wish to restrict ourselves to only reversible procedures. The system should deal with each object a high level of abstraction, rather than being concerned with the logistics of passing appropriate commands to all subobjects.

Object interaction is implemented by designing the script so that the geometry of interacting objects has been properly expanded when a particular step in the script is reached. Additional categories of methods that support this interaction include:

1) Geometric information:
   inquire, inform, and respond
2) Geometric modification of another object:
   request and response

5. Examples

These procedural model enhancements have been built into a new modeling and display system written in the object oriented language, C++ [19]. C++ does not provide message passing, but does have class structure with inheritance of methods. For procedural models, and especially for subdivision, the inheritance mechanism of object oriented languages is an invaluable asset. Since any of the three components of a subdivision procedure for a class of objects may be inherited from its superclass, we have tried to write our procedures as generic methods.

Two examples illustrate the principles outlined above. First consider the example of a road winding through wooded terrain (figure 5). Three dissimilar procedural models are used to generate the geometry. We model the terrain using stochastic subdivision of triangles. The road is modeled by a roadbed section swept along a spline curve. For convenience, the spline path is recursively subdivided into straight line segments. The sweep operator is actually applied to the straight segments. Trees are modeled using a straightforward growth model similar to that described in [18].

The dominance rules in this example are straightforward. Both road and terrain dominate trees since trees must lie outside the roadway, and the tree elevation is determined by the terrain. The interaction between the road and the terrain is not as simple because the relative dominance is not static. At the coarsest level, the road must conform to the terrain since roads follow the lay of the land. At a finer level, however, the terrain is bulldozed to conform to the road. This is represented by the terrain dominating the road at low levels of subdivision, and just the reverse at high levels of subdivision.

Figure 5. Foggy morning

Figure 6 shows only the road and terrain to illustrate a special case of interlocked hierarchies. For this example the subdivision procedures are not executed in lock-step fashion. Instead, each procedure executes a fixed number of steps independently before checking for interference with neighboring objects. As the road is built, a three level tree is constructed whose nodes contain bounding box information about parts of the road. At the root is the extent of the entire road. At the second level are nodes with information about pairs of control points. At the lowest level are extents of individual straight road segments formed by subdividing the spline path of the road.

Links from terrain triangles into the tree of bounding box information are updated during triangle subdivision. A link is maintained if the bounding box of a triangle overlaps a

Figure 6. Fractal terrain and road

bounding box of the road (figure 7). In the data base for this scene there are 108 initial triangles of which 1680 are still active at subdivision level 3. (The subdivision procedure discards triangles that will not be visible in the final image.) Comparing the bounding boxes for each of these triangles against the 180 straight line segments of the road (only some of which are visible) would involve over 300,000 checks. However, at this point only 228 triangles were potentially in conflict with the road and 3653 bounding box checks were used to determine which triangles were actually in conflict with the road.

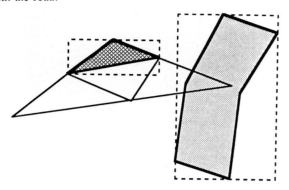

Figure 7. Road and terrain bounding box check

The second example is the champagne bottle scene, shown in figure 8. This example demonstrates how scripts may be used to synthesize various surface characteristics. Bezier subdivision was applied to the control points defining the glass part of the bottle. The foil at the top of the bottle was created by applying Bezier subdivision followed by a stochastic subdivision step. The ground surface was created with conversions between B-spline, Bezier, and stochastic surface representations. Advantages of this representation are that it generates proper silhouette edges and requires minimal input. Extremely complex surfaces may be defined with little effort.

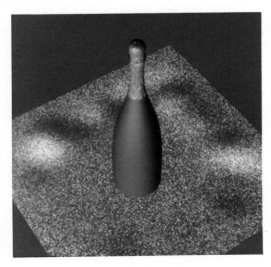

Figure 8. Champagne bottle with foil wrapper

6. Open Questions

There are a number of questions that we have not adequately answered. In the first place, with the notion of scripts and changes of representation there can be no "convergence" to a well defined curve or surface. For the same reason we have no adequate way to deal with non-local effects. Particle systems, for instance, which do maintain a hierarchy, are non-local since they expand with each generation. We have no way to prune message paths in either case.

There are also unsolved problems in defining rules that govern the procedural models. These include rules for automatic construction of scripts as well as dominance rules.

Acknowledgments

This work was supported in part by Schlumberger-Doll Research. Mary Ranade and Lee Westover implemented some of the procedure models. Andrew Glassner and Marco Valtorta were early participants in the project. Henry Fuchs continues to provide insight and encouragement. Tim Rentsch and Jeff Friedberg were involved in many helpful discussions about object-oriented programming. Finally, we thank Tom Cargill and Kye Hedlund for their help with C++.

References

[1] Badler, N.I. *Design of a Human Movement Representation Incorporating Dynamics.* University of Pennsylvania. 1984.

[2] Blinn, James F. "Generalization of Algebraic Surface Drawing," *ACM Transactions on Graphics,* 1, No. 3 July 1982 pp. 235-256.

[3] Bloomenthal, Jules "Modeling the Mighty Maple," *Computer Graphics,* 19, No. 3 July 1985 pp. 305-311.

[4] Catmull, Edwin E. "A Subdivision Algorithm for Computer Display of Curved Surfaces," Ph.D. Diss. University of Utah December 1974.

[5] Clark, James H. "A Fast Algorithm for Rendering Parametric Surfaces," *Supplement to the Proceedings of SIGGRAPH '79,* August 1979.

[6] Csuri, Charles, personal communication, 1985.

[7] Fournier, Alain, Don Fussell, and Loren C. Carpenter "Computer Rendering of Stochastic Models," *Communications of the ACM,* 25, No. 6 June 1982 pp. 371-384.

[8] Hedelman, Harold, personal communication, 1982.

[9] Kahn, K. "An Actor-Based Computer Animation Language," in *Proceedings of the ACM-SIGGRAPH Workshop on User-Oriented Design of Computer Graphics Systems,* Pittsburgh, PA: October 1976.

[10] Lane, Jeffrey M., Loren C. Carpenter, James F. Blinn, and Turner Whitted, "Scan Line Methods for Displaying Parametrically Defined Surfaces," *Communications of the ACM,* 23, No. 1 January 1980 pp. 23-34.

[11] Lane, Jeffrey M., and R.F. Riesenfeld, "A Theoretical Development for Computer Generation and Display of Piecewise Polynomial Surfaces," *IEEE Transactions on Pattern Analysis and Machine Intelligence,* PAMI-2, No. 1 January 1980 pp. 35-46.

[12] Mandelbrot, Benoit *Fractals: Form, Chance, and Dimension.* San Francisco: W.H. Freeman, 1977.

[13] Newell, Martin E., "The Utilization of Procedure Models in Computer Synthesized Shaded Images," Ph.D. Diss. University of Utah 1975.

[14] Perlin, Ken, "An Image Synthesizer," *Computer Graphics,* 19, No. 3 July 1985 pp. 287-296.

[15] Reeves, William, "Particle Systems - A Technique for Modelling a Class of Fuzzy Objects," *ACM Transactions on Graphics,* 2, No. 2 April 1983 pp. 91-108.

[16] Reeves, William T., and Ricki Blau, "Approximate and Probabilistic Algorithms for Shading and Rendering Structured Particle Systems," *Computer Graphics,* 19, No. 3 July 1985 pp. 313-322.

[17] Reynolds, Craig, "Computer Animation with Scripts and Actors," *Computer Graphics,* 16, No. 3 July 1982 pp. 289-296.

[18] Smith, Alvy Ray, "Plants, Fractals, and Formal Languages," *Computer Graphics,* 18, No. 3 July 1984 pp. 1-10.

[19] Stroustrup, Bjarne *The C++ Programming Language.* Addison-Wesley, 1986.

[20] Zeltzer, David, "Representation and Control of Three Dimensional Computer Animated Figures," Ph.D. Diss. Ohio State University August 1984.

A Consistent Hierarchical Representation for Vector Data

Randal C. Nelson
Hanan Samet

Computer Science Department
Center for Automation Research
University of Maryland
College Park, MD 20742

Abstract:

A consistent hierarchical data structure for the representation of vector data is presented. It makes use of a concept termed a *line segment fragment* to prevent data degradation under splitting or clipping of vector primitives. This means that the insertion and subsequent deletion (and vice versa) of a vector leaves the data unchanged. Vectors are represented exactly and not as digital approximations. The data is dynamically organized by use of simple probabilistic splitting and merging rules. The use of the structure for implementing a geographic information system is described. Algorithms for constructing and manipulating the structure are provided. Results of empirical tests comparing the structure to other representations in the literature are given.

CR Categories and Subject Descriptors: E.1 [**Data**]: Data Structures - trees; I.3.3 [**Computer Graphics**]: Picture/Image Generation - display algorithms; I.3.5 [**Computer Graphics**]: Computational Geometry and Object Modeling - object representations; geometric algorithms

General Terms: Algorithms, Data Structures

Additional Key Words and Phrases: vector data, quadtrees, hierarchical data structures, polygonal representations

I. Introduction

Quadtrees are a useful structure for representing certain types of geometric or geographic data. In particular, point and region data have simple and natural representations which allow the efficient performance of operations involving locality of reference, geometric calculations such as area computation, and set operations such as region intersection. The representation of line data, on the other hand, is more complicated. Several hierarchical structures based on quadtrees have been proposed, all with certain drawbacks, and none with the

natural elegance of the adaptations representing points and lines. Our study reviews the hierarchical representation of vector data in the particular context of a geographic information system, but most of our requirements would be necessary in any application where vector data is important. A good vector representation should have the following properties. First, the data structure must represent vectors precisely rather than as digital approximations. This includes the ability to accurately represent any number of vectors intersecting at a single point. Secondly, the structure must allow the data to be updated consistently. For example, insertion and subsequent deletion of a vector should leave the data unchanged. As a more complex example, it should be possible to compute the intersection of a set of vectors with a region, and then restore the information to its original state by performing a union with the complement of the original intersection. This operation involves splitting and reassembling vector primitives. Thirdly, the structure should allow the efficient performance of primitive operations such as insertion and deletion of vector data elements, and should facilitate the performance of more complex operations such as edge following, intersection with a region, or point-in-polygon though these are somewhat application-dependent. Previous hierarchical representations for vector data have been deficient in one or more of these areas.

In this paper, we develop a data structure for the representation of vector data which has the properties described above. Section II contains a brief overview of quadtrees, while section III reviews quadtree structures for storing vector data. Section IV presents a new data structure termed a PMR quadtree and shows how it can deal with line segment fragments. Section V describes a simple implementation of the PMR quadtree while section VI reports on empirical tests. Conclusions and suggestions for future work are presented in section VII.

II. Quadtrees as Geometric/Geographic Data Structures

The quadtree [Same84b] is a hierarchical, variable resolution data structure which recursively subdivides the plane into blocks based on some decomposition rule. The technique is general and can be applied to three (octrees) and higher dimensional spaces. It may be considered as a member of a general class of hierarchical data structures based on spatial decomposition which includes k-d trees [Bent75], bintrees [Know80, Same85a], and other structures. A distinction is frequently drawn between those structures in which the subdivision boundaries are determined by the data as in the classical point quadtree [Fink74], and those in which the boundaries are pre-determined by the data structure as in the region quadtree [Klin71]. The latter is sometimes termed "regular decomposition", and the structures considered in this paper are of this type.

Because of their explicitly spatial nature, quadtrees are well suited for the representation of geometric data. The simplest example is the region quadtree where an image consisting of a set of discrete regions is represented by recursively quartering the image until every block is uniform in color. In a typical binary image, the number of blocks or leaf nodes in such a representation can be considerably less than the number of pixels in an array representation of the same image. Since many operations can be performed on a quadtree in time proportional to the number of nodes, it may be advantageous in terms of speed to manipulate data in quadtree form. Furthermore, the quadtree contains information regarding the large-scale structure of the data which is not present in a low-level representation such as an array. For point data, an analogous structure, termed the PR quadtree is formed by recursively quartering the plane until no block contains more than one data point.

We have used the above representations for areal and point data in a prior implementation of a geographic information system [Same85d]. Such simple schemes do not, however, work well for vector data. For example, attempting to divide the plane until each subdivision contains only one vector element leads to an unbounded decomposition if two vectors intersect. This reflects a basic property of lineal data. Namely, while point and area data can be adequately represented by a hierarchical decomposition of space that stores only a single piece of information per block, a similar representation of vector data requires the ability to store an arbitrary amount of data per node. Specifically, for a one item per node representation to work, the amount of information needed to describe a block must decrease as the size of that block is reduced. An intrinsic property of lineal data however, is that large amounts of information can be concentrated at a single location (e.g. when several vectors intersect at the same point). No amount of subdivision will reduce this information. Thus it is not surprising that hierarchical representation of vector data should be more difficult than point or areal data. To set our problem in a proper perspective, we review in the following, several recent proposals for the hierarchical representation of vector data that have appeared in the literature.

III. Quadtree Structures for Storing Line Data

1. The MX Quadtree

The MX quadtree [Hunt79], is probably the simplest way of representing line data, and is a region quadtree in which lines are represented by regions which are one pixel wide. It can be viewed as a quadtree representation of a chaincode. Its advantages are its relative simplicity, and the ability to represent (more or less) arbitrary space curves. Disadvantages include lack of exact representation, extreme locality of reference, large storage requirements since every point on a line is stored as a separate pixel, and lack of any structure related to the lineal nature of the data.

2. The Line Quadtree

The line quadtree [Same84a] is also based on the region quadtree, and represents curves by the boundaries of the encoded regions. This is accomplished by storing additional information about the edges of the blocks. It has the advantages of a relatively simple structure, the ability to combine region and boundary data, and is somewhat less local than the MX quadtree. The primary disadvantages are the fact that it is limited to rectilinear curves which demarcate regions, and the lack of structure based on lineal nature of data.

3. The Edge Quadtree

The edge quadtree was originally developed by Shneier [Shne81] as a method of approximating an edge in an image by recursively splitting space into quadrants until each block contains at most a single section which can be approximated by a line segment. This scheme deals only with single segments, and hence some modification is necessary to make it suitable for representing multiple intersecting lines. A variant described in Rosenfeld *et al.* [Rose83] known as the linear edge quadtree achieves this by using the decomposition rule "split until no block intersects more than one line segment or until the resolution limit is reached". Nodes containing more than one segment at the highest resolution are assigned a special type (point nodes), and a count of the number of lines intersecting the block is associated with the node. Thus point nodes indicate those places where the vectors constituting the data are too close together to be resolved. Line segments are stored in the other nodes by recording their local intersection with the edges of the block. Advantages include the ability to represent arbitrary collections of line segments, some structure based on the lineal nature of the data, and a representation that stores only one item per node (as opposed to the methods requiring the use of variable size nodes described later in this paper). Major disadvantages are the complexity of the representation and consequent difficulty of performing operations, loss of information at intersections due to the use of single a special value to label such nodes, locality of reference, and loss and degradation of information caused by separately calculating the intersection of the data segment with every block through which it passes.

4. PM quadtrees

The PM quadtree was developed by Samet and Webber [Same85c] and refers to a group of structures which store linear data in the form of line segments. The basic idea is to use some splitting rule to recursively partition the plane into quadrants, and to store with each block all the segments passing through it. This generally requires the use of variable size nodes, and for some splitting rules, the depth of decomposition generated may exceed the resolution of the segment endpoints by a considerable factor. Samet and Webber [Same85c] describe the structures resulting from three decomposition rules, which they refer to as PM1, PM2, and PM3.

The PM1 quadtree is defined by the rule "quarter until every block contains a single segment endpoint, or else it intersects just one segment, or else it is empty". The main drawback of the PM1 quadtree is that it has very bad worst case behavior in terms of the maximum depth and the number of nodes which may be generated. A one item per node variation called the segment quadtree is described by Samet [Same85b].

The PM2 quadtree is defined by the rule "quarter until every block contains a single segment, or else all segments intersected by it have a common endpoint, or else it is empty" It has better worst-case behavior than the PM1 formulation in terms of maximum depth, but this depth is still considerably higher than the resolution of the segment endpoints.

The PM3 quadtree uses the rule "quarter until no block contains more than one endpoint". The segments passing through each block are then recorded in the node. Note that the splitting rule is just the PR rule applied to the endpoints of the line segments. The rule for the PM3 quadtree is the simplest of the three, and despite the fact that it does not refer to vectors as lineal objects, but only to their endpoints, it produces the most usable structure of the three. Figure 1 depicts a set of line segments and its PM3 quadtree. Note that the PM quadtrees essentially solve the problem of how to represent vector data exactly in a hierarchical structure. The price is the cost of implementing variable size nodes.

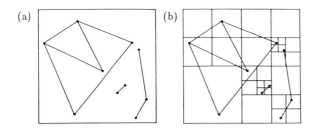

Figure 1. (a) Set of line segments and (b) corresponding PM3 quadtree.

5. Edge EXCELL

A slightly different method called *edge* EXCELL is described by Tamminen [Tamm83]. It is based on a regular decomposition that splits the cells of a grid alternately along different dimensions. A grid directory is used to map the cells into storage areas of fixed capacity (buckets) which may reside on disk. In each bucket are stored the segments that intersect the corresponding cell. When a bucket associated with a single cell overflows, every cell in the grid is split along one dimension. Overflow buckets are used to handle the case when more segments intersect at a point than can be contained in a bucket. *Edge* EXCELL is similar to the PM quadtree in that it attempts to divide space into bins containing a manageable amount of information, however it differs in that it uses fairly large bucket sizes (i.e greater than 10 data elements), while the various PM quadtrees use splitting rules which result in a low average occupancy.

IV. The PMR quadtree and fragments.

The structure that we propose uses a variant of the PM quadtree, henceforth referred to as the *PMR quadtree* as the means of controlling the amount of information stored per node. We also generalize the concept of a line segment to represent vector data in a manner that is exact and does not degrade under operations which cause a vector feature to be split or clipped. This generalization is referred to as a *fragment*.

The PMR quadtree (for PM Random) is based on the observation that any rule that divides up the line segments among quadtree blocks in a reasonably uniform fashion can be used as the basis for a PM-like quadtree. In fact, unless it is required by the application, the structure need not be uniquely determined by the data. Probabilistic splitting rules can be used as easily as any other. For instance, a rule such as "If the number of segments in a block exceeds n when a segment is added, split it once" in conjunction with a corresponding deletion rule could be used to dynamically maintain a collection of line segments.

The PMR quadtree uses a pair of rules, one for splitting and one for merging, to dynamically organize the data. The splitting rule, invoked whenever a line segment is added to a node, states "if the number of segments in the node exceeds n (four in the particular example studied,) then split the node once into quadrants". The corresponding merging rule, invoked when a segment is deleted, states "merge while the number of distinct line segments contained in the node and its siblings is less than or equal to n (four) " Figure 2 shows the construction of a PMR quadtree with the threshold n equal to two, for the segments in Figure 1. Note in figure 2b, that the insertion of segment 7 causes two blocks to split (the NW and NE quadrants) since the capacity of each of these blocks was exceeded by its insertion. Since a node is split only once when the insertion of a segment causes the threshold n to be exceeded, a node may contain more than n segments. However, except in the unusual case where many segments share an endpoint, the node occupancy is unlikely to exceed the threshold by much. This scheme differs from the structures previously considered here in that the quadtree for a given data set is not unique, but depends on the history of manipulations applied to the structure. Certain types of analysis are thus more difficult than with uniquely determined structures. On the other hand, this structure permits the decomposition of space to be based directly on the lineal data stored locally. The PMR quadtree was chosen for this reason.

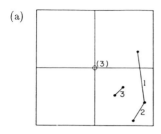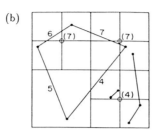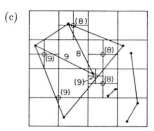

Figure 2. Building PMR quadtree from segments of Figure 1 with threshold equal to two. (a) Three segments have been inserted causing the plane to be quartered once as indicated by the small circle, (b) Segments 4-7 inserted causing three blocks to split, (c) Segments 8 and 9 inserted causing five more blocks to split.

We now address the problem of how to clip a segment in such a way that the operation may be reversed without data degradation should the missing portion be reinserted. In geographical applications, segment truncation arises when a line map is intersected with an area. Since the borders of the area may not correspond exactly with the endpoints of the segments defining the line data, certain segments may be clipped. Such an intersection is illustrated in Figure 3. The partial line segment produced is referred to as a *fragment* and the artificial endpoints produced by such an intersection are referred to as *cut points*. The problem reduces to that of representing fragments. One possible solution is to represent a fragment by introducing new, intermediate endpoints at the cut points, creating a whole new segment. In continuous space, a new segment which is colinear with the original one, but has at least one different endpoint, can be exactly represented. In discrete space (e.g., as a result of the digitization process), this is not always possible because the continuous coordinates of the cut point do not, in general, correspond exactly to any coordinates in the discrete space. If the new line segment is represented approximately in the discrete space, then the original information is degraded, and the pieces cannot reliably be rejoined. In addition, if an intermediate point is introduced to produce new line segments, then the new line segment descriptor must be propagated to all remaining blocks containing the original segment. This is likely to be a very time-consuming operation.

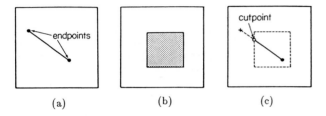

Figure 3. Definition of a fragment (c) from the intersection of a segment (a) with a region (b).

An alternative solution is to retain the description of the original segment, and use the spatial properties of the quadtree to specify what portions of the segment are actually present. The underlying insight is that a node may contain a reference to a segment, even though the entire segment is not present as a lineal feature. Rather, the segment descriptor contained in a node can be interpreted as implying the presence of just that portion of the segment which intersects the corresponding quadtree block. Such an intersection of a segment with a block will be referred to as a *q-edge*, and the original segment will be referred to as the *parent segment*. The presence or absence in the quadtree of a particular q-edge is completely independent of the presence or absence of q-edges representing other parts of the parent segment. Thus lineal features corresponding to partial segments (i.e., fragments) can be represented simply by inserting the appropriate collection of q-edges. Since the original descriptors are retained, a lineal feature can be broken into pieces and rejoined without loss or degradation of information. In the quadtree structure, q-edges are combined to represent arbitrary fragments of line segments. Since they all bear the same segment descriptor, they are easily recognizable as deriving from the same parent segment. This solves the problem of how to split a line or a map in an easily reversible manner. The use of this principle to represent the lineal feature produced by the intersection of Figure 3 is shown in Figure 4.

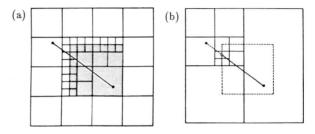

Figure 4. Representation of fragment of Figure 3 using a collection of q-edges. (a) Region quadtree for area with line segment superimposed, (b) set of five q-edges composing fragment.

The PMR quadtree can be used to represent a collection of fragments by slightly modifying the splitting and merging rules to reflect the insertion and deletion of fragments instead of line segments. The splitting rule which is invoked whenever a fragment is introduced into the structure now states "quarter until no block contains a cut point in its interior (i.e., first localize the cut points), and then once more if a block contains more than n (four) q-edges." The merge condition is now invoked both when a fragment is deleted, and when one is inserted (since a fragment may be inserted which restores the larger segment of which it is a part) and states "merge while there are n (four) or fewer distinct parent segments in the four sibling blocks and the q-edges are continuous through the block produced by the merge". Q-edges satisfying this last condition are said to be *compatible*. For example, see figure 5a where q-edges a,b and c are compatible, whereas in figure 5b, q-edges a and b are incompatible. Figure 6 shows a set of fragments produced by the intersection of the segments of Figure 1 with an area, and depicts the corresponding PMR quadtree when n is equal to two.

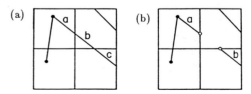

Figure 5. Sibling blocks containing (a) compatible and (b) incompatible sets of q-edges.

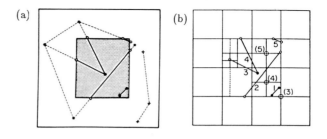

Figure 6. (a) Set of five fragments induced by the intersection of a region with the segments of Figure 1. (b) PMR-f quadtree with bucket size equal to two, for fragments of Figure 9 inserted in indicated order. The three circled splits were caused by exceeding the threshold. All others are necessary to localize the cut points of the fragments.

The above procedure is stated in terms of arbitrary fragments considered as abstract objects, but in practice some method is needed for specifying a fragment concretely. The easiest method is to restrict ourselves to the insertion and deletion of the restricted set of fragments corresponding to the intersection of line segments with all potential quadtree blocks. We will term these *q-fragments* in view of their similarity to q-edges. Arbitrary fragments can be specified to the resolution of the tree in terms of component q-fragments which thus form a set of building blocks. Note that a given fragment may be represented by different collections of q-edges in different quadtrees. The particular collection of q-edges that results from the insertion of any fragment depends upon the structure of the tree. Precise algorithms for insertion and deletion of q-fragments in PMR trees are given in the next section.

V. Implementation and algorithms.

The PMR quadtree was implemented in a geographic information system as part of an ongoing investigation into the use of of hierarchical data structures in the representation and processing of cartographic information of which only a brief description is given here. For a detailed description see [Same85d]. Since quadtrees are based on spatial decomposition, and geographical information is intrinsically spatial in nature, it was felt that quadtrees would be particularly appropriate as a basic data structure for this application. The current system includes representations and primitive operations which can be used to efficiently handle queries such as "report all wheat-growing regions within 50 miles of the Mississippi River".

Because of the large amount of information contained in geographic features, most of the data must be maintained in secondary storage. In the database system, this is achieved by use of a structure called a linear quadtree [Garg82], which is a list of the quadtree leaf nodes in the order that would be produced by a preorder traversal of the tree. The leaf nodes are represented by a pair of numbers collectively termed a *locational code*. The first number corresponds to the level of the node in the quadtree. The second is composed of a sequence of two bit directional codes that give the path from the root of the quadtree to the leaf. This process is equivalent to taking the x-y coordinate of the pixel in one corner of the leaf and interleaving the bits. The ordered list is maintained on disk as a B-tree [Come79] which is brought into core a few pages at a time. This organization enables the efficient execution of any operation that can be performed by traversing the quadtree in preorder including calculation of area, overlay, display, and connected component analysis. In fact almost any task which can be performed one scan line at a time in an array representation can be done during a single traversal in a quadtree. The B-tree structure is maintained by a kernel of primitive functions which allows the user to manipulate the structure as if it were an ordinary quadtree. The system represents areal and point data as (linear) region and PR quadtrees respectively. The similarity of these two data structures allows easy implementation of operations involving multiple data types -- for example locating all the cities with population greater than 5,000 within 20 miles of wheat-growing regions in Texas.

Since line data constitute a third major cartographic data type, a line representation is desired which is similarly compatible. The search for such a structure led us to the development of the PMR quadtree and the idea of fragments.

The first question is how to implement the variable size nodes. Since the number of line segments in a node is potentially unbounded, a true variable-length storage scheme must be used. For pointer-based quadtrees, linked lists are one possibility. An alternative is a variant of a binary tree structure that reflects the position of the segments within the block (see Samet and Webber [Same85c]). The second suggestion seems to be unnecessarily complicated for our application. One property of the PMR quadtree is that, although the maximum number of q-edges occurring in a node is potentially unbounded, the average occupancy remains low. For random vectors, it can be shown that the expected value is less than n if $n > 1$. In our empirical tests, with $n = 4$, the average occupancy remained less than 3 in all cases. The low average occupancy makes a linear search through the q-edges of a node practical. For linear quadtrees, ordered by the locational codes of their leaf nodes, the simplest way of implementing variable node sizes is to duplicate locational codes. This is the method used in our application. The q-edges intersecting a node are represented by a pointer to a record describing the parent segment. All q-edges with the same parent share this descriptor, which avoids unnecessary duplication of information.

We now present algorithms for the insertion and deletion of q-fragments in the PMR quadtree. At this point we should emphasize, the terminological distinction between q-edges and q-fragments. We use the term q-edge, to refer to the information content of a PMR quadtree node. Every node in the PMR quadtree contains zero or more q-edges representing the intersection of line segments with the corresponding quadtree block. We use the term q-fragment, on the other hand, to refer a member of a convenient set of primitive fragments, which just happen to be the the intersections of line segments with potential quadtree blocks. The block is conceptual in that it may not correspond to a leaf node in the quadtree into which the q-edge is being inserted. The block may correspond to a node deeper than any that exist in the tree, in which case the plane must be further subdivided. On the other hand, the block may correspond to a gray node in the quadtree in which case, several q-edges must be inserted.

We assume that a PMR quadtree is represented as a collection of pointers to records of type *node*. These conceptual nodes may contain a variable amount of information since a node may contain several q-edges. We also assume some basic routines for manipulating the structure. In the following N is a pointer to a quadtree node, L is a pointer to a record representing a line segment, and B refers to the locational code of a quadtree block. INSTALL(L,N) installs a q-edge in node N corresponding to the intersection of line segment L with the node N. REMOVE(L,N) removes q-edge corresponding to the intersection of L with N from node N (if it exists there). SPLIT(N) splits leaf node N into quadrants. MERGE(N) merges leaf node N with its siblings if they are leaf nodes. FIND(B) takes a block and returns a pointer to the corresponding node n in the tree if it exists, or to the smallest subsuming node if it does not. SPLITCOND(N) returns true iff node n contains more than (four) q-edges. MERGECOND(N) returns true iff node N is a leaf node all of whose siblings are leaf nodes, and the siblings contain (four) or fewer parent segments, and their q-edges are compatible. SON(B, direction) returns the locational code of the block which is the son of B in the given direction. SIZE(N) returns the size of a node N or block B.

Insertion of a q-fragment, say F representing the intersection of line segment L with block whose locational code is B is accomplished as follows.

(1) If B corresponds to a leaf node then F is installed, and the node is checked for splitting or merging. Merging can occur if the inserted q-edge restores a larger fragment. An example of this is shown in Figure 7.

(2) If B corresponds to a gray node, then the q-fragments corresponding to the intersection of L with the sons of B are inserted recursively. Figure 8 shows this procedure.

(3) If B is subsumed by a leaf node, say N, then N is quartered until a leaf node is produced which corresponds to B, and F is then installed as in case 1. This process is illustrated in Figure 9.

   (a)   (b)   (c)   (d)

Figure 7. Insertion in PMR quadtree of a q-fragment which causes merging of blocks. (a) Quadtree before insertion, (b) q-fragment to be inserted, (c) insertion produces sibling blocks with compatible q-edges, (d) Structure after merging.

(a)   (b)   (c)

Figure 8. Insertion in PMR quadtree. Large q-fragment is inserted by decomposing it into smaller q-fragments. (a) Original quadtree, (b) q-fragment to be inserted, (c) q-fragment broken into three, smaller q-fragments whose sizes match those of extant blocks.

(a)   (b)   (c)

Figure 9. Insertion in PMR quadtree of small q-fragment into large block. (a) Original quadtree, (b) q-fragment to be inserted, (c) block quartered until size matches q-fragment.

More formally, we have:

recursive procedure INSERT(L,B);
/* Insert the q-fragment corresponding to the intersection of line segment L with the quadtree block whose locational code is B into the PMR quadtree */
begin
  value pointer line L;
  value locationcode B;
  pointer node N;
  quadrant I;
  N ← FIND(B);

if SIZE(N) = SIZE(B) **then**
  begin
    INSTALL(L,N);
    if SPLITCOND(N) **then** SPLIT(N)
    else if MERGECOND(N) **then** MERGE(N);
  end
else if SIZE(N) < SIZE(B) **then**
  begin
    for I **in** {'NW', 'NE', 'SW', 'SE'}
      do INSERT(L, SON(B,I));
  end
else
  begin
    while SIZE(N) > SIZE(B) **do**
      begin
        SPLIT(N);
        N ← FIND(B);
      end;
    INSTALL(L,N);
    if SPLITCOND(N) **then** SPLIT(N)
    else if MERGECOND(N) **then** MERGE(N);
  end;
end;

Deletion of a q-fragment, say F, representing the intersection of a line segment L with a block whose locational code is B, is accomplished by a similar procedure. Deletion of a q-fragment is interpreted as erasing a portion of the parent segment.

(1) If B corresponds to a leaf node which contains F, then the reference to F is removed and a check for merging is made on the node and its siblings.

(2) If B corresponds to a gray node, then the q-edges formed by intersecting L with the sons of B are deleted recursively.

(3) If B is subsumed by a leaf node, then that node is quartered until a leaf node is produced which corresponds to B, and F is deleted as in 1.

More formally, we have

recursive procedure DELETE(L,B);
/* Delete the q-fragment corresponding to the intersection of line segment L with the quadtree block whose locational code is B from the PMR quadtree */
begin
  value pointer line L;
  value locationcode B;
  pointer node N;
  quadrant I;
  N ← FIND(B);
  if SIZE(N) = SIZE(B) **then**
    begin
      REMOVE(L,N);
      if MERGECOND(N) **then** MERGE(N);
    end
  else if SIZE(N) < SIZE(B) **then**
    begin
      for I **in** {'NW', 'NE', 'SW', 'SE'}
        do DELETE(L, SON(B,I));
    end
  else
    begin

```
while SIZE(N) > SIZE(B) do
  begin
    SPLIT(N);
    N ← FIND(B);
  end;
  REMOVE(L,N);
  if MERGECOND(N) then MERGE(N);
  end;
end;
```

VI. Tests and Comparisons

In order to evaluate the performance of the proposed line representations, tests were run using geographic data on four different structures: MX, edge, PM3, and PMR quadtrees. PM3 quadtrees were implemented using fragments in a manner analogous to our PMR implementation. The first two, as discussed in earlier sections of this paper, have deficiencies that ultimately make them unsuitable for the desired application. However, enough can be done with them to allow a meaningful comparison to be made for some operations. In particular, if the performance of the PM methods is far worse than that of methods known to be deficient other ways, we must ask whether the gain is worth the cost. The following tests were made.

(1) Time required to build the quadtree structure.
(2) Comparison of the storage requirements of the different representations.
(3) Time required to perform an intersection with an area.
(4) Comparison of the effect of different values for the split threshold n for PMR quadtrees.

Three different lineal data sets were used in the tests. The data are in the form of connected line segments and correspond to maps of three different geographic features: a railroad line, a city boundary, and a road map for the city. The first is very simple and contain only 16 segments. The city boundary is a simple closed curve containing 64 segments. The road map is fairly complex and contains 764 segments (figure 10). The vector endpoints were digitized onto a 512 x 512 grid which is the size of the space used for the experiments.

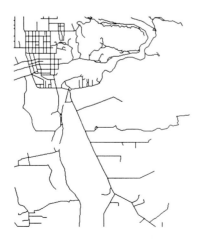

Figure 10. Set of 764 line segments consituting road map.

1. Building test.

The building algorithm essentially tests the efficiency of insertion into the structure. The three maps were built for each of the four structures. Results are displayed in Table 1. Utime refers to the actual runtime of the algorithm. The data indicate that none of the methods is overwhelmingly superior in terms of insertion efficiency, but the PMR representation has a definite if irregular lead in most cases. In the case of the road map, which represents the most realistic data set, the MX, edge, and PMR representations are more or less equivalent, and about 30% faster than the PM3.

2. Tree sizes.

The final size of the structure is important because it is the form in which the information is stored within the system. To a lesser extent, the size is important because many of the algorithms run in time proportional to the number of nodes (i.e., the size) of the quadtree. However, the constants of proportionality may differ between different representations, so a comparison in this respect is not very meaningful without additional information. The results are tabulated in Table 1 for the three maps and methods. The term "leaves" refers to the number of quadtree leaf nodes for the MX and edge quadtrees, and to the sum of the number of q-edges and the number of empty nodes for the PM quadtrees. A quadtree leaf and a q-edge pointer occupy the same amount of storage, so the numbers represent comparable quantities. The term "qnodes" refers to the number of nodes in the PM methods and is included to provide a feeling for the fullness of the nodes and to support the claim that the average occupancy is indeed small (less than three for all examples here), for realistic geographic data sets.

Table 1: Building times and sizes				
Map	Structure	Utime	Leafs	qnodes
railroad	MX	2.21	2101	-----
	edge	.63	301	-----
	PM3	.63	92	70
	PMR	.30	35	19
city	MX	2.62	2347	-----
	edge	2.25	835	-----
	PM3	2.36	310	214
	PMR	1.28	151	70
road	MX	22.55	19699	-----
	edge	20.48	7723	-----
	PM3	29.38	3939	2350
	PMR	19.03	2078	874

Examination of the results reveals a steady decrease in the required storage from MX to edge to PM3 to PMR. The PMR representation is at least eight times more efficient in its use of storage than the simple MX in all the cases tested, but both PM techniques improve the storage efficiency significantly over the other two techniques. This improvement can be explained by noting that the PM quadtrees use one-dimensional primitives which can extend over distances of many pixels rather than the pixel by pixel representation that is used by the MX method exclusively, and by the edge method when segments approached each other. It should be mentioned that these results are for collections of complete line segments since no cut-points were involved in the original maps. The presence of cut-points in the data would be expected to reduce the storage efficiency, since further decomposition would be required to localize them.

3. Intersection test.

The intersection function is a high level geographic computation which involves processing the entire data structure. In the case of the PM quadtrees, it tests the efficiency of the fragment representation, because the previously intact line segments are now cut where they cross an area boundary. Because the PM/fragment methods enable the performance of operations not possible with the local methods (e.g., reassembling split lines without degradation of data) it is not entirely clear that the different intersection computations are comparable: however, the results may give a general idea of the practicality of high level operations. The intersections were performed using the roadmap as the lineal data set (the others being too small to provide a reasonable intersection,) and three binary maps and their complements, represented in the form of area quadtrees, as templates. The use of the complements is intended to permit the effects of the size and shape of the templates to be distinguished from the overall efficiency of the different algorithms. This precaution is necessary because the intersection algorithm used with the PM structures works differently than the one used with the two other methods, and is affected differently by changing the shape of the template. In particular, the intersection procedure for the MX and edge quadtrees works by inserting into a blank map all linear sections that intersect the template, while the procedure for the PM quadtrees works by erasing the sections of the line map which do not intersect the template. It turns out that insertion and deletion of q-edges are operations of comparable complexity. For a map produced by erasing portions of a preexisting map, the number of deletions corresponds to the number of insertions necessary to produce the complementary map since the same q-edges are involved. Hence it is more appropriate to compare the intersections of the first two representations with the complementary intersections of the PM/fragment representations.

The three templates used are referred to as center, stone, and pebble, and represent a floodplain in register with the road map, and unrelated binary images derived from thresholded photographs of stones and pebbles respectively. Only the floodplain map has any geographic relevance. The other two were used with the intention of giving the system a more stringent, if less realistic, test. In particular, the degree of fragmentation induced by the pebble map probably exceeds any that would normally arise in a geographic application.

The results of the tests are given in raw form in Table 2, and are apparently ambiguous. In some cases the PM methods take much longer than the MX and edge schemes, but in others they take less time (though not correspondingly so). This inconsistency is due to the complementary effect of the different intersection algorithms discussed above. Table 3 reorganizes the data so that the appropriate complements are compared, and a consistent trend is now apparent. The time needed to perform an intersection generally increases from MX to edge to PM3 to PMR with the PM methods taking somewhere around twice as long as their competitors. Note that the order in which the intersection times increase is the same in which the structure sizes decrease suggesting that we are observing a time versus space trade-off.

Table 2 also gives the sizes of the structures representing the intersections. Comparing the sizes of the resulting maps reveals that, as predicted above, the improvement in storage requirements from MX to PMR is less dramatic than when no cut points were present. The degree of fragmentation varies, but in the case of intersections with the pebble map and its complement, it is probable that few if any of the original segments are intact. Since additional splitting is required to localize the fragment ends, the representation is not as efficient as for data that contains no cut points. The improvement is still present, however, with the PM methods generally requiring between one half and one quarter of the space of the MX, and significantly less than the edge quadtree. The order of decreasing sizes from MX to PMR which was noted for the segment data remains the same.

Table 2: Intersection times and sizes				
Intersection	Structure	Utime	Leafs	qnodes
road & center	MX	4.10	3094	-----
	edge	5.60	1759	-----
	PM3	15.50	1019	874
	PMR	14.60	910	775
road & centercomp	MX	16.90	17314	-----
	edge	14.50	8320	-----
	PM3	6.83	4275	2677
	PMR	8.02	2568	1402
road & stone	MX	4.90	3397	-----
	edge	8.70	2344	-----
	PM3	22.40	2011	1774
	PMR	28.10	1853	1651
road & stonecomp	MX	19.70	17776	-----
	edge	19.60	8803	-----
	PM3	15.30	4684	3244
	PMR	22.00	3270	2122
road & pebble	MX	11.45	9022	-----
	edge	17.25	5653	-----
	PM3	32.20	4530	3760
	PMR	47.00	4034	3370
road & pebblecomp	MX	16.95	13564	-----
	edge	20.80	7459	-----
	PM3	30.20	5086	4078
	PMR	42.00	4250	3436

Table 3: Reordered intersection times		
Intersection	Structure	Utime
road & center	MX	4.10
	edge	5.60
road & centercomp	PM3	6.83
	PMR	8.02
road & centercomp	MX	16.90
	edge	14.50
road & center	PM3	15.50
	PMR	14.60
road & stone	MX	4.90
	edge	8.70
road & stonecomp	PM3	15.30
	PMR	22.00
road & stonecomp	MX	19.70
	edge	19.60
road & stone	PM3	22.40
	PMR	28.10
road & pebble	MX	11.45
	edge	17.25
road & pebblecomp	PM3	30.20
	PMR	42.00
road & pebblecomp	MX	16.95
	edge	20.80
road & pebble	PM3	32.20
	PMR	47.00

At first glance, the results seem disappointing because we have come to expect, since so many quadtree algorithms can be made to run in time proportional to the number of nodes, that a decrease in the size of a structure will imply a corresponding decrease in execution time for operations performed using that structure. There is however, no reason to expect this property to hold across different structures, since the amount of work done per node will certainly differ. On the other hand, the increased execution time is by no means severe enough to damage the value of the representation. This is especially true in light of the fact that the PM/fragment structures have capabilities and a certain elegance that the MX and edge quadtrees completely lack. This is worth a certain price.

4. Different splitting thresholds.

In our implementation of the PMR quadtree, we chose $n=4$ as the threshold at which to split a node. It was clear from the start that both very low and very high thresholds would degrade the performance of the structure. For low splitting thresholds, say one or two, the storage requirements would tend to be high, since a large amount of splitting would take place in a futile attempt to separate intersecting vector features. Conversely, a high average occupancy would unduly increase the amount of effort involved in processing each node, the extreme example being a single node containing a list of all the vector features, which would completely nullify any benefits obtained from the spatial decomposition. We initially selected a threshold of four because that was the greatest number of roads likely to intersect at a single point. Tests were run for thresholds of 1,2,4,8,16 and 32 on two data sets: the road map, and a collection of 100 randomly intersecting line segments. The segments for the road map form a planar graph, but no such restriction was imposed upon the random segments of the second data set.

The times and sizes for the building and intersection algorithms are given in tables 4 and 5. For the roadmap, the results are as expected. There is a slow decrease in building time, and a rapid decrease in storage requirements as the threshold increases. This is not surprising since generally less decomposition is being done. For the intersection algorithm, the time increases for both high and low thresholds as predicted, with a minimum at $n=4$. The storage requirements of the PMR quadtree representing the intersection decrease to an asymptotic value as the threshold increases. This is the point at which all decomposition is due to the localization of fragment endpoints, and further changes in the threshold consequently have no effect.

The results for the random segments are very similar. The optimal threshold for the intersection algorithm is 8 instead of 4, but the difference is very small. The somewhat greater sensitivity of the structure storage requirements to the threshold is due to the fact that the road map contains many very short segments with the result that there are fewer opportunities for merging when the threshold is increased. The fact that the performance of PMR quadtree is similar for radically different types of vector data, suggests that it would provide a robust, general vector representation.

Table 4a: Results of building PMR road map using different thresholds.			
Threshold	Utime	Leaves	Qnodes
1	26.9	5765	3745
2	22.5	4082	2404
4	16.6	2078	874
8	14.7	1396	346
16	13.7	1145	163
32	15.6	1001	73

Table 4b: Intersection of PMR road map with center using different thresholds.			
Threshold	Utime	Leaves	Qnodes
1	14.7	1069	925
2	13.5	968	829
4	12.0	910	775
8	13.8	897	763
16	17.8	895	760
32	22.0	895	760

Table 5a: Results of inserting 100 random segments using different thresholds			
Threshold	Utime	Leaves	Qnodes
1	31.1	9189	6508
2	20.4	5970	3433
4	11.6	3031	1114
8	6.3	1407	262
16	4.2	763	79
32	3.4	452	25

Table 5b: Intersection of 100 random segments with center using different thresholds.			
Threshold	Utime	Leaves	Qnodes
1	23.5	2496	2131
2	17.9	2159	1804
4	16.1	1880	1582
8	15.8	1807	1540
16	19.3	1774	1531
32	27.2	1774	1531

VII. Conclusions

The PMR quadtree used to store segment fragments provides a hierarchical vector representation that satisfies the conditions set forth at the beginning of this paper. It is exact (i.e., non digitized). It allows consistent updating of the data, and permits primitive vector features to be manipulated as well as cut or clipped and reconstructed without data degradation. It facilitates efficient insertion and deletion of vector elements, and the performance of high level operations such as area intersection. Since the endpoints of the vectors are not used to direct the spatial decomposition, both planar and non-planar graphs can be efficiently represented.

The basic technique, is not however, limited to representing lineal data in two dimensions. The idea of using probabilistic splitting and merging rules to recursively decompose the space and dynamically organize the data into bins of manageable average size is a powerful general notion. The PMR quadtree generalizes immediately to the representation of lines or faces in three or more dimensions. For some recent work involving PM quadtrees in 3 dimensions, see [Ayal85, Carl85, Fuji85]. Moreover, the object represented by the q-edge need not be a line segment, but could be any entity for which there exists a descriptor, and which has definite spatial extent. The representation of lineal data could be extended for example, by having "generalized q-edges" represent the intersection of the blocks with cubic splines rather than simply with line segments. As another example, consider an image processing environment where a generalized q-edge could represent the presence or absence of a proposed object in the block. Several hypotheses could be maintained simultaneously, and updated as processing progressed. As a third example, the generalized q-edge could represent the intersection of a rectangular region with the block in a system for VLSI design rule checking.

To sum up, the PM quadtrees using fragments provide a conceptually clean representation for lineal data which explicitly addresses its one-dimensional character. For the geographic information system, the structures compare favorably in performance with the cruder MX and edge quadtrees in cases where they can be compared, and resolve the problems of loss of information and degradation of data which encumbered the latter. Finally, the structures have the potential for use as a general representation in any application where the spatial relationship of objects is important.

Acknowledgments This work was supported in part by the National Science Foundation under Grant DCR–83–02118. We have benefited greatly from discussions with Clifford A. Shaffer and Robert E. Webber.

References

1. [Ayal85] - D. Ayala, P. Brunet, R. Juan, and I. Navazo, Object representation by means of nonminimal division quadtrees and octrees, *ACM Transactions on Graphics 4*, 1(January 1985), 41-59.

2. [Bent75] - J.L. Bentley, A survey of techniques for fixed radius near neighbor searching, SLAC Report No. 186, Stanford Linear Accelerator Center, Stanford University, Stanford, CA, August 1975.

3. [Carl85] - I. Carlbom, I. Chakravarty, and D. Vanderschel, A hierarchical data structure for representing the spatial decomposition of 3-D objects, *IEEE Computer Graphics and Applications 5*, 4(April 1985), 24-31.

4. [Come79] - D. Comer, The Ubiquitous B-tree, *ACM Computing Surveys 11*, 2(June 1979), 121-137.

5. [Fink74] - R.A. Finkel and J.L. Bentley, Quad trees: a data structure for retrieval on composite keys, *Acta Informatica 4*, 1(1974), 1-9.

6. [Fuji85] - K. Fujimura and T.L. Kunii, A hierarchical space indexing method, *Proceedings of Computer Graphics '85*, Tokyo, 1985, T1-4, 1-14.

7. [Garg82] - I. Gargantini, An effective way to represent quadtrees, *Communications of the ACM 25*, 12(December 1982), 905-910.

8. [Hunt79] - G.M. Hunter and K. Steiglitz, Operations on images using quad trees, *IEEE Transactions on Pattern Analysis and Machine Intelligence 1*, 2(April 1979), 145-153.

9. [Klin71] - A. Klinger, Patterns and Search Statistics, in *Optimizing Methods in Statistics*, J.S. Rustagi, Ed., Academic Press, New York, 1971, 303-337.

10. [Rose83] - A. Rosenfeld, H. Samet, C. Shaffer, and R.E. Webber, Application of hierarchical data structures to geographical information systems phase II, Computer Science TR 1327, University of Maryland, College Park, MD, September 1983.

11. [Same84a] - H. Samet and R.E. Webber, On encoding boundaries with quadtrees, *IEEE Transactions on Pattern Analysis and Machine Intelligence 6*, 3(May 1984), 365-369.

12. [Same84b] - H. Samet, The quadtree and related hierarchical data structures, *ACM Computing Surveys 16*, 2(June 1984), 187-260.

13. [Same85a] - H. Samet and M. Tamminen, Efficient component labeling of images of arbitrary dimension, Computer Science TR-1480, University of Maryland, College Park, MD, February 1985.

14. [Same85b] - H. Samet, C.A. Shaffer, and R.E. Webber, The segment quadtree: a linear quadtree-based representation for linear features, *Proceedings of Computer Vision and Pattern Recognition 85*, San Francisco, June 1985, 385-389.

15. [Same85c] - H. Samet and R.E. Webber, Storing a collection of polygons using quadtrees, *ACM Transactions on Graphics 4*, 3(July 1985), 182-222.

16. [Same85d] - H. Samet, A. Rosenfeld, C.A. Shaffer, R.C. Nelson, Y-G. Huang, and K. Fujimura, Application of hierarchical data structures to geographic information systems: phase IV, Computer Science TR-1578, University of Maryland, College Park, MD, December 1985.

17. [Shne81] - M. Shneier, Calculations of geometric properties using quadtrees, *Computer Graphics and Image Processing 16*, 3(July 1981), 296-302.

18. [Tamm83] - M. Tamminen, Performance analysis of cell based geometric file organizations, *Computer Vision, Graphics, and Image Processing 24*, 2(November 1983), 168-181.

A MONTAGE METHOD: THE OVERLAYING OF THE COMPUTER GENERATED IMAGES ONTO A BACKGROUND PHOTOGRAPH

Eihachiro Nakamae, Koichi Harada and Takao Ishizaki
Hiroshima University
Saijo, Higashi-Hiroshima
Hiroshima 724, Japan

Tomoyuki Nishita
Fukuyama University
Higashimura, Fukuyama
Hiroshima 729-02, Japan

ABSTRACT

A system of computer programs has been established to generate high quality montage image of considerable usefulness in architectural simulation which combine computer-generated images and photographed background pictures.

Traditionally, there are two methods of creating architectural montages: (1) an artist paints new buildings onto a background scene usually generated photographically, and (2) a three-dimensional scale model is created to simulate the whole landscape, and this model is then photographed. The montage method described here combines aspects of both traditional montage methods with significant improvement in accuracy and reduction of time and cost of preparation. Specifically, a digitized photograph is used as a background scene onto which is superimposed a 3D computer-generated image of a new building. The outstanding points of the new method are:

(i) The shading and shadows of each computer generated image are calculated with higher accuracy, (ii) the fog effect is taken into account, and (iii) a new anti-aliasing technique improves the quality of the final montage image.

CR Categories and Subject Descriptors: I.3.3[Computer Graphics]:Picture/Image Generation -- display algorithm; I.3.5[Computer Graphics]: Computational Geometry and Object Modelling -- curve, surface, solid and object representations; I.3.7[Computer Graphics]: Three-Dimensional Graphics and Realithm -- color, shading, shadowing and texture; I.4.3[Image Processing]: Enhancement -- sharpening and deblurring; I.4.6[Image Processing]: Segmentation -- region growing, partitioning; I.4.8[Image Processing]: Scene Analysis -- depth cues; J.4 [Social and Behavioral Sciences]: Sociology

General Terms: Algorithms, Measurement

1. Introduction

In order to assess the potential impact of a new construction on local environments, it is very important to understand what is going to happen to viewing angles and local lighting/shadows if new buildings are constructed. Assessment grows more important and more difficult as the number and scale of the new buildings increases.

Traditionally, two methods have been used for attacking this problem: (1) A landscape where new construction occurs is photographed, and an artist paints the new building(s) onto this picture. (2) A 3D scale model is made to gauge the influence of the new buildings on their surroundings.

The major difficulty of the second method is that it is expensive even though it offers three-dimensional investigation. And it should be noted that every part of the model is artificial. Though the first method is less costly, the montage is totally affected by the artist's personal preference.

Modern computer graphics techniques offer a viable solution to this problem. In 1979, Uno et al.[1] proposed a general purpose graphics system that was used to create simple image compositions. In 1980, Feibush et al.[2] overlaid an imaginary house onto a background using a complex database composed of many polygons and textures. In 1984, Porter et al.[3] presented an interesting approach (Alpha channel method) to the digitized composition problem that allows processing of complicated three-dimensional images.

Image compositions in these earlier studies have been investigated chiefly from the viewpoint of anti-aliasing. The montage system in this paper includes the following unique characteristics along with the anti-aliasing processing:

(1) The ratio between the maximum illuminance due to the sun beam [4] and the ambient illuminance of each computer generated image described in an early paper by the authors is calculated by using information contained in the background picture. This enables superior simulation of natural shading and shadows.

(2) Atmospheric moisture effects (fogginess) is added to simulate various weather conditions. In the new method, the fog effects are processed by using exponential functions[5]. These functions are determined with a sophisticated algorithm based on the illuminance information

contained in the background picture. This makes the montage more reliable and applicable for wider range of environment impact assessment.

2. Overlaying of Computer-Generated Images onto a Background Photograph

2.1 Schematic Description of Proposed Method

The method consists of the following five steps:

(1) The data for computer-generated building images are prepared.

(2) The land where the buildings will be constructed is photographed. This picture is processed with an A/D converter; geometric transformation (translation, rotation, etc.) are carried out to fit the photographic image on a CRT screen.

(3) The computer-generated images and the photographed background scene are matched from the viewpoint of geometry and adjusted by calculating the control parameters (the coordinates of the camera position, the view angle, the ambient illuminance and the fogginess).

(4) The computer generated images are overlaid on the background scene and displayed on the CRT. Hidden-surface removal, anti-aliasing and fog calculations are implemented at this stage.

(5) The foreground scene in front of the superimposed computer-generated image is re-displayed.

Further explanation of Steps (3), (4) and (5) is given below.

2.2 Geometric Matching Between Computer-Generated Images and Background Scene

The view reference point (a point existing on the object at the center of the photograph) and the viewpoint (the camera location) must be designated to carry out projection mapping. The object point is easily known by tracing the position of this point on a geophysical map.

However, the viewpoint is not easily determined if the camera is set on an airplane for instance. The least square method (see Appendix) may be used to estimate the viewpoint comparing several points on the photograph with their actual position coordinates on a map.

The size of the perspective plane is aligned with that of the photograph by selecting approximate horizontal and vertical angles; these angles are calculated based on the focal length of the camera lens and the size of the photograph. They can also be determined by tracing the objects existing at the edge of the photograph on a map. The photographs are assumed to have been taken with a standard (55mm) or telephoto lens to avoid the distortion caused by wide angle lenses.

2.3 Shading

The position of the sun must be determined from the photograph's time and date as well as the longitude and latitude of the camera position, in order to correctly calculate the shading of buildings and the shadows they cast in the simulated montage image. Let the angle between the x-axis (that defines the computer-generated image) and the southern direction be β and the hour angle be τ ($\tau=0$ deg. corresponds to the noon and $\tau=15$ deg. indicates one hour later). Furthermore, let ϕ and δ denote the longitude and the solar declination, respectively. The direction toward the sun is determined by:

$$\begin{bmatrix} x_\tau \\ y_\tau \\ z_\tau \end{bmatrix} = \begin{bmatrix} \cos\beta & -\sin\beta & 0 \\ \sin\beta & \cos\beta & 0 \\ 0 & 0 & 1 \end{bmatrix}$$

$$\times \begin{bmatrix} -\cos\delta\sin\phi & 0 & \sin\delta\cos\phi \\ 0 & \cos\delta & 0 \\ \cos\delta\cos\phi & 0 & \sin\delta\sin\phi \end{bmatrix} \begin{bmatrix} \cos\tau \\ \sin\tau \\ 1 \end{bmatrix} \quad (1)$$

Once the direction of the sun is determined, shadows and shading are calculated by traditional methods. The shading on each object is described by:

$$E = I\cos\alpha + E_h \quad (2)$$

where I, $\cos\alpha$ and E_h stand for the intensity of sun light, the cosine of the angle between the surface normal and the direction vector toward the sun and the ambient illuminance, respectively. For simplicity, specular reflection is neglected.

For montage generation, the ratio between E_h and I, called H, is important because the ultimate aim is to match computer-generated images to the background scene. First, H is calculated for the background scene by using the method explained below. Then, the computer generated images are designed so that their H values are equal to that of the background image.

Two walls of a building in the background scene are chosen (one is preferred to face the shadow side), and their intensity level is detected (this quantity is proportional to the illuminance and the reflectance). H is then calculated as:

$$H = (D_2\cos\theta_1 - D_1\cos\theta_2)/(D_1 - D_2), \\ \cos\theta_i (i=1,2) \geq 0 \quad (3)$$

where D_1, D_2 are illuminance on each wall. θ_1 and θ_2 denote the angle between the direction vector toward the sun and the surface normal of each wall surface, respectively.

If there is no such building, a pilot box (a white box is useful for this purpose) may be set in the vicinity of the camera to serve as a reference for ambient illuminance.

Since the ambient illuminance is affected by the surrounding objects, H varies depending on the object position. H should be calculated for several points and the average value of these calculation results is used.

2.4 Fog Effects

In general an object far from the viewpoint seems to lose its color and tone because of atomospheric moisture effects. If these effects are not taken into account, the new buildings, computer-generated images, do not match the photographed background pictures.

The reduction rate of color and tone depends on the various factors such as seasons, weather conditions and time. This fact means that the informations of the reduction rate should be obtained from the background picture, even though it is already known that the color and tone of each object changes exponentially with respect to its distance from the viewpoint [5].

A new method has been established to determine this exponential function based on the background picture: The color and tone become gray as the distance becomes large. Let red-, green- or blue-component of the illuminance at a point in the picture be C_e (e=r,g,b, respectively). If the point moves from the viewpoint to the infinite point, the apparent color C'_e of it approaches exponentially to a color which depends on the background picture. This color is called the standard color F_e. The apparent color C'_e is therefore given by:

$$C'_e = (1-\exp(-x/R_e))(F_e - C_e) + C_e,$$
$$e = r,g,b \qquad (4)$$

R_e (standard distance) and F_e are determined as follows: At least, three sampled points are designated on the photograph; more sampled points help refine the final result. These points should be selected on objects which are considered to share a color (trees, for example) but stand at different distances from the viewpoint. The illuminance on these points, which is defined as the average value in the vicinity of each point, is detected on the photograph. The distance to each of the points should be obtained by using the geophysical map. Data points are plotted on a illuminance-distance plane (see Fig.1). The least mean square measure is used to give the most appropriate exponential function from these data.

A simpler method is to use a pair of objects. These objects are assumed to possess different colors and locate at a near position (x=0 in Eq.(4)) and at the distance x. Let A'_e and B'_e be the colors of the pair of objects at the distance x. Then, these colors are given with their original colors A_e and B_e (the color at a near position of each object) as:

$$A'_e = K_e(F_e - A_e) + A_e,$$
$$B'_e = K_e(F_e - B_e) + B_e,$$
$$K_e = 1 - \exp(-x/R_e), \qquad (5)$$
$$e = r,g,b$$

By solving a simple system of equations, the standard distance R_e (which dominates the change of each color with respect to the distance) and the standard color F_e is determined by:

$$F_e = (A_e B'_e - B_e A'_e)/(A_e - A'_e - B_e + B'_e),$$
$$R_e = -x/\log_e[(F_e - A'_e)/(F_e - A_e)] \qquad (6)$$

The fogginess of an image heavily depends on the weather conditions when the photographs are taken. Therefore, the requirement to add or even remove the fog in the photographed scenes might occur in order to observe the montage image under the different conditions.

Strictly speaking, a background scene should be processed in a three-dimensional space to know the exact fog effect. Since this is almost impossible, the next best approximation is useful: Each object on the background scene is described with a combination of planes. The distance between the objects and the viewpoint is calculated by using this approximated image. In the case of Fig.2, mountains (A through D) and a grove of trees (E) are approximated with vertical planes. F and G are processed with horizontal planes. The road (H) and two banks of earth (I and J) are treated as convex polyhedra.

A cursor or a tablet is used to interactively divide the background scene into several parts, and each part is checked whether it should be approximated with vertical planes, horizontal planes or polyhedra. The distance from the viewpoint is also specified at this step.

Because each part consists of planes, Eq.(4) may be applied to calculate the fog effects at each point. It should be noted that the longer the standard distance, the smaller the fog effect, and vice versa.

2.5 Anti-Aliasing

It is well known that the diagonal edges of objects displayed on a raster-scan type CRT are jagged. In some cases, moire patterns appear; e.g. the same shaped objects are set periodically. These undesireable phenomena called 'aliasing' make the computer-generated images unnatural against the background scene.

The anti-aliasing for montage methods should be different from other usual ones because: (i) the background scene includes pixels which in general change pixel by pixel, and (ii) image overlay operation is performed several times (overlay process initiates from the further scene, and ends at the closest scene, or foreground).

This first characteristic ((i) above) excludes the use of filters that work based on more than one pixel. If these filters were used, the resulting image would be very vague. This second characteristic ((ii) above) increases calculation cost, so a simpler filter is preferred over more complicated filters, such as the conical filter or Gaussian filter[2].

The Alpha channel method[3] is useful for anti-aliasing when making extremely complex montages requiring many overlay loggers. However,

SIGGRAPH '86

anti-aliasing is only really required along the
edges of each computer-generated image. Hence,
for simple montages such as discussed here, the
following easy anti-aliasing method is suggested:

The color at each pixel on the CRT screen is
first read out. The color of the background scene
is determined pixel by pixel based on this
information. Then, a modified two-dimensional
Fourier window (box window) is activated. The
detailed explanation is:

A pixel is approximated with a unit square
shown in Fig. 3. This square is divided into n
parts. S_0 is an actual scan line. Each of other
lines within the pixel is called a virtual scan
line (VSL). The color of this pixel is determined
according to the product of the length of the
image on each VSL S_ℓ ($\ell=1,2,...,n$) and the
illuminance of this image. Each product is added
with a proper weight to decide the pixel color:
Let m objects exist within the pixel (i,j). The
background scene color at this pixel is supposed
to be $B_{i,j}$ (this vector consists of three
components that correspond to red, green and
blue). Furthermore, let $L_{f,\ell}$ and $b_{i,j,\ell}$ stand for
the visible interval on the VSL of the object O_f
and the background scene, respectively. The color
$C_{i,j}$ of the pixel (i,j) is calculated according to
the trapezoidal integration rule as:

$$C_{i,j} = \sum_{\ell=1}^{n} d_\ell (b_{i,j,\ell} B_{i,j} + \sum_{f=1}^{m} L_{f,\ell} C_f),$$

$$d_\ell = \begin{cases} 1/n; & 0 < \ell < n \\ 1/2n; & \ell=0,n \end{cases}$$

(7)

where d_ℓ indicates the weight factor. C_f is the
color of object O_f.

2.6 Removal of Computer-Generated Images Hidden by Foregrounds

A basic problem of this overlay method is
that the inserted computer-generated images might
hide the scene which exists in front of them. To
avoid this drawback, the scene which is supposed
to exist in front of the computer-generated images
is interactively designated with a cursor or a
tablet, and the images inside the designated area
are overlaid again. The boundaries of each
designated area are depicted with straight lines
or splines[6] -- the former is useful for
buildings, and the latter to mountains or trees.

The aliasing problem mentioned above also
occurs when the foregrounds are superimposed onto
the computer-generated images. In this case, the
boundaries of the foregrounds become jagged. This
problem is serious especially when the foregrounds
cross the objects, which consist of straight
boundaries (buildings, for example). The anti-
aliasing method is also applicable here: If a
pixel includes the boundaries of a foreground, its
color is determined based on (i) the area of the
foreground, (ii) the background color and (iii)
the color of the computer-generated image within
this pixel. The color of the pixel is determined
considering the intersection of the boundary
(straight line or spline) of the image and each
VSL.

3. Implementation

Fig. 4 indicates R, G and B intensity
variation with respect to the distance. Trees at
various distance from the viewpoint are selected
from the original background scene. Actual R, G
and B intensity calculation was carried out by
averaging each small region, about ten pixels,
within a group of trees. The exponential function
described in Section 2.4 was determined in this
way. The exponential functions in Fig. 3 is used
for the second example.

Fig. 5 shows the outputs of the proposed
method. (a) is the background scene. (b) depicts
the overlay of the computer-generated images onto
the background scene, and the foreground scene in
front of the superimposed computer-generated image
has been re-displayed. However, anti-aliasing and
the distance from the viewpoint are not taken into
account. Therefore, the windows of the buildings
seem uneven, and the contrast of the building far
from the viewpoint looks too strong because the
inserted computer-generated images do not match
their surroundings.

In (c), anti-aliasing and distance are
considered, but there are no shadows from the new
buildings. As a result, the building near the
viewpoint seems to stand above the earth level.
In (d), the shadows are cast properly on the
ground up to a grove of trees and a house near the
right side.

In (e), the fog effect is activated. The
buildings seem to be natural due to this effect.
In (f), the fog effect is removed. The mountains
look as if they are too close. The
computer-generated images match their surroundings
in cases (d), (e) and (f).

Figures 5(g), (h) and (i) demonstrate another
set of examples. (g) corredponds to (d) in the
previous example (anti-aliasing, the distance from
the viewpoint and the shadows are all considered).
(h) and (i) show the cases when the fog effect is
activated and when it is removed, respectively.
Note that the difference between (g) and (i) is
not so clear, while (f) is very different from
(d). This is simply because the weather condition
in (d) was better (fog was thinner) than that in
(f).

The fog effect is more apparent in (j).
Upper-left is the original background scene.
Other pictures demonstrate the fog effect. Four
buildings in upper-right are set on different
distance planes; the greater the distance of the
building from the viewpoint, the stronger the fog
effect. The fog effect is removed in lower
right.

In (k), four different colors are assigned to
the bridge. This is another application of the
proposed method to assess the visual impact [8] of
new construction on its surroundings.

Calculations were carried out on a TOSBAC
DS600 computer and GRAPHICA M508 color graphic
display (512x512 pixels, 8-bit each for R, G and
B).

4. Conclusion

The proposed method produces useful montages
because:

210

(1) The fog effect increases the sense of perspective in the montages, and it permits simulation of various weather conditions.

(2) The shading and shadows of the computer generated images help a montage match to the background scene.

(3) The new anti-aliasing technique enables cost-effective high quality display of objects which might include narrow vertical parts; e.g. electric light poles or chimneys.

Further improvement should enable:

(1) The correction of the distortion which appears on the photograph due to the use of a wide-angle lens.

(2) The computer image generation of roadside trees and/or flower beds.

(3) Processing for the light that comes from buildings.

Of these improvements, (1) requires complicated geometric transformation. The clue to achieve (2) is found in Ref.[7]. (3) is important when a night view is considered.

5. Acknowledgments

The background scenes were prepared with image scanners installed at GRAPHICA Inc. and Government Industrial Research Institute, Chugoku. The computer-generated images were created according to data supplied by Kajima Corporation. We are grateful to Laurin Herr for his discussions. Special thanks to Tsuyoshi Tokoro for his skillful computer operation.

APPENDIX Location of Viewpoint

The ultimate aim is to estimate the coordinate of the viewpoint. This point is defined by R(the distance between the viewpoint and the view reference point), θ (the azimuth angle) and ϕ (the elevation angle). n sampled points are selected on the picture for calculating the viewpoint. 3-D coordinate of these points, (x_i,y_i,z_i), $i=1,2,...,n$, may be obtained on the geographical map.

The coordinate of these points on the picture, (M_{xi},M_{yi}), along with the above 3-D coordinates are used for calculating the location of the viewpoint based on the following equation:

$$e_{xi} = f_i(R,\theta,\phi) - M_{xi} ,$$
$$e_{yi} = g_i(R,\theta,\phi) - M_{yi} ,$$
$$f_i(R,\theta,\phi) \triangleq f(R,\theta,\phi,x_i,y_i,z_i) , \qquad (A1)$$
$$g_i(R,\theta,\phi) \triangleq g(R,\theta,\phi,x_i,y_i,z_i) ,$$
$$i = 1,2,\cdots,n \ (n \geq 3)$$

In Eq. (A1), $f(g)$ and $e_{xi}(e_{yi})$ mean the relation function which maps the points in the 3-D space onto the 2-D picture coordinates and the difference between the mapped coordinates and its measured coordinates on the picture, respectively.

The best viewpoint estimation is described as the minimization problem of:

$$Q = \sum_{i=1}^{n} (e_{xi}^2 + e_{yi}^2) \qquad (A2)$$

Partially differentiating this value with respect to R, θ and ϕ, the following system of equations is given:

$$\begin{bmatrix} A_{RR} & A_{R\theta} & A_{R\phi} \\ A_{\theta R} & A_{\theta\theta} & A_{\theta\phi} \\ A_{\phi R} & A_{\phi\theta} & A_{\phi\phi} \end{bmatrix} \begin{Bmatrix} -dR \\ -d\theta \\ -d\phi \end{Bmatrix} = \begin{Bmatrix} B_1 \\ B_2 \\ B_3 \end{Bmatrix}$$

$$A_{jk} = \sum_{i=1}^{n} (a_j^i a_k^i + b_j^i b_k^i) ,$$
$$B_j = \sum_{i=1}^{n} (a_j^i E_{xi} + b_j^i E_{yi}) , \qquad (A3)$$
$$a_e^i = (\partial f_i / \partial e)_{R=R_0,\theta=\theta_0,\phi=\phi_0} ,$$
$$b_e^i = (\partial g_i / \partial e)_{R=R_0,\theta=\theta_0,\phi=\phi_0} ,$$
$$e = R,\theta,\phi ,$$
$$E_{xi} = f_i(R_0,\theta_0,\phi_0) - M_{xi} ,$$
$$E_{yi} = g_i(R_0,\theta_0,\phi_0) - M_{yi}$$

Appropriate values for R, θ and ϕ are set for initiating the iteration. On each iteration, the estimated value of the viewpoint (R_0,θ_0,ϕ_0) is replaced to the value (R,θ,ϕ) obtained by the following equation.

$$R = R_0 - dR ,$$
$$\theta = \theta_0 - d\theta , \qquad (A4)$$
$$\phi = \phi_0 - d\phi$$

The iteration continues until dR, dθ and dϕ become small enough.

REFERENCES

1 S.Uno and H.Matsuka,"A General Purpose Graphic System for Computer Aided Design," Computer Graphics, vol.13, no.2,1979, pp.25-32

2 E.A.Feibush, M.Leroy and R.L.Cook,"Synthetic Texturing Using Digital Filters," Computer Graphics, vol.14, no.3, 1980, pp.294-301

3 T.Porter and T.Duff,"Composing Digital Images," Computer Graphics, vol.18, no.3,1984, pp.253-259

4 T.Nishita and E.Nakamae,"A Perspective Depiction of Shaded Time," Proc. of 4th Int. Symp. on the Use of Comp. for Env. Eng. Related to Build.,1983, pp.565

5 B.J.Schachter,Computer Image Generation, John Wiley & Sons.,New York, 1983

6 C.de Boor,Practical Guide to Splines, Springer-Verlag, New York, 1978

7 R.Marshall, R.Wilson and W.Carlson,"Procedure Models for Generating Three-Dimensional Terrain," Computer Graphics, vol.14, no.3,1980, pp.154-162

8 T.W.Maver, C.Purdie and D.Stearn," Visual Impact Analysis -- Modelling and Viewing the Natural and Built Environment," Comput. & Graphics, vol.9, no.2, 1985, pp.117-124

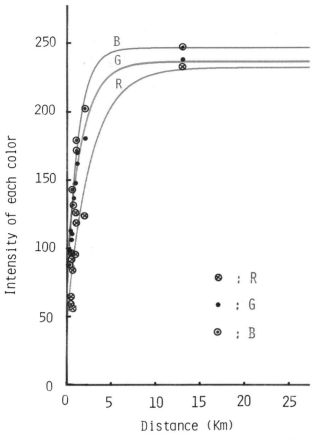

Fig. 1 Intensity variation with respect to the distance.
          This Figure is referred along with Fig.4 (see Section 4).

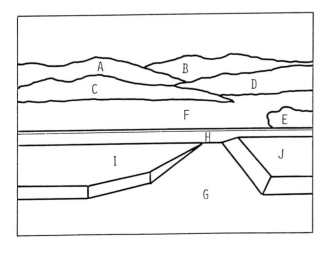

Fig. 2 Partition of the image for fog effect processing.

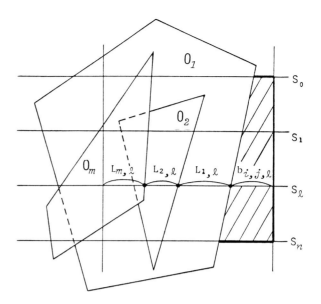

Fig. 3 Anti-aliasing operation in one pixel.

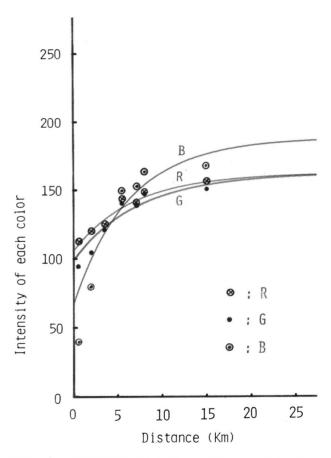

Fig. 4 Intensity variation with respect to the distance. This figure was given from the first background scene.

(a)

(b)

(c)

(d)

(e)

(f)

Fig. 5 (continued)

(g)

(h)

(i)

(j)

Fig. 5 Examples. Explanations are given in the text.

(k)

TWO BIT/PIXEL FULL COLOR ENCODING

Graham Campbell*　Thomas A. DeFanti**　Jeff Frederiksen
Stephen A. Joyce　Lawrence A. Leske　John A. Lindberg
and Daniel J. Sandin**

ABSTRACT

Realism in computer graphics typically requires using 24 or more bits/pixel to generate an image. This paper describes a method developed by the authors called "Color Cell Compression" or "CCC" that preserves at least a limited animation and local update capability yet yields extraordinary-looking color images in approximately two bits/pixel independent of image complexity. Three intermediate methods of compressing images to six, four and three bits/pixel respectively are also described. The CCC encoding process for a 640 x 480 image averages 11 seconds on a VAX 11/750, however, the CCC method does permit real-time decoding of these images using software look-up tables and conventional display hardware. The three intermediate methods may also be decoded in real time but have the added advantage of requiring only 3-4 seconds for encoding on a VAX 11/750.

CR Categories: I.3 Computer Graphics; I.31 Hardware Architecture - - Raster display devices; I.32 Graphics Systems; I.4 Image Processing; I.42 Compression (coding).

I.0.　INTRODUCTION

CCC was orignally developed to facilitate storing images in read-only memory (ROM) for systems that would have to pass serious ruggedness tests. This ruled out rotating memory sub-systems and since ROM is of course relatively expensive, compared to rotating memory media, nearly any amount of preprocessing costs are justified to reduce the chip count.

Run-length encoding is a popular method to use to store and transmit image data, easy to encode and decode. However it is efficient only if the image has reasonably long spans of identical pixels, not a feature of scanned-in and anti-aliased images. The encoding and decoding can be done by hardware permitting real-time animation yet the need for and presence of significant runs of same-color pixels severely limits the ability to do smooth shading, texture mapping, and anti-aliasing. See [10] for details on ANIMA II, a system that implements these ideas rather fully.

Aside from run-length encoding, compression of color images to 2 bits/pixel or better can be accomplished using transform coding [2]-[5]. Transform coding requires that (a) a two dimensional mathematical transform of an image block be performed, (b) discard some of the coefficients, (c) efficiently code the remainder of the coefficients, and (d) store/transmit. Decoding requires that the inverse transform be performed making this method inherently complex at both the compression and decompression stages. The Hadamard transform is the simplest transform method to implement since the matrix consists of ±1's thus only additions are required [5]. However since each of the compressed blocks represent a mathematical transform, this can introduce problems at the common edges of blocks which can complicate local updating.

The CCC algorithm for the compression of color images uses as a starting point the block truncation coding (BTC) algorithm for black and white images as developed by Delp and Mitchell [1]. A recent extension of BTC to color may be found in [12]. Equivalent work was carried out in Japan [7]-[9]. The BTC algorithm is presented and then the following color image compression

---

*　Dept. of Computer Science, Illinois Institute of Technology.

**　Electronic Visualization Laboratory, Univ. of Illinois at Chicago, m/c 154, Box 4348, Chicago, IL　60680.

Other authors are currently independent consultants.

techniques are described;

1) the BTC algorithm as extended to 24-bit color images (photos 3, 6, 10) which provides compression of images to 6 bits/pixel (photo 4),

2) an intermediate CCC technique which provides compression to 4 bits/pixel,

3) an intermediate CCC technique which provides compression to 3 bits/pixel and

4) the CCC technique which provides good quality images at approximately 2 bits/pixel (see photos 1,2,5,8,9,11).

2.0. THE BTC ALGORITHM

BTC uses a moment-preserving quantizer rather than depending upon underlying statistical distributions as do transform methods. An image is divided into n x n pixel blocks (n = 4 in our implementation), each of whose pixels are individually quantized to two levels, a and b such that the block sample mean η and variance σ^2 are preserved. If $X_1, X_2,....,X_n$ are the original sampled values within a given block, then the sample mean is defined as

$$\eta = (1/N) \sum_{i=1}^{N} X_i = \bar{X} \qquad (1)$$

and the sample variance is defined as

$$\sigma^2 = (1/N) \sum_{i=1}^{N} X_i{}^2 - \eta^2 = \bar{X^2} - \bar{X}^2 \qquad (2)$$

A threshold X_{th} is set to the sample mean $\bar{X}$ and a 16-bit bitplane M is created where a binary 1 indicates that the corresponding value in the original block is equal to or greater than X_{th} and a binary 0 indicates that the corresponding value is less than X_{th}. Another method for selecting X_{th} which offers slightly improved performance is given in [1] and [11].

It has been shown [1] that sample moments $\bar{X}$ and $\bar{X}^2$ are preserved by using the quantizer levels

$$a = \eta - \sigma \sqrt{(q/p)}$$
$$\qquad (3)$$
$$b = \eta + \sigma \sqrt{(p/q)}$$

where q and p are the number of pixels above and below the sample mean, respectively. Pixels below the sample mean are quantized to level a and the others to level b. For each block, a, b, and a bitplane M (one bit per pixel to select quantizer level a or b) are transmitted. Using 4 x 4 pixel blocks and 8 bits for each of a and b, and 16 bits for the bitplane M, the data rate is 2 bits/pixel. The value η and σ could be transmitted instead of a and b but this requires that (3) be computed at the receiver. There is advantage in transmitting η and σ in that different quantization levels could be used for η and σ. If 6 bits and 4 bits were assigned to η and

σ respectively then the date rate is reduced to 1.675 bits/pixel at the cost of computing (3) at the receiver and some decrease in quality [1].

3.0. SIX BITS/PIXEL COMPRESSION USING BTC

The BTC method as described above can be applied to color images by applying the BTC technique to each of the R,G, and B color planes. This results in three 32-bit vectors for each corresponding cell and provides good quality images at six bits/pixel. (See photos 1 and 2, 3 and 4.) All the images in this paper (except photo 9) are taken from videotape; whatever benefits of seeing the images on a high quality monitor are reduced to those artifacts that still come through as normally viewed by humans. The difference between 24-bit and 6-bit images can be discerned on a high quality monitor but the viewing distance must be less that for normal television viewing.

4.0. CCC ALGORITHM

CCC encoding provides color images equivalant to the quality of the 6/bit pixel technique described in section 3.0 but requires only 2 bits/pixel plus a fixed size look-up of 256 x 3 x 8 = 6144 bits. CCC encoding uses a BTC type binary bitmap of the luminance values of a cell to partition the corresponding cells of the R, G, and B components into two areas. Subsequently, after selecting 256 appropriate colors, each cell is represented by this 16-bit bitmap and two 8-bit pointers into a table containing 256 entries, each entry representing a 24-bit (R,G,B) color. The detailed steps are presented below.

4.1 An image is decomposed into R,G,B, and Y (NTSC luminance) planes and then each plane is divided into cells of 4 x 4 pixels. The luminance values are obtained from

$$y(i) = .30 \times r(i) + .59 \, g(i) + .11 \, b(i) \qquad (4)$$

4.2 A sample mean as per (1) is obtained for each cell of the Y plane and this value is used to partition each Y cell into two areas of high and low luminance. Each pixel with a luminance value greater than the sample mean is represented by a binary 1 and each pixel with a luminance less than or equal to the average is represented by a binary 0. This results in a 16-bit binary bitmap M for each cell. The sample variance (2) is not used.

4.3 The bitmap M is used to partition the pixels of each of the corresponding R,G, and B cells into two distinct groups. A color is then chosen for each partition that best represents the colors within that partition. This is accomplished with equations (5) and (6).

The set of equations for the 0's partition:

$$r_0 = 1/m \sum_{i=1}^{m} r(i)$$

$$g_0 = 1/m \sum_{i=1}^{m} g(i) \qquad (5)$$

$$b_0 = 1/m \sum_{i=1}^{m} b(i)$$

where m is the number of pixels (colors) in the 0's partition.

The set of equations for the 1's partition.

$$r_1 = 1/(16-m) \sum_{i=m+1}^{16} r(i)$$

$$g_1 = 1/(16-m) \sum_{i=m+1}^{16} g(i) \qquad (6)$$

$$b_1 = 1/(16-m) \sum_{i=m+1}^{16} b(i)$$

Each cell of the original image has now been reduced to a 16-bit binary bitmap M and two 24-bit vectors, each vector representing three 8-bit color values. The 16-bit binary bitmap M specifies where the two representative colors are located within the cell. This information is written to a temporary file TEMP. At this point the image has been compressed to 4 bits/pixel.

4.4 The 8-bit values for R, G, and B are quantized to 5 bits. Three 5-bit values can be stored in two bytes, thus at this point each 4 x 4 cell of the original image is described by a 16-bit binary bitmap and two 15-bit vectors for a total of 46 bits. The image has now been compressed to slightly under 3 bits/pixel. From a practical point of view the 16th bit in each of the two bytes of storage used for the three 5-bit color values would be used to enhance one of the colors or could be used as a mode bit. The image at this point has been compressed to 3 bits/pixel.

4.5 The following steps are carried out to obtain 256 colors most representative of the original image.

   (a) A color histogram which is indexed by color and contains corresponding color frequency of occurence values is created and is sorted into ascending order by color.
   (b) All frequency information for

identical colors are combined so that the histogram contains only unique color frequency pairs. The ordering by color is maintained.
(c) The histogram data is processed to select 256 colors which best represent the range of colors present in the original image. Heckbert [6] devised a method called "Median Cut" which accomplishes this in an elegant manner. (Simply by choosing the most frequently occuring colors results in images as shown in photo 7.) A look-up table is created consisting of the 256 colors represented by 8 bits for each of the R, G, and B values.

4.6 The file FINAL is created by replacing each of the 24-bit vectors representing the R,G,B components in the file TEMP with an 8-bit value pointing at the color in the look-up table which best matches the 24 bit color in each partition of each cell. The look-up table is appended to the file FINAL. A possible option is to use the bitmap values, 0 or 1, to each index one of two 256 entry tables providing a choice of 512 values. There would be some duplication of colors in the two tables since a color in a 1's partition in a given cell could be the same color in the 0's partition in another cell. At this point the image has been compressed to 2 bits/pixel plus the look-up table. The encoding process is complete.

5.0. DISCUSSION OF CCC ALGORITHM

The CCC algorithm is based on the observation that in normal images change in chrominance almost always indicates a change in luminance as well. A practical reason for this is that most computer (and video) images are meant to be viewable on black and white television (e.g. blue lettering on a red background of same luminance would not be readable on a black and white television). The NTSC signal allocates far more of its bandwidth to luminance than to chrominance so that adjacent colors of the same luminance do not have sharp vertical edges.

The color space of camera-digitized or synthetic images is often as high as 24 bits/pixel, or 8 bits for each of red, green and blue. For natural images digitized at a spatial resolution of 640 by 480 pixels, the number of distinct colors produced is typically 30,000 or less, which is about ten pixels per color for this image resolution. Many synthetic images, and certain natural images such as rainbows will produce a distinct color for nearly every pixel of the ditital image. This level of color resolution, however, is seldom discernable by the human eye. For the vast majority of images encountered, 5 bits each of red, green, and blue (15 bits total) is sufficient both computationally and aesthetically.

The reduction of the R, G, and B values from 8 bits to 5 bits reduces the size of the histogram in 4.4, this has important consequences for the production of large numbers of CCC encoded images, since the number of distinct colors to be processed is reduced by up to an order of magnitude, typically to around 5000 colors.

A wide range of 24-bit RGB images and 15-bit RGB quantizations of the same images have been approximated to 256 colors or less with look-up tables generated by the median cut process. The results have been acceptable, with no difference in quality using either the 24-bit or the 15-bit histogram as the source. This same conclusion applies to the CCC encoded versions of the very same images.

The CCC encoding method essentially introduces large color "jaggies" but retains the luminance information fairly well. This is true for the 6, 4, 3 and 2 bit cases. It rather poorly encodes the case where more than two colors exist in a cell, as when three different color vectors intersect. Nevertheless, the images produced look much better than we originally predicted given the limitations of the CCC method.

CCC has the same desirable property of frame buffers, that is, each area on the screen has a unique area in memory containing the information describing that area. Thus to update a CCC sub-image, one only needs to change the corresponding blocks. Colors for the replacement blocks must be in the look-up table. When using CCC in a dynamic environment, i.e. modifying parts of the image, it is desirable to median cut to less than 256 colors thus allowing for the creation of new colors or to reserve certain values for matting purposes.

6.0. IMPLEMENTATION CONSIDERATIONS

The implementation of CCC is straightforward in that the algorithm is computationally simple. CCC can be implemented using integer arithmetic and still generate acceptable images. The histogram building and the median cut algorithm in the compression phrase are time-consuming but not inordinately so. A 640 by 480 image may be processed in 11 seconds on a VAX 750. The 6 bit/pixel BTC method, and the 4 and 3 bit/pixel intermediate CCC methods do not require the histogram construction or median cut algorithm and therefore will run in 3-4 seconds on the VAX 11/750. This includes the time for loading the 640x 480x3 bytes from disk storage. CCC offers a distinct economic advantage over the compression techniques for many applications in that the decompression phase consists solely of a table look-up operation. Software decoding could be implemented on any microcomputer which has display hardware with a capability of 256 colors chosen from a larger palette.

The CCC encoding algorithm as implemented requires slightly over one megabyte of memory for code and data, most of which is used for the median cut tree, the initial 640 x 480 x 24 bit image and the associated blocks which are gener-

ated. The first stage of compression, 4.3, reduces memory requirements by 75% but approximately 270K of this freed up memory is used by the median cut algorithm.

7.0. APPLICATIONS

7.1 Animation Considerations

Standard film animation for cartoons is "done on two's", that is, twelve frames per second. Real time playback of 320 x 480 CCC images requires a transfer rate of
12 x 320 x 480 x 2 = 3,686,400 bits/second. Adding 73,728 bits for twelve 768 byte lookup tables results in a required transfer rate of 3,760,128 bits or 470,000 bytes per second. Current microcomputer hard disks have a transfer rate of 5,000,000 bits or 625,000 bytes per second. Allowing for "no data" space on the disk tracks and head movement it means that a 30 megabyte hard disk, now standard on the IBM AT, could store and display in real time approximately 60 seconds of animation.

Full size 640 x 480 CCC images require a transfer rate of 940,000 bytes per second for animation purposes. This is well within the transfer rate of conventional hard disks on mini and larger computers.

Much of the interest in developing CCC came from the idea of storing digital images (and program information) on videodisks, essentially a giant ROM, albeit analog. The teletext industry provides access to encoding and decoding chips which store 256 bits/line of video or 15,360 bytes/frame, assuming 480 active lines. This is 460,800 bytes per second. The calculations above indicate that the real-time play-back of 320 x 480 pixel images is possible using CCC.

Digital encoding provides some advantages over conventional NTSC encoding;

1) Analog video loses 3 db per copy made, digital nothing.
2) Panning an analog image requires that an entire frame be retransmitted each update; digital panning requires that only the edge(s) in the direction of the pan be transmitted.
3) High resolution images, say 1024 x 1024, may be encoded; not possible with analog NTSC.
These advantages apply to any digital encoding technique; CCC requires one-twelfth the storage of conventional 24-bit quantized R, G, B, images.

7.2 Electronic Shopping and Image Transmission in General

A potential application of CCC is electronic shopping. In such a system the editing and coding of the images takes place at a central facility, and the images are then transmitted to possibly thousands or tens of thousands of viewers for display, preferably with the addition of spoken comment, via cable. The advantage of CCC in this type of application, aside from the reduction in storage requirements and data rates, is the minimal cost of the decoding hardware, which must be supplied in large quantities. The same hardware could be used to provide "slide and sound" shows on a variety of subjects on a demand basis.

The previous paragraph describes one-to-many applications; CCC would also be useful on a one-to-one basis. For instance a graphics arts shop could transmit a compressed version of a sample color picture to a customer for review and approval of changes in layout and content. A typical 640 x 480 color image can be compressed to 620,000 bits thus the image could be transmitted in approximately one minute over a 9600 bit-per-second phone circuit. Again in such an application the major computational and memory requirements are at the producer site, the consumer site only requires implementation of a look-up table aside from the conventional display electronics.

Many-to-many applications are also conceivable in teleconferencing where an image representing each speaker's face could be encoded and distributed to all participants for display. (See photo 9). Only the image representing the person talking would remain "live" and be transmitted to the other conferees. The entire image could of course be utilized to display a drawing requiring higher resolution.

8.0. CONCLUSIONS

The CCC algorithm for compressing color images has been described. The potential saving of 22/24 or approximately 90% of storage or transmission costs is particularly attractive in consumer or personal graphics applications. Furthermore CCC encoding of an image guarantees that the encoding results will not change in size with image complexity. Also any change to the image not requiring a change of the color lookup tables can be effected on a purely local basis, an important consideration when updating parts of encoded images. A further advantage of the CCC algorithm is that it is easily implemented with conventional display hardware and micro-computers, and the decoding is particularly easy to implement.

ACKNOWLEDGEMENTS

The authors wish to thank the Bally Corporation for several years of support, Ed Catmull and Pat Cole at Lucasfilm Ltd. for some early help in demonstrating the CCC ideas, and John Whitney Jr. of Digital Productions, Inc. for supplying some of the test images.

REFERENCES

[1] E.J. Delp and O.R. Mitchell, "Image compression using block truncation coding,", IEEE Trans. Commun., vol. COM-27, Sept. 1979.

[2] W.K. Pratt and H.C. Andrews, "Fourier transform coding of images, "Proc. Hawaii Inter. Conf. System Sciences, Jan. 1968.

[3] P.A. Wintz, "Transform picture coding," Proc. IEEE, vol. 60, no. 7, pp. 809-820, July 1972.

[4] W. Chen, C.H. Smith, and S. Fralick, "A fast computational algorithm for the discrete cosine transform, "IEEE Trans. Commun., pp. 1004-1009, Sept. 1977.

[5] H.J. Landau and D. Slepian, "Some computer experiments in picture processing for bandwidth reduction, "Bell Syst. Tech. Journal, vol. 50, pp. 1525-1540, May-June 1971.

[6] Paul Heckbert, "Color image quantization for frame buffer display," SIGGRAPH 1982 Proceedings, pp. 297-307.

[7] T. Kishimoto, E. Mitsuya, and K. Hoshida, "An experiment of still picture coding by block process" (in Japanese), Nat. Conf. of the Inst. of Elec. and Commun. Eng. of Japan, March 1975, no. 974.

[8] T. Kishimoto, E. Mitsuya, and K. Hoshida, "An experiment of still picture coding by block processing" (in Japanese), Nat. Conf. of the Inst. of Elec. and Commun. Eng. of Japan, March 1978, no. 975.

[9] T. Kishimoto, E. Mitsuya, and K. Hoshida, tech. group of commun. systems of the Inst. of Elec. and Commun. Eng. of Japan, pp. 63-69, July 1978.

[10] R.J. Hackathorn, "ANIMA II: A 3-D color animation system," 1977 SIGGRAPH Proceedings, pp. 54-64.

[11] D.R. Halverson, "On the implementation of a block truncation coding algorithm, IEEE Trans. Commun., Vol Com-30, No. 11, pp. 2482-2484, Nov. 1982.

[12] M. Lena and O.R. Mitchell, "Absolute Moment Block Truncation Coding and its Application to Color Images," IEEE Trans. Commun., Vol.Com-32, No. 10, October 1984, pp. 1148-1157.

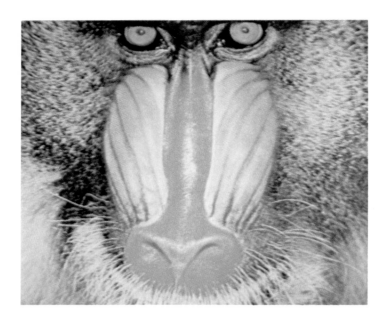

Photo 1: 512x480x2 bits/pixel CCC Image

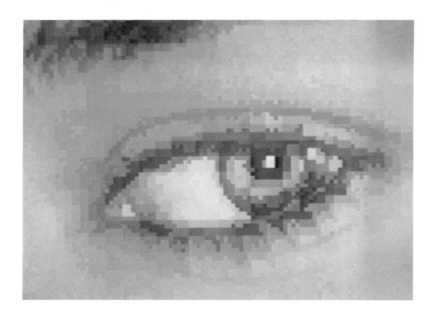

Photo 2: Detail of Photo 8. 2 bits/pixel
         CCC Image

Photo 3:   512x480x24 bits/pixel Image

Photo 4:   512x480x6 bits/pixel 3-color
BTC Image

Photo 5:   512x480x2 bits/pixel CCC Image

Photo 6: 512x480x24 bits/pixel Image

Photo 7: 512x480x2 bits/pixel CCC Image
          showing the most 'popular'
          256 colors

Photo 8: 512x480x2 bits/pixel CCC Image
          colors selected with median
          cut algorithm

Photo 9:   Potential Application of CCC
(Assume faces are different)

Photo 10:   512x480x24 bits/pixel Image
(Courtesy of Digital Productions,
copyright 1984, Digital Scene
Simulation(SM). All rights
reserved.)

Photo 11:   512x480x2 bits/pixel CCC Image
Note the re-introduction of
jaggies on sharp edges.
(Courtesy of Digital Productions,
copyright 1984. Digital Scene
Simulation(SM). All rights
reserved.)

Hairy Brushes

by Steve Strassmann
Computer Graphics and Animation Group
MIT Media Laboratory
Cambridge, Massachusetts
Arpanet: straz@media-lab.mit.edu

Abstract

Paint brushes are modeled as a collection of bristles which evolve over the course of the stroke, leaving a realistic image of a *sumi* brush stroke. The major representational units are (1) Brush: a compound object composed of bristles, (2) Stroke: a trajectory of position and pressure, (3) Dip: a description of the application of paint to a class of brushes, and (4) Paper: a mapping onto the display device. This modular system allows experimentation with various stochastic models of ink flow and color change. By selecting from a library of brushes, dips, and papers, the stroke can take on a wide variety of expressive textures.

1 Introduction

The "brushes" used in conventional computer painting systems are far simpler than real paint brushes. Usually no more than automated rubber stamps, they build up images by placing repeated copies of some static or simply derived pattern. Some systems offer "airbrushes," which simulate a spray of ink by painting pixels in a circular region around the brush.

This paper describes an investigation into a far more realistic model of painting. The image left by a sopping wet brush or crumbly crayon dragged erratically across a sheet of textured paper can be generated by a representation which keeps track of the physical properties of the materials. This work is useful not only to artists who want to paint intractively, but also for automated rendering of natural (or nonrealistic) scenes. As techniques like ray-tracing extend the ability of computers to render scenes with photographic exactitide, there will be a complementary advancement of techniques which allow computers to *suggest* scenes with artistic abstraction.

1.1 Previous work

In Whitted [11], an unchanging anti-aliased image is dragged to draw a smooth glossy tube. Paint systems using input devices with three or more degrees of freedom (say, position and pressure) allow the user to vary some parameter of the brush pattern (say, radius or hue of a solid circle) as they paint. Lewis [5] describes stochastic and frequency-domain representations of texture, but these techniques do not adequately render the effects at the boundaries of discrete strokes.

Greene [4] describes an input device called the "drawing prism" which digitizes the image of a real brush (or other object) making optical contact with a transparent prism. Although the resulting images are realistic, the system has no representational abstraction higher than the pixel level. The system described in this thesis simulates a brush stroke using a hierarchy of representation, allowing repeatability and experimentation at many levels of control.

1.2 Sumi-e Painting

This research was inspired by the traditional Japanese art known as *sumi-e*. Although there are a wide variety of *sumi-e* painting styles, one seems a particularly good candidate for computer simulation. Paintings in the *bokkotsu* style are characterized by a few well-placed strokes on a light background. Pictures with hundreds or more strokes may become practical some day, but for now *bokkotsu sumi-e* is appealing as a model because evocative pictures may be made in black and white, and with only a few strokes. The *bokkotsu* style emphasizes the quality of each stroke; this focuses the attention on the processes and materials involved in the construction of each stroke.

Figure 1: An example of *Sumi-e*: "Shrimp and Leaf"

An example of computer-generated *sumi-e*[1] can be seen in Figure 1. The picture is one frame from an animated sequence (described below in Section 6). It contains 17 strokes, each defined as a spline with between 3 and 8 control points. It is anti-aliased, and was generated on an 8-bit 640 × 480 pixel frame buffer. The design was drawn free-hand by the author, interactively, using a mouse.

2 The Representation

The key to a successful implementation is choosing the right representation. In attempting to simulate brushes, there is a broad spectrum of possible representations, ranging from the simple to the complex, which would have a corresponding degree of realism and computational expense. In this section, I discuss the basic representational units and my reasons for choosing them.

2.1 The Objects

All of the code is written in Zetalisp using *flavors*, an object-oriented programming style. The basic representational units are therefore flavors, or classes of objects. This creates a useful modular abstraction which allows the user to deal with the many parameters of drawing in a managable and structured hierarchy.

They are:

1. Brush - a compound object composed of bristles
2. Stroke - a trajectory of position and pressure
3. Dip - a description of the initial state of a class of brushes
4. Paper - a mapping onto the display device

Bristles, which do a lot of the work of the brush, are also objects in their own right, but their description and definition is intimately connected with that of the brush.

2.1.1 The Brush

A brush can be thought of as a one-dimensional array of bristles, each of which has its own ink supply and position relative to the brush handle. Thus, the brush has a one-dimensional "footprint" (like a windshield wiper), and is moved so that it is always perpendicular to the path of the stroke.

As the brush is moved through the trajectory specified by the stroke, two periodic computations are performed:

- The state of each bristle is updated.

  Updating the bristles consists of evaluating one or more code fragments ("rules") which modify the color, ink quantity, relative position, or any other property for each bristle.

- An image computed from the bristles is transferred to the paper.

  A single bristle contributes to the image only if two conditions both hold: it is applied to the paper with

sufficient pressure, and it has ink remaining. A droplet of ink corresponding to that bristle's color at that point in time is added to the paper by sending a message to a paper object (see Section 2.1.4).

Each bristle has a color: for *sumi* the color is simply a shade of gray, represented as a fraction between 0 and 1. It is assumed that all the ink on a given bristle is of the same color; however, neighboring bristles may be of different colors.

2.1.2 The Stroke

A stroke is a set of parameters (e.g. position and pressure) which evolve as a function of an independent variable. This may be thought of as elapsed time, or the distance along the stroke; any monotonically increasing variable will do. I call this variable "time", and represent it with the symbol S (since T already has a special meaning in LISP). Its value is an approximation of the distance along the stroke.

Since there is no special input hardware (other than a keyboard and a mouse) currently attached to our Lisp machines, the shape of the stroke is determined by a spline of 2D coordinates specifed using the mouse, clicking once to specify each control point. For each control point, the user can specify the pressure manually with the keyboard. The spline itself is a connected series of line segments sufficiently small to give the illusion of a smooth curve.

Position and pressure samples and the splines derived from them are stored in the "stroke" object. The user can edit an incorrect stroke, or select a different brush or dip for the same trajectory.

2.1.3 The Dip

In traditional Oriental painting and calligraphy, a complex texture of color and uneven distribution of ink can be applied to the brush. This can set up the patterns of light and darkness which can make a simple straight stroke look like a cylindrical segment of smooth bamboo, or make a cliff rising out of the ocean seem to be covered with moss on top. By separating the abstraction of dip from brush, one can use the same brush for a wide variety of strokes and effects, just as in real *sumi*. If one selects a particular brush and stroke, one can experiment with different dips to achieve exactly the desired effect.

Since moving a brush through a stroke uses up the ink and can change the position and color of the bristles, the dip must carry enough information to restore the brush to its initial state (or a sufficiently similar state), so that strokes can be repeated. This can be anything from using a simple rule to storing an explict snapshot of the state of each bristle. Such a rule is a procedure which has access to parameters such as the position of each bristle within the brush, or user-specified parameters like blotchiness or smoothness. Dipping a brush executes the procedure and/or copies the stored bristle parameters. Randomness can be introduced at the time of creating the dip, and/or at each act of dipping.

2.1.4 The Paper

The paper object is responsible for rendering the ink as it comes off the brush. As each bristle decides to imprint itself, it sends a message to the paper indicating its position and other relevant parameters. The paper then reacts, usually by

---

[1]Pronounced *soo-me-ay*, it comes from the Japanese words "sumi," the black ink used in calligraphy, and "e," meaning picture. Sato's work [8] has many examples and discusses the history, symbolism, and techniques of traditional and modern *sumi-e*. It includes the famous *Mustard Seed Garden Manual of Painting*, a compendium of 1000 years of *sumi-e* experience and technique first published in China in 1679.

rendering a single dot of appropriate color at the appropriate point.

The paper concept is useful because it presents an abstraction which allows the system to run on frame buffers of various resolutions and depths. An arbitrary texture can be mapped over the stroke in several ways to simulate textured papers (see Section 4.5), using an algorithm similar to conventional texture-mapping. The paper abstraction also has the potential of modelling such effects as the wetness or absorptive properties of real paper, but I have not yet implemented such behavior. I discuss some of the possibilities in Section 7.5.

Currently, the user can draw on frame buffers with either 1, 8, or 24 bits per pixel, at either NTSC (640×480) or high (1280×1024) resolution. Papers of arbitrarily higher resolution can be simulated because of the super-sampling patch provided for anti-aliasing (see Section 3.2).

2.2 Why this representation?

Although I have identified four major abstractions and a host of effects (described in Section 4) which can be created with them, it is still too early to pin down their exact specifications. Rather than design a system which exactly emulates, say, a camel hair brush dipped in a particular brand of india ink, I chose to design a framework in which many categories of paint-like media can be expressed.

Anyone who has ever walked into an art store can attest to the fact that – to the novice – there seems to be a bewildering number of degrees of freedom to control in artistic media. It is important to choose a representation that is modular for the following reasons:

- The user can become familiar with a small repertoire of familiar tools. For example, different brushes can be used and re-used over the same stroke to explore various effects. A certain dip or paper, once perfected, can be saved for later use.

- Since the simulation is based on a modular and hierarchically organized set of effects, aspects of the simulation can be replaced or augmented with more sophisticated algorithmic models as they are developed.

- The same picture can be rendered at many levels of complexity, from quick drafts to final images, by selectively "turning on" different effects independently of each other.

3 The Implementation

This section describes the computation of the brush's motion. Earlier work involved brushes with two-dimensional footprints, but I found I could save a great deal of computation without much loss of generality using a 1D footprint. A discussion of the issues leading to this decision, plus the details of the implementation with the 2D footprint is in [10].

The stroke is defined by the user as a list of position and pressure samples. Both position and pressure are interpolated using a cubic spline to yield a series of nodes (Figure 2). The width of the stroke is computed for each node by a function of the pressure at that node, and the region between two nodes is covered by a quadrilateral defined below.

Figure 2: A stroke defined by 4 control points with intervening nodes generated by a cubic spline. The area covered by the stroke is approximated by quadrilaterals.

Once the quadrilateral is found, a generalized polygon interpolation algorithm is used to assign each pixel within that polygon

- its position in "time" along the stroke, and

- the bristle which passes nearest to it.

The former is used to sort the pixels in the order that the brush sweeps over them, and the latter is used to compute the color for that pixel.

It is important to note that conventional polygon-filling algorithms are not useful to me here. This is because I need to draw each pixel *in chronological order* in order to capture the evolution of the bristles as they move along the stroke.

3.1 Details

The user first specifies the stroke path. This is represented as the N nodes $(X, Y, P, S)_i$ for $i = 0, \ldots, (N - 1)$. The values X, Y, and P represent position and pressure. S is an approximation of the distance traveled along the curve, where $S_0 = 0$. The brush's center moves along the line segments connecting consecutive nodes $(X, Y)_i$, as computed by Bresenham's algorithm [7] for drawing line segments.

On a system with no continuous pressure-sensitive input device, the path may be derived from a cubic spline with n control points. Each point is a triple $(x, y, p)_j$ specifying location and pressure at the jth point. A fourth value approximating the distance along the curve, s_j, is computed for that point.

$$s_0 = 0, \quad s_j = \sum_{k=1}^{j} \sqrt{(x_k - x_{k-1})^2 + (y_k - y_{k-1})^2}$$

From this, two 2D cubic splines are created. One comes from $(x, y)_j$ and generates $(X, Y)_i$, the other from $(p, s)_j$ and generates $(P, S)_i$.

Let us call two such nodes A and B. Between them, a segment $(\overline{AB})$ is created. If $\overline{AB}$ is not the last segment, the next point is called C.

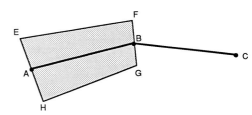

Figure 3: Construction of the polygon connecting nodes A and B.

For each segment, a quadrilateral ($EFGH$) is constructed which has the following properties [Figure 3]:

- A bisects $\overline{EH}$
- B bisects $\overline{FG}$
- $\left|\overline{EH}\right|$ is the width computed from the pressure at A
- $\left|\overline{FG}\right|$ is the width computed from the pressure at B
- $\overline{FG}$ bisects $\angle ABC$.

One exceptional case is when the lines $\overline{EH}$ and $\overline{FG}$ actually intersect [Figure 4]. This can happen if $\overline{AB}$ is relatively short compared to the width $\overline{EH}$. Since the polygon interpolation algorithm I use insists on being handed vertices in clockwise order, one cannot simply pass on the quadrilateral $EFGH$. I call this the "bow-tie" case, and I handle it by partitioning the bow tie into two triangles, and rendering each one independently. Note that one cannot simply swap the offending vertices, since the chronological order of the vertices must be preserved.

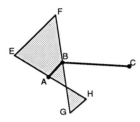

Figure 4: The annoying bowtie case.

Once the polygon's vertices are found, three properties are generated for each pixel using 2D interpolation algorithm.

1. Its position on the frame buffer (X, Y). This is generated in the course of the interpolation.

2. Its position along the stroke (S). This is done by interpolating (S_A, S_B, S_B, S_A) on polygon $EFGH$.

3. Its position across the brush (B). This is done by interpolating $(1, 1, 0, 0)$ on polygon $EFGH$.

As the pixels are generated, they are sorted chronologically (by S) into a temporary array of length $(S_B - S_A)$. Then, as the brush moves and updates, all pixels belonging to that portion of the stroke can be drawn. For each pixel, its abstract brush position B (where $0 \leq B \leq 1$) is used to determine the nearest responsible bristle(s).

3.2 Anti-aliasing

Although the stroke is broken into polygons, one cannot merely anti-alias the polygon edges, since the brush could theoretically change anywhere, at any time; i.e. every pixel could be an edge. So, anti-aliasing is done by supersampling. The brush draws on a patch of virtual paper at a higher resolution than the frame buffer. For each polygon, a 2D array the size of the polygon's bounding-box is allocated, and the corresponding image of the paper is copied to the patch. This idea is similar to the high-resolution patch used in [11], except that the brush's image cannot be pre-computed like Whitted's, since it is constantly changing. The polygon is rendered at high resolution onto the patch, which is then sampled and copied back to the frame buffer.

3.3 Efficiency

The computational time consumed by the algorithm can be separated into two parts:

- The serial part; this is the computation of the stroke geometry, e.g. computation of the polygon vertices and edges.

- The parallel part; this can be broken into two parts:
  - Each bristle executes the evolution rules to determine its next state.
  - Each pixel consults the brush to determine what color it should become.

From running several informal timing benchmarks, it seems that about 90% to 99% of the computation on a serial machine is occupied by the parallel part of the algorithm, except for pathologically small strokes and brushes. Thus, although the polygon-vertex computation seems complex, it occupies an insignificant amount of time compared to the rendering.

Of the parallel part, the ratio of time between the two parts is very much a function of how big the brush is, as measured both in bristles and in pixels. Another important factor is the complexity of the evolution rules.

4 Effects

In this section, I will describe some of the effects one can control by changing different parameters of the simulation. Although there may seem to be a bewildering myriad of parameters to control, it's important to recognize that each parameter has an intuitively recognizable function, and its effect on the image can be appreciated with a minimum of experimentation.

4.1 Ink Quantity

The ink supply on each bristle is assumed to be a reservoir of a finite quantity of fluid, which gets replenished each time the brush is dipped. The quantity is decreased as the brush moves through the stroke, and eventually the bristle runs out. When the quantity drops to zero, that bristle no longer contributes to the image on the paper.

If a scratchy breakup at the tail of each stroke is desired, the dip should put just the right amount of ink on the brush, including selecting a few bristles to be short-changed so they run out early [Figure 5]. If the stroke is known at the time of the act of dipping, its length is used to help determine the quantity of ink deposited on the bristles. There are parameters which control how many bristles get short-changed, and by how much, either as a fraction of the total stroke length or in units of absolute distance.

Figure 5: Different quantities: (A) 50% of the bristles are approx. 33% dry. (B) 75% of the bristles are approx. 50% dry.

4.2 Ink Color

Each bristle has a color: for *sumi* the color is simply a shade of gray, represented as a fraction between 0 and 1. It is assumed that all the ink on a given bristle is of the same color; however, neighboring bristles may be of different colors.

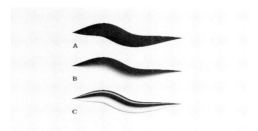

Figure 6: Different colors: (A) Constant (B) Linear (C) User-specified

The distribution of color across the brush may be specified as constant, or a linear ramp from one value to another, or as an explicit list of arbitrary values [Figure 6]. Although this distribution must be specified for the beginning of the stroke, there are several ways of thinking about how the color evolves over the stroke:

- A distribution is specified for both the start and end of the stroke. At any point in the middle of the stroke, the color of a given bristle is linearly interpolated between the starting and ending values specified for it [Figure 7 A, B]. This idea may be extended to generalized distribution samples at arbitrary points in the stroke.

- From the starting distribution, diffusion may be simulated by smoothing the colors of neighboring bristles [Figure 7 C,D]. Each bristle updates its color according to a partial interpolation. For example, if

  - C_{i_t} is the color on the ith bristle at time t,
  - D is a speed-of-diffusion parameter between 0 and 1 (1 is rapid diffusion),
  - and the bristles are assumed to be regularly spaced,

  Then $C_{i_{t+1}} = C_{i_t}(1 - D) + \left(\frac{C_{i-1_t}+C_{i+1_t}}{2}\right) D.$

- A generalized evolution algorithm can be supplied [Figure 7 E, F]. The color on a bristle may be a function of brush pressure, distance from the origin, or even the quantity of the ink remaining (see Section 4.3).

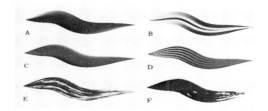

Figure 7: Color effects: (A) Start/end interpolation from one ramp to another (B) Interpolation from spike to notch (C) Fast color diffusion ($D = .5$) (D) Slow diffusion ($D = .1$) (E) Random (Brownian) evolution of color (F) "Ink stealing" evolution of quantity.

In addition to or instead of the above phenomena, a pattern can be texture-mapped onto the stroke (see Section 4.5).

Once the color of the ink on the bristle is decided, the color to place on the paper must be computed. The paper may already be colored due to either the paper's natural texture or previously deposited ink. The user may supply a *color combination function* of two or three inputs to be evaluated each time a given bristle attempts to draw on a particular pixel of the paper; the inputs are the ink color (C_i), the color of the paper at the point to be drawn upon (C_p), and an optional value derived from the texture-mapping array, if there is one.

For *sumi* the default function used is a very simple one: the darkness at the intersection of several strokes is assumed to equal the darkness of the darkest stroke (e.g. $C_{p_{t+1}} = \max(C_{i_t}, C_{p_t})$)

4.3 Evolution of Quantity and Color

Jostling of neighboring bristles sometimes transfers ink among them; this affects both the quantity and color of the bristles concerned. This is modeled by thinking of the brush as a cellular automaton [12] with a small procedure (rule) for quantity and color transfer. As the brush moves across the page a bit at a time, all bristles repeatedly execute the same rule, which can refer to the parameters of each bristle and its immediate neighbors. It may compute a new value for any of that bristle's parameters and modify it accordingly.

For example, one rule can allow a near-dry bristle to run out of ink, then temporarily "discover" a new supply (either by stealing from a neighbor, or just conjuring it out of nowhere) to create islands of ink and whitespace in the middle of the stroke [Figure 7 F]. Incorporating an element of randomness into the rules can give rise to rich textures. On the other hand, avoiding randomness may be necessary in applications like some kinds of animation, where the user wants the complex texture of stroke to be consistent from frame to frame (see Section 6).

4.4 Pressure

The pressure on a particular bristle is a function of the geometry of the brush and the overall pressure on the brush at a certain point in the stroke.

Changing the applied pressure during the stroke can have two different kinds of effects:

- *Spreading.* Pressing harder can spread the bristles further apart.

- *Contact.* Pressing harder can bring more bristles into contact with the paper.

Under spreading, each bristle's distance from the brush center is an arbitrary function of the applied pressure. By default, distance is linearly proportional to pressure, but some interesting effects can be demonstrated by exploring other relationships [Figure 8].

One can also consider that greater overall pressure brings more bristles into contact with the paper [Figure 9]. A value is assigned to each bristle which represents the minimum brush pressure necessary to bring it into contact with the paper. For example, to simulate a round brush of radius 1, each bristle gets a pressure-threshold proportional to the arcsine of its distance from the center of the brush.

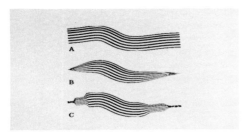

Figure 8: Spreading under pressure: (A) Constant width (B) Width ∝ pressure (C) Width quantized by user-supplied function

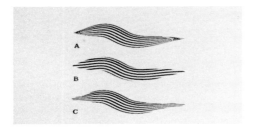

Figure 9: Two interpretations of pressure: (A) More pressure spreads bristles (B) More pressure brings more bristles into contact (C) A combination of these two effects.

Intermittent contact with the paper near the pressure threshold is simulated by adding a rule which causes perturbations (either overall, or for individual bristles) in two paramete:

- Changing the brush's pressure implies one's hand is oscillating.

- Changing the the pressure-threshold of a bristle implies the geometry of the brush is changing.

Although these parameters have different meanings, the image ultimately depends on the difference between them; so it doesn't matter which modified as long as one is consistent. A more realistic test for determining contact might take into account the orientation of the brush and hysteresis (stickiness).

4.5 Texture Mapping

Some interesting effects can be realized by mapping a texture onto the image of the stroke [Figure 10]. There are at least two ways of computing the mapping:

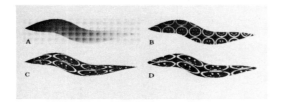

Figure 10: Texture mapping: (A) Textured paper (B) Textured by smiley-face paper (C) Texture mapping with spreading bristles (D) Texture mapping with pressure-threshold bristles.

- A rectangular array representing the texture of the paper is mapped by a straightforward flat tiling. When a bristle attempts to draw ink of a certain color on a given pixel, the array element corresponding to that pixel is used.

- A one or two dimensional array is mapped along the long axis of the stroke (this is only used in the implementations where the brush has a one-dimensional footprint). The array element used corresponds to how far along the stroke the brush has travelled. For example, a simple 1D texture (say, a sine wave) mapped onto a curvy stroke gives the impression of banding similar to a raccoon's tail. If the texture map is two-dimensional, the bristle's radial distance from the brush center is used to compute the array index in the second dimension.

Once a value is supplied by the texture array, it is used in the user-supplied color combination function (see Section 4.2). For *sumi* the texture value is a number (usually a fraction between 0 and 1) which is multiplied by the ink color to selectively attenuate it before applying it to the paper.

5   The User Interface

The prototype system is not intended to be a general-purpose paint program. As such, it lacks most of the useful functionality and well-designed user interface users have come to expect from paint programs. Instead, effort was concentrated on exploring new rendering algorithms and effects.

5.1   System specifics

The system runs on a Symbolics 3600 Lisp Machine with a $1280 \times 1024 \times 24$ bit frame buffer, configured for 8-bit per pixel grayscale. All of the code is written in Zetalisp using *flavors*, using an object-oriented programming style. The rules which govern the evolution of the brush are pieces of Lisp code ("methods" in Zetalisp) associated with a particular flavor of brush. These rules are executed as the brush moves along its path, and the code in them can freely refer to and modify any parameters.

5.2   Drawing

The prototype system takes up to a minute or two to render a stroke, depending on brush complexity and the supersampling ratio for anti-aliased strokes. Although this is too slow for real-time interactive drawing, the user enters and edits the strokes' paths interactively. The input consists of discrete samples of position and pressure, which are then smoothed using a cubic spline by the rendering algorithm. The user uses a mouse to position the points of the stroke with one hand, while the other hand specifies the pressure with the keyboard.

The user can dynamically select from among 16 different levels of pressure by pressing combinations of four keys on the standard keyboard. The cursor responds to this in real time by growing or shrinking accordingly, depending on the pressure-to-width algorithm selected by the user.

6 Animation

One of the most important motivations for this work is the hope that creating reproducible brush strokes will allow paintings to be animated.

The code supporting animation right now is rather crude. It is basically a two-dimensional keyframing system which allows the user to specify key shapes of brush strokes as they change over time. The position and pressure of each control point of the stroke is interpolated between the key frames, using a spline for non-periodic motion and a generalized sinusoid for periodic motion. The same brush and dip is used for any given animated stroke.

The shrimp shown in Figure 1 was animated from four key frames, spline interpolated over the total 92 frame sequence. Each frame took about one minute to render. With the antennae and legs waving around, the tail kicking, and the ripples flowing away from the leaf, the resulting animation is very lifelike.

7 Further work:

7.1 Better input methods

Without an input device as expressive as a real brush, the current environment isn't very user friendly. There are many kinds of input devices offering three or more degrees of freedom which might be adapted for manually entering strokes. At the MIT Media Lab, we are exploring force sensitive touchscreens [6], LED-based body trackers [3], and magnetic pointing devices [9]. Other possible input devices include touch-sensitive tablets [2] and the drawing prism [4].

7.2 Better rendering hardware

With the advent of parallel computers, the drawing of the most sophisticated of strokes should be possible in real time. This is because almost all of the computation in the algorithms described here are local, that is, dependent only on an immediate neighborhood of bristles or pixels, and thus is well-suited to implementation on machines using parallel architectures.

7.3 Exploring rules

More experimentation is needed to build a good-sized library of rules. Hopefully, subjective properties like "blotchiness", "dryness", or "clumpiness" can be controlled by adding a rule and setting a parameter or two. New kinds of rules will result in innovative brushes, as well as realistic models of traditional watercolor brushes.

7.4 Real color

For simplicity, I stayed with monochrome ink even though the frame buffer I used has full 24 bit color. A useful extension would be to allow the user to experiment with a virtual brush laden with various colors. A more complicated rule would describe the behavior of paint mixing. Real electronic paint can change color as a function of thickness of application or chemical reaction with the brush, paper, or other strokes.

7.5 Paper effects

The wetness and absorptive properties of the ink or paper can be described by specifying the area of the paper covered by each bristle, and an ink redistribution function associated with the paper. The former corresponds to the pre-filtering and the latter to post-filtering steps in anti-aliasing. In addition to the usual blurring (low-pass filter) operations, one could use a simple asymmetrical fractal to simulate the forked bleeding that capillary action sometimes causes on dry papers.

7.6 Splatter

A bit of splatter from a heavily-laden brush with stiff bristles pulled briskly around a corner might be represented as a rule which gets activated when the brush velocity or accelleration surpasses a certain threshold. It then places a fractal distribution of splattered, fuzzy dots on the paper as a function of the ink supply, trajectory, and pressure on the brush.

7.7 Music and painting

An appealing analogy to the stroke is the contour of a musical note over time. Each stroke is a set of time-varying parameters (like position and pressure, or loudness and timbre). A cluster of strokes can evoke a recognizable image, much as a collection of notes create a chord or arpeggio.

Occasionally, when I am asked about the limits of realism in my simulation, I am reminded of similar questions asked of builders of electronic instruments. The answer, of course, is that there is room in electronic media for both accurate reproduction of physical phenomena, and for creative exploration with totally new forms of expression which take advantage of the differences inherent in the new media.

7.8 3D strokes

Perhaps the strokes themselves can be liberated from the 2D quality of paper, and a technology of 3D paintbrushes can be realized. Non-computer techniques come to mind, including sweeping a lit taper through a room to leave a trail of smoke, or "drawing" in an aquarium filled with a viscous gel using a long hypodermic filled with ink. All the issues of describing the evolution of texture through the stroke remain. With stereoscopic displays [9] or computer-generated holograms [1], one will be able to create tenuous sculptures far more delicate than currently possible. One could even imagine folding translucent paper into origami shapes which define plane fragments on which these brush strokes lie.

8 Conclusion

To get realistic brush strokes, one must simulate the phenomena which gives rise to them. The tough part is modeling the behavior of individual bristles, which we do with rules which execute each time the brush moves. To produce an anti-aliased image, the brush's image is drawn onto a small patch which is sampled and incrementally copied to the page.

When an animal, plant, or river can be represented by a few deft strokes, perhaps under some circumstances a brush representation can replace a polyhedral one. Whereas polyhedra are good representations of analytic objects, and polygonal fractals are good for largely amorphous ones, there is a middle classification of things too rich for one and too structured for the other. Given the computational complexity and storage expense of representing a warm, fuzzy bunny as a skeleton of faceted polyhedra covered with skin polyhedra and particle generated hair, perhaps representing it instead as a collection of brush strokes would result in faster rendering, more compact storage, and a more aesthetically appealing image.

9   Acknowledgements

This work was supported in part by a grant from Apple Computer, Inc., and an equipment loan from Symbolics, Inc. Karl Sims suggested the use of and provided the polygon interpolation routine.

References

[1] Benton, Stephen A., "Holographic Displays — A Review," *Optical Engineering* **14,** 5, Sept-Oct 1975.

[2] Buxton, W., Hill, R., and Rowley, P., "Issues and Techniques in Touch-Sensitive Tablet Input," *Computer Graphics* **19,** 3, July 1985, pp. 215-224.

[3] Ginsberg, C., and Maxwell, D., "Graphical Marionette," *Proc. ACM SIGGRAPH/SIGART Workshop on Motion*, April 1983, pp. 172-179.

[4] Greene, Richard, "The Drawing Prism: A Versatile Graphic Input Device," *Computer Graphics* **19,** 3, July 1985, pp. 103-110.

[5] Lewis, John-Peter, "Texture Synthesis for Digital Painting," *Computer Graphics* **18,** 3, July 1984, pp. 245-251.

[6] Minsky, Margaret, "Manipulating Simulated Objects with Real-world Gestures using a Force and Position Sensitive Screen," *Computer Graphics* **18,** 3, July 1984, pp. 195-203.

[7] Rogers, David F., "Procedural Elements for Computer Graphics," McGraw-Hill, New York, 1985.

[8] Sato, Shozo, "The Art of *Sumi-e*" (in English), Kodansha International, Tokyo, 1984.

[9] Schmandt, Chris, "Spatial Input/Display Correspondence in a Stereoscopic Computer Graphic Workstation," *Computer Graphics* **17,** 3, July 1983, pp. 253-257.

[10] Strassmann, Steve, "Hairy Brushes in Computer-Generated Images," M.S. Thesis, MIT Media Laboratory, June 1986.

[11] Whitted, Turner, "Anti-aliased Line Drawing Using Brush Extrusion," *Computer Graphics* **17,** 3, July 1983, pp. 151-156.

[12] Wolfram, Stephen, "Cellular Automata as Models of Complexity," *Nature* **311,** 4, 1984, pp. 419-424.

Snap-Dragging

Eric Allan Bier
Dept. of EECS
UC Berkeley
Berkeley, CA 94720

Maureen C. Stone
Xerox PARC
3333 Coyote Hill Rd.
Palo Alto, CA 94304

Abstract

We are interested in the problem of making precise line drawings using interactive computer graphics. In precise line drawings, specific relationships are expected to hold between points and lines. In published interactive drawing systems, precise relationships have been achieved by using rectangular grids or by solving simultaneous equations (constraints). The availability of fast display hardware and plentiful computational power suggest that we should take another look at the ruler and compass techniques traditionally used by draftsmen. Snap-dragging uses the ruler and compass metaphor to help the user place his next point with precision, and uses heuristics to automatically place guiding lines and circles that are likely to help the user construct each shape. Snap-dragging also provides translation, rotation, and scaling operations that take advantage of the precision placement capability. We show that snap-dragging compares favorably in power and ease of use with grid or constraint techniques.

CR Category: I.3.6 [Methodology and Techniques, Interactive techniques]

Additional Keywords: Interactive design, geometric construction, constraint systems

1. Introduction

Artists drawing technical illustrations often require that precise relationships are held among picture elements. For example, certain line segments should be horizontal, parallel, or congruent. In the past, interactive illustration systems have provided techniques such as grids and constraints to facilitate precise positioning. Both of these techniques have significant limitations. Grids provide only a small fraction of the desired types of precision. Constraints, while very powerful, require the user to specify additional structures that are often difficult to understand and time-consuming to manipulate. Our interactive technique, *snap-dragging*, is a compromise between the convenience of grids and the power of constraints.

Snap-dragging is based on the familiar idea of snapping the display cursor to points and curves using a gravity function. The new idea is that a set of *gravity-active* points, lines, and circles called *alignment objects* are automatically constructed from hints given by the user plus heuristics about typical editing behavior. The result is a system with as much power as a ruler, compass, protractor, and T-square drafting set, but with little time spent in moving the tools and setting up the constructions.

Snap-dragging can be seen as an extension of the idea of gravity-active grids, used in illustrators such as Griffin [Stone80], Gremlin [Opperman84], MacDraw® [MacDraw84], and Star® Graphics [Lipkie82], or as a simple form of constraint solver, used in systems such as Sketchpad [Sutherland84], ThingLab [Borning79], and Juno [Nelson85]. As in a grid system, the cursor may snap to gravity-active objects provided by the system. However, the set of gravity-active objects is richer, and varies with the current scene and the operation being performed. As in a constraint-based system, points can be placed to satisfy angle, slope, and distance constraints. However, with snap-dragging, constraints are solved two at a time, with the user explicitly controlling the placement of each point, and the constraints are forgotten as soon as they are used, rather than becoming part of the data structure.

Snap-dragging is currently implemented as part of the Gargoyle two-dimensional illustrator, running in the Cedar programming environment [Swinehart85], on the Xerox Dorado high-performance personal workstation [Pier83]. All figures in this paper were created with Gargoyle.

In Section 2 we will present snap-dragging in more detail. Section 3 is an analysis of design issues for geometric precision techniques: comparing grids, constraints, and snap-dragging. Section 4 presents more detail on the implementation of snap-dragging. Section 5 summarizes our results.

2. Snap-Dragging

This section describes how snap-dragging is used to construct shapes and perform transformations. In Gargoyle, a special point called the *caret* can be placed, with precision, using gravity. The caret is distinct from the *cursor*; the cursor always moves with the mouse, while the caret can stray from the cursor if a gravity-active object attracts it. The caret is the source of precision. When control points are added to a scene, they are always placed at the position of the caret. Positioning operations use the position of the caret as a parameter.

When one control point of an object is moved, affected line segments are adjusted, in real time, using a technique called rubber-banding [Newman79]. Transformed objects are smoothly dragged into position. The user specifies which region of the scene and which kinds of alignment objects are of interest. The system automatically constructs alignment objects of that kind in the requested region. Alignment objects are visible only when the user is in the process of moving a point or object, and are drawn in gray so they may be easily distinguished.

Figure 1 shows how a user would adjust a point in an existing triangle to make the base horizontal. In figure 1(a), the user has activated horizontal alignment lines, and picked up a vertex with the caret. In figure 1(b), the user drags the vertex until it snaps onto one of the alignment lines. When the operation is finished, the alignment lines will disappear.

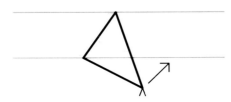

Figure 1(a) Picking up a vertex with the caret.

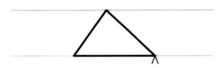

Figure 1(b) Snapping the caret onto an alignment line.

Figure 2 demonstrates construction of an equilateral triangle, 3/4 inch on a side, with its base at 15 degrees to the horizontal. Constructing the triangle takes six steps:

1) Activate lines of slope 15 degrees (click on a menu).

2) Activate 3/4 inch circles (click on a menu).

3) Place the lower left vertex. A 3/4 inch alignment circle appears centered on the new vertex, and an alignment line sloping at 15 degrees appears passing through the new vertex.

4) Place the second vertex at one of the intersections of the circle and the 15 degree line. Figure 2(a). A second alignment circle appears, centered on the second vertex.

5) Place the last vertex at the intersection of the two circles. Figure 2(b).

6) Invoke a close polygon command, or place a fourth vertex on top of the first. Since the operation is finished, the alignment objects disappear to allow the artist to inspect the shape. Figure 2(c).

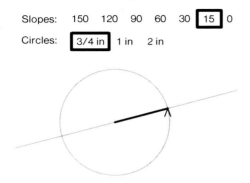

Slopes: 150 120 90 60 30 [15] 0

Circles: [3/4 in] 1 in 2 in

Figure 2(a) The user places the first two points of an equilateral triangle with side of length 3/4 inch and with its base at 15 degrees. A 3/4 inch alignment circle and a 15 degree alignment line appear.

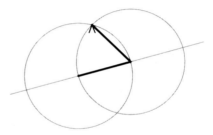

Figure 2(b) Another circle appears. The last vertex is placed at the intersection of the two circles.

Figure 2(c) The triangle is closed and all alignment lines disappear.

The whole process takes six keystrokes and all but two of these would be needed to draw any triangle. Note that in a grid system, it is impossible to construct an equilateral triangle, and in most constraint systems, only a triangle with a horizontal base would be easy to construct.

Once an object has been created, it can be translated, rotated, scaled, and combined with other objects. The ability to position the cursor on alignment objects makes it easy to perform these operations with precision. Each transformation is performed in three steps. First, the objects to be transformed are selected. Second, the caret is placed at an initial position in the scene, usually on a selected scene object or alignment object. Third, the selected objects are smoothly transformed using the displacement between the original position of the caret and the new (constantly updated) position of the caret to determine the current transformation. Like the original caret position, the new caret position can be snapped to alignment objects. We will discuss the operations translate, rotate, and scale in more detail next.

2.1 Translation

When performing translation, we simply add a displacement vector (old caret - new caret) to the original position of each selected object to get its new position. We move one polygon P to touch another polygon Q by selecting P, placing the caret at a point on P, and snapping the caret onto a point on Q. Figure 3 shows how point-parameterized translation can be used to align two rectangles; the caret is snapped onto a vertex, A, and then onto a 90 degree line in this example.

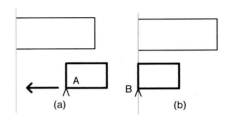

Figure 3 An example of translation parameterized by two points (A and B). (a) The caret snaps onto point A on the object. (b) The user then drags and snaps the caret onto a vertical alignment line at point B. A single vertical alignment line appears because the user has expressed an interest in the left edge of the fixed rectangle.

2.2 Rotation

The center of rotation, called the *anchor*, is placed by positioning the caret and invoking the Drop Anchor command. During rotation, the angle of rotation is kept equal to the angle through which the displacement vector (old caret - new caret) has moved from its initial position. If we initially position the caret on a point A of the selected object, then the anchor, the point A, and the caret remain collinear throughout the rotation. Consider the example in figure 4. We place the anchor point at the base of an arrow, place the caret initially onto its tip (point A), and drag the caret to the object we would like the arrow to point to (point B).

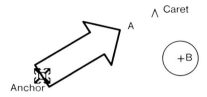

Figure 4(a) The caret, which was initially placed on point A, has been dragged to an arbitrary position. Anchor, A, and caret are kept collinear.

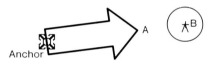

Figure 4(b) When the caret is placed on point B, the arrow points at it; Anchor, A, and B are collinear.

2.3 Scaling

The anchor point is also used as the center of scaling. The scale factor is the ratio of the magnitudes of the new caret displacement vector (caret - anchor) to the original caret displacement vector. This transformation can be used to scale one object until one of its dimensions matches a dimension of another object. In figure 5 the square is enlarged to fit onto an edge of the hexagon.

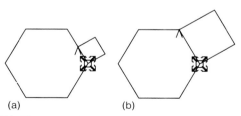

Figure 5(a) The anchor is fixed on one corner of the square and the caret is positioned on the adjacent corner. **(b)** The square is scaled as the caret is dragged to the vertex of the hexagon.

3. Design Issues for Geometric Precision Tools

The ideal tool is powerful but easy to use. Good tool design, therefore, requires a compromise between functionality and user interface complexity. We measure the functionality of a geometric precision tool by examining which geometric relationships can be expressed directly. These relationships must be weighed against the total number of commands the user must learn and the time taken to specify all the arguments and invoke each command.

Ease of use involves more than the reduction of commands and

keystrokes. A system that is easy to use will be predictable, require user input in proportion to the difficulty of the task, and be free from catastrophic failures that destroy hours of work. We will show that snap-dragging makes it easy to reach these goals.

In this section, we will describe the sets of relationships we use to define the power of a geometric tool, and describe some important factors in making a system easy to use. In the process, we will compare snap-dragging to grids and constraints.

3.1 Geometric Power

Our approach to the problem of making precise line drawings has been to assume that the designer will define shapes by carefully placing points rather than by sketching and aligning afterwards, which is the method used by Pavlidis and VanWyk [Pavlidis85]. Our design philosophy focuses the design issues on methods for positioning points, and especially on the issue of positioning a new point with respect to the other points in a scene or with respect to the boundaries of the drawing space. Whether or not a picture is actually produced by placing one point at a time, we can measure the power of a geometric design system, particularly a polygon-based one, on the point-to-point relationships (e.g., distance, slope, angle) that its user can express. We describe a taxonomy of point-to-point relationships and a taxonomy of geometric constructions and use them to compare grid, constraint, and snap-dragging systems.

One way to organize the point-to-point relationships that a user might want is by the set of affine transformations that preserve a given relationship. We use six groups of transformations in the classification scheme shown in figure 6. Each group is a subset of the group above it. They are: general affine transformations (called the affine group in algebra texts); combinations of scaling, rotation, and translation (the extended similarity group); combinations of scaling and translation; combinations of rotation and translation (the Euclidean group); pure translation (the group of translations); and the identity transformation. The point-to-point relationships that can be preserved under these transformations are parallelism (which includes collinearity), angles, ratios of distances, slopes, distances, vectors, and coordinates. Each relationship in figure 6 is invariant to the group named in its box, and to all those groups below it. We call these the *seven basic relationships* because, when a designer scales, rotates, and translates shapes to assemble an illustration, he can count on these relationships to be maintained.

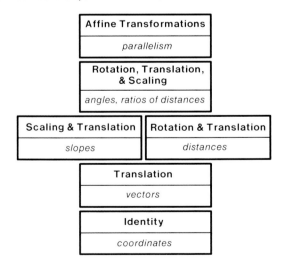

Figure 6 A taxonomy of our seven basic geometric relationships. Relationships appear in the bottom half of each box. Each relationship is invariant to the transformations listed in the top half of its box and to all transformations below its box.

One way to organize geometric constructions is by the number of points in the construction. We view a construction as a function that takes a set of points as arguments and returns a point or curve in the plane. The number of point arguments that a construction takes has a direct bearing on the user interface; constructions involving more points will take more work to specify or will require more guesswork on the part of the tool. However, constructions that take many point arguments can potentially be more powerful than those that take fewer. The seven basic relationships can be produced using constructions that take only zero, one, or two points as arguments. One way to do this is:

Group 0: No points are needed as arguments. Construct a line of known *x coordinate*, or known *y coordinate*.

Group 1: One point, A, is needed. Construct a circle of points that are a known *distance* from A, construct a line through A of known *slope*, or construct a point at a known *vector* (distance *and* slope) from A.

Group 2: Two points, A and B, are needed. Construct lines that are a known *angle* from segment AB, construct lines that are *parallel* to AB at a known distance, or construct the midpoint of AB. Midpoints are a special case of the *ratio of distances* relationship.

Each relationship can be expressed using a different construction group. For instance, parallelism can be created with a Group 3 construction:

Group 3: Three points, A, B, and C, are arguments. Construct a line, parallel to A and B, that passes through C.

Our taxonomies of relationships and constructions highlight the limitations of grid systems. A grid is the computer graphics equivalent of graph paper. When the grid is turned on, all points placed by the user will be forced to land on the intersection points of the rules of the graph paper (figure 7). This gives us only a discrete set of absolute coordinates. Only a subset of the possible coordinates, distances, and slopes can be built, and only those that are aligned with the grid axes are easy to specify. Operations in Group 2 and higher order groups are particularly difficult to achieve since the chances are small that a larger set of points will satisfy a precise relationship *and* lie on the grid.

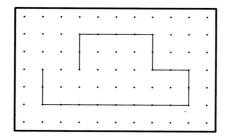

Figure 7 An object with horizontal and vertical lines is constructed with a grid system.

Constraint-based systems can potentially provide all of the relationships mentioned above and more. For instance, the Juno constraint-based illustrator [Nelson85] provides some Group 1 constructions (for horizontal and vertical), and some Group 3 constructions (for parallel and congruent). The user selects as many as four points at a time and then specifies the new relationship between them that the system should enforce. An example is shown in figure 8. Not only are a larger set of relationships possible than with the other two approaches, but many constraints can be solved simultaneously. Constraint-based illustrators are typically very powerful by our metric.

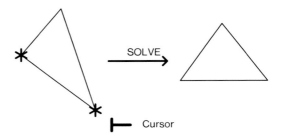

Figure 8 A Juno user touches two points with a T-square shaped cursor to add a horizontal constraint. After the constraint solver is invoked, a new triangle is drawn.

Snap-dragging, as implemented in Gargoyle, provides only Group 1 and 2 constructions. We felt this was an appropriate balance between power and ease of use. Providing more complex relationships would stretch the capabilities of snap-dragging; the technique relies on being able to guess what relationships will be useful, and there would be too many groups of three or more points to make guessing possible. Snap-dragging is generally less powerful than constraints and more powerful than grids.

3.2 Ease of use

To be easy to use, a system should be predictable, require user input in proportion to the difficulty of the task, and be free from catastrophic failures that destroy hours of work. In this section we focus on how the properties of geometric precision schemes affect these aspects of system design.

3.2.1 Predictability and User Confidence

A system is predictable if the designer can confidently predict the results that each action will have on the state of his illustration. A predictable system will provide commands at the right semantic level to help the user concisely express his intent, and will provide good feedback when the intent has been captured. Too low a semantic level requires the user to perform tasks that take too many steps, which is tedious and unreliable. Too high a level results in operations that are hard to learn and understand.

Superficially, grid systems are predictable. The grid itself is a visible reminder of the active constraints. The mechanism of a grid, however, provides no straightforward way to express relationships as simple as specific distances or angles. For example, a user trying to construct a 45 degree line has to express this idea in primitive terms: move 5 points over and 5 points up. To be sure the angle is correct, he may need to count grid points several times. So while a grid is easy to use, it may not inspire confidence that a particular relationship is satisfied because it provides control at too low a level.

Constraint-based systems tend to be difficult to control. A set of simultaneous non-linear equations almost always has multiple solutions. Many points may be moved at once to reach a solution, drastically altering the scene. Presenting and controlling all the constraints and possible solutions is a formidable user interface problem. Some constraint-based systems do not attempt to describe the constraints graphically, relying on a textual description and letting the user correlate the text with the geometry. In any case, getting the constraints correct can be more like debugging code than like graphical editing.

With snap-dragging, one point is moved at a time, and all constraints are represented as visible lines and circles so that the constraints remain simple and visible. We believe snap-dragging presents commands at the correct semantic level, providing the same operations that a designer would use to describe the construction.

3.2.2 Appropriate User Input

A system makes appropriate use of user input if a small change to the picture always requires a short period of designer time. The amount of work required to produce a design must be measured not only in keystrokes but in the amount of effort it takes to make use of the design tools. Most systems do well at providing local optimization of keystrokes by taking advantage of *coherence* in the editing session, providing ways to free the user from repeatedly indicating that the same relationship and/or values are needed in a sequence of editing steps. However, in systems that are optimized for specific directions, such as horizontal and vertical, or that limit precise editing to a discrete grid, a significant amount of planning and extra construction may be needed for precise editing to proceed at all stages of the design.

Grid systems are both quantized and optimized for constructions that align with the edges of the page. To maintain precise control throughout the editing session, the designer must plan ahead to make sure that all his vertices can be placed on grid points. For example, if an arrowhead is to be attached precisely to the middle of the edge of a rectangle, the rectangle must be an even number of grid units long, and the designer must take this into account when the rectangle is created. Otherwise, it may be necessary to change the size of the rectangle when the arrowhead is added, which may require further changes to the picture.

Constraint-based systems often include direction-specific constraints such as horizontal and vertical. A shape defined using these constraints cannot be rotated without either changing or violating the constraints. Editing the constraints to make them consistent with the new rotation requires the user to change the constraint network everywhere the horizontal and vertical constraints are used. It is possible to design a shape with only a single mention of absolute orientation so that it can be rotated by altering that one constraint. However, designing such a re-orientable shape requires extra planning and effort.

The most important feature of an alignment paradigm based on points and geometric constructions is that it works equally well at arbitrary scales and rotations. The transformation independence in Gargoyle comes from three sources. First, Gargoyle treats all angles and scaling factors in an equivalent fashion; it is just as easy to align the base of the triangle in figure 2 with a 15 degree line as it would be to make the base horizontal. Second, Gargoyle implements relationships that are preserved under scaling and rotation, as described in section 3.1 above; if the designer uses one inch circles to build a shape with one inch features, he can rotate the object and then continue to edit it without difficulty. Third, Gargoyle allows the user to set the scaling unit to an arbitrary value. If the designer uses 1 inch circles to create a shape, and later scales the shape, he cannot use his one inch circles to modify the shape further. However, if the designer can temporarily alter the scaling unit, multiplying it by the same factor used to scale the object, the "one inch" circles will again line up with the shape, allowing it to be edited in place. This is like fitting the grid to an object in a grid-based system, instead of moving the object back onto the grid.

We believe that the transformation independence of snap-dragging is the most significant advantage it has over grids and constraints in reducing the work needed to make an illustration.

3.2.3 Preventing Catastrophic Failures

Catastrophic failure occurs when a short sequence of actions can destroy large amounts of work, requiring the user to redo significant parts of the design. Such failures include scaling by zero, constraint solutions that collapse several lines or points together, and accidental deletions. In addition, it is a catastrophic failure if, late in the illustration process, a problem is uncovered that requires significant rework of pieces of the illustration. These problems include shapes moved prematurely off a grid, designs that are incorrectly quantized, subsections of a design that don't fit together, constrained objects that can't be rotated, and other failures of planning. We feel snap-dragging is a good methodology for preventing both types of catastrophic failures.

Most work losses can be prevented by good feedback and by the ability to undo an action. Snap-dragging provides visible feedback for transformations as they occur. Likewise, undo operations and incremental checkpoints of the system state are easy to implement since each operation makes a small change and leaves the scene objects in a well-defined state.

Failures of planning can never be completely eliminated but a tool that is transformation-independent is clearly more adaptable than one that provides its full power only in specific directions, such as horizontal and vertical, and specific scale units, such as multiples of the grid spacing. Errors can be corrected in place, independent of orientation. Shapes can be combined and adjusted independent of the original orientation or size. Overall, we feel that snap-dragging offers a significantly better compromise between power and ease of use than grids or constraints.

4. Snap-Dragging Implementation Details

In this section we will provide more detail about three important aspects of snap-dragging: how we decide which alignment objects are active, how allowing the user to measure existing geometric relationships can increase the utility of alignment objects, and how we get snap-dragging to work in real time.

4.1 Choosing Alignment Objects

Ruler and compass constructions have traditionally been performed by adding one circle or one line to the scene at a time. With computer-aided illustration this approach involves specifying a number of points and invoking a construction command for every line or circle that is desired. In Gargoyle, we try to reduce the effort spent on constructions by constructing many alignment objects at the same time. Our technique takes advantage of two kinds of *coherence* in a design session: often consecutive changes will be made to the same region of the illustration (*spatial* coherence), or the changes will involve similar construction operations (*construction* coherence). If little coherence is present, we provide several ways to turn off alignment object construction. Below, we discuss the creation of alignment objects in detail.

We motivate the construction of multiple alignment objects with two examples. First, consider a user who is interested in extending a mesh of equilateral triangles. He knows that he will be adding edges at 0, 60, and 120 degrees, and that he will be placing new vertices relative to existing triangle vertices. He might ask Gargoyle to construct, at each vertex of the existing triangles, three lines of slopes 0, 60, and 120 degrees (see figure 9).

Figure 9 The designer adds another segment to a mesh of equilateral triangles. The alignment lines are shown in gray.

Figure 10 The user builds the inner polygon at an offset of 1/4 inch from the outer polygon. Alignment lines, constructed 1/4 inch from each edge of the outer polygon, are shown in gray.

Now consider a second construction. The user would like to add a polygon that is 1/4 inch from an existing polygon. He might request the construction of all lines that are 1/4 inch away from the existing edges, as shown in figure 10.

The user requests the construction of alignment objects in two steps. First, the user identifies those vertices and segments in the scene at which the alignment lines should be constructed. These vertices and segments are said to be *hot*. Next the user specifies the types of construction to be performed. In the examples, the user asks for lines with specified slopes and lines at a specified offset.

Figure 11 illustrates the process by which alignment objects are computed by Gargoyle. Those vertices and segments that the user has made hot are combined with other vertices and segments suggested by heuristics. The resulting vertices and segments are called the *triggers*; each of them will trigger the construction of a-lignment objects. From this set, the system removes any vertices or segments that are currently being dragged or rubber-banded, so that all alignment objects will be stationary. Finally, the list of user-specified constructions is consulted. Each specified construction that takes a vertex as an argument *fires* once per vertex, and each specified construction that takes a segment as an argument fires once per segment, creating the final set of alignment objects.

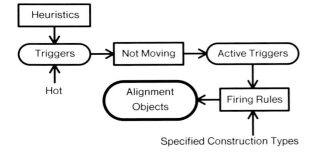

Figure 11 The process of computing the alignment objects.

Below, we give examples of heuristics that we have found useful for augmenting the set of triggers and describe the set of construc-tions that we have implemented.

We can often save the user the trouble of explicitly making ob-jects hot and cold by inferring the region of interest from his actions. One such inference follows from Observation 1:

> **Observation 1**: When the user moves one point of a polygon, he will often want to align it with other parts of that same polygon.

A Gargoyle heuristic has been implemented from this observa-tion. When the heuristic is activated and the user modifies a

polygon, Gargoyle uses as triggers the set of vertices and segments of that polygon. Additional vertices and segments are used as triggers only if the user has explicitly made them hot.

When polygons are being repositioned rather than modified, we cannot use Observation 1. Instead, we rely on a second observation:

> **Observation 2**: When a polygon is translated, rotated, or scaled in entirety, the resulting operation is often performed to make that polygon touch an existing polygon.

No heuristic for augmenting the set of triggers follows from this ob-servation. Instead, the observation suggests that it is important for the scene objects themselves to be gravity-active. In Gargoyle, all scene objects are always gravity-active unless they are being dragged or rubber-banded.

In Gargoyle, we have implemented five types of construction to be used with snap-dragging. Two types of construction are triggered by vertices, and three types of construction are triggered by segments. They are:

> **Vertex Constructions**: Construct a line of a specified slope through the vertex, or construct a circle of a specified radius centered on the vertex.

> **Segment Constructions**: Construct the two lines (one on each side) that are parallel to the segment, at a specified distance from it, or construct the two lines (one from each end) that make a specified angle with the segment, or construct the midpoint of the segment.

From the five constructions, we have most of the power of the seven basic relationships. The vertex constructions give us *slope* and *distance*. The segment constructions give us *parallel* lines, *angles*, and one form of *distance ratio* (midpoint). *Vectors* can be made by using slope and distance constructions at the same time. Vertical and horizontal lines at known x and y coordinates are not triggered by vertices or segments but can be requested by a separate mechanism.

The user activates alignment objects by selecting the appropriate slopes, radii, angles, and offset distances from menus, and by turning midpoint construction on or off. New values can be added to the menus by typing them in or by measuring existing slopes, radii, angles, and offset distances in the scene (see section 4.2).

It is important to note that the system is not really guessing which alignment lines to construct; it is acting on requests from the user. We found this was essential for user acceptance. A large number of alignment objects can quickly become overwhelming. We provide several ways for the user to disable the alignment objects: gravity can be turned off, so that the alignment objects do not attract the caret; all hot objects can be made cold; all selected slopes, radii, angles, and offset distances can be deselected; and the heuristics can be turned off.

4.2 Measuring

It is clear how to use our alignment objects to construct line segments of known slope or known length. However, it is less clear how to perform constructions involving relative values such as making line B parallel to line A, where the slope of line A is unknown. One technique that is easy for the programmer to implement and easy for the user to understand, is to allow the user to measure scene quantities.

To make two segments parallel, for example, it suffices to measure the slope of one segment and then adjust the other segment to have the same slope. Solving the problem in this way takes about the same number of keystrokes as it would take to set up and solve the constraint in a constraint-based system, where the user would point at both segments, choose the parallel constraint, and invoke the constraint solver. Figure 12 shows the use of measuring to make one segment parallel to another.

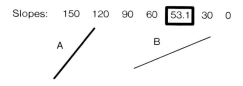

Figure 12(a) Measure the slope of line A, 53.1 degrees, and add it to the menu. Activate alignment lines of this slope.

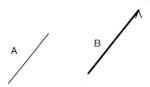

Figure 12(b) Snap one end of segment B onto the new 53.1 degree alignment line to make B parallel to A.

In Gargoyle, the distance between a pair of points, the slope between a pair of points, the angle made by three points, and the distance from a point to a line can be measured and added to the appropriate menu by placing the caret successively on the points of interest and invoking a measuring command.

4.3 Performance

Snap-dragging requires significant rendering and computing resources. Each time the user begins a new operation, all alignment objects must be displayed in less than a second. During transformations, affected objects must move smoothly as they are dragged into position. An additional real-time computational burden is the calculation of points of intersection among all alignment objects whenever the set of alignment objects changes. How can these computations be performed in a reasonable amount of time?

One observation is that the set of alignment objects doesn't usually change much from one moment to the next. Making a vertex hot will add a few alignment objects. Beginning to drag an object will remove any alignment objects that were triggered by its segments and vertices. It makes sense to keep a scan-converted version of the alignment lines around and make small changes to that. Furthermore, we know which line slopes and circle radii are currently of interest. These lines and circles can be scan-converted in advance and then stamped onto the screen as a block of pixels when they are needed. This is already a practical solution for bi-level displays and will become so for color displays.

The problem of smooth motion during dragging is addressed in many commercial systems. Common solutions include reducing detail during dragging (show only a bounding box), or rendering the moving objects into a bitmap that is repeatedly repositioned. These same tricks can be used for snap-dragging.

Calculating the points of intersection of the alignment lines and circles is not particularly time consuming. However, finding the intersections of alignment objects with scene objects and of scene objects with scene objects can be time consuming, since scene objects can be spline curves and other complicated shapes. This cost can be reduced by using spatial sorting techniques (bounding boxes or grids) and by computing only on demand; the intersection calculation can be performed only when both the scene object and the alignment line are within the gravity field of the caret. This same trick can be used to compute the intersections of scene objects with themselves.

5. Conclusion

There are three construction techniques used in computer illustration systems. Grid systems have been commercial successes because they are easy to learn and implement. Constraint-based systems are constantly discussed in the literature because of their great power. We have shown that ruler and compass style construction systems are a viable compromise. Most of the advantages that we claim for snap-dragging are advantages of the ruler and compass approach. In particular, it handles a wide range of alignment types, works at any rotation and scaling, and provides constraints that are easy to add, delete, and modify.

These ideas are beginning to show up in commercial products. Qubix Graphics Systems has begun to demonstrate a technical illustration workstation that employs the ruler, compass, and protractor paradigm.

The obvious drawback of a construction approach is that setting up the constructions may take a long time. Snap-dragging tries to reduce construction time by taking advantage of the repetition that is present in many constructions; often the same slope or distance is needed repeatedly or a polygon's vertex is aligned with other vertices of that same polygon. We believe that snap-dragging is almost as easy to learn as grids, while providing most of the power of constraint systems.

While ruler and compass construction is not inherently computationally expensive, snap-dragging is; many alignment objects must be drawn and many intersection points must be computed. However, the computational requirements are bounded, because the user will turn off alignment objects when the screen becomes too cluttered. Improvements in graphics hardware will make the technique feasible in low-cost workstations in the near future.

Below, we include a number of pictures that have been produced with Gargoyle. Currently, only straight line and arc scene objects are implemented. Figure 13, "Gargoyle Hacker", shows some of the types of precision that snap-dragging makes possible. The fingers of the gargoyle and many of the lines in its wings are parallel even though at odd angles. The bands on the arm are parallel and end exactly on the arm. The gargoyle's pedestal contains a piece of a hexagon. Snap-dragging can be used for traditional ruler and compass constructed letters, as illustrated in figure 14, and for less conventional letters as illustrated in figure 15.

5.1 Future work

Work is in progress to extend snap-dragging to the editing of free-form curves and to three-dimensional objects.

We can easily introduce curves such as Bezier splines that are controlled by points, since we can already place points precisely. In addition, we would like to extend our system to make alignments based on the local tangent to a curve to provide a simple way to position objects on curves themselves, without using control points.

One of the motivations for our work on interactive two-dimensional editing is to develop better ways to edit objects quickly in three-dimensions. In three dimensions, the grid approach is impractical because drawing a full three dimensional grid puts so many lines on the screen that the user has trouble identifying the proper grid point, and notifying the system of the point chosen. Constraint-based approaches are also difficult to use. Some progress has been made in MIT's Mechanical Engineering Department towards using constraints in three dimensions to alter dimensions in mechanical assemblies [Lin81] [Serrano84]. It is more difficult to use constraints to provide a quick-sketch capability. In three dimensions, there is an explosion of degrees of freedom that need to be constrained, requiring a large number of constraints. A modified version of snap-dragging may be successful in providing a precise three-dimensional quick-sketch capability.

Acknowledgments

Eric Bier gratefully acknowledges support from an AT&T Bell Laboratories fellowship and from a Xerox PARC research internship. Both authors are indebted to Xerox PARC for the research environment which made this work possible. We would also like to thank Ken Pier for his many contributions to Gargoyle and for his helpful comments on this paper. Finally, thanks to Subhana Menis for meticulous proof-reading under pressure.

References

[Borning79] Alan Borning. *Thinglab – A Constraint-Oriented Simulation Laboratory.* Revised Ph.D. thesis, Report SSL-79-3, Xerox PARC, Palo Alto, CA 94304, July 1979. Also available as Stanford CS Dept. Report STAN-CS-79-746.

[Goines82] David Lance Goines. *A Constructed Roman Alphabet.* David R. Godine, publisher. 306 Dartmouth Street, Boston MA 02116. 1982.

[Lin81] V. C. Lin, D. C. Gossard, and R. A. Light. Variational geometry in computer-aided design. *Computer Graphics* 15(3):171-177, August 1981. SIGGRAPH '81 Proceedings.

[Lipkie82] Daniel E. Lipkie, Steven R. Evans, John K. Newlin, and Robert L. Weissman. StarGraphics: an object-oriented implementation. *Computer Graphics* 16(3):115-124, July 1982. SIGGRAPH '82 Proceedings.

[MacDraw84] MacDraw Manual. Apple Computer, Inc. 20525 Mariani Ave., Cupertino, CA 95014. 1984.

[Nelson85] Greg Nelson. Juno, a constraint-based graphics system. *Computer Graphics* 19(3):235-243, July 1985. SIGGRAPH '85 Proceedings.

[Newman79] William M. Newman and Robert F. Sproull. *Principles of Interactive Computer Graphics,* chapter 12. McGraw Hill, second edition, 1979.

[Opperman84] Mark Opperman. A Gremlin Tutorial for the SUN Workstation. Internal document, EECS Department, UC Berkeley, Berkeley CA 94720.

[Pavlidis85] Theo Pavlidis and Christopher J. VanWyk. An automatic beautifier for drawings and illustrations. *Computer Graphics* 19(3):225-234. SIGGRAPH '85 Proceedings.

[Pier83] Kenneth A. Pier. A retrospective on the Dorado, a high-performance personal computer. Proceedings of the 10th Symposium on Computer Architecture, SigArch/IEEE, Stockholm, pages 252-269, June 1983.

[Serrano84] David Serrano. MATHPAK: An interactive preliminary design system. Master's thesis, MIT Mechanical Engineering Department, 1984.

[Swinehart85] Daniel C. Swinehart, Polle T. Zellweger, and Robert B. Hagmann. The structure of Cedar, SIGPLAN Notices 20(7):230-244, July 1985. Proceedings of the ACM SIGPLAN 85 Symposium on Language Issues in Programming Environments.

[Stone80] Maureen Stone. How to use Griffin. Internal Memo, Xerox PARC, 3333 Coyote Hill Rd, Palo Alto CA 94304. 1980.

[Sutherland84] Ivan E. Sutherland. Sketchpad, a man-machine graphical communication system. In Herbert Freeman, editor, *Tutorial and Selected Readings in Interactive Computer Graphics,* pages 2-19. IEEE Computer Society, Silver Spring, MD, 1984. Reprinted from AFIPS 1963.

Figure 13 The Gargoyle Hacker. (drawn by Maureen Stone)

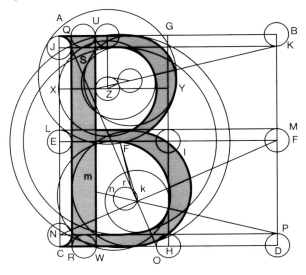

Figure 14 A constructed Roman letter B. The steps of the construction were taken from a book of constructed Roman letters, by David Lance Goines [Goines82]. (drawn by Eric Bier)

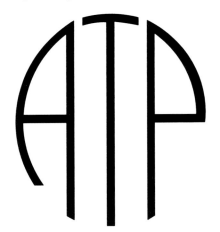

Figure 15   A logo for the Ridge Vineyards Advanced Tasting Program. (drawn by Ken Pier & Maureen Stone)

A Multitasking Switchboard Approach to User Interface Management

Peter P. Tanner[†], Stephen A. MacKay, Darlene A. Stewart,
and Marceli Wein

Laboratory for Intelligent Systems
National Research Council of Canada
Ottawa, Ontario K1A 0R8 Canada

Abstract

A Switchboard model of user input management is presented which takes advantage of opportunities afforded by a multitasking multiprocessor programming environment. This model further separates application programming from the programming of the interaction dialogues as compared with conventional user interface management systems. It also provides powerful tools for implementing parallel forms of input, is suitable for managing interaction in window-based systems, and is very flexible.

The paper describes this Switchboard model and its implementation on top of the Harmony operating system, as well as discussing some of the graphics support needed for the model.

CR Categories and Subject Descriptors: D.1.3 [**Programming Techniques**]: Concurrent Programming; D.2.2 [**Software Engineering**]: Tools and Techniques — *user interfaces*; D.4.1 [**Operating Systems**]: Process Management — *concurrency, multiprocessing/multi-programming, synchronization*; D.4.7 [**Operating Systems**]: Organization and Design — *real-time systems*; I.3.2 [**Computer Graphics**]: Graphics Systems — *distributed/network graphics*; I.3.4 [**Computer Graphics**]: Graphics Utilities — *graphics packages, software support*; I.3.6 [**Computer Graphics**]: Methodology and Techniques — *device independence, ergonomics, interaction techniques.*

General Terms: Algorithms, Design, Human Factors.

Additional Keywords and Phrases: input model, message passing, parallel input, user interface management systems, workstations.

[†] current address: Computer Graphics Laboratory
University of Waterloo
Waterloo, Ontario N2L 3G1 Canada.

NRC number: 25635

ISBN   0-89791-196-2

Introduction

The development of Adagio, a workstation to support research in intelligent robotics, draws on current research in multitasking/multiprocessing, window management, and user interface management and thereby leads to a novel approach to the programming model of the workstation.

Adagio is implemented as a large number of cooperating tasks (currently about 50 tasks are simultaneously active at any one time). Each of these tasks is associated with one of: a screen window, a tablet window, a scarce resource such as a device or data structure, or alternatively, acts as a courier between other tasks.

One of the tasks, the Switchboard, is responsible for connecting tasks which consume input to tasks which produce it. This responsibility extends to coordinating the flow of input so that fresh input is available, that redundant input is discarded, that tasks are provided with connections to the devices they require at task creation or on request, and that these connections are closed when a task is destroyed.

After discussing the goals of the Switchboard approach to user input management, this paper describes the Switchboard model — illustrating the multitasking approach, the window management facility and the user interface possibilities. Most importantly, the paper will show that these three concepts are complementary and lead to the development of a powerful user interface management system (UIMS), notable both for its flexibility and its support for parallel user input.

Input Management Goals

The design of the software that supports the computer-human interface has been greatly influenced by the ideas and goals put forward by researchers in User Interface Management Systems (UIMS's) [10, 15]. Studies of UIMS approaches have established the advantages of separating the application from the interaction programming, where this interaction programming is done using the assistance of a UIMS. Because a UIMS permits rapid prototyping, an iterative style of specifying the interactive dialogue is encouraged. The implementor may try out several possible interaction techniques on potential users, evaluate them, and then select the one that is the most appropriate. In addition to providing an easy prototyping capability, UIMS designers strive to make a variety of input techniques available to the implementor.

The goals for Adagio's input control include:
- the separation of interaction programming from application programming
- the availability of easily modifiable connections between the

input requirements of the application and the input devices (we use the term *device* to mean either a physical or a virtual device)

• a facility that encourages the implementation of several input streams, all active in parallel

Multitasking

Tasking Model

The Switchboard UIMS model is based on and depends on Harmony, a multitasking realtime operating system with rapid intertask message passing developed at the National Research Council of Canada [7]. A program in Harmony is typically composed of many tasks. A task is often used as one would use a subroutine in a conventional O/S, except that an instance of the task must be explicitly created, and once it has been created it executes independently of, and in parallel with, the task that created it. (Executing in parallel is, of course, only strictly possible on a multiprocessor — the current implementation of Adagio runs on a single processor. Harmony, however, is a multiprocessor operating system where the tasking operations are accomplished in a uniform manner whether the tasks involved are on the same or different processors, so few problems are foreseen for the planned expansion to a multiprocessor).

Tasks communicate and synchronize with each other using the send-receive-reply mechanism. The primitives are similar to those used in Thoth, the forerunner of Harmony, described previously at SIGGRAPH by Beach et al [1], although Harmony supports variable length messages rather than being limited to fixed length messages for task communication. In brief, a task may send information or may send a request for information to another task with the blocking _Send primitive. The recipient of the message, which receives the message with a _Receive or a _Try_receive, unblocks the sender by replying using the _Reply primitive. The _Receive primitive causes the receiving task to block if no incoming messages are queued; _Try_receive, on the other hand, never blocks. With either receive primitive, the programmer can specify whether a message may be accepted from any task or from some specific task. Note that a task need not reply to the previous message it received before receiving the next; replies may be issued in any order and at any time the recipient sees fit.

A message passing system such as Harmony makes a multitasking approach to programming feasible as the programmer is provided with an easy to use and intuitive tasking model whose message passing and other tasking operations are accomplished very rapidly. A send-receive-reply sequence in Harmony takes about 1 ms. Beach et al [1] demonstrate the value and effectiveness of the multitasking message-based approach for building an interactive application. As will be described below, the multitasking environment makes possible a much closer relationship among windows and lays the groundwork for the Switchboard UIMS.

Servers

In addition to facilitating the use of many small tasks, Harmony encourages the use of *servers* to provide various sorts of services, such as the managing of scarce resources. These servers, all individual and separate tasks, are modelled on the *administrator* concept [6]. An administrator normally does not send messages (it only receives and replies to requests), and it often relies on one or more worker tasks (which send it requests for work to do) to manipulate the resource it owns and to perform major computations, freeing up the administrator task to process the *client* requests as quickly as possible. The scarce resources controlled by Adagio servers include input devices,

data structures, and the graphics display list. The Switchboard itself, as will be illustrated below, is a server.

An illustrative example of a server is the one used to manage tablet input (Figure 1). Clients of the Tablet Server, which are of course tasks themselves, each send messages requesting tablet input from a specific window. These requests are responded to when the tablet pen is in the appropriate window, but held for later, thus blocking the client, when the pen is in another window. A worker task, the Tablet Notifier, which communicates directly with the Tablet Interrupt Handler, sends a message to the Tablet Server whenever the pen changes significantly in position or status. The Tablet Server, following the administrator concept, is never blocked from processing requests. It is always either waiting for a request or processing one. The request processing may result in zero or more replies, not necessarily including one to the sender.

If a server wishes to communicate with another server, it usually does so through a *courier* which it may create for the purpose. Such couriers are used between the Switchboard and the device servers.

Servers provide for a highly structured design with controlled access to resources. The server concept simplifies complex systems and is fundamental in the design of Adagio.

Window Management

Windows

The implementation of windows in the Adagio system reflects Adagio's goals of supporting robot simulation and programming. In many window-based systems, windows are viewports for disjoint applications, some disjoint to the degree that each window runs a different shell or instance of the operating system. On the other hand, all Adagio windows assist in the single job of creating and manipulating a data structure defining the robot, its environment, and the robot's tasks. Consequently there is a much tighter coupling among the windows.

Because Adagio is implemented on an Adage 3000, a high performance raster graphics device with 24 bits per pixel, the difficulties involved in rasterops and the large memory requirements for such a system led to the use of a tiled window approach rather than the use of overlapping windows. (This decision is supported by the experimental work of Bly and Rosenberg [2]).

There are two fundamentally different types of windows supported by the Adagio system, one for text and 2D symbolic graphics, the second for the display of three dimensional views of the robot and its environment. Using the multitasking approach, there is a single task associated with each 2D window, whether it be a menu window, a virtual device echo

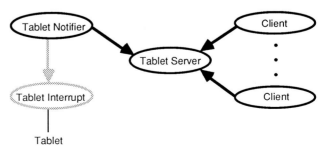

Figure 1. The Tablet Server. (Note that arrow-heads point away from the task making the request.)

window (described below under Virtual Devices) or some other interaction window. Because each 3D window displays a graphic representation of the current state of the single data structure describing the robot and its environment and, with the multitasking approach to the workstation, it is quite feasible that more than one task would need to update or query the structure representing the 3D geometric data, a single task, the Data Structure Server, is given control over what is to be displayed in all the 3D windows.

The Data Structure Server

To guarantee a tight coupling between the 3D windows and the data structure they display, and to prevent corruption of the data from concurrent accesses, the data structure is known only to a single task, the Data Structure Server. All requests for data structure updates and for information from the data structure are fielded by the Data Structure Server (Figure 2). This serialization of accesses to the data structure is not considered a bottleneck because of the low amount of processing performed by the Data Structure Server for each request.

Any update that requires a modification of the screen image is forwarded by the Data Structure Server to the Graphics Server (described below). To avoid blocking the Data Structure Server, these updates are passed via the Display List Courier. When a major portion of the graphics data structure must be sent to the Graphics Server for the creation of the display list, this is done by sending a pointer to the structure, thus making the structure temporarily known to another task. (Such sharing of a data structure can always be done among tasks running in the same processor. It can also be done among tasks executing in different processors of a multiprocessor with shared memory.) Until the Display List Courier reports the completion of the screen update, the Data Structure Server will satisfy only 3D data information requests. Requests to change the data will be held until it is safe to do so.

The Graphics Server

Both the Data Structure Server and the 2D window tasks request modifications to the display by sending messages to the Graphics Server. This server replaces the graphics subroutine package traditionally used in a single-task graphics program. Running as an independent task with the role of managing the frame buffer and the Adage bitslice processor, the Graphics Server handles three classes of request messages — window management messages, 2D graphics messages, and 3D graphics messages (Figure 3).

Window management messages come from three distinct sources. The Window Manipulator task, as the coordinator of the arrangement of windows on the display, requests changes in

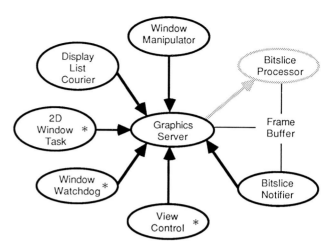

Figure 3. The Graphics Server. (* denotes that there may be multiple instances of the task.)

the positions of windows. View Control tasks are responsible for requesting changes in the viewing parameters associated with each window. Window Watchdog tasks ask that they be informed (via a _Reply) of any changes to their respective windows.

The 2D graphics messages request text or symbolic output to be directed to the screen window associated with the requesting task. The server is responsible for translating from the virtual coordinate system of the requestor to the screen coordinates of its window. If required, the messages to a window may be stored and then reinterpreted if the window is modified in size, or if a picture segment that potentially blocks other segments is moved. This is different from many other tiled window systems that require the application running in the window to become involved with the redraw of a window that has been changed in size.

The 3D graphics messages are in the form of commands for the Graphics Server to modify the display list. The display list is in turn interpreted by the Adage bitslice processor to render the 3D image into the frame buffer [8]. The microcode running in the bitslice processor is not strictly speaking a Harmony task, using shared memory for communication rather than the send-receive-reply message passing primitives. However, it can still be viewed externally like any other independent Adagio task. The Graphics Server acts as an *agent* task, as described by Plebon and Booth [11], for the task running in the bitslice processsor, providing an interface to the other processor and managing the communication between and the shared resources of the two processors. Because requests for the bitslice processor to update the display list are buffered by the Graphics Server until the bitslice is ready to begin another update, client tasks requesting the services of the Graphics Server do not remain blocked for long. To prevent the Graphics Server from wasting time monitoring the shared memory, a worker task, the Bitslice Notifier, is responsible for checking the condition of the bitslice processor and informing the Graphics Server when the bitslice processor has finished.

The display list supports multiple views of a single environment where these views may differ in their viewpoints as well as their display parameters. Using different display parameters for different 3D windows permits, for example, the posting of shaded images of the robot in one window and a simple stick figure of only the axes of rotation of each of the joints in another — both rendered from the same display list.

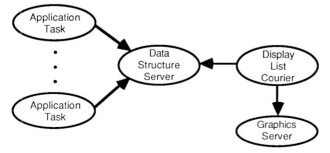

Figure 2. Task structure for 3D graphics.

The Switchboard

Introduction

The Switchboard model of interactive programming has, for its goal, the handling of user input in a multitasking window-based environment. It was therefore designed to handle many sources of user input (be they physical or virtual devices), and to properly direct each input to the appropriate task, selected from the many tasks that may request input.

The idea of several tasks requesting input through a single program entity is not new. Enderle, in his Seeheim workshop report on the interface of the UIMS to the application [4], describes the relationship shown in Figure 4 — a UIMS funnelling input to a set of application modules executing in parallel. Conventional operating systems provide a mechanism through which input device information flows to several tasks. However, the restricted nature of this flow and the difficulty in developing abstractions of input that easily coexist results in a far less flexible situation than is provided by the Switchboard model. These difficulties have, for example, resulted in the paucity of implementations of the full GKS level 2C input model [12]. The Switchboard, together with Harmony, provides a more appropriate base for a UIMS.

The Switchboard is a task that communicates with both clients (tasks requiring input from user controllable peripherals) and device couriers (tasks that provide this input) (Figure 5). Clients are often application tasks in that they use information from the input peripherals in order to determine how to carry out their assigned functions. Device couriers, on the other hand, provide a link between the Switchboard and the device servers or handlers. In the message passing paradigm, the courier alternates between sending requests to the server to acquire input values, and sending messages to the Switchboard to report these values. The device servers and the Switchboard are never request-blocked, as they never send messages, they only receive them and reply to them.

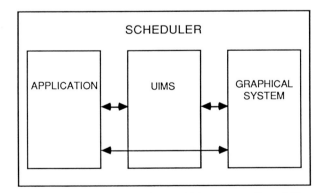

Figure 4. UIMS structure for parallel processes (from [4]).

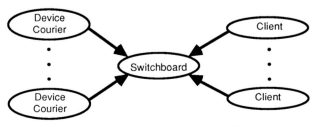

Figure 5. The Switchboard task.

The role of the Switchboard is to manage the connections between clients and device couriers. When a client requests a connection to a certain device, it is the Switchboard that determines to which courier it will be connected. (This association of device and task can be done at either link time or run time.) The Switchboard then directs the subsequent communication between the client and the device courier.

Input Example

To illustrate how a Switchboard input communication proceeds, imagine a user wishing to control the viewpoint of a specific window using a trackball. After the user has used an interactive menu-based dialogue to specify this connection, the Switchboard starts transmitting the trackball information from the Trackball Courier to the Window Viewpoint task, an example of a View Control task (Figure 6).

Messages are then passed along this communication path in the following manner:
1. The Trackball Courier requests input from the Trackball Server.
2. The Trackball Server holds its reply, thus blocking this path, until the trackball has moved a significant amount since the previous input request. A reply containing the current trackball data is then passed to the Trackball Courier.
3. The Trackball Courier sends the data on to the Switchboard.
4. The Switchboard forwards the data to the client task which had requested the connection to the trackball (Window Viewpoint). This forwarding is in the form of a reply to a READ_REQUEST message from the Window Viewpoint task.
5. The Window Viewpoint task then calculates what the new viewing transformation should be, and sends this to the Graphics Server. After the Graphics Server replies, the Window Viewpoint task again makes a READ_REQUEST to the Switchboard.
6. On receipt of the READ_REQUEST, the Switchboard replies to the Trackball Courier, thus releasing it to try to get more input from the Trackball Server.

When the user is ignoring the trackball, this connection uses almost no CPU time, only that required for the server to monitor the trackball. What is more significant for both programmer and user is that this connection is independent of other tasks running on the system both in terms of the setup of the information flow and the subsequent timing of the flow. This connection may be made at any time during an interactive dialogue, and, once made, the trackball will control the viewpoint of the window no matter what the user is doing with the window. He may be using one application module to define a robot, switch to

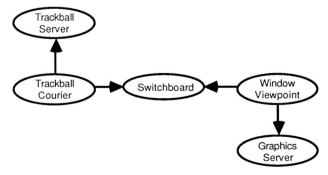

Figure 6. Example of Switchboard mediated use of a trackball.

another to specify a robot movement, then use a third to view a simulation of the movement, during which time his connection will remain in force and be usable. The application modules are unaware of the connection, they are dealing only with the modification of data bases, and not with how the data is to be displayed.

Switchboard Functionality

The Switchboard, following the administrator model, processes incoming messages. A client sends the Switchboard READ_ REQUEST messages asking for input from any of the devices to which it is connected as well as messages requesting that new connections be established between itself (the client) and other devices. Device couriers, on the other hand, send messages containing *significant* input from their respective devices. The functioning of the Switchboard is then best explained by describing its reactions to the arrival of its various messages.

Input message arrival: The Switchboard has access to information about each input message that arrives and about each courier with which it corresponds. Each input structure (there are different structures depending on whether the input is a valuator, a 2D or 3D locator, a string, etc.) has, as a header, the structure IN_STD (Figure 7). In addition, each task corresponding with a server such as the Switchboard is registered with that server, and this registration results in a connection record being created. The Switchboard can look up the connection record for a device courier which includes a pointer to an instance of the COURIER structure (Figure 8).

Task selection: On the arrival of an input message, the Switchboard must select the task to which the message will be forwarded. There is not necessarily a simple one to one, courier to client correspondence as perhaps has been implied to this point. Three types of task selection are possible. If the courier is a TASK_COURIER, it is indeed the case where a single client task has requested a connection to a specific device. This client's ID is listed in the TASK_INFO portion of the COURIER structure.

The Switchboard, based on UIMS concepts, supports the idea of application modules being called on by the system to perform specific application functions [4, 15], often in response to menu selections by the user. This results in a relaxation of the concept of the client task to that of a *client set*. A client set is a set of application tasks called upon to perform certain duties. The client set tasks for a window form a task stack controlled by the menu system associated with that window (described by Tanner et al [14]). For any particular window, the *input active* task (the task ready to accept input) is on top of the task stack for the client set. Input directed at the window will therefore be sent to this top task. Device couriers whose messages are to be treated in this way are of type CLIENT_SET_COURIER.

The final method of task selection is necessitated by the existence of only a single keyboard and a single button box at the workstation. Ideally, one would prefer to have a keyboard for each window, but this is physically impractical. To compensate, a keyboard icon is placed on the screen. All keyboard input and certain button box selections (such as HELP and UNDO) are sent to the client (or client set) associated with the window displaying the keyboard icon. (This still results in the problem, particularly during debugging, that one cannot type to tasks not associated with a window.) Couriers for the keyboard and the button box are of type SYSTEM_COURIER. In this case the client (set) associated with the window containing the keyboard icon is chosen.

Message queueing or forwarding: If the selected task is waiting for input when the input message arrives, the message is simply forwarded to that task, thus unblocking it, and the ID of the courier is placed in the client's TASK_INFO structure. The courier itself is not replied to and so remains blocked. If the selected task is busy processing input from some other device, the input message is placed in a FIFO queue linked to the client's TASK_INFO structure, and again the courier remains blocked.

Client's READ_REQUEST: When a client has finished processing an input message, it requests new input from the Switchboard. On receipt of this request, the Switchboard

```
struct IN_STD
    {
        uint_16          MSG_SIZE;          /* message size - in all Harmony messages */
        int_16           MSG_TYPE;          /* message type - in all Harmony messages */
        struct IN_STD    *IN_NEXT;          /* to link to next input in list */
        struct IN_STD    *IN_PREV;          /* to link to previous input in list */
        uint_32          *IN_WINDOW;        /* window pointer */
        uint_32          IN_COURIER_ID;     /* ID of courier providing input */
        int_16           IN_VIRTUAL_ID;     /* device ID known to client */
        uint_32          IN_CONNECTION;     /* Connection ID for the Switchboard */
    };
```

Figure 7. The header for all input messages.

```
struct COURIER
    {
        struct COURIER     *COU_NEXT;           /* pointer to next courier in list */
        struct COURIER     *COU_PREV;           /* pointer to previous courier in list */
        union START_MSG    *COU_START_MSG;      /* start-up message for the courier */
        struct CLIENT_SET  *COU_CLIENT_SET;     /* pointer for CLIENT_SET_COURIER */
        struct TASK_INFO   *COU_TASK_INFO;      /* pointer for TASK_COURIER */
        uint_16            COU_TYPE;            /* CLIENT_SET_COURIER, TASK_COURIER,
                                                   or SYSTEM_COURIER */
    };
```

Figure 8. The COURIER structure.

replies to the device courier associated with the input that the task received in its previous request, thus unblocking the courier. This is to say that a courier, on presenting the Switchboard with input, is blocked until not only the client has received the input, but until it has processed the data and then asked for more. This prevents the problem of input coming in faster than it can be handled.

After freeing the courier, the Switchboard either replies to the client with input from the input queue (logging the ID of the courier of the new input) or, if the queue is empty, logs the fact that the client is waiting, and blocks it by not replying to it.

Task Destruction: In Harmony, when a task is destroyed, all servers to which it is connected are informed. The Switchboard, on the death of a client, discards all pending input and replies to all blocked device couriers for that client, after destroying those couriers associated exclusively with the dying task.

In addition to these message handling capabilities, the Switchboard is also responsible for creating and destroying tasks as a service for the menu servers. It can be thought of as being responsible for many of the services normally assigned to a conventional operating system, but with the ability to carry out these operations in a highly flexible manner, more suited to multitasking.

Switchboard Attributes

Parallel Input

As most of us have two hands and two feet, and as we are capable of using more than one of these appendages at the same time, a fact normally ignored by interactive systems designers, we can certainly make use of more than one input device at a time [3, 13].

Implementation of parallel input with several devices active at the same time is achieved in two complementary ways. First, several application tasks can be executing at any one time, each reacting to the inputs from one or more devices. This is called *simultaneous input* because the user may control several different things simultaneously. Second, each of these application tasks can receive input from any of several input devices to which a connection was established through the Switchboard. In this case, referred to as *user's-choice input*, the task can offer the user more than one device with which to perform a single operation, the choice of which to use being entirely left up to the user, e.g. type point coordinates to define a point, or alternatively, use the tablet to define a point. The manner in which a task requests input encourages the programmer to offer the user alternative input techniques. Adagio's implementation of this second form of parallelism modifies the programmer's model of input. This is an attempt to break away from the idea that the user input is a single stream that can be parsed. In Adagio, as mentioned before, the only input instruction available to application tasks is READ_REQUEST. This request is always sent to the Switchboard which replies with a message containing input from any one of the devices to which the task is connected or with a system message.

The underlying model of READ_REQUEST is an elaboration of the model present in GKS level 2C [12]. GKS specifies three modes of implementing input: request, await event, and sample. The first is the classical FORTRAN approach in a time-sharing environment, and is of no interest here. The second mode permits a task to await an input event that is triggered by operator action. In this await event mode, a task can wait for the next event produced by one of a number of

devices. However, the task will only be given the device values, such as tablet coordinate values, when the corresponding device is triggered. In the case of a tablet, the trigger would be the push of the puck button. The third mode permits the task to loop, sampling one or more input devices repetitively. In our model these latter two modes are merged. Devices make available the most recent value, as in sample mode, but only if that value is *significantly* different from the previous sample (akin to event mode).

Taking the example of a regular application task associated with a window on the screen, it is, by default, connected through the Switchboard to the tablet and to the keyboard. It may also have requested connections to other devices (Figure 9). Inputs from these devices are then passed on to the application task as replies to READ_REQUESTs. A courier that provides input to the Switchboard is blocked from fetching more input until the application task has accepted its previous input message, processed it, and requested input again. One consequence is that the system menu manager may well receive input from the terminal keyboard instead of the tablet. This possibility encouraged the implementor to allow the user to make his selections with either device — giving the user two ways of accomplishing the same thing.

Because a program is made up of many tasks, not all the input to the entire program is interleaved in a single stream; only the input for each task is. Therefore the merging of input directly supports the making of several devices available to control some single aspect of the system.

Delivering all input to each task through a common interface is an experiment which we hope will result in a different attitude among programmers and in better styles of interaction.

System Commands

Tasks that consume input are programmed to expect this input from any of a number of devices — the choice of which device to use at any time is the user's. In addition to input data there are system commands that must be sent asynchronously to these tasks. These commands include such messages as SUSPEND (a task may be suspended when the user wishes to work on something else, and then resume the operation), RESUME, COMMIT_SUICIDE (the user has called for the cessation of the current operation and the task must now stop

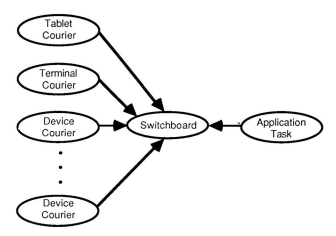

Figure 9. An application task (or Switchboard client) corresponding to a screen window is connected, through the Switchboard to the tablet, a terminal, and possibly to other input devices.

what it was doing and clear away any side-effects before dying), UNDO, and HELP. In all cases, system command messages are put into the client task's input stream so that they are passed on to the task as if they were input messages. In addition to simplifying the application programming, this technique also forces the programmer to handle each of these messages. At the very least, the programmer must consciously decide to include code that ignores the messages — although COMMIT_SUICIDE may not be ignored.

Of course, all these commands are the direct or indirect result of some user action. However, they are actions on devices not specifically connected with the receiving task necessitating their being treated separately with additional mediation by the Switchboard.

Aging of input

One may note that input may remain queued during the time a client is processing input from another device, thus possibly resulting in delayed response to user actions. The possibility of such delay is handled on the servers' side of the Switchboard by ensuring that each value from a device that is sent along the communication path reflects an accumulation of changes to the device since the previous reading. On the clients' side, the problem is usually minimized by the small amount of processing required to respond to most inputs. In the case of computing intensive tasks, the client is programmed as an *overseer* which creates a worker task that actually performs the calculations. The overseer can then respond to input as it deems fit. In particular, an overseer can react to the COMMIT_SUICIDE or UNDO system commands in the input stream by killing the worker it has created, and removing its unfinished work.

Multiwindow Tablet

A tasking mechanism for a multiwindow approach to the tablet illustrates a typical use of the Switchboard. The tablet, a single input device, must be viewed by a window-based system as a set of virtual locator devices, one device for each window, and one for the tracker if the tablet tracker is to be independent of the application tasks (see MacKay and Tanner [9] for a description of the tracker model). To accomplish this, an instance of the Tablet Courier task is created for each window. This task, knowing its allocated tablet real estate, logs a connection with the Tablet Server giving it this information. The Tablet Server will then feed the courier tablet values when the puck or pen is in the appropriate tablet window, and let it know when the user moves on to another window [14]. The Tablet Courier then forwards these input values to the Switchboard, which, knowing to what this courier is connected, will forward the input in turn to the appropriate client task (Figure 10). The Tablet Courier is responsible for translating from the tablet coordinates provided by the Tablet Server, to the coordinates of the window-based virtual tablet. For 3D windows, the courier must provide the definition of a line in three-space represented by the tablet position. The Tablet Courier performs frequent non-blocking _Try_receive's to determine if its Window Watchdog task has sent it a message indicating a new viewing transformation for its window. All consumers of tablet information are unaware of the area on the screen or the tablet they occupy and of the viewing transformations for the 3D windows they may be modifying through the Data Structure Server and the Graphics Server.

Sharing of a Single Device

The Switchboard model illustrates two methods of using a single device simultaneously for several clients. The keyboard, with a single courier, has its input directed by the Switchboard to the client associated with the window in which the keyboard

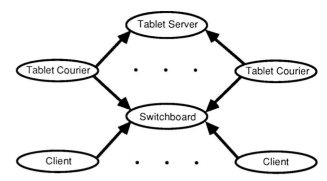

Figure 10. Window based communications between the Tablet Server and the Switchboard.

icon rests. The tablet, on the other hand, has a courier for each window. Each Tablet Courier requests, from the Tablet Server, pen or puck input from a specific region. The courier can then make a window specific transformation of the data before passing it on to the Switchboard.

Both methods are extensible to other devices. One could have device icons for directing input from other devices to specific windows although the screen clutter problem is a limiting factor. Couriers for button boxes or sets of potentiometers might request input from different subsets of the buttons or pots, leaving it to the device server to reply to the appropriate courier when a device is used.

Techniques such as these are essential for multitask implementations of interactive dialogues.

Virtual Devices

Device couriers have been described, up to this point, as tasks that forward input device values to the Switchboard. There is nothing implicit in the system that forces a courier to seek these inputs from an actual device server. Couriers that create user input following some predefined pattern, or that retrieve stored input from a previous session are quite possible. A particularly useful extension to the device courier idea permits the implementation of more complex virtual devices. Virtual devices such as the tablet-based virtual devices described by Evans et al [5] may be implemented in a manner quite invisible to the task that makes use of the resulting values.

To illustrate possible implementations with an example, one can consider a virtual device program that takes locator values and simulates a slider. Figure 11 shows this virtual device acting as a Switchboard client in that it sends a request to the Switchboard for input from the tablet when the pen is in the virtual device's window. After processing the locator input and updating the device echo on the screen, it then acts as a device courier by sending the virtual valuator input to the Switchboard which forwards it to the second client. This client had requested

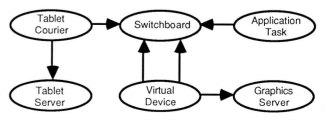

Figure 11. Virtual device implementation.

a connection to a valuator, but the decision of which valuator to use was made at the Switchboard (and hence easily modifiable). The client is ignorant of what physical or virtual device the input is from, save that it is from valuator X as the association was made either by the interaction designer or by the user through an earlier interactive dialogue.

Conclusion

In many ways, interactive graphics and realtime systems have much in common. Consequently, it is reasonable that a realtime operating system be used as the basis for interactive graphics. In realtime work, the processors must be able to respond in a reasonable way to inputs that are sent to them asynchronously from a variety of sources. Although much early work in interactive programming modelled the user as a file that could be read, the realtime model is far more appropriate. The user can, and will, send inputs to a task when he sees fit and using the device he sees fit. In essence, the user is unpredictable.

The Switchboard is an appropriate vehicle for linking a multitasking environment to this set of asynchronous inputs. It, together with the multitasking capability, provides the flexibility to handle parallel input — both the use of several devices to control several parameters simultaneously, and the offering of a choice of several devices to control a single parameter. The Switchboard provides a basis for the implementation of a rich variety of virtual devices allowing, for example, a single device to be used as a set of devices. This approach is particularly useful for interacting with multiwindow systems. It also provides, as does any good model, a design aid where new possibilities of device-task communication become apparent.

In addition, the Switchboard simplifies the implementation of logically consistent interactions. For example, control of window viewing parameters and values in the data structure is independent of the application tasks running in the system. Consequently, the definition of the interaction control remains in effect from one application to the next.

As presented in this paper, the concept of multitasking extends to the entire application. Thus it represents a major restructuring of the application program. However, the process can also be evolutionary, whereby the Switchboard and the Harmony kernel could be embedded in a dedicated processor. The rest of the application program could then remain in the more traditional form on the workstation host processor.

The multiprocessor capabilities of the Switchboard and Harmony permit the implementation of the ideal form of time-sharing, whereby all the processors time-share the user rather than users time-sharing a processor.

Bibliography

[1] Beach, R.J., Beatty, J.C., Booth, K.S., Fiume, E.L., and Plebon, D.A. The message is the medium: Multiprocess structuring of an interactive paint program. *Computer Graphics* 16, 3 (July 1982), 277-287.

[2] Bly, S.A. and Rosenberg, J.K. A comparison of tiled and overlapping windows. *Proc. CHI'86 Human Factors in Computing Systems*, Boston (Apr. 1986), 101-106.

[3] Buxton, W.A.S. There's more to interaction than meets the eye. *User Centered System Design, New Perspectives in Human Computer Interaction*, D.A. Norman and S.W. Draper (Ed.), Lawrence Erlbaum Associates, Hillsdale, NJ (in press).

[4] Enderle, G. Report on the interface of the UIMS to the application. in [10], 21-29.

[5] Evans, K.B., Tanner, P.P., and Wein, M. Tablet-based valuators that provide one, two, or three degrees of freedom. *Computer Graphics* 15, 3 (Aug. 1981), 91-97.

[6] Gentleman, W.M. Message passing between sequential processes: the reply primitive and the administrator concept. *Software Pract. & Exper.* 11,5 (May 1981), 436-66.

[7] Gentleman, W.M. Using the Harmony operating system. Report of DEE, National Research Council of Canada, NRCC-ERB-966, Ottawa, Ont. (Dec. 1983, revised May 1985).

[8] Loo, R. ARIA — A near-real-time graphics package. M.Math Thesis, Univ. of Waterloo, Dept. of Computer Science (1986).

[9] MacKay, S.A. and Tanner, P.P. Graphics tools in Adagio, a robotics multitasking multiprocessor workstation. *Proc. Graphics Interface '86*, Vancouver (May 1986), 98-103.

[10] Pfaff, G.E. (Ed.). *User Interface Management Systems, Proc. Seeheim Workshop on User Interface Management Systems, Nov. 1983*, Springer-Verlag, Berlin (1985).

[11] Plebon, D.A. and Booth, K.S. Interactive picture creation systems. Univ. of Waterloo, Dept. of Computer Science, CS-82-46 (Dec. 1982).

[12] Rosenthal, D.S.H., Michener, J.C., Pfaff, G., Kessener, R., and Sabin, M. The detailed semantics of graphics input devices. *Computer Graphics* 16, 3 (July 1982), 33-43.

[13] Tanner, P.P. and Wein, M. Parallel input in computer-human interaction. *Proc. 18th Annual Meeting, Human Factors Association of Canada*, Hull, Quebec (Sept. 1985), 141-144.

[14] Tanner, P.P., Wein, M., Gentleman, W.M., MacKay, S.A., and Stewart, D.A. The user interface of Adagio, a robotics multitasking multiprocessor workstation. *Proc. 1st International Conference on Computer Workstations*, San Jose (Nov. 1985), 90-98.

[15] Thomas, J.J. and Hamlin, G.H. Graphical input interaction technique workshop summary. *Computer Graphics*, 17, 1 (Jan. 1983), 5-30.

Creating Highly-Interactive and Graphical User Interfaces by Demonstration

Brad A. Myers
and
William Buxton

Dynamic Graphics Project
Computer Systems Research Institute
University of Toronto
Toronto, Ontario, M5S 1A4
Canada

ABSTRACT

It is very time-consuming and expensive to create the graphical, highly-interactive styles of user interfaces that are increasingly common. User Interface Management Systems (UIMSs) attempt to make the creation of user interfaces easier, but most existing UIMSs cannot create the low-level interaction techniques (pop-up, pull-down and fixed menus, on-screen "light buttons", scroll-bars, elaborate feedback mechanisms and animations, etc.) that are frequently used. This paper describes Peridot, a system that automatically creates the code for these user interfaces while the designer *demonstrates* to the system how the interface should look and work. Peridot uses rule-based inferencing so no programming by the designer is required, and Direct Manipulation techniques are used to create Direct Manipulation interfaces, which can make full use of a mouse and other input devices. This allows extremely rapid prototyping of user interfaces.

CR Categories and Subject Descriptors: D.1.2 [**Programming Techniques**]: Automatic Programming; D.2.2 [**Software Engineering**]: Tools and Techniques - *User Interfaces*; I.2.2 [**Artificial Intelligence**]: Automatic Programming - *Program Synthesis*; I.3.6 [**Computer Graphics**]: Methodology and Techniques.

General Terms: Human Factors.

Additional Key Words and Phrases: Programming by Example, Visual Programming, User Interface Design, User Interface Management Systems, Graphical User Interfaces, Direct Manipulation.

1. Introduction

This paper discusses Peridot, a new User Interface Management System (UIMS) currently under development, that can create graphical, highly interactive user interfaces. Peridot stands for Programming by Example for Real-time Interface Design Obviating Typing. It is implemented in Interlisp-D [Xerox 83] on a Xerox DandeTiger (1109) workstation, and allows the user interface designer to create user interfaces by *demonstrating* what the user interface should look like and how the end user will interact with it. This approach frees designers from having to do any programming in the conventional sense, and allows them to design the user interface in a very natural manner. The general strategy of Peridot is to allow the designer to *draw* the screen display that the end user will see, and to perform actions just as the end user would, such as moving a mouse, or pressing a mouse button or keyboard key. The system attempts to guess (or *infer*) the relationship of that action to existing elements of the user interface based on context, and asks the designer if the guess is correct. If so, a piece of code is generated by the system that will handle this action for the end user. If incorrect, other reasonable guesses are tried, or the designer can explicitly specify the relationship.

The guesses are encoded as simple condition-action rules, and the generated code is put into small parameterized procedures to help ensure a structured design of the resulting system. The screen displays and interactions depend on the values of the parameters to the procedures. The procedures created by Peridot can be called from application programs or used in other user interface procedures created by demonstration.

Many user interface designers now draw, typically on paper, scenarios (or "story boards") of how the user interface (UI) will look and act. Unfortunately, it is difficult to get a feeling for how a system works from the paper descriptions, and customers of the user interface are not able to investigate how the system will work. Peridot enhances the design process by supporting extremely rapid prototyping with little more effort than drawing the scenarios on paper. In addition, the user interfaces produced by Peridot are expected to be efficient enough for use in the actual end systems.

Another motivation for this style of specifying user interfaces is that it should be possible to allow non-programmers to design *and implement* the interfaces. This will allow professional UI designers (sometimes called "User Interface Architects" [Foley 84]) and possibly even end users, to design and modify user interfaces with little training and without conventional programming. Virtually all textual UI specification methods are too complicated and program-like to be used by non-programmers [Buxton 83].

The *Direct Manipulation* style of user interfaces [Shneiderman 83][Hutchins 86], where the user typically uses a mouse to select and manipulate objects on the screen, has become very popular (and possibly even predominant) for modern computer systems. Unfortunately, there are virtually no tools available to help develop the low level interaction techniques that support these interfaces, so almost all are laboriously programmed using conventional programming languages. It is well documented in the literature how expensive this process is [Williams 83][Smith 82]. This limits the amount of prototyping possible, and therefore the quality of the interfaces. Existing tools to help build user interfaces, called User Interface Management Systems (UIMSs) [Thomas 83][Olsen 84][Pfaff 85], have not provided a powerful and flexible way to conveniently generate the interaction techniques for these styles of interfaces. In particular, few systems have allowed Direct Manipulation techniques to be used to create the interfaces [Shneiderman 86].

All UIMSs are restricted in the forms of user interfaces they can generate [Tanner 85]. Peridot is only aimed at graphical, Direct Manipulation interfaces. For example, Peridot should be able to create interfaces like those of the Apple Macintosh [Williams 84]. Peridot does not help with textual command interfaces or with the coding of the semantics of the application. The set of interfaces it will produce is rich enough, however, to be very interesting and of practical use for commercial systems.

In summary, the goals of Peridot are that:

1) interaction techniques for Direct Manipulation interfaces should be supported,

2) the system should be easy to use for the designer and require little or no training,

3) the designer should not have to write programs,

4) the interface should be visible at all times as it is developed and changes should be immediately apparent,

5) the *behavior* of the interface should also be created in a Direct Manipulation manner and it should run in real time (points 4 and 5 provide for extremely rapid prototyping), and

6) the system should create run-time code that is efficient enough for use in actual application programs.

This paper presents the design and implementation of the demonstrational aspects of Peridot. A longer report providing more detail and covering other aspects is in preparation [Myers prep]. Throughout this paper, the term "designer" is used for the person creating user interfaces (and therefore using Peridot). The term "user" (or "end user") is reserved for the person using the interface created by the designer.

2. Background and Related Work

Tanner and Buxton [Tanner 85] present a model of User Interface Management Systems that identifies a number of separate parts (see Figure 1). Peridot is aimed mainly at the "module builder" aspects, but it also covers the "system glue" and "run-time support" components.

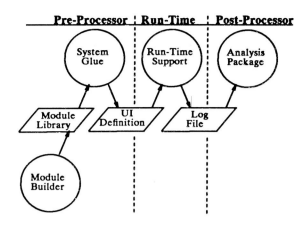

Figure 1.
Model for User Interface Management Systems (from [Tanner 85]).

The "module builder" creates a library of specific interaction techniques. Some systems, such as the Macintosh ToolBox [Apple 85] and the routines that come with most modern window managers [Myers 84][Tesler 81], are essentially the library portion by itself. Using a library has the advantage that the final UI will look and act similarly to other UIs created using the same library, but clearly the styles of interaction available are limited to those provided. In addition, the libraries themselves are often expensive to create. A few UIMSs, such as Syngraph [Olsen 83] and Squeak [Cardelli 85], are designed to help with the creation of the interaction techniques that make up the library, but the indirect and abstract methods used by these programs have proved difficult to use. Peridot attempts to make this process more direct.

Many (probably most) UIMSs concentrate on combining ("gluing") the modules together after they have been created, since it is often non-trivial to write the programs that coordinate the interaction techniques. This is evidenced by the need for the MacApp system to help write programs that use the Macintosh ToolBox. Some, such as Menulay [Buxton 83] and Trillium [Henderson 86], allow the designer to see the design as it is created, but most require that the specification be in a textual language (e.g. [Hayes 85][Jacob 85]). Although a number of modern UIMSs allow the layout of the screen to be specified in a Direct Manipulation manner, virtually all still require the interaction to be specified in an abstract, indirect way, such as using state transition networks. Peridot allows Direct Manipulation to be used for both.

The power in Peridot comes from the use of a new approach to user interface design. The principles of *Programming by Example* and *Visual Programming* have been adapted to allow the designer to demonstrate the desired user interface graphically. These principles are defined, and a comprehensive taxonomy of existing systems that use them is presented, in [Myers 86]. "Visual Programming" (VP) refers to systems that allow the specification of programs using graphics. "Programming by Example" (PBE) systems attempt to infer programs from examples of the data that the program should process. This inferencing is either based on examples of input-output pairs [Shaw 75][Nix 86], or traces of program execution [Bauer 78][Biermann 76b]. Some systems that allow the programmer to develop programs using specific examples do not use inferencing [Halbert 81 and 84][Lieberman 82][Smith 77]. For example, SmallStar [Halbert 84] allows users to write programs for the Xerox Star office workstation by simply performing the normal commands and adding control flow afterwards. Visual Programming systems, such as Rehearsal World [Gould 84], have been successful in making programs more visible and understandable and therefore easier to create by novices.

Peridot differs from these UIMSs and programming systems in that it applies Programming by Example and Visual Programming to the specific domain of graphical user interface specification. Tinker [Lieberman 82] has similar aims, but it does not provide inferencing, and code is specified in a conventional, textual manner in LISP. Early inferencing systems were rather unsuccessful since they often guessed the wrong program and it was difficult for the programmer to check the results without thoroughly studying the code [Biermann 76a]. In limited domains, PBE has been more successful, for example, for editing in the Editing by Example system [Nix 86]. Other systems that are relevant to the design of Peridot are those, such as [Pavlidis 85], that try to "beautify" pictures by inferring relationships among the picture elements (such as parallel and perpendicular) and modifying the picture to incorporate them.

3. Sample of Peridot in Action

The best way to demonstrate how easy it is to create a user interface with Peridot is to work through an example. Due to space limitations, we will take a simple interaction: a menu of strings. The operations discussed in this example will be further explained in the following sections. First, however, we present the Peridot screen.

When using Peridot, the designer sees three windows and a menu (see Figure 2). The menu, which is on the left, is used to give commands to Peridot. The window at the top shows the name of the current procedure, the name of its arguments, and *examples* of typical values for those arguments. The window in the center shows what the user will see as a result of this procedure (the end user interface), and the window at the bottom is used for prompting the designer and for messages. For debugging Peridot itself (and for the very few designers that will be interested), the system can be configured to display the generated code in a fourth window. Currently this code is presented in LISP, but creating a more readable form is possible in the future. The displayed procedure and the picture are always kept consistent, so if the picture is edited, the code is changed, and when the code changes, the picture is also updated. It is not necessary for the designer to view or use the code to perform any operations in Peridot.

Figure 3 shows the steps that can be used to create a procedure that handles a menu with a grey drop shadow. First, the designer types the name for the procedure, ("MyMenu"), the name for the parameters ("Items"), and an example of a typical value for each parameter (the list: ("Replace", "Move", "Copy", "Delete", "Delete All", "Help", "Abort", "Undo", "Exit")). Next, the designer draws a grey box for the shadow and then a black box for the background slightly offset from it (see Figure 3a). These commands are given using the Peridot command menu and a mouse. The system guesses that the black box should be the same size as the grey one and at an offset of 7 in X and Y. The designer confirms that this is correct. Next, (in Figure 3b)

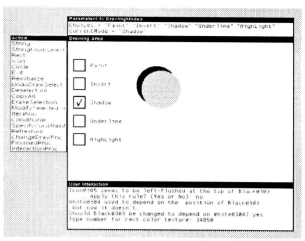

Figure 2.

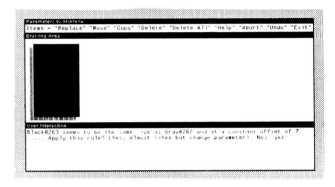

Figure 3a.

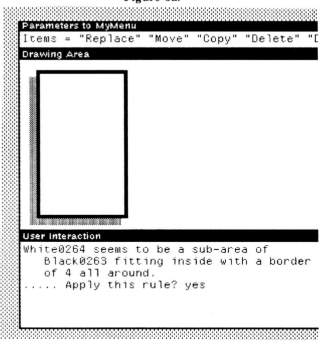

Figure 3b.

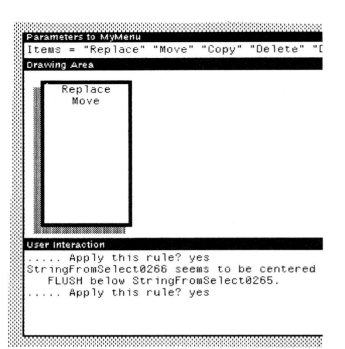

Figure 3c.

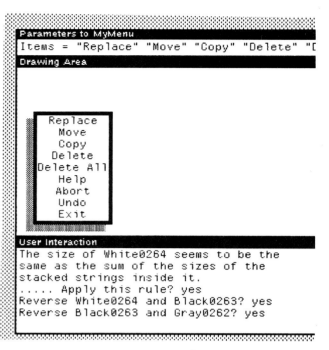

Figure 3e.

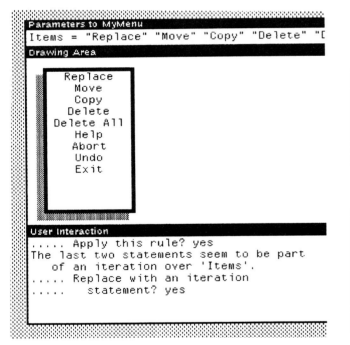

Figure 3d.

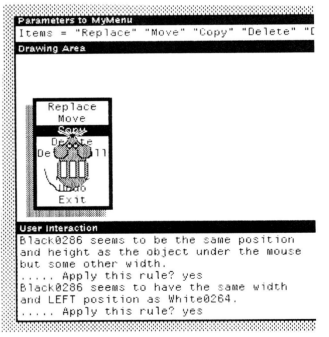

Figure 3f.

A sequence of frames during the definition of a menu interaction technique. (The pictures for 3b-3f have been expanded to be more readable.) In 3a, the shadow and background are drawn (and the system infers that they should be the same size). In 3b, a white area is nested inside the background, and in 3c the first two elements of the parameter are copied to the top of the white rectangle. Peridot notices that they are stacked vertically, and that they are part of an iteration. The rest of the iteration is executed in 3d. The size of the white rectangle is then changed to be just big enough to include all the strings and the system changes the black and grey rectangles accordingly 3e. In 3f, the interaction is being defined using the "simulated mouse."

a white box inside the black one is drawn, and the system adjusts it to be a constant 4 pixels all around, after confirmation from the designer. Next, (in Figure 3c) the first item in the argument ("Replace") is copied to the top of the white rectangle, and the system asks if it should be centered at the top. Peridot makes this assumption because the string was placed approximately centered in the box, as shown in Figure 3c. If the string had been placed left-justified in the box instead, then Peridot would have asked if the string should be left-justified. The system asks the designer to confirm every assumption because sometimes the placing is ambiguous. Next, the second string, "Move", is copied below "Replace" and the system guesses that it is also centered. Since the first two elements of a list have been placed on the screen, the system guesses that the entire list might be desired, so it asks the designer if there should be an iteration to display all elements of the list. After the designer confirms this (in Figure 3d), the system executes the rest of the iteration and changes the code to be a loop. Finally, (in Figure 3e) the designer adjusts the size of the white rectangle to be approximately the size of the strings, and the system asks if the rectangle should be adjusted to fit exactly around all the strings. The sizes of the black and grey rectangles are then automatically adjusted to be proportional to the size of the white rectangle. This completes the presentation aspects of the menu (Figure 3e). It should be remembered that the code being generated does not depend on the specific example values for the parameter; any list of strings will work correctly.

To specify the *interaction* (behavior) of the user interface for the menu, the designer uses an icon that represents the mouse. First, this "simulated mouse" is moved over one of the menu items, and then the designer draws a black rectangle over that item in INVERT drawing mode (see Figure 3f). Peridot infers that the box should be the same height and Y position as the string, and the same width and X position as the white box. The designer then moves the simulated mouse off to the side and erases the black rectangle. Peridot infers that the box should be erased when the mouse is no longer over an object. The designer can perform this action on another string, or explicitly specify an iteration, and the code that handles highlighting is completed. Now the designer "presses" one of the simulated mouse's buttons and specifies, using a Peridot command, that the object under the mouse is returned. From this, the system infers that the procedure should be exited upon button press. The MyMenu procedure is now complete.

Although the textual description of the designer's actions is clumsy, only about ten actions had to be performed to create this procedure (plus confirming Peridot's 12 guesses). Once created, the picture or interaction can be edited, and the menu can used as part of other user interfaces.

4. General Principles of Peridot

One problem with all demonstrational systems is that the user's actions are almost always ambiguous. The system cannot usually know *why* the person did a particular action. This is especially true when the system attempts to infer a general case from a particular example. For instance, when an item is selected, does the user mean that particular item, an item with a similar name, an item at that particular place on the screen, an item with the same type as the selected one, or an item with some other property? Early inferencing systems attempted to solve this problem by guessing and requiring the user to go back later and check the generated code. Non-inferencing systems, such as Halbert's system for the Xerox STAR workstation [Halbert 81 and 84], require the user to explicitly specify why objects were chosen. Peridot, on the other hand, tries to guess what the designer intends by an action, but, to avoid the problems of earlier systems, always asks the designer if each guess is correct. It is expected that the guesses will usually be correct, which will save the designer from having to specify a great deal of extra detail and from having to know a programming language to express those details. In addition, it is easy to check for errors since the results of all actions and inferences are always immediately visible on the screen.

Any graphical user interface is composed of two parts: the *presentation* or layout, which defines what pictures are on the screen, and the *interaction* or behavior, which determines how these pictures change with user actions. As shown in the previous example, these are specified separately in Peridot. The pictures that Peridot currently supports are: rectangles filled with various grey shades, text strings, filled circles, and static pictures drawn with other programs (e.g. icons)[1].

Peridot uses inferencing in three different ways. First, it tries to infer how various objects in the scene are related graphically. When the designer draws an object, it usually has some implied relation with other objects that have already been drawn. For example, a box might be nested inside another box, or a text string centered at the top of a box. If the picture was simply a static background that never changed, it would not be important for the system to notice these relationships. In Peridot, however, the pictures usually depend on the parameters to the procedure that generate them. For example, the size of the box around a menu might depend on the number of items in the menu and the width of the largest item. Peridot must therefore infer the meaningful relationships among objects from the drawings that the designer produces. This object-object inferencing is described in section 5.1.

The second type of inferencing used by Peridot is to try to guess when control structures are needed. For example, when the designer displays the first two elements of a list, Peridot infers that the entire list should be displayed and will generate an iteration. Conditionals are also inferred for special cases and exceptions. For example, a check-mark might be displayed to show the current value of a set of choices (as in Figure 2). Iterations and conditionals are discussed in sections 5.2 and 5.3 respectively.

The final type of inferencing used by Peridot is to try to guess when actions should happen during the execution of an interaction. For example, a highlight bar might be displayed when the left mouse button goes down. This type of inferencing is described in section 6.

---

[1] Straight and curved lines, and individual pixels should be easy to add in the future, if needed.

5. Specifying the Presentation of a User Interface

When specifying the presentation of a user interface, the designer is mainly interested in placing graphics on the screen. During this process, however, Peridot is constantly watching the objects to see what object-object relationships there are, and whether some objects drawn would properly be part of an iteration or conditional.

The designer may draw an object on top of another object. Depending on the drawing function in use, the second object may obscure parts of the first object. This is obvious in Figure 3e, where the black rectangle obscures some of the grey rectangle, the white rectangle obscures part of the black one, and the text obscures part of the white one. For this reason, Peridot never changes the order for drawing objects (although the designer is allowed to do this, of course). The calculation order may be changed, however, if a property of an object to be drawn later is needed. For example, in Figure 3e, the width of the strings are needed to calculate the width of the white rectangle even though the rectangle must be drawn first. Peridot insures that the calculation is done in the correct order before the drawing commences.

5.1. Inferring Object-Object Relationships

The object-object relationships that are inferred deal with the position and size properties of the objects. The other properties (color, value, font, etc.) are assumed to be constant unless the designer explicitly specifies that they should depend on some other object or parameter. In the example of section 3 above, the colors of the rectangles were constant, but the values for the strings were explicitly specified to depend on the parameter "Items" (by selecting "Replace" and "Move" in the parameter window and using the "StringFromSelect" menu command).

Each object-object relationship that can be inferred is represented in Peridot as a simple *condition-action rule*. Each rule has a test that determines if the relationship is appropriate (the *condition*), a message to be used to ask the designer whether the rule should be applied, and an *action* to cause the objects to conform to the rule. The Appendix lists some sample rules from Peridot. The rules are currently expressed in LISP so the designer will not be able to add new rules. It is very easy, however, for a LISP programmer to modify the rule set.

Since the rules specify very low level relationships (e.g. that a string should be centered inside a box), there appear to be a small number of rules required to handle existing interfaces. In an informal survey of a number of Direct Manipulation interfaces, about 50 rules seemed to be sufficient. In order to allow for human imprecision, however, some leeway must be given to the designer as to the placement and size of objects, so the drawings will not be exact. For example, the designer may want one box to be inside another box with a border of 3 pixels all around, but actually draw it with a border of 5 on one side and 2 on another. Therefore the tests in Peridot for whether to apply a particular rule have thresholds of applicability. Unfortunately, this means that the same drawing may pass more than one test. The *conflict resolution strategy* is simply to order the tests based on restrictiveness (the most demanding tests are first) and based on the heuristically determined likelihood of their being appropriate. This ordering is changed based on the types of the objects being tested, since, for example, it is much more likely for a text string to be centered at the top of a box than for another box to be.

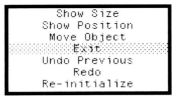

Figure 4.
The grey rectangle is the same height and Y position as the string "Exit" and the same width and X position as the white rectangle.

When the designer draws an object and a rule's test succeeds, Peridot queries the designer whether to apply the rule using the rule's message (see the lower window in Figures 3a-3f). If the system has guessed wrong, the designer answers "no" and the system will try to find a different rule that applies. If the system is correct, the designer may still want to modify parameters of the rule. For example, the system may decide that a box is inside another box with a border of 13 pixels all around, and the designer may decide to use 15 pixels instead. Of course, it may be the case that no rule is found or that the appropriate rule is skipped because the designer has been too sloppy in the original drawing and the rule's test fails. In this case, the designer will usually modify the drawing so that the test will succeed, but it is also possible to explicitly pick a rule to apply.

Most rules in Peridot relate one object to one other existing object[2]. The designer can explicitly specify two objects to apply rules to, but normally the relationships are inferred automatically when an object is created. In this case, the other (existing) object is found by searching through all the other objects in a certain order. When defining the *presentation* of the user interface, the order is: (1) the selected object (the designer can explicitly select an object to apply the rules to), (2) the previous object that was created, and (3) the objects in the vicinity of the new object. When defining the *interaction* portion of the user interface, the order for checking is: (1) the selected object, (2) the object under the simulated pointing devices (see section 6), and (3) the objects in the vicinity of the new object. The system stops searching when an object and a rule are found that completely specifies all of the positional and shape properties of the new object.

Occasionally some of an object's properties may depend on one object and other properties depend on a different object. For example, the highlight bar in a menu may have the same height and "y" value as the string, but the same width and "x" as the surrounding box (see Figure 4). To handle this case, there are rules in Peridot that only define some of the properties of objects. These rules are marked as "incomplete" so that Peridot knows to try additional rules on other objects to handle the rest of the properties (in the Appendix, rule "Rect-same-size" is incomplete).

[2] There are a small number of special rules that test a *group* of objects. This is necessary, for example, to make the size of a box depend on the sum of the sizes of all the items inside it.

Peridot will infer relationships among objects no matter how they are created. Therefore, the same rules will be applied whether an object is created from scratch, by copying some other object, or by transforming an existing object. Since Peridot generalizes from the *results* of the operations, and not *traces* of the actions like many previous Programming by Example systems, it provides much more flexibility to the designers and allows user interfaces to be easily edited. For example, if the designer makes an error when drawing an object or wants to change an existing object, he can simply correct it and Peridot will automatically apply the rules to the new version.

The relationships that Peridot infers can be thought of as *constraints* [Borning 79][Olsen 85] between the two objects. Although the relationships are inferred in one direction (e.g. object R2 depends on object R1), the reverse dependency is also remembered so the relationships can be automatically reversed, if necessary. For instance, the width of the white rectangle in the example of section 3 originally depended on the width of the black rectangle (Figure 3b). When it is later changed to depend on the width of the widest string (Figure 3e), Peridot automatically reverses the constraint with the black rectangle so *black* rectangle's width depends on the *white* rectangle, and similarly for the grey and black rectangles.

Usually, the first object tested is the correct one to apply rules to and the first rule whose test succeeds covers all of the properties of the object. Even when multiple comparisons are required, however, the rule checking occurs without any noticeable delay. If the delay were to increase in the future, this would still not be a problem since the rules are checked at design time (not when the user interface is used by end users), so some delays are acceptable. The advantage of using inferencing rather than requiring the designer to explicitly specify the relationships is that much less knowledge is required by the designer. This is because the designer does not have to know how to choose which of the 50 possible relationships apply and what the parameters to those relationships are.

5.2. *Inferring Iterations*

A recognized problem with all Direct Manipulation systems is that repetitive actions are tedious. For example, if a procedure takes a list of strings to be displayed, the designer does not want to have to individually demonstrate where to display each one. Therefore, Peridot watches the designer's actions to try to infer when two previous actions might be part of a loop. If they appear to be, it queries the designer as to whether a loop is intended. If so, the statements are replaced with a loop statement, and the rest of the loop is executed. As an example, if the designer copies the first two strings from a list of strings and displays them stacked vertically (as in Figure 3c), Peridot asks the designer if the rest of the strings should be displayed in the same manner. If the designer agrees, Peridot calculates how to display the rest of the strings in a similar manner as the first two (as in Figure 3d) and the code for the procedure is automatically changed.

Clearly, this assumes that the objects will be related in some linear fashion, and it will not handle some types of layouts. For example, it will not handle the items of the menu being spaced exponentially, or only displaying every third menu item. Our claim is that these unusual layouts are extremely rare in *real* user interfaces and Peridot will have good coverage without them.

Currently, Peridot infers iterations when the first two elements of a list are displayed[3]. Other objects may also be involved in the iteration, however. For example, in Figure 2, there are black boxes and white boxes for each string taken from the list. Peridot therefore will also include these in the iteration.

5.3. *Inferring Conditionals*

Conditionals are important in user interfaces for specifying *exceptions* and *special cases*. As an example of an exception, a procedure might display a list of strings vertically. However, if one of the strings is a list, then the first element of the list might be the string to be displayed, and the rest of the list might be a sublist to select from after this element is selected. With special cases, the designer wants something extra to happen when certain conditions are met. For example, a check mark may signal the current value from a set of choices, as in Figure 2.

For conditionals, the designer needs a way to specify what to look for to signal the condition (the "IF" part) and what action or actions to perform (the "THEN" part). Peridot supports this by having the designer specify the general case as described above, and giving the "Conditional" command to Peridot. The designer then selects the item that is an exception or special case. For an exception, Peridot tries to infer why it is different, and for a special case, it tries to infer when the graphic should occur. The conditions that are noticed are:

- one value has a different type (e.g. a list versus an atom, or a number rather than a string),
- one is an empty string, or
- numerical properties such as equal to, greater than, or less than zero.

Alternatively, the designer can specify that the value of a parameter should determine whether the conditional should apply. For example, the parameter CurrentMode in Figure 2 determines when to display the check mark.

After Peridot knows the "IF" part, it then allows the designer to demonstrate the "THEN" part, if it is not already displayed, using the same techniques as for any other picture.

Naturally, after a conditional statement is specified, Peridot re-executes the code to insure that the picture is consistent with the new procedure. This causes any additional places where the condition applies to be displayed correctly, which should help the designer spot any errors in the conditional.

6. Specifying the Interaction for a User Interface

One of Peridot's primary innovations is to allow the interaction portion of a user interface to be specified by demonstration. This operates in a similar manner to the presentation component. The major change is the addition of input devices which can determine when actions should take place and the parameters for those actions.

---

[3] It will be easy to also allow the designer to explicitly specify that an iteration should occur for some integer number of times, where the integer may be constant or depend on the value of some variable.

(a)   (b)

Figure 5.
A simulated "mouse" pointing device with three buttons. The device can be moved by pointing at the "nose" (using a real pointing device), and the buttons can be toggled by pressing over them. In (b), the center button is pressed over the word "replace".

Ideally, the designer would simply use the various input devices in the same manner as the end user, but this has three main problems. First, all of the end user's devices may not be available to the designer (for example, in designing the user interface for a flight simulator). Second, some of the input devices are also used for giving commands to Peridot, so disambiguating actions meant for Peridot from those that the end user will perform is difficult. Third, it may be difficult to keep the input device in the correct state (e.g. with a button held down or at a certain location) for the entire time it takes to specify the actions. Therefore, Peridot uses *simulated* devices by having a small icon for each input device (see Figure 5). The designer can move these and toggle "buttons" to indicate what the end user will do with the real input devices.

In addition, it is necessary to have a mode in which the designer can demonstrate what will happen using the *actual* input devices. Although often more clumsy, this is necessary when there are time dependencies, such as with double-clicking or with animations that should happen at a particular speed[4]. In this case, there will be "start watching" and "stop watching" commands to tell Peridot when actions signify what the end user will do and when they are Peridot commands.

When specifying the interaction portion of the user interface, the designer typically moves a simulated input device or changes the status of one of its buttons, and then performs some operation, such as moving an object or drawing a new object. Peridot then creates a conditional statement that is triggered when the input device state or position changes. Of course, there will always be ambiguities (e.g. is the new position significant because it is over an object or because it is no longer over the previous object?) so the designer is always queried to confirm Peridot's guess. Iterations (e.g. perform this until a button is hit), exceptions, and special cases are all be supported for controlling the interaction.

Just as what the end user *sees* is always visible to the designer, what the end user will *do* can also be executed at any time. The designer simply enters execution mode, and the procedure so far is executed. The designer can either use the simulated or the real devices while in execution mode.

7. Current Status

The design and implementation of Peridot are not complete as of the time of this writing (May, 1986). The inferencing mechanisms in Peridot are working, and the presentation component is mostly complete: object-object inferencing is working, iterations are inferred, as shown in Figures 2 and 3, and conditionals are designed but not implemented, although they are expected to be a straightforward extension. For the interaction component, the correct inferences are being made, but the code generation is not implemented.

8. Future Work

In addition to finishing the implementation of the parts of Peridot that are described here, other aspects of Peridot will be developed. Connections with application programs will use "active values," which behave like continuously evaluated procedures. These can be updated by either the interface or the application and the other will be immediately notified so it can make the appropriate updates.

The designer can easily edit the presentation of an interface after it has been created, but it is a difficult unsolved problem how to allow editing of the interaction component. To support multiple input devices operating in parallel [Buxton 86], multiple processing for procedures and constraints will be added. In addition, multiprocessing and constraints should allow animations and complex echoing and feedback to be specified using Peridot. Peridot will also be tested with a number of different user interface designers to ensure that the same guesses about relationships apply to different people.

9. Conclusions

Although not yet completed, Peridot already is capable of producing a variety of graphical, highly interactive user interfaces. Both the presentation (layout) and interaction (behavior) of these Direct Manipulation interfaces can be created in an extremely natural, Direct Manipulation manner. For example, Peridot can now create light buttons (as in Figure 2), menus (Figure 3), and toggle switches. Automatic inferencing is used to free the designer from having to specify most of the properties of objects. Constant feedback through queries, and continuously making the results of actions visible, helps insure that all inferences are correct. When fully implemented, Peridot should be able to handle the user interfaces of state-of-the-art graphical programs, such as those on the Apple Macintosh and other Direct Manipulation systems, including Peridot's own user interface. Extremely rapid prototyping should be possible, as well as generation of the actual code used in the final user interfaces. Peridot should also be easy enough to use so that even end users will be able to modify the user interfaces of programs. In its present form, Peridot has already demonstrated that the application of rule-based inferencing and Programming by Example techniques to User Interface Management Systems has tremendous potential.

---

[4] It is also intended in the future to allow designers to specify timing dependencies by constraining actions to a clock as in Rehearsal World [Gould 84].

Appendix: Sample rules

This appendix shows the form of three rules used in Peridot. The rules are shown in a LISP-like form, with the arithmetic presented in the normal infix notation to make it more readable. The TEST part determines whether the rule should be applied, the MSG is used to ask the designer for confirmation, the ACTION enforces the rule, and the SPECIFIES field tells which of the graphical properties of the object are covered by the rule. The actual rules in Peridot are slightly more complicated.

```
Rect-same:
    TEST:       (AND ((abs (R1.left - R2.left)) < THRESHHOLD)
                     ((abs (R1.bottom - R2.bottom)) < THRESHHOLD)
                     ((abs (R1.width - R2.width)) < THRESHHOLD)
                     ((abs (R1.height - R2.height)) < THRESHHOLD) )
    MSG:        (CONCAT R1.name
                " seems to be the same size and position as "
                R2.name ".")
    ACTION:     (SETQ R2.left "Fetch R1.left")
                (SETQ R2.bottom "Fetch R1.bottom")
                (SETQ R2.width "Fetch R1.width")
                (SETQ R2.height "Fetch R1.height")
    SPECIFIES: ALL

Rect-same-size-with-same-offset:
    TEST:       (AND ((abs (R1.left - R2.left)) < BigTHRESHHOLD)
                     ((abs (R1.bottom - R2.bottom)) < BigTHRESHHOLD)
                     ((abs (R1.width - R2.width)) < SmallTHRESHHOLD)
                     ((abs (R1.height - R2.height)) < SmallTHRESHHOLD)
                     ((abs ( (abs (R1.left - R2.left)) -
                             (abs (R1.bottom - R2.bottom)) )) < SmallTHRESHHOLD) )
    MSG:        (CONCAT R1.name " seems to be the same size as "
                R2.name " and at a constant offset of "
                (SETQ offset (ave ((abs (R1.left - R2.left)) -
                                   (abs (R1.bottom - R2.bottom)))))
                ".")
    ACTION:     (SETQ R2.left (CONCAT "Fetch R1.left + " offset))
                (SETQ R2.bottom (CONCAT "Fetch R1.bottom + " offset))
                (SETQ R2.width "Fetch R1.width")
                (SETQ R2.height "Fetch R1.height")
    SPECIFIES: ALL

Rect-same-size:
    TEST:       (AND ((abs (R1.width - R2.width)) < THRESHHOLD)
                     ((abs (R1.height - R2.height)) < THRESHHOLD) )
    MSG:        (CONCAT R1.name " seems to be the same size as "
                R2.name " but in an unrelated place.")
    ACTION:     (SETQ R2.width "Fetch R1.width")
                (SETQ R2.height "Fetch R1.height")
    SPECIFIES: (width height)
```

ACKNOWLEDGEMENTS

First, we want to thank Xerox Canada, Inc. for the donation of the Xerox workstations and Interlisp environment. This research was also partially funded by the National Science and Engineering Research Council (NSERC) of Canada. For help and support with this paper, we would like to thank the SIGGRAPH referees, and Bernita Myers, Peter Rowley, Ralph Hill, and Ron Baecker.

REFERENCES

[Apple 85] Apple Computer, Inc. *Inside Macintosh.* Addison-Wesley, 1985.

[Bauer 78] Michael Anthony Bauer. *A Basis for the Acquisition of Procedures.* PhD Thesis, Department of Computer Science, University of Toronto. 1978. 310 pages.

[Biermann 76a] Alan W. Biermann. "Approaches to Automatic Programming," *Advances in Computers*, Morris Rubinoff and Marshall C. Yovitz, eds. Vol. 15. New York: Academic Press, 1976. pp. 1-63.

[Biermann 76b] Alan W. Biermann and Ramachandran Krishnaswamy. "Constructing Programs from Example Computations," *IEEE Transactions on Software Engineering.* Vol. SE-2, no. 3. Sept. 1976. pp. 141-153.

[Borning 79] Alan Borning. *Thinglab--A Constraint-Oriented Simulation Laboratory.* Xerox Palo Alto Research Center Technical Report SSL-79-3. July, 1979. 100 pages.

[Buxton 83] W. Buxton, M.R. Lamb, D. Sherman, and K.C. Smith. "Towards a Comprehensive User Interface Management System," *Computer Graphics: SIGGRAPH'83 Conference Proceedings.* Detroit, Mich. Vol. 17, no. 3. July 25-29, 1983. pp. 35-42.

[Buxton 86] William Buxton and Brad Myers. "A Study in Two-Handed Input," *Proceedings SIGCHI'86: Human Factors in Computing Systems.* Boston, MA. April 13-17, 1986.

[Cardelli 85] Luca Cardelli and Rob Pike. "Squeak: A Language for Communicating with Mice," *Computer Graphics: SIGGRAPH'85 Conference Proceedings.* San Francisco, CA. Vol. 19, no. 3. July 22-26, 1985. pp. 199-204.

[Foley 84] James D. Foley. "Managing the Design of User-Computer Interfaces," *Proceedings of the Fifth Annual NCGA Conference and Exposition.* Anaheim, CA. Vol. II. May 13-17, 1984. pp. 436-451.

[Gould 84] Laura Gould and William Finzer. *Programming by Rehearsal.* Xerox Palo Alto Research Center Technical Report SCL-84-1. May, 1984. 133 pages. A short version appears in *Byte.* Vol. 9, no. 6. June, 1984.

[Halbert 81] Daniel C. Halbert. *An Example of Programming by Example.* Masters of Science Thesis. Computer Science Division, Dept. of EE&CS, University of California, Berkeley and Xerox Corporation Office Products Division, Palo Alto, CA. June, 1981. 55 pages.

[Halbert 84] Daniel C. Halbert. *Programming by Example.* PhD Thesis. Computer Science Division, Dept. of EE&CS, University of California, Berkeley. 1984. Also: Xerox Office Systems Division, Systems Development Department, TR OSD-T8402, December, 1984. 83 pages.

[Hayes 85] Philip J. Hayes, Pedro A. Szekely, and Richard A. Lerner. "Design Alternatives for User Interface Management Systems Based on Experience with COUSIN," *Proceedings SIGCHI'85: Human Factors in Computing Systems.* San Francisco, CA. April 14-18, 1985. pp. 169-175.

[Henderson 86] D. Austin Henderson, Jr. "The Trillium User Interface Design Environment," *Proceedings SIGCHI'86: Human Factors in Computing Systems.* Boston, MA. April 13-17, 1986. pp. 221-227.

[Hutchins 86] Edwin L. Hutchins, James D. Hollan, and Donald A. Norman. "Direct Manipulation Interfaces," *User Centered System Design*, Donald A. Norman and Stephen W. Draper, eds. Hillsdale, New Jersey: Lawrence Erlbaum Associates, 1986. pp. 87-124.

[Jacob 85] Robert J.K. Jacob. "A State Transition Diagram Language for Visual Programming," *IEEE Computer.* Vol. 18, no. 8. Aug. 1985. pp. 51-59.

[Lieberman 82] Henry Lieberman. "Constructing Graphical User Interfaces by Example," *Graphics Interface, '82*, Toronto, Ontario, March 17-21, 1982. pp. 295-302.

[Myers 84] Brad A. Myers. "The User Interface for Sapphire," *IEEE Computer Graphics and Applications.* Vol. 4, no. 12, December, 1984. pp. 13-23.

[Myers 86] Brad A. Myers. "Visual Programming, Programming by Example, and Program Visualization; A Taxonomy," *Proceedings SIGCHI'86: Human Factors in Computing Systems.* Boston, MA. April 13-17, 1986. pp. 59-66.

[Myers prep] Brad A. Myers. *Applying Visual Programming with Programming by Example and Constraints to User Interface Management Systems.* PhD Thesis, Department of Computer Science, University of Toronto, Toronto, Ontario, Canada. In progress.

[Nix 86] Robert P. Nix. "Editing by Example," *ACM Transactions on Programming Languages and Systems.* Vol. 7, no. 4. Oct. 1985. pp. 600-621.

[Olsen 83] Dan R. Olsen and Elizabeth P. Dempsey. "Syngraph: A Graphical User Interface Generator," *Computer Graphics: SIGGRAPH'83 Conference Proceedings.* Detroit, Mich. Vol. 17, no. 3. July 25-29, 1983. pp. 43-50.

[Olsen 84] Dan R. Olsen, Jr., William Buxton, Roger Ehrich, David J. Kasik, James R. Rhyne, and John Sibert. "A Context for User Interface Management," *IEEE Computer Graphics and Applications.* Vol. 4, no. 2. Dec. 1984. pp. 33-42.

[Olsen 85] Dan R. Olsen, Jr., Elisabeth P. Dempsey, and Roy Rogge. "Input-Output Linkage in a User Interface Management System," *Computer Graphics: SIGGRAPH'83 Conference Proceedings.* San Francisco, CA. Vol. 19, no. 3. July 22-26, 1985. pp. 225-234.

[Pavlidis 85] Theo Pavlidis and Christopher J. Van Wyk. "An Automatic Beautifier for Drawings and Illustrations," *Computer Graphics: SIGGRAPH'85 Conference Proceedings.* San Francisco, CA. Vol. 19, no. 3. July 22-26, 1985. pp. 225-234.

[Pfaff 85] Gunther R. Pfaff, ed. *User Interface Management Systems.* Berlin: Springer-Verlag, 1985. 224 pages.

[Shaw 75] David E. Shaw, William R. Swartout, and C. Cordell Green. "Inferring Lisp Programs from Examples," *Fourth International Joint Conference on Artificial Intelligence.* Tbilisi, USSR. Sept. 3-8, 1975. Vol. 1. pp. 260-267.

[Shneiderman 83] Ben Shneiderman. "Direct Manipulation: A Step Beyond Programming Languages," *IEEE Computer.* Vol. 16, no. 8. Aug. 1983. pp. 57-69.

[Shneiderman 86] Ben Shneiderman. "Seven Plus or Minus Two Central Issues in Human-Computer Interfaces," *Proceedings SIGCHI'86: Human Factors in Computing Systems.* (closing plenary address) Boston, MA. April 13-17, 1986. pp. 343-349.

[Smith 77] David Canfield Smith. *Pygmalion: A Computer Program to Model and Stimulate Creative Thought.* Basel, Stuttgart: Birkhauser, 1977. 187 pages.

[Smith 82] David Canfield Smith, Charles Irby, Ralph Kimball, Bill Verplank, and Erik Harslem. "Designing the Star User Interface," *Byte Magazine,* April 1982, pp. 242-282.

[Tanner 85] Peter P. Tanner and William A.S. Buxton. "Some Issues in Future User Interface Management System (UIMS) Development," in *User Interface Management Systems,* Gunther R. Pfaff, ed. Berlin: Springer-Verlag, 1985. pp. 67-79.

[Tesler 81] Larry Tesler. "The Smalltalk Environment," *Byte Magazine.* August 1981, pp. 90-147.

[Thomas 83] James J. Thomas and Griffith Hamlin, eds. "Graphical Input Interaction Technique (GIIT) Workshop Summary." ACM/SIGGRAPH, Seattle, WA. June 2-4, 1982. in *Computer Graphics.* Vol. 17, no. 1. Jan. 1983. pp. 5-30.

[Williams 83] Gregg Williams. "The Lisa Computer System," *Byte Magazine,* February 1983, pp. 33-50.

[Williams 84] Gregg Williams. "The Apple Macintosh Computer," *Byte Magazine.* February 1984. pp. 30-54.

[Xerox 83] Xerox Corporation. *Interlisp Reference Manual.* Pasadena, CA. October, 1983.

An Object-Oriented User Interface Management System

by
John L. Sibert, William D. Hurley and Teresa W. Bleser
The George Washington University

Abstract

The George Washington User Interface Management System (GWUIMS) has been designed as a test bed for comparing user interface models, as a tool for rapidly prototyping highly interactive graphic user interfaces,and as a vehicle for investigating the applicability of knowledge-based technology to user interface design. The GWUIMS was designed and implemented using the object-oriented programming paradigm and consists of a variety of object classes representing different levels of abstraction. Responsibility for lexical, syntactic, and semantic levels of both input parsing and feedback are distributed throughout these classes. We include a description of the GWUIMS and a brief scenario to demonstrate its capabilities. A description of the implementation is followed by a discussion of the future application of knowledge representation techniques and the evolution towards an intelligent assistant for the user interface designer.

Introduction

The George Washington User Interface Management System (GWUIMS) provides a framework for investigating different user interface models and the feasibility of knowledge-based assistance for the user interface designer. It also serves as an interactive tool for developing realistic user interface prototypes.

Models of the user interface fall into two broad categories. The more frequently used of these contains the **linguistic** models which view the interface as a dialog between user and computer. Although they provide a valuable framework for focusing on issues that occur within the semantic, syntactic, and lexical levels of the dialog, linguistic models encourage the designer to view each of these levels in isolation. In addition, they have limitations when used to specify interactive graphics or direct manipulation interfaces. The second category, **spatial** models includes interactive graphic or direct manipulation models. Spatial models lack straightforward syntactic mechanisms for sequencing events such as those provided by linguistic models.

We feel that good user interfaces normally incorporate both linguistic and spatial components. Therefore, though we chose to adopt an inherently spatial object-oriented paradigm, we include the linguistic model by defining the boundaries of the lexical, syntactic, and semantic levels of the interface language within objects. Each boundary between two levels is embodied in a specialized object class with sufficient knowledge about adjacent linguistic levels to accomplish its function.

Our design has roots in a continuing tradition in user interface management systems, which, although not given its current name until 1982 (Kasik 1982), goes back at least to Newman's "Reaction Handler" (Newman 1968) and has recently been exemplified by (Olsen et al 1985) and (Green 1985), both of which use some object-oriented concepts.

Another influence is the development of object-oriented programming, dating from the Simula language (Dahl and Nygaard 1966) and popularly known in Smalltalk (Goldberg 1984). Object-oriented programming has been intimately related to graphics for some time; concepts can be recognized in Anson's device model (Anson 1982), as well as in other recent interactive graphics applications (Foley and McMath 1986, Beach et al 1982, and Lipkie et al 1982 to name a few).

Also related is work in specification of interactive interfaces using formal grammars (Reisner 1981, Bleser and Foley 1982, and Jacob 1983). Such formal specifications allow rigorous analysis of interactive dialogs prior to implementation. Moreover, an interactive dialog so specified can be viewed as an automaton, providing a straightforward flow of control mechanism for a UIMS. Many of the UIMSs which have been built have in fact incorporated such a dialog specification (Olsen 1985, Kasik 1982, Kamran 1983).

Finally, we are applying artificial intelligence techniques to the design and management of user interfaces. Previous examples include (Roach et. al. 1982, Cochran and Stocker 1985) and the frame-like aspects of COUSIN (Hayes et.al. 1985). We are primarily interested in incorporating knowledge-based tools into the interface designer's toolkit to act as assistants.

We have designed our UIMS according to the object paradigm, in contrast to an object-oriented implementation of a design based on another model. It is also implemented in an object-oriented language, a locally enhanced (Hurley 1985) Flavors environment(Weinreb and Moon 1980) running on Franz Lisp. In the following sections we describe our system, give an example of its use, and discuss its implementation.

The GWUIMS

The current version of the GWUIMS is the most recent in a series of UIMSs developed at The George Washington University. Its immediate predecessor (Sibert and Hurley 1984), was a system based on a dialog specified as an augmented transition network (ATN), the equivalent of a context sensitive grammar. Our conversion to an object paradigm was driven by the desire to treat various components of the system as autonomous entities, as well as the desire to gradually substitute more intelligent components as we learn what they should contain and how to build them. In this section we provide an overview of our object-oriented UIMS design, after defining our particular use of objects and object-oriented programming.

Objects in the GWUIMS

There are numerous versions of the object-oriented abstraction and probably as many different sets of terminology; for example see (Stefik and Bobrow, 1986). This section defines our use of the terminology.

We define an **object** as an entity with **attributes** and **relationships** with other objects (e.g. an object for a temperature gauge might include attributes describing its temperature range, size, color, danger level, etc. while the value of a relationship could be the identity of an alarm object). The behavior of an object is embodied in **methods** which are procedures for performing activities (these would include graphics routines to display the temperature dial). All activity in an object-oriented system is caused by communication between objects. Objects communicate by sending **messages** to other objects requesting information from them, or requesting them to exhibit some form of behavior (e.g. another object in the system can send a message to the temperature gauge requesting it to display itself).

We define different **classes** of objects and each object is an **instance** of one class. Each instance of a class has the same methods as all other instances of that class; it differs from other instances only in the values of its attributes and relationships. For example, the temperature gauge described above is an instance of the class graphic_object. The following pseudo code defines the class:

Class: graphic_object;
Attributes: color, font, linestyle, position, visibility, hot_spot_extent, pickability, vector_list, text_list, pix_rect_list;
Relationships: graphic_object_list;
Methods: display, make_invisible, change_position;
Messages: none;

The only relationship defined is a list of graphic objects making it possible to build object hierarchies. The graphic object originates no messages, it only responds to messages to perform its methods, and forwards messages to the objects on its list. Attributes and relationships are both implemented as instance variables. In addition to the methods listed above, graphic objects share with all objects certain common behavior such as adding, setting, and retrieving attribute values.

We gain several advantages from this object paradigm. First, it provides a natural mechanism for representing our system at several levels of abstraction since an object may be anything from a very high level concept, such as an icon construction tool, to a very low level concept, such as an input device driver. The designer of a user interface may wish to work at very different levels of abstraction depending on whether a new interaction technique is being developed or an interface to an application such as a CAD system is being designed. A second advantage is the ease with which simple objects can be combined into more complex objects, making it possible for us to define new components of a system interactively by building them from existing objects. A third advantage is the inherent flexibility of systems defined in terms of message passing protocols. It is easy for us to add new capabilities to the system without extensive recoding. Finally, the object paradigm allows us to relegate design constraints (for our UIMS implementation, not for user interfaces designed using it) imposed by hardware and operating systems, to low levels of the implementation.

With the object paradigm in mind, we are now ready to examine the structure of the GWUIMS.

Overview

Figure 1 is an upper level view of our system. The box labeled *USER INTERFACE* represents a collection of objects which will be described later; at this point it is taken as a black box. In addition to the *USER INTERFACE* , the system consists of representation objects (R_objects), interaction objects (I_objects), and application objects (A_objects). The arrows in Figures 1-3 indicate allowed message paths. For example, a representation object may only send messages to an interaction object or to objects within the *USER INTERFACE*, and it receives messages only from the same set of objects. This design restriction on message paths is a means of enforcing a logical separation between different linguistic levels within the UIMS. Messages are forced to pass through objects which incorporate boundaries between levels (see Figure 1).

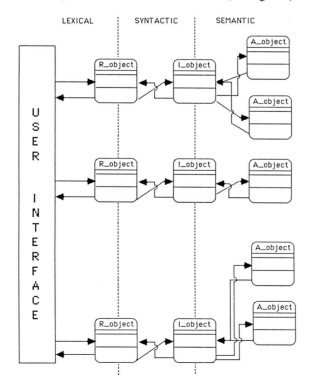

Figure 1: Overview of the GWUIMS

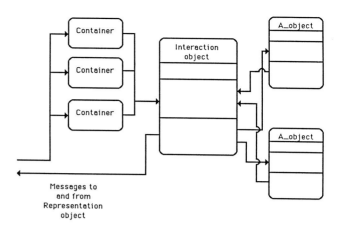

Figure 2: An Interaction Object and Containers

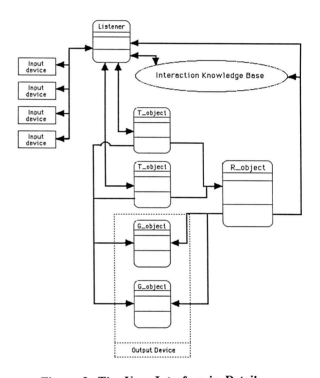

Figure 3: The User Interface in Detail

Our system architecture is partly a reaction to earlier work at GW, (Feldman and Rogers 1982 , Kamran and Feldman 1983) which maintained a strict logical separation between the lexical, syntactic and semantic levels of the user computer interface. We are convinced that it is not possible to build systems which handle semantic errors and feedback intelligently if we maintain a strict separation between the lexical/syntactic domain in the UIMS on the one hand, and the semantic domain of the application on the other (Sibert, Belliardi and Kamran 1985). Our current design embodies these boundaries between levels within objects, so that an object's behavior can depend on information about more than one level.

The A_objects on the right in Figure 1 embody the semantics of the application. For prototyping user interfaces, the A_objects are simulators which are parameterized to simulate some aspect of an application's behavior. To use our system with a real application, the procedural code and data structures of the actual application must be packaged into A_objects. The difficulty of doing this with an existing application clearly varies with the structure of the application code.

The A_objects may send messages to and receive messages from the interaction objects (I_objects), which encapsulate the syntactic/semantic boundary. I_objects have some general knowledge of the application semantics, but the implementation of these semantics is completely within the A_objects. Typically, an I_object sends a message to an A_object requesting that it perform its function, supplying it with any data or parameters it might need. The A_object sends messages to an I_object informing it of results or errors which may affect the future flow of control of the application or which need to be displayed.

The representation object (R_object) is responsible for determining how information is to be displayed to the end user and for partially verifying the syntax of any input from the end user before passing it on to the interaction object (see the section on input parsing for more details of the R_object's role). R_objects embody the boundary between the lexical and syntactic levels of the UIMS.

Now let us take a more detailed look at how information is handled within the interaction object. Figure 2 gives a detailed view of the structure of an interaction object. Among its relationships is a list of **containers**. We use the term container collectively to refer to six classes of objects: **items**, **slots**, and **results**, which may be either **active** or **passive**. The purpose of these containers is to hold information for transmission in both directions between the user interface and the application. The contents of an item are determined at design time and cannot be altered by the user at run time. This is analogous to menu items or button values which can be selected but not changed by the user. The contents of a slot may be modified at run time by the user, while the contents of a result may be altered by the application. This distinction is based on the observation that the tasks of selecting, entering information, and reporting results are conceptually different to the interface designer.

Active containers are subclasses of passive containers. A passive container can be selected or filled, but does nothing to cause a message to be sent to the application. In contrast, an active container, when selected or filled, causes a message to be sent to a pre-specified A_object asking it to perform its function. It is therefore selection of an active item or filling an active slot which causes something to happen in the application domain. In this respect our UIMS is similar to COUSIN (Hayes et. al. 1985).

Containers can be filled or selected as a result of messages sent by either application or representation objects (the latter as a result of end user actions). By filling or selecting an active results container, the application can influence flow of control. Results contents can also be sent to an R_object for ultimate display to the end user.

When an active container is accessed, it sends a message to an I_object identifying the A_object which is to perform its function, and providing a list of containers. The I_object in turn sends a message to the appropriate A_object including information needed by the A_object to carry out its action. This message path allows the I_object to extract the necessary information from the container list. At the same time, the I_object provides partial semantic error checking by making sure that the message is complete and semantically correct. As an example of the inheritance relationship between active and passive containers consider the following item class definitions:

> **Class:** active_item;
> **Attributes:** none;
> **Relationships:** Application_object_id,
>   Interaction_object_id, parameter_container_list;
> **Methods:** change_flag;
> **Messages:** send [interaction_object_id invoke_action
>   (application_object_id parameter_container_list)];
> **Component_objects:** passive_item;

Notice that the active item has a component object from which it inherits attributes, relationships and methods. The component object, a passive item, is defined as:

> **Class:** passive_item;
> **Attributes:** status, value, select_flag;
> **Relationships;** representation object_id;
> **Methods:** change_value, augment_value, change_status,
>   change_flag;
> **Messages:** none;

An active item inherits all methods of a passive item. Note the redefinition of the change_flag method (which is responsible for selecting and deselecting items) for the active_item class. The active item must recognize that its select flag has been set in order to send its message; therefore it requires a different method. The active item has a message which it can send to an I_object. All messages in our system have the same syntax:

send
  [destination_object_id
  method_name
  (argument_list)].

In this example, the only message an active item can send is to an interaction object requesting it to exercise its "invoke_action" method. The message provides it with the name of the A_object which can carry out the specified semantic action and a list of containers which hold the parameters the A_object requires.

Encapsulating the semantic/syntactic boundary allows an I_object to have some intelligence concerning the way in which the syntax and semantics interact. For example, an I_object could have access to rules enabling it to infer a reasonable action to take based on a semantic error message from the application. The error may require the respecification of a series of parameters by the end user. In this case, the I_object would empty the appropriate containers and send a message to a specified R_object, requesting it to provide an appropriate prompt to the end user.

Figure 3 opens the user interface black box seen in Figure 1, illustrating the relationships between an R_object and the components of the user interface. The R_object controls the visual form of the end user's display by sending messages to graphic objects (G_objects). Everything that can be displayed is a G_object. A G_object receives messages which control attributes such as visibility, color, position, etc. G_objects may also send messages to other G_objects allowing us to establish object hierarchies.

Each R_object receives messages from one or more technique objects (or T_objects). T_objects represent the lexical level of input and feedback for a given user interface design. They are controlled by an object called the listener. There is only one instance of a listener object. Its role is to interpret input from the currently enabled set of physical input devices and pass the input on to the appropriate T_object. The listener carries out this task by parsing the input based on a representation of the current interface, as described in the next section. This representation is maintained in the interaction knowledge base so named because it contains rules, constraints, and state specifications which various objects can

use to modify their behavior. (Currently the contents of the knowledge base are minimal; one of our major goals for the future is to increase them.) Each object is responsible for keeping this knowledge base current. For example, whenever an R_object is "activated" (made available for interaction) or "de- activated", it updates the knowledge base.

Input Parsing in the GWUIMS

An important responsibility of the UIMS is understanding and verifing input from the end user. The domain of this input parsing ranges from recognizing and providing dynamic feedback for mouse movements, to validating sentences for correct syntax and semantics. In the GWUIMS, this parsing is distributed among the following objects: the listener, T_objects, R_objects, and I_objects.

At the lowest level, parsing responsibility is shared by the listener and the T_objects. The listener, using both the identity of the source physical device and the type and value(s) of the input, determines for which R_object the input is intended and which T_object should control further parsing. It does this using a generalized extent test applied to the input and a data structure contained in the knowledge base. This data structure includes extent definitions and physical device associations for all currently active R_objects as well as all of their associated G_objects and is similar to those found in window managers.

The listener hands both control and the input over to the appropriate T_object which completes this low level of parsing by identifying the G_object whose sensitivity-extent includes the input. At this point, the T_object receives input directly from the device driver level and provides lexical feedback until either the context of the input changes and control is passed back to the listener, or an event occurs causing the T_object to send a message to the listener. The message identifies the current G_object and includes any additional input information, such as a text string, or numeric input from a keyboard, which the T_object has gathered. The listener forwards the message to the previously identified R_object. At this point the "lexical analysis" phase of the parse is complete.

The next phase of parsing is handled by the R_object and consists of checking a set of parameterized rules in the knowledge base against a set of parameter values which the I_object owns. An example of this sort of rule is:

only k of n entities may be concurrently selected;

The parameters **n** and **k** are attributes of the R_object which have been set previously, probably at interface design time. A common example is the popularly known "radio button" , where selection of one button causes a previously selected button to be automatically deselected.

Once the R_object has satisfied its constraints, it sends a message to one or more containers filling, selecting, or deselecting them. The destination is known to the R_object because of a correspondence, established at design time, between each selectable G_object and a fillable/selectable container. At this point, further parsing becomes the responsibility of the I_object which receives a message from the container.

The I_object completes the syntactic level parsing begun by the R_object. Recall from the preceding section that containers gather information by being filled/selected until an active container requests the I_object to perform a semantic action. The I_object then verifies the completeness of the parameter list for the A_object which actually performs that action, and sends a message to the A_object.

This overview has introduced the major object types in our UIMS and described the general nature of their relationships to each other, as well as describing the sequence of events in input parsing. In the next section we present a more detailed example of the system in use to help clarify these relationships.

Direct Manipulation Using GWUIMS

For the following scenario, we will present first the actions of the system from the perspective of the user/designer followed by a description of the internal actions of the UIMS which are responsible for the observed behavior. The problem is to customize a bank of "soft" (virtual) buttons starting from a default template. It is intended to reveal some of the capabilities of the GWUIMS but is by no means representative of the only style of design it supports.

Customizing an Object: Designer's View

As our scenario begins, we have already selected the button bank shown in Figure 4 from a set of templates. We now have a number of options available. We may directly change the button bank by moving or resizing it. To move it we simply position the cursor somewhere along the top border, press and hold the mouse button while we move the mouse, and release it when we wish to "drop" the button bank in a new position. Dynamic feedback is provided by a drag box.

We may also modify the contents of the button bank. The numbers in Figure 4 are labels for the buttons. By clicking on a number, we indicate that we wish to change that label. The old

label disappears and we may now enter a new label by typing it at the keyboard. We terminate entry of a new label by simply moving the cursor elsewhere and beginning a new action. Some modifications require a further selection. If the mouse button is pressed and held while the cursor is over the currently selected button, a menu with alternative feedback specification for button selection appears. While continuing to hold the button down, we move the cursor vertically over the feedback menu, causing different feedback options to be temporarily displayed at the button labeled 1, showing us how the newly selected feedback will look on the button bank itself. When we release the button, the currently displayed option becomes the new selection feedback technique. For this example we decide to change the feedback from a dot in the center of the button (the default) to a completely filled in button and to change the labels from numbers to letters.

What the System Does:

In the preceding section, three specific actions were discussed: moving the button bank, changing labels, and changing the feedback specification. Each of these is handled somewhat differently by the system. Moving the button bank is handled primarily within a T_object. The listener object recognizes that the mouse button is depressed while the cursor is over the button bank and hands control over to the T_object responsible for managing, shaping and moving menu objects. The T_object remains in control as long as the button is held down. It recognizes that the cursor is located over some part of the bank other than one of its corners and so it creates a "drag box" for feedback. Every time it receives an updated cursor position, it moves the drag box. When the button is released,

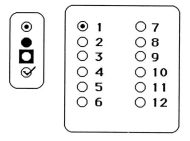

Figure 4: Feedback Selections

the T_object sends a message to the R_object for the button bank, informing it of the position change. The R_object sends messages to its G_objects telling them to disappear and reappear in their new locations. The I_object is not involved since this is a purely syntactic change.

Changing the label's appearance is similar to the position change except that it is handled entirely by the T_object since it is solely a lexical level change. The technique recognizes that one click over a label means that the label is to be replaced and manages the details of causing the portion of the G_object representing the label to disappear. It also accepts the keyboard input for the replacement label and causes it to be displayed. The T_object communicates directly with the G_object to change the contents of the text string for the label.

The feedback specification is at the lexical level in the context of the button bank, but it is part of the semantics of the designer's interface. Therefore, changing it cannot be handled by a T_object alone, since it requires the use of the appearing menu. The change involves an additional I_object and R_object, associated with the appearing menu, as well as those for the button bank. The following code fragment shows the messages for this example:

```
{ specific objects used in this example are}
T_object_one        { menu selection using mouse}
T_object_two        { dynamic feedback change}
R_object_one        { button bank }
I_object_one        { button bank}
R_object_two        { appearing menu }
I_object_two        { appearing menu }
A_object_one        { initiate feedback selection }
A_object_two        { complete feedback selection }
A_item_id           { an arbitrary active item }
G_object_id         { an arbitrary graphic object }


send { from T_object_one }
  [Listener, selected,
   (G_object_id)]

send  { from Listener  }
  [R_object_one, selected,
   (G_object_id)]
send { from R_object_one }
  [A_item_id, change_flag,
   (selected)]
send
  [I_object_one, invoke_action,
   (A_object_one, A_item_id)]
send
  [A_object_one, invoke_action,
   (A_item_contents)]
send
  [I_object_two, activate, ()]
```

```
send
  [R_object_two, activate,()]
send { a list of G_objects }
  [Listener, activate, (G_object_list)]


{ at this point the listener awaits input from      end user }


send { a list of G_objects  }
  [T_object_two, activate,(input_data)]


{the T_object dynamically changes the feedback   by sending
messages to appropriate G_objects   until the button is released
   then a selection    message is sent via the listener }


send {selection from appearing menu}
  [R_object_two, selected, (G_object_id)]
send {correlated with G_object_id}
  [A_item_id, change_flag,
   (selected)]
send
  [I_object_two, invoke_action,
   (A_object_two, A_item_id)]
send
  [A_object_two, invoke_action,
   (A_item_contents)]
send
  [R_object_one, change_value,
   (feedback_specification)]
```

When the mouse button is pressed over the currently highlighted soft button, a message is sent through the R_object and I_object for the button bank to the A_object in the designer's interface application responsible for changing feedback selection. That A_object, in turn, sends a message to the R_object associated with the appearing menu which activates itself as described above. The T_object then changes the feedback in the button bank by interacting directly with the G_objects. When the button is released, the T_object sends a message via the listener to the R_object associated with the appearing menu indicating which object on the appearing menu has been selected. The message is passed on to the I_object which selects an active item corresponding to the new feedback specification. Finally an action is initiated which sends a message to the R_object for the button bank requesting a change of feedback specification.

It is clear that this example includes many redundant messages. We do this purposely to force a complete specification of the interaction technique. For use at run time, the redundant messages may be removed to improve performance.

Actions and Values: Designer's View

At this point, we have a button bank for which we have specified a location, new labels, and a new selection feedback. However, we have not yet associated any meaning (semantics) with the buttons. There are two types of meanings we can associate with pressing a button. One is to cause some action to occur while the other is to cause some value to be set. When the designer positions the cursor over a button and double clicks (clicking twice in rapid succession), the menu shown in Figure 5 appears. This menu has three parts. The first is a list of all actions currently known to the system. In the event that

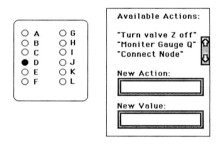

Figure 5: Specifying a Semantic Action

there are too many actions to fit conveniently on the menu, it may be paged using the bar on the right. Selection of one of these actions will causeit to be bound immediately to the soft button. No compilation is necessary, the button bank is live and may be tested throughout the design process. The designer can now single click on that soft button. If an A_object embodying the semantics for that action exists and all necessary parameters for the action are specified, the action will occur. If the action does not exist because the application object necessary to carry it out has not yet been created or there are missing parameters, the system will issue a warning message to the designer.

The second part of the menu is a box within which the designer can enter a new action name, while the third is a similar box for specifying a value. In this example we position the cursor over the value box and type in a value, terminating by pressing the "return" key. The appearing menu disappears and we are free to continue customizing the button bank.

What the System Does:

The double click causes the T_object to send a message "awakening" the R_object for the appearing menu in Figure 5. The system behaves in much the same way as it did when specifying a new selection feedback. When an action is selected from the list or entered in the new action field, a message is sent through the R_object and I_object associated with the appearing menu to an A_object which sends a message to the I_object for the button bank, instructing it to bind the specified action to the selected item and to make it an active item. If a value is specified, a message is sent over the same route, instructing the I_object to bind the value to the selected item and to make it passive.

Summary

This scenario illustrates some of the power of our system. The example of interactive feedback specification illustrates a composite interaction technique built from primitive objects. The technique is built by specifying attribute and relationship values for the objects involved. Only the A_objects require any procedural code and it is simple, consisting of a test on the value of A_item_contents followed by the dispatch of a message to the appropriate I_object or R_object.

A second example is the run-time binding of actions to buttons or menu items and their immediate availability. This makes possible dynamic, incremental testing of pieces of the user interface as they are being built and facilitates rapid interface prototyping.

Implementation of the GWUIMS

The GWUIMS is implemented on a Sun microsystems workstation using a locally developed programming environment built on top of Franz LISP with Flavors. The programming environment, which we call the metasystem because of the knowledge it has about systems developed with it, includes a number of extensions to Flavors which we found necessary for implementation of our UIMS. These extensions include:

1. It is possible to save the current state of a system and all of its components to secondary storage. This is clearly critical for incremental development and customizing of user interface designs as described above.

2. When a class is redefined, the metasystem can immediately and automatically modify all existing instances of

that class. This is essential to the system's ability to expand over time with a minimum of additional programming.

3. The system automatically generates unique identifiers for all instances. This feature is necessary to avoid ambiguity internally, but does not prevent the user/designer of the GWUIMS from assigning arbitrary names.

In addition to these capabilities which are required for the current implementation of the GWUIMS, the metasystem provides us with a good framework for knowledge acquisition, exploratory development, and iterative growth. This framework is crucial to our plans for adding design knowledge and reasoning to the system.

Unfortunately, with our limited hardware and software configuration, the Flavors environment does not provide sufficient execution speed for highly interactive graphics Accordingly, the T_objects, listener and graphics display primitives are all implemented in the C programming language. For further detail see (Sibert, Hurley and Bleser 1986) which includes complete description of the semantics and syntax of all objects in the system and (Hurley 1985) which describes our object-oriented programming environment.

Conclusions and Future Evolution

When we set out to build this system, we had several goals in mind. First and foremost was developing a capability for realistic prototyping of highly interactive graphic user interfaces. We are currently using our system in this manner, and plan to build increasingly more sophisticated prototypes as our experience with the system grows and as we add more interaction techniques. We have been concentrating on mouse and keyboard oriented techniques but hope to add techniques using touch screens, several different graphic tablets, and both voice and character recognition.

Another goal of our work has been to investigate the applicability of the linguistic model of the user interface. We have for some time felt that this model is limited in its ability to describe the natural use of interactive graphics in user interfaces. In this work we focused on defining the boundaries of the lexical, syntactic and semantic levels of the interface "language" in terms of objects, rather than as strictly defined interfaces. Each interface between two levels is embodied in an object with sufficient knowledge about both levels to handle their interface intelligently. For example, embodying the syntactic/semantic boundary in the I_object allows many

situations requiring knowledge of both syntax and semantics such as semantic error handling and semantic feedback to be handled within the UIMS in a manner specified by the dialog designer rather than the application programmer.

Localization of these boundaries within objects is also important for our approach to our longer term goal of developing knowledge-based "assistants" to aid the designer of user interfaces. We intend to develop assistants first in two specific areas: semantic error handling and selection of natural interaction techniques for given application tasks. Within our current model the first of these assistants fits at the same level of abstraction as an I_object and the second at the level of an R_object.

We are currently developing knowledge representations and knowledge acquisition techniques to enable us to add these assistants to our system. The reader familiar with knowledge representation may have noticed the similarity between our objects (most apparent in the I_object) and frames with procedural attachment. This similarity is not coincidental since we have consciously designed our system to include an expansion of our current simple knowledge base. We are still in the early stages of this enhancement and cannot predict with certainty where it will lead. Ultimately we intend for the GWUIMS to develop into a true partner for the user interface designer; at present we are working on understanding it as a tool.

Acknowledgements

The work reported in this paper was supported in part by the National Aeronautics and Space Administration under contract NAS5-27585. In addition , we are grateful for thoughtful and detailed editorial comments from Jerry Farrell , Jim Foley, and Linda Sibert.

Bibliography

Anson Edward. 1982. The Device Model of Interactive Computer Graphics. *Computer Graphics.* 16,3:107-114.

Beach, R.; Beatty, J., Booth, K., Plebon, D. and Fiume, E. 1982. The Message is the Medium: Multiprocess Structuring of an Interactive Paint Program. *SIGGRAPH'82 Conference Proceedings,* 277-287.

Bleser, T., and Foley J. (1982, March). Towards specifying and evaluating the human factors of user-computer interfaces. *Proc. Human Factors in Computer Systems*

Buxton, W.; Lamb, M.R.; Sherman, D.; and Smith, K.C., 1983. Towards a comprehensive user interface management system. *Computer Graphics.* 17(3), 35-42.

Cochran, Duane r., and Stocker, Frederick R. 1985. RIPL; An Environment for Rapid Prototyping with Intelligent Support. *SIGCHI Bulletin.*

Dahl, O.J., and Nygaard, K. 1966. SIMULA - An Algol-based Simulation Language. *Communications of the ACM.* 9: 671-678.

Feldman, M.B., and Rogers, G.T. (1982, March) Toward the design and development of style-independent interactive systems. *Proc. Human Factors in Computer Systems .* 111-116.

Foley, James D.; and McMath, C.F. 1986. Dynamic Process Visualization. Forthcoming issue of *Computer Graphics and Applications.*

Foley, James D.; van Dam, A. 1982. *Fundamentals of Interactive Computer Graphics.* Addison-Wesley, Reading, Massachusetts.

Goldberg, Adele. 1984. Smalltalk-80. The Interactive Programming Environment. Addison-Wesley, Reading Mass.

Green, Mark. 1985. The University of Alberta user interface management system. *Computer Graphics .* 19(3), 213.

Hayes, P.; Szekely, P.; and Lerner, R. 1985. Design Alternatives for User Interface Management Systems Based on Experience with COUSIN. *Human Factors in Computing Systems, Chi'85 Proceedings.* 169-175.

Hurley, W.D. 1985. An Enhanced Flavors Environment for Prototyping and Knowledge Acquisition. GWU-IIST-85-24. George Washington University

Jacob, R.J.K. 1983. Using formal specifications in the design of a human-computer interface. *CACM .* 26(4), 259-264.

Kamran, Abid, and Feldman, Michael B. 1983. Graphics programming independent of interaction techniques and styles. *Computer Graphics* 17(1), 58-66.

Kasik, David J. 1982. A user interface management sytem. *Computer Graphics.* 16(3), 99-106.

Lipke, D.; Evans, S.; Newlin, J.; and Weissman, R. 1982. Star Graphics: An Object-Oriented Implementation. *SIGGRAPH'82 Conference Proceedings.* 115-124.

Newman, William. 1968. A System for Interactive Graphical Programming. SJCC 1968. Thompson Books. Washington D.C. 47-54.

Olsen, D.R. Jr., and Dempsey, E.P. 1983. SYNGRAPH: a graphical user interface generator. *Computer Graphics .* 17(3), 43-50.

Olsen, D.R., Jr.; Dempsey, E.P.; and Rogge, R. 1985. Input/output linkage in a user interface management system. *Computer Graphics .* 19(3), 191-197.

Reisner, P. 1981. Formal Grammar and Human Factors design of an interactive graphics system. *IEEE Transactions on Software Engineering.* SE-7(2), 229-240.

Rentsch, T. 1982. Object-oriented programming. *SIGPLAN Notices* 17(9), 51-57

Roach, J., Pittman, J., Reilly, S., and Savarese, J. 1982. A Visual Design Consultant. *Proc. of the IEEE Systems, Man, and Cybernetics Conf.* Seattle Wash.

Sibert, J.L.; Belliardi, R.; and Kamran, A. 1985. Some Thoughts on the Interface Between UIMS and Application Programs. User Interface Managment Systems, . Springer Verlag. 183-189.

Sibert, J.L., and Hurley W.D. 1984. A prototype for a general user interface management system. GWU-IIST Report 84-47.

Sibert J.; Hurley, W.D.; and Bleser T. 1986. "User Interface Prototyping System: Design Document".GWU-IIST Report 86-1. George Washington University Institute for Information Science and Technology, Washington D.C.

Stefik, M. and Bobrow, D. 1986. Object-oriented programming: themes and variations. AI Magazine 6(4), 40-62.

Weinreb, D. and Moon, D. 1980. Flavors: Message Passing in the Lisp Machine. MIT AI Laboratory Memo No. 602.

Ray Tracing Complex Scenes

Timothy L. Kay
James T. Kajiya
California Institute of Technology
Pasadena, CA 91125

Abstract

A new algorithm for speeding up ray-object intersection calculations is presented. Objects are bounded by a new type of extent, which can be made to fit convex hulls arbitrarily tightly. The objects are placed into a hierarchy. A new hierarchy traversal algorithm is presented which is efficient in the sense that objects along the ray are queried in an efficient order.

Results are presented which demonstrate that our technique is several times faster than other published algorithms. Furthermore, we demonstrate that it is currently possible to ray trace scenes containing hundreds of thousands of objects.

Keywords: Ray tracing, extent, bounding volume, hierarchy, traversal

1 Introduction

Our purpose in studying ray tracing is to develop techniques for synthesizing complex, realistic images. We have two primary requirements; the rendering program must produce images of the highest possible quality, and it must be able to handle hundreds of thousands or millions of objects.

Rubin and Whitted [Rubin 80] determined that their program spent most of its time computing ray-object intersections in order to calculate which object was visible for a given ray. The performance worsened linearly as the number of objects in the scene increased. To improve performance, they proposed placing simple bounding volumes around each object in their database. If a given ray failed to intersect the bounding volume for a particular object, the object needed no further consideration. This way, they avoided many ray-object intersection calculations. By grouping objects hierarchically and placing a bounding volume encompassing the extent of all children at each node of the hierarchy tree, the majority of the ray-bounding volume intersection calculations could also be avoided. Rubin and Whitted chose rectangular solids as bounding volumes. To improve tightness, they deformed the rectangular solids with an affine matrix, thereby requiring a matrix-vector multiply before the ray-bounding volume test could be performed.

Weghorst, et. al. [Weghorst 84] proposed and benchmarked a similar scheme. Notably, they studied the use of different types of bounding volumes in a single hierarchy.

Concurrently but independently, Glassner [Glassner 84] and Kaplan [Kaplan 85] and more recently Fujimoto, et. al. [Fujimoto 86] studied a different approach to the problem. Whereas Rubin and Whitted and Weghorst created bounding volumes to surround their objects, Glassner and Kaplan divided their objects into cells of an octree. As a ray passed through space, the octree data structure rejected any objects trivially far away from the ray. A significant feature of the Glassner-Kaplan algorithm is that it considered objects along a given ray roughly *in the order that they occurred along the ray*. A major drawback of this space-partitioning approach is that any particular object might end up in more than one octree cell, potentially requiring a ray to be intersected with the same object more than once.

In this paper we partition objects rather than space. We present a new type of bounding volume for which a ray intersection requires very little computation. Unlike previously described bounding volumes, ours have the advantage that they can be made to fit the convex hull of an object arbitrarily tightly in exchange for a slower intersection computation.

We present a new algorithm for traversing a hierarchy of such bounding volumes. The algorithm is ef-

© 1986   ACM 0-89791-196-2/86/008/0269 $00.75

ficient in the sense that, for a given type of bounding volume and a given ray, the objects are queried in a well-defined, efficient order regardless of the hierarchy.

The results section compares our method to recently-published work and finds that our algorithm is roughly three times faster. More importantly, our technique has proven capable of rendering scenes containing over one hundred thousand objects. This enabled us to compute two sequences for the SIGGRAPH '84 Omnimax film *The Magic Egg* and the piece *Trees* in the SIGGRAPH '85 film show.

2   Object Extents

The *extent* of an object is the region of space occupied by the object. For the sake of computational simplicity, we wish to bound each object in a volume that is simpler than the object itself. If a ray-extent intersection is significantly faster than a ray-object intersection, the results of the ray-extent intersections can be used to prune a majority of the expensive ray-object intersections. If a ray does not hit an object's bounding volume, then clearly it will miss the object itself.

In choosing bounding volumes for arbitrarily complex objects, two opposing constraints must be balanced. If a bounding volume fits an object loosely, many rays that hit the bounding volume will miss the object. If a bounding volume describes an object's extent precisely, very few ray-object intersection calculations will be wasted. By this criterion alone, the best bounding volume for an object is the object itself. On the other hand, intersecting rays with simpler bounding volumes requires fewer calculations. This constraint suggests that simple spheres, ellipsoids and rectangular solids are good bounding volumes. For example, Rubin and Whitted and Toth [Toth 85] used rectangular solids to describe object extents, while Weghorst used a mixture of objects such as rectangular solids and spheres.

With respect to the tightness versus speed tradeoff, the bounding volumes now presented can be tailored to suit the particular scene being rendered.

2.1   Bounding Volume Description

We bound objects with parallelopipeds constructed of planes. An arbitrary plane in 3-space is described implicitly by the equation

$$Ax + By + Cz - d = 0. \qquad (1)$$

Geometrically, Equation 1 describes a plane with normal vector $\hat{P}_i = \begin{pmatrix} A \\ B \\ C \end{pmatrix}$ lying d units from the origin.

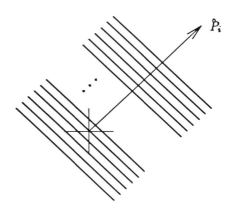

Figure 1: The set of planes defined by $\hat{P}_i$

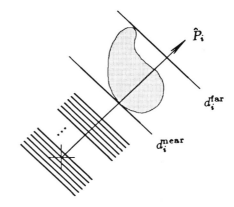

Figure 2: Planes corresponding to $\hat{P}_i$ that bound an object

If the normal vector $\hat{P}_i$ is fixed, leaving the distance d free to vary, Equation 1 then describes the set of all planes normal to $\hat{P}_i$. See Figure 1. Out of any such set we choose two planes that bound a given object. See Figure 2. Significantly, we can describe these two planes by exactly two real numbers d_i^{near} and d_i^{far}, the values of d for the two planes. We call the region in space between such planes a *slab*. The normal vector defining the orientation of a slab is termed a *plane-set normal*.

Different choices of plane-set normals $\hat{P}_i$ yield different bounding slabs for an object. The intersection of a set of bounding slabs yields a bounding volume. In order to create a closed bounding volume in 3-space, at least three bounding slabs must be involved, and they must be chosen so that the defining normal vectors span 3-space. For the sake of simplicity, the examples in the figures are presented in 2-space, in which a minimum of two vectors will span. The generalization to 3-space requires the addition of a third coordinate to each vector; the equations generalize without modification. Figure 3a shows an object bounded by slabs with nor-

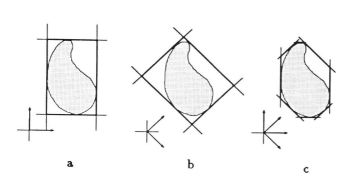

Figure 3: Bounding an object using various normals

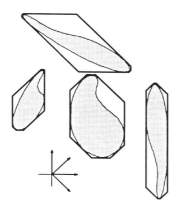

Figure 4: Objects bounded by a fixed set of normals

mals $\begin{pmatrix} 1 \\ 0 \end{pmatrix}$ and $\begin{pmatrix} 0 \\ 1 \end{pmatrix}$. Figure 3b shows the same object bounded using normals $\begin{pmatrix} \frac{\sqrt{2}}{2} \\ \frac{\sqrt{2}}{2} \end{pmatrix}$ and $\begin{pmatrix} \frac{\sqrt{2}}{2} \\ \frac{-\sqrt{2}}{2} \end{pmatrix}$. Figure 3c shows the same object bounded using all four normals.

A realistic scene will contain millions of objects. Storing plane-set normals and corresponding d^{near} and d^{far} for each object would require a great deal of memory and, as we will soon see, a great deal of computation. Therefore, we choose our plane-set normals in advance, independent of the particular objects to be bounded. This will restrict our choices of bounding volumes, but will allow us to describe them by a small set of numbers. Figure 4 shows several objects bounded by volumes restricted to preselected plane-set normals.

The plane-set normals $\begin{pmatrix} 1 \\ 0 \\ 0 \end{pmatrix}$, $\begin{pmatrix} 0 \\ 1 \\ 0 \end{pmatrix}$ and $\begin{pmatrix} 0 \\ 0 \\ 1 \end{pmatrix}$ define rectangular solid bounding volumes whose faces are perpendicular to the coordinate axes. The plane-set

normals $\begin{pmatrix} \frac{\sqrt{3}}{3} \\ \frac{\sqrt{3}}{3} \\ \frac{\sqrt{3}}{3} \end{pmatrix}$, $\begin{pmatrix} \frac{-\sqrt{3}}{3} \\ \frac{\sqrt{3}}{3} \\ \frac{\sqrt{3}}{3} \end{pmatrix}$, $\begin{pmatrix} \frac{-\sqrt{3}}{3} \\ \frac{-\sqrt{3}}{3} \\ \frac{\sqrt{3}}{3} \end{pmatrix}$ and $\begin{pmatrix} \frac{\sqrt{3}}{3} \\ \frac{-\sqrt{3}}{3} \\ \frac{\sqrt{3}}{3} \end{pmatrix}$ define eight-sided parallelopipeds.

Bounding volumes constructed using a larger number of plane-set normals will bound objects more tightly. For example, Figure 13 shows a tree for which we wish to compute bounding volumes. Figure 8a shows the bounding volumes created using the first three normals mentioned in the previous paragraph. Figure 8b shows the volumes formed using all seven normals.

2.2   Computing Bounding Volumes

The d_i^{near} and d_i^{far} values are simply the endpoints of the extent of the projection of the object onto the normal $\hat{P}_i$.

A modeling transformation is associated with each object in the database. This transformation must be taken into account because the bounding volumes exist in world space. We will treat a modeling transformation as a three-by-three matrix M and a translation vector T. We describe the bounding volume calculation for several types of objects.

Example 1. Polyhedra

A polyhedron is defined by a collection of vertices $\begin{pmatrix} x_j \\ y_j \\ z_j \end{pmatrix}$. We compute the bounding volume for the polyhedron by computing the bounding volume enclosing these vertices. There are three steps.

1. The bounding volume belongs in final world coordinates, the vertices must be transformed by M.

$$\begin{pmatrix} x_j' \\ y_j' \\ z_j' \end{pmatrix} = M \begin{pmatrix} x_j \\ y_j \\ z_j \end{pmatrix} + T.$$

2. Each vertex is projected onto each $\hat{P}_i$.

$$d_{ij} = \left(\hat{P}_i \right)^T \begin{pmatrix} x_j' \\ y_j' \\ z_j' \end{pmatrix}.^1$$

3. Corresponding to each $\hat{P}_i$, compute

$$d_i^{near} = \min \{d_{ij}\}$$

and

$$d_i^{far} = \max \{d_{ij}\}.$$

---

[1] A row vector followed by a column vector denotes dot product.

Example 2. Implicit surfaces

Spheres and other implicit surfaces must be approached differently. We wish to compute bounds for the set of points $\begin{pmatrix} x \\ y \\ z \end{pmatrix}$ which satisfy the implicit equation of the surface. We will first treat the transformation by M and then account for T afterwards.

After transforming by M, we project each point onto $\hat{P}_i$. The transformation and projection yield

$$f\begin{pmatrix} x \\ y \\ z \end{pmatrix} = \hat{P}_i^{\mathrm{T}}\left(M\begin{pmatrix} x \\ y \\ z \end{pmatrix}\right).$$

We apply the associative property.

$$f\begin{pmatrix} x \\ y \\ z \end{pmatrix} = \left(\hat{P}_i^{\mathrm{T}}M\right)\begin{pmatrix} x \\ y \\ z \end{pmatrix}.$$

If we let

$$\begin{pmatrix} A \\ B \\ C \end{pmatrix} = \left(\hat{P}_i^{\mathrm{T}}M\right)^{\mathrm{T}} = M^{\mathrm{T}}\hat{P}_i,$$

we can rewrite f as

$$f\begin{pmatrix} x \\ y \\ z \end{pmatrix} = Ax + By + Cz. \tag{2}$$

Here we have a scalar field constrained by the implicit equation, and we wish to find the minimum and maximum values assumed by f. Problems of this type can be solved readily using the method of Lagrange multipliers (see [Apostol 69]).

Next we account for the translation T. We need to translate each $\left(d_i^{\mathrm{near}}, d_i^{\mathrm{far}}\right)$ pair by the length of the component of T parallel to $\hat{P}_i$, which is simply $T \cdot \hat{P}_i$.

For example, the implicit equation of a sphere is

$$x^2 + y^2 + z^2 - 1 = 0. \tag{3}$$

The method of Lagrange multipliers tells us that the extrema occur when

$$\begin{pmatrix} A \\ B \\ C \end{pmatrix} = \lambda \begin{pmatrix} 2x \\ 2y \\ 2z \end{pmatrix}.$$

Substituting back into Equations 2 and 3 gives

$$f\begin{pmatrix} x \\ y \\ z \end{pmatrix}\Bigg|_{x^2+y^2+z^2-1=0} = \pm\sqrt{A^2 + B^2 + C^2}.$$

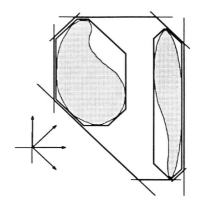

Figure 5: The bounding volume of two bounding volumes

The contribution of T to the position of each slab is $T \cdot \hat{P}_i$. Combining the contributions from M and T yields

$$\left(d_i^{\mathrm{near}}, d_i^{\mathrm{far}}\right) = \left(T \cdot \hat{P}_i - \left|M^{\mathrm{T}}\hat{P}_i\right|, T \cdot \hat{P}_i + \left|M^{\mathrm{T}}\hat{P}_i\right|\right).$$

Example 3. Compound objects

The bounding volumes for compound objects such as booleans (constructed as unions, intersections and subtractions of other objects) can be calculated by first computing bounding volumes for each subobject. These bounding volumes can then be combined. As Figure 5 demonstrates, the bounding volume of two bounding volumes is simply the pairwise minimum of each d_i^{near} and the pairwise maximum of each d_i^{far} value.

For example, the branches of the trees in the results section are cylinders with a sphere at each end. A branch's bounding volumes is computed as a combination of the two sphere's bounding volumes. We can ignore the bounding volume of the cylinder because it is guaranteed to lie within the combined bounding volume of the two spheres.

2.3 Ray-Volume Intersection

The intersection algorithm presented here is similar in spirit to that of Cyrus and Beck [Cyrus 78].

A ray intersects with a slab to yield an interval along the ray. To compute this interval, we intersect the ray

$$R = \hat{a}t + b \tag{4}$$

with the each of the two planes bounding the slab. The solution of this intersection in terms of the ray parameter t is computed by substituting the ray Equation 4 into the plane Equation 1 yielding

$$t = \frac{d_i - \hat{P}_i \cdot b}{\hat{P}_i \cdot \hat{a}}. \tag{5}$$

The computation for both planes is identical, and each provides one endpoint to the interval along the ray. Care must be taken to orient the two endpoints correctly. If the denominator of Equation 5 is less than zero, then the roles of the near and far values must be reversed. Also, in the event that this dot product is close to zero, the division in Equation 5 might cause an overflow (or division by zero). We will provide a solution to this problem later.

To compute the intersection of a ray with a bounding volume, we compute the intersection of the ray with each slab, and then compute the intersection of these intervals. We compute the intersection of the intervals by computing the maximum of the near values and the minimum of the far values.

If the ray happened to miss the bounding volume, then t^{near} will be larger than t^{far}. Otherwise we have the value of t at the two intersections of the ray with the bounding volume. These values are useful as estimates of the position of the object along the ray.

2.4   Cost of Intersection

By counting operations in Equation 5 we see that each ray-slab intersection requires four dot products, two subtracts and two divides when taking both planes into account. These numbers must be multiplied by the number of slabs involved in each bounding volume, and a minimization and a maximization must be done across the slabs.

But we have determined our choice of plane-set normals a priori. For a given ray, we can compute the dot products to be used in all calculations just once. If there are many ray-bounding volume intersections associated with each ray, and this is generally the case, the expense of the dot product computation will be of little significance. Furthermore, at the time that the dot products are precomputed, we can calculate the reciprocal of the denominator of Equation 5 and replace the divide with a multiply. Before taking its reciprocal, though, the value must be checked for the possibility of overflow or divide by zero. If this is the case, a large number can be used in place of the reciprocal. [2]

$$t = (d_i - S)T.$$

where $S = \hat{P}_i \cdot b$ and $T = \frac{1}{\hat{P}_i \cdot a}$.

The new computation requires two subtracts, two multiplies and a comparison for each slab contributing to the bounding volume. The calculation is now very fast.

---

[2] Let M be the square root of the largest number representable by the machine. If we restrict the database to lie within a sphere of this radius, centered at the origin, then we can safely replace the reciprocal with M and avoid overflows.

The expense of a ray-bounding volume intersection grows linearly with the number of slabs used to bound an object. A slight modification improves performance. Most rays miss most bounding volumes by a wide margin. When this occurs, the intersection of the different ray-slab computations will be empty after no more than three slabs are processed. Therefore, the interval intersection calculation should be done in tandem with the ray-slab intersection calculation. If the intersection becomes empty, the rest of the ray-slab intersections can be ignored.

3   Object Hierarchies

While a large savings can be obtained by placing each object in a bounding volume, the cost of computing an image remains proportional to the number of objects in the image. A much larger savings can be achieved by creating a hierarchy of objects. We define the extent of a particular node in the hierarchy to be the combined extent of all that node's children. For each such node we compute a bounding volume. Then if a ray misses the bounding volume at a given node in the hierarchy, we can reject that node's entire subtree from further consideration. Using a hierarchy causes the cost of computing an image to behave logarithmically in the number of objects in the scene.

In creating a hierarchy, we require one fundamental operation on bounding volumes. We must be able to compute the bounding volume of a particular node in the hierarchy tree given the bounding volumes of that node's children. The volume enclosing two other bounding volumes is simply the minimum of the d_i^{near} and the maximum of the d_i^{far} values for the pair of bounding volumes in question.

3.1   Hierarchies

There are many schemes for constructing a hierarchy. Some are easy to implement and fast to execute, while others might be sophisticated and consume large amounts of computer time. There are several interrelated properties that would seem to distinguish a good hierarchy from a bad one.

- Any given subtree should contain objects that are near each other. "Nearness" is relative, but the lower the subtree is with respect to the entire hierarchy, the "nearer" objects should be.

- The volume of each node should be minimal.

- The sum of the volume of all bounding volumes should be minimal.

- The construction of the tree should concentrate on the nodes nearer the root of the tree. Pruning a branch of the tree there allows a large subtree to be remove from further consideration, whereas pruning one lower down removes just a few bounding volumes and objects from further consideration.

- The time spent constructing the hierarchy tree should more than pay for itself in time saved rendering the image.

The simplest hierarchy involves almost no computation, and gives no consideration to the "nearness" criterion. Taking the objects in the order that they are described, we simply create a tree with a fixed branching ratio using a bottom-up construction. This construction does moderately well with regard to nearness if the database is modeled in a coherent fashion.

We could spend additional computer time to construct a better hierarchy. A *median-cut* scheme will help group near objects together even if they aren't modeled coherently. The scheme constructs a binary tree in a top-down fashion. At each level all the objects in the database are sorted by their x coordinate. The objects are then partitioned at their median. This defines which objects belong on each side of the tree. The process is repeated recursively, except that at each level the objects are sorted and partitioned on a different coordinate axis.

The previous algorithm attempts to group objects based on their nearness to each other, but it does so along one dimension at a time. It might do better to group objects in along three dimensions at once by employing an octree. This preprocessing step would be very similar to the one described in [Glassner 84] or [Kaplan 85]. The difference is that, if an object stradles two or more octree cells, it is arbitrarily placed in exactly one of them. Furthermore, after the preprocessing is completed, the octree is used solely to define the hierarchy; each object must still be assigned a distinct bounding volume.

4 Hierarchy Traversal

We present a traversal algorithm whose output is insensitive to the manner in which the hierarchy is constructed. This traversal algorithm bears similarities to the fractal intersection algorithm of Kajiya [Kajiya 83]. We will assume that the type of bounding volume to be used has has been fixed *a priori*. We demonstrate that for any ray there is a preferred order with which to query the objects in the database.

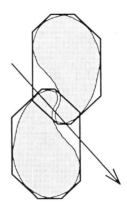

Figure 6: The ray tracing program must compute two object intersections

The intersection of a ray with an object's bounding volume yields two numbers. We call the nearer number the *estimated distance* of the object along the ray. For a given ray, a bounding volumes will assign a unique estimated distance to each object in the database. These numbers impose a total order on the objects which defines the best order to search the database to resolve the ray's intersection.

The first object in the preferred order is not necessarily the one in which we are interested. Figure 6 demonstrates that the first object is not always the visible object. The best we can do is to proceed through the objects in order and compute ray-object intersections. If we find an object that intersects the ray at a point closer than the remaining objects' distance estimates, then the object in question is the visible object.

The hierarchy traversal algorithm presented in Figure 7 will search the database in the total order just defined. Because objects are queried in the same order regardless of the object bounding volume hierarchy, the difference between a poorly constructed hierarchy and a good one is slight. Given a poor hierarchy, the program will spend more time computing ray-bounding volume intersections. *The performance of the rest of the program (ray-object intersections, shading calculations) will be unaffected.*

The traversal algorithm searches the hierarchy tree, but unlike a depth first or breadth first search, it traverses the hierarchy tree in an order derived while the traversal is in progress. A *candidate* node is one whose bounding volume is known to be in the path of the ray, but whose children have yet to be interrogated. We keep track of candidate nodes in a priority queue, implemented as a heap (see [Aho 74] or [Sedgewick 83]). The heap guides the search by selecting the candidate with the smallest nonnegative distance estimate.

We have found that the use of a heap is essential to

We are given a ray
Compute dot products and reciprocals (section 2.4)
Let t = distance to the nearest object hit so far
Initialize $t = +\inf$
Let p contain a pointer to the nearest object hit so far
Initialize p = nil
While heap is non-empty and distance to top node $< t$
  Extract candidate from heap
  If the candidate is a leaf
    Compute ray-object intersection
    If ray hits candidate and distance $< t$ then
      t = distance
      p = candidate
    Endif
  Else
    For each child of the candidate
      Compute ray-bounding volume intersection
      If the ray hits the bounding volume
        Insert the child into the heap
      Endif
    Endfor
  Endif
Endwhile

Figure 7: Traversal algorithm

the efficiency of the algorithm. In previous implementations it was found that a tremendous amount of time was spent in sorting routines. A heap does a better job while consuming much less computer time.

5 Results

The ray tracing scheme just described has been under development for several years. A primitive version was used to compute the *Space Colony* and *Saturn Flyby* sequences from the SIGGRAPH '84 Omnimax film *The Magic Egg*.

A revised version of the program was used to compute *Trees,* which was shown at the SIGGRAPH '85 Film Show. Figure 9 is a frame from this movie. The *Trees* database contains about 110,000 objects.

The ability to compute these two movies demonstrates the feasibility of our algorithms. We expect to ray trace a scene containing at least one million objects by the end of 1986.

The test images represent an increasing sequence of scene compositions and complexities. With Figure 10 we attempt to duplicate a test case in Glassner's paper. The pyramid is constructed of 1024 triangles. Figure 11 contains four copies of the pyramid from Figure 10. Figure 12 contains 2 superquadrics [Barr 81] and 400 tiles each composed of 6 faces. Figure 13 contains a base polygon and a single tree composed of 1271 branches. Figure 14 contains the same objects as Figure 13 in

	Pyramid ** 4	Pyramid ** 5	Super-quadric	Tree Branches	Tree Leaves	Trees
Objects	1024	4096	2402	1272	7455	110000+
Lights	1	1	2	1	1	1
Pixels	262	262	262	262	262	262
Color Rays	263	263	263	263	263	263
Shadow Rays	37	34	410	135	155	
Total Rays	300	297	673	398	418	
Rays that Hit	43	41	241	151	206	
Object Int.	521	330	841	354	983	
B. V. Int.	2810	3678	44802	18491	33783	2880000@
Time 4381 sec	980	1033	5147	2429	4116	
(sec/ray)	.00327	.00348	.00765	.00610	.00985	
(sec/ray that hit)	.02276	.02523	.02138	.01608	.01998	

All pixel, ray and intersection counts are in thousands.

@ Computed on a 3081 using an early version of the code.

Table 1: Timing data

addition to 6184 polygonal leaves.

All images were computed on an IBM 4381/Group 12 using Amdahl UTS, a version of Unix/System V. Depending on the scene, a 4381 benchmarks 3.5-4.0 times faster than a Vax 11/780 running Berkeley Unix 4.2. The pictures were computed at 512 by 512 pixel resolution. For the sake of the presentation, all images in this publication were antialiased using 4 by 4 subsampling. The samples were then filtered using an eight-lobe, windowed sinc function. The values reported in Table 1 correspond to the same images computed with one sample per pixel.

It is reasonable to present the benchmarks in terms of atomic actions rather than as execution times for pictures of some arbitrary size. Since we are concentrating on the ray casting aspects of ray tracing, we report the speed of the program in units of seconds per ray.

Table 1 contains the statistics for the test images. Timings are given in seconds, seconds per ray, and seconds per object-hitting ray. The time per ray value changes drastically with each image. When the amount of visible background increases, there are more rays that miss the world. These rays require very little computation and thereby bias the statistics. We ignore these rays by keeping track of the object-hitting rays. While the time per ray changes a great deal from image to image, the time per object-hitting ray stays relatively constant.

In their recent papers, Glassner and Weghorst report execution times for their ray tracing programs. We had hoped to do an in-depth comparison of the speeds of their implementations with ours. Despite our efforts, we have found that there are too many unknown factors involved. In the hopes of establishing a basis for future comparison, we offer our databases to anyone who wishes to put their programs through its paces. Furthermore, we welcome discussions regarding which benchmarks would be most informative.

The few comparisons we can make between Glassner's data and our own seem to suggest that our method is significantly faster. We managed to faithfully reproduce only one of his models. We recomputed our version on a Vax/780 for the sake of comparison. Glassner program used 8700 seconds of Vax/780 time to render his "recursive pyramid" of Figure 10, while our implementation took 2706 seconds. Because the viewpoints differed slightly, he shot 352322 rays to our 298588. Taking this into account, we can conclude that, for this particular image, our program runs 2.6 times faster than his.

We can increase the number of plane-set normals beyond the required three. Figure 8 demonstrates that objects can be bounded very tightly in this fashion. The pyramid benchmark ran the fastest when the combined normals of an octahedron were combined with a single additional normal pointing upwards.

When ray tracing on a supercomputer, a larger number of plane-set normals is very advantageous. In that environment, the traversal algorithm may be vectorized, and the incremental cost of additional plane sets is minimal.

6   Conclusion

As databases become increasingly complex, the time spent computing the visible object for a ray becomes the dominant concern. We have presented a new algorithm for speeding up this process.

7   References

[Apostol 69] Apostol, Tom M., *Calculus*, Volume II, Wiley, New York, 1969, pp. 314-318.

[Barr 81] Barr, Alan H., "Superquadrics and Angle Preserving Transformations," *Computer Graphics and Applications,* 1(1).

[Cook 84] Cook, Robert L., Thomas Porter and Loren Carpenter, "Distributed Ray Tracing," Computer Graphics, 18(3), July 1984, pp. 137-145.

[Cyrus 78] Cyrus, M. and J. Beck, "Generalized two and three dimensional Clipping," Computers and Graphics, 3(1), 1978, pp. 23-28.

[Fujimoto 86] Fujimoto, Akira, Takayuki Tanaka, and Kansei Iwata, "ARTS: Accelerated Ray-Tracing System", IEEE Computer Graphics and Applications, 6(4), April 1986, 16-26.

[Glassner 84] Glassner, Andrew S., "Space Subdivision for Fast Ray Tracing," IEEE Computer Graphics and Applications, 4(10), October, 1984, pp. 15-22.

[Kaplan 85] Kaplan, Michael R., "The Uses of Spatial Coherence in Ray Tracing," ACM SIGGRAPH '85 Course Notes 11, July 22-26 1985.

[Kay 86] Kay, Timothy L., M.S. dissertation in preparation.

[Kajiya 83] Kajiya, James T., "New Techniques for Ray Tracing Procedurally Defined Objects", Computer Graphics, 17(3), July, 1983, pp. 91-102.

[Rubin 80] Rubin, Steve M. and T. Whitted., "A Three-Dimensional Representation for Fast Rendering of Complex Scenes," Computer Graphics 14(3), July 1980, pp. 110-116.

[Sedgewick 83] Sedgewick, Robert, *Algorithms*, Addison-Wesley, Reading, 1983, pp. 127-142.

[Toth 85] Toth, Daniel L., "On Ray Tracing Parametric Surfaces," Computer Graphics 19(3), July 1985, pp. 171-179.

[Weghorst 84] Weghorst, Hank, Gary Hooper, and Donald P. Greenberg, "Improved Computational Methods for Ray Tracing," ACM Transactions on Graphics, 3(1), January 1984, pp. 52-69.

[Whitted 80] Whitted, Turner, "An Improved Illumination Model for Shaded Display," Communications of the ACM, 23(6), June 1980, 343-349.

Figure 8a

Figure 8b

Figure 9

Figure 10

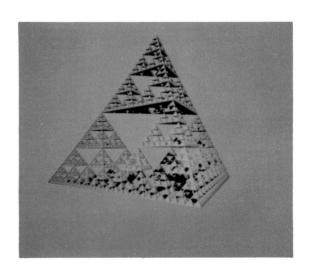

Figure 11

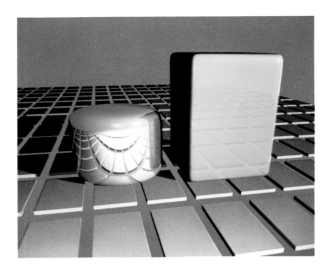

Figure 12

Figure 13

Figure 14

Ray Tracing
Parametric Surface Patches
Utilizing Numerical Techniques and Ray Coherence

Kenneth I. Joy
Murthy N. Bhetanabhotla

Signal and Image Processing Laboratory
Computer Science Division
Department of Electrical and Computer Engineering
University of California, Davis

Abstract

A new algorithm for ray tracing parametric surface patches is presented. The method uses quasi-Newton iteration to solve for the ray/surface intersection and utilizes ray-to-ray coherence by using numerical information from adjoining rays as initial approximations to the quasi-Newton algorithm. Techniques based upon object space subdivision are used to insure convergence to the correct intersection point. Examples are given of the use of the algorithm in scenes containing Bézier surface patches. Results show that a significant number of ray/surface intersections on these parametric surface patches can be found using very few iterations, giving a significant computational savings.

Categories and Subject Descriptors: I.3.3 [**Computer Graphics**]: Picture/Image Generation; I.3.5 [**Computer Graphics**]: Computational Geometry and Object Modeling ; I.3.7 [**Computer Graphics**]: Three-Dimensional Graphics and Realism

General Terms: Algorithms

Additional Key Words and Phrases: Computer graphics, ray tracing, visible-surface algorithms, parametric surfaces, quasi-Newton methods.

1. Introduction

Ray Tracing is a powerful yet simple approach to image generation. It has its roots in the works of Appel [1] and Bouknight and Kelley [4], but most current implementations are based upon the results of Whitted [28], who specified a method to accurately determine the light propagation throughout a scene, including reflections, refractions from transparent surfaces and shadows. The method has become the primary vehicle from which highly realistic imagery is generated.

The primary computational burden of the algorithm is the calculation of the intersection of a ray and a surface. Typically, for complex scenes modeling complex lighting effects, anti-aliasing or motion blur [6, 9, 21], this calculation must be performed millions of times. Direct methods of calculation have

© 1986   ACM 0-89791-196-2/86/008/0279 $00.75

been found for several surface types, including spheres, polygons [28], cylinders and volumes of revolution [20], Steiner Patches [22] and bicubic surface patches [19]. Numerical techniques have been employed in the calculation for certain algebraic surfaces [3, 16] and for parametric surface patches [26, 25].

Reducing the number of ray/surface intersection calculations has been addressed by several authors [8, 13, 14, 18, 24, 27, 28]. Object space subdivision [8, 13, 14, 18] divides the scene into cells, each holding information as to the surfaces that intersect the cell. A fast method is then given for tracing the rays through the cells, only performing intersections with those objects which are contained in the intersected cells. Hierarchical definition of the data using bounding volumes [27] has also been shown to be useful.

This paper also focuses on numerical techniques to calculate the intersection of a ray and surface, specifically quasi-Newton methods. These methods accelerate the steepest-descent technique for function minimization by using computational history to generate a sequence of approximations. We describe this technique in section 2. Section 3 describes the application of the quasi-Newton algorithm to the process of ray tracing and develops a minimal set of information that is needed in the iteration. The integration of this "computational history" into a ray coherence scheme is discussed in section 4 and an adaptation of an object space subdivision scheme used to implement the ray coherence is given in section 5. Implementation details and Examples are contained in sections 6 and 7.

2. Quasi-Newton Methods

Given a non-negative function $F : \mathbf{R}^n \dashrightarrow \mathbf{R}$ and an initial approximation $x^{(0)}$, Newton's method for finding a local minimum of $F(\mathbf{x})$ generates a sequence of points,

$$\mathbf{x}^{(k+1)} = \mathbf{x}^{(k)} - s^{(k)}\left[\mathbf{J}^{(k)}\right]^{-1}\mathbf{g}^{(k)}$$

where

- $\mathbf{g}^{(k)} = \nabla F(\mathbf{x}^{(k)})$, the gradient of F at $\mathbf{x}^{(k)}$,
- $\mathbf{J}^{(k)} = \nabla^2 F(\mathbf{x}^{(k)})$, the Hessian matrix of F evaluated at $\mathbf{x}^{(k)}$, and
- $s^{(k)}$ is a scalar satisfying

$$s^{(k)} = \min_{s}\left(F(\mathbf{x}^{(k)} - s\left[\mathbf{J}^{(k)}\right]^{-1}\mathbf{g}^{(k)})\right)$$

The convergence of the method is better than linear (i.e. *superlinear*), and under certain, very strict, conditions on the structure of the function F and its derivatives, second order convergence can be achieved (see [7]).

This method, unfortunately, exhibits two main computational bottlenecks. First, methods or formulas must be supplied by which $\mathbf{J}^{(k)}$ can be evaluated and inverted at each iteration. Second, the calculation of $s^{(k)}$, which is usually accomplished by a "line search" (see [7]), must be exact in order to achieve superlinear convergence. These problems can be avoided in the class of *quasi-Newton methods*. These methods use an initial estimate and computational history to generate a symmetric, positive definite, estimate $\mathbf{H}^{(k)}$ to $[\mathbf{J}^{(k)}]^{-1}$ at each step rather than performing the computation work of evaluating and inverting $\mathbf{J}^{(k)}$. Thus, given an initial approximation $\mathbf{x}^{(0)}$ and an initial estimate $\mathbf{H}^{(0)}$ of the inverse Hessian, the quasi-Newton methods generate a sequence of points

$$\mathbf{x}^{(k+1)} = \mathbf{x}^{(k)} - s^{(k)}\mathbf{H}^{(k)}\mathbf{g}^{(k)} \qquad (1)$$

and a sequence of updates to the approximate inverse Hessian

$$\mathbf{H}^{(k+1)} = \mathbf{H}^{(k)} + \mathbf{D}^{(k)}$$

where the correction $\mathbf{D}^{(k)}$ is derived from information collected during the last iteration. We note that this is a generalization of the *simple Newton Iteration* discussed by Toth [26], which can be obtained by setting $s^{(k)} = 1$ and $\mathbf{H}^{(k)} = \mathbf{H}^{(0)}$ in equation (1). This method clearly has computational advantages over the conventional Newton's method in that only first derivatives are required, and no matrix inversions need be calculated.

Procedures for updating the approximate inverse Hessian $\mathbf{H}^{(k)}$ have been a active topic of research in nonlinear optimization theory for a number of years. The update used in this research, and found to work well in practice, was developed independently by Broyden [5], Fletcher [11], Goldfarb [15] and Shanno [23] and is referred to as the *BFGS update*. It is given by the following:

Theorem (BFGS)

Let $\mathbf{y}^{(k)} = \mathbf{g}^{(k+1)} - \mathbf{g}^{(k)}$, $\sigma^{(k)} = \mathbf{x}^{(k+1)} - \mathbf{x}^{(k)}$, and

$$r = \frac{(\sigma^{(k)})^T \mathbf{y}^{(k)}}{(\sigma^{(k)})^T \mathbf{y}^{(k)} + (\mathbf{y}^{(k)})^T \mathbf{H}^{(k)}\mathbf{y}^{(k)}}$$

and define

$$\mathbf{H}^{(k+1)} = \mathbf{H}^{(k)} + \frac{(\sigma^{(k)} - r\,\mathbf{H}^{(k)}\mathbf{y}^{(k)})(\sigma^{(k)} - r\,\mathbf{H}^{(k)}\mathbf{y}^{(k)})^T}{(\sigma^{(k)} - r\,\mathbf{H}^{(k)}\mathbf{y}^{(k)})^T \mathbf{y}^{(k)}} \\ + (r-1)\frac{\mathbf{H}^{(k)}\mathbf{y}^{(k)}(\mathbf{y}^{(k)})^T \mathbf{H}^{(k)}}{(\mathbf{y}^{(k)})^T \mathbf{H}^{(k)}\mathbf{y}^{(k)}} \qquad (2)$$

Then, $\mathbf{H}^{(k+1)}$ is positive definite and symmetric, and the quasi-Newton iteration (1) converges superlinearly. In fact, the iteration converges superlinearly even with inexact line searches.

Proof : See [5, 11, 15, or 23], or for a more general treatment see [7]

The fact that superlinear convergence is achieved with inexact line searches implies that exhaustive searches for the exact minimum on the line are not needed. In practice results have also shown the value of taking the full Newton step ($s^{(k)} = 1$) when close to the actual solution. Therefore line searches used with quasi-Newton iteration have evolved to the following form (see [7, 23]).

Let $f(s) = F(\mathbf{x}^{(k)} - s\,\mathbf{H}^{(k)}\mathbf{g}^{(k)})$, and set α to a small positive value, then

- If $f(1) < f(0) + \alpha f'(0)$, then set $s^{(k)} = 1$.
- if $f(1) \geq f(0) + \alpha f'(0)$, then fit a cubic polynomial to the four values $f(0)$, $f(1)$, $f'(0)$, and $f'(0)$, find the unique minimizer $\hat{s}$ of this cubic, and set $s^{(k)} = \hat{s}$

This minimizer can be calculated by the following procedure. Let

$$a = f'(0) + f'(0) - 2f(1) - 2f(0)$$
$$b = 3f(1) + 3f(0) - 2f'(0) - 2f'(0)$$

then

$$\hat{s} = \frac{-b + \sqrt{b^2 - 3af'(0)}}{3a}$$

This search takes a maximum of only two function evaluations and two derivative evaluations. In general, the cubic fit is usually done only once to get the algorithm "on track". The full Newton step is then done on subsequent iterations.

In general, these quasi-Newton methods have been shown to perform better than Newton's method. The total number of iterations to reach a solution may be greater in the quasi-Newton case, but the decreased number of function evaluations allow a better overall performance.

3. Applying Quasi-Newton Methods to Ray Tracing

Given the parametric surface

$$\mathbf{S}(u,v) \quad : \quad \begin{cases} x(u,v) \\ y(u,v) \\ z(u,v) \end{cases}$$

and a ray, defined by the anchor $\mathbf{P} = (x_p, y_p, z_p)$, and the unit direction $\mathbf{R} = <x_r, y_r, z_r>$, we obtain the square of the distance from the surface to the ray by

$$F(u,v) = |\mathbf{V}|^2 - (\mathbf{V}\cdot\mathbf{R})^2$$

where

$$\mathbf{V} = \mathbf{S}(u,v) - \mathbf{P}$$

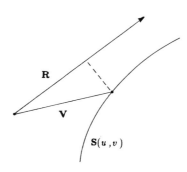

Distance from a Point on the Surface to a Ray
Figure 1

In a more verbose form, this becomes

$$F(u,v) = (x(u,v) - x_p)^2 + (y(u,v) - y_p)^2$$
$$+ (z(u,v) - z_p)^2 - t^2$$

where t, the distance along the ray to the point where the minimum is achieved, is given by $\mathbf{V} \cdot \mathbf{R}$, i.e.

$$t = x_r(x(u,v) - x_p) + y_r(y(u,v) - y_p) + z_r(z(u,v) - z_p)$$

If a local minimum of F is zero, then this corresponds to a point where the ray intersects the surface. Those points where F is a minimum, but where $F > 0$, indicate that the ray misses the surface by a finite distance. This is actually desirable in that the algorithm will still converge near "silhouette edges" of surface, but will give a non-zero minimum.

Given an initial estimate $(u^{(0)}, v^{(0)})$ to the closest point of intersection, we can use a quasi-Newton iteration, with a BFGS update procedure, to solve for the point where the minimum of F exists. We have $\mathbf{g}^{(k)} = \begin{pmatrix} \frac{\partial F}{\partial u} \\ \frac{\partial F}{\partial v} \end{pmatrix}$, where The partial of F with respect to u is given by

$$\frac{\partial F}{\partial u}(u,v) = 2\left[\frac{\partial \mathbf{S}}{\partial u} \cdot \mathbf{V} - t\frac{\partial \mathbf{S}}{\partial u} \cdot \mathbf{R} \right]$$

$$= 2\frac{\partial \mathbf{S}}{\partial u} \cdot (\mathbf{V} - t\mathbf{R})$$

$$= 2\frac{\partial \mathbf{S}}{\partial u} \cdot (\mathbf{S} - (\mathbf{P} + t\mathbf{R}))$$

and, similarly, the partial of F with respect to v is given by

$$\frac{\partial F}{\partial v}(u,v) = 2\frac{\partial \mathbf{S}}{\partial v} \cdot (\mathbf{S} - (\mathbf{P} + t\mathbf{R}))$$

and the iteration proceeds as

- Assume $\mathbf{H}^{(0)}$ and $\begin{pmatrix} u^{(0)} \\ v^{(0)} \end{pmatrix}$ are given.
- Iterate the following
    - Set $\mathbf{d}^{(k)} = -\mathbf{H}^{(k)}\mathbf{g}^{(k)}$
    - Calculate an acceptable value for $s^{(k)}$, by using a line search in the direction $\mathbf{d}^{(k)}$

    - Set $\sigma^{(k)} = s^{(k)}\mathbf{d}^{(k)}$
    - if $|\sigma^{(k)}| < \epsilon$, where ϵ is some preset tolerance, then terminate the algorithm and return $\mathbf{x}^{(k)}$ as the solution.
    - Set $\mathbf{x}^{(k+1)} = \mathbf{x}^{(k)} + \sigma^{(k)}$
    - Update $\mathbf{H}^{(k)}$ by the BFGS update of equation (2)

We note that $\mathbf{H}^{(k)}$ is a 2×2 symmetric matrix. Thus it requires only 5 real numbers, including $u^{(0)}$, $v^{(0)}$, and 3 values for the approximate inverse Hessian, to be stored and updated to perform the quasi-Newton iteration. Each iteration requires one function evaluation and one gradient evaluation, plus the number of evaluations in the line search, and the few sums and multiplications that are needed to update the approximate inverse Hessian.

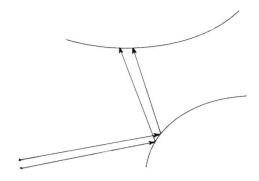

Ray Coherence
Figure 2

4. Utilizing Ray Coherence

The use of coherence in ray tracing algorithms has been discussed by several authors [28, 27, and 24]. It can be observed that in most scenes, groups of rays follow nearly the same path from the eye, striking the same objects. When calculating the ray/surface intersections, the probability is high that two adjoining rays coming from the eyepoint will strike the same surface, and will intersect the surface in the same general area. The same is true for adjoining reflected (refracted) rays that hit the same surface (see Figure 2). Therefore, in a large number of cases, the ray/surface intersection calculations should be nearly identical.

If it can be determined that a ray potentially strikes a parametric surface S, we can exploit ray coherence by setting the initial approximation $(u^{(0)}, v^{(0)})$ and $\mathbf{H}^{(0)}$ in the quasi-Newton iteration to be the the parametric values (u,v) and approximate inverse Hessian $\mathbf{H}$ calculated on the final iteration by the quasi-Newton algorithm for the last ray to hit the surface. If we require the two rays to be at the same relative position in the ray tree, originate from the same surface, and intersect S in the same neighborhood, then (u,v) should be an excellent approximation to the minimum of F required by the ray/surface intersection calculation In addition, $\mathbf{H}$ should be an accurate approximation to the inverse Hessian at the intersection point, and convergence of the quasi-Newton method should be rapid.

Unfortunately, even if adjoining rays satisfy the above properties, we cannot insure that the iteration converges to the

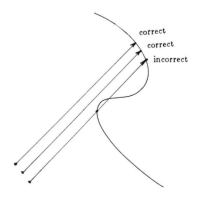

correct
correct
incorrect

Iteration to an Incorrect Intersection.
Figure 3

correct solution (see Figure 3). In order to solve this problem, we resort to a space subdivision technique to restrict the ray coherence utilization to a limited area of object space and to insure that two rays that are "close" intersect the surface in the same general neighborhood.

5. Space Subdivision Methods

Object space subdivision methods have been recently developed [14, 13, 18, 8] for the purpose of limiting the ray/surface intersection calculations by restricting the calculations to only those objects that lie near the ray. As a preprocessing step, object space is subdivided into a set of cells, each cell acting as a bucket containing information as to the objects in the space that intersect the cell. A fast method is then used to determine an ordering of the cells that intersect the ray. The ray can then be tested against each object in the relevant cells until an object is intersected, or no intersection is found. The use of such algorithms can significantly reduce the number of ray/surface intersections that must be calculated.

The algorithms of Glassner [14] and Kaplan [18], which are essentially equivalent, are most appropriate for use in restricting the ray coherency. These algorithms subdivide the space into an octree of cells and can proceed to an arbitrary tree depth. This data base of cells, created to limit the number of ray/surface intersection calculations, can also be utilized to assist the ray coherence usage of the quasi-Newton iteration.

We classify the 3-tuples ($\mathbf{S}$, C_1, C_2) according to the ray/surface intersection calculation for rays that are anchored in cell C_1, pass through cell C_2, and are to be tested against surface $\mathbf{S}$. This 3-tuples are classified into the following types (see Figure 4).

- Type 1 -- For any ray that is anchored in C_1 and passes through C_2, it can be determined that equation (4) has a unique minimum for the portion of the surface $\mathbf{S}$ contained in the cell.
- Type 2 -- For some ray anchored in C_1 that passes through C_2 a silhouette edge exists on the surface $\mathbf{S}$ with respect to the ray, and it can be determined that equation (4) has either a single minimum, with $F > 0$, or two local minima, each with $F = 0$, for all rays with anchor in C_1 and passing through C_2.
- Type 3 -- This type includes all rays that cannot be classified as either type 1 or 2.

These 3-tuples are classified only if a ray encounters a cell that contains one or more parametric surfaces, and no classification has previously been calculated.

Within cells with rays of Type 1, the algorithm uses the ray coherence to assist in the calculation of the intersection. Within cells with rays of type 2, there may be two intersections to choose from. Ray coherence can again be used, but extra checking must be done to insure that the numerical algorithm does not calculate an incorrect intersection. This can be done by examining the normal vector to the surface at each point calculated and comparing it with previous values. Within cells of type 3, the ray coherency cannot be used, and an alternate intersection algorithm must be utilized. As rays move across adjacent cells, ray coherency can still be utilized if the adjacent cells are of the same type.

The calculations to classify a ray are expensive, but only need to be calculated infrequently. We have implemented a subdivision technique that works adequately, but is somewhat slow. In order to minimize the number of type 3 classifications, we require the preprocessing step to continue to subdivide cells that contain surfaces until the curvature of the surface multiplied by the diagonal of the cell is less than a preset tolerance.

6. Implementation Issues

As with all numerical based algorithms care must be taken to insure the validity of the information used by the iteration. In particular, it is possible that the smallest eigenvalue of the matrix $\mathbf{H}^{(k)}$ will approach zero. In this case, if the eigenvalue is too small, the matrix can be replaced with the identity matrix and the iteration can continue. Similar action is taken if truncation errors cause the matrix $\mathbf{H}^{(k)}$ to become non-positive definite. In this case, one of the eigenvalues becomes negative. Detection of these problems is simple in that $\mathbf{H}^{(k)}$ is a 2×2 matrix, and the eigenvalues are trivial to determine.

There are fairly intricate relationships between the many tolerances needed to implement this algorithm. If the cell size is too large, then virtually all cell/surface 3-tuples are of type 3, and no ray coherency may be used. If the tolerance used to stop the quasi-Newton algorithm is too small, then the algorithm may take many iterations to converge, negating the benefits of ray coherence. We have found the following tolerances to be acceptable

- The quasi-Newton algorithm continues until

$$| \sigma^{(k)} | \ < \ .00001 *diag\,(O)$$

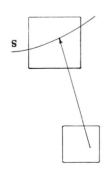 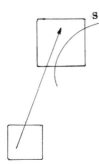 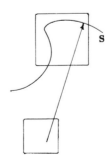

Type 1   Type 2   Type 3
                      Figure 4

where $diag(O)$ is the length of the diagonal of a box surrounding the object space.

- When determining the octree of cells, cells that contain parametric surfaces continue to be subdivided until

$$|K| * diag(cell) < .01$$

where K is the maximum curvature of the surface in the cell (see [10]).

- Two rays are "close" if the angle between the direction vectors is less than 5 degrees and the anchors lie in the same cell.

For rays that are classified in cell/surface 3-tuples of type 3, we currently have implemented a variation of Toth's algorithm [26] to calculate the intersections. This method is also used if the numerical calculations fail to converge after 10 iterations.

7. Examples

Figures 5, 6 and 7 illustrate the use of the algorithm on scenes containing several Bézier patches. Statistics for the renderings are given in Tables 1 and 2.

Figure 5 consists of 60 shiny spheres reflected in a surface consisting of 16 Bézier patches. The picture was generated at 512×512 resolution, with no anti-aliasing. Figure 6 consists of a lamp generated using 310 Bézier surface patches. The picture was generated to a resolution of 512×512 using supersampling to produce an anti-aliased image. Figure 7 consists of the lamp, rendered with full reflection, refraction and shadows. Four point light sources (three representing the light bulb) were used to illuminate the scene. Supersampling was again utilized to produce the anti-aliased image.

We note that in all cases over 90% of the ray/surface intersection calculations performed with the quasi-Newton method converge in less than three iterations. The algorithm also performed significantly better on the supersampled images.

8. Conclusions

In this paper, we have introduced methods of applying quasi-Newton iteration to the problem of intersecting a ray with an arbitrary, parametrically defined surface patch. The method takes minimal storage, and converges rapidly to a solution even near silhouette edges. The BFGS updating formula gives a method by which previously calculated inverse Hessian matrices, $\mathbf{H}^{(k)}$, can be utilized to give excellent initial approximations for the iteration for adjoining rays. Thus we can utilize ray coherence by using calculated values from one ray as initial approximations for the quasi-Newton iteration at an adjoining ray. Convergence has been shown to be excellent, with over 90% of the intersection calculations accomplished in two iterations or less.

The ray-cell classification scheme is an integral part of the algorithm. Currently it has been implemented by subdivision techniques, and faster algorithms are currently being investigated. Better classification schemes should yield additional improvements to the algorithm.

9. Acknowledgments

The authors would like to thank the Computer Research Group and the Computer Graphics Group at Lawrence Livermore National Laboratory for their support. Nelson Max, Chuck Grant, Brian Cabral and Mike Gwilliam made many helpful comments on an early version of this paper.

This research was supported in part by a grant from Lawrence Livermore National Laboratory, Contract 5607805.

10. Bibliography

[1]. Appel, A., "Some Techniques for Shading Machine Renderings of Solids," *Proc. AFIPS Spring Joint Computer Conf.*, Vol. 32, 1968, 37-49.

[2]. Blinn, J.F., "Computer display of curved surfaces," Ph.D. dissertation, Department of Computer Science, University of Utah, December 1978.

[3]. Blinn, J.F., "A generalization of algebraic surface drawing," *ACM Trans. on Graphics,* Vol 1, No. 3, July 1982, 236-256.

[4]. Bouknight, J., and K. Kelley, "An Algorithm for Producing Half-Tone Computer Graphics Presentations with Shadows and Movable Light Sources," *Proc. AFIPS Spring Joint Computer Conf.*, Vol. 36, 1970, 1-10.

[5]. Broyden, C.G., "The convergence of a class of double-rank minimization algorithms," Parts I and II, *J.I.M.A. 6,* 76-90, 222-236.

[6]. Cook, R.L., T. Porter and L. Carpenter, "Distributed ray tracing," *Computer Graphics 18*, No. 3, (Proceedings of SIGGRAPH/84), July 1984, 137-144.

	Figure 5	Figure 6	Figure 7
Rays Traced	1,600,000	1,200,000	4,750,000
Patch Intersections	463,000	480,000	1,808,000
Convergence in			
1 Iteration	59.2%	69.1%	74.2%
2 Iterations	34.9%	26.7%	21.8%
3 Iterations	3.0%	2.3%	1.5%
4 Iterations	0.4%	0.1%	0.2%
5 Iterations	0.2%	0.1%	0.2%
6 Iterations	0.1%	0.1%	0.1%
>6 Iterations	0.3%	0.2%	0.2%
Alternate Method Required	1.9%	1.7%	1.8%

(Percentages given are of total patch intersections)

Numerical Statistics

Table 1

	Figure 5	Figure 6	Figure 7
Total Number of Cells	3116	5145	5145
Cell Classification			
Type 1	96.0%	87.6%	88.4%
Type 2	3.8%	12.2%	11.4%
Type 3	0.2%	0.2%	0.2%

Cell Classification

Table 2

[7]. Dennis, J.E., and R.B. Schnabel, *Numerical Methods for Unconstrained Optimization and non-Linear Equations* Prentice-Hall, Englewood Cliffs, NJ, 1983.

[8]. Dippé, M.A.Z., and J. Swensen, "An adaptive subdivision algorithm and parallel architecture for realistic image synthesis," *Computer Graphics 18*, No. 3, (Proceedings of SIGGRAPH/84), July 1984, 149-158.

[9]. Dippé, M.A.Z. and E.H. Wold, "Antialiasing through stochastic sampling," *Computer Graphics 19*, No. 3, (Proceedings of SIGGRAPH/85), July 1985, 69-78.

[10]. Faux, I.D., and M.J. Pratt, *Computational Geometry for Design and Manufacture* Ellis Horwood, Chichester, 1982.

[11]. Fletcher, R., "A new approach to variable metric algorithms," *Computer Journal 13*, 317-322.

[12]. Fletcher, R., *Practical Methods of Optimization,* John Wiley & Sons, Chichester, England, 1980.

[13]. Fujimoto, A., T. Tanaka and K. Iwata, "ARTS: Accelerated Ray Tracing System," *IEEE Computer Graphics and Applications* Vol. 6, No. 4, April 1986, 16-26.

[14]. Glassner, A.S., "Space subdivision for fast ray tracing," *IEEE Computer Graphics and Applications 4*, No. 10, November 1984, 15-22.

[15]. Goldfarb, D., "A family of variable metric methods derived by variational means," *Math. Comp. 24*, 23-26.

[16]. Hanrahan, P., "Ray tracing algebraic surfaces," *Computer Graphics 17*, (Proceedings of SIGGRAPH/83), No. 3, July 1983, 83-86.

[17]. Joy, K.I., "On the use of quasi-Newton methods in ray tracing parametric surface patches," Technical Report CSE-85-10, Computer Science Division, Department of Electrical and Computer Engineering, University of California, Davis, October, 1985.

[18]. Kaplan, M.R., "Space tracing: a constant time ray tracer," 1985 SIGGRAPH Tutorial on State of the Art in Image Synthesis, July, 1985.

[19]. Kajiya, J.T., "Ray tracing parametric patches," *Computer Graphics 16*, (Proceedings of SIGGRAPH/82) (3), 1982, 245-254.

[20]. Kajiya, J.T., "New techniques for ray tracing procedurally defined objects," *ACM Trans. on Graphics 2*, No. 3, July 1983, 161-181.

[21]. Lee, M.E., R.A. Redner and S.P. Uselton, "Statistically optimized sampling for distributed ray tracing," *Computer Graphics 19*, No. 3, (Proceedings of SIGGRAPH/85), 61-68.

[22]. Sederberg, T.W., and D.C. Anderson, "Ray tracing of Steiner patches," *Computer Graphics 18*, No. 3, (Proceedings of SIGGRAPH/84), July 1984, 159-164.

[23]. Shanno, D.F., "Conditioning of quasi-Newton methods for function minimization," *Math. Comp. 24*, 657-664.

[24]. Speer, L.R., T.D. DeRose and B.A. Barsky, "A theoretical and empirical analysis of coherent ray-tracing," *Proceedings of Graphics Interface 85*, May, 1985, 1-8.

[25]. Sweeney, M.A.J. and R.H. Bartels, "Ray Tracing Free-Form B-Spline Surfaces", *IEEE Computer Graphics and Applications* Vol. 6, No. 2, February 1986, 41-49.

[26]. Toth, D.L., "On ray tracing parametric surfaces," *Computer Graphics 19*, (Proceedings of SIGGRAPH/85), No. 3, July 1985, 171-179.

[27]. Weghorst, H., G. Hooper and D.P. Greenberg, "Improved computational methods for ray tracing," *ACM Trans. on Graphics 3*, No. 1, January 1984, 52-69.

[28]. Whitted, T., "An improved illumination model for shaded display," *CACM*, Vol. 23, No. 6, June 1980, 343-349.

Figure 5

Figure 7

Figure 6

Ray Tracing Deformed Surfaces

Alan H. Barr

California Institute of Technology

Pasadena, CA 91125

ABSTRACT:

A collection of new methods for ray tracing differentiable surfaces is developed. The methods are general, and extend the set of "ray-traceable" surfaces suitable for use in geometric modeling. We intersect a ray $\underline{\ell} = \underline{a}t + \underline{b}$, $t > 0$ with a parametric surface $\underline{x} = \underline{f}(u, v)$, and with implicit surfaces $f(x, y, z) = 0$. A smooth surface is treated as a deformation of a flat sheet; the intersection problem is converted to a new coordinate system in which the surfaces are flat, and the rays are bent. We develop methods for providing good initial estimates of the parametric intersection values, and a "closeness criterion," to reduce computation. These same criteria help us substitute a set of simpler surfaces for the more complex surface. The parametric method produces the intersection values of u, v, and t. These are suitable for shading calculations and for mapping textures onto the surface; they can also produce the local coordinate frame values, suitable for anisotropic lighting models.

Keywords: Ray tracing, deformations, hierarchical sampling

1. Introduction

Ray-traced images are created by numerically simulating the behavior of photons impinging on a mathematical film plane, through the principles of geometric optics. The ray tracing approach has been one of the most successful techniques to date in creating high fidelity computer generated images, and is becoming progressively more practical due to the increasing speed and decreasing cost of computation.

Almost all of the surfaces found in ray traced images have been mathematically simple, chiefly due to the complexity of the intersection algorithm, and the numerical intensity of the computation. Planes and quadric surfaces are amongst the simplest of these surfaces, requiring the solution of linear and quadratic equations respectively for the ray intersections. Recently, biquadratic surfaces such as Steiner patches, and bicubic surfaces have become tractable (see [KAJIYA 82], [SEDERBERG 84], and [TOTH 85]). For the most part, these surfaces have been the traditional geometric modeling primitives used in ray traced scenes.

The methods in this paper are developed for ray tracing differentiable surfaces more general than the above. Objects which do not have differentiable surfaces, however, such as three dimensional density functions (clouds), and fractal surfaces (mountains), are outside the domain of this article. See [BOUVILLE 85], [KAJIYA and VON HERZEN 84], [KAJIYA 83].

The traditional geometric modeling primitives are well suited to modeling static shapes, such as rigid machine parts. They are not so ideal, however, for compactly representing objects whose shapes change as a function of time, such as the shapes of flexible materials, biological forms, and the blending of shapes. The simple primitives are either too limited (as are spheres) in that they cannot model many of the desired shapes, or else are too fine grained (as are polygons and bicubic patches) in that they require large quantities of data that human beings find difficult to manipulate.

New geometric modeling primitives are needed to help us control the formation and behavior of flexible objects. These primitives could permit a more succinct representation of a wider range of objects than is currently available. The computational intensity of modeling and rendering with the new primitives should not overwhelm the other benefits of their use. Deformed surfaces have a potential role in the endeavor to create such primitives; the methods of this paper can be used to efficiently render the surfaces.

2. Inverse methods in Ray Tracing

The parametric *ray intersection problem* is to find values of u, v, and t such that the three dimensional ray $\underline{\ell}(t)$ and the parametric surface $\underline{f}(u,v)$ satisfy

$$\underline{f}(u,v) = \underline{\ell}(t). \qquad (2.1)$$

We create a "difference space" by choosing $\underline{D}(u,v,t)$ to be the difference of the two functions, i.e.,

$$\underline{D}(u,v,t) \equiv \underline{f}(u,v) - (\underline{a}t + \underline{b}). \qquad (2.2)$$

The intersection problem becomes that of finding the roots of

$$\underline{D}(u,v,t) = 0. \qquad (2.3)$$

There are two coordinate systems (other than the conventional modeling space) which we will use to set up the equations for this problem.

The first coordinate system is *parameter space*, or "$\underline{U}$ space," in which we obtain three dimensional difference vectors $(D_1, D_2, D_3)^T$ as a function of u, v, and t, via Equation 2.2.

The inverse coordinate system is called *difference space* or "$\underline{D}$ space," in which we obtain parametric values of $(u,v,t)^T$ as a function of difference values D_1, D_2, and D_3.

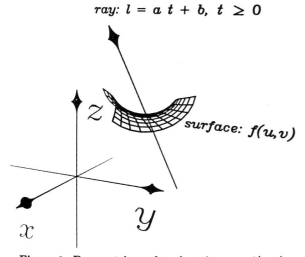

ray: $l = a\,t + b$, $t \geq 0$

surface: $f(u,v)$

Figure 1. Parametric surface function $\underline{x} = \underline{f}(u,v)$ and ray $\underline{x} = \underline{a}t + \underline{b}$, in Cartesian space.

$\underline{D}$ space is a *deformation* of $\underline{U}$ space (see [BARR 84]). Each point in a three dimensional region in $\underline{U}$ space is mapped to a corresponding point in a three dimensional region of $\underline{D}$ space, via Equation 2.2. Figure 2 shows the mapping from a rectangular region of $\underline{U}$ space to a region of $\underline{D}$ space.

A way to visualize the transformation from $\underline{U}$ space to $\underline{D}$ space is as follows: at each value of t, the image of a $u - v$ region is a portion of the original surface $\underline{f}(u,v)$, translated in space by the amount $\underline{a}t + \underline{b}$. As t increases, this portion of the surface is translated parallel to vector $\underline{a}$, sweeping out a region of space.

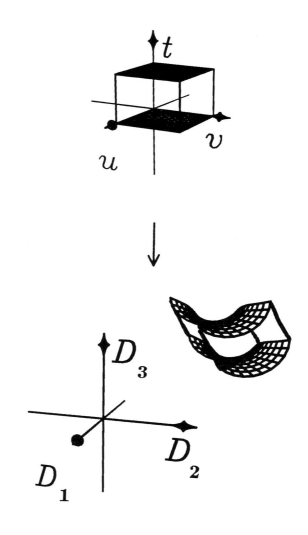

Figure 2. A rectangular region of $\underline{U}$ space maps to a corresponding region of $\underline{D}$ space via (2.2)

There is a fundamental fact at the heart of the method. In $\underline{D}$ space, i.e., difference space, we *know* where the solution is: it's at the origin, where the difference vector is $(0,0,0)^T$. We will derive a method to compute the $\underline{U}$ space value which corresponds to $(0,0,0)^T$ in $\underline{D}$ space, inverting Equation 2.2. This gives us the intersection values of u, v, and t we seek.

3. Derivation: Parametric Method

In this section, we assume that a point $\underline{U} = (u_1, v_1, t_1)^T$ is given, which approximates the solution values of u, v, and t.

First, we map this point to $\underline{D}$ space, by creating the initial difference vector

$$\underline{\mathcal{F}}_1 = \underline{D}(u_1, v_1, t_1). \tag{3.1}$$

from the initial values of u, v, and t.

Second, we create a "difference curve" $\underline{d}(s)$, connecting the initial difference vector $\underline{\mathcal{F}}_1$ to $(0,0,0)^T$ in $\underline{D}$ space.

The inverse image of the difference curve $d(s)$ is a parametric curve $\underline{\mu}(s)$ in $\underline{U}$ space called the "solution curve." The endpoint of $\underline{\mu}(s)$ which corresponds to $(0,0,0)^T$ yields the solution values of u, v, and t (see Figures 3a and 3b). The difference curve $\underline{d}(s)$ can be any piecewise smooth curve in $\underline{D}$ space which terminates at the origin, for which the inverse image exists.

We will examine the case for two different choices of $\underline{d}(s)$.

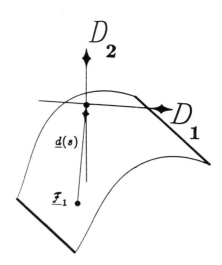

Figure 3a. A region of D space and the difference curve $\underline{d}(s)$

The above equations can be modified slightly by allowing s to be considered a function of an independent parameter ξ.

$$D(\mu_1(s(\xi)), \mu_2(s(\xi)), \mu_3(s(\xi))) = \underline{\mathcal{F}}_1 s(\xi) \tag{3.5}$$

Formulation 1:

One such curve, for which the inverse image can exist, is:

$$\underline{d}(s) = s\underline{\mathcal{F}}_1, \qquad s : 1 \Rightarrow 0 \tag{3.2a}$$

The above curve starts at the initial difference vector $\underline{\mathcal{F}}_1$, where $s = 1$, and ends when $s = 0$, at $(0,0,0)^T$.

The solution curve $\underline{\mu}(s)$ starts at the initial point (u_1, v_1, t_1).

The solution is obtained when $s = 0$, i.e, at $\mu(0)$, as long as the inverse image of $d(s)$ exists continuously along the segment. This is a continuation method for solving the intersection problem.

So, how do we find the solution curve $\underline{\mu}(s)$, which deforms to the difference curve $\underline{d}(s)$? Where does the above curve have a unique inverse image in $\underline{U}$ space?

We do this by expressing the condition that the deformation of the solution curve $\underline{\mu}(s)$ is equal to $\underline{d}(s)$. Thus,

$$D(\mu_1(s), \mu_2(s), \mu_3(s)) = \underline{\mathcal{F}}_1 s \tag{3.4}$$

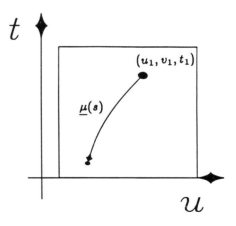

Figure 3b. The corresponding region of $\underline{U}$ space and the solution curve $\underline{\mu}(s)$

We compose the above functions, and consider u, v, t, and s, without loss of generality, to be functions of ξ.

$$\underline{D}(u(\xi), v(\xi), t(\xi)) = \underline{\mathcal{F}}_1 s(\xi). \tag{3.6}$$
$$u(\xi_1) = u_1$$
$$v(\xi_1) = v_1$$

$$t(\xi_1) = t_1$$

$$s(\xi_1) = 1$$

A geometric interpretation of the above equation exists, which uses the original world space, without the explicit reference to the other two coordinate systems. We expand the definition of $\underline{D}(u, v, t)$ in Equation 3.6, and note that u, v, t, and s are functions of ξ with the previously stated initial conditions.

$$\underline{f}(u, v) - (\underline{a}t + \underline{b}) = \underline{\mathcal{F}}_1 s \qquad (3.7)$$

This equation states that as s goes from one to zero, u, v, and t change in such a manner that the difference vector (joining the ray and the surface) gets smaller in magnitude, but maintains its parallelism to $\underline{\mathcal{F}}_1$. Thus, these values of u and v constrain $\underline{f}(u, v)$ to lie in the plane containing both $\underline{a}$ and $\underline{\mathcal{F}}_1$. This plane contains the initial point $\underline{\ell}(t_1)$ on the ray and the initial point $\underline{f}(u_1, v_1)$ on the surface.

The parameter t goes along the ray in direction $\underline{a}$, while s is the proportion of the length of the vector joining the surface and the ray (parallel to the difference vector $\underline{\mathcal{F}}_1$). When $s = 1$, the distance is 100 percent of $|\underline{\mathcal{F}}_1|$.

The intersection curve on the surface is equal to the solution curve (as a function of s) plus the ray position at each t value.

Formulation 2.

Another curve, for which the inverse image can exist, is

$$d(s, t) = s(t(\underline{A} - \underline{a}) + \underline{B})$$

As s goes from one to zero, $d(s, t)$ goes to zero.

The equation analogous to Equation 3.6, is

$$\underline{D}(u(\xi), v(\xi), t(\xi)) = s(\xi)(t(\xi)(\underline{A} - \underline{a}) + \underline{B}). \qquad (3.8)$$

$$u(\xi_1) = u_1$$

$$v(\xi_1) = v_1$$

$$t(\xi_1) = t_1$$

$$s(\xi_1) = 1$$

where

$$\underline{B} = \underline{D}(u_1, v_1, t_1) - (\underline{A} - \underline{a})t_1.$$

This formulation will prove to be an improvement over the previous formulation, for suitable choices of the $\underline{A}$ vector.

4. Creating and Solving the Initial Value Problems

Formulation 1:

We take the derivative of Equation 3.6 with respect to ξ.

$$\frac{\partial \underline{D}}{\partial u}u' + \frac{\partial \underline{D}}{\partial v}v' + \frac{\partial \underline{D}}{\partial t}t' = \underline{\mathcal{F}}_1 s' \qquad (4.1)$$

where $'$ signifies $d/d\xi$.

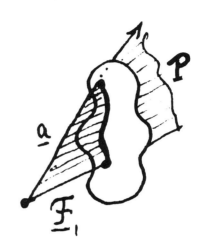

Figure 4. The plane P of Formulation 1, and the image of the solution curve in modeling space

Thus, from Equation 2.2,

$$\frac{\partial \underline{f}(u, v)}{\partial u}u' + \frac{\partial \underline{f}(u, v)}{\partial v}v' - \underline{a}t' = \underline{\mathcal{F}}_1 s'. \qquad (4.2a)$$

so, using subscripts to denote partial derivatives,

$$\underline{f}_u u' + \underline{f}_v v' - \underline{a}t' = \underline{\mathcal{F}}_1 s'. \qquad (4.2b)$$

where

$$u(\xi_1) = u_1$$

$$v(\xi_1) = v_1$$

$$t(\xi_1) = t_1$$

$$s(\xi_1) = 1$$

We wish to convert this into an initial value problem and solve it to find values such that $s(\xi_0) = 0$, (thus showing that the ray hits the surface) or else show that such values do not exist (showing that the ray does not hit the surface).

Rewriting Equation 4.2 b in matrix form, we obtain

$$\left(\underline{f}_u, \underline{f}_v, -\underline{a}\right) \begin{pmatrix} du/d\xi \\ dv/d\xi \\ dt/d\xi \end{pmatrix} = \underline{\mathcal{F}}_1 ds/d\xi \qquad (4.3)$$

We let the matrix $J = \left(\underline{f}_u, \underline{f}_v, -\underline{a}\right)$.

We divide both sides of equation 4.3 by $ds/d\xi$, and obtain

$$\begin{pmatrix} du/ds \\ dv/ds \\ dt/ds \end{pmatrix} = J^{-1} \underline{\mathcal{F}}_1 \qquad (4.4)$$

If the right hand side of the above equation satisfies a "Lipschitz condition" on its dependent variables (see Appendix A), then it is guaranteed that a solution exists, and that the solution is unique. Effectively, this means that the right hand side must be continuous, and its various partial derivatives be bounded, in the region of $\underline{U}$ space under consideration.

Equation 4.4 is valid in all regions where the determinant of the matrix J does not approach zero. The determinant is given by

$$detJ = -\left(\underline{f}_u \times \underline{f}_v\right) \cdot (\underline{a}) \qquad (4.5)$$

Since $\underline{f}_u \times \underline{f}_v$ is the normal vector to the surface (although it is not necessarily the unit normal), Equation 4.4 is valid as long as the dot product of the ray direction $\underline{a}$ and the normal vector is never zero as the independent parameter s goes from 1 to 0. (Note that the determinant would be zero if $\underline{f}_u$ or $\underline{f}_v$ were identically zero, such as at the north pole of a sphere).

In other words, Equation 4.4 becomes unusable as the vector $\underline{a}$ becomes tangent to the current surface position $\underline{f}(u,v)$, near the silhouette edges of the surface. We also will not use 4.4 if it would cause the values of t to decrease, so we can know if the ray has missed the surface by going out of the range in t. The equation is adequate for those parts of the surfaces where $\underline{f}_u$, $\underline{f}_v$, and $\underline{a}$ are nonzero and bounded, and the absolute value of the determinant $|detJ| > \epsilon > 0$. The Lipschitz bound we need is provided by the constant ϵ. We terminate solving this differential equation if $|detJ| < \epsilon$ or $detJ$ changes sign as a function of s.

We are free to use the extra degree of freedom in Equation 4.2b: we switch the s and t terms as follows:

$$\underline{f}_u du/d\xi + \underline{f}_v dv/d\xi - \underline{\mathcal{F}}_1 ds/d\xi = \underline{a} dt/d\xi \qquad (4.6)$$

Thus, dividing by $dt/d\xi$,

$$\left(\underline{f}_u, \underline{f}_v, -\underline{\mathcal{F}}_1\right) \begin{pmatrix} du/dt \\ dv/dt \\ ds/dt \end{pmatrix} = \underline{a} \qquad (4.7)$$

The matrix J for this equation is given by

$$J = \left(\underline{f}_u, \underline{f}_v, \underline{\mathcal{F}}_1\right).$$

We can express equation 4.7 via:

$$\begin{pmatrix} du/dt \\ dv/dt \\ ds/dt \end{pmatrix} = J^{-1}\underline{a} \qquad (4.8)$$

This equation is valid for values of t where the absolute value of the determinant of the matrix $J > \epsilon$, and $detJ$ does not change sign as a function of t.

The determinant is given by

$$detJ = -\left(\underline{f}_u \times \underline{f}_v\right) \cdot (\underline{\mathcal{F}}_1) \qquad (4.9)$$

We solve this equation looking for values of u, v, and t such that $s \leq 0$.

Thus, Equation 4.8 is valid as long as the absolute value of the dot product of the initial surface direction $\underline{\mathcal{F}}_1$ and the normal vector does not approach zero. As before, this equation becomes singular as the vector $\underline{\mathcal{F}}_1$ becomes tangent to the current surface position $\underline{f}(u,v)$.

So, what happens where both criteria fail? For instance, our initial approximation can cause $\underline{\mathcal{F}}_1$ to be virtually parallel to $\underline{a}$, so there will be no advantage to switching between the two equations. In this circumstance, the matrices of both equations are singular. We can create a differential equation with a Lipschitz condition even if this occurs, using orthogonal projection of the terms in Equation 4.2b, but it is preferable to use Formulation 2.

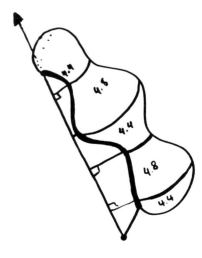

Figure 4.1. Regions of validity of the equations
Use Eqn 4.4 if t increases in it
Use Eqn 4.8 to force t to increase otherwise

Formulation 2:

The difference curve $d(s, t)$ in this formulation depends on both s and t.

We analyze equation 3.8, to examine its behavior at the silhouette edges.

$$\underline{D}(u(s), v(s), t(s)) = s(t(\underline{A} - \underline{a}) + \underline{B}) \qquad (4.11)$$

We take the full derivative of equation 4.11 with respect to s, and obtain:

$$\left(\underline{f}_u, \underline{f}_v, -\underline{a}(1-s) - s\underline{A}\right) \begin{pmatrix} du/ds \\ dv/ds \\ dt/ds \end{pmatrix} = \underline{\mathcal{E}}(s, t) \quad (4.12)$$

where $\underline{\mathcal{E}}(s, t) = s(\underline{D}(u_1, v_1, t_1) + (t - t_1)(\underline{A} - \underline{a}))$.

The matrix

$$J = \left(\underline{f}_u, \underline{f}_v, -\underline{a}(1-s) - s\underline{A}\right)$$

$$det J = -(f_u \times f_v) \cdot (\underline{a}(1-s) + s\underline{A})$$

The absolute value of this determinant must be larger than ϵ, and $det J$ must not change sign as a function of s.

If we let the normal vector be designated by

$$\underline{N} = (\underline{f}_u \times \underline{f}_v),$$

we see that

$$det J = \underline{N} \cdot ((1-s)\underline{a} + s\underline{A})$$

The linearly interpolated ray $(1-s)\underline{a} + s\underline{A}$ must not approach being tangent to the surface. The linearly interpolated ray lies between the ray vector direction $\underline{a}$ and the user-specified vector $\underline{A}$; the interpolated ray points in the direction of vector $\underline{A}$ when $s = 1$, and becomes the ray direction $\underline{a}$, as s approaches 0.

A few choices exist for the user-specified vector $\underline{A}$. If the ray direction $\underline{a}$ is far from being tangent to the surface (i.e., far from being perpendicular to the normal vector), then a good choice for $\underline{A}$ is one of the previous ray directions fired at the surface. We would set the initial values u_1 and v_1 to be the previous intersection values of u and v with the surface. We need to make sure that the interpolated vector does not become tangent to the surface.

On the other hand, if the ray direction $\underline{a}$ is close to being tangent to the surface, we can let the user-specified vector $\underline{A}$ be the initial normal vector, which is given by

$$\underline{N}_1 = (\underline{f}_u \times \underline{f}_v)|_{(u=u1, v=v1)}$$

Thus, if

$$\underline{A} = \underline{N}_1$$

$$det J > 0$$

as long as

$$N \cdot N_1 s > N \cdot a(1 - s).$$

This will be true if

$$N \cdot a < 0,$$

or if

$$\frac{s}{(1-s)} N \cdot N_1 > |N \cdot a|.$$

5. Making the Methods Practical

In the previous section, we have stated some of the conditions under which the intersection equation is guaranteed to have a unique solution. We could use a numerical differential equation solution method such as Gear's method for solving stiff ordinary differential equations (see [GEAR 71], [GUPTA et al 85] and [RALSTON and RABINOWITZ 78] for a description of stiff differential equations and solution methods). However, most of us would prefer almost anything to numerically solving a potentially stiff differential equation at each of the million points or so in a ray traced scene.

We will make slight modifications to the methods, and obtain robust and fast solution techniques. This includes methods for obtaining good starting points and termination conditions. We want to avoid any unnecessary numerical overhead that we can, without sacrificing picture quality.

Obtaining Starting Values:

The starting values are best obtained by preprocessing the surface, and subsequently intersecting the ray with a hierarchical bounding volume such as those found in [KAY 86]. In addition, each portion of the surface is defined to have its range of u and v; each bounding box needs to have access to this range (stored from the preprocessing step when the bounding volumes were made). In addition, each bounding box needs to remember at least one parametric point (u_1, v_1) and its position in space $\underline{f}(u_1, v_1)$. The starting values for t are obtained at ray tracing time, by intersecting the ray with the convex bounding volume, and selecting the closer t value. Like many iterative techniques, we can converge to the solution more quickly with better starting points.

A "Closeness Criterion"

We can save computation time if we compute the image only to the needed degree of accuracy. We need to make the image accurate within some specified fraction ρ of a pixel (a suggested value is 1/20th of a pixel).

We can calculate τ, the absolute spatial tolerance (a three dimensional distance) for the ray to be within a fraction of a pixel of the surface.

This is achieved by finding the *total length* in space that fits within the camera's view at the actual distance of the object, dividing by the number of pixels in an edge (yielding the length in space per pixel), and then multiplying by the tolerance ρ (to obtain the absolute length in space per fraction of a pixel). The exact equation depends on the camera model we are using.

For instance, for a "look-from, look-at, field-of-view" camera model (see Figure 5.1),

$$\tau = \frac{2\rho X sin(\theta/2)}{N} \qquad 5.1$$

where X is the distance from the eye (i.e., the lookfrom vector) to the surface, *theta* is the total field of view, and N is the number of pixels across the image (choose the larger of the two values N_{rows} and $N_{columns}$ if the image is not square). The trigonometric analysis is usually quite tractable for more advanced camera models.

The above analysis is satisfactory for ray tracing environments which calculate single ray-surface intersections. The tolerance for a pair of interacting surfaces is equal to the sum of the tolerances of the two surfaces.

$$\tau_{pair} = \tau_{Surf1} + \tau_{Surf2}.$$

Thus, when we are checking for self shadowing, the net tolerance doubles, since the surface is interacting with itself.

If we require reflections from concave surfaces, or refractions through convex surfaces, the effective field of view may need to change in the above equation. Convex reflections and concave refractions are already sufficiently accurate (although we may want to loosen the tolerance if we can).

It is possible to make a "ray tracing microscope" by modeling the appropriate lenses, which can magnify any surface feature by an arbitrary amount, and we need to calculate tolerances for these situations automatically; the full analysis of this, however, is left to a future paper.

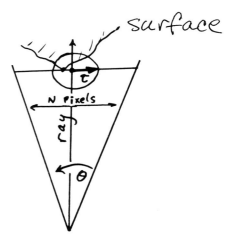

Figure 5.1. Camera Geometry
for the closeness criterion

The Fundamental Coefficients of the Surface

For some intersection algorithms, we want to create our bounding boxes such that a single tangent plane approximates the surface within the forementioned tolerances. This is not quite a polygonal approximation to the surface, in that there are no polygon edges to be connected together. In addition, we wish to obtain the actual u and v values on the surface (within some fraction of a pixel), so that we can calculate normal vectors, coordinate frames for anisotropic lighting models (see [KAJIYA 84]), and the like, without doing normal vector interpolation. We simply rely on the closeness criterion and the bounding box intervals to guarantee our intersection accuracy.

To do this, we need to get an estimate of the maximum distance of a point on the tangent plane to the surface. If the surface is too curved, we will recursively subdivide into subregions until each part is flat enough to be approximated by a single tangent plane. The net distance of a point on the tangent plane to the surface $\underline{f}(u, v)$ can be approximated by

$$h = \frac{1}{2}(D^{(0)}(\Delta u)^2 + 2D^{(1)}\Delta u \Delta v + D^{(2)}(\Delta v)^2,$$

where $D^{(0)}$, $D^{(1)}$, and $D^{(2)}$ are the fundamental coefficients to the surface, and are given by

$$D^{(0)} = \underline{N} \cdot \underline{f}_{uu}$$

$$D^{(1)} = \underline{N} \cdot \underline{f}_{uv}$$

and

$$D^{(2)} = \underline{N} \cdot \underline{f}_{vv}$$

where $\underline{N}$ is the *unit* normal vector. Subscripts denote partial derivatives.

ALGORITHM 1: *Tangent Plane Method.*

Large Memory requirements, short time per ray.

Preprocessing:

1. Divide the unit parameters of the surface into n by m parametric regions.

2. Place bounding volumes on each of the portions of the surface. In addition, each box should retain the range of the u and v parameters that it is bounding. If a theoretical bound is not available on the surface type you are using, you can numerically sample the remembered subregion to create the boxes.

3. For each bounding volume, we know the worst case distance (the closest distance of the box to the eye). Use this to calculate τ, to obtain the absolute distance tolerance for a ray-surface intersection to be accurate within a fraction of a pixel.

4. Calculate the fundamental coefficients of the surface, $D^{(0)}, D^{(1)}, and D^{(2)}$. Store the u_1, v_1 center of the patch, the function and partial derivative values $\underline{f}(u_1, v_1)$, $\underline{f}_u$ and f_v in the bounding box data structure. This will give us the information for the tangent plane to the surface.

5. For the worst case points in the bounding box's parametric region calculate h, to estimate the worst case distance of the tangent plane to the surface.

6. If $\tau < h$ for any of the worst case parametric points, subdivide the parametric region, and recursively repeat steps 2 through 6, until all of the bounding boxes contain a tangent plane which is completely within the specified tolerance to the surface.

Ray intersection:

1. Shoot a ray at the bounding boxes.

2. If a ray misses the boxes, we have not hit the surface. Go on to the next ray.

3. Otherwise, if the ray hits the box, obtain the minimum and maximum t value which hits the bounding box. Look up the range of u and of v for this particular box, and the starting point (u_1, v_1).

4. Solve Equation 4.4 using one step for the whole interval, via Euler's method. Euler's method will intersect accurately with the tangent plane.

$$\begin{pmatrix} u \\ v \\ t \end{pmatrix}_{new} = \begin{pmatrix} u_1 \\ v_1 \\ t_{min} \end{pmatrix} - \left(\underline{f}_u, \underline{f}_v, -\underline{a}\right)^{-1} \underline{\mathcal{F}}_1$$

Do not solve if the determinant is less than ϵ.

5. Calculate $d = |f(u, v) - at - b|$

6. The ray hits the surface only if $d < \tau$ and the values of u, v, and t lie within the u,v, t limits for the box.

ALGORITHM 2: *Tangent Biquadratic Surfaces.*

Medium Memory, Medium time per ray

Preprocessing:

1, 2, 3. The first three steps are identical to the previous algorithm.

4. Calculate and store the u, v center of the patch, the function and partial derivative values $\underline{f}(u, v)$, $\underline{f}_u$, f_v, and estimates of $\underline{f}_{uu}$, f_{uv} and $\underline{f}_{vv}$ in the bounding box data structure. The biquadratic approximation for the surface is

$$\underline{bi}quad(u, v) = f(u_1, v_1) + \underline{f}_u(u - u_1) + \underline{f}_v(v - v_1)$$

$$+\frac{1}{2}(\underline{f}_{uu}(u - u_1)^2 + 2\underline{f}_{uv}(u - u_1)(v - v_1) + \underline{f}_{vv}(v - v_1)^2$$

5. For the worst case points in the bounding box's parametric region calculate the worst case distance of the tangent biquadratic to the surface. If this cannot be performed analytically, set $h = max(|biquad(u, v) - f(u, v)|$

6. If $\tau < h$ subdivide the parametric region, and recursively repeat steps 2 through 6. This guarantees that we have accurate enough biquadratic approximations.

Ray intersection:

1. Shoot a ray at the bounding boxes.

2. If a ray misses the boxes, we have not hit the surface. Go on to the next ray.

3. Otherwise, if the ray hits the box, obtain the minimum and maximum t value which hits the bounding box. Look up the range of u and of v for this particular box, and the starting point (u_1, v_1).

4. If the ray hits the box, we solve the intersection of the ray with the biquadratic surface, obtaining a value of u, v and t. See [KAJIYA 82], [SEDERBERG 84], and [TOTH 85]).

5. Calculate $d = |f(u, v) - at - b|$

6. The ray hits the surface only if $d < \tau$ and the values of u, v, and t lie within the u,v, t limits for the box.

ALGORITHM 3: *Differential equation method*

Low Memory requirements, Large time per ray

Preprocessing:

1, 2, 3. Same as Algorithm 1.

4. Calculate and store the u, v center of the patch, the function and partial derivative values $\underline{f}(u, v)$, $\underline{f}_u$ and f_v in the bounding box data structure.

Ray intersection:

1. Shoot a ray at the bounding boxes.

2. If a ray misses the boxes, we have not hit the surface.

3. Otherwise, if the ray hits the box, obtain the minimum and maximum t value which hits the bounding box. Look up the range of u and of v for this particular box, and the starting point (u_1, v_1).

4 a. Solve Equation 4.8. until the magnitude of the term on the right hand side in Equation 3.8 is less than τ, i.e.,

$$h = |s(t(\underline{A} - \underline{a}) + \underline{B})| < \tau$$

This means that s does not have to go all of the way to zero, but can stop at

$$s_{min} = \frac{\tau}{|(t(\underline{A} - \underline{a}) + \underline{B})|}.$$

4 b. If $det J$ changes sign, or $|det J| < \epsilon$, *subdivide the patch within the bounding box*, repeat the preprocessing and ray intersections on these bounding boxes, until the ray hits the surface, or misses the boxes.

5. The ray hits the surface only if $h < \tau$ and the values of u, v, and t lie within the limits for the box.

Figure 5.2. Bounding volumes on the surface

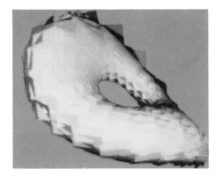

Figure 5.3. Tangent solution planes to the surface

6. Implicit Surfaces

We want to intersect a ray

$$\underline{\ell} = \underline{a}t + \underline{b}, \quad t > t_0, \tag{6.1}$$

and an implicit function

$$f(x, y, z) = 0 \tag{6.2}$$

which represents a surface.

We let $t = t_1$ from a nearby bounding box intersection.

We let s go from 1 to 0, in the equation

$$f(\underline{a}t + \underline{b}) = f_1 s \tag{6.3}$$

Taking the total derivative with respect to ξ :

$$(f_x a_1 + f_y a_2 + f_z a_3)t' = f_1 s' \tag{6.4}$$

Thus,

$$t' = \frac{f_1}{f_x a_1 + f_y a_2 + f_z a_3} s' \tag{6.5}$$

We solve this differential equation as before, stipulating that t always increase as ξ repeatedly goes from 1 to 0. The equation is valid when

$$(f_x a_1 + f_y a_2 + f_z a_3) \neq 0, \tag{6.6}$$

i.e., when

$$\begin{pmatrix} f_x \\ f_y \\ f_z \end{pmatrix} \not\perp \begin{pmatrix} a_1 \\ a_2 \\ a_3 \end{pmatrix}. \tag{6.7}$$

In other words, this equation is valid in much the same circumstances as the parametric equation: the normal vector to the surface must not be perpendicular to the ray.

If the denominator in Equation 6.4 is too small, or crosses zero, we can use the equation

$$s' = \frac{f_x a_1 + f_y a_2 + f_z a_3}{f_1} t' \tag{6.8}$$

We can force t to increase as before, choosing between

$$s' = 1 \tag{6.9}$$

$$t' = \frac{f_1}{f_x a_1 + f_y a_2 + f_z a_3}$$

$$t' = -1 \tag{6.10}$$

$$s' = -\frac{f_x a_1 + f_y a_2 + f_z a_3}{f_1}$$

Summary

A few new methods to ray trace differentiable surfaces are developed, for both parametric and implicit surfaces. The method is suitable for locally deformed surfaces, because the partial derivatives are directly available for these surface types. For parametric functions, the local coordinate frame values, which are required for anisotropic lighting and reflection models, are obtained easily as a function of u and v by direct evaluation of $\underline{f}_u$ and $\underline{f}_v$. Some of the methods fare badly when f_v or f_u goes to zero, such as at the north pole of a parametric sphere. Such surfaces can be repaired using the concept of coordinate charts from differential geometry, to avoid these types of singularities, or else using some of the other proposed methods.

Acknowledgements

I would like to thank Steve Gabriel and Jim Kajiya for helpful discussions during the development of this method, and to Tim Kay for his assistance with the implementation and the figures.

References

A.H. Barr "Global and Local Deformations of Solid Primitives", SIGGRAPH '84 Conference Proceedings.

C. Bouville, "Bounding Ellipsoids for Ray Fractal Intersections," SIGGRAPH '85 Conference Proceedings

Gear, C.W., *Numerical Initial Value Problems in Ordinary Differential Equations*, Prentice Hall, 1971.

G. Gupta, R. Sacks-Davis, P.E. Tischer, "A Review of Recent Developments in Solving Ordinary Differential Equations," Computing Surveys, Vol 17, No. 1, March 1985.

J.T. Kajiya, "Ray Tracing Parametric Patches ," SIGGRAPH '82 Conference Proceedings.

J.T. Kajiya, "New Techniques for Ray Tracing Procedurally Defined Objects," SIGGRAPH '83 Conference Proceedings.

J.T. Kajiya, B. Von Herzen, "Ray Tracing Volume Densities," SIGGRAPH '84 Conference Proceedings.

J.T. Kajiya, "Anisotropic Reflection Models," SIGGRAPH '85 Conference Proceedings.

T.L. Kay, "Issues in Ray Tracing Complex Scenes," M.S. Thesis, to be completed, 1986.

T.L. Kay, "Ray Tracing Complex Scenes" Conference Proceedings, SIGGRAPH '86.

A. Ralston, P. Rabinowitz, *A First Course in Numerical Analysis*, McGraw Hill, 1978.

T. Sederberg, "Ray Tracing Steiner Patches," Conference Proceedings, SIGGRAPH '84.

M. Spivak, *Differential Geometry*, Publish or Perish Press, 1975.

D. Toth, "On Ray Tracing Parametric Surfaces," SIGGRAPH '85 Conference Proceedings.

Figure 6. Preliminary Implementation Results

Appendix A. Theoretical Considerations

We state the well-known existence theorem, stated in [GEAR] which guarantees that an initial value problem has a unique solution.

Existence Theorem. If $\underline{G}(\underline{u}, \xi)$ is a *continuous* function of ξ and satisfies the Lipschitz condition in $\underline{u}$ in the region $0 \leq \xi \leq b$, $-\infty \leq u_i \leq \infty$, then there exists a unique differentiable function $\underline{u}(\xi)$ such that

$$\underline{u}(0) = \underline{u}_{initial} \qquad (Theorem\,A.1)$$

and

$$d\underline{u}/d\xi = \underline{G}(\underline{u}, \xi). \qquad (A.2)$$

By definition, $\underline{G}(\underline{u}, \xi)$ satisfies the Lipschitz condition on a region R if there exists a constant L such that

$$\|\underline{G}(\underline{u}, \xi) - \underline{G}(\underline{u}^*, \xi)\| \leq L\|\underline{u} - \underline{u}^*\| \qquad (A.3)$$

where $\underline{u}$ and $\underline{u}^*$ are within the region R.

Adaptive Precision in Texture Mapping

Andrew Glassner

Department of Computer Science
The University of North Carolina at Chapel Hill
Chapel Hill, North Carolina 27514

Abstract

We introduce an adaptive, iterative technique for obtaining texture samples of arbitrary precision when synthesizing a computer-generated image. The technique is an improvement on the sum table texturing method. To motivate the technique we analyze the error properties of the sum-table method. Based on that analysis we propose using a combination of tables independently or together to obtain a better estimate, and analyze the error properties of such methods. We then propose a new technique for obtaining texture samples whose accuracy is a function of the texture and the image. As part of this technique we propose the use of an auxiliary table which contains local estimates of the texture variance. We show how the iteration of a given sample may be controlled by values from this table. We then analyze the error in this method, and present images which demonstrate the improvement.

General Terms: Algorithms, Graphics
Keywords: Textures, Sum Tables, Iteration, Adaptive Refinement, Variance
CR Categories: I.3.3 Picture/Image Generation; I.3.7 Three-Dimensional Graphics and Realism

1.0   Introduction

Synthetic texturing was first introduced by Catmull [Catm75]. Since that time there has been considerable interest in the correct and efficient application of texture to surfaces.

A popular use of texturing has been to apply color detail to surfaces. In this sense, textures have been used to simulate painted images [Blin76]. Another use of textures has been to simulate shape detail that would be inefficient or difficult to model directly, either through normal perturbation [Blin78], or displacement mapping [Cook84].

Some techniques for generating textures that have been discussed in the literature are stored look-up tables [Blin76], procedural routines [Gard84], and multi-dimensional methods [Peal85]. Texture has also been incorporated into synthesized images as a post-process, either to enhance the understanding of shapes [Schw83], or to generate special effects [Perl85].

Many image synthesis systems build an image by rendering pieces of surface (such as a polygon) one at a time. The pieces may be combined with previous pieces as they are rendered in a Z-buffer [Suth74] or an A-buffer [Carp84]. Alternatively, entire images may be merged after rendering [Port84], [Duff85]. In all of these schemes, the texturing process is usually one of *inverse mapping* [Feib80].

The problem of texturing may be expressed in many ways, with varying degrees of theoretical and practical considerations. A popular model which is theoretically incomplete but often visually acceptable is to assign a texture value to a pixel based on the average value of the texture within the surface region seen by that pixel. This is the model we use in this paper.

In general, a pixel may be considered to be a small window looking onto a surface. When texture is applied to that surface, the inverse viewing transform is invoked to find the projection of the pixel onto the surface (in practice, we usually project only the four corners of the rectangular pixel). We now want to know where those surface points sit in the texture. Often, the axes of two-dimensional textures are referred to as (u,v). These four (u,v) pairs (one for each pixel corner) then describe a quadrilateral in that table. If we are rendering a very warped surface, it is possible that this quadrilateral will not be convex; in such a case we usually use the convex hull for the rest of the process. We then find an average texture value inside that quadrilateral. This average value is returned to the renderer as the average particular property of that surface seen from that pixel.

In [Will83] Williams described the *mip map*, which pre-computed averages of square regions of texture at a variety of different resolutions. In [Crow84] Crow described the *sum table*, which can provide the average value in any rectangle oriented parallel to the texture axes. The sum table is usually used to find the average texture value in the smallest oriented rectangle enclosing the mapped pixel. The texture value returned by a sum table is usually more accurate than that from a mip map, due to its ability to sample a region that more tightly encloses the texture-space image of the pixel. Sum tables have been studied in the field of probability theory as *joint cumulative probability distribution functions* on two variables [Ross76].

Both mip maps and sum tables provide a great speedup over direct averaging for every pixel, especially when the texture area covered by the pixel is large. Although sum tables are superior to mip maps, they can still present artifacts. In particular, texture outside the pixel but within the enclosing rectangle is included in the average. It is possible that the area inside the pixel is very small compared to its bounding rectangle; thus texture from outside the pixel may dominate the final average. If this extraneous texture contributes substantially to the final average, the texture value applied to a pixel may be substantially wrong.

The texture-sampling problem can be expressed mathematically by writing the average value g as a nonlinear convolution of a filter kernel h with a texture function f [Andr77]. If we knew the correct filter to apply to the texture for a given sample, we could simply convolve the texture and the filter to obtain:

$$g_{region} = \iint h(x - \xi, y - \eta) \, f(\xi, \eta) \, d\xi \, d\eta$$

The assumption behind sum tables is that the filter h can be approximated by a unit-height filter which is 1 inside the bounding box of the texture-space image of the pixel, and 0 outside of that box (see Figure 1a).

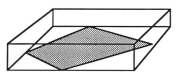

(a) The filter used in rectangular sum tables has unit height over the bounding box of the pixel's texture-space image.

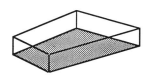

(b) We suggest a better filter would have unit height only over the texture-space pixel itself.

Figure 1

In this paper we present an improvement on the sum table technique which allows us to compensate for errors that arise from the inclusion of texture which lies outside the pixel. We will give methods to construct a filter which is 1 only inside the transformed pixel, and 0 everywhere else (see Figure 1b). Our conjecture is that this filter will provide superior results over the standard sum table bounding box filter. We present methods for obtaining this improved filter to different degrees of precision. Our technique is also iterative and adaptive, allowing us to perform only as much extra work as the image requires.

2.0 Terminology

When we refer to *texture space*, we mean that coordinates are to be interpreted as positions in the texture function. If the function is two dimensional, we call the axes u and v. When we transform a screen pixel into a corresponding quadrilateral in texture space, we call the new quadrilateral the pixel's *texture-space image*. The convex hull of this quadrilateral we will call the *inverse-mapped pixel*, or for convenience simply the *mapped pixel*. The four points that comprise a mapped pixel may form a quadrilateral, triangle, line, or single point. For simplicity, we will call the shape formed by a mapped pixel a *general quadrilateral*.

For a given region R in texture space, we will designate its area by R_a, the sum of all its values (its integral) by R_Σ, and its average value R_Σ / R_a as R_v.

We will sometimes illustrate texture operations by determining a color for a pixel, but the texture may actually be supplying any surface parameter. When we do speak of color from textures, we imply that three texture tables are accessed simultaneously (holding the red, green, and blue components of the texture color).

3.0 Fixed Polygon Approximation

When we build a sum table, each entry receives the summation of all the values in the original texture within some fixed region, oriented with reference to that entry. The traditional region used in a sum table is a rectangle. In a rectangular sum table each table entry contains the sum of the texture values between its corresponding position in the texture and the texture origin. We may extend the utility of the sum table by integrating under other shapes. The sum table is valuable because of its ability to provide the average value under a fixed region of variable size and position. However, the orientation and shape of the region must remain fixed throughout the table. Thus, we may quickly find the average value within any fixed region with a sum table, but each change in the desired shape or orientation of the region will require a new table. We will call the integration region provided by a sum table that table's *fundamental region*. Note that the region we integrate under to build a sum table is of the same shape as the fundamental region provided by the table.

The values returned by a sum table may be composed with one another to create an average value for a region with a shape other than the table's fundamental region. This may be achieved with simple linear combinations of the values returned by the table and the areas of the queried regions. Figure 2 shows an example of finding the average value in the region bounded by a letter E in a sum table with a rectangular fundamental region. The desired region is E, the enclosing rectangle is R, and the extra spaces are A, B, and C. We can express E_v, the average value in E, as

$$E_v = \frac{E_\Sigma}{E_a} = \frac{R_\Sigma - A_\Sigma - B_\Sigma - C_\Sigma}{R_a - A_a - B_a - C_a}$$

which may be generalized as

$$E_v = \frac{R_\Sigma - \sum_{i=1}^{n} (region_i)_\Sigma}{R_a - \sum_{i=1}^{n} (region_i)_a}$$

We will investigate a variety of techniques for finding the average value in regions other than a table's fundamental region. To compare these techniques it is helpful to have a measure of how much error may exist in the final value. To compare these different techniques we use the *relative error* measure:

$$\epsilon_{relative} = \left| \frac{\text{desired value} - \text{obtained value}}{\text{desired value}} \right|$$

It is a bit more difficult to decide what we ought to measure. It would be nice to include the texture data itself in our comparison of texture estimation schemes. However, the only aspect of the different techniques that remains unchanged over different textures is the area averaged by that technique for a given mapped pixel. Thus, our measured values will be the area we want in our final region (whose contents are averaged to obtain a final value), and the area of the region we actually get from each technique.

Let us first analyze the area errors from the rectangular sum table. Figure 3a shows a screen pixel which has mapped into a diamond in texture space. The bounding box encloses twice as much area as the interior of the diamond. Let us call the side of the bounding box L. Then the length of one side of the diamond is $L\sqrt{2}/2$, so the diamond's total area is $L^2/2$. The relative area error in this case is

$$\epsilon_{rectangle-table} = \left| \frac{L^2/2 - L^2}{L^2/2} \right| = 1$$

One solution to this problem is to augment the rectangular sum table with a *diamond* sum table. This is simply a rectangular sum table built at a 45° angle relative to the standard rectangular sum table. When this combination is presented with a mapped pixel, based on the geometry of the pixel we determine which of the two tables to use for the texture estimate. Consider this combination of sum tables applied to Figure 3b, which shows a rectangle canted at a 22.5° angle to the table sides. We want the area inside the rectangle; this is the area of the bounding box minus the four outer triangles:

$$desired\ area = L^2 - 4 \left[\frac{1}{2} \left(\frac{3}{4}L \right) \times \frac{1}{4}L \right] = \frac{5}{8}L^2$$

$$\epsilon_{diamond-table} = \left| \frac{(5/8)L^2 - L^2}{(5/8)L^2} \right| = \frac{3}{5}$$

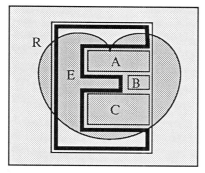

We can easily combine elements from a sum table to find the average of a shape other than the table's fundamental region.

Figure 2

For comparison with the other techniques analyzed in this paper, let us find the relative error of the worst cases for these tables. Figure 3c shows the worst case for the rectangular table (a thin quadrilateral at 45°), and Figure 3d shows the worst case for the combined tables (a thin quadrilateral at 22.5°). Under the combined tables, if the mapped pixel's bounding box is not square, we call the shorter side L and the longer side nL. The respective errors are:

$$\epsilon_{rectangle} = \left| \frac{L - L^2}{L} \right| = |1 - L|$$

$$\epsilon_{rectangle-or-diamond} = \left| \frac{nL - nL^2}{nL} \right| = |1 - L|$$

Note that the errors in the worst case are the same, so the addition of the diamond table hasn't really earned us anything in general.

We have just seen one approach to improving estimates provided by a rectangular sum table: maintain a table with a different fundamental region and use it where the rectangular table's estimates would be at their worst. Another way to improve a texture estimate is to remove regions of texture we don't want included in our sample. We are not limited to a rectangular fundamental region for these subtracted regions. If we maintain a second table with a different shape, we may find it easier to remove unwanted areas.

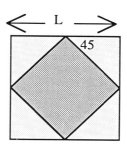

(a) A bad case for rectangular sum tables.

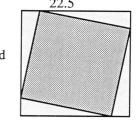

(b) A bad case for combined rectangular and diamond tables.

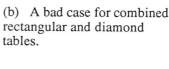

(c) A worst case for rectangular sum tables: a degenerate quadrilateral at 45 degrees.

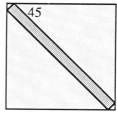

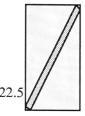

(d) A worst case for combined rectangular and diamond tables: a degenerate quadrilateral at 22.5 degrees.

Figure 3

Let us choose triangles as the fundamental region for such an auxiliary sum table. Recalling the above statements on sum tables, we may pick any fixed shape of triangle we like, but we may only have one such shape per table. Let's choose 45° right triangles, with the sides adjacent to the right angle lined up parallel to the sides of the sum table. It may appear that we need four sum tables, one for each orientation of the right angle. However, we can get by with just two triangle tables and the rectangle table. The trick is that when we want a triangle we don't have we can find its bounding box and subtract the triangle we do have. The ability to remove these triangular regions allows us to draw a generalized octagon around a mapped pixel, and obtain the average within this octagon, as shown in Figure 4a.

The worst case for the rectangle-plus-triangles scheme is when the sides of the mapped pixel make 22.5° angles with the sides of the bounding box. Figure 4b demonstrates the degenerate form of this worst case, whose error may be expressed as:

$$\epsilon_{triangle} = \left| \frac{nL - \left(nL^2 - 2\left(\frac{1}{2}L^2\right)\right)}{nL} \right| = \left| 1 - \frac{1}{2}L \right|$$

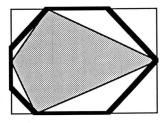
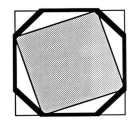

(a) A general case.

(b) A worst case: all triangles are 45-45-90.

Mapped pixels approximated by 45 degree octagons.

Figure 4

This error is still linear in L, but grows half as quickly as for the combined rectangle-or-diamond table error.

We might want to improve our texture estimate further by iteratively removing more triangles of smaller size from the unwanted region. However, we would need to know when to stop. We would also like to be able to stop as soon as practical; that is, remove no more regions than the image and the texture require to provide acceptable results. In the following section we examine a method to provide a stopping point for such an iteration.

We should also mention that one can interpolate to sub-table values in the sum table, using techniques such as bilinear interpolation. Indeed, this interpolation is required to generate alias-free images. It does not save us from the kinds of oversampling errors mentioned above, however, unless carried to an extreme (as briefly discussed in Section 5).

4.0 Estimation of Local Texture Complexity

We have seen that we can improve the texture estimate (or at least the area sampled) by iteratively removing extraneous regions from the first approximation made with the bounding box. However, we noted that a stopping point is required that will enable us to stop iterating when the sampled value is sufficiently accurate for that pixel.

To achieve this goal we create a new table: the *variance table*. The variance table contains a local estimate of the variance of the texture at each texture position in the table. For a color texture, we can estimate local variance by looking at the 3×3 neighborhood around each texture entry, finding the mean color $(\bar{r}, \bar{g}, \bar{b})$, and computing:

$$est.\ variance = \frac{\sum_{i=1}^{8} \left[(r_i - \bar{r})^2 + (g_i - \bar{g})^2 + (b_i - \bar{b})^2 \right]}{8}$$

To use the variance table, first convert it into a rectangular sum table. When a pixel is mapped into image space, we estimate the variance in that pixel before computing the texture value. We estimate the average variance by finding the total variance inside the bounding box of the mapped pixel and dividing by the area of the bounding box.

Using this technique, we can find an estimate of the average amount of high-frequency information inside the mapped pixel, and use that information to control how much work we need to do to get a good texture estimate. Figure 5 shows a sample texture (before conversion into a rectangular sum table), along with some sample mapped pixels. Note that mapped pixel A is in a region with no local variance; the average value inside the bounding box is exactly the same as the average value inside the mapped pixel. In this case we should do no more work than that involved in looking up the bounding box. However, mapped pixel B is in a very busy area. We would like a very careful estimate of the area inside the mapped pixel in this case.

In the next section we will show how to use the estimated variance to control the accuracy of the sampled pixel.

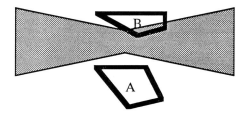

We can approximate A coarsely, but we will want a very careful estimate for B.

Figure 5

5.0 Adaptive Polygon Approximation

In the texturing operation we desire an estimate of the average value within a general quadrilateral. One way to derive this estimate is to approximate a non-rectangular shape with rectangles. There are at least two ways to do this: additive and subtractive synthesis. We will briefly discuss additive synthesis, and then focus on subtractive synthesis for the remainder of this paper.

The image of the pixel in texture space is usually some form of quadrilateral. This quadrilateral could be scan-converted in texture space, creating a set of spans defined by one constant co-ordinate and a pair of the other co-ordinates defining the endpoints. Each such "scanline" can be looked up in the sum table. This would require one sum table access for as many lines as one cares to generate. If the quadrilateral is enclosed in a box with height L, this would require L table lookups. Alternatively, one may approximate the actual region with a set of smaller rectangles. Let us use K rectangles and apply them to the worst case (Figure 4c). Each rectangle would be L/K high by nL/K wide. Thus, the error would be

$$\epsilon_{additive-synthesis} = \left| \frac{nL - K \left(\frac{L}{K} \times \frac{nL}{K} \right)}{nL} \right| = \left| 1 - \frac{L}{K} \right| \quad (1)$$

Let us now look at subtractive synthesis. We will call the area within the quadrilateral representing a mapped pixel the *internal region*, while the total area outside the quadrilateral but within the bounding box is the *external region*. We may obtain an estimate of the average value in a general quadrilateral by first estimating the average value in its bounding box, and then removing rectangles from the exterior region. We call each removed rectangle a *bite*.

To maximize the benefit of removing bites from the exterior region we should insure that we remove the largest possible bite remaining at each step. We must also be able to identify this largest bite quickly and efficiently, since it is an operation we may perform many times for every pixel.

Bite identification is a two-step process. The first step partitions the exterior region into a set of geometric primitives, or *fragments*. The second step finds the largest available rectangular region and removes it from the set. The first step is performed once per pixel, while the second step is executed once each time we want to refine our texture estimate for a given pixel.

We chose rectangles and right-angled, table-aligned triangles for the fragments. These shapes are attractive because the area of their largest bite is easy to compute, and their extents require the storage of only four co-ordinates. The largest bite in a rectangle is the entire rectangle, and it may be stored by just its two diagonal corner points. The largest bite in a triangle is the rectangle with one corner at the right angle and the other at the midpoint of the hypotenuse, and it may be stored by its right-angle vertex and two side lengths. When a rectangle is removed it is simply deleted from the set. When a triangle is removed it is deleted from the set, and the two smaller remaining triangles are added, as shown in Figure 6.

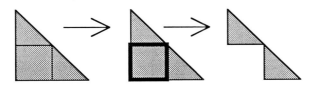

When we take a bite out of a triangle, we remove the largest rectangle it encloses. Two smaller triangles remain.

Figure 6

We have developed an iterative technique that partitions the exterior region into rectangles and triangles. At several points in this approach we need to find the orientation of a point with respect to a line. We can find which side of the line the given point is on by examining the sign of the line equation when solved for the point. We can compute this efficiently for a point A and a line from $P0$ to $P1$ by finding the sign of

$$d = (P1_x - P0_x)(A_y - P0_y) + (P1_y - P0_y)(P0_x - A_x)$$

We first tag each point of the quadrilateral with a bit field indicating whether it lies on each of the four edges or its bounding box (points on a corner are marked by both edges). We look for three special cases before proceeding farther. Special case 1 holds if no points are corner points; then we must have the case illustrated in Figure 7. Special case 2 holds if all points are corner points; then the quadrilateral is a rectangle or a single point, and we have one of the two cases illustrated in Figure 8 (either way there is no exterior region to be partitioned). Special case 3 holds if we only have corners on a diagonal, and the other points lie along this line. We check for this case by first looking at all the corners; if we only have diagonally opposite corners we then find the sign of the distance of the other two points from that line. If the sign of both distances is 0, then they all lie along a line, and the partitioning is as illustrated in Figure 9.

If all 4 corners of the mapped pixel are on the edges of the bounding box, then the pixel must have this form: a right triangle in each corner of the bounding box.

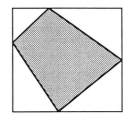

Figure 7

If all four corners of the pixel are on the corners of the bounding box, there are only these two situations:

(a) when the mapped pixel is a rectangle with non-zero area.

(b) holds when the mapped pixel degenerates into a single texture point.

Figure 8

When the mapped pixel is a degenerate line across the diagonal of its bounding box we partition the bounding box into two triangular regions of equal size, indicated A and B.

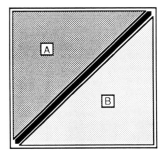

Figure 9

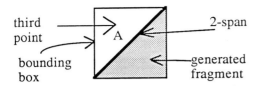

If the 2-span forms a diagonal of the bounding box we examine a third point (A); if possible this point is chosen to lie off the line formed by the 2-span. Based on the direction of the 2-span and the postition of A, we can tell which triangle to create as a fragment.

If the 2-span travels from edge to edge, then it must cut off a corner. We can deduce from the rules that created the 2-span that the rest of the polygon must lie away from that corner. We thus create the fragment triangle between the corner and the 2-span.

(a)　　　　　　Figure 10　　　　　　(b)

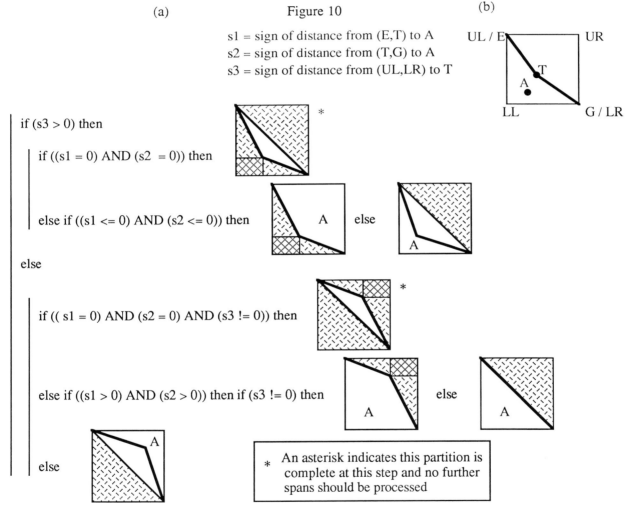

When we process a 3-span, we need a variety of values to help us create the fragments. We compute the sign of the distance from the middle point of the 3-span (denoted T) to each of the two corners not included in the 3-span. We also want to know if the fourth point A is on the same side of both segments of the 3-span. To this end we compute the distance from A to each of the two line segments. We then process the 3-span as shown above. The same process is followed for 3-spans on the other diagonal, with appropriate re-labelling. On each partitioning diagram we show the location of the fourth point A, determined by the algorithm, to show how the convex hull is automatically determined as we process the span.

Figure 11

If none of these special cases holds, we partition the region with an iterative procedure. We start with a corner point and fix a direction to pick up the remaining points (clockwise around the original pixel works fine). We then look at the edge information for next point around the quadrilateral.

If this second point is on an edge, we call this pair of points a *2-span*. We pick one of the other two points as an auxiliary point and call it point *A*; if possible, we pick *A* to lie off the line formed by the 2-span. We then find the sign of the distance from this point to the line formed by the 2-span. If both points of the 2-span are corner points, then we create partitions as shown in Figure 10a, otherwise we create partitions as shown in Figure 10b.

If this second point is not on an edge, then we examine the next point in turn. If this third point is on an edge, we call the trio a *3-span*, and *A* is assigned the remaining point. If the first and last points of the 3-span are corners we create partitions as shown in Figure 11, otherwise we re-label the points as shown in Figure 12 and then create the partitions shown in Figure 11.

If this third point is not on an edge, we then take the fourth point and call the quartet a *4-span*, and partition it as shown in Figure 13.

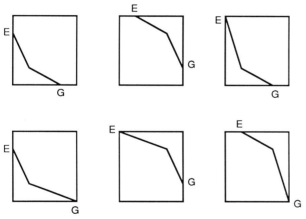

If the endpoints of a 3-span are not corners, then we label them according to these conventions and use the algorithm of Figure 11.

Figure 12

A 4-span necessarily spans opposite diagonals of the bounding box. If both of the other points are on the same side of the diagonal we partition the box into these 6 fragments.

If the two non-corner points in a 4-span are not on the same side of the diagonal, then we derive the convex hull and partition the regions outside it into 6 fragments using this scheme.

Figure 13

If the point at the end of the most recently classified span is not the same point we started with, we use last that point as the start of a new span and continue walking around the points of the quadrilateral. When we return to our starting point, we will have walked around the entire outside of the mapped pixel, partitioning the region between its convex hull and its bounding box into triangles and rectangles. The partitioning algorithm is summarized in the Appendix.

We are then prepared to remove bites from the external region, as guided by this partitioning. The process is recapitulated in Figure 14. Figure 14a shows a mapped pixel, 14b shows its decomposition into triangles and rectangles, 14c shows the removal of the first bite, and 14d shows the removal of the first six bites.

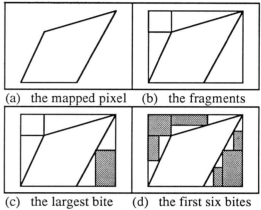

| (a) the mapped pixel | (b) the fragments |
| (c) the largest bite | (d) the first six bites |

Figure 14

It is informative to compute the area error left after each step in the refinement of the estimate. A worst-case general quadrilateral consists of a line from one corner of its bounding box to its diagonal opposite. Let us label the shorter side (if there is one) as L, and the longer side as nL. Both regions around L have equal area; let us take the largest bite out of one of them. The area left after this bite is now

$$desired = nL^2 - \left(\frac{L}{2} \times \frac{nL}{2} \right) = \frac{3nL^2}{4}$$

Thus the relative error is

$$\epsilon_{one-bite} = \left| \frac{nL - \left(3nL^2/4 \right)}{nL} \right| = \left| 1 - \frac{3}{4}L \right|$$

Similar reasoning for other numbers of bites leads us to a piecewise-linear approximation to the curve 2^{-n}, with exact matches where n is an integer. We thus arrive at the general formula for the error after k bites:

$$\epsilon_{adaptive}(k) = \left| 1 - \left(\frac{3\left(2^{\lfloor \log_2 k \rfloor} \right) - k - 1}{4^{\lfloor \log_2 k \rfloor}} \right) L \right| \quad (2)$$

This formula gives us a relationship (albeit a little complex) between the number of rectangular bites taken from the area and the resulting relative area error. Since this analysis was carried out for the worst case, if we take enough bites to meet this error for any situation we are guaranteed a maximum bound on the relative error.

The variance table and the results of Equation 2 are used to determine a maximum bound on the number of bites we need to take from a sample. We simply use a linear relationship between the range of variance and the range of error, adjusted to err on the side of over-refining.

6.0 Implementation and Results

The implementation of the technique was written to run in either of two environments: on a VAX-11/780 running UNIX BSD4.2, or within the Adage/Ikonas RDS-3000 raster graphics engine. To this end, the code was written in gia2 [Bish82], a dialect of C.

The implementation used to generate the pictures partitions the external regions with the iterative span classification technique. The generated rectangles and triangles (or *fragments*), are kept in a doubly-linked list. Each entry in the list contains the co-ordinates needed to describe the fragment, the area of the largest bite it contains, and a pair of forward and backward pointers. Bites are taken from the sample until no fragments with non-zero area remain, or the maximum number of bites (as determined from the average variance) have been taken.

It is most efficient to pre-allocate memory for storage of the fragment list. An upper bound on the size of the list is the maximum number of starting fragments (6) plus the maximum number of bites (because each triangle bite adds one triangle to the list). When there are no more entries left to fill in the list we simply discard the fragments we can't accommodate. The maximum number of bites can be found from the last entry in the error/bite correspondence table (discussed below). In the current implementation an upper limit of 80 bites is imposed, so the fragment list has 86 entries.

Equation 2 expresses the allowable error, in terms of the number of bites taken. We want the opposite relation, i.e. how many bites to take given a particular error. To compensate for this problem we create a table indexed by tolerable error. When we have a maximum allowable error (derived from the variance map) we scan this table for the first entry with an error value less than the allowable error. The associated number of bites is the value we use to terminate the refinement.

It is interesting to note that the three color tables and the variance table can all be stored in a single square array. We used 256 × 256 tables, arranged in a 512 frame buffer as a two-by-two matrix.

As a demonstration of the new technique case we present Figure 15, which shows images of a black-and-white checkerboard in perspective. In the lower-left is the image generated by standard sum tables. As the checkerboard nears the horizon the sum table image blurs into a grey band. In the lower-right is the image generated by the technique described in this paper. The black and white squares of the checkerboard near the horizon are still resolvable, especially as we sight along the diagonals. Above each checkerboard is an enlargement of the square region indicated in red.

Figure 16 is an image which was generated along with the bottom-right image of Figure 15. It shows how many bites were taken on a pixel basis. Black indicates no bites were taken; a whiter entry indicates a larger number of bites. Pure white indicates 21 bites for this image. Note that the iterative technique only executes where the standard sum table would not provide a good estimate.

Figure 17 shows the same checkerboard receding at a 45° angle to the axes of the pixels.

Table 1 summarizes the number of rectangular sum table samples taken for the two images. Recall that the division operation needed to derive an average from a sum and an area is still executed only once per pixel in the new technique.

Figure 15

Figure 16

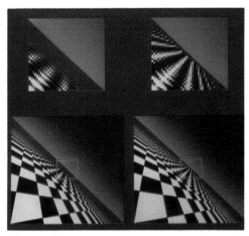

Figure 17

	Figure 15	Figure 17
Rectangle samples in standard sum table	50,176	65,536
Rectangle samples in new technique	76,942	88,774
Relative increase	1.5334	1.3545

Experimental Costs of New Technique and Sum Tables

Table 1

7.0 Discussion and Future Work

The use of the variance map to determine how many bites to take in an estimate seems to be a good approximation, but it's not ideal; in fact it can lead to estimates which are much higher than they ought to be. A better way to determine which bite to take would be to take the Fourier transform of all the possible bites at each step, and choose the bite with the maximum energy under its transform. The drawback to this scheme is clearly the high computational cost involved in taking the transforms and evaluating their energy. It would be interesting to examine techniques to get a quick estimate on these values.

It would be nice if we could remove bites from the concave portions of concave mapped pixels, rather than work with their convex hulls. It would be interesting to look for other fragment shapes that had the storage and simplicity characteristics of oriented rectangles and oriented right triangles, but could also give us a handle on approximating concave mapped pixels.

It should be noted that there is an inherent limit on the theoretical precision of this technique. As mentioned in Section 1.0, we are not performing an ideal filtering of the texture when we derive our estimate. Our first major assumption was to use rectangular, abutting "Fourier windows" to control our examined texture region. Our second assumption was to effectively sample the texture with a delta function, instead of a proper filter. These assumptions usually produce good results in synthesized images. However, after a certain point further refinement of the texture estimate by the techniques presented here will not come closer to a theoretical value. This theoretical drawback does not seem to detract from the general usefulness of the technique.

It is true that the complexity measure described in this paper is best for textures with large homogeneous areas (such as checkerboards!). Complex textures will have very high values throughout the variance map. This isn't too bad, since we will usually will want very accurate estimates of complex textures. But this is another reason that a better complexity estimator than the variance would be valuable.

We have investigated another way to determine the partitions of a mapped pixel and its bounding box. We have found that there are 25 types of box-bounded convex quadrilaterals. If we can quickly determine to which of the 25 types a given mapped pixel corresponds, we can have the entire partitioning immediately. We hope to follow this line of thought farther.

The techniques described in this paper can be extended in a straightforward way to sum tables of 3 or more dimensions. In the 3d case we would remove right pyramids and right parallelpipeds from our bounding right parallelpiped to refine the texture estimate. The fragmentation code would be considerably more complex.

8.0 Acknowledgements

Several of the ideas in this paper were considered independently by Ken Perlin [Perl86]. Specifically, he investigated three-dimensional tables for the triangular tables discussed in Section 3, using two axes for u and v and the third for the free angle.

Thanks go to my advisor Henry Fuchs for his enthusiastic support. Thanks also go to my fellow students in the UNC-CH Computer Graphics Lab, whose expertise and insight contributed greatly to this work. Many of the ideas and results in this paper grew out of conversations with Greg Abram, Phil Amburn, Larry Bergman, John Gauch, Eric Grant, Jeff Hultquist, Marc Levoy, Chuck Mosher, and Lee Westover. Comments on this paper were offered by several of the above and Bobette Eckland.

Special thanks go to Jeff and Mary Hultquist, who volunteered to assist me in the final production of this paper. The excellent layout and pasteup are entirely due to their talents and friendship.

9.0 References

[Andr77] Andrews, H.C., and Hunt, B.R., "Digital Image Restoration," Prentice-Hall, Inc. (1977)

[Bish82] Bishop, G., "Gary's Ikonas Assembler Version 2," UNC-CH Computer Science Department Technical Report, June, 1982

[Blin76] Blinn, J., and Newell M.E., "Texture and Reflection in Computer Generated Images," CACM 19, 10 (Oct 1976)

[Blin78] Blinn, J., "Simulation of Wrinkled Surfaces," *Computer Graphics*, vol. 12, no. 3, August 1978

[Catm75] Catmull, E., "Computer Display of Curved Surfaces," *Proc. IEEE Conference on Computer Graphics, Pattern Recognition, and Data Structure*, May 1975.

[Carp84] Carpenter, L., "The A-buffer, an Antialiased Hidden Surface Method," *Computer Graphics*, vol. 18, no. 3, July 1984

[Cook84] Cook, R., "Shade Trees," *Computer Graphics*, vol. 18, no. 3, July 1984

[Crow84] Crow, F., "Summed-Area Tables for Texture Mapping," *Computer Graphics*, vol. 18, no. 3, July 1984

[Duff85] Duff, T., "Compositing 3-D Rendered Images," *Computer Graphics*, vol. 19, no. 3, July 1985

[Feib84] Feibush, Levoy, M., Cook, R., "Synthetic Texturing Using Digital Filters," *Computer Graphics*, vol. 14, no. 3 July 1980

[Gard84] Gardner G., "Simulation of Natural Scenes Using Textured Quadric Surfaces," *Computer Graphics*, vol. 18, no. 3, July 1984

[Peal85] Peachey D., "Solid Texturing of Complex Surfaces," *Computer Graphics*, vol. 19, no. 3, July 1985

[Perl85] Perlin, K., "An Image Synthesizer," *Computer Graphics*, vol. 19, no. 3, July 1985

[Perl86] Perlin, K., private communication.

[Port84] Porter, T., and Duff, T., "Compositing Digital Images," *Computer Graphics*, vol. 19, no. 3, July 1985

[Ross76] Ross S., "A First Course in Probability," MacMillan Publishing Co, Inc. (1976)

[Schw83] Schweitzer D., "Artificial Texturing: An Aid to Surface Visualization," *Computer Graphics*, vol. 18, no. 3, July 1984

[Suth74] Sutherland, I., Sproull, R., Schumaker, R., "A Characterization of Ten Hidden-Surface Algorithms," *Computing Surveys*, vol. 6, no. 1, March 1974

[Will83] Williams L., "Pyramidal Parametrics," *Computer Graphics*, vol. 18, no. 3, July 1984

Appendix: derivation of the partitioning algorithm

The figure below shows the possible spans that may arise in a mapped pixel. When we consider edge information some spans become unrealizable; these are marked X. For example, the fifth span on the first row must have the given partitioning; if the quadrilateral had any points inside the shaded triangle the endpoints of the span would be corners. Sometimes we need another point of the polygon to decide which side of the span to partition. This point is chosen to lie off the line(s) formed by the span, if possible, and is marked ● in this diagram.

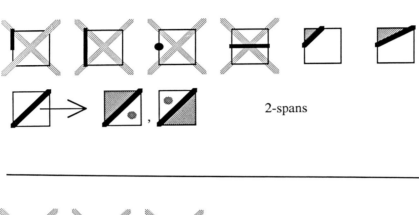

2-spans

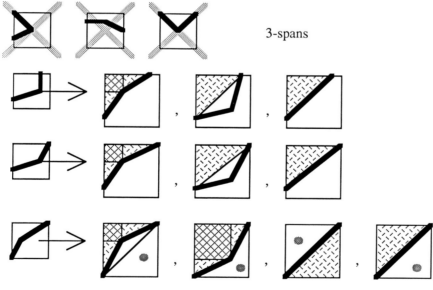

3-spans

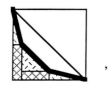 , ,

4-spans

Anti-Aliasing in Topological Color Spaces

Kenneth Turkowski

CIMLINC, Inc.
Menlo Park, CA

ABSTRACT

The power of a color space to perform well in interpolation problems such as anti-aliasing and smooth-shading is dependent on the topology of the color space as well as the number of elements it contains.

We develop the *Major-minor* color space, which has a topology and representation that lends itself to simple anti-aliasing computations between elements of an arbitrary set of colors in an inexpensive frame store.

CR Categories and Subject Descriptors: I.3.3 [**Computer Graphics**]: Picture/Image Generation - *Display algorithms*; I.3.7 [**Computer Graphics**]: Three-Dimensional Graphics and Realism - *Color, shading, shadowing, and texture*; I.4.1 [**Image Processing**]: Digitization - *Quantization*

General Terms: Algorithms, Theory

Additional Keywords and Phrases: anti-aliasing, smooth shading, topology, computation, color, color map, color spaces, frame buffer.

1. Introduction

As color graphics hardware becomes widely available, it is being used in more applications with different requirements. Many of these cannot be met with the default 8 colors available with 3 bits per pixel, so most general-purpose graphics systems come with 6, 8, or 24 bits per pixel, as well as a color map to tailor the set of colors to the particular application.

This extra flexibility brings with it a curse, though; it is difficult to choose a good working set that allocates most of the available colors in a useful way [10] [26] [14] [12] [24]. There is a desire, then, to find a systematic way of choosing colors by imposing structure on the color map. The resultant set of available colors is a *color space*, and its structure the *topology*.

2. Anti-Aliasing

Aliasing is a phenomenon that manifests itself as jagged borders in computer-generated images. The term *aliasing* comes from the field of discrete signal processing, in which higher frequencies become aliased as, and indistinguishable from, lower frequencies in the signal if the sampling rate is not high enough. The frequency that is twice that of the maximum in the signal is known as *the Nyquist frequency*, and is the lowest rate at which the signal can be sampled without exhibiting any aliasing artifacts. The Shannon (Nyquist) Sampling Theorem states that the signal can be *perfectly*

reconstructed from its samples only if the samples are taken at a rate higher than the Nyquist frequency [16] [18]. The continuous signal is reconstructed by passing the samples through a *reconstruction filter*. The ideal low-pass filter specified by the sampling theorem is not physically realizable, but it can be approximated by a digital-to-analog (D/A) converter followed by an analog $\sin(x)/x$ correction filter [27] [7]. To assure that the signal is properly bandlimited *before* sampling, it is passed through an *anti-aliasing filter*.

Computer graphics is concerned with sampling a mathematical model of an image (a *two*-dimensional signal) on a rectangular array of points. These points, as well as their quantized value, are called *pixels*, or picture elements.

The sharper or more detailed an image is, the higher its spatial frequency content. Sharp edges occur at the border of graphical primitives (e.g. polygons and lines) when their colors are substantially different from the scene around them.

Aliasing at sharp edges and small objects can be avoided by computing, at each pixel, an appropriately weighted average of the colors of every object in the neighborhood of the pixel [6]. These anti-aliasing computations produce colors that are different than the colors of the objects in the model. If they are not *perceptibly* different than colors already available, no additional colors need be introduced. In general, though, the color space should be augmented with a few colors relatively close to those produced by the anti-aliasing calculations.

Closeness of colors can be determined by measuring the perceptual difference between them. The sensitivity of the human visual system to color differences varies throughout the spectrum [30] though, so we instead use a simpler, uniform model for comparing colors.

3. Metric Color Spaces and Interpolation

3.1. The RGB Color Space

The Young-Helmholz theory of color [1] states that there are three basic colors (red, green, and blue), and three kinds of cones in the eye, each most sensitive to one of these three primary colors. By the tristimulus theory of color representation [18], we can use these three colors as a basis for a Cartesian three-space. Every color can then be represented as an ordered triple (r,g,b), whose components indicate the relative amounts of each primary to be added together.

The three colors to which the eye is most sensitive are not the only ones that can be used as primaries. *Any* three colors can be used as a basis, as long as they are linearly independent [17]. By linearly independent, we mean that one of the colors cannot be formed by adding appropriate amounts of the other two colors. This point is important, because the three primaries in a color graphics monitor are not in general the same as those of the eye.

Like the physically separate cones in the eye, there are physically separate dots of colored phosphor integrated into an array on the screen of the monitor. The light emitted from these dots is spatially filtered (i.e. *added*) because the distance between adjacent dots cannot be resolved by the eye at normal viewing distances.

3.2. Blending Colors

The basic operation involved in anti-aliasing [28] as well as that for smooth-shading [9] is a color interpolation illustrated by the following blending equation:

$$C = (1-\alpha)B + \alpha F \qquad (1)$$
$$= B + \alpha(F-B)$$

where α is a parameter that varies between 0 and 1, and C is a color that is interpolated between B and F, nominally the background and foreground colors.

The metric qualities of a color space affect the ease with which this interpolation can be done.

3.3. Gamma Correction

In order for linear interpolation to work correctly in our Cartesian color space, the luminance values of each of the primaries must be linear. The computer graphics monitor has a nonlinearity, however, between its driving signals and the resultant intensity. Both this and the nonlinear response of the eye can be compensated for adequately through the use of *gamma-correction* [5]:

$$V_o = V_i^{\frac{1}{\gamma}} \qquad (2)$$

where both V_o and V_i range between 0 and 1, and γ is fixed for a given monitor, usually in the range 1 to 2.2. This introduces a gain greater than unity for low brightness levels and a gain less than unity for higher levels.

This gamma-correction can be implemented by either analog or digital means. If it is analog, then it must be recalibrated for each different type of monitor, unless it resides in the monitor itself. Digital gamma correction is implemented when computing the values to load into the color map, and is much easier to change with a computer program than it is to adjust a nonlinear analog circuit with a screwdriver. A digital implementation is also more attractive because it can include other compensation, such as that necessary when the final medium is film [4]. The drawback is that the intensities may be further quantized if there are not enough entries in the color map. For example, when mapping a linear 8-bit range to an 8-bit D/A converter with a gamma correction of 2, {252, 253, 254, 255} will map into {254, 254, 255, 255}. For γ in the range [1, 2] then, at least one additional bit of output (i.e. 9) is necessary in order to maintain the same number of distinct levels.

3.4. Interpolation in Cartesian Three-Space

With appropriate compensation (gamma, etc.) the three primaries are independently linear, i.e. α units of red results in a color that is α times as bright as one unit of red, etc. Linear interpolation (eq. 1) in three-space then takes the form of linear interpolation in each primary component separately:

$$\begin{bmatrix} r_C \\ g_C \\ b_C \end{bmatrix} = \begin{bmatrix} r_B \\ g_B \\ b_B \end{bmatrix} + \alpha \left\{ \begin{bmatrix} r_F \\ g_F \\ b_F \end{bmatrix} - \begin{bmatrix} r_B \\ g_B \\ b_B \end{bmatrix} \right\} \qquad (3)$$
$$= \begin{bmatrix} r_B \\ g_B \\ b_B \end{bmatrix} + \begin{bmatrix} \alpha(r_F-r_B) \\ \alpha(g_F-g_B) \\ \alpha(b_F-b_B) \end{bmatrix} = \begin{bmatrix} r_B + \alpha(r_F-r_B) \\ g_B + \alpha(g_F-g_B) \\ b_B + \alpha(b_F-b_B) \end{bmatrix}$$

In a digital frame store only a finite number of colors can be represented, so that the above interpolation will be quantized. It is not necessarily desirable that this quantization occur on a componentwise basis. There are many frame stores that do not have enough bits per pixel to allow acceptable quantization in each primary separately. Therefore, symbolic encodings of colors are frequently used to place intermediate colors at appropriate locations in the color space.

4. Different Requirements for Smooth Shading and Anti-Aliasing

One class of images is that which consists of a limited number of different colored objects with anti-aliased borders.

Another features smooth shading between one color and another, to simulate the effect of lighting on a curved object [9] [2] [3].

The requirements for these are quantitatively different. Psychophysical experiments [18] have determined that at least 64 levels (6 bits) of grey-scale are required between light and dark in order for gradual, but quantized changes between colors to be imperceptible.

On the other hand, 4 levels (2 bits) of grey-scale work remarkably well for anti-aliasing, with appropriate gamma correction and reconstruction filtering [fig. 1a, 1b]. Adding more levels makes visual improvements mostly for edges near horizontal, vertical and 45 degrees [fig. 1c].

Few practitioners use both smooth-shading and anti-aliasing, because more computational effort is required, and because the color space is more expensive to accommodate both of these simultaneously. Anti-aliasing is most often applied to lines and sharp edges, whereas smooth-shading is applied to the interior of polygons and patches. Realistic images, of course, would use both.

Certainly one can perform anti-aliasing in a color space designed for smooth-shading, since there are more than enough levels of grey-scale. However, since the additional levels do not make remarkable improvements in quality, they could be better used to introduce more colors into the color space, or else eliminated entirely to reduce the cost of the system.

By abstracting the features of a particular class of images, the cost of hardware and computation can be reduced with an appropriate choice and encoding of a topological color space.

5. Color Space Topology

The existence and density of colors between other colors is an indication of the coarseness or fineness of the topology.

Loosely, the relationship or similarity between colors induces a topology [21] [13] in the color space. The more similar two colors are, the smaller the distance between them. When two colors are close to each other (i.e. the distance between them is small), they are called neighbors. The degree of similarity between a set of neighbors establishes a partial ordering among them†. The set of partially ordered sets of colors is called a *color space topology*. Therefore, given a color space topology, there exists a set of partially ordered sets of colors (possibly null) that interpolate between two given colors.

One elementary topology is one in which *all* colors are neighbors of each other; all color spaces with this topology are equivalent to one in which all colors are black. This is the *trivial* [21] or *indiscrete* topology, and has no practical applications. Below, we list some of the more useful color space topologies and their features.

6. Some Useful Color Space Topologies

6.1. The Discrete Topology

One topological color space quite widely used is one in which each color has *no* neighbors other than itself; this means that all colors are considered to be equally different. This is known as the *discrete* [21] topology [fig. 2], and permits no anti-aliasing, giving rise to jagged borders between colors. This space can be likened to an artist's palette, with a carefully chosen, but unrelated, set of colors available to compose the picture.

Since there are no intermediate colors available for interpolation, computations in this color space are particularly simple, taking the form of a simple conditional that chooses the background color if $\alpha < \frac{1}{2}$, and the foreground color if $\alpha > \frac{1}{2}$. This is particularly attractive, since most of the other color spaces require a multiplier to implement the blending equation (eq. 1).

6.2. The Layers Topology

This topology is analogous to several layers of superimposed transparencies, with each layer contributing some feature to the total image. Commonly, one bit is assigned to each layer, although there is nothing to preclude more than one bit per layer to accommodate anti-aliasing on each layer. A color is assigned to each layer, and when all layers are inactive, the resulting color is black, or some other *base* color. When only one layer is active, the result-

---

† Using *distance* to establish a partial ordering actually results in a *metric* space; a *topological* space uses the more general notion of *open sets*. The open sets (or neighborhoods) of each point in the space are partially ordered by inclusion.

ing color is the color corresponding to that layer. When more than one layer is active, the resultant color is some appropriate *combination* of the colors corresponding to each of the active layers. This topology is often used in the design of integrated circuits and printed circuit boards, to show the different layers.

The anti-aliasing features between active layers are non-uniform and rarely utilized. Therefore the computations in practice are similar to that of the discrete topology.

6.3. The Integer Topology

The next topology is that based on the integers, where 0 corresponds to a color at one extreme ("sepia") and MAX (e.g., 255 with 8 bits/pixel) to another (the other, "tan"), with all other colors linearly interpolated between the extremes ("shades of grey") [fig. 3]. Operations performed on colors in this space have exactly the same properties as the integers. This is a powerful color space, capable of anti-aliasing and smooth-shading, but can do so in just one color range.

6.4. The Full-Color Topology

Extending the integer color space to three dimensions by Cartesian product yields a quantized full color space. This is rich enough in colors and topology to represent realistic-looking images. However, with 8 bits per primary, each pixel requires 24 bits, which may be too expensive for some applications.

One can represent a full color space in fewer bits only with coarser quantization. Approximately uniform color space quantization in 8 bits would give 6 or 7 levels per primary. With 9 bits per pixel, each primary could have 8 levels (3 bits/primary), in a representation more suitable for computation. Similarly for 6 bit pixels, with 2 bits/primary. All of these are acceptable for anti-aliasing between 8 colors that are combinations of 3 arbitrarily-chosen primaries. If the standard primaries are chosen, we can anti-alias between black, white, red, green, blue, yellow, cyan, and magenta.

There are many three-dimensional coordinate systems for representing color, besides the primaries red, green, and blue (RGB). Some of these are simple linear transformation of the RGB axes: the XYZ system primaries developed by the Commission Internationale de l'Eclairage (CIE); the CIE-UCS (*Uniform Chromaticity Scale*) primaries UVW; and the YIQ and YUV systems used for NTSC and PAL color television transmission respectively [17]. Others are nonlinear: the CIE-recommended L*a*b* *uniform perceptual* system for reflected light; the CIE-recommended L*u*v* *uniform perceptual* system for additive light [19]; the hexcone HSV system (hue, saturation, value); the triangle HSL system (hue, saturation, and brightness) [22]; the double hexcone HLS system (hue, lightness, and saturation) [8].

6.5. The Disjoint Segment Topology

Suppose we choose arbitrary pairs of colors, and assign quantization only to several points between them [fig. 4] With 2 bits choosing the color segment, and 6 bits measuring the distance between end points of the chosen segment, we have 4 color ranges, with 64 values (suitable for smooth-shading) in each range. We cannot, however, anti-alias between segments, because they may be disjoint.

Segment		Value					
1	0	5	4	3	2	1	0

6.6. The Star Topology

By stipulating that the color ranges share a common color, we produce a topology with a path between any two colors. If one endpoint of each range is common, we have the star topology [fig. 5]. This color space has the property that it is possible to anti-alias between two color ranges (rays) by first going through black (or other chosen common color). The result is that all shapes are outlined in black, a desirable effect in television, which makes letters and other symbols legible on any color background. This topological color space, with the self-matting (outlined) property, has been called the *tint fill* color space, and has been widely used in video paint systems and two-dimensional animation [25] [23].

Tint		Value					
1	0	5	4	3	2	1	0

One can trade off the number of ranges with the number of quantization levels in each range by partitioning the code word differently: 16 ranges with 16 levels per range, 64 ranges with 4 levels per range, etc. With less levels, a smaller multiplier is needed for interpolation.

7. The Color Net Topology

The limitation of the star topology that all objects are outlined in black, may be objectionable for certain applications. It is desirable to develop a color space with a topology that allows anti-aliasing between any two arbitrary colors. The model for this color space is a net, with connections between every pair of nodes [fig. 6].

Let the nodes of the net be called primary colors, and the colors on the branches between the primaries be called secondaries. The number of secondaries desired can be chosen chosen arbitrarily.

The following table [29] shows the total number of quantization levels (Q) required given the desired number of primaries (N) and secondaries (s) between each pair of primaries. Note that the number of branches (b) required to link the primaries is a function of the number of primaries only. In addition, the total number of secondaries needed is equal to the number of secondaries desired between every pair of primaries multiplied by the number of branches needed to connect every pair of primaries. The number of quantization levels needed then is the sum of the number of primaries and the total number of secondaries.

$$b = \frac{1}{2}\binom{N}{2} = \frac{N(N-1)}{2} \qquad (4)$$

$$Q = N + s\frac{N(N-1)}{2} \qquad (5)$$

Number of Primaries N	Branches b	Quantization Levels Required (Q) for a Given Number of Secondaries (s)			
		s = 1	s = 2	s = 4	s = 6
2	1	3	4	6	8
3	3	6	9	15	21
4	6	10	16	28	40
5	10	15	25	45	65
6	15	21	36	66	96
7	21	28	49	91	133
8	28	36	64	120	176
9	36	45	81	153	225
10	45	55	100	190	280
11	55	66	121	231	
12	66	78	144	276	
13	78	91	169		
14	91	105	196		
15	105	120	225		
16	120	136	256		

2 secondaries/branch gives an anti-aliasing capability equivalent to 2 bits per pixel, and 6 secondaries/branch is equivalent to 3 bits per pixel (check the cases with 2 primaries). Note that, for 2 secondaries per branch, some of the required number of quantization levels are powers of two. This suggests that there might be a good way to encode these colors.

7.1. The Major-minor Colorspace

There is an elegant way of representing colors with two secondaries between each pair of primaries. Given the ordered pair (M,m), let M be called the Major component of the color, and m the minor. Those colors along the diagonal [fig. 9], where $M = m$, are purer than the rest, and can be called primary colors. The others $(M \neq m)$ are mixtures of two primary colors M and m, and so are secondary colors. The weights assigned to the Major and minor components should sum to one, and if the weights are $\frac{2}{3}$ and $\frac{1}{3}$, then the secondary colors are uniformly spaced between the primaries.

This set of colors can be represented as follows:

$$code = N_{pri} * M + m \qquad (6)$$

where N_{pri} is the number of primaries, M is the code number for the Major component, and m is the code for the minor.

When the number of primaries, N_{pri}, is a power of two, the multiplication is simply a shift, giving a representation of the form:

Major Component				Minor Component			
3	2	1	0	3	2	1	0

This simplifies anti-aliasing computations considerably; bit field extraction and insertion take the place of the more expensive division and multiplication.

For example, suppose we have a 4-bit datum, partitioned up into 2 2-bit fields.

Major Component		Minor Component	
1	0	1	0

In each of these 2-bit fields we can encode one of four numbers: 0, 1, 2, or 3. Let

    0 represent orange,
    1 represent blue,
    2 represent brown,
    and 3 represent green.

In traversing the colors from blue to green, we have

    (1,1) blue (a primary color)
    (1,3) greenish blue
    (3,1) bluish green
    (3,3) green (a primary color)

Similarly, for the paths leading to the other primaries orange (0,0) and brown (2,2).

Note that 2-, 4-, 6-, and 8-bit codes permit anti-aliasing between 2, 4, 8, and 16 colors, respectively. This implies that half the bits specify the color, and the other half are used for anti-aliasing between those colors.

7.2. Computation with the Major-minor Color Net Representation

If α is a number between 0 and 1 inclusive, then it can be represented as a fixed-point fraction, with 00...0 representing 0 and 11...1 representing 1. The most significant 2 bits of α can then be used to choose the new Major and minor components from the foreground and background Major and minor components. The 2 bits for α represent 0, $\frac{1}{3}$, $\frac{2}{3}$, and 1. Using the symbols F_1 and F_0 as the major and minor components of the foreground, B_1 and B_0 as the major and minor components of the background, and C_1 and C_0 as the major and minor components of the interpolated color (eq. 1), respectively, we have the following results for the various values of α:

α	C_1	C_0
00 (0)	B_1	B_0
01 ($\frac{1}{3}$)	B_1	F_1
10 ($\frac{2}{3}$)	F_1	B_1
11 (1)	F_1	F_0

This blending works as follows: with (α=00 or 11) the full background or foreground, respectively, is passed through. With α in between, though, some combination of the foreground and background is used; the effect is as if the foreground and background colors are first truncated to the nearest primary, and then interpolated according to α.

This blending computation is very simple, requiring no multiplications whatsoever, and can be easily implemented in hardware with a multiplexer [fig. 7].

7.3. Properties of the Major-minor Color Space

The simplest Major-minor color space is called monochrome with 2 bits/pixel, even though two colors (usually black and white) define it. 00 represents black, 11 white, 01 dark grey, 10 light grey. This space can also be considered to have a coarsely quantized integer topology. All of the properties of this 2-bit/pixel monochrome color space can be generalized to the Major-minor color space, if one considers it to be a 2-*digit* color space, where the radix of the digits can be larger than 2.

In particular, 4 quantization levels allow one to shift the apparent location of a line approximately one-third of a pixel to either side of the center, as illustrated by the following sequence:

0	1	0	0	Energy on the left pixel
0	$\frac{2}{3}$	$\frac{1}{3}$	0	Energy shifts to the right
0	$\frac{1}{3}$	$\frac{2}{3}$	0	Energy shifts more to the right
0	0	1	0	Energy on the right pixel

This triples the linear positional resolution of a computer-generated image.

The Major-minor color space has proved most useful in anti-aliasing of engineering drawings [fig. 8] where the different colors represent different types of lines in different stages of editing. The quality is especially noticeable on curves.

A convenient way of representing the colors in a Major-minor space is in a square array, much like a plaid [fig. 9]. The primary colors lie along the diagonal, and the intermediate colors are found in the overlapping horizontal and vertical strips going through the two primaries.

8. Extensions to the Major-minor Color Space

8.1. The Major-minor-subminor Color Space

Let us look at a generalization of the Major-minor color space by adding another "digit". This Major-minor-subminor color space corresponds to 3 bits/pixel, representing the colors in a cube with the primary colors along the cube's diagonal.

Major			Minor			Subminor		
2	1	0	2	1	0	2	1	0

In this representation, the Major component has a weight of $\frac{4}{7}$, the minor $\frac{2}{7}$ and the subminor $\frac{1}{7}$. Between primaries there are 6 secondary colors, yielding anti-aliasing quality corresponding to 3 bits. As a bonus, there are tertiary colors interpolating between secondary and primary colors: 6 new tertiaries for each set of three primaries [fig. 10].

The computation is nearly as simple as the Major-minor case:

α	C_2	C_1	C_0
000	B_2	B_1	B_0
001	B_2	B_1	F_2
010	B_2	F_2	B_1
011	B_2	F_2	F_1
100	F_2	B_2	B_1
101	F_2	B_2	F_1
110	F_2	F_1	B_2
111	F_2	F_1	F_0

The interpretation for these calculations in hardware is as follows: The foreground and background colors are contained in shift registers, and their outputs are multiplexed together, controlled by successive bits of α. The most significant bit of α chooses where the most significant (Major) component of the result comes from. Whichever source (F or B) was chosen is shifted up by the width of that component; i.e., once a component is used, it is shifted out of the way so that the lower order components can contribute. This technique extends readily to representations with more components as long as either F or B is a primary.

8.2. Vector Number Systems

Each of the fields in these color spaces has a binary weight based on its position in the code. This is not unlike the familiar number systems, except that these "digits" represent vectors in color three-space.

Figure [11] illustrates the set of colors that interpolate three primaries in a 4-digit vector number system. Note that the topology of the 3-digit number system is embedded within that of the 4-digit, and that the topology of the 2-digit (Major-minor) is embedded in that of the 3-digit, with the same type of self-similarity as fractals [15]. Since this is a 4-digit system, there is a possibility of another color participating in the interpolation as well, so a tetrahedron would more accurately represent the set of all combinations of four colors. The vertices of the larger tetrahedron would then be composed of smaller tetrahedrons, etc., in a similar way as the triangle vertices are composed of smaller triangles.

One apparent property of these color spaces is that there is an ever-widening hole in the middle. This is a result of the binary weighting of the vectors in the number system. This seems to limit the usefulness of the color space. But the original impetus behind the design of the color net topology was to interpolate between any two primaries, and the vector number system topologies do this very well, so the interior colors should be considered a bonus.

The 6-digit vector number system with 2 bits per digit (total of 12 bits) is rich enough to do smooth-shading (64 levels) and anti-aliasing between 4 primaries.

9. Advantages

The value of some of the color space topologies presented here is lessened somewhat by the low cost of memory. However, there are other factors that still keep the Major-minor and other schemes attractive:

Power Consumption

A full color system not only requires more memory chips, but usually incorporates a hardware multiplier to accelerate computation; Major-minor only requires a multiplexer.

Ease of Computation

It is simple to implement algorithms for the discrete and layers color spaces, because choice of color is a binary one: either a pixel is on a line or polygon, or it is not. The Major-minor decisions are slightly more involved (4-way), but still relatively simple. They are also immune to overflow and the resultant color wraparound. Full-color interpolation sometimes exhibits errors due to rounding, e.g. the value 256 does not fit into an 8-bit pixel, and results in the totally incorrect value 0; most implementations follow interpolation by saturation to guard against this.

Symbolic Interpolation

The computations for every color space except the full-color proceed without regard to the actual primary colors used; the aesthetic qualities of the image can be changed without recomputation by a simple change of the color map.

Interpolation in Uniform Perceptual Color Spaces

Robertson and O'Callaghan [19] show that linear interpolation in the uniform color spaces L*a*b* and L*u*v* is superior to the more common RGB and HSL. Simulating this in RGB requires costly nonlinear computations at each pixel, whereas the symbolic color spaces need only perform this once when generating the colormap.

Bleeding

When a full-color anti-aliased line is drawn repeatedly at the same location, it exhibits a bleeding effect, in which the line gets wider and more jagged. This can easily be overcome in the Major-minor, discrete, and layers color spaces.

10. Implementation

The color space topologies outlined in this paper have been implemented by the author in the microcode of a color graphics controller, with support for several interpolation functions (e.g. *mix*, *erase*). These functions currently work with unary and binary operations on rasters, and line drawing, with partial support for polygons. Current products make use of the discrete, Major-minor, and star topologies simultaneously in an 8-bit frame store.

11. Conclusions

Topology is an important characteristic of a color space, and has a direct implication on the types of pictures that can be represented. The topological properties of some of the more common color spaces have been evaluated for their suitability in anti-aliasing and smooth-shading problems.

The color net color space has been developed to allow anti-aliasing between arbitrary colors at a minimum cost, which requires twice as many bits as a system without anti-aliasing. The Major-minor representation for this color space provides a simple way to perform the calculations, one that could easily be implemented in hardware. The quality of anti-aliasing is found to be equivalent to two bits per pixel, which seems to be sufficient for most applications.

In an 8-bit frame store, the vector number color spaces span a range from 2-bit anti-aliasing between 16 arbitrary colors, to 5-bit shading between 3 arbitrary colors.

12. References

[1] Branley, Franklyn M. *Color from Rainbows to Lasers*, Thomas Y. Crowell Co., New York, 1978

[2] Bui-Tuong, Phong. "Illumination for Computer-Generated Pictures," *Communication of the ACM*, vol. 18, no. 6, June 1975, pp. 311-317

[3] Catmull, E. E. "A Subdivision Algorithm for Computer Display of Curved Surfaces," University of Utah Computer Science Department, UTEC-CSc-74-133, December 1974, NTIS A-004968/Ad/A-004973

[4] Catmull, E. "A Tutorial on Compensation Tables," SIGGRAPH '79 Proceedings, published as *Computer Graphics*, vol. 12, no. 3, August 1978, pp. 348-353

[5] Conrac Division, *Raster Graphics Handbook*, Conrac Corporation, Covina, California, 1980

[6] Crow, F. C. "The Aliasing Problem in Computer-Generated Shaded Images," *Communications of the ACM*, vol. 20, no. 11, Nov. 1977, pp. 799-805

[7] Drewery, J. O. "The zone plate as a television test pattern," BBC Res. Dept. Report # BBC RD 1978/23, July 1978

[8] Foley, James D. and van Dam, Andries. *Fundamentals of Interactive Computer Graphics*, Addison-Wesley Publishing Co., Reading, Mass., 1982

[9] Gouraud, H. "Continuous Shading of Curved Surfaces," *IEEE Transactions on Computers*, vol. C-20, no. 6, June 1971, pp. 623-628

[10] Heckbert, Paul. "Color Image Quantization for Frame Buffer Display," SIGGRAPH '82 Conference Proceedings, published as *Computer Graphics*, Vol. 16, No. 3, July 1982, pp. 297-307

[11] Hochberg, Julian E. *Perception*, Prentice-Hall, Englewood Cliffs, New Jersey, 1964

[12] Joblove, George H. and Greenberg, Donald. "Color Spaces for Computer Graphics," SIGGRAPH '78 Conference Proceedings, published as *Computer Graphics*, Vol. 12, no. 3, August 1978, pp. 20-25

[13] Kelley, J. L. *General Topology*, Van Nostrand, New York, 1955

[14] Lehar, A. F., and Stevens, R. J. "High-Speed Manipulation of the Color Chromaticity of Digital Images," *IEEE Computer Graphics and Applications*, February 1984, pp. 34-39

[15] Mandelbrot, B. B. *The Fractal Geometry of Nature*, Freeman, San Francisco, 1982

[16] Oppenheim, Alan V. and Schafer, Ronald W. *Digital Signal Processing*, Prentice-Hall, Inc., Englewood Cliffs, New Jersey, 1975

[17] Pearson, D. E. *Transmission and Display of Pictorial Information*, Halsted Press, A Division of John Wiley & Sons, Inc., New York, 1975

[18] Pratt, William K. *Digital Image Processing*, John Wiley & Sons, New York, 1978

[19] Robertson, Philip K. and O'Callaghan, J. F. "The Generation of Color Sequences for Univariate and Bivariate Mapping," *IEEE Computer Graphics and Applications*, Vol. 6, No. 2 (Feb. 1986), 24-32.

[20] Rogers, David F. *Procedural Elements for Computer Graphics*, McGraw-Hill Book Co. pp. 92-101

[21] Royden, H. L. *Real Analysis*, Macmillan Publishing Co., Inc., New York, 1963

[22] Smith, Alvy Ray. "Color Gamut Transform Pairs," SIGGRAPH '78 Conference Proceedings, published as *Computer Graphics*, Vol. 12, no. 3, August 1978, pp. 12-19

[23] Smith, Alvy Ray. "Tint Fill", SIGGRAPH '79 Conference Proceedings, published as *Computer Graphics*, August 1979, pp. 276-283

[24] Smith, Alvy Ray. *YIQ vs. RGB*, Technical memo no. 9, Computer Graphics Lab, New York Institute of Technology, April 1979

[25] Stern, Garland. "SoftCel - An Application of Raster Scan Graphics to Conventional Cel Animation," SIGGRAPH '79

Conference Proceedings, published as *Computer Graphics*, August 1979, pp. 284-288

[26] Stevens, R. J., Lehar, A. F., and Peterson, F. H. "Manipulation and Presentation of Multidimensional Image Data Using the Peano Scan," *IEEE Transactions on Pattern Analysis and Machine Intelligence*, Vol. PAMI-5, No. 5, Sept. 1983, pp. 520-526

[27] TRW Digital Signal Processing seminar notes

[28] Turkowski, Ken. *Color Space Quantization*, CADLINC Internal Memo, January 1983.

[29] Turkowski, Kenneth. "Anti-Aliasing through the Use of Coordinate Transformations," *ACM Transactions on Graphics*, Vol. 1, no. 3, July 1982, pp. 215-234

[30] Wyszecki, G. and Stiles, G. S. *Color Science*, Wiley, 2nd edition, 1982

Fig. 1a. 1 bit of grey-scale. These images were produced on a 1024x792 display and were compensated for a gamma of 1.8. The right-hand portion magnifies the left by a factor of 4 using pixel replication.

Fig. 1b. 2 bits of grey-scale.

Fig. 1c. 8 bits of grey-scale.

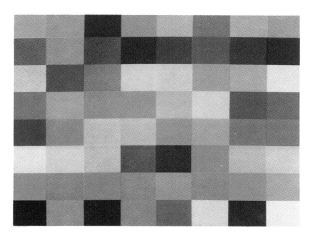

Fig. 2. The discrete color space topology.

Fig. 3. The integer topology.

Fig. 4. The disjoint segment topology.

Fig. 5. The star topology.

Fig. 6. The Major-minor color net topology, with 2 secondary colors interpolating each pair of the 4 primary colors.

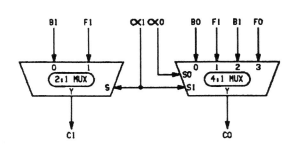

Fig. 7. Hardware interpolation in Major/minor color space.

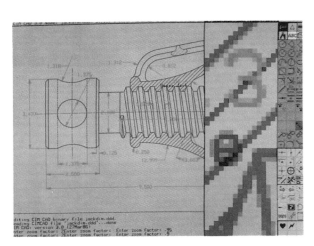

Fig. 8. An engineering drawing, drawn in a Major-minor color space, with inset showing detail of pairwise anti-aliasing between 4 primary colors.

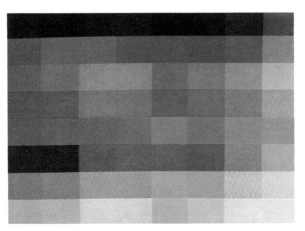

Fig. 9. The Major-minor color plaid. Each row has the same Major component, each column has the same minor component, and the primary colors lay along the main diagonal, where the Major component is equal to the minor component.

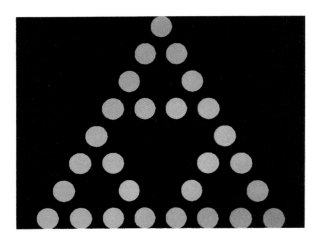

Fig. 10. The Major-minor-subminor topology, with 6 colors interpolating each pair of the 3 primary colors. The tertiary colors in the interior of the triangle are bonus colors augmenting the color net.

Fig. 11. The set of colors interpolating 3 primaries in a 4-digit vector number system.

FILTERING BY REPEATED INTEGRATION

Paul S. Heckbert †

Pacific Data Images
Sunnyvale, CA

ABSTRACT

Many applications of digital filtering require a space variant filter - one whose shape or size varies with position. The usual algorithm for such filters, direct convolution, is very costly for wide kernels. Image prefiltering provides an efficient alternative. We explore one prefiltering technique, *repeated integration*, which is a generalization of Crow's *summed area table*.

We find that convolution of a signal with any piecewise polynomial kernel of degree $n-1$ can be computed by integrating the signal n times and point sampling it several times for each output sample. The use of second or higher order integration permits relatively high quality filtering. The advantage over direct convolution is that the cost of repeated integration filtering does not increase with filter width. Generalization to two-dimensional image filtering is straightforward. Implementations of the simple technique are presented in both preprocessing and stream processing styles.

CR Categories: I.3.3 [**Computer Graphics**]: Picture/Image Generation – *display algorithms;* I.3.7 [**Computer Graphics**]: Three-Dimensional Graphics and Realism – *color, shading, shadowing, and texture;* I.4.3 [**Image Processing**]: Enhancement – *filtering.*

General Terms: algorithms, theory.

Additional Key Words and Phrases: space variant filter, convolution, texture mapping, blur.

INTRODUCTION

Filtering is one of the most common operations in signal processing, image processing, and raster image synthesis. Its applications include image enhancement, low pass filtering (blurring), antialiasing for image warping and texture mapping, and special effects. The fundamental filtering operation is convolution, in which a weighting function or *kernel* is passed over the input signal and a weighted average is computed for each output sample.

---

† Current address: Pixar, P.O. Box 13719, San Rafael, CA 94913

The most straightforward filtering method is *direct convolution*, in which a weighted average is computed anew for each output sample. For a discrete signal of length M and a filter of width W, the number of operations required by direct convolution is $O(MW)$. The method is thus very expensive for wide kernels.

When the kernel's shape is independent of position the filter is called *space invariant*. Under these conditions we can use Fourier convolution: the signal and kernel are transformed to the frequency domain using an FFT, these are multiplied together, and an inverse FFT is computed [Brigham74]. The cost of this algorithm is $O(M \log M)$. Since the cost is independent of kernel width, Fourier convolution is the preferred method for wide, space invariant kernels.

Many applications demand a *space variant* filter, however, one for which the kernel varies with position. Such applications include nonlinear image warps, texture mapping, and depth of field filtering. Since Fourier convolution is inapplicable, direct convolution is usually used for space variant filtering [Feibush80]. This can be extremely slow for wide kernels, however.

An example from image synthesis will illustrate the problem. In texture mapping, texture images are stored in parametric surface coordinates and projected to the screen by modeling and viewing transformations [Heckbert86]. For proper antialiasing it is necessary to filter the texture area corresponding to each screen pixel [Feibush80]. But the transformations can cause these texture areas to be arbitrarily large (imagine a pixel containing the horizon of an infinite plane). Using direct convolution, accurate filtering of such pixels can be prohibitively expensive. In order to make high quality texture filtering practical we must find alternative techniques to direct convolution.

We are interested in wide kernels for another reason: in general, high quality low pass filters are wide. The ideal low pass filter, a sinc, has infinite width, but we must use finite width approximations to it in practice [Bracewell78].

The Problem

We would like to find efficient algorithms for performing space variant filtering with the criteria (a) cost independent of kernel width, and (b) enough kernel shape control to allow high quality filtering.

A general approach to this problem is signal prefiltering, in which the signal (or image) is preprocessed so that filtering with arbitrary width kernels can be performed in constant time [Heckbert86]. Two data structures have been proposed for this purpose: pyramids and integrated arrays.

Pyramid methods are common in image processing for a variety of purposes [Rosenfeld84], and in image synthesis for texture filtering [Dungan78], [Williams83]. Pyramids are ideal when the access kernel closely matches the kernel used in creating the pyramid, but can be awkward otherwise. Filtering of rectangular areas is inconvenient on pyramids created with square filters.

We will explore an alternative prefiltering technique, the integrated array, which was proposed by Perlin and Crow [Perlin85], [Crow84]. While they focused on applications of the technique for texture mapping and image blurring, our emphasis is on the theory behind the technique.

We begin with filtering of 1-D signals and later generalize to 2-D images.

ONE-DIMENSIONAL FILTERING

An unweighted average is equivalent to convolution with a box. The average value of a signal f between a and b is:

$$\int_a^b f(x)dx = \frac{F(b)-F(a)}{b-a}$$

where F is the indefinite integral of f, evaluated either symbolically or numerically. This formula can be used to convolve f with a box of width W if we choose $a=x+W/2$ and $b=x-W/2$. Computation with this formula is very attractive: for a discrete sequence f we precompute its partial sum F and do merely two table lookups, one subtraction, and one divide per output value. The cost is independent of kernel width, and the width can vary with position. This formula is thus a constant cost space variant filter, albeit a low quality one.

Can we generalize the above formula to higher quality filters? First let's look at some of those filters.

Repeated Box Filters

Consider a box kernel of width W:

$$box_W(x) = \begin{cases} 1/W & |x|<W/2 \\ 0 & |x|\geq W/2 \end{cases}$$

When a box is convolved with itself n times, we call the result a *repeated box filter*:

$$box^{*n} = box*box* \cdots *box \quad (n\ times)$$

where '*' denotes convolution and the superscript $*n$ denotes n-fold convolution.

The repeated box filters are commonly used in both signal processing and computer aided geometric design, although there has been little cross-pollination to date [Hou78], [Goldman83]. In the field of splines these functions are known as the uniform b-spline basis functions [Gordon74]. Figure 1 and the table below summarize the shapes, properties, and common names for low order box filters / b-splines.

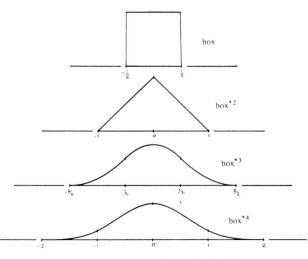

Figure 1: repeated box filters of order 1-4

order	degree	filter name	spline name	continuity
n=1	0	box, Fourier	nearest neighbor	none
n=2	1	triangle, Bartlett	linear interp.	C^0 (value)
n=3	2	parabolic	quadratic b-spline	C^1 (slope)
n=4	3	Parzen	cubic b-spline	C^2 (accel.)

The filters we have mentioned can be ranked in quality as follows: box $<$ box^{*2} $<$ box^{*3} $<$ ... $<$ gaussian $<$ sinc. By the Central Limit Theorem, as n increases the repeated box filters broaden and approach a gaussian in shape [Bracewell78].

Integration and Differentiation

Perlin showed how unweighted averaging can be generalized to repeated box filtering [Perlin84].

We'll need a few convolution identities:

$$f*g = g*f$$
$$(f*g)*h = f*(g*h)$$
$$\int(f*g) = (\int f)*g$$
$$(f*g)' = (f')*g$$

Repeated application of the latter two identities implies that the convolution of f with g is equivalent to convolution of the nth integral of f with the nth derivative of g:

$$f*g = (\int^n f(x)dx)*(\frac{d^n g}{dx^n}) = f_n*g_{-n} \tag{1}$$

where a subscript n on a function denotes n-fold integration and a subscript $-n$ denotes n-fold differentiation, a notation we will use henceforth. We will usually regard f as the signal and g as the filter kernel. This formula is especially useful when g_{-n} is a simple kernel such as a train of impulses.

An elegant proof of this identity employing Fourier transforms has been suggested by Perlin [Perlin84]. We write a Fourier transform pair as: $f(x) \longleftrightarrow F(\omega)$ [Bracewell78]. Noting that integration in the spatial domain corresponds to division by $i\omega$ in the frequency domain and differentiation in the spatial domain corresponds to multiplication by $i\omega$ in the frequency domain,

$$f_1(x) \longleftrightarrow F(\omega)/(i\omega)$$
$$f_{-1}(x) \longleftrightarrow i\omega F(\omega)$$

we can write:

$$f(x)*g(x) \longleftrightarrow F(\omega)G(\omega)$$
$$\parallel \qquad\qquad\qquad \parallel$$
$$f_n(x)*g_{-n}(x) \longleftrightarrow \frac{F(\omega)}{(i\omega)^n}(i\omega)^n G(\omega)$$

Reading these equations in clockwise order, we take the Fourier transform of the upper left to arrive at the upper right. Multiplying and dividing by $(i\omega)^n$ in the lower right changes nothing, but when we take its inverse Fourier transform we get the result at lower left. Equality of the spectra (on the right) implies equality of the signals (on the left). Q.E.D.

Repeated Box Filtering by Repeated Integration

By taking the nth derivative of an nth order box filter we will simplify it significantly:

$$g_{-n} = (box^{*n})_{-n} = (box')^{*n}$$

The derivative of a box is a train of two impulses with opposite signs (figure 2, top), a very simple filter for convolution purposes.

To proceed we switch to the discrete domain. We define the kth integral (partial sum) of f to be:

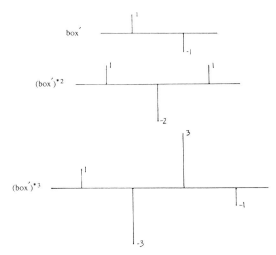

Figure 2: the nth derivative of an nth order box filter is an impulse train

$$f_k(x) = \sum_{t=0}^{x} f_{k-1}(t)$$

where $f_0 = f$. We can write the derivative of a box as:

$$\text{box}'_W(x) = [\delta(x+W/2) - \delta(x-W/2)]/W$$

where $\delta(x)$ is a discrete impulse function, defined to equal 1 for $x=0$ but zero elsewhere.

When convolved with itself n times, box'_W creates a sequence of $n+1$ impulses each spaced W units apart (figure 2):

$$(\text{box}'_W)^{*n}(x) = W^{-n} \sum_{i=0}^{n} (-1)^i \binom{n}{i} \delta(x+(n/2-i)W) \qquad (2)$$

Convolving this with the integrated array:

$$f * \text{box}_W^{*n} = f_n * (\text{box}'_W)^{*n} = W^{-n} \sum_{i=0}^{n} (-1)^i \binom{n}{i} f_n(x+(n/2-i)W)$$

since convolution with an impulse selects a single sample point: $f(x)*\delta(x-a)=f(x-a)$. In summary, we can convolve with an nth order box using $n+1$ samples of the integrated array f_n.

We have therefore succeeded in generalizing the box filtering algorithm to repeated box filters. Perlin called this a *selective image filter*, because it allows blurring by a different amount at each sample. Below is a basic implementation:

Implementation of Repeated Box Filtering

Setup requires integration of f n times:

```
for k := 1 to n
    for x := 1 to M-1
        f[x] := f[x-1] + f[x]
```

After setup, computation of each filtered sample requires $n+1$ accesses to the integrated array:

```
sum := 0
for i := 0 to n
    sum := sum + -1^i * comb(n,i) * f[x+(n/2-i)*W-n/2]
result := sum / W^n
```

In most implementations the order n of the filter will be fixed and the above loop can be unrolled. In order to allow x and W to have non-integer values all accesses to the integrated array **f** should be replaced by a linear interpolation between adjacent array entries, but Crow points out that this refinement is only needed for small kernels [Crow84].

Integration and Convolution

The techniques developed so far allow efficient convolution with repeated box filters, but none others. By studying the filter equivalent to repeated integration we can gain a deeper understanding of our new tool and thereby learn how to design other efficient filters.

Convolution with a step function is equivalent to integration, so n-fold convolution with a step is equivalent to n-fold integration. If we define δ_n, the nth order *ramp function*, as a step function δ_1 convolved with itself n times [Papoulis62]:

$$\delta_n = \delta_1 * \delta_1 * \cdots * \delta_1 = \delta_1^{*n}$$

then the relation between convolution and integration can be written:

$$f * \delta_n = f_n * \delta_0 = f_n \qquad (3)$$

An equivalent definition of δ_n is the nth integral of an impulse δ_0. Equation (3) is a special case of the Riemann-Liouville integral [Lavoie76].

Graphs of the ramp functions are shown in figure 3. Their formulas are:

$$\delta_n(x) = \begin{cases} x^{n-1}/(n-1)! & x \geq 0 \\ 0 & x < 0 \end{cases}$$

The ramp functions allow us to relate convolution with a polynomial kernel to convolution with an impulse, and thereby generalize repeated integration filtering to a wide variety of kernels.

Equations (1) and (3) suggest that we can choose the kernel g to be a superposition of translated ramp functions:

$$g(x) = \sum_i c_i \delta_{k_i}(x-x_i)$$

Note that we allow different orders of ramp functions to be mixed. The kernel can be designed at unit width and then scaled to width W using the formula $g(x/W)/W$. To scale ramp functions use the rule $\delta_n(ax)=a^{n-1}\delta_n(x)$.

For a kernel expressed as a sum of ramp functions, repeated integration filtering is performed by:

$$f*g = f_k * g_{-k} = \sum_i c_i f_{k_i}(x-x_i) \qquad (4)$$

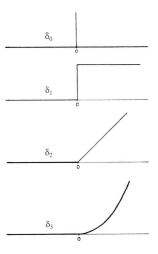

Figure 3: ramp functions of orders 0-3

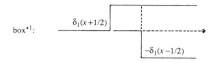

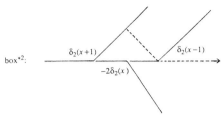

Figure 4: superposition of ramp functions to create
first and second order box filters

Once we have expressed a filter as a sum of ramp functions the repeated
integration formula can be read off simply by substituting f_k for δ_k.

The repeated box filters are easily described in terms of ramp functions:

$$\text{box}_W^{*1} = W^{-1}[\delta_1(x+W/2) - \delta_1(x-W/2)]$$

$$\text{box}_W^{*2} = W^{-2}[\delta_2(x+W) - 2\delta_2(x) + \delta_2(x-W)]$$

as shown in figure 4, and, in general,

$$\text{box}_W^{*n} = W^{-n}\sum_{i=0}^{n}(-1)^i \binom{n}{i}\delta_n(x+(n/2-i)W)$$

The latter equation can be proven either by induction or by integrating
equation (2) n times. The original definition of b-splines used an
equivalent formula [Schoenberg46, p.70].

Arbitrary Polynomial Kernels

Equation (4) allows us to convolve with filters other than repeated boxes
efficiently. In fact, any piecewise polynomial kernel can be expressed as
a sum of ramp functions, and thereby convolved using repeated integration.

For example, the Overhauser or Catmull-Rom cubic spline is often used
for filtering in image processing (where it is known as parametric cubic
convolution) [Catmull74], [Park83]. It can be expressed using a combination of ramp functions of orders 3 and 4 (quadratic and cubic):

$$3\delta_4(x+2) - 12\delta_4(x+1) + 18\delta_4(x) - 12\delta_4(x-1) + 3\delta_4(x-2)$$

$$-\ \delta_3(x+2)\ +\ 2\delta_3(x+1)\qquad\quad -\ 2\delta_3(x-1)\ +\ \delta_3(x-2)$$

Repeated integration filtering with this kernel requires retention of both
3rd and 4th order integrated arrays in memory.

Filtering On-The-Fly

The algorithm above can be summarized as:

(1) integrate signal as a preprocess
(2) convolve with impulse train with spacing W

Under some circumstances the signal is too large to hold in memory at
one time, or it is desirable to filter in real-time as a stream process. This
can be accomplished by reversing the order of operations [Perlin85]:

(1) convolve signal with impulse train
(2) integrate

This swap is analogous to the identity $f_n * g_{-n} = (f * g_{-n})_n$.

An implementation of filtering on-the-fly for repeated box filters is given
below:

```
initialize diff array
for x
    input f[x+n*W/2]
    sum := 0
    for i := 0 to n
        sum := sum + -1^i * comb(n,i) * f[x+(n/2-i)*W-n/2]
    diff[n] := sum
    for i := n-1 to 0 step -1
        diff[i] := diff[i] + diff[i+1]
    output diff[0] / W^n
```

This is a generalization of the well-known add-incoming, subtract-
outgoing box blur algorithm [Schowengerdt83]. The **f** array above can
be stored as a circular buffer of length nW, so the memory requirements
are minimal. This method of filtering on-the-fly is limited, however, to
fixed values of W, so it is space *invariant*.

Cost Analysis

A cost comparison demonstrates the efficiency of filtering by repeated
integration. Consider a signal of length M convolved n times with a box
filter of width W. Using direct convolution n times the cost would be
$O(nMW)$. Using repeated integration filtering, the setup time and convolution time are both $O(nM)$. For more general kernels the time cost is
proportional to the number of terms in its ramp representation. The maximum number of terms for a piecewise polynomial of degree $n-1$ with K
singularities is nK.

One of the disadvantages of repeated integration filtering is the storage
cost of integrated arrays. For a signal of length $M=2^r$ with b bits per
sample, integration n times requires a dynamic range of $nr+b$ bits. For
example, an 8-bit signal of length 1024 has $b=8$ and $r=10$, so the
number of bits needed for $n=1, 2, 3,$ and 4 is 18, 28, 38, and 48, respectively.

Such large dynamic ranges are not required when the filter width is limited, however. The variable **sum** in the implementations above has a
dynamic range of $n\log_2 W+b$ bits, so if we use modulo arithmetic with at
least this number of bits the standard evaluation formula will work perfectly. This trick is helpful if we know an upper bound on W a priori.
Imposing a limit on width weakens one of the principal advantages of
repeated integration filtering, however.

The best storage technique is probably a hybrid of full $(nr+b)$ and limited $(n\log_2 W+b)$ dynamic range arrays. We can store most of the data
at a low dynamic range (say 16 bits) and record changes in higher bits of
the integrated array in a sparse array of full dynamic range (say 32 or 64
bits). With this scheme, only very wide kernels require the full range
array to be consulted.

TWO-DIMENSIONAL FILTERING

The methods above generalize quite simply to two dimensions. The signal f must be integrated along each dimension:

$$f_{k,l}(x,y) = \sum_{u=0}^{x}f_{k-1,l}(u,y) = \sum_{v=0}^{y}f_{k,l-1}(x,v) \quad \text{where } f_{0,0}=f$$

and evaluated at a grid of sample points. For a separable kernel

$$g(x)h(y) = \sum_i c_i\delta_{k_i}(x-x_i) \sum_j d_j\delta_{l_j}(y-y_j)$$

the convolution is

$$f * gh = \sum_i\sum_j c_i d_j f_{k_i l_j}(x-x_i, y-y_j)$$

Note that the orders of integration in x and y can be different.

Convolution with an nth order box requires $(n+1)^2$ array accesses. First
order box filtering is equivalent to Crow's *summed area table* [Crow84].

Figure 5: unfiltered image (order 0)

Figure 9: motion blurred text: filtering in x with the biased triangular kernel $\delta_2(x+1) - \delta_2(x-1) - \delta_1(x-1)$:

Figure 6: box filtering (order 1)

Figure 10: point sampled (order 0)

Figure 7: triangle filtering (order 2)

Figure 11: box filtered (order 1)

Figure 8: filtering with Catmull-Rom spline

Figure 12: triangle filtered (order 2)

Perlin has used second order filtering for a number of applications [Perlin85]. The grids of coefficients for low order filters are shown below:

	$n=1$	$n=2$	$n=3$
$n=0$			-1 3 -3 1
	-1 1	1 -2 1	3 -9 9 -3
1	1 -1	-2 4 -2	-3 9 -9 3
		1 -2 1	1 -3 3 -1

It is desirable to use higher order integration, $n \geq 2$, in order to minimize artifacts. The first order filter, a box, generates fairly strong horizontal and vertical mach bands, as shown in figure 6. As the order n is increased, the x and y cross sections converge toward a gaussian, and because of the gaussian's separability, contours of the two-dimensional filter converge toward circularity. In figure 7, second order filtering has eliminated the mach bands. Third and higher order box filters are nearly the same.

Figure 8 demonstrates Catmull-Rom filtering of text. New filter kernels are easy to test: figure 9 illustrates the use of biased kernels to simulate a common artistic stylization of motion blur. The space variant application of texture mapping is shown in figures 10-12. Note that the improvement from zeroth order (point sampling) to first order (box filtering) is much greater than the improvement from first order to second order (triangle filtering). These images were computed at far lower than normal resolution in order to clearly depict the filtering effects.

Repeated integration filtering in multiple dimensions is not limited to separable kernels. One can simply superpose several kernels to construct new ones. For texture mapping one would like to filter arbitrarily oriented ellipses [Greene86]. This is possible with repeated integration filtering, but it appears that for non-rectilinearly oriented areas the number of array samples required increases with the ellipse eccentricity.

For high resolution images it is sometimes impossible to store an entire image in memory at once. In such cases the stream oriented filtering algorithm is helpful, since it can perform a high quality blur using a buffer of only nW scan lines. Of course, if the kernel is separable, the convolution could also be done in two passes, one horizontal and one vertical: $f*g*h$.

Storage Cost in 2-D

The dynamic range of 2-D integrated arrays is quite substantial. For a $2^r \times 2^r$ monochrome image with b bits per pixel, 2-D integration n times yields $2nr+b$ bits per array element. For example, an 8-bit 512x512 image has $r=9$ and $b=8$, so 26 bits are required for $n=1$ (box filtering, a.k.a. summed area table), 44 bits are needed for $n=2$ (triangle filtering), 62 bits for $n=3$ (parabolic filtering), and 80 bits for $n=4$ (cubic filtering).

As mentioned earlier, however, we need not store the entire integrated array at full dynamic range. To compact the summed area table, Crow suggested that the image be divided into blocks, say 16x16 in size, and that a mini 16-bit limited range integrated array be created for each [Crow84]. In addition, the totals for each block are integrated to form a sparse 32-bit full range array. Unfortunately, this makes integration of a rectangular area rather cumbersome, as it is no longer simply a matter of sampling the four corners (see Crow's comments on wraparound). For large kernels the number of samples required increases in proportion to the side length of the rectangle, but for kernels of limited size the full range array is unnecessary and the number of samples is constant. In either case the asymptotic cost is less than that of direct convolution, which grows in proportion to the *area* of the rectangle.

Using the hybrid storage technique, therefore, the storage cost for integrated arrays is about 2 times that of the original image. Another prefiltering technique, the image pyramid, has a storage factor of only 1.33 [Heckbert86].

CONCLUSIONS

By relating convolution and integration we have generalized definite integration to weighted averaging and thereby developed efficient algorithms for space variant filtering with any piecewise polynomial kernel. Since its cost is independent of filter width, the repeated integration filter is clearly more efficient than direct convolution for wide kernels. The method generalizes easily to the two dimensional domain. Its possible applications are numerous, including audio signal processing, image blurring, nonlinear image warps, motion blur, antialiasing, texture mapping, and depth of field filtering.

Further work is needed on storage economization and two-dimensional kernel shape control. In addition, alternatives to unweighted preintegration and independent integration in x and y should be explored.

Compared to standard pyramid techniques, repeated integration filtering gives greater filter shape control and hence higher quality but at higher storage cost [Crow84], [Heckbert86]. The use of arbitrarily oriented elliptical filters on image pyramids promises to improve pyramidal filtering quality, however [Greene86]. A definitive comparison between various space variant filtering methods has yet to be made.

ACKNOWLEDGEMENTS

The original idea of filtering by repeated integration is due to Ken Perlin. A fertile environment for discussing such topics was provided by Pat Hanrahan and the 3-D Systems Group at NYIT's Computer Graphics Lab. Thanks also to the enthusiastic bunch at PDI, and their addictive Marvin Gaye theme song.

REFERENCES

Bracewell, Ronald N., *The Fourier Transform and Its Applications,* McGraw-Hill, New York, 1978.

Brigham, E. Oran, *The Fast Fourier Transform,* Prentice-Hall, Englewood Cliffs, NJ, 1974.

Catmull, Edwin E., and Raphael Rom, "A Class of Local Interpolating Splines", *Computer Aided Geometric Design,* Robert Barnhill and Richard Riesenfeld, eds., Academic Press, New York, 1974, pp. 317-326.

Crow, Franklin C., "Summed-Area Tables for Texture Mapping", *Computer Graphics,* (SIGGRAPH '84 Proceedings), vol. 18, no. 3, July 1984, pp. 207-212.

Dungan, William, Jr., Anthony Stenger, and George Sutty, "Texture Tile Considerations for Raster Graphics", *Computer Graphics,* (SIGGRAPH '78 Proceedings), vol. 12, no. 3, Aug. 1978, pp. 130-134.

Feibush, Eliot A., Marc Levoy, and Robert L. Cook, "Synthetic Texturing Using Digital Filters", *Computer Graphics,* (SIGGRAPH '80 Proceedings), vol. 14, no. 3, July 1980, pp. 294-301.

Goldman, Ronald N., "An Urnful of Blending Functions", *IEEE Computer Graphics and Applications,* vol. 3, Oct. 1983, pp. 49-54.

Gordon, William J., and Richard F. Riesenfeld, "B-spline Curves and Surfaces", *Computer Aided Geometric Design,* Robert Barnhill and Richard Riesenfeld, eds., Academic Press, New York, 1974, pp. 95-126.

Greene, Ned, and Paul S. Heckbert, "Creating Raster Omnimax Images from Multiple Perspective Views Using The Elliptical Weighted Average Filter", *Computer Graphics and Applications,* June 1986.

Heckbert, Paul S., "Survey of Texture Mapping", *Graphics Interface '86,* May 1986.

Hou, Hsieh S., and Harry C. Andrews, "Cubic Splines for Image Interpolation and Digital Filtering", *IEEE Trans. Acoustics, Speech, and Signal Processing,* vol. ASSP-26, no. 6, Dec. 1978, pp. 508-517.

Lavoie, J. L., Thomas J. Osler, and R. Tremblay, "Fractional Derivatives of Special Functions", *SIAM Review,* vol. 18, pp. 240-268, 1976.

Papoulis, R., *The Fourier Integral and its Applications,* McGraw-Hill, New York, 1962.

Park, Stephen K., and Robert A. Schowengerdt, "Image Reconstruction by Parametric Cubic Convolution", *Computer Vision, Graphics, and Image Processing,* vol. 23, no. 3, Sept. 1983, pp. 258-272.

Perlin, Kenneth, personal communication, Jan. 1984.

Perlin, Kenneth, "Course Notes", *SIGGRAPH '85 State of the Art in Image Synthesis seminar notes,* July 1985.

Rosenfeld, A., *Multiresolution Image Processing and Analysis,* Leesberg, VA, Springer, Berlin, 1984.

Schoenberg, I. J., "Contributions to the Problem of Approximation of Equidistant Data by Analytic Functions", *Quart. Applied Math,* vol. 4, 1946, pp. 45-99, 112-141.

Schowengerdt, Robert A., *Techniques for Image Processing and Classification in Remote Sensing,* Academic Press, New York/London, 1983.

Williams, Lance, "Pyramidal Parametrics", *Computer Graphics,* (SIGGRAPH '83 proceedings), vol. 17, no. 3, July 1983, pp. 1-11.

Panels

Computer Graphics in Scientific Animation

Chair: Pauline Ores (New York University Medical Center)

Panelists: James F. Blinn (Jet Propulsion Laboratory)
                   Don Stredney (Cranston/Csuri Productions, Inc.)
                   Craig Upson (Digital Productions)

The production of computer-generated scientific animation is an important and expanding activity within research organizations as well as companies which specialize in the production of computer graphics. Developments in medical imaging, computer graphic modeling and turnkey animation systems have increased the scope of this type of animation, enabling it to effect changes in the fields of education, science, medicine, pharmacology and entertainment.

The panelists address such topics as design issues in communicating scientific information, modeling organic forms, the use of research data for modeling and animation, insights for research that can be gained in the process of visualization and future developments in scientific animation.

The Future of Window Systems

Chair: David S. H. Rosenthal (Sun Microsystems)

Panelists: John Butler (Microsoft)
Jim Gettys (MIT)
Brad Meyers (University of Toronto)
Larry Tesler (Apple Computer)

Window systems have become a part of life for users and programmers of both PCs and workstations. But both have to live with systems that are often complex and incompatible with one another. The complexity of the user interface appears in the number of options expressing the user's preferences, and the incompatibility in the differences both between systems and between applications in one system. The complexity of the programmer interface appears in huge manuals and libraries, and the incompatibilities are evident to anyone trying to port applications between window systems.

A panel of window system developers and standards representatives address the questions of whether the complexities and incompatibilities are inevitable, and what is being done to reduce them.

Computer Graphics Application and Systems Trends in the Japanese Printing Industry

Chair: Laurin Herr (Pacific Interface, Inc.)

Panelists: Yoshihiko Azuma (Dainippon Printing Co., Ltd.)
Takeo Fukuzawa (Texnai, Inc.)
Masa Imakage (Independent media artist and researcher)

This panel provides an overview of the market for computer graphics in the Japanese printing industry, discusses system and application trends including implications for computer aided publishing (CAP), and presents recent examples of both commercial and artistic print output. Particular attention is paid to some of the fundamental problems facing vendors and users in Japan, including:

- Need for very high resolution fonts containing thousands of characters (Kanji), simultaneous access to multiple fonts and horizontal/vertical writing.
- User interface design for technicians and artists with limited English language abilities, limited computer experience and limited familiarity with keyboards of any type.
- Development and utilization of more compact, less expensive systems.

Applications of Interactive Digital Image Processing

Chair: Tom Brigham (New York Institute of Technology)

Panelists: Nancy Burson (Independent)
                   David Kramlich (Face Systems)
                   Ralph Weinger (Color Systems Technologies)
                   Lance Williams (Computer Graphics Laboratory)

This panel session presents and discusses new uses of digital image processing techniques in commercial and artistic applications. Members of the panel present their own work, review the precedents of image manipulations, and identify applications where digital image processing is not now, but could be, applied. These techniques are placed on a historical continuum pointing toward future possibilities. The panel discusses applications such as facial image composite development, plastic surgery previewing and colorization of original black and white films. Reference is made to the issue of interaction and the creative/production process.

An Application Overview of Program Visualization

Chair: Ronald Baecker (University of Toronto)

Panelists: Marc Brown (Brown University)
                   Ralph L. London (Tektronix, Inc.)
                   Aaron Marcus (Aaron Marcus and Associates)

Program visualization is the use of the technology of interactive computer graphics and the crafts of graphic design, typography, animation and cinematography to enhance the presentation and understanding of computer programs. Program visualization is related to but distinct from the discipline of visual programming which is the use of various two-dimensional or diagrammatic notations in the programming process.

The panel attempts to present a broad overview of program visualization as an emerging and significant application of computer graphics. Topics include: an introduction to program visualization; the role of graphic design; the enhanced presentation of program source text; the effective use of diagrams; the animation of program execution; interacting with the program as an animated object; the design of systems to produce visualizations automatically from minimally changed program source; applications of program visualization; and open problems and research frontiers.

Hardware versus Software

Chair: Carl Machover (Machover Associates Corp.)

Panelists: Nick England (Trancept Systems)
               Clifford Hirsch (Genigraphics GP)
               Ian Hirschhorn (SUPERSET, Inc.)
               Anders Vinberg (ISSCO)

This panel considers the assertion that workstations incorporating special devices — coprocessors, array processors, tiling engines, geometry engines — offer hardware solutions to specific functions that are more effective than traditional software solutions. However, not all practitioners agree with that contention. Some people believe that performance, flexibilty and price are compromised by incorporating unique hardware solutions. In a sense, issues that the graphic field has faced for the last three decades are being reconsidered. Early on, the battle of hardware-versus-software character generators, hardware-versus-software vector generators and hardware-versus-software wireframe rotators was sought. Today, people are suggesting putting drafting packages on a chip.

This panel brings together proponents of both points of view to discuss arguments and to forecast where each path might lead.

Color Issues in the User Interface Design

Chair: Aaron Marcus (Aaron Marcus and Associates)

Panelists: Michael Arent (Aaron Marcus and Associates)
               Barbara Meier (Brown University)
               JoAnn M. Taylor (Tektronix, Inc.)

Rapid growth of sophisticated color displays has put programmers in a difficult decision-making situation. Developers and users want to know what colors to select and how to design with color as a powerful tool for communication in the user interface. Unfortunately most programmers have little expertise in the science, theory or application of color. Color selection is often made subjectively with no consideration of the physiological or psychological effects on the user. Graphic design factors such as legibility and readability are often ignored.

This panel addresses key issues in color from three points of view: (1) the physiological, psychological and human factors perspective, (2) the information-oriented graphic design perspective and (3) the perspective of the builder of an expert system for color selection in the user interface currently being designed at Brown University.

Ramifications of Integrating Computing into the Creative Process in the Arts

Chair: Joan Truckenbrod (The School of the Art Institute of Chicago)

Panelists: Darcy Gerbarg (New York City School of Visual Arts)
Cynthia Goodman (Guggenheim Museum)
Rus Grant (Massachusetts Institute of Technology)

New directions in artistic expression are emerging as artists integrate computing systems into the creative process. Artists working with computer-related devices probe the nature of this electronic medium and its relationship to the creative process. However, the ramifications of pursuing creative work in this context raise significant pact does this technology have on the artist, the creative process and the final artwork? Does the computing environment function like a template that predisposes the creative process and the nature of the artwork? Does the computer act as a catalyst, stimulating creative thought? How will the artwork be effected by the nature of computing and the various input, processing and output devices?

As we pursue new directions in artistic expression, it is essential to address these issues in order to develop an in-depth understanding of the "context of computing" and its effect on creative expression.

Computer Animation in the Fifth Generation

Chair: David Zeltzer (Massachusetts Institute of Technology)

Panelists: Norman Badler (University of Pennsylvania)
Gary Demos (Digital Productions)
Henry Fuchs (University of North Carolina at Chapel Hill)
Alan Kay (Apple Computer)

Beyond the steadily increasing visual complexity and realism of computer-generated animation, recent research in computer graphics, artificial intelligence, robotics, VLSI and supercomputing will have a profound impact on the way we think of computer graphics and animation, and on the human computer interface.ication of artificial intelligence to computer animation, and discuss the importance of integrating both robotics and knowledge engineering technologies in computer animation systems to give the full power of computer animation to both expert and non-expert users.

The "Vivarium" project is discussed, which deals with a class of interactive learning tools aimed at developing models of biological habitats and animal behavior that can be used to drive animated simulations of evolutionary processes. A VLSI-based graphics system called PIXEL-PLANES, which is capable of generating shaded views of objects for real time animation, is described. Finally, the panel discusses the impact of supercomputers, such as the Cray XMP, on computer animation.

Knowledge-Based Computer Graphics:
Intersections of AI and Computer Graphics

Chair: Marek Holynski (Massachusetts Institute of Technology)

Panelists: Alan Borning (University of Washington)
                  Steven Feiner (Columbia University)
                  Mark Friedell (Harvard University)
                  Fanya Montalvo (Massachusetts Institute of Technology)

As graphic interaction becomes more complex, present computer graphics technology for managing such interaction becomes increasingly inadequate. Knowledge-based graphics systems, using domain-specific knowledge, may be the key. Knowledge-based graphics systems tie the meaning of a picture to its graphics representation and support the user in deciding about graphics presentation. Artificial intelligence techniques organize and manipulate knowledge specific to graphics in the form of semantic networks, rules and constraints. This panel considers the following topics: recent work on constraint-based graphics; rules for determining the objects to be shown in a picture; matching levels of abstraction to the user's need to control detail; graphical definitions of new kinds of constraints and the use of constraints in a "viewing and filtering" model of user interfaces; a general framework for the graphic input problem, i.e., how to recognize potentially ambiguous input; problems of reference in graphic interaction; adaptive graphics interfaces; application of inductive learning techniques for an effective visual representation; inference reasoning for scene composition.

Application of Array Processors
for Imaging, Graphic, and Simulation Processing

Chair: John Montelione (Mercury Computer Systems)

Panelists: Robert Bennett (Star Technology)
                  Stephan Cannon (Floating Point Systems)
                  Barry Isenstein (Mercury Computer Systems)
                  Thomas Litrenta (Numerixs)

As a computational coprocessor, array processors are utilized to off-load general purpose computers for the performance of sophisticated algorithms in images, graphics and simulation processing. Advancements in computer technology (for pipelined architectures), shared memory implementation and VLSI arithmetic processors have dramatically changed the utility and performance/price ratio of array processors. This, in turn, has resulted in widespread usage of array processors in applications as diverse as optical inspection, electronic publishing, seismic data analysis, medical imaging and mapping, reconnaissance and solids modeling and finite element analysis.

The panel session focuses primarily on four principal issues in the utilization of array processors:

● Applications/algorithms which can benefit from array processors.

● Programming issues.

● Tightly vs. loosely coupled interface to host computer.

● Performance "Mflop ratings" vs. actual throughput.

A secondary issue the panel addresses is emerging technologies in co-processor design.

Notes

Index

Image Credits

PROCEEDINGS FRONT COVER

Views II
Peter Oppenheimer
© Copyright 1986 by P. Oppenheimer, NYIT/CGL, Old

TITLE PAGE

Two Kinds of Dimples
Shinichi Kasahara
© Copyright 1986 by S. Kasahara-Kajima Corp., Tokyo, JAPAN

PROCEEDINGS BACK COVER

1 **The Beams of Light in the Foggy Night**
   Eihachiro Nakamae
   Hiroshima University, JAPAN

2 **Untitled Fractal**
   Richard Voss
   IBM, Yorktown Heights, NY.

3 **Traditional Room**
   D. Thalmann
   © Copyright 1986 by MIRALab, Université de Montréal, CANADA

4 **Shrimp and Leaf**
   Steve Strassmann
   © Copyright 1986 by Steve Stassmann-MIT Media Lab, Cambridge, MA

5 **Mobius Gears**
   Michelle L. Amato
   © Copyright 1986 by Cranston/Csuri Productions, Inc., Columbus, OH

6 **Untitled**
   Robert L. Bowers Jr.
   © Copyright 1986 Robert L. Bowers Jr. CGRG, Ohio State University, Columbus OH.

7 **Grand Canyon**
   Craig Upson
   © Copyright 1986 by Digital Scene Simulations (sm) Digital Productions, Los Angeles, CA